W. Murray Bradford
Glenn B. Davis

Strategies for Business
and Professional People

THE PRENTICE HALL
BUSINESS
TAX DEDUCTION
MASTER GUIDE
1986 EDITION

Prentice Hall Press · New York

First Prentice Hall Press Edition
A Division of Simon & Schuster, Inc.
Simon & Schuster Building
Rockefeller Center
1230 Avenue of the Americas
New York, New York 10020

PRENTICE HALL PRESS is a trademark of Simon & Schuster, Inc.

Manufactured in the United States of America

Library of Congress Cataloging in Publication Data

Bradford, W. Murray.
    Business tax deduction master guide.

    "A Spectrum Book."
    Bibliography
    Includes index.
    1. Income tax—United States—Deductions.   I. Davis,
Glenn B.
HJ4653.D4B68 1984   343.7035'23   84-24815
ISBN: 0-13-694035-8   347.303523
       0-13-694027-7 (pbk.)

Contents

HOW THIS BOOK WILL REDUCE YOUR INCOME TAXES AND YOUR FEAR OF A TAX AUDIT

You need this book if you spend money to make money. If you are self-employed, an outside sales professional, in a profession, serving as a consultant, conducting a second business, the owner-employee of a small corporation, a partner in a partnership, or in any other capacity that requires you to pick up the tab for your own business expenses, you need this book.

This book is a practical, down-to-earth guide with two primary purposes: (1) to reduce your income taxes, and (2) to reduce your fear of the IRS.

When you pick up the tab for your own business expenses, you have almost magic tax advantages because of your treatment as a business. Unfortunately, many of those tax advantages may not have been properly explained to you. Tax books often quote the rhythmless, jargon-loving authors of the Tax Code or the deadly bureaucratese of the IRS's Regulations. Such books may cure your insomnia, but they won't increase your tax know-how.

This book is designed to help you, not just to regurgitate the law. We've limited the book to business deductions so that we could get down to the gut issues and tell you not only what is required, but how to do it.

While reading this book you will find yourself actually enjoying taxes. Of course, you'll be saving money, and that will make enjoyable reading even more enjoyable. By reading this book you will learn

- At least 31 write-offs that you have probably overlooked.
- How to identify, write off, and document your legitimate business tax deductions.
- How to evaluate the benefits of incorporating and to protect your benefits from IRS attack.
- How to locate and cuddle a tax advisor.
- How to handle an IRS audit.

In this taxing life of ours, there is one investment you can stand on—your paperwork. If you want to shrink your income tax burden, you will have to put forth more effort. You cannot expect the improbable: that by reading this book you will automatically

Preface

reduce your income tax burden. Under our nation's tax laws, you are guilty until you prove yourself innocent. You must develop supporting records to prove that you are "not guilty."

Your supporting records may be causing you tax anxieties. Neurotic taxpayers believe that their tax records will not stand up to IRS scrutiny. Accordingly, such taxpayers understate their tax deductions and are fearful of taking many deductions that are rightfully theirs. Furthermore, this insecurity makes them afraid of an IRS audit.

This book will help you overcome your tax anxieties by showing you practical ways to support your tax deductions. You will learn many time-saving record-keeping techniques. In many cases, it will reduce your *taking care of taxes* time and increase your *taking care of business* time. A four- to eight-week test, for example, could be used in the right circumstances to substantiate your annual business mileage. This is easier than keeping a detailed log 365 days a year. Similarly, a test approach could be used to prove where you spend your time working, and that in turn could lead to a massive conversion of your nondeductible personal automobile mileage to deductible business automobile mileage. Using the techniques in this book, one taxpayer converted 154 daily personal miles to business miles. That increased his business write-offs by $7,700!

Your results may not be as dramatic, but they *will* be dramatic. Your record-keeping will become almost fun as you watch your write-offs multiply.

Good record-keeping swells all of your business write-offs. Salary payments to a spouse or child, entertainment expenses, investments in business assets, education expenses, payments to baby-sitters to allow you to work—to name just a few—are all fertile sources of tax refunds. Keeping good records not only *protects* your write-offs against IRS attack, it actually *increases* your write-offs! You will see why as you read this book.

Doesn't my tax advisor take care of my taxes? No. It's easy to turn the most competent tax advisor into a buffoon! Simply supply sketchy, incorrect, or downright bad information. There's an old computer expression: "Garbage in, garbage out." Nowhere is

that expression more applicable than in the preparation of tax returns.

"My accountant takes care of my taxes" is a popular myth, which we equate to a doctor taking care of bodies or a mechanic taking care of cars. Just as you must take care of your own body and your own car, you must also take care of your own taxes. You must understand the basics of your own tax situation. You must know what records to keep and how to keep them. And you must know when to seek your tax advisor's counsel before entering a transaction.

This book will help you make better use of your accountant. You will be able to bring in better numbers and more complete information, to ask more questions, and to obtain better advice.

How big is your tax bite? It's bigger than it needs to be—and getting bigger all the time. The IRS has its marching orders: collect more money to help shrink that bulging deficit. Congress is looking for new ways to get into your pockets. Even with President Reagan's tax cuts, you will probably share a greater and greater percentage of your income with the tax collector to maintain your standard of living.

That's just one reason why it's important for you not to overpay your income taxes. A single, self-employed taxpayer earning only $5,000 in taxable income must give 25.3 cents of the next dollar earned to the Federal Government before buying food. State income taxes do not help this food shortage.

This book will show you how tax brackets work and how tax savings are achieved within brackets. If you are self-employed, you will learn that the write-offs discussed in this book will reduce your self-employment income as well as your taxable income.

Some commonly overlooked dawn-to-dusk tax deductions: This book tells you how to keep records on a daily basis to achieve the common tax benefits that arise every day you are in the business of trying to make money. It will show what is deductible, how to support it, and how to put it in your tax return. We've simplified what those bureaucrats at the IRS have written and have made this book easy to read, understand, and apply.

This book is filled with goodies to reduce your tax bite. Here are just 30 of the many tax-saving techniques covered:

1. How to write off the cost of entertaining colleagues, clients, and prospects in your home.

2. How to write off the business portion of Dutch treat lunches.

3. How to determine if a meal is a deductible business meal.

4. How to take the investment tax credit on your automobile, desk, lamp, file cabinet, carpet, drapes, auto fix-up equipment, and other items you may have considered personal.

5. How to establish the business purpose and tax-deductible expenses for skiing trips, hunting trips, and similar social activities.

6. How to write off the cost of entertaining your spouse.

7. How to meet the $^{51}/_{49}$ test for deducting dues paid to country clubs, social clubs, fraternal clubs, and other types of athletic clubs.

8. How to write off educational expenses that maintain or improve your business skills.

9. How to travel for business with pleasure, and still write off your travel expenses.

10. How to pay the lowest estimated taxes without incurring any penalties.

11. How to establish a tax-free retirement plan to reduce your income taxes, whether you are self-employed or operate a corporation.

12. How to increase your cash return from a retirement plan.

13. How to get the most from an Individual Retirement Account (IRA).

14. How to write off the expenses of an office in your home.

15. How to write off business assets in your home even if you don't qualify for a home office deduction.

16. How you can covert nondeductible commuting mileage to 100 percent deductible business mileage.

17. How to double your automobile expense deduction by using actual expenses instead of lousy IRS standard mileage rates.

18. How to trade in or sell your automobile to reduce taxes.

19. How to apply the new cost recovery rules (formerly known as depreciation) to get the maximum write-offs from your automobile.

20. How to apply the new cost recovery rules to uncommon business assets.

21. How to get a tax refund for a business loss.

22. How to take the dependent and child care credit.

23. How to save tax dollars through income averaging.

24. How to amend (change) your prior years' taxes.

25. How to turn your business gifts into entertainment expenses and take larger write-offs.

26. How to pay your dependent child a deductible wage instead of a nondeductible allowance.

27. How to compensate your hard-working spouse and save taxes at the same time.

28. How to make December a time of big tax savings.

29. How to get extra cash out of your corporation without an extra tax bite.

30. How fringe benefits pay some of your personal expenses with untaxed dollars.

This book will explain not only why these items are overlooked, but also how to develop supporting documentation to make your deductions stick. You must get certain key pieces of documentation to support specific deductions. Documentation requirements vary from asset to asset and from expense to expense.

This book will show you how to apply the "magic words" to your everyday tax situation to obtain better-documented deductions. It will demonstrate the specific types of support you need for each type of write-off and some easy ways to get those documents. It will explain the interrelationship between supporting documents, and how all the supporting elements must build an audit trail leading to your business purpose. This book also will show you how to report deductions in your tax return to reduce your chances of selection for an IRS audit.

Tax myths that are frequently misapplied: When you are out there in the money jungle, you will hear a number of tall tales regarding income tax deductions. Acting on such tales can be a fatal mistake—especially now, because the IRS has been armed with new weapons to attack taxpayers who take dubious write-offs. This book will show you how to separate dubious from actual tax deductions and how to avoid being trapped by tax myths.

Have you ever heard people say that they use their cars 100 percent of the time for business? You will be unhappy to learn that this statement is, in most cases, a myth. In fact, such a statement will normally lead taxpayers into the arena of substantial tax problems. If someone tells you to use a corporation to get a 100 percent deduction, watch out—that could put you in double tax jeopardy. You could end up paying twice as much tax as you should.

Many chapters of this book will explore myths associated with tax write-offs. Once the myths are properly dismissed, the chapter will explain how to achieve your desired tax result, but without the pitfalls inherent in the myth. Following are just a few of the many myths explored throughout this book:

- Why 100 percent business usage of your automobile is improbable.
- Why failure to use the magic words to record all five elements of substantiation will cost you entertainment expenses.
- Why IRS audits do not always result in additional taxes.
- Why your business gifts are limited to $25.
- Why estimated tax underpayments don't have to result in tax penalties.
- How the $25 receipt rule for travel and entertainment is often misapplied to other expenses.
- Why business mileage percentages are usually incorrect.
- Why the investment tax credit is overlooked by 90 percent of the individuals who prepare their own tax returns.
- Why most entertainment expenses for sporting events and theater performances are improperly documented.
- How the IRS uses repair bills and other documents to negate your business mileage claim.
- Why canceled checks are almost useless as the only support for your business tax deductions.
- Why your tax preparer is not a tax advisor.
- Why your tax advisor can only be as effective as you allow.

The myths are explored in detail, and then the actual facts are explained succinctly and lucidly to aid your comprehension.

Why we wrote this book: We searched high, low, and in between to find a book that explains your business tax write-offs in plain English but in enough detail for you to put your knowledge to work on a practical, day-

to-day basis. We know without a doubt that you are looking for a ready reference source. We know you need a reference source that's easy to understand and to apply, whether you're using a tax advisor or preparing your own tax return. This book is it.

We've avoided the unnecessary use of tax jargon and we've set tax examples in everyday situations. Tax professionals use tax jargon because that's what they're familiar and comfortable with. Unfortunately, many professionals communicate with you using that same jargon. This book will help you to understand that jargon and to use your tax advisor more effectively. Throughout this book you will learn the "magic" tax words that will help you to understand the tax laws and apply them to your everyday situations.

You will benefit from this book in four principal ways:

1. You will put more money in your pocket, not only by reducing your tax burden, but by financial planning as well. Accordingly, we have provided you with worksheets and materials that you can apply to your situation.
2. You will understand how numbers fit into your tax return. Accordingly, we have explained how to fill out tax forms and have given you simplified instructions to assit you in either preparing your own return or understanding what your tax preparer has done for you.
3. You will hurdle the tax jargon barrier, understand tax words, and apply the words to fit your situation. Accordingly, we use examples and illustrations of tax laws, tax hints, supporting documents, and diary pages.
4. You will get a basic knowledge of the tax laws that apply to you and how they apply to you.

A final word: After you have taken care of food, lodging, and clothing, what is your largest expense? It may be the support of your silent business partner, the tax collector. Moreover, inflation is changing the nature of that partnership agreement so that the unwelcome silent partner gets a bigger cut every year.

This book was written to reduce your tax burdens and the partnership take of the tax collector. It will lessen your fear of your tax-collecting partner because it will show you how to establish your tax records. It is written in an informative, practical style that tells not only what can be done but how to do it. We believe *this book will save worries, time, and money.*

If you've ever read IRS instructions and gotten a headache, you will be even more disgruntled to find out that the instructions offer no cure for your tax problem. It seems these days that the principal manifestation of tax books, especially those printed by the IRS, is vagueness. Meanwhile, you are out there in the money jungle yearning to control your tax situations.

There are hundreds of exceptions, counterexceptions, and elections contained in the Internal Revenue Code. It is practically impossible for a citizen to understand what's happening. The IRS has embarked on an extensive program to simplify tax forms and instructions and Congress has attempted, although rather feebly, to simplify its mandates. The results so far are good, but they offer a threadbare cure for a momentous problem that has multiplied over three decades to its present proportions.

In this chapter, we explain how two magic words must fit every business deduction. We help you analyze your business position for possible tax deductions, and we explain why a part-time business can provide some additional tax deductions. We even walk through the tax rate schedules and help you determine your effective tax bracket. We explain why

hobby losses can destroy your tax deductions and how losses from real businesses can put extra money in your pockets. We explain what to do when you make a mistake on a prior year's return and how to fix it. We explain the new Social Security law and the impact it has on your present business situation. Finally, we show you a sure-fire way to measure the tax savings from incorporation.

MAGIC WORDS THAT MAKE EXPENSES DEDUCTIBLE

Almost every business tax deduction available to you is subject first to the "ordinary and necessary" test before it has any chance whatsoever of resulting in a deductible business expense. Entertainment and travel deductions must first pass the "ordinary and necessary" test. Your automobile deduction is dependent on use of the automobile in your "ordinary and necessary" course of business.

"Ordinary and necessary" was once found by the Senate Finance Committee to result in entertainment expenses being allowed as tax deductions even though their connection with a trade or business was quite remote. The committee further stated that if even a slight

1

How to Put Tax Law to Work for You

business purpose existed, entertainment expenses generally were fully deductible under the "ordinary and necessary" test. Webster may disagree with the Senate Finance Committee, but judicial interpretations have followed this line of reasoning in areas other than entertainment expenses for quite some time. This is not to suggest that you should be looking for remote business expenses, but it does add vision to the meanings given the terms "ordinary and necessary."

The term "ordinary" has been applied somewhat as Webster would have desired. It has been interpreted by the courts to mean *customary*, *usual*, and *normal* business practices. Webster might kick his coffin, however, if he heard the tax interpretation of the term "necessary." Long-standing precedent has held this term to include expenses that are *helpful*, *needed*, and *appropriate*. Obviously, there has been a little seepage since Webster wrote his book.

Actually, Congress intended a certain vagueness with the terms "ordinary and necessary" because all tax deductions are predicated on the "facts and circumstances" of a particular taxpayer. What's necessary to one taxpayer in a particular circumstance may include what is helpful. Therefore, if you can answer any one of the following questions "yes," you may have a sound basis for a business deduction:

- Is the expense helpful to your pursuit of profit?
- Is the expense needed for you to make money?
- Is the expense appropriate to your pursuit of business?

Every business expense must have a direct (versus remote) relationship to your existing business pursuits to qualify as an ordinary and necessary expense. In determining whether an expense is ordinary and necessary (or direct or remote), that vast gray area is decided on the basis of your facts and circumstances.

To use the words "ordinary and necessary" to your advantage, you must determine if the expenses are helpful or needed, or usual and normal. These interpretations open new horizons as to what those two magic words really mean for tax purposes.

USING THE MAGIC WORDS TO DEDUCT BUSINESS EXPENSES

Our nation's income tax is based on gross income from all sources, less certain specified deductions allowed by the Internal Revenue Code. Deductions fall into general classes such as "ordinary and necessary business expenses." The deductibility of a business expense is determined by three basic requirements:

- It must be incurred in your trade or business.
- It may not be a capital expenditure, although such expenditures are often deductible through mechanisms known as depreciation, recovery, and amortization.
- It must be ordinary and necessary.

While mumbling about the innumerable complexities in the Internal Revenue Code, the Supreme Court stated that the determination of directly related and ordinary and necessary is a question of pure fact.

Proving the facts: This book will emphasize the importance of keeping appropriate records of your business expenses. The burden of proof, as you will learn in the documentation section, is totally on you, the taxpayer. The Internal Revenue Service is not required to prove that you did not incur a claimed expense.

The determination of an ordinary and necessary expense is usually a question of fact. Your records must first establish and then support your facts.

Adequate records put you in a position to prove your ordinary and necessary business expenses. Once you prove that vital element, you need only prove that you were in business and that you paid your business expenses, rather than the expenses of someone else. The upcoming examples will explain and further elaborate on these points.

Rule: No deductions are allowable for personal, living, or family expenses.

Example: A railroad conductor was able to convince the tax court that his watch was necessary for his pursuit of business (that is, earning his salary), and he was allowed to deduct the cost of watch repairs.

Result: A wristwatch is usually considered a personal asset. It is not tax deductible under the long-established and well-embedded tax principle that no deductions are allowed for personal, living, or family expenses. Hundreds of taxpayers have lost deductions for depreciation or repair to watches. The railroad conductor, however, was able to establish that in his circumstances his watch was necessary to his business. Obviously, he had to have records and evidence to support the use of his watch in his business. But with good records, he was able to convince the tax court.

Rule: Payments of ordinary and necessary business expenses must benefit your business, as opposed to someone else's.

Example: Cloud, an attorney, was the sole owner of a corporation that had some outstanding interest and tax obligations. Cloud paid the expenses of his corporation out of his own pocket rather than the corporation's; he was denied a tax deduction because the expenses were not owed by him. There was no evidence that nonpayment by the corporation would have impaired Cloud's professional reputation or caused him to lose clients.

Result: Cloud was caught in a trap that millions of taxpayers are setting for themselves today. When you establish a solely owned corporation, the corporation must own its assets and pay its bills. Similarly, you are not allowed to pick up the tab for a relative or a partnership. Both relatives and partnerships must pay their own expenses.

Rule: There must be a business reason for incurring the expense.

Example: Two partners in a dry-cleaning business took quarterly fishing trips and claimed the expenses as ordinary and necessary business expenses. The tax court disallowed the deductions because the partners failed to establish a business relationship be-

tween the fishing trips and the dry-cleaning business.

Result: There must be some causal relationship between the incurrence of an expense and an expected business benefit. The rules on fishing trips are twofold. First, you must prove that the expense was an ordinary and necessary business expense. Second, as you will see in Chapter 3, you must write down five elements of substantiation for each entertainment expense. Moreover, a fishing trip is subject to special rules for entertainment associated with business. The rules require documentation of business discussions before or after the entertainment to justify the expense. Otherwise, the IRS may think that the business purpose is fishy.

You will learn in Chapter 3 that a certain amount of tax planning is necessary to deduct the cost of fishing trips. But millions of taxpayers each year properly document such trips and are allowed tax deductions.

The business benefit rule is also demonstrated by the sole proprietor who paid a minister for business advice and prayed that it would be considered a necessary expense. The court disallowed the deduction because the minister had only hazy notions of what constituted business, gave spiritual solutions, and had no prior business experience.

Your business establishes your right to be paid off with tax deductions. You must be in business to claim an ordinary and necessary business expense. Being in business may include earning a salary. You may incur business expenses in your status as an employee that are needed to retain your salaried status. A second business may qualify for deductible expenses as well as a first business. Being in business simply means that you're out to make a profit. Whether or not you are actually making a profit is irrelevant, but you must be trying.

For tax purposes, you could even be operating a business that is illegal under state law. We're not recommending you do so but are merely pointing out that business is business. And when business makes money, the tax collector wants a share.

Example: Tinsley operated a numbers game and was allowed deductions for his telephone, his rent, and the business portion of his car expenses.

Tinsley, of course, had to pay some taxes, and that's why he was allowed certain deductions. Had he been paying for protection from racketeers, those payment woul not have been deductible under Federal tax law. Similarly, bribes to government officials are considered contrary to public policy and are not deductible.

Interrelationship with personal expenses: When business assets are used for both business and personal purposes, you must have evidence to support business usage. An automobile is a good example of a business asset that may be used for both business and personal activities. In such a case, you must have documentation to prove that the asset was used in business.

Example: Butz, a self-employed taxpayer, maintained an office in his home. He claimed tax deductions for lawn maintenance expenses around his home. The court ruled that lawn care expenses were not deductible as ordinary and necessary business expenses. It was rare for Butz to have a client or business associate to his home office. He had no lawn surrounding a separate entrance to the office. Overall, the expenditures for lawn care were attributable to the maintenance of Butz's personal residence and not to that of his home office.

Magic words: If you are not doing something in the ordinary and necessary course of business, your possibility of getting a tax deduction is slim. Expenses that are helpful, appropriate, needed, or usual qualify under the "ordinary and necessary" test, provided that you are in business.

To assure that you are not being nudged away from equal opportunity in determining what is an ordinary and necessary business expense, each chapter of this book devotes time to defining the terms "ordinary and necessary" in the context of a particular deduction. This discussion will open new vistas for many expenses which, until now, you may have considered personal or not business related. You'll find this book permeated with the magic

words that will help you make more money after taxes.

HOW TO ANALYZE YOUR BUSINESS POSITION FOR TAX DEDUCTIONS

Achieving maximum tax savings is a year-round, daily activity. Nowhere is this truer than in business, and remember, you are in business if you are pursuing a salary, commissions, fees, or any other compensation that will help you make a living. Since your individual facts and circumstances determine the nature of your deductible expenses, much depends on the nature of the product or service you are selling and on how you go about making a living. In this section, we will explore various activities from dawn to dusk for their tax-reductive possibilities.

Tax deductions arise from three principal areas of your business life. First, *people*—your prospects, clients, contacts, and colleagues—give rise to tax deductions. Second, *physical assets*—your automobile, calculator, special clothing, and other items—give rise to tax deductions and tax credits. Third, *expenses*—your continuing education, paper, pens, and repairs—give rise to tax deductions.

When the day of reckoning comes, your facts and circumstances will determine how the people you know, the assets you use, and the expenses you incur are judged according to the IRS's prescribed standards for tax-deductibility.

The people you know: Who are the people you know and meet, and how do they give rise to tax deductions? First, you have prospects—the people you seek in your quest for the dollar. If you sell real estate, for example, your prospects would include neighbors, friends, relatives, members of the country club, parking lot attendants, grocery check-out personnel, and possibly even your maid. By maintaining a prospect list, you begin laying the foundation for building a tax-reductive file.

All expenses from finding a prospect to making a sale are valid business expenses. Your prospect file will contain the names of good friends, bad friends, neighbors, and others with whom you maintain business and personal relationships. Although tax law disallows personal, living, and family expenses, that does not negate business expenses associated with friends; it merely requires you to keep better records of business activities. In your business, a neighbor or good friend may be a better prospect than a cold call you receive at the office.

Example: Mattson used her neighbors to launch a terrific career in real estate. Twice a week, she had dinner parties for six neighborhood couples. At the dinner parties, she showed photographs of a new neighborhood development, gave comparable sales prices to each of the couples, showed them how their homes could be sold at a tidy profit, and assured them that the new community offered similar schools and recreational facilities. By the end of the year, Mattson had spent more than $12,000 on home entertainment expenses. Her gross income directly attributable to this home entertainment was in excess of $35,000. Mattson incurred valid business expenses by selling to personal acquaintances.

Mattson had to avoid some early fumbles in the documentation game in order to secure her deduction. For instance, she had to list the individuals entertained. Because the entertainment took place in her home, she needed a record of the business discussions that took place. There is a tax presumption that entertainment in the home is for personal rather than business purposes. Mattson overcame that presumption with two lists, one of prospects and the other of revenue-producing clients. The integration of the two lists established that her entertainment took place in the normal and ordinary course of business and disclosed a direct business benefit.

Medical doctors often have contacts with other medical doctors as a source of patients. A specialist depends mightily on referrals from doctors in general practice. For a medical doctor, developing referral sources is part of everyday business.

Example: King, an ulcer specialist, entertains 20 different doctors who are in general practice. King maintains a list of all referral sources, using his new patients' cards to obtain the data. Whenever he entertains one of his referral sources, King thanks the referring doctor and mentions the names of the patients. King's audit trail between referral sources and actual referrals is an excellent document to establish that his entertainment took place in the ordinary and necessary course of business. The fact that he entertains to obtain such referrals is established by the relationship between the referrals and the individuals entertained.

On some chilly winter evening, sit down and go through your personal telephone book to identify those individuals with whom you have business contact. Then, as you're reading the chapters in this book, note how the deductions pertain to that list of contacts. If you are hoping for shrinkage in your tax bite, you must develop an eye for tax deductions that fall within the parameters of your facts and circumstances.

The assets you use: There are a number of physical assets located in your home that you may use for either personal or business purposes. Usually, there is no problem whatsoever in identifying business assets found in the office. It's when they are located in the home that there is a problem identifying them as possible business assets.

If you own and use an automobile for both business and personal use, it's immediately recognized as a business asset because of its inordinate expense. But if you own an automobile, you will have a number of related assets, even if you're not particularly fond of getting all greasy and dirty fixing your own car. Common examples include trickle chargers, battery cables, socket sets, screwdrivers, and tire pumps. At least a portion of the cost of these items qualifies as a deductible expense or possibly as a depreciable asset, depending on the cost. If the equipment is used on two automobiles, you will have to make an allocation between the two cars based on personal and business mileage. More details on these allocations are contained in Chapter 5.

If you work at home, you probably sit at a desk. Whether or not you take a home office deduction, the desk is a business asset. It should be capitalized and depreciated. If you're sitting at a desk, it's likely that there's a lamp near that desk. Possibly you have some books in a bookcase. There may be a file cabinet next to the desk, and shades over the windows. Next time you're sitting at your desk write down all the business assets that are located there.

You may have some hobbies that are interwoven with your business activities. You could, for example, be a camera buff who needs to use the camera for both business and personal activities. The portion of the camera equipment used for business activities represents a business asset, providing you document the business usage.

Example: Lamb purchases camera equipment costing $800 for business and personal use. He maintains a log of film used, which discloses the number of personal versus business photographs he takes during a year. On the basis of this log, Lamb has a valid allocation formula for capitalizing and depreciating the business portion of the camera equipment. In addition, the formula provides a basis for the investment tax credit.

The expenses you incur: If you are an owner-employee of a small business, a self-employed individual, an outside salesperson, or an employee who picks up the tab for many business expenses, you will purchase business supplies in personal environments. Trips to the grocery store for paper, pencils, and pens may be combined with your personal grocery shopping. Such trips present two tax problems: First, if you do not write down the purchase soon after leaving the grocery store, you will forget it; and second, you must actually identify the items purchased for business on the grocery bill.

The problem is compounded if you report expenses as an employee or partner. If you are a partner in a partnership, for example, the partnership must reimburse you for partnership expenses. If you are the owner-employee of your corporation, you must have the corporation reimburse you for expenses. Direct payments by you on behalf of a partnership or a corporation are not deductible. Expenses must be paid by the taxable entity entitled to the deduction.

When looking for out-of-pocket expenses, take a survey for a few days while you work. What books are you reading that help you in your business? By asking this simple question, you will identify not only deductible

books, but deductible magazines and other materials as well.

Most individuals have an ear for business. Often the ear is employed at home using the residential telephone. But to obtain a deduction for the residential telephone, you must have some type of record to prove to the IRS that it's actually used in business. A simple but effective record is to establish a log for several test periods during the year. In the log, record the number of calls made for business and those made for personal purposes. List individual names next to the telephone calls made to business prospects and clients. Then if the IRS ever attacks your deduction for telephone expenses, your efforts (about 700 seconds) will pay a dividend.

If you are hoping for deflation in tax liability, you must pay attention to how you conduct your business affairs. For most of us, conducting business involves combining business activities with a certain element of personal activities. The business portion must be separated. You must have documents that support your business portion, unless you have a real taste for risk.

Take two hours and think of the things you do for business. Think of how your business interplays with the way you live. A small expenditure of time will give you the happy dilemma of deciding how many new tax deductions you want.

AVOID THE "HOBBY" CLASSIFICATION

The IRS considers business to be an "activity carried on for livelihood or for profit." An activity can be fun and still be a business, provided the profit motive is present and some type of economic activity has taken place. Failure to establish your activity with a profit motive will leave you thrashing about for tax deductions.

It's entirely possible to have more than one business. Moonlighting for salary, profit, or even fun is treated as a business if you do it regularly. The IRS says that a business must make a regular effort to make money. This effort to make money is what separates a business from a hobby—an activity engaged in purely for personal satisfaction.

You do not want your activities to be considered a hobby. Such a classification will result in denial of any losses you incur in that business and limit your total deductions to the total revenue produced. Under the hobby classification, if you make money, you are taxed. If you lose money, the IRS will not subsidize your hobby.

If you make a tiny bit of money, the hobby loss rule will put your nonbusiness activity into Schedule A of your tax return, not a desirable classification in itself. Once it is positioned in Schedule A, your hobby income is further hampered by the following two rules.

1. Amounts already allowable as itemized deductions (mortgage interest and property taxes) are deductible in full regardless of your hobby activities.
2. Expenses that would be allowable as business expenses if your activity were not classed as a hobby are allowable only to the extent of your hobby income. Any excess is forever lost in the sewer of unwarranted tax deductions.

The first business deductions allowable against hobby income are those that *do not* reduce the basis of your property, such as depreciation, recovery, and amortization. If you have hobby income after deducting such expenses, then depreciation, recovery, and amortization are allowable.

The IRS will seldom claim that you have a hobby when you are making money. However, you have a problem when you are losing money. The IRS thinks you enjoy losing money. If you are losing money in a part-time activity that involves recreational and pleasurable travel, the IRS will quickly insist that such part-time activities are hobbies and that you had no intention of making a profit, just an intention of having fun. The IRS is paranoid about people having fun.

The IRS seldom considers earning a salary to be fun. It's when you have your own trade or business that the IRS thinks you are having a good time. If you happen to have some type of second business, such as a distributorship, the IRS may again raise the "hobby" issue. Remember, when a new activity produces taxable income, no extra tax problems arise. When you make money, you are treated the same as any full-time business and all of the tax strategies and tax deductions highlighted in this book are fully applicable.

Profit motive: When you start a new business, even a second business, you will probably need a good supply of tranquilizers. Often, you will need to do a little belt tightening and grit your teeth while getting started. You can be sure the IRS will come bouncing along a short time after you start to see how its interest in your income is coming along. If no payoff is available, the IRS will make you an offer that's hard to refuse.

This offer will be as follows: "Make a profit and pay some taxes in any two of the first five years you are in business, and you can deduct your business losses." In most cases, this proposition gives the IRS a "lock" (in racetrack terms, a sure bet) on your money. Earn a profit, and get taxed. Fail to earn a profit, and you lose business deductions. You get in on this IRS lock by filing IRS Form 5213. With this filing, you agree to make a profit in any two of the first five years or eat your losses.

The IRS lock is known as the "presumption of profit" rule. The IRS will allow you to deduct your business losses during your start-up phase if you are willing to state that you will make a profit in two of the first five years to qualify your activities as a business. When you fail the "presumption of profit," your activities are deemed a hobby and you obtain no deductions in excess of hobby income.

As part of this agreement, the IRS will not examine your business or hobby during the five-year period, because during that time the IRS does not know if you have a business or a hobby. Your invitation for audit is delivered later, after the IRS is sure you have a hobby.

If you find the IRS's proposition under the "presumption of profit" rule to your liking, you may take advantage of it by completing IRS Form 5213. IRS instructions for this form state that if you have more than one activity for which you want to make the election, you may do so if you submit a separate form for each activity. You are allowed to submit this form up to three years after the due date for the return in which you reported your business activity.

You may have gotten the idea that we are not fond of Form 5213. That's almost true. If you have a lock because you have made a profit in two years, we suggest that you file Form 5213 to cash in on your lock. When the issue is in doubt, however, we strongly suggest that you consider the alternative method.

The alternative: Rather than use the "presumption of profit" rules, a taxpayer may set out to appeal to the IRS's wisdom. As you would expect, this requires feeding the frantic demands of the IRS for pieces of paper. IRS regulations specify that all relevant factors are to be taken into account in determining whether or not a profit motive is present in an activity. The regulations give a listing of what are considered possible relevant factors, but they also state that no one factor is determinative, and that all the facts and circumstances with respect to the activity are to be taken into account. Following are some of the factors that could be useful in proving your profit motive:

- Carrying on the activity in a businesslike manner.
- Maintaining complete and accurate books and records.
- Developing expertise in the business and its activities.
- Expending substantial time and effort conducting the activity.
- Having a sound prior business track record.
- Establishing a history of your business's profits and losses.
- Having the financial means to carry out your business plans.
- Keeping elements of personal pleasure and recreational activities inherent in the business to a minimum.

These factors simply mean that "you gotta wanna make money." The regulations further point out that you need not be smart or even have a reasonable expectation of making a profit. Your activities must indicate, however, that you entered into the activity or continued it with the *objective* of making a profit. It is possible to have a profit objective when there is only a very small chance of making a large profit. Thus, it may be found that an investor in a wildcat oil well who incurs very substantial expenditures is in the venture for profit even though the expectation of profit might be considered unreasonable.

One significant factor in determining profit motive is the amount of time spent by a taxpayer in carrying on the activity. Substantial personal or recreational aspects will be looked at as a boondoggle unless you spend time and energy on the activity itself. If you have withdrawn from another occupation to devote most of your energies to this activity, you obviously intend to make some money to provide for your livelihood. In the absence of complete withdrawal, you may work at an activity on a regular basis—for example, in a second business that takes 10 to 20 hours a week—and still have a profit motive.

The term *profit* encompasses appreciation in the value of assets as well as operating profit. You may intend to derive a profit from operations, but even if no profit from the operation occurs, you may expect to make an overall profit because of appreciation in the value of land and buildings used in the activity. In looking at your profit motive, the IRS considers the full value of appreciation even though a portion of the appreciation may not be subject to tax because of favorable capital gain treatment.

Start with a projection: You have a business, not a hobby, when you have an "expectation of profit." When you start a new business, buy a rental property, or enter into any transaction for profit, you should project your taxable income and loss at that time. Generally, you make such a projection before deciding to enter into an activity.

The original projection should form the nucleus for your tax file. Add to that file all documents you obtain during your search for information and add diary notations as to the experts from whom you sought advice.

Important hint: Keep track of the time you spend pursuing your "profit-seeking—property-seeking" activity. Throughout this book we discuss the importance of keeping a daily diary. While reviewing the chapters on travel, entertainment, automobile, and home office, note the types of diary entries that are made. You will want to make similar types of diary entries, and especially keep track of the time you spend taking care of your *new* "profit-seeking" activities.

Exhibit 1-1 contains an example of the

EXHIBIT 1-1. Projected Taxable Income and Loss at Time of Purchase (Example Computation).

FACTS: Yesterday, Bailey purchased a residential rental unit. The unit was subject to the "antichurning" rules; therefore, Bailey had to use the old depreciation rules for tax purposes. To establish her profit motive, Bailey prepared the following economic analysis three days before she made her offer on the property.

OPERATING EXPENSES

Year	Rental Income	Interest	Taxes	Depreciation	Other	Total	Rental Loss
1	$ 7,200	$12,000	$1,200	$5,760	$1,000	$19,960	$12,760
2	7,500	11,750	1,200	5,299	1,000	19,249	11,749
3	7,800	11,450	1,250	4,875	1,000	18,575	10,775
4	8,400	11,100	1,250	4,485	1,000	17,835	9,435
5	9,000	10,700	1,300	4,126	1,000	17,126	8,126
Totals	$39,900	$57,000	$6,200	$24,545	$5,000	$92,745	$52,845

Estimated Net Gain When Property Is Sold:

Value at date of sale; original cost of $90,000 appreciating at an annual rate of 11 percent for five years	$152,000
Less estimated selling expenses	− 11,000
Expected net proceeds	$141,000
Less tax basis of property at date of sale ($90,000 original cost less depreciation of $24,545)	− 65,455
Gain on sale of property	$ 75,545

Net Result For Period Property Is Owned:

Gain on sale of property	$ 75,545
Losses on rental of property	− 52,845
Net gain from purchase, rental, and sale	$ 22,700

projected taxable income Bailey expects from the purchase of a residential rental unit. The projection was prepared at the time Bailey purchased the property. Each year thereafter, she compares her projections with actual operating results. She also does all the other things we discussed. Bailey is in an excellent position to establish her profit motive. Regardless of activity, the projection is the starting point.

The IRS will not outlaw your tax deductions when you are making taxable income. The benefit of proving that your activity is a business (not a hobby) is that should you be a loser in business, you will be a winner with your tax refund.

HOW TO TURN A BUSINESS LOSS INTO A TAX REFUND

When your deductible business expenses exceed your taxable income for a tax year, you have incurred a net operating loss for that year. That's good, at least for tax purposes. It's certainly better than getting deathly ill and having medical bills that exceed your income for the year. You have only one year to claim your medical expenses, but with a net operating loss, you have almost two decades to reap the benefits.

Once you've incurred a business loss, you may have created a tax deduction called the "net operating loss deduction." This deduction is available as a direct offset against your gross income for up to 18 other taxable years. Unlike medical deductions, you get to carry the net operating loss around. The net operating loss deduction is a business deduction. This is true regardless of whether or not you were engaged in a trade or business in the taxable year to which you carry the loss. You need not itemize deductions in order to claim a net operating loss deduction because the deduction is taken from your gross income.

The net operating loss deduction allows you to offset your taxable income in the three years preceding your loss year and in the 15 years following your loss year. There is a specific order in which the loss must be used, which we'll discuss in a moment. But first, it's important to note that you may carry the loss around during the refund period until you claim tax refunds for the entire loss.

Your 18-year period of benefit from a net operating loss starts three years before you incur the loss. Your first option is to carry the net operating loss deduction back to the third year preceding your loss year. If the loss is not totally used in that year, you may carry any excess to the second year preceding your loss year. If you have not used the loss at the end of the second year preceding the loss year, you may carry any unused loss to the first year preceding the loss year. If, after carrying the loss back to the three preceding tax years, you still have some left over, you may start to carry it forward for 15 years. During the carry-forward period, you apply the net operating loss to the first tax year following your loss year, then to the second, and on through to the fifteenth year.

If for some reason you had a shortfall three years before your loss year, you may elect to carry the loss forward and forgo the carry-back period. The election to carry the loss forward only is irrevocable. You must reap the benefits in the fifteen-year carry-forward period or lose some of your loss. To elect not to carry the loss back, you must attach a statement to your tax return for the tax year in which you incurred the loss. Exhibit 1-2 contains a statement for this purpose. You must make the election at the time you file your tax return, and you may not amend your return for the election. Thus, you file the election when you *know* that you

will achieve greater tax savings by carrying the loss forward.

The time for advice: When you have incurred a net operating loss for a tax year, it's a good idea to spend some extra money with your tax advisor. The cost of that advice is also deductible, but its main purpose is to make sure that you get the full tax refund. Computations for the net operating loss carry-back and carry-forward are, as you can imagine, somewhat complicated. There's also a good deal of strategy involved in taking maximum advantage of your ill fortune.

When you report a loss in your Form 1040, the IRS will not ring your bell and tell you that you have a refund due; you must ask for it. If you have elected to carry the loss forward, you attach a computation of your loss carry-forward to each carry-forward return until the loss is used.

If you want a refund for taxes you paid in prior years, you have two choices. First, you may ask for a "quickie" refund by submitting Form 1045 (individual) or Form 1139 (corporate) within 12 months after the end of the tax year in which you incurred the net operating loss. The advantage to Form 1045 or 1139 is that the IRS will act on the claim within 90 days.

Second, if you are in no particular hurry to get your money, you may file for a refund by submitting Form 1040X (individual) or Form 1120X (corporate), an amended return. This is the same form you use to change your prior years' tax returns.

HOW TO CHANGE PRIOR YEARS' TAX RETURNS

Suppose that while reading this book you find a tax deduction for a prior year that you overlooked. Further suppose that your supporting records are adequate to substantiate that deduction. What can you do?

Tax law allows you to file a claim for refund if you overpaid your taxes because you somehow overlooked an allowable deduction or credit. You have three years from the date you filed your return to claim a refund. If you filed early, the three years is measured

---

EXHIBIT 1-2. Statement of Taxpayer Who Elects to Carry a Net Operating Loss Forward Only.

Example—Note to Tax Return

Taxpayer hereby elects to carry the net operating loss embodied in this tax return to future years. Taxpayer understands that this election precludes carrying the net operating loss back to the prior three years.

---

from the due date—for most individuals, April 15. For example, assume that you discover an error in your 1983 tax return, which was originally filed March 3, 1984. You may claim a refund anytime between the date of original filing and April 15, 1987.

If, for some reason, you procrastinated and did not file and pay your taxes within one year after the due date, you have two years from the time you actually paid to file for a refund. For example, if you didn't file and pay your 1983 taxes—due April 15, 1984—until July 1, 1985, you have until July 1, 1987, to claim a refund.

If you never bothered to file a return at all, but you did pay your taxes, you have two years from the payment date to claim a refund. For example, if you paid your 1983 taxes on April 15, 1984, but didn't file a return, you have until April 15, 1986, to claim a refund. (We strongly suggest that you pay your taxes *and* file your return on time, however.)

Refund claims are filed with the Internal Revenue Service Center where you sent the return you are now changing.

Sleeping dogs: Most tax professionals agree that filing a refund claim will increase your chances of receiving an audit invitation. The IRS has not commented either way, except to state that the filing of a refund claim will cause your tax return to take another trip through the computer. If your return made the trip some time ago, you may be better off letting sleeping dogs lie, especially if you have some "soft spots" in your return.

Keep in mind that audits are triggered by the nature of your entire tax return, including amendments of your return for a refund or extra payment of tax. You could end up paying more income taxes if you made a mistake

on a prior return and later file an amended return that subjects your tax return to an increased possibility of audit selection. When faced with the question of whether to amend or not to amend, you will have to base your decision on how your entire return falls together and how well you have supported your deductions. Don't file an amended return if you're relying on dazzling footwork to explain your deductions.

When you file an amended return—and you should file one for all your rightful deductions—you will be happy to find that interest is paid on many refund claims. Interest starts with the filing date for your return, or the date you paid your tax, and runs until 30 days preceding the date of the check. The interest rate in effect from February 1, 1982, to January 1, 1983, was 20 percent. From January 1, 1983, until June 30, 1983, the rate was 16 percent. The rate from July 1, 1983, until December 31, 1984, was 11 percent. From January 1, 1985 to June 30, 1985 the rate was 13%. The rate returned to 11% from July 1, 1985 to December 31, 1985. From January 1, 1986 to June 30, 1986 the rate is 10%. So in addition to getting your tax refund at whatever tax bracket you were in, you will also receive interest on your refund.

HOW TO DETERMINE YOUR TAX BRACKET AND ITS TAX EFFECT

Exhibit 1-3 contains the tax rate schedules for married individuals filing joint returns in taxable years 1982, 1983, and 1984. Under our nation's progressive tax system, you are taxed in brackets. The first $3,400 you earn is taxed at the rate of zero percent for a zero

EXHIBIT 1-3. Tax Rate Schedules for Married Individuals Filing Joint Returns.

Taxable income	1982 Pay +	1982 % on Excess*	1983 Pay +	1983 % on Excess*	1984 Pay +	1984 % on Excess*
0 – $3,400	– 0 –	– 0 –	– 0 –	– 0 –	– 0 –	– 0 –
$3,400 – 5,500	– 0 –	12	– 0 –	11	– 0 –	11
5,500 – 7,600	$252	14	$231	13	$231	12
7,600 – 11,900	546	16	504	15	483	14
11,900 – 16,000	1,234	19	1,149	17	1,085	16
16,000 – 20,200	2,013	22	1,846	19	1,741	18
20,200 – 24,600	2,937	25	2,644	23	2,497	22
24,600 – 29,900	4,037	29	3,656	26	3,465	25
29,900 – 35,200	5,574	33	5,034	30	4,790	28
35,200 – 45,800	7,323	39	6,624	35	6,274	33
45,800 – 60,000	11,457	44	10,334	40	9,772	38
60,000 – 85,600	17,705	49	16,014	44	15,168	42
85,600 –109,400	30,249	50	27,278	48	25,920	45
109,400 –162,400	42,149	50	38,702	50	36,630	49
162,400 –215,400	68,649	50	65,202	50	62,600	50
215,400 – . . .	95,149	50	91,702	50	89,100	50

*Tax on amount by which taxable income exceeds base amount, i.e., $8,000 exceeds $7,600 by $400, the 1982 tax would be $610.

tax. The next $2,100 you earn is taxed at 11 percent in 1984 for a total tax of $231. The next $2,100 you earn is taxed at 12 percent for a total tax of $252. If you add the $231 and $252 you arrive at $483, the base amount for the next tax bracket.

Exhibit 1-4 illustrates the above discussion. It shows how each bracket or earnings level is taxed at a specified rate and how the Bolens' total tax of $7,132 is computed. You will notice that the rates in Exhibit 1-4 are the same as those in Exhibit 1-3, but instead of using the tax rate schedules for the computation, we merely used the tax brackets in Exhibit 1-4. The significance of looking at taxes in tax brackets is that savings are achieved in brackets. If the Bolens can find $2,000 of additional deductions, they will save Federal income taxes at the 33 percent rate.

The last bracket in Exhibit 1-4, 33 percent, is found by taking the difference between $37,800 and the next lower bracket of $35,200. Every dollar earned in this bracket is taxed at the 33 percent rate. The Bolens earned $2,600 subject to tax at the 33 percent rate.

Ignore effective tax rate: The Bolens' effective tax rate was 18.86 percent ($7,132 divided by $37,800). This is a meaningless rate. It merely reflects the total tax paid on the total earnings. Tax savings are effected at the bracket rates. That's what makes them so valuable. Each dollar of additional tax deductions you can locate produces a return based on your last tax bracket.

If you are subject to state income taxes, you will be sliding down a similar scale.

Note at the bottom of Exhibit 1-4 that the total taxes paid by the Bolens reflect the Federal income tax, the Social Security tax, and the state income tax. If the Bolens lived in Washington, D.C., and earned their taxable income from self-employment, their total tax rate on the last dollar earned would have been 55.3 percent. If they had operated as a one-person corporation or a closely held corporation, their total tax rate would have been 57.7 percent. It's not difficult to arrive at the 50 percent tax bracket when you combine and think of all the taxes you pay.

EXHIBIT 1–4. How Tax Brackets Work.

TAX BRACKET COMPUTATIONS DETERMINE YOUR TAX

EXAMPLE: Henry Bolen files a joint tax return with his wife and they pay tax on $37,800 computed as follows:

EARNINGS LEVEL	TAX RATE	TAX
$ 3,400	0%	-0-
2,100	11	$ 231
2,100	12	273
4,300	14	602
4,100	16	656
4,200	18	756
4,400	22	968
5,300	25	1,325
5,300	28	1,484
2,600	33	858
$37,800		$7,132

18.86%
Effective Tax Rate

TOTAL TAXES PAID BY THE BOLENS

	EMPLOYEE		SELF-EMPLOYED		ONE-PERSON CORPORATION	
	Dollars	*Rate*	*Dollars*	*Rate*	*Dollars*	*Rate*
Federal income tax	$ 7,132	33.00%	$ 7,132	33.00%	$7,132	33.00%
Social Security tax	2,533	6.70%	4,271	11.30%	5,179	13.70%
State (D.C.) income tax	3,358	11.00%	3,358	11.00%	3,358	11.00%
	$13,023	50.70%	$14,761	55.30%	$15,669	57.70%

94 PERCENT INCREASE IN SELF-EMPLOYMENT TAXES

The self-employment tax is a Social Security tax for people who work for themselves. It is similar to the Social Security tax withheld from the pay of wage earners, except that it is much greater.

The Social Security tax is based on the premise that some day you will reap the rewards of Social Security. Your payments of self-employment tax contribute to your coverage under our nation's Social Security system. Even if you are currently receiving benefits under Social Security, you'll still have to pay the self-employment tax.

The amount on the bottom line of Schedule C is the amount subject to both self-employment taxes and income taxes. You take the bottom line of your Schedule C and transfer that number to IRS Schedule SE to compute your self-employment tax.

One person—two businesses: If you operate more than one business, you will generally fill out one Schedule C and that total will be the amount subject to the self-employment taxes.

Two persons—two businesses: If your spouse operates a separate self-employed business, each of you must fill out separate Schedule Cs and separate Schedule SEs for your separate businesses.

Tax increase: For 1983, your self-employment tax was 9.35 percent of the first $35,700 of self-employment earnings, or a maximum tax of $3,338. In 1985, you paid 11.8 percent of the first $39,600. By 1989 you will pay $6,484 (13.02 percent of the first $49,800).

These numbers represent a 94 percent

increase in the self-employment tax from 1983 to 1989. This results from the combination of increased tax rates under the new law and estimated increases in the earnings ceiling, i.e., the amount of income subject to the tax. Exhibit 1-5 charts the rate increase and estimated increase in the earnings ceiling.

Effect of tax credit: The rates shown in Exhibit 1-5 are net figures. The self-employment tax rate will be the same as the combined rate for employers and employees, but you will get a credit against the tax. For example, the 1985 rate is 14.1 percent. You will *not* pay the full 14.1 percent, however, because you will get a credit of 2.3 percent. Thus, you will pay 11.8 percent. But the full 14 percent will be credited to the Social Security Trust Funds.

Where will the extra 2.3 percent come from? From the general Treasury, where the rest of our taxes go. For example, if your 1986 self-employment income is $30,000, your self-employment tax will be figured at 14.3 percent, or $4,290. But you get a credit of 2 percent of $30,000, or $600, so your net tax will be $3,690. The remaining $600 will be earmarked for the Social Security Trust Funds and paid from other tax revenues.

SOCIAL SECURITY TAX RATES FOR EMPLOYERS AND EMPLOYEES

Compared to the self-employed, employers and employees were treated pretty well by the new law. Rates increased from 13.4 percent in 1983 to 13.7 percent in 1984. By 1989, the rate will be 15.02 percent. The numbers represent a dollar increase of 56 percent over the next six years. Exhibit 1-6 charts the increases.

NEW TAX ON SOCIAL SECURITY BENEFITS

Beginning in 1984, up to one-half of Social Security benefits are taxed. The tax applies only if one-half of the benefits plus certain other income exceeds a base amount. If the tax applies, the taxable portion is added to gross income on the regular income tax return, Form 1040.

Base amount: For married taxpayers filing jointly, the base amount is $32,000. For married persons who file separately but live together at any time during the year, the base amount is zero. For all other taxpayers, the base amount is $25,000.

Other income: The other income that's added to one-half of the Social Security benefits is called "modified adjusted gross income." Bas-

---

EXHIBIT 1-5.   Self-Employment Tax Increases Through 1989.

YEAR	TAX RATE[1]	EARNINGS CEILING[2]	MAXIMUM TAX[3]
1983	9.35%	$35,700	$3,338
1984	11.30%	37,800	4,271
1985	11.80%	39,600	4,673
1986	12.30%	42,000	5,166
1987	12.30%	44,100	5,424
1988	13.02%	46,800	6,093
1989	13.02%	49,800	6,484[5]

[1]Tax rates shown are net figures. After 1983, the self-employment tax rates are equal to the combined employer/employee rates, but a credit is allowed to reduce the net tax rate to the figures shown above.
[2]The figures for 1987 through 1989 are projections of the Board of Trustees of the Social Security Trust Funds.
[3]The figures shown are rounded to the nearest whole number.
[4]The six-year increase from 9.35% to 13.02% is an increase of 39.25%.
[5]The six-year increase from $3,338 to $6,484 is an increase of 94.25%.

EXHIBIT 1-6. Social Security Tax Rates Through 1989 for Employers and Employees—Combined Rates.

YEAR	TAX RATE	EARNINGS CEILING[2]	MAXIMUM TAX[3]
1983	13.40%	$35,700	$4,784
1984	13.70%[1]	37,800	5,179
1985	14.10%	39,600	5,584
1986	14.30%	42,000	6,006
1987	14.30%	44,100	6,306
1988	15.02%	46,800	7,029
1989	15.02%	49,800	7,480

[1]This figure reflects a 0.3% credit allowed against the employee's portion of Social Security tax. This credit applies in 1984 only.

[2]The figures for 1987 through 1989 are projections of the Board of Trustees of the Social Security Trust Funds

[3]The figures shown are rounded to the nearest whole number.

ically, this means your regular adjusted gross income, except for the new deduction for two-income families, plus tax-exempt interest. (Adjusted gross income is your gross income minus business deductions, IRA contributions, moving expenses, and certain other items. It's the number shown at the bottom of page 1 of Form 1040 (Line 32, usually).

Amount taxed: After adding the modified adjusted gross income to one-half of your Social Security benefits, subtract the base amount from the total. If there is any excess, the tax applies. The amount to include in gross income is one-half of this excess amount, but never more than one-half the Social Security benefits.

Example 1: Smith received $8,000 of Social Security benefits in 1986, and had other income of $23,000, which we will assume is also Smith's "modified adjusted gross income." (Smith had no adjustments or tax-exempt interest.) Smith adds one-half of his benefits, $4,000, to the $23,000 of other income, for a total of $27,000. Since Smith is unmarried, his base amount is $25,000, which he subtracts from $27,000 to get $2,000. One-half of this $2,000, or $1,000, is the amount Smith must include in his gross income in 1986.

Example 2: Assume instead that Smith had other income of $30,000. When the $4,000 (one-half of Smith's Social Security benefits)

is added, the total is $34,000. The excess over Smith's $25,000 base amount is $9,000. One-half of $9,000 is $4,500. However, since the maximum amount included in income is one-half of the Social Security benefits, Smith includes only $4,000 (one-half of $8,000) in his gross income. Exhibit 1-7 contains a brief worksheet showing you how to figure the amount to include in your gross income.

Indirect tax on tax-exempt interest: Because tax-exempt interest is included in the formula for taxing Social Security benefits, it may be taxed indirectly. In example 2 above, if Smith's modified adjusted gross income consisted solely of tax-exempt interest, he still would have been taxed.

NEW SOCIAL SECURITY TAX ON DEFERRED COMPENSATION

Under some tax-free retirement plans, employees may elect to receive cash instead of having the employer put money into the retirement plan. If the employee elects the cash, the regular income tax applies, but if the employee elects to have the money put into the retirement fund, the money is not taxed currently. This election is available under profit-sharing and stock bonus plans. The plans are sometimes called "Section 401(k) plans," since they are authorized by Section 401(k) of the Internal Revenue Code. This option may also

---

EXHIBIT 1-7. Figuring Amount of Social Security Benefits Included in Income.

The Social Security Amendments of 1983 added a provision that makes Social Security benefits subject to income tax after 1983. A short worksheet is shown below. But always remember this:

A MAXIMUM OF ONE-HALF OF YOUR SOCIAL SECURITY BENEFITS
WILL BE INCLUDED IN YOUR INCOME.

Now, let's look at the worksheet.
STEP ONE

1.	Adjusted gross income (Line 32, Form 1040)	_____
2.	Plus: Tax-exempt interest	_____
3.	Plus: Deduction for married couples who both work (Schedule W)	_____
4.	Plus: One-half Social Security benefits	_____
5.	Add Lines 1 through 4	_____
6.	Less: $25,000 (or $32,000 if married filing jointly)	$[25,000]
7.	Excess of Line 5 over Line 6— *If zero, nothing is included in income*	_____

STEP TWO

8.	One-half amount on Line 7	_____
9.	One-half Social Security benefits	_____
10.	Lesser of Line 8 or Line 9— This is amount added to income	========

---

be offered as part of a "cafeteria plan," in which employees have a choice of benefits.

Beginning in 1984, money set aside under this type of plan—whether a straight-cash versus deferred-compensation plan or a cafeteria plan—counts as wages for Social Security purposes. The income tax exclusion will continue to apply.

Example: You receive $20,000 of cash wages and elect to have your employer put $3,000 into your retirement account. $20,000 is subject to income tax, but $23,000 is subject to Social Security tax.

Nonqualified deferred compensation plans: Often used as supplements for tax-free retirement plans, nonqualified deferred compensation plans allow employees to avoid current income tax, although employers get no deduction until the money is actually paid to the employees. Under the new law, any deferred compensation is subject to Social Security tax when the employee performs the services, unless the money is subject to a "substantial risk of forfeiture" at that time.

For example, if the money would be forfeited unless the employee worked for another two years, it would be subject to a substantial risk of forfeiture. As soon as the money is no longer subject to the substantial risk of forfeiture, it will be subject to Social Security tax. In the case just mentioned, the deferred amount would be subject to Social Security tax in two years, after the risk of forfeiture passed.

HOW TO ANALYZE
THE DECISION TO INCORPORATE

There is a lot of hyperbole about the benefits of incorporating. Before you take the plunge, make absolutely certain that you see the results in hard black and white numbers.

If you have already taken the plunge and you want to analyze the merits, make sure you see each operating year in hard black and white numbers.

During recent years, the tax benefits of being incorporated versus operating as a partnership or Schedule C taxpayer have changed considerably. Also, there are no hard and fast rules that make incorporation a good idea for one person and not a good idea for another person. It all depends on each person's particular facts and circumstances.

Exhibit 1-8 contains the type of analysis that you should see regarding your operations. Essentially, your tax advisor should illustrate the bottom line benefits of operating as a corporation compared to using some other form of business. That's the only known way to be sure that you're conducting your business in the proper mode.

One-person corporations: If you presently operate or are thinking of operating your business as a one-person corporation, an analysis similar to that in Exhibit 1-8 should take your tax advisor no more than an hour to prepare. Moreover, you should think of a one-

EXHIBIT 1-8. Overall Dollar Comparison Between Sole Proprietorship and Corporation (One Operating Year).

	SOLE PROPRIETOR	ONE-PERSON CORPORATION
Personal taxable income:		
Professional fees and commissions	$160,000	$160,000
Business deductions	(40,000)	(40,000)
New deductions because of incorporation:		
Extra legal and accounting fees		(2,000)
Payroll taxes (Social Security and unemployment)		(2,375)
Medical insurance and reimbursement plan		(2,000)
Group life insurance plan		(500)
Retirement plan contribution		(22,625)
Salary		(90,500)
Taxable business income	$120,000	-0-
Keogh plan contribution	(15,000)	
Salary		90,500
Itemized deductions	(12,150)	(12,000)
Exemptions	(3,000)	(3,000)
Total personal taxable income	$ 89,850	$ 75,500
Spendable cash:		
Taxable income	$ 89,850	$ 75,500
Personal exemptions	3,000	3,000
Income taxes	(32,374)	(25,300)
Social Security taxes	(3,029)	(2,170)
Nondeductible medical costs	(1,850)	
Nondeductible group life insurance	(500)	
Total spendable cash	$ 55,097	$ 51,030

$4,067 Decrease

	SOLE PROPRIETOR	ONE-PERSON CORPORATION
Economic earnings:		
Net spendable cash	$ 55,097	$ 51,030
Retirement savings	15,000	22,625
Total economic earnings	$ 70,097	$ 73,655

$3,558 Increase

person corporation as one person having two tax pockets. First, you have your personal tax pocket. Second, you have your corporate tax pocket. If money is left in your corporation, you must determine how you will get it to your personal pocket. Thus, the analysis should be extensive enough to show how you can spend the money.

Complications caused by employees: If you have employees, there are significant differences between operating as a sole proprietorship and operating as a corporation. In various sections of this book, we will deal with employee complications. But for purposes of obtaining an economic analysis of your business form, get the employee complications in hard black and white numbers. What you want and must have in order to make intelligent decisions are the bottom line numbers. Your tax advisor can provide them—but will only when asked.

You may have to incorporate: If you operate a business which produces substantial liability for the owners, good legal advice may necessitate operating as a corporation. There are two people who should be involved in your incorporation decision: your attorney and your accountant.

Always obtain an economic analysis: Your situation will be different from that depicted in Exhibit 1-8. You may or may not be able to put more money into a corporate pension plan. You may or may not be able to discriminate against employees. You could obtain the benefits of a medical insurance and reimbursement plan, if Congress doesn't change the law. There are a number of advantages and disadvantages, but all can be defined in terms of economic benefits. See them in black and white.

Working example: Exhibit 1-8 is based on an analysis of Lucky Lumbuck. Lucky is 45 years old, married to Lucy, and has one teenage daughter, Laurie. Lucky's earnings come from professional fees and commissions. His net self-employment income (bottom line from his Schedule C, Form 1040) is $120,000. He has no employees and he makes annual contributions of $15,000 to his Keogh plan.

No corporate income: Exhibit 1-8 shows taxable business income of zero for Lucky's corporation. If money were left in the corporation, it would have been subject to corporate tax. If Lucky wanted the money from the corporation in the form of a dividend, he would have paid income tax on the dividend distribution. That's double taxation. Furthermore, if the money were left in the corporation, the IRS could attack and state that Lucky was the true earner of the income, not the corporation.

Eventually, you will want the money from the corporation. Therefore, your analysis of benefits should be based on the life expectancy of the corporation. This may entail a more detailed analysis than the one in Exhibit 1-8, but it will provide the bottom line benefits. Future dollars should be discounted for inflation. Your tax advisor is well trained to make these computations.

Increase in retirement plan contribution: Under the corporate form, Lucky was able to put $22,625 into his retirement plan. As the sole proprietor, the maximum contribution in 1983 would have been $15,000.

In 1984 and later years, the maximum contributions to either a self-employed or corporate plan are in all material respects the same. Thus, retirement plan contributions are not a factor under current law.

Extra legal and accounting fees: Lucky is very busy with his professional activities and is not much interested in keeping his own books, or taking care of his own legal matters. Legal and accounting fees vary widely depending on the scope of the services rendered and the nature and complexity of your corporation. Lucky's fees fall at the lower end of the fee spectrum, which we estimate to range from $2,000 to $6,000.

Caution: Forming a corporation on a "do-it-yourself" basis in an attempt to minimize or eliminate legal and accounting fees is, at best, a hazardous endeavor. Your attention to form and detail is extremely important if you are to avoid any IRS attacks on your corporation.

Payroll taxes: As a self-employed individual, Lucky paid $3,029 in Social Security taxes. As a corporation, he will pay not only increased Social Security taxes, but also unemployment taxes, and that will increase his payroll tax liability by $1,516. As a corporation, Lucky pays $2,375 in corporate payroll taxes and $2,170 in personal Social Security taxes that are withheld from his personal paychecks. Moreover, the corporate form not only increases Lucky's payroll taxes, but it also increases the administrative paperwork involved in filing quarterly and annual payroll reports for the taxing authorities.

Medical insurance and reimbursement plan: As an individual, Lucky received a $150 tax deduction for all of his medical expenses. As a corporation, Lucky is able to deduct $2,000—an increase of $1,850.

Individuals deduct medical expenses, but (and it's a big but) only to the extent qualified medical expenses, net of any insurance reimbursements, exceed certain percentages of adjusted gross income.

Medical expenses paid by a one-person corporation on behalf of its one Lucky employee and his family are allowed as ordinary and necessary business expenses to the corporation. Thus, as a corporation you could establish a medical reimbursement plan to cover not only your medical and dental expenses, but also those of your family.

Group-term life insurance: If Lucky paid for his own life insurance under the group policy, the payments would not be deductible. However, because Lucky's corporation pays the premium, the amount is deductible to the corporation, even though Lucky is the beneficiary of the policy. Corporations are allowed to provide up to $50,000 of group-term life insurance coverage to employees without including the premium cost in the employee's taxable income.

Reduction in spendable cash: The bottom line for Lucky in his first operating year as a corporation is a $4,067 decrease in his standard of living. Lucky's spendable cash decreased because he put $7,625 more in his retirement plan than he could have if he had not incorporated. Lucky's economic earnings increased by $3,558 during his operating year. In the long run, the increase in retirement savings may more than offset the present value of the decrease of spendable cash. Again, Lucky's tax advisor will be able to work out the details. You need to go to your tax advisor to get comparable information.

Analyzing changes in spendable cash: Once your tax advisor has prepared an overall dollar comparison between operating your business as a sole proprietorship and a corporation, you will be in a position to analyze the changes in your spendable cash. Exhibit 1-9 shows a typical analysis. Note how the decrease in Federal income taxes resulting from incorporation amounts to $7,074 if an additional contribution is made to the retirement plan. If there is no additional contribution to the retirement plan, and Lucky contributes $15,000 for retirement, the decrease in Federal income taxes will amount to $3,338. The bottom line of this comparison is that spendable cash decreases by $4,067 with the additional contribution and by only $178 with no increased contribution to the retirement fund.

By analyzing the changes in your spendable cash, you can determine what types of activities you desire for the year. This is called tax planning. Proper tax planning is predicated on looking at numbers, and you should meet with your tax advisor at least once a year to analyze the numbers.

EXHIBIT 1-9. Analysis of Changes in Spendable Cash.

	ADDITIONAL CONTRIBUTION TO RETIREMENT FUND	NO INCREASE IN RETIREMENT FUND
Change causing an increase in spendable cash:		
Decrease in Federal income taxes	$ 7,074	$ 3,338
Changes causing a decrease in spendable cash:		
Increase in social security and unemployment taxes	1,516	1,516
Extra legal and accounting fees	2,000	2,000
Increase in retirement fund	7,625	-0-
Total decrease	11,141	3,516
Decrease in spendable cash	$ 4,067	$ 178

TAX REDUCTION CHECKLIST

IRS publications to be obtained:

- Publication 535—*Business Expenses and Operating Losses*
- Publication 583—*Information for Business Taxpayers—Business Taxes, Identification Numbers, Recordkeeping*
- Publication 334—*Tax Guide for Small Business*
- Publication 556—*Claims for Refund, Examination of Returns, and Appeal Rights*
- Publication 533—*Self-Employment Tax*
- Publication 17—*Your Federal Income Tax*

Ordinary and necessary business expenses depend on:

- Your individual facts and circumstances.
- Your being in business versus having a hobby.
- Whether the expense has a relationship to your business activities. It must be helpful, needed, appropriate, customary, usual, or normal for you to incur the expense in your business.
- The expense being yours, versus your corporation's or relative's.

Spend a few hours analyzing your business situation:

- Determine who the people are that you do business with, including your prospects, clients, patients, contacts, colleagues, friends, and neighbors.
- Survey the physical assets you use for both business and personal purposes and establish a business basis for deductions.
- Conduct a brief inventory of the expenses you incur on a daily basis. Consider your trips to the grocery store, office supply stores, and other stops where you may purchase both business and personal items.

Make sure your business is not a hobby:

- If you're making money, you have no problem.
- Avoid IRS Form 5213 unless you have a lock on making a profit in any two of the first five years.
- You may use relevant factors in proving your profit motive rather than the "presumption of profit" rule.
- If you fail the profit motive, you may not deduct any operating losses for a hobby.

How business losses may result in tax refunds:

- When your business deductions exceed your business income you may create a new deduction known as the "net operating loss deduction."
- You have 18 years to reap the benefits of your net operating loss deduction.
- The net operating loss deduction may be carried back three years and forward 15 years.
- You may elect to forego the carry-back years and only carry forward the net operating loss deduction.

You may change your prior years' tax returns by:

- Filing Form 1040X or 1120X.
- Making corrections to your past three years' open tax returns using Form 1040X or 1120X.
- Using Form 1045 or 1139 for "quickie" refunds of net operating loss deductions and other carry-backs.

Social Security taxes are rising:

- 1986 rate for self-employed is 12.3 percent—up from 9.35 percent in 1983.

- 1989 rate for self-employed is projected to be 13.02 percent.
- Employer/employee rate for 1986 is 14.3 percent—up from 13.4 percent in 1983.
- Employer/employee rate for 1989 is projected to be 15.02 percent.
- Social Security benefits are taxed beginning in 1984.
- Certain deferred compensation arrangements are now subject to Social Security tax.

How to analyze the decision to incorporate or disincorporate:

- See a comparison of results in hard black and white numbers.
- Have your tax advisor prepare the analysis—it's complicated.
- Make sure analysis deals with spendable cash.

Let's start with the presumption that at this very moment, the IRS is preparing an invitation for you. We agree that there is a certain amount of morbidity in this presumption, but it sets the stage for the reason why good records are required to substantiate your tax deductions. The IRS may be noodling around with your tax return, muttering about some of your deductions and wondering if there is any deceptive practice on your part.

We know you will not be delighted to receive the invitation. And we know you will be enraged to find out that the IRS thinks you might cheat on your taxes. But to begin at the beginning, you are *assumed* to be cheating on your taxes unless you can prove otherwise.

Contrary to an impression that is widespread even among newcomers to our country, you are *not* innocent until proven guilty. The founding fathers of our tax system declared you guilty until you prove you are innocent. Proof is available only in the form of your supporting records and other corroborative evidence.

The IRS has prepared a publication to help you prove that you are not guilty of cheating—Publication 552, *Recordkeeping For Individuals and a List of Tax Publications*. It profoundly directs: "You must maintain records that will enable you to prepare a correct tax return." After some elaboration, the publication goes on to imply that keeping records can also save you money. You may cagily anticipate that we have some objections to this wonderful IRS publication. We can only say that it must be looked at in light of the biggest lie in this land of ours: "We are from the government, and we are here to help you."

The central theme of Publication 552, as in numerous other IRS publications, is that the law does not require any particular *kinds* of records. This so-called "help" continues through a paragraph with phrases such as: "However, you must keep sales slips, invoices, receipts, canceled checks, stock brokerage statements, Forms W-2, W-2P, and 1099, and other documents that prove the amounts you show on your return as income, deductions, and credits."

You will find that you need to keep records of your nontaxable income to prove that it was not taxable. As you will find out shortly, you must keep five specific types of records, including the business reason why you entertained or traveled. You must also keep supporting records to prove that the entries in your appointment book or other records are accurate.

The problem with Publication 552 and other IRS publications is that they simply don't

2

How to Establish
Your Tax Deductions
With Good Records

tell you *enough*. If you read several IRS publications, you *might* learn enough to stay out of hot water. But you *won't* learn enough to actually *cut your tax burden*.

If all of this sounds a bit overwhelming, it should, because that is what we intended. Record-keeping is a burden—your burden—and you have only two choices. You can choose not to keep records and end up paying considerably more tax than you should, perhaps sharing as much as 50 percent of your revenue with the government. Or you can keep records that will establish the validity of your business expenses, prove that you're not cheating, and substantially increase your disposable income.

This chapter will help you establish a simple system for substantiating your business tax deductions. It explains how a diary is used and the necessity for receipts and canceled checks. It reveals the necessity of corroborative evidence and how to obtain it. Finally, it sets the stage for each chapter of this book by showing you how various records intertwine with the substantiation requirements.

WHY CONGRESS REQUIRES DOCUMENTATION

Congress, in spite of what you may have heard, has passed some smart laws. The documentation requirements surrounding your income tax are no exception. Congress knew that people tend to move away from pain or at least from activities that inflict pain. Record-keeping is considered painful to many taxpayers, but avoidance of that pain (by not keeping records) produces more money for the Treasury, reduces our Federal deficit, and provides other good kinds of benefits for the government.

In 1962 Congress considered outlawing all business travel and entertainment deductions. Public criticism focused on entertainment expenses. Congress was faced with the problem of either outlawing entertainment deductions altogether or just making them more difficult to come by. Opting for the second choice, Congress saved legitimate business deductions by enacting strict documentation requirements. Unless your deductions are properly documented, the IRS can totally disallow them.

The exact travel and entertainment requirements enacted in 1962 and since amended are contained in Chapters 3 and 4 of this book. A discussion of how the entire record-keeping system works to save you money follows in the next section of this chapter.

HOW DOCUMENTATION GIVES YOU TAX DEDUCTIONS

You might assume that the only way out of the requirement to keep supporting records is not to claim any deductions. Wrong. You must still keep records to prove that not all of your bank deposits are taxable income. The IRS would be more than happy to forget about your business expenses, but it is still very interested in your business income, your non-business income, and any other revenues you earned or deposits you made into your bank account, slipped under your bed, or buried in your backyard.

We assume you are interested in reducing your taxes. To obtain that objective, you must be armed to face the IRS gladiators in their arena. Deductions draw their attention, and most assuredly the day will come when you'll receive your personal invitation to explain your understanding of the Internal Revenue Code.

Before getting into specific requirements and a definite record-keeping system, let's explore the axiom that the human mind is fallible. If you suffer from the human element of forgetfulness, at least periodically, you can bet that your handicap is costing you some tax money along the way. Failure on your part to record your tax deductions at or near the time they're incurred will probably result in one of two situations, neither of which is beneficial to you. First, your failure to record your tax deductions at or near the time they're incurred violates the rules and could result in disallowance by the IRS. Second, your oversight may lead you to forget to make a claim for the deduction.

We thus approach the record-keeping problem with a two-pronged argument: If you fail to list your tax deductions, you will forget to take them; if you fail to write down your deductions on a timely basis, the IRS will not allow them.

A word about last minute support: You may know or have heard of a creative taxpayer who claims to initiate all supporting documents in just one sitting on April 14th. You may even hear such a person espouse the virtues of this system, saying that it increases deductions and saves time. We would be derelict if we did not point out that the IRS has observed this pestilence throughout the land.

One creative taxpayer, for example, filled out a business diary record at the end of the year. Various pens, pencils, and markers were used to make the entries. Coffee stains were appropriately added to certain pages, and other pages were dragged through the dump. Agatha Christie would have been proud. The physical appearance of the document was magnificent.

The IRS examiner opened the diary, looked through all the entries, and then noticed that the copyright date of the book was one year subsequent to the tax year. Copyright dates usually follow the year of publication, and therefore this diary could not have been published at the time the taxpayer claimed to have made the entries.

Last minute documentation is *not* a wise approach to record-keeping.

COMMON DOCUMENTATION PROBLEMS THAT DESTROY TAX DEDUCTIONS

It's the system that supports your tax deductions. You could, for example, have all the canceled checks and receipts in the world and still fail to prove legitimate tax deductions. Receipts and canceled checks merely prove that you purchased something, not what was purchased.

You may have heard the popular myth that you need to keep your supporting documents only for three years. That's wrong. It is true that the IRS may audit any of your past three years' tax returns, and that you must have supporting documents to prove what's contained in those returns. Therein lies the heart of the problem: Do you have anything in those three years' returns that was purchased prior to the time they were filed?

If you buy a house, for example, you must keep all the records to show how much you paid for it and what you spent for improve-ments. If you sell the house, buy another one, and rollover the gain, you must have records for both houses to support the tax basis in the new property.

Suppose that while reading this book your house burns down. You would be entitled to a casualty loss on the house itself and on its various contents. The only catch is that you must have records to support how much you paid for the items you're trying to deduct. If your records are destroyed in the fire, you have another problem.

The only excuse for not having records is that God took them. If God caused the fire, you have a chance. If you're indicted for arson, however, the story becomes much longer and more complicated than we care to discuss here. In effect, the only excuse for not having records is that God, or someone quite close, took your records and won't give them back. Claiming that your records were lost or stolen by a human being only leads the IRS to the presumption that there is something wrong with your tax return. Allowable deductions for years in which you have no records will be substantially less than for years in which you have the proper supporting documentation.

IRS Publication 552 contains the statement, "Your records must be kept as long as they are important to any Internal Revenue law." This means that you must have records of all your business and personal deductions for a minimum of three years, unless you are cheating on your return. Cheaters are required to keep records forever.

Whether you're cheating or not, you must keep records supporting the cost of all assets you hold during the three years that your tax returns are open. You may need records on your house, your automobile, your clothing, and any gifts or heirlooms you receive. For gifts and heirlooms passed through the family, you should find out (as gauche as this may sound) how much the donor paid for the item. If it was passed down through the line, your basis may go all the way back to your great-grandfather. Sadly, there is no adjustment for inflation.

In one tax case, Robert Ingersoll was quoted as saying, "From the voiceless lips of the unreplying dead there comes no word." Take a quick inventory of all the items you received recently from relatives who you expect to die soon. You may need such records to prove the basis of your property.

If you receive property from an estate, your record of basis is determined by the estate. Generally, your basis for tax purposes is the fair market value of the property at either the date of death or as of a date six months after death. Make sure you keep the notice of estate value for your tax records.

RECORD RETENTION PERIODS

The IRS says that you must have records for as long as such records are important to any Internal Revenue law. That can produce some confusion. From a practical standpoint, you should consider keeping tax records indefinitely.

Exhibit 2-1 contains the statutory periods for keeping tax records. Generally, such records must be kept for three years. However, for property used in your business, you should keep records for as long as you own the property and for your three open tax years after disposition. An "open tax year" begins on the date your return was filed, or due, whichever is later, and continues for three statutory years.

If you purchase property for personal use, you should keep records for as long as you own the property. If sale of the property, such as your personal residence, could result in a taxable event, you should keep records for as long as you own the property and for three years after the taxable event.

Why keep records of property held for personal use? If you sell jewelry at a gain, the gain is taxable. If you sell a personal car at a gain, the gain is taxable. If you do a lot of entertaining, the IRS could invoke the Sutter rule against you and disallow the personal cost of your meals.

Special rule for income averaging: If you income average, you need tax records for the three based period years that are averaged. The IRS can change any of the base years in the averaging period. Thus, if you income average, keep tax records for the "three base period years" that are averaged.

WHY "PACK RATS" PAY LESS TAX

Lack of adequate information enables the IRS to keep sniping at your deductions.

You will be far better prepared to fire the opening shot if you maintain all receipts that might have any relationship, at any time, to your tax return. All grocery bills, for example, should be saved if you have children. You are allowed an exemption for each dependent child, as long as you can prove that you support that child. Children eat groceries, and grocery bills will help establish the cost of the food.

One of the best systems is to retain all receipts for a period of three years. After three years, you may eliminate the receipts for purchases of items not in your home, on your body, in your car, or taken by the children. This will put you in a position to support all of your current deductions. Should you be subject to examination, you may find a few deductions you overlooked. With receipts and corroborative evidence, you are in a position to assert the additional deductions when the need arises.

WHY CAMERA BUFFS PAY LESS TAX

Your receipts, correspondence, appointment book, and other evidence may not be all they're cracked up to be. Good camera sessions can offer credibility to otherwise incredible records.

Take pictures of your business parties, your home, your office, your automobile, and all your valuable assets. Photographs come in handy when substantiating inventories of assets, inventories of friends, and the general way you conduct your personal and business life.

Photographs of your home will establish additional evidence if you ever suffer a casualty loss. If the photographs were taken near the time when you took a physical inventory of your assets or had an appraisal (which you should have periodically), you will be in a strong position to assert that the assets were actually

EXHIBIT 2-1. Record Retention Periods.

GENERAL RULE: You must keep records in sufficient detail to establish the amount of income, deductions, and credits shown in any tax or information return. You must keep them available for IRS inspection for as long as the contents may become material in the administration of any tax law.

FLOWCHART OF GENERAL RULE

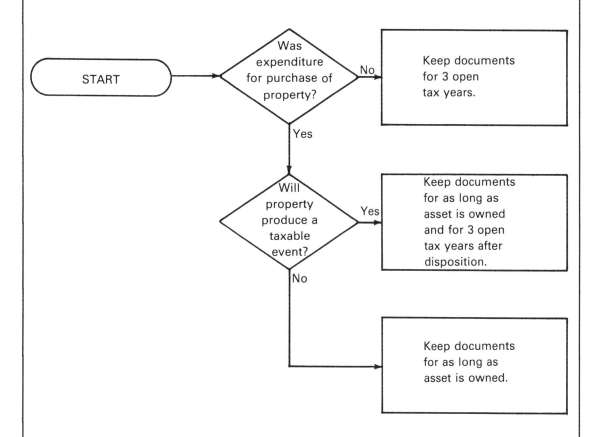

THREE-YEAR RULE: Generally, all income taxes must be assessed within three years from the date the return was filed, or due, whichever is later.
EXTENSION BY AGREEMENT: The statute of limitations can be extended by a written agreement between you and the IRS.
SIX-YEAR RULE: If you omit an amount in excess of 25 percent of gross income shown in the return, a six-year limitation period applies.
NO LIMITATION RULE: If you fail to file a return, or file a fraudulent return, there is no statute of limitations.

destroyed by a casualty. You will have corroborated the entries from the appraiser and from your inventory, adding credibility to your tax file.

WHY CANCELED CHECKS ARE TERRIBLE TAX EVIDENCE

There is manifested in our land the great belief, mostly undisputed, that a canceled check is adequate tax evidence. Think about that for a moment. What does a canceled check prove?

Say that you wrote "RX prescriptions" in the memo section of a check to a drugstore. Will the canceled check prove that you paid the drugstore for prescription drugs?

Observe the situation through the ever-watchful eyes of the IRS. If you actually purchased garden supplies, would the drugstore refuse to take your check because it contained the inscription "for drugs"? No, the drugstore clerks will accept your check no matter what you write in the memo section. So what has the canceled check accomplished? It has proven that you paid the drugstore for a purchase, nothing more.

Do you need to keep canceled checks at all? Yes, you need the canceled checks to prove that you paid for the items purchased. After all, what's to stop you from sitting outside the drugstore and collecting all the receipts that no one else wants? It's the combination of the canceled check with the receipt that proves you actually purchased prescription drugs at the drugstore. However, even that may not be enough.

Again, look through IRS eyes at a situation where a taxpayer has paid a drugstore for thousands of dollars worth of prescription purchases, properly backed up by receipts. What if the taxpayer had no other medical expenses, no expenses for seeing a doctor or lying in a hospital, and no evidence of missing organs or limbs? Obviously, as an IRS auditor you would want to know more.

The total system of record-keeping is important. All the evidence must lead the auditor to the same conclusion you reached. Significant receipts for prescription drugs, unaccompanied by illness or other evidence of drug need, would surely lead you to the conclusion that something was wrong.

What then are canceled checks, by themselves, good for? Contributions are one area of your return where canceled checks usually provide sufficient supporting evidence. But even here, there have been some exceptions to the rule.

One taxpayer claimed church contributions in excess of $500 per week, but the canceled checks showed odd amounts. On one Sunday, for example, the canceled check was for $521.49, and on the following Sunday it was for $577.44. The IRS examiner looking at this case was a little distraught by these large figures to begin with, but the odd amounts created even more suspicion.

The auditor called the pastor of the church to find out about this overly generous parishioner. The pastor went on at great length about what a fine person the taxpayer was; how much he helped the church, even teaching Sunday School; and what a terrific family man he was. During the course of these laudatory comments, the pastor stated that every Sunday the taxpayer helped with the collections. After counting the stipends, the taxpayer would sort out checks, pledges, and cash contributions. Every Sunday, "in order to reduce the chances of burglary," the taxpayer would issue a check for all cash contributions and take the cash for use in his business.

Thus, the alert IRS auditor uncovered a case of fraud. The dishonest taxpayer paid fines and penalties and faced a prison term.

It's the total system that creates tax deductions, not just a canceled check or a receipt, or even a combination of canceled checks and receipts.

THE SELDOM APPLIED, OFTEN ABUSED, $25 RECEIPT RULE

The entertainment and travel rules, discussed in depth in Chapters 3 and 4, substitute a certain amount of receipt collecting for more pencil pushing. The rules do not require receipts for expenditures of less than $25, except for lodging, where all receipts are required to prove that you've actually been away from home overnight. The trade for this relaxation, however, is the need to pinpoint the specific business reasons why entertainment or travel took place. For entertainment expenses you must record *who, where, when,* and *what,* at or near the time the entertainment occurred. The four *w*'s are used to substantiate

- Cost
- Time
- Description
- Business relationship
- Business purpose

The travel rules contain similar requirements in which you have to write down why you took the trip, how long it lasted, and the business purpose.

The unfortunate part of the $25 receipt rule for travel and entertainment is that it is often misapplied to other types of expenses. If you went to the supply store and bought staples costing $1.10 and then had a $22.50 lunch with a client, you would need a receipt for the staples, but no receipt would be required for the lunch. In trade for not needing the luncheon receipt, however, you must record the five elements of substantiation.

If you find the $25 receipt rule confusing, the easiest way to overcome this confusion is to obtain receipts for every possible expenditure, then write down the business purpose for the expenditure at the time it was made. That way, you will have a double-entry record that will help substantiate your deductions.

A SIMPLE SYSTEM: SHOEBOX AND APPOINTMENTS

The documentation system we are about to describe assumes that you're not crazy about the idea of keeping lots of receipts. You do not iron your money for neatness, and you do not have a penchant for keeping records.

If you are in business, you usually have some type of book, piece of paper, or other document where you write down your appointments. If you have an appointment next week, you log it somewhere.

Never throw away the record you use to keep track of your appointments. It's the beginning of a type of journal that establishes your business activities. All other documents you use to support your tax return will emanate from and depend on the appointment

book. The more travel, entertainment, or other deductions you have, the more imperative it becomes to have an appointment book.

The appointment book is the imperative, but all of the surrounding documents are important in establishing the credibility of your tax deductions. Exhibit 2-2 contains an illustration of a documentation system. The focal point of the system is the appointment book. All other documents tie into the appointment book, so it becomes, in the end, a business journal.

The diagram in Exhibit 2-2 shows communication links between the appointment book and

- Receipts
- Canceled checks
- Photographs
- Activity logs
- Monthly summaries
- Retrieval systems

Assuming you've written the names of your business acquaintances, prospects, customers, and others in your appointment book, all of the surrounding data will support your business activities for a day. If you take a client to lunch, for example, the supporting receipt will establish that the lunch occurred. The canceled check, even for a credit card statement, will prove that you actually paid for the lunch. But receipts, canceled checks, and the appointment book by themselves are frequently inadequate to take advantage of some tax rules.

A deduction for an office in the home is one example where you need much more than just receipts, canceled checks, and an appointment book. To take the deduction, you must prove that the office is used exclusively for business. You should have photographs in your file to show the room arrangement, proving that you actually set up an area for exclusive business use. The deduction also depends on using the office in the normal course of business. A guest book goes a long way to establish that you actually did meet and greet clients, prospects, patients, or customers in your home office. You must also prove that you used it on a regular basis. An activity log (an embellishment of the appointment book) helps es-

EXHIBIT 2-2. A Documentation System.

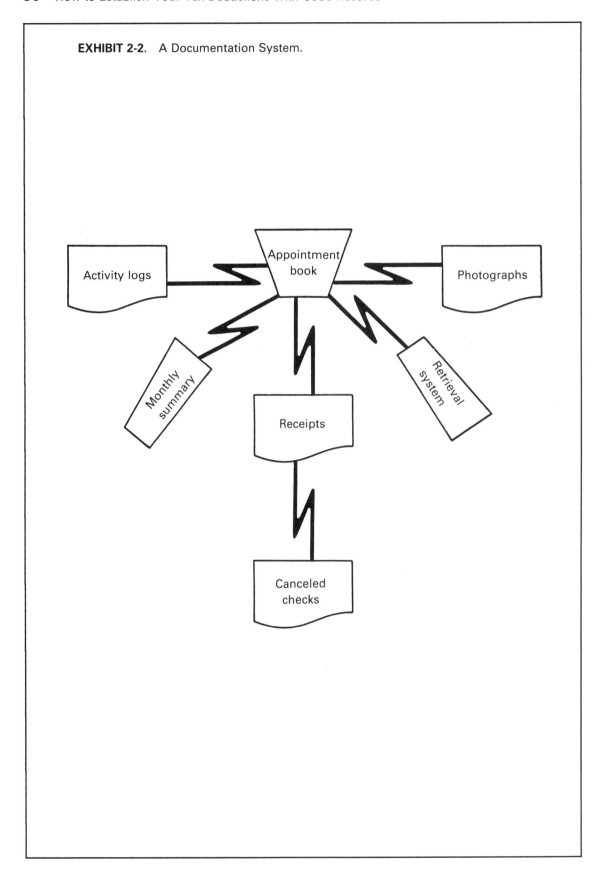

tablish the actual time spent working from your home office and the types of activities that took place. For this deduction, explained in Chapter 8, the appointment book is merely a central recording document. The real support for the deduction comes from photographs, guest books, and activity logs. Receipts and canceled checks prove only what you paid for, not how you used an item or how it entered into your business activities.

Exhibit 2-3 illustrates how receipts and canceled checks are only part of establishing a business travel deduction. It's the entire system that establishes the deduction. To take a deduction for travel expenses, you must pass two tests. First, the trip must be planned for the primary purpose of conducting business in the ordinary and necessary course of your business activities. Second, you must have the necessary receipts and record the specific elements of substantiation required by law for all business trips.

The primary purpose for your business trip is proved by showing intent. Correspondence with clients, registration for a seminar, and other such elements would prove that you were planning the trip for business purposes. If a side trip is to be taken, the business portion of the trip should be planned beforehand in order to establish that the primary purpose of the trip is not pleasure, with business merely incidental.

Once a trip plan is firm, it's a good idea to write the dates in your appointment book. This entry merely corresponds with documents that establish your primary purpose.

Once you're actually on the trip, you are required by the IRS to obtain receipts for all hotel bills. The reason, quite simply, is to prove to the IRS that you were actually out of town overnight. The IRS would also like to know if you went alone or with someone else. Lodging receipts normally show the number of occupants in the room. If there was more than one, the IRS may suspect other activities.

You are also required to have receipts for all expenditures in excess of $25. Usually your airline ticket will cost more than this, and the ticket will prove that you did indeed travel to the destination listed on your lodging receipt. The airline ticket, the hotel bill, and other receipts for $25 or more merely prove that you spent some money. Your appointment

book establishes the business activities that took place on the trip. You are required by law to list why you took the trip, and the appointment book will establish whether you spent those days on business or pleasure. The receipts, the entries in your appointment book, and any resulting actions comprise the complete record-keeping system.

Whether a business trip is successful or not makes no difference as far as your deduction is concerned. After a trip, however, you should have some of the following items: orders; correspondence thanking people for the opportunity to meet them; handbooks from a seminar; agendas from a convention; and notes of your activities related to business.

We mentioned earlier that IRS Publication 552 does not offer any particular guidance on required types of records. After reading that document, taxpayers are left in the lurch as to what's actually needed. IRS examiners are put in no better position. Look at this statement from the IRS Audit Manual on proper records: "The determination of whether any particular taxpayer has maintained adequate records . . . is a matter of judgment based on the facts and circumstances of the particular case." We judge this statement to be somewhat incomplete with respect to record-keeping requirements.

We are also insistently reminded that we are solely responsible for proving our tax deductions. That's why each chapter of this book explains the type of records required to support a particular deduction. Entertainment expenses require one type of documentation, for example, while a deduction for an office in the home requires a different system of documentation. The business automobile, being somewhat more mobile than your home, requires another type of record. If all of these records leave you somewhat breathless, you will be happy to know that after reading this book you will be prepared to put together a perfect documentation system.

The appointment book: The central point of your documentation system is the appointment book. Appointment books are usually rather feeble documents because they list only appointments in the future. To have a sound system, you must strengthen your appointment book by marking down the names of all

EXHIBIT 2-3. How Corresponding Documents Support Business Travel (Example).

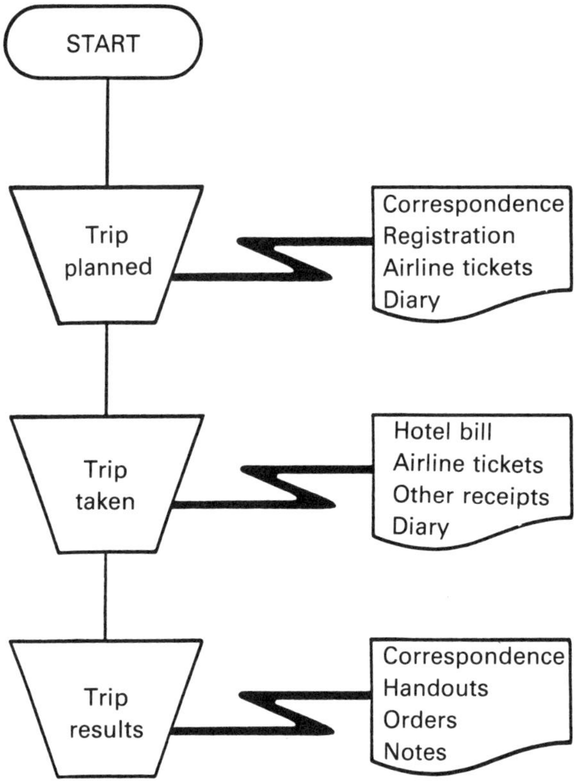

```
                    ┌──────────────┐
                   (    START       )
                    └──────┬───────┘
                           │
                    ╱──────┴───────╲        ┌─────────────────┐
                   │     Trip       │╱╲╱╲   │ Correspondence  │
                    ╲   planned     ╱        │ Registration    │
                     ╲─────┬───────╱         │ Airline tickets │
                           │                 │ Diary           │
                           │                 └─────────────────┘
                    ╱──────┴───────╲        ┌─────────────────┐
                   │     Trip       │╱╲╱╲   │ Hotel bill      │
                    ╲    taken      ╱        │ Airline tickets │
                     ╲─────┬───────╱         │ Other receipts  │
                           │                 │ Diary           │
                           │                 └─────────────────┘
                    ╱──────┴───────╲        ┌─────────────────┐
                   │     Trip       │╱╲╱╲   │ Correspondence  │
                    ╲   results     ╱        │ Handouts        │
                     ╲─────────────╱         │ Orders          │
                                             │ Notes           │
                                             └─────────────────┘
```

business contacts you have each day. This way, your journal puts you in a position to articulate a more complete business schedule.

The appointment book is the focal document. It should show all meetings and contacts with business associates, prospects, clients, patients, or any other individuals with whom you do business. Such a record will come in handy in a number of ways. Failure to record this information can result in your doom.

For example, the appointment book can support your business activities if your entertainment deductions are questioned. Entertainment deductions are claimed in light of the eventuality that the expenditures could result in a profit. In other words, you may entertain prospects to turn them into clients, and you may entertain clients to get new orders.

Let's assume that you're new in business, and that you have developed 100 prospects whom you entertain. When you first started, none of the prospects increased your revenue, and all of your expenditures were one-way. About six months after you made contact and entertained your first prospects, however, they became customers. You continued to entertain those who became customers, and they gave you new prospects. Your appointment book will put you in a position to substantiate this cycle. You could list the 100 prospects, and then show how 10 became clients, and how those 10 eventually gave you 30 new prospects.

Your system must have a cyclical effect. Receipts should support expenditures made for business purposes, and they in turn are supported by entries in the diary. These entries are then corroborated by contracts or other revenue-producing transactions. It may take 25 prospects to generate one client, but expenditures made prospecting are just as deductible as expenditures made on clients.

You must have a total system. Without it you do not have the ability to sell the IRS on your business position. Most tax patsies are doomed in the snows, because their systems do not make any sense. Having receipts for $1,000 of office supplies does not prove you're in any type of business. You must have other evidence to support your claim that you're actually in business.

Any major reductions in your income tax are usually based on one of two happenings. Either you can properly document all of your legitimate deductions or you can spend lots of money to make sure that you show extra deductions for the year. This second choice will cause you to needlessly spend a lot of extra money, and possibly to lose some of it. We rate the option of losing money rather low on the reality quotient.

REIMBURSED EXPENSES OF EMPLOYEE

If you employ other individuals and reimburse them on the basis of an expense account, your employee reimbursed expenses must be supported just as described in all chapters of this book. Your employee does not have to report the expenses or reimbursements for income tax purposes. The employer is responsible for all supporting records.

Employees who do not submit expense accounts: If you are an employee who does not account to your employer for amounts spent on travel, transportation, entertainment, or other expenses, you are entitled to claim "employee business expenses" as a tax deduction providing such expenses *had to be incurred under your employment arrangement*. Thus, if you are in this situation, make sure that you have an employment agreement that clearly states what types of expenses you will be expected to incur and for which you will not be reimbursed.

Partial reimbursement: If you are an employee whose business expenses exceed the amount of your reimbursements and you wish to deduct the excess, you must file a statement with your tax return showing: (1) the total of your reimbursements, and (2) the nature of your occupation, the number of days spent away from home on business, and the total expenses paid or incurred. The expenses must be broken down into components such as transportation, meals and lodging while away from home overnight, entertainment expenses, and other business expenses. Use Form 2106 for reporting such expenses.

Caution—have an employment agreement: If you are in a situation where you are reimbursed for some, but not all expenses, make sure that you have an agreement with your employer which clearly states what type of expenses you are expected to incur on behalf of your employer, and that your salary is considered adequate for you to absorb such expenses. Failure to have such an agreement will often result in disallowance of valid employee business expenses.

Per diem or mileage allowances: An employee is deemed to have made an accounting to his employer if the employee's per diem allowance does not exceed the greater of $44 or the maximum per diem rate authorized to be paid by the Federal Government in the locality in which the travel is performed and if the employee's mileage allowance does not exceed 20 cents per mile. The per diem allowance generally paid by the Federal Government is greater than $44 per day. At one time, the Federal Government allowance for Birmingham, Alabama, was $67 per day and the rate for New York City was $75 per day. If you would like to obtain the Federal Government rates for all localities, your local IRS office has a copy of the latest rates.

Reimbursement policy: An employer's reimbursement policy regarding employee expenses is a critical factor in determining whether certain types of expenses incurred by the employee can be deducted at all.

Several courts have denied employees deductions for automobile expenses where the employer would have reimbursed the employee for such expenses if the employee had submitted a claim. The deductions were disallowed. The expenses were those of the employer, not the employee; accordingly, the expenses were not necessary to the employee's business of being an employee.

If as an employee you have individuals working under you, and your employer expects you to but will not reimburse you for entertaining such employees, make sure you have an employment agreement that clearly states you are expected to entertain and maintain good relations with your subordinates. The absence of such an agreement will cause you to lose valid entertainment deductions.

WHY A CORPORATE RESOLUTION IS ESSENTIAL FOR STOCKHOLDER/EMPLOYEES

If you are a stockholder in a one-person or closely held corporation, you should think of yourself as one taxpayer with two tax pockets. First, you have the corporate tax pocket. Second, you have your personal tax pocket. The IRS has two tax pockets to attack.

If you have two tax pockets, you should have an agreement between them. The agreement should first cover the compensation arrangement between you and your corporation. Second, the agreement should cover the expense reimbursement understanding between you and your corporation.

There is a general tax law that says you cannot pay expenses on behalf of another and receive a deduction for such expenses. Thus, you cannot pay the expenses of your corporation, nor can your corporation pay your expenses.

Example: You operate your business as a one-person corporation. You incur $10,000 of travel expenses on behalf of your corporation. You deduct the expenses on your personal tax return as "employee business expenses." The expenses are not deductible by you. They are corporate expenses, not employee business expenses.

Corporate resolution is the cure: If you had an employment agreement with your corporation and that agreement specified that your salary or other expense reimbursement was to cover expenses incurred on behalf of the corporation, you would be able to deduct the $10,000 of travel expenses as "employee business expenses."

Agreement avoids double taxation: Assume you were reimbursed by the corporation for the $10,000 of travel expenses, but that you failed to properly document your travel expense deductions as specified in Chapter 4. The IRS audits the corporate tax return and disallows the $10,000 travel expense deduction. Moreover, the IRS deems the $10,000 travel expenses as a personal benefit to you and calls the $10,000 expense reimbursement a "constructive dividend." You pay tax on the $10,000. Thus, both you and your corporation are taxed.

If the employment agreement with your company had a "reimbursement obligation" that was also expressed in your corporation's bylaws, you could avoid the double taxation problem. If an expense were disallowed to your corporation because it was not properly documented, your agreement would specify that you would have to reimburse the corporation for such disallowed expenses. Thus, in the above case your corporation would still be denied the $10,000 travel expense deduction, but you would *not* pay tax on the $10,000 because you would have to repay it to your corporation. Thus, you have only one disallowance and you avoid double taxation.

If you operate your business as a one-person or closely held corporation, you must observe corporate formalities or you will put yourself at a supreme disadvantage if you are ever audited by the IRS. You should have corporate resolutions covering your employment agreement, your compensation, your expenses, and other aspects of the corporate business. Such agreement should be in writing between you and your corporation, enforceable under state law, and impose a duty on the board of directors to enforce such arrangements.

WHY GOOD RECORD-KEEPING IS MORE IMPORTANT THAN EVER

Although Congress in 1985 backed off from the "contemporaneous records" requirement passed in 1984, you must have complete records for:

- Traveling expenses (including meals and lodging while away from home, as well as local transportation).
- Entertainment expenses.
- Business gifts.
- Business use of automobiles (and other transportation property), entertainment or recreation property, computers, and other property listed in future IRS regulations. The type of property Congress had in mind was any property used partly for business purposes and partly for personal purposes.

Stiff penalties for noncompliance: If you claim tax benefis and you don't have the required records, you will be socked with a negligence penalty. The negligence penalty is five percent of your tax underpayment.

It gets worse. Congress, when it passed the 1984 law, hinted that the absence of adequate records is tax fraud!

How to comply: We assume the foregoing discussion has piqued your interest in learning how to comply with the new rules. It's easy. Here's how.

Just keep a tax diary—every day of the year. Our employer, the Tax Reduction Institute, publishes a tax diary, which in our somewhat biased opinion we regard as the world's best. The examples of good record-keeping that fill this book use the Tax Reduction Diary. Regardless of what diary you use, you must: (1) know what information to record and (2) record that information on a timely basis.

TAX REDUCTION CHECKLIST

IRS publications to be obtained:

- Publication 552—*Recordkeeping For Individuals and a List of Tax Publications*
- Publication 583—*Information for Business Taxpayers—Business Taxes, Identification Numbers, Recordkeeping*
- Publication 17—*Your Federal Income Tax*

Supporting documents required: The IRS says you must keep the following records to produce and prepare a complete and accurate income tax return:

- Receipts.
- Canceled checks.
- An appointment book.
- Corroborative evidence such as correspondence, activity logs, or guest books.

Record-retention periods:

- All records must be maintained for three open tax years.
- Records must be maintained to support all items you still own or use that are more than three years old.
- It's a good idea to keep all receipts during the three open years, even those not required to support your tax return.
- If you sell one house, buy a new house, and rollover the gain, you must keep records on both the old and new houses so that you can establish your tax basis.
- If your gross income is understated by more than 25 percent, you must keep records for the last six years.
- Cheaters must keep everything forever.

Common documentation pitfalls:

- Canceled checks, standing alone, are not good tax evidence.
- The $25 receipt rule applies only to travel and entertainment deductions.
- You need more than canceled checks and receipts—an appointment book is imperative, as are other supporting documents such as correspondence.
- Failure to establish travel and entertainment expenses contemporaneously with the activity will destroy the deductions.

The shoebox and appointment system:

- Make your appointment book your central recording document.
- Write names of all business acquaintances in the appointment book.
- Use receipts and canceled checks to support expenditures recorded in the appointment book.
- Summarize the appointment book on a monthly basis.
- Establish a business trail of correspondence, contracts, and other corroborative evidence to support your receipts, canceled checks, and appointment book.

Special rules for employees:

- Employers are responsible for record-keeping.
- Employees who claim employee business expenses should have an employment agreement which specifies the expenses that will be reimbursed, if any, and the types of expenses the employee is expected to incur on behalf of the employer.

Special rules for stockholder/employees:

- Employment agreement is essential.
- Double taxation is possible if deductions are not supported.
- Reimbursement obligation agreement can avoid double taxation.
- Corporate payments must be made by corporation and individual payments must be made by individual.

Business entertainment is a must for most professionals. In fact, it's your best promotional tool . . . and it's tax deductible.

Entertainment expenses might be one of the most misused and misunderstood sections of the Internal Revenue Code. This part of the law requires you, the taxpayer, to substantiate your entertainment expenses by doing lots of pencil pushing. Your tax advisor can't be very helpful in this area of tax law. In fact, here you must guide your tax advisor.

Entertainment expenses are constantly monitored by the ever-watchful eyes of the IRS. There are many reasons for this, but perhaps most important is the fact that entertainment should be fun. If it's fun, it must have some personal purpose as well as a business purpose. Playing golf, for example, is inherently a personal activity and sometimes even fun; however, it can also be a business activity. It's the fun aspect of entertainment expenses that creates IRS suspicion. The IRS doesn't believe in fun.

WHY YOUR ENTERTAINMENT EXPENSES ARE PROBABLY UNDERSTATED IN YOUR TAX RETURN

The Tax Reduction Institute (TRI), our employer, conducts periodic taxpayer surveys in connection with its audience profiles for spe-

cific tax workshops. When TRI asked 20,000 workshop participants about specific entertainment deductions, a surprising lack of knowledge emerged. Lack of taxpayer knowledge always benefits the IRS.

In one of the surveys, TRI asked a professional group if business meals with prospects (potential clients) were deductible. The surprising answer from over 35 percent of this group was that such meals were not deductible. That's wrong! Business meals with prospects are just as deductible as business meals with clients and customers.

Another common failing, according to TRI workshop surveys, is the human element of forgetfulness. If you take someone out to dinner on June 10, are you going to remember on April 15 how much you spent? Probably not. Yet the survey showed that over 40 percent of the 20,000 professionals who attended seminars last year maintained no diary or other type of daily tax record.

Failure to keep a daily diary or some other type of tax record will not only result in an understatement of your business lunches and dinners, but you will generally forget such legitimate deductions as taxi fares, coat checks, and valet parking expenses.

The circulation of horror stories among taxpaying groups constitutes another inherent reason why entertainment expenses are

How to Increase Your Tax-Deductible Entertainment Expenses

often understated. The IRS has audit plans for specific groups of taxpayers. Those who have high entertainment expenses are audited more often than those who have low entertainment expenses. Consequently, the IRS will audit many individuals in the same profession during the same year, creating talk about disallowed deductions. This results in much misinformation and more conservative reporting by taxpayers in subsequent years. Crafty on the part of the IRS? Yes. Effective? Definitely!

WHY ENTERTAINMENT EXPENSES INCREASE YOUR CHANCES OF AN IRS AUDIT

Do you like to see good customers keep coming back? Certainly, don't we all? Well, the IRS is no different.

The IRS has unmasked many naughty taxpayers who fail to meet the five rules of substantiation for entertainment expenses. This puts the IRS in a position to disallow their deductions. Disallowances result in more money for the Treasury, and makes the IRS look good, since it is one of the few government agencies that pays for itself.

The documentation rules surrounding entertainment expenses are not only onerous, but exacting. Estimates don't count! When you fail to comply with the rules of proof, your testimony—even if accepted by a judge as truthful—will not be sufficient to support your entertainment expense deductions. Estimates are not allowed. Your documentation also must be timely—recorded at or near the time the entertainment took place.

Documentation is difficult and exacting. The IRS has been paying close attention to the documentation of entertainment deductions. Recently, the North Carolina Association of Certified Public Accountants sent a letter of protest to their congressman. In the letter, they stated, "Since 1979, we have found examinations by Internal Revenue agents of travel and entertainment expenses . . . to be harsh, punitive, lack consistency and any reasonable rationale."

Further research also uncovered other accountants who were complaining that the IRS

is paying too much attention to the documentation requirements for entertainment expenses.

The unfortunate fact is that the IRS is simply enforcing the law as written. So, if you are incurring deductible travel and entertainment expenditures, make sure you follow the rules for documentation discussed in this chapter.

MAGIC WORDS, AND EASY WAYS TO DOCUMENT YOUR BUSINESS MEALS AND MEET THE FIVE SUBSTANTIATION REQUIREMENTS

"I did it my way" won't work with the IRS. For an entertainment expenditure to be deductible, it must pass the "ordinary and necessary" business test and then the substantiation test. The substantiation requirements are stiff, and strictly enforced. Failure to meet them will result in loss of valid tax deductions for your entertainment expenses.

Only one approach meets the specific requirements of the IRS regulations. Each expenditure for entertainment must be proven using the five basic elements which follow.

1. Cost: The cost of each entertainment expenditure must be recorded some place. When the cost is $25 or more, documentary evidence such as a receipt, voucher, or credit card copy must be retained.

2. Time: The time is the date when the entertainment took place. When entries are made in a diary-type document, the date on the diary page is adequate support for time.

3. Description: The nature and place of the entertainment ("business meal at the Dirty Nail") must be described. When a charge slip or receipt is obtained, the nature and place are usually self-evident.

4. Business purpose: Of the five elements, this is the most important. The exact nature of the business discussion or activity must be stated. Be specific, but brief. If no business is discussed, your "purpose" for arranging the meal should be described. All entertainment expenditures other than "quiet business meals" must have a clear description of the business discussion.

5. Business relationship: The IRS wants you to identify the person or persons entertained. Their names, occupations, official titles, and other corroborative information establishing a business relationship should be included. In many cases the person's name with the word "prospect" would be sufficient to establish both the business relationship and the business purpose of a meal.

Again, it is imperative that you meet the five elements of substantiation. The easiest way to get labeled a naughty taxpayer by the IRS is to fail to record all five elements. Missing only one could cost you that legitimate deduction.

When must you record the information: IRS regulations require that you record the elements of your entertainment expenditures at or near the time such expenditures are incurred. Timely recording ensures the maximum deduction for entertainment expenses. If entries are made later, you will not be in compliance with the tax law requirement to keep adequate records. The IRS assumes a lack of total recall.

Records for substantiating entertainment expenses should be maintained in an account book, diary, statement of expenses, or similar type of record (supported by receipts, when required) sufficient to establish the five elements of an entertainment expenditure.

Generally, you will want to record the information the day the entertainment occurred.

You are not required to duplicate information reflected on a receipt or other record. When both records are used, the receipt complements entries in the diary and vice versa.

There are various ways to record your entertainment expenditures; the scope of your present business activity should determine the method best suited to your individual needs. Choose that method from the numerous examples in this chapter.

Magic words: *Prospect* and *client* are two magic words, because these words are all-encompassing, yet both clearly establish a business relationship.

Choose one specific business item to establish your business purpose. Remember, for a "quiet business meal" no business discussion need take place to have a tax deduction. But if a business discussion does take place, record

it and make sure that you delineate the specific topic of discussion.

Entertainment expenditures must be incurred in the ordinary and necessary course of business to be deductible. Effectively, you must expect to make some money because of the entertainment. When you describe a specific element of the discussion or purpose for the entertainment, you must put yourself in a position to prove a profit motive.

Example: Jones sells real estate to make a living. When entertaining Peters, a prospect, Jones discusses numerous properties that are available for sale. In his diary or on his charge slip, Jones writes, "Purchase of 1649 Fourth Place and other properties."

Result: Jones has put himself in a perfect position to substantiate the business benefit expected from the entertainment. He discussed a specific property, 1649 Fourth Place, and if he had made a sale, he would have received a commission.

THREE BASIC TYPES OF ENTERTAINMENT

Your deductible entertainment expenses will fall into one of the following three categories:

1. Quiet business meal: A quiet business meal must take place in the ordinary and necessary course of business. It must occur in conditions conducive to a business discussion. However, no business discussion need take place—that's what makes it "quiet." The five elements of substantiation must be met.

2. Directly related entertainment: Directly related entertainment must take place in surroundings conducive to a business discussion. It is arranged for the purpose of conducting specific business and a substantial business discussion takes place. It is different from a quiet business meal in that a substantial business discussion actually takes place. The five elements of substantiation must be met for directly related entertainment.

3. Associated entertainment: Associated entertainment, also called goodwill entertainment, takes place in a nonbusiness setting. No business discussion occurs during the entertainment. The entertainment *follows or precedes* a substantial and bona fide business discussion, which usually takes place the same day as the entertainment. There must be a link between the business discussion and the entertainment for the purpose of generating goodwill. The five elements of substantiation must be met and linked to the business discussion.

In the succeeding sections of this chapter, we will discuss the three types of entertainment and expand on the definitions. We will also show you how to document each type of entertainment.

WHY YOU HAVE MORE BUSINESS MEALS THAN YOU THINK

To deduct the cost of a business meal, you must meet two tests:

- The cost of the business meal must be incurred in the ordinary and necessary course of your business; and
- You must meet the five elements of substantiation to deduct the cost of the business meal.

Congress once labeled "ordinary and necessary entertainment expenses" to mean any entertainment expense that had a "slight" business element. The courts have consistently held that the terms *ordinary* and *necessary* include any one of the following expenses: helpful, needed, appropriate, customary, usual, or normal.

The definitions still apply to business meals. There are two basic types of tax business meals. First, there is the "quiet business meal." Second, there is the "directly related business meal." Business meals may also occur in a variety of settings, such as a restaurant, a country club, or your home. To be deductible, a business meal need only be incurred in the ordinary and necessary pursuit of your business activities.

Well then, what are your normal types of business activities? What individuals must you meet and know in order to make money?

Example: Curtis sells real estate full time. In order to make sales, he must meet prospects, who later become clients and ultimately give referrals to other prospects.

Question: Who are Curtis's prospects?

Answer: Just about everyone. Actually, Curtis may have to go through twenty prospects to find a client. But the lifeblood of Cur-

tis's real estate sales is his list of prospects; they are part of the ordinary and necessary conduct of his business. Therefore, entertaining prospects is appropriate to his line of work.

In fact, in Curtis's situation, one would have to ask how he could have a lunch or dinner that was not tax deductible, since almost everyone is a prospective client.

The starting point for determining your deductible business meals is to find out what is included in the ordinary and necessary course of your business. Doctors, for example, depend on referrals, often from other doctors, to obtain new patients. Attorneys depend on other attorneys, banks, accountants, and others for referrals.

If you depend on referrals, prospects, or others as a source of your business and you have a substantial number of business meals, it is a good idea to establish a matrix that identifies the prospects you had to go through to find a client. The chart in Exhibit 3-1 provides a good example of how Brady, a medical doctor, obtains the majority of his clients. The chart establishes that the lifeblood of Brady's business is referrals and that the more he entertains the more referrals he obtains.

The chart in Exhibit 3-1 applies to all entertainment, not just business meals. Also, Brady must record the five elements of substantiation involved in each entertainment.

What if no business results? Dr. Brady entertained Dr. Cole four times in 1983 and no business resulted. Is the entertainment still deductible? Absolutely. Dr. Brady's purpose in entertaining Dr. Cole was to establish Dr. Cole as a referral source. The fact that it did not work out does not mean there was no business purpose.

Dr. Brady also entertained Dr. Wallin in 1984 and 1985. Six entertainments resulted in no referrals. The expenses in entertaining Dr. Wallin are still just as deductible as the expenses of entertaining Dr. Allen, who brought in all kinds of revenue. Deductibility depends on intent and purpose. It does not depend on results.

No business need be discussed: An often overlooked section of the Internal Revenue Code is the "quiet business meal" exception. Under this exception, you are allowed to de-

EXHIBIT 3-1. Chart for Tracking Sources of Business (Example).

FACTS: Brady, a medical doctor, practices at a clinic and obtains the majority of his clients by referral. He develops the following chart to prove the importance of referrals to his economic health.

1983

Prospective Referral Source	Times Entertained	Patients Referred	Revenue Received
Dr. Allen	2	8	$ 5,100
Dr. Barton	4	3	500
Eli Brison	3	6	4,300
John Bush	5	1	50
Dr. Cole	4	0	0
Dr. Feller	1	7	7,200
Dr. Katz	2	6	4,700
Liz Murphy	3	15	18,010
Dr. Oliver	2	5	2,131
Jim Steele	3	1	5,415
Dr. Wallin	0	0	0
Other referrals	0	18	9,000
Walk-ins	0	11	7,000
Totals	29	81	$63,406

1984			1985		
Times Entertained	Patients Referred	Revenue Received	Times Entertained	Patients Referred	Revenue Received
6	21	$23,421	8	17	$ 23,916
4	3	711	3	8	8,416
3	11	685	2	16	7,594
3	15	29,614	9	2	314
4	13	11,619	1	22	19,986
3	2	4,214	1	6	1,092
5	11	16,434	4	5	1,461
7	3	4,617	5	26	35,916
2	14	2,871	8	6	5,117
3	1	50	1	2	1,561
1	0	0	5	0	0
0	29	23,416	0	35	17,615
0	18	6,819	0	51	29,682
41	141	$124,471	47	196	$152,670

duct the cost of food and beverages served to an individual in an atmosphere conducive to business discussion, even though no business is discussed.

Example: Wilson, a life insurance agent, meets a client for lunch to discuss the client's policy base and maintain a valuable referral source. Wilson and his client drink seven martinis and end up taking taxis home, never getting around to a business discussion.

Result: Wilson has a valid tax deduction provided that he meets the five elements of substantiation.

To avail yourself of this "quiet business meal" exception, you must have the food or beverage furnished for the primary purpose of furthering your trade or business and not primarily for a social or personal reason. The business purpose is generally shown by the present or potential relationship or the guest who is entertained. A medical doctor specializing in stomach pains could entertain a general practicing doctor for the sole purpose of obtaining referrals. Actual referrals need not be discussed, nor obtained, during the entertainment. The mere presence of the guest can indicate that the purpose was referrals.

Meeting the five elements of substantiation: Exhibit 3-2 contains an example of how Warin, an attorney, records the five elements of substantiation for a lunch with Rogers. Warin records the cost of all entertainment in his daily appointment book (the pocket accounting system described in an advertisement in the back of this book).

Hint: Note that Warin recorded the cost of a taxi to and from the Palm restaurant where lunch had taken place. Had Warin relied on just the receipt to take his tax deduction, he would have overlooked the taxi fares. Use a diary to record all of your entertainment expenses to avoid overlooking expenses connected with the entertainment. Moreover, record the information the day the entertainment occurs to ensure compliance with the contemporaneous and timely recording requirements.

You already have a diary: If you record your appointments in advance in a date book, you have the beginnings of a business diary. Many times, a simple update of your appointment notation is all that is necessary. If Warin, the attorney in Exhibit 3-2, had arranged the lunch with Rogers a week in advance, a notation of that appointment would have been made in Warin's diary. It may have stated, "Lunch, Palm restaurant, Rogers." After the lunch, all Warin had to do was write the business reason and cost of the lunch under the appointment entry in the diary.

Business setting: The IRS regulations state that the food or beverages must be served in surroundings "conducive to business discussions." This means that the surroundings must not contain substantial distractions to business discussions, such as a floor show.

A breakfast, lunch, or dinner meeting in a restaurant, hotel dining room, eating club, or similar establishment would satisfy the "conducive surroundings" test. Similarly, a drink served in a cocktail lounge or hotel bar without distracting influences would meet this requirement. On the other hand, business distractions would generally be present in nightclubs, at sporting events, and in large cocktail parties or sizeable social gatherings.

Directly related business meals: Many of your business meals will be what tax law calls "directly related." You will want such meals if you want to deduct the cost of activities which could follow a business meal, such as taking someone to the theater. A meal is directly related if it is arranged for the purpose of conducting specific business and a substantial business discussion takes place.

Essentially, a business meal is directly related if during the meal you actively pursue something that will make you money either the day of the business meal or sometime in the future.

Exhibit 3-3 shows how Smith, a real estate salesperson, uses a charge card receipt to record a "directly related" business meal with Jones.

The entry Smith makes at the bottom of the charge receipt meets the five elements of substantiation and Smith does not have to duplicate any of that information in a daily diary. The charge receipt standing by itself is adequate support for this business meal deduction.

The meal is directly related because Smith actively pursues the sale of a specific property, 1549 Fourth Place. By bringing a copy of the property description and showing it to Jones during lunch, Smith *actively* tries to sell Jones the property. It turns out that Jones is not interested in that property or others which Smith brings up; nevertheless, the meal is directly related to Smith's business. Thus, not only is the business meal deductible, but if Smith had taken Jones to the theater after the meal, the theater tickets would have been deductible as well. We'll discuss this in more detail in the "associated with" entertainment section of this chapter.

The IRS requires you to keep a record of entertainment expenses contemporaneously with the entertainment. A charge slip provides you with three elements of support already. When the establishment fills out the credit card it will give you the name of the

EXHIBIT 3-2. Recording Business Meals in a Diary (Example).

FACTS: Warin, an attorney, takes Rogers, an accountant, to lunch. During lunch, Warin and Rogers discuss Sunday's ball game. Rogers is not Warin's client, but he has referred several clients in the past and Warin would like to obtain his business.

ENTRY IN WARIN'S DIARY:

Tax Reduction Diary	Circle Month & Day	JAN FEB MAR APR MAY JUN JUL AUG SEP OCT NOV DEC SUN MON TUE WED THU FRI SAT	**15**

TRANSPORTATION

To Do (Priority)		Automobile	Gas & Oil	12		
☐		Check One	Repairs/Main. Wash/Wax	13		
☐		☐ Local	Insurance Tags/Licenses	14		
☐		☐ Out-of-Town	Auto Lease Other	15		
☐		Circle Car #				
☐		1 2 3	Total	17		
☐			Parking & Tolls	19		
☐		**Hired Transportation**	Airfare	21		
☐		Check One	Skycaps	22		
		☒ Local	Auto Rental	23		
Appointments	Automobile Mileage Bus / Per	☐ Out-of-Town	Bus/Taxi Subway	24	4	00
8:00			Total	25	4	00

TRAVEL

8:30						
9:00		Where (City) Where _ _ _ _ _ _	Breakfast	31		
9:30		Where _ _ _ _ _ _	Lunch	32		
10:00		Where _ _ _ _ _ _	Dinner	33		
10:30		Why (Business Reason)	Lodging	34		
11:00			Tips/Laundry	35		
11:30			Other	36		
12:00 Rogers — Palm			Total	37		

ENTERTAINMENT

12:30		Who (Name & Title)	Breakfast	41		
1:00		Rogers, CPA	Lunch	42	24	00
1:30		Where Palm Rest.	Dinner	43		
2:00		Wash. DC	Cocktails	44		
2:30		Why (Business Reason)	Associated	45		
3:00		Referral Source	Home/Other	46		
3:30		Prospect	Total	47	24	00

EDUCATION

4:00		Institution/Sponsor	Tuition	71		
4:30		Location	Books	72		
5:00			Supplies	73		
5:30		Subjects	Total	74		

RESULTS: DEDUCTIBLE BECAUSE DIARY ENTRY MEETS TESTS 1 AND 2.

TEST 1—Ordinary and Necessary Course of Business: Yes, Warin is accomplishing two things. First, the lunch is a form of advertising and may sway Rogers to become a client. Second, Warin is maintaining a referral source.

TEST 2—Meets Five Elements of Substantiation: Yes, as follows:

1. **Cost:** Recorded "$24.00" in diary. No receipt or other support is necessary.
2. **Time:** Warin's diary page has the date at the top of each page.
3. **Description:** "Lunch—Palm Restaurant" recorded in diary adequately describes the type of entertainment.
4. **Business purpose:** "Prospect" and "referrals" define reason for lunch. Since lunch is a "quiet business meal" no discussion of business was needed to make the lunch deductible.
5. **Business relationship:** Same as purpose. Often elements 4 and 5 are intertwined and self-evident.

EXHIBIT 3-3. Using a Charge Card Receipt to Record Business Meals (Example).

FACTS: Smith, a real estate salesperson, takes Jones, a prospect, to lunch. Smith and Jones discuss several properties and have a good time; however, Jones does not purchase or even agree to look at a property.

ENTRIES ON CHARGE SLIP:

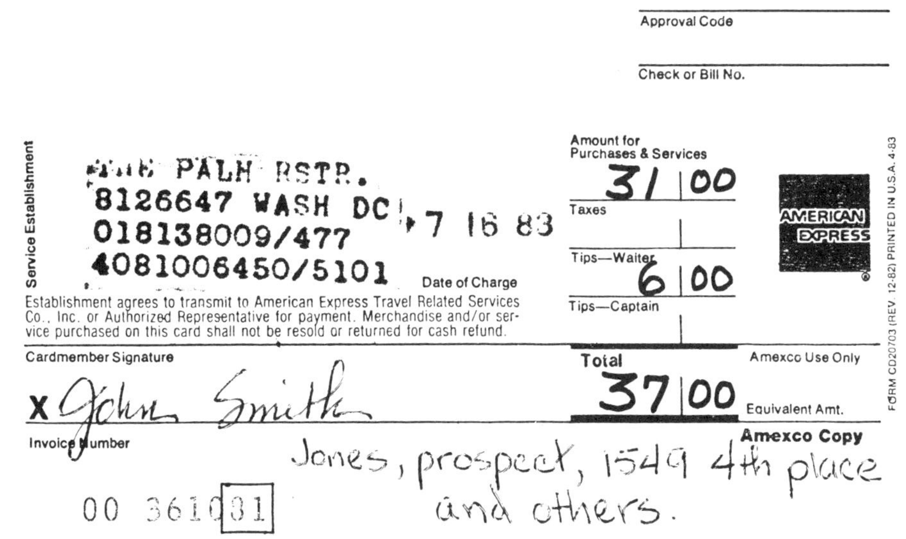

Approval Code

Check or Bill No.

```
THE PALM RSTR.
8126647 WASH DC    7 16 83
018138009/477
4081006450/5101    Date of Charge
```

Service Establishment

Establishment agrees to transmit to American Express Travel Related Services Co., Inc. or Authorized Representative for payment. Merchandise and/or service purchased on this card shall not be resold or returned for cash refund.

Amount for Purchases & Services **31 00**

Taxes

Tips—Waiter **6 00**

Tips—Captain

Cardmember Signature

X *John Smith*

Invoice Number

00 361081

Total **37 00**

Amexco Use Only

Equivalent Amt.

Amexco Copy

Jones, prospect, 1549 4th place and others.

FORM CO20703 (REV. 12-82) PRINTED IN U.S.A. 4-83

RESULTS: DEDUCTIBLE BECAUSE TESTS 1 and 2 ARE PASSED.

TEST 1—Ordinary and Necessary Course of Business: Yes, Smith must prospect to make money. It may take ten, twenty, or even thirty prospects to find a client.

TEST 2—Meets Five Elements of Substantiation: Yes, as follows:

1. **Cost:** Restaurant recorded "$37.00" at the time of purchase. Amount exceeds $25.00; therefore, a receipt is required and the charge slip is an adequate receipt.
2. **Time:** Restaurant recorded date on charge slip. Date and time are synonymous under this regulation.
3. **Description:** Obviously lunch from charge record.
4. **Business purpose:** Attempt to sell a specific property, among others.
5. **Business relationship:** Prospect.

Hint: Record amount from charge slip in diary to assure deduction and jog memory as to other expenses such as coat check, valet parking, and taxis.

---

restaurant, the date, and the amount. All you have to do is supply the name of the person entertained, and business purpose and relationship. Generally, this can be accomplished in less than ten words.

Hint: If you use an American Express or other type of charge card where the service establishment gives you a carbon of the charge ticket, write the elements of support on the face of the charge slip so that it will be reproduced on the carbon copy. This little trick provides "proof" of contemporaneous recording.

The best record-keeping combination: If you use only a daily diary to record your expenses, you will have difficulty "proving" that you recorded the information on a timely basis (contemporaneously with the activity). If you use only charge card receipt carbon copies to support your entertainment expenses, you will forget many of the expenses connected with your entertainment. The best bet is to use a combination of the charge card receipt and diary as illustrated in Exhibit 3-4.

Had Perry used only the charge card to record the business lunch, he may have forgotten the taxis and the coat check.

When Perry signed the credit card receipt, he noted the name "Day—referral relations" at the bottom of the charge card receipt. He duplicated that information in his daily diary where the expense was recorded. The duplicate entry is not necessary for IRS

EXHIBIT 3-4. Using a Charge Card Receipt and Diary Combination to Record Business Meals (Example).

FACTS: Perry, a medical specialist, takes Day, a general practice medical doctor, to lunch to maintain a referral source.

ENTRY IN PERRY'S DIARY:

Tax Reduction Diary

Circle Month: JAN FEB MAR APR MAY JUN / JUL AUG SEP OCT NOV DEC

& Day: SUN MON TUE WED THU FRI SAT

15

To Do (Priority)

☐
☐
☐
☐
☐
☐
☐

Appointments (Automobile Mileage: Bus | Per)

Time	Appointment
8:00	
8:30	
9:00	
9:30	
10:00	
10:30	
11:00	
11:30	
12:00	
12:30	
1:00	Day – Palm
1:30	
2:00	
2:30	
3:00	
3:30	
4:00	
4:30	
5:00	
5:30	
6:00	
6:30	
7:00	
7:30	
8:00	
8:30	
9:00	

TRANSPORTATION

Automobile — Check One: ☐ Local ☐ Out-of-Town; Circle Car # 1 2 3

Item	No.	Amount
Gas & Oil	12	
Repairs/Main. Wash/Wax	13	
Insurance Tags/Licenses	14	
Auto Lease Other	15	
Total	17	
Parking & Tolls	19	

Hired Transportation — Check One: ☐ Local ☐ Out-of-Town

Item	No.	Amount
Airfare	21	
Skycaps	22	
Auto Rental	23	
Bus/Taxi Subway	24	
Total	25	

TRAVEL — Where (City): Where ______ / Where ______ / Where ______; Why (Business Reason)

Item	No.	Amount
Breakfast	31	
Lunch	32	
Dinner	33	
Lodging	34	
Tips/Laundry	35	
Other	36	
Total	37	

ENTERTAINMENT — Who (Name & Title): Day MD; Where: Palm Rest. Wash. DC; Why (Business Reason): Referral Relations See chart of referrals

Item	No.	Amount
Breakfast	41	
Lunch	42	24 00
Dinner	43	
Cocktails	44	
Associated	45	
Home/Other (Coat check)	46	2 00
Total	47	26 00

EDUCATION — Institution/Sponsor; Location; Subjects

Item	No.	Amount
Tuition	71	
Books	72	
Supplies	73	
Total	74	

MISCELLANEOUS

Club	1	2	3
Direct			
Personal			
Associated			

Each day a club is used, place one X in one box.

Business Gifts — Description of gift

Item	No.	Amount
Club Dues 1 2 3 (Circle One)	80	
Office Supplies & Postage	90	
Dues & Publications	91	
Interest	92	
Wages	93	
Rent	94	
Repairs	95	

Exhibit 3-4. *continued*

CHARGE CARD RECEIPT:

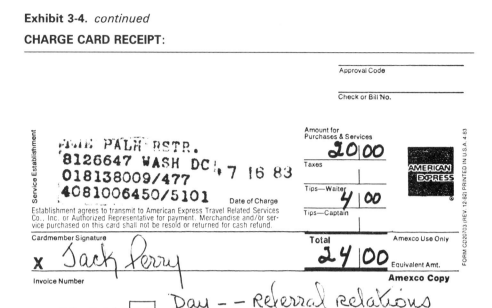

RESULTS: DEDUCTIBLE BECAUSE COMBINATION OF DIARY ENTRY AND CHARGE CARD RECEIPT PASS TESTS 1 and 2.

TEST 1—Ordinary and Necessary Course of Business: Yes, Perry is maintaining active relations with a referral source, the lifeblood of obtaining new patients.

TEST 2—Meets Five Elements of Substantiation: Yes, as follows:

1. **Cost:** Restaurant records "$24.00" on charge card and Perry maintains a copy for the shoebox.
   Note: No receipt is necessary because cost is less than $25.
2. **Time:** Date is recorded twice, once on charge card receipt and once at the top of appointment book page.
3. **Description:** Lunch from diary and restaurant name from both diary and charge card receipt.
4. **Business purpose:** Lunch with a referral source from diary entry.
5. **Business relationship:** Evident from purpose—referral source.

regulations; however, from a practical standpoint it is desirable. The IRS auditor will be looking at the diary first, and the receipt second. If the diary contains all the necessary information, in good form, the auditor spends little time on your entertainment expenses. Moreover, when the auditor looks at the carbon copy which duplicates the information, the entertainment expense audit may be put to rest at that point.

WHY YOU SHOULD KEEP TRACK OF NONDEDUCTIBLE PERSONAL MEALS

Assume that it's a beautiful Saturday afternoon, and you're at home relaxing in the shade with a wonderful book. You get hungry, run to the refrigerator, and grab a piece of chicken left over from last night's dinner. Should you record in your diary, "piece of chicken, 72 cents"?

The answer is yes! There are two basic reasons why it's important to record the cost of personal meals. First, there's a rule on "Dutch treat" business meals that allows you to deduct the business portion of your own tab when you go Dutch treat for business reasons. Second, the "Sutter rule" may act to disallow a portion of your business meals when such meals absorb substantial amounts of your typical personal living expenses.

Save all grocery bills: If you are ever subject to an IRS collection effort on your business meals, you will find grocery bills to be a handy item. Grocery receipts put you in a position to show how much it costs to eat at home, either alone or with the family. But we hope you never need the grocery bills to fend off the IRS.

You need grocery receipts to build your deductions under the Dutch treat rule and to repel any applications of the Sutter rule. We will talk about the Dutch treat business meals in the next section of this chapter; meanwhile, let's discuss the Sutter rule.

Sutter rule: The Sutter rule is associated with a court case in which Sutter, a doctor practicing industrial medicine, claimed ordinary and necessary business expenses for the cost of lunches while attending Chamber of Commerce meetings. The cost of these lunches was disallowed because there was no evidence that the cost of such meals was greater than the cost of his personal meals. The court held that the Chamber of Commerce lunches cost about the same as personal lunches and that Sutter could overcome the personal expense portion only by "clear and detailed evidence" that the amount spent for the lunches was in excess of what he would have incurred for personal purposes.

The IRS has consistently stated that it will limit application of the Sutter rule to "abuse cases" involving taxpayers who claim deductions for substantial amounts of personal living expenses. Application of the Sutter rule appears to be a matter of administrative convenience for the IRS. If it has the whim to invoke the Sutter rule, IRS will be upheld by the court and the IRS knows that. Therefore, the only protection for taxpayers is the ability to prove that business meals cost more than personal meals.

Protect yourself with an average personal meal cost: Since the IRS has a rule which it may or may not enforce against you, your best protection is to have the evidence ready to repel any IRS attacks. If you generally go to lunch as a means of developing your customer base, write the cost of personal lunches in your daily diary. You will want to record at least 30 personal lunch days, so you will probably have to record personal lunches for a period longer than a straight 30 days. The 30-day recording will provide you with solid protection for your business lunches. Exhibit 3-5 contains an example of how Peck, a garment salesman, records the cost of personal lunches in his appointment book.

Example: You take a customer out to dinner and spend $40—$20 for you and $20 for the customer. If you cannot prove an average personal meal cost, the IRS could invoke the Sutter rule and disallow $20. If you have a personal meal average cost of $8, the Sutter rule could limit your deduction to $32. However, the IRS says it will not enforce the Sutter rule except in cases of so-called abuse. *Result*: The entire $40 is deductible.

What is abuse? The IRS used whim to define abuse.

Example: Fenstermaker usually ate lunch with two other company executives at a nearby hotel or at some other restaurant in town. Many times other company employees or outside consultants joined them to discuss business over lunch. The executives paid for the meals and received reimbursement from their companies. They never included the reimbursements in income. The IRS attacked them under the Sutter rule.

Result: The court ruled that the lunches were legitimate business meals. But, since none of the executives could show that his lunch expenses exceeded what he would have spent on a nonbusiness lunch, the court held the full cost of the lunches as nondeductible by the corporations and includable in the income of the executives, a double-jeopardy penalty we'll discuss in more detail later.

Further, the executives argued that the IRS had departed from its long-standing policy of applying the Sutter rule only in "abuse" cases. The court saw no merit in that argument. According to the court, the IRS cannot change the basic rule of nondeductibility of personal expenses. Further, the court stated that the IRS is not bound to follow its own statement of applying the Sutter rule only to so-called abuse cases. The IRS may treat the Sutter rule any way it likes in any tax year. Now, that's whim!

Best approach: Always deduct 100 percent of the expenses for picking up the tab for anyone else. The IRS has stated that it will continue to allow a deduction for 100 percent of business meals, and that it will apply the Sutter rule only in abuse cases. Nevertheless, you will want to keep track of your personal lunches just in case the IRS gets whimsical.

HOW TO DEDUCT THE BUSINESS PORTION OF DUTCH TREAT BUSINESS MEALS

When you and a business associate go to lunch and you pick up the entire tab for the two of you, you are generally allowed a tax deduction for 100 percent of the tab. But what happens when you and a business associate go to lunch and each person pays his or her own way?

You will be pleased to know that any cost of a Dutch treat business lunch in excess of personal lunch expenses is tax deductible.

Example: Peck, a garment salesperson, goes to lunch with Nelson, a prospective customer. Peck and Nelson share the tab. Peck's portion comes to $17.

Result: Peck has had a Dutch treat lunch. He picked up his share of the tab. Peck also has evidence (his 30-day test) supporting an average personal lunch cost of $3. Thus, Peck has a deductible Dutch treat business lunch of $14 ($17 minus $3).

When Peck has a business lunch, he usually goes to a sit-down restaurant. When he has a personal lunch, he usually goes to a fast-food restaurant, spending considerably less. For 30 consecutive days, Peck keeps track of his personal meals at the fast-food restaurants

by writing in his appointment book the name of the restaurant, its location, and the amount spent. His average cost for such personal lunches on working days amounts to $3.

Result: When Peck has a Dutch treat business lunch, he subtracts the $3 from whatever amount he paid for his share of the lunch. Exhibit 3-6 contains an example.

Is it worth it? You decide. Peck has 40 Dutch treat business lunches during the year. His average excess cost is $14. His deductible Dutch treat business lunches amount to $560.

Breakfast, lunch, and dinner: When dinners and breakfasts are involved as well as lunches, and these meals are consumed in restaurants, the recording procedures are the same as those in Exhibit 3-5. When such meals are eaten at home, however, the task becomes more complicated. There are basically two ways to compute the cost of personal meals consumed at home. First, you could write down the actual items consumed and determine the cost of each item. Two eggs for breakfast, when a dozen eggs cost $1.20 would cost 20 cents ($1.20 divided by 12 times 2). If you need to determine actual costs only a few times during the year, you should consider writing down the individual items consumed.

The second method uses actual grocery bills to make an allocation by members of the family. If, for example, the grocery bill for a week amounts to $150 and there are four people in the family, your computation may be quick and dirty. You can determine, for example, that the average cost of groceries for a week is $37.50 per person ($150 divided by 4). Since the grocery bill is for a week, you can determine that the average daily cost is $5.36 ($37.50 divided by 7). You can then allocate the average daily cost to each of the three meals consumed at home, or you may simply divide the average daily cost by three to determine an average meal cost of $1.79 ($5.35 divided by 3).

Once you've made computations of your average personal meal cost, you are in a position to record the cost of Dutch treat business meals, and deduct them.

EXHIBIT 3-5. Recording the Cost of Personal Lunches (Example).

FACTS: Peck, a garment salesperson, records the cost of personal lunches in his appointment book to substantiate his usual personal lunch costs. Such entries put Peck in a position to deduct Dutch treat lunches, and neutralizes the effect of the Sutter rule, if it is invoked by the IRS.

ENTRY IN APPOINTMENT BOOK:

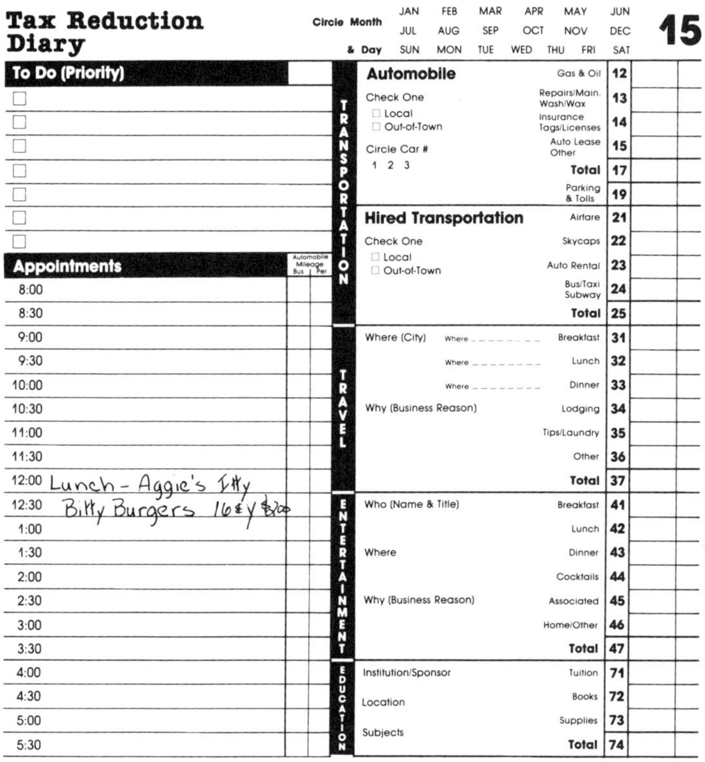

Tax Reduction Diary			
Circle Month JAN FEB MAR APR MAY JUN / JUL AUG SEP OCT NOV DEC **15**			
& Day SUN MON TUE WED THU FRI SAT			

Appointment book page showing Transportation, Travel, Entertainment, and Education sections. Handwritten entry at 12:00: "Lunch – Aggie's [?]" and at 12:30: "Bitty Burgers 16$ [?] $.00"

RESULT: Peck has evidence of a personal lunch.

AVOIDING COMMON MISTAKES IN RECORDING ASSOCIATED ENTERTAINMENT

"Associated" entertainment takes place in a non-business setting but occurs for business reasons.

An entertainment activity is associated with the active conduct of your trade or business when you *show there is a clear business purpose for the expenditure, and the activity is linked to a substantial and bona fide business discussion.* Thus, the principal character or aspect of the combined entertainment and business activity must be the active conduct of business. This requirement, however, does not make you spend more time on business than on entertainment.

What is associated entertainment? The "associated with" entertainment rules apply to

EXHIBIT 3-6. Recording the Cost of a Dutch Treat Lunch (Example).

FACTS: Peck, a garment salesperson, goes to lunch with Nelson, a prospective client, for the purpose of making Nelson a customer. Both Nelson and Peck pay their own way—go Dutch treat.

ENTRY IN DIARY:

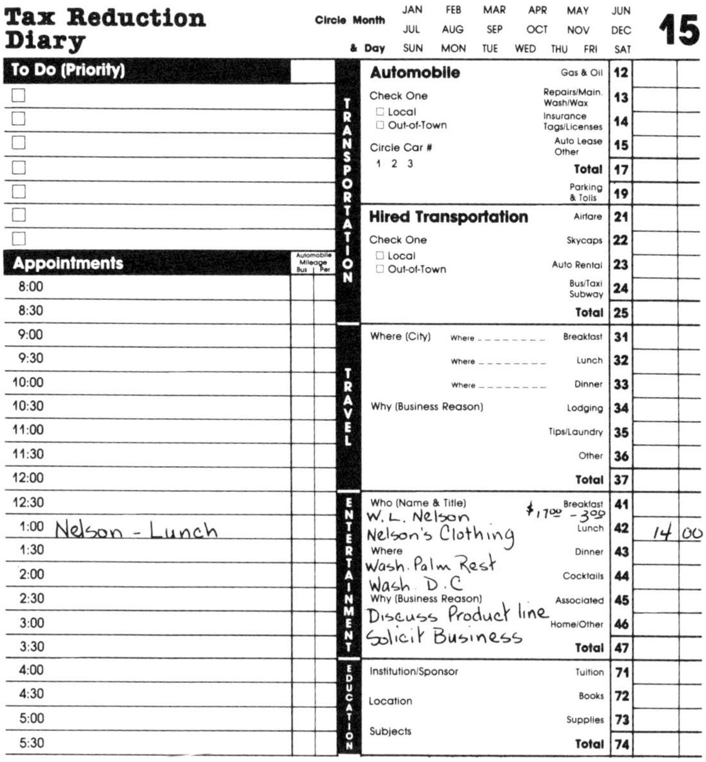

Tax Reduction Diary

Circle Month: JAN FEB MAR APR MAY JUN / JUL AUG SEP OCT NOV DEC
& Day: SUN MON TUE WED THU FRI SAT

15

To Do (Priority)

☐
☐
☐
☐
☐
☐
☐

Appointments (Automobile Mileage: Bus | Per)

8:00
8:30
9:00
9:30
10:00
10:30
11:00
11:30
12:00
12:30
1:00 Nelson - Lunch
1:30
2:00
2:30
3:00
3:30
4:00
4:30
5:00
5:30

TRANSPORTATION

Automobile — Check One: ☐ Local ☐ Out-of-Town; Circle Car # 1 2 3

Gas & Oil	12	
Repairs/Main. Wash/Wax	13	
Insurance Tags/Licenses	14	
Auto Lease Other	15	
Total	17	
Parking & Tolls	19	

Hired Transportation — Check One: ☐ Local ☐ Out-of-Town

Airfare	21	
Skycaps	22	
Auto Rental	23	
Bus/Taxi Subway	24	
Total	25	

TRAVEL

Where (City) Where ________ Where ________ Where ________
Why (Business Reason)

Breakfast	31	
Lunch	32	
Dinner	33	
Lodging	34	
Tips/Laundry	35	
Other	36	
Total	37	

ENTERTAINMENT

Who (Name & Title) W. L. Nelson — Nelson's Clothing
$17.00 - 3.00
Where Wash. Palm Rest — Wash. D.C
Why (Business Reason) Discuss Product line — Solicit Business

Breakfast	41	
Lunch	42	14 00
Dinner	43	
Cocktails	44	
Associated	45	
Home/Other	46	
Total	47	

EDUCATION

Institution/Sponsor
Location
Subjects

Tuition	71	
Books	72	
Supplies	73	
Total	74	

RESULTS: DEDUCTIBLE BECAUSE DIARY ENTRY MEETS TESTS 1 AND 2.

TEST 1—Ordinary and Necessary Course of Business: Yes, Nelson is a prospect and Peck was pursuing Nelson's business.

TEST 2—Meets Five Elements of Substantiation: Yes, as follows:

1. **Cost:** The deductible business portion is $14.00. Cost is less than $25.00; therefore, no receipt is required. Personal meal costs average $3.00 and are supported by diary entries.
2. **Time:** Peck's diary page has the date at the top.
3. **Description:** Business lunch at Joe & Mo's.
4. **Business purpose:** Evident from relationship of Nelson.
5. **Business relationship:** Prospect, owner of clothing store.

entertainment that takes place at nightclubs, golf courses, theaters, or sporting events, on hunting trips, fishing trips, or ski trips, and in other places where there is little possibility for a business discussion during the entertainment activity. To obtain the deduction, you must establish a clear linkage between the entertainment activity and the substantial business discussion. Generally, the entertainment must take place on the day of the business discussion.

You must demonstrate that you actively engaged in a business meeting, business discussion, or negotiation of a business transaction to obtain a deduction for associated entertainment.

Caution—goodwill entertainment only is not deductible: Entertainment not directly following or preceding a "substantial and bona fide business discussion" does not qualify for deduction when the only business benefit is goodwill. Goodwill entertainment, such as playing golf with a customer, can be deducted only if such entertainment is "associated."

Example: Lennon, a lawyer, threw a birthday party where two-thirds of the guests were his clients and law partners. At the party, no business discussions took place, and Lennon had not seen many of the guests for several days or even weeks. The court held that the party was not associated with business and disallowed any deduction.

The IRS does not define the phrase "substantial and bona fide business discussions." It relegates this issue to a determination of the facts and circumstances. Effectively, this means that you must have more than a passive possibility of doing business. You must enter into a negotiation or discussion for the specific purpose of generating a business benefit—the possibility of making money. An actual business benefit is not necessary, but attempt is.

Once you have met the "substantial and bonafide business discussion" test, you are entitled to encourage further goodwill in business through associated entertainment. The idea is to allow you to use such entertainment to obtain new business or to encourage the continuation of an existing business relationship.

Also, once you have met this requirement, you need not be present during the entertainment activity itself. You may, for example, send your clients to the theater by themselves and still take a deduction under the "associated with" rules.

A common mistake: The entry in your diary must clearly indicate when and where the substantial and bona fide business discussion took place. Remember, it does not take place during the entertainment. The entertainment either precedes or follows a substantial and bona fide business discussion, usually in a setting separate from that of the discussion. Exhibit 3-7 contains an example of how associated entertainment must be recorded to substantiate a deduction. In the example, a specific business contract was negotiated in the office at 3 o'clock in the afternoon. Later that same day, directly following and linking the contract signing, the goodwill entertainment took place. The linkage between the entertainment and the business discussion must be established. Generally, the business discussion and entertainment must take place on the same day. When that's not possible, the goodwill entertainment will be allowed when there are good reasons why the entertainment did not take place on the day of the business discussion. For example, if you conduct substantial negotiations with business associates from out of town and entertain them the evening before the business discussions, the entertainment will qualify as "directly preceding."

When entertainment is associated with the active conduct of your trade or business, you must record the five elements of substantiation. In addition, you must record:

- The date and duration of the business discussion that preceded or followed the associated entertainment.
- The place where the business discussion was held.
- The nature of the discussion, its purpose, and the benefit derived or expected from the discussion.
- The identity of the persons entertained who participated in the business discussion.

EXHIBIT 3-7. Recording "Associated With" Entertainment (Example).

FACTS: Murphy negotiated a contract with Smith during the day and that evening took the Smiths to the theater.

ENTRIES IN DIARY:

Tax Reduction Diary				
Circle Month	JAN FEB MAR APR MAY JUN			
	JUL AUG SEP OCT NOV DEC	**15**		
& Day	SUN MON TUE WED THU FRI SAT			

To Do (Priority)

☐
☐
☐
☐
☐
☐
☐

Appointments

		Automobile Mileage Bus | Per
8:00		
8:30		
9:00		
9:30		
10:00		
10:30		
11:00		
11:30		
12:00		
12:30		
1:00		
1:30		
2:00		
2:30		
3:00	Smith – widget contract	
3:30		
4:00		
4:30		
5:00		
5:30		

TRANSPORTATION

Automobile

Check One	Gas & Oil	12
☐ Local	Repairs/Main. Wash/Wax	13
☐ Out-of-Town	Insurance Tags/Licenses	14
Circle Car #	Auto Lease Other	15
1 2 3	**Total**	17
	Parking & Tolls	19

Hired Transportation

Check One	Airfare	21
☐ Local	Skycaps	22
☐ Out-of-Town	Auto Rental	23
	Bus/Taxi Subway	24
	Total	25

TRAVEL

Where (City) Where _ _ _ _ _ _	Breakfast	31
Where _ _ _ _ _ _	Lunch	32
Where _ _ _ _ _ _	Dinner	33
Why (Business Reason)	Lodging	34
	Tips/Laundry	35
	Other	36
	Total	37

ENTERTAINMENT

Who (Name & Title) Mr and Mrs RC Smith Widget buyers	Breakfast	41	
	Lunch	42	
Where Kennedy Center Palm Rest Wash DC	Dinner	43	117 | 00
	Cocktails	44	16 | 00
Why (Business Reason) Build Goodwill	Associated	45	72 | 00
Smiths Purchased widgets –	Coats Home/Other	46	6 | 00
see Contract file	**Total**	47	211 | 00

EDUCATION

Institution/Sponsor	Tuition	71
Location	Books	72
	Supplies	73
Subjects	**Total**	74

RESULTS: DEDUCTIONS FOR "ASSOCIATED WITH" ENTERTAINMENT SUBSTANTIATED BECAUSE:

1. A substantial and bona fide business discussion occurred on the same day as the associated entertainment.
2. The associated entertainment had a business purpose to generate goodwill and enhance business relations.
3. The five elements of substantiation were met. Receipt for dinner contains name of restaurant. Receipt for theater is kept, also.

When the associated entertainment follows directly related entertainment, both the associated and directly related entertainment are deductible. Directly related entertainment refers to a situation where an active business discussion takes place during the entertainment and meets the "substantial and bona fide business discussion" test.

Definition of directly related entertainment: You meet the "directly related entertainment" test when the entertainment relates to the active conduct of your trade or business. To meet this test, you must show that

- You had more than a general expectation of deriving income or some business benefit other than goodwill.
- You actively engaged in business discussions during the entertainment period with the person being entertained.
- The principal character or aspect of the combined business and entertainment was the transaction of business.

You are not required to show that business income or other business benefit actually resulted from each and every entertainment expenditure that is directly related. You must merely show how you intended to derive a specific business income or other business benefit and that you actively pursued such income or benefit, unless circumstances outside your control precluded your making such advances.

According to the IRS, when entertainment takes place on hunting or fishing trips or on pleasure boats, the conduct of business is not considered to be the principal character or aspect of the combined business and entertainment unless you, the taxpayer, are able to prove otherwise.

Directly related entertainment occurs in a clear business setting. When you entertain a group of business associates and display or create discussion of your business products, and when there is no meaningful personal or social relationship between the persons entertained and yourself, you have entered the world of a clear business setting. In effect, a group session must have as its principal purpose either business publicity or actual discussion of business products.

The IRS presumes that there is little or no possibility of engaging in an active conduct of business in certain entertainment places. Meetings at nightclubs, theaters, sporting events, or essentially social gatherings such as cocktail parties are presumed to preclude the possibility of engaging in the active conduct of business. Also, when you meet with a group that includes persons who are not business associates, at places such as cocktail lounges, country clubs, golf clubs, athletic clubs, or vacation resorts, the IRS presumes that there is little possibility that you will be able to engage in the active conduct of business. In such situations, this presumption may be overcome by establishing that you did engage in substantial business discussions during the entertainment. A notation of the actual business discussion must be made in your diary.

In meeting the directly related test, you must prove that when you committed yourself to the expenditure, you had more than a general expectation of deriving some income or other business benefit, and that you actively engaged in discussions trying to procure that benefit. You need not actually realize a benefit, nor do you need to spend more time trying to procure the benefit than you spend entertaining, but you must actively pursue the benefit.

Example: Patterson, a business consultant, meets Calvert, a prospective client, for lunch at the country club. At the time Patterson committed himself to the lunch, he intended to discuss a new computer program with Calvert. During lunch he discussed the computer program, showed charts, and reviewed costs. Calvert declined the offer.

Result: Patterson's expenditure for lunch is deductible as directly related entertainment. Although the business lunch would have been deductible under the "quiet business meal" rules had he not intended a specific business discussion, the active pursuit of business during a specific entertainment qualifies the business meal as directly related entertainment.

The advantage of directly related entertainment over that of a quiet business meal is that Patterson may now take Calvert to the golf course and deduct the cost of the golf as "associated" entertainment. Thus, both the golf and the lunch are deductible.

TEN PRACTICAL ILLUSTRATIONS OF DEDUCTIBLE ENTERTAINMENT

So far, we have covered the rules for quiet business meals, directly related entertainment, and associated entertainment. The following examples will help clarify the various nuances of these rules.

Example 1: You take Jones, a referral source, to dinner. Your purpose in taking Jones is to maintain Jones as a referral source. During dinner, you never get around to discussing business.

Result: You have a quiet business meal deduction.

Example 2: You wait three weeks before recording the five elements of substantiation for the quiet business meal with Jones.

Result: You are in direct violation of the contemporaneous recording requirement, and you will be denied an otherwise valid deduction (assuming the IRS catches you).

Example 3: Your best friend is a referral source who has increased your income by $5,000 during the year. You entertain your friend in your home every Saturday evening for the purpose of asking for new referrals. The cost of the home entertainment for the year amounts to $2,500.

Result: You have a valid tax deduction for the $2,500 cost of entertaining your friend.

Example 4: Tuesday, you discuss and obtain a nice contract from Smith. Friday, you take Smith to the theater.

Result: No deduction, you have violated the "associated with" rules for having the business discussion on the same day as the associated entertainment.

Example 5: You take Nelson to a business lunch and spend $22. In your diary, you write, "Nelson—lunch—$22—prospect."

Result: No deduction—you failed to write down the place where the entertainment occurred. We assume your diary contains the dates at the top of each page. The only element you are missing is the place where the lunch took place.

Example 6: Some business prospects arrive in town Tuesday evening. You take them to the ball game and a nightclub. All day Wednesday, you have substantial and bona fide business discussions. Wednesday night, you're back at the nightclub and another ball game.

Result: The ball game and nightclub are deductible as associated entertainment expenses.

Example 7: You have prospective local customers come to your office during the day for lengthy discussions. That evening you take them out to dinner and to the theater.

Result: The dinner and theater are deductible as associated entertainment expenses.

Example 8: Nelson, an out-of-town customer, comes to your city for a vacation. You not only pay for the vacation, but you take Nelson to the local night spots each night. Nelson is your largest customer and spends hundreds of thousands of dollars with you each year.

Result: No deductions. The entertainment did not precede or follow any substantial business discussion; therefore, it is not associated with the active conduct of your business.

Example 9: You attend a business convention. During breaks and after the meetings, you entertain business associates and prospects.

Result: The cost is deductible.

Example 10: You write a check for $80 to cover the cost of a business dinner. In the memo section of the check, you record all five elements of substantiation.

Result: Sorry, no deduction. A cancelled check is not a receipt. A credit card charge slip is a receipt.

TAX DEDUCTIONS FOR ENTERTAINING IN YOUR HOME

Who are your prospects? How do you get referrals? Do you ever entertain prospects or referral sources in your home?

Odds are that you do entertain these people in your home and that you are overlooking an important business expense. This expense is not only sizeable, but it is money that you spend whether or not you read this book. This expense is the business cost of home entertainment.

Surveys conducted among 20,000 professionals and small businesspersons who have attended TRI seminars indicate that all were eligible for home entertainment deductions, but fewer than 20 percent claimed the deductions properly. The surveys revealed that the average lost deductions for failing to claim home entertainment properly amounted to $1,800 per person!

Several important court cases have helped define the rules for deducting the cost of home entertainment. In this section we will discuss the new ramifications and help you increase your home entertainment deductions.

We will explain:

- Why the Internal Revenue Service doesn't believe you entertain in your home;
- Why quiet business meals are not allowed as often as home entertainment deductions;
- How home entertainment deductions can be claimed as "associated with" entertainment;
- Why all home entertainment should be "directly related" to your business to assure deductions; and
- Recent court cases that clarified many of the rules for deducting the cost of home entertainment.

No one looks forward to visits from the IRS. We have innate fears that our record-keeping is sloppy and that a close look at our tax returns will surely uncover something wrong. Moreover, most people are aware that the more deductions a person claims, the higher the chances of audit. On the other hand, the fewer deductions a person claims, the more taxes the IRS collects.

There must be some trade-off, but what is it? It isn't nearly as difficult as you might think. Simply claim all the deductions to which you are legally entitled—nothing more and nothing less. This includes home entertainment.

Our goal in this section is to help you claim as a deduction the valid cost of your business home entertainment. However, please note that if you increase the size of your home entertainment deduction, you increase the probability that the IRS will audit your tax return.

The IRS likes to audit entertainment expenses because specific documentation rules must be followed for every entertainment expenditure. Failure to meet the specific requirements spelled out in this chapter could negate otherwise valid entertainment deductions. To the IRS's delight, many folks are lax about the necessary documentation.

Several rules for deducting the cost of entertainment are unusual. If you fail to understand and apply these rules, you can lose deductions.

Three kinds of deductible entertainment could take place in your home. First, you could have a quiet business meal, wherein you need not have a business discussion but merely the intention of securing a business benefit. Second, you could have a directly related business meal, which means that you must discuss business. Third, you could have associated entertainment, in which you never intended to discuss, and you did not discuss, business during the entertainment.

Your home is conducive to a business discussion if there is a clear showing that the expenditure was commercially rather than socially motivated. The phrase "clear showing" is meant to purge any absorption of personal expenses. Moreover, that phrase means that to be deductible, most home entertainment must be directly related.

You do not need to spend more time trying to conduct business than you spend entertaining your guests. If, for example, your purpose is to obtain a referral and you ask for a referral and receive it, you can devote the rest of the evening to entertaining and that entertainment will qualify as directly related entertainment. Even if you ask for but fail to get a prospect's name, the entertainment is directly related.

You must secure or attempt to secure a specific business benefit as a result of home entertainment. If that is not your purpose, the entertainment still may be deductible under the "associated with" entertainment rules.

Spouses: If you entertain a business guest, your meal and the meal of the business guest are tax deductible. But what happens when your guest brings his or her spouse and you bring your spouse? Under tax law, your spouse is deemed to be closely connected to you and the spouse of your business guest is deemed to be closely connected to that guest. Under the closely connected rule, you are allowed to deduct the cost of feeding all four.

As absurd as it may seem, the IRS considers the local pub a clear business setting but considers your home not to be a clear business setting. Accordingly, when you entertain at home, you are required to establish a clear business motive. For most taxpayers, that eliminates quiet business meals. So far, Howard is the only exception.

How Howard won quiet business meals at home: Howard took his home entertainment expenses out on a ledge with the judge. In the judgment of the IRS, Howard was not entitled to deduct the cost of home entertainment. He didn't like or agree with the judgment, so Howard took his case to court and won.

Howard was a corporate executive in the communications business who incurred expenses for hosting private dinner parties at home. He deducted those expenses as business expenses. The guests were prominent people from politics, business, journalism, publishing, theater, and other fields. They ranged from prominent office holders to a presidential press secretary, and included many persons affiliated with Howard's news business. Most of the guests were professional rather than social acquaintances of his, although in some instances both elements existed. The dinners for which Howard took the home entertainment deductions occurred approximately once a month, almost always on a weekday evening. In addition, Howard often hosted dinner parties at home for social reasons, the cost of which he did not deduct as a business expense.

Hint: If you are deducting home entertainment, keep track of social entertainment as well.

Howard's first argument was that his home entertainment expenses constituted an ordinary and necessary business expense that was not barred by the disallowance provisions for directly related entertainment. The IRS made the exact opposite argument. The court agreed with Howard.

The court stated that tax law allows the deduction for all ordinary and necessary expenses paid or incurred during the taxable year in carrying on a trade or business. Thus, the expenditures must have been "necessary" in that they were "appropriate and helpful" to Howard's business. The expenses must have been "ordinary" in that they were "normal and natural" expenditures under the specific circumstances. The court concluded that Howard's purpose for the dinners was to provide an opportunity to discuss developments and ideas with people who were prominent in their professions. As a result, Howard was able to keep abreast of topics that were important to him in his business and he was able to establish contacts that would be useful sources of information in the future.

The IRS contended that the home entertainment deductions were barred by the "directly related" provisions of the tax law. Howard maintained that the dinners fell within the "business meal" exception. The court agreed (for the first time) that the business meals fell within the quiet business meal exception. In other words, business need not be discussed specifically or be directly related for the home entertainment expenses to qualify for deduction.

The court concluded that Howard's home was an appropriate place for business discussions and that the quiet business meal exception was available. Howard convinced the court that he invited business guests to his home because his home was more conducive to the kind of discussions he wanted to stimulate than a public place would be, especially since many of his guests were well known. By inviting a group of eight to ten people to his home, Howard could talk with all of them and inquire discreetly about subjects and ideas helpful to him in his business.

Because of the time and circumstances of the dinners, as well as the individual and collective professional interests of the few guests invited, it was clear that the infrequent business dinners were "commercially rather than socially motivated" and were "for the primary purpose of furthering the taxpayer's trade or business and did not primarily serve a social or personal purpose." The court found the quiet business meal exception available to Howard for a variety of reasons. The primary reason was that Howard established the problem of entertaining in public places. (Public places are less private than the confines of the home, and in your home you do not need to worry about long ears at the next table.) Also, Howard established a business purpose for the entertainment.

Howard would have had no trouble at all with his deduction if he had established the home entertainment as directly related to his business. With directly related entertainment, there is no question about commercial rather than social motivation. Therefore, if you desire to claim a deduction for home entertainment expenses, try to make that entertainment directly related to your business, because such a relationship is easier to prove.

Exhibit 3-8 shows how to record a business meal served at home. Note the change of test 1 from "ordinary and necessary" to a "clear showing of commercial motivation."

Howard was entertaining groups which

EXHIBIT 3-8. Recording a Business Meal Served at Home (Example).

FACTS: Steel, a commissioned office salesperson, has just received a new product line. He invites Leon, a customer, and his spouse over for dinner for the purpose of selling the new product line.

ENTRY IN DIARY:

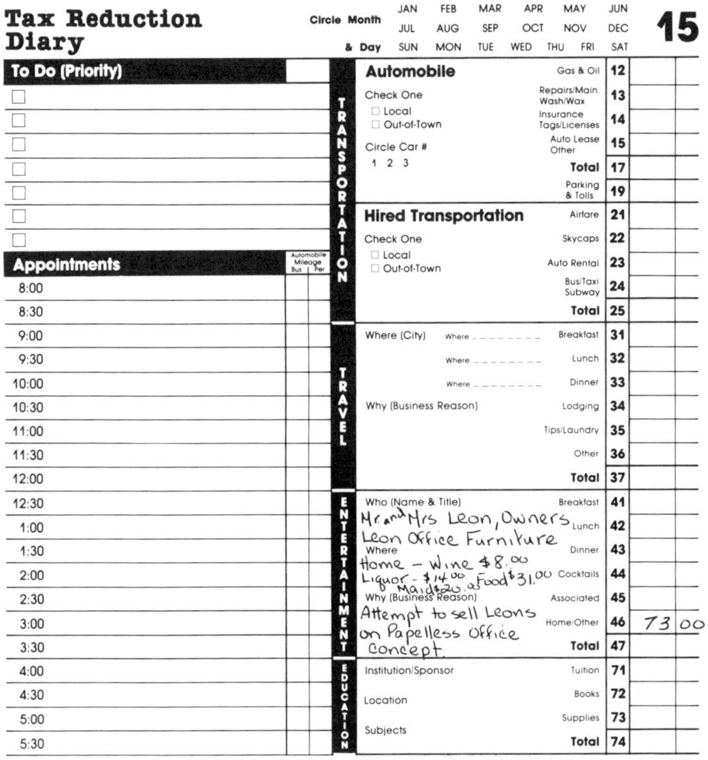

EXHIBIT 3-8. *continued*

RESULTS: DEDUCTIBLE BECAUSE STEEL PASSES TESTS 1 AND 2.

TEST 1—Clear Showing of Commercial Motivation: Yes, Steel definitely had a business reason for having the Leons to dinner; the introduction of a new product line. Furthermore, he actually engaged in substantial discussions about the line and showed pictures and brochures. He did not sell the new line to Leon, nor did he have to in order to establish the deduction.

Caution: Note how the "ordinary and necessary" test is expanded for a quiet business meal to include a clear commercial motivation.

TEST 2—Meets Five Elements of Substantiation: Yes, as follows:

1. **Cost:** Steel has receipts to back up all costs entered in the diary, even those under $25.00. Reason: Home entertainment is treated harshly by the IRS and receipts prove helpful.
2. **Time:** Date at top of diary page.
3. **Description:** "Dinner at home" adequately describes entertainment function.
4. **Business purpose:** Attempt to sell a specific product to Leon.
5. **Business relationship:** Current customer and prospect for new product line.

Spouses: Note that Steel deducted the costs for his and Leon's spouses. See "How to Deduct the Cost of Entertaining Your Spouse" later in this chapter for details on how this was accomplished.

---

ranged in size from eight to ten people. Had the groups been any larger, Howard would have been hard pressed to claim that he had active business discussions with the people. Group entertainment is subject to special rules and is much more difficult to establish.

Dr. Roush was a dentist who attempted to deduct the cost of several parties but lost his case in court. He attempted to deduct the cost of parties and luncheons given for clients and friends to promote the goodwill of his dentistry business. The luncheons and parties that Roush claimed included a birthday party and a party for his daughter's college friends.

The court said that it could not find any business reason for allowing these parties as a deduction. The court was particularly upset by Roush's claimed deduction for a luncheon of Mrs. Roush and one of her friends. Obviously, these three claimed deductions alone cast huge shadows of doubt over the allowability of Roush's home entertainment expenses.

Roush's other failing was claiming the deductions built goodwill. The court ruled that obviously goodwill is an element of any professional occupation, but it does not follow that all activities promoting goodwill are necessarily deductible. To be deductible, such activities must meet the rigid requirements of tax law for "associated with" entertainment. Roush failed on all counts.

To obtain the deduction for the birthday party, Roush would have had to establish that the birthday party was a clear commercial setting. The mere fact of the birthday party precludes such an assertion in almost every case. But there are ways to establish a clear business setting when many people are present.

The simplest and most convenient way to turn a group party into directly related entertainment is to create a display or other mechanism that will generate a discussion of your product, service, or other business purpose for the party. The IRS holds that the creation of a business discussion can be used to establish a clear business setting.

If you are entertaining a group of people, your home is not an atmosphere conducive to a business discussion. Large cocktail parties and sizeable social gatherings are considered distractions and therefore are held not to be the kind of surroundings generally conducive to business discussions.

To obtain a deduction for entertaining a group of business associates, clients, or future prospects, you must establish that the recipients of the entertainment knew you had no significant motive for incurring the expenditure for entertainment other than directly furthering your business. When entertaining groups, it helps if you have no meaningful personal or social relationship with the persons you are entertaining.

You also must prove that the group entertainment was for more than the promotion of "goodwill."

Thus, when you entertain a group, you must make your home a clear business setting.

For example, a taxpayer establishes a clear business setting when he creates a discussion of his products. When he has a display of products or wares, generally there is no problem substantiating a deduction for home entertainment. Handout materials are a valuable aid to help establish this requirement.

To establish a clear business setting, people visiting the taxpayer's home must know that he intends to discuss business. If he can prove that entertainment at his home resulted in a discussion of his business products, he has established that critical clear business setting. To create such a discussion, an agenda of the evening's activities may be necessary to ensure that people know there's a display in the back of the room.

Remember, if you entertain a group of people in your home, you must establish a clear business setting. The fire power of a display is that it generates business discussions. The fire power of an agenda is that it establishes the element of intent, since the agenda is made up before the entertainment begins.

Example: Baisey sells real estate for a living. His display consists of a bulletin board with photographs of six investment properties currently for sale. Below each photo, Baisey has a summary of investment benefits. Baisey sends invitations to 16 couples to attend a cocktail party. Each invitation notifies the invited guests that not only will they have cocktails and fun, but a complete display of the best investment properties in town will be available for viewing at the party. When the party is in progress, Baisey makes a short announcement regarding the display.

Baisey takes a photograph during the party that shows the display and some of the people. He gets the photograph processed by a firm that puts the processing date on the photo. Thus, Baisey establishes the vintage of the photograph.

He also keeps a copy of the invitation and writes in his diary the name of each person who attended the party. Baisey has all his bases covered.

IRS regulations require that you record the elements of your entertainment expenditures at or near the time such expenditures are incurred. Timely recording ensures the maximum deduction for entertainment expenses. If entries are made later, the IRS assumes a lack of total recall, and you will not be in compliance with the requirement to keep adequate records.

Exhibit 3-9 shows how Ritter records the cost of group entertainment at home. His description includes both the type of entertainment and where it occurred ("cocktail party at home"). Ritter also lists all the names of the individuals who attended the party. Then, in the expense side of his daily diary, he breaks down the components of the cocktail party into beverages, food, maid, and bartender.

EASY REVIEW OF DEDUCTIBLE BUSINESS MEALS

Exhibit 3-10 contains a flowchart for deducting business meals. Since you have a variety of business meals which are deductible, the flowchart will help you determine what documentation is required for each business meal.

From a practical standpoint, there should be no difference between a meal served in a restaurant and a meal served in your home. Yet, IRS positions and court cases definitely establish a difference. You will want meals at home to be primarily "directly related." When you have a meal in a restaurant, that meal can be "quiet."

If you go Dutch treat, you must have your average meal cost recorded in order to take the excess business portion as a business expense. If you pick up the tab for all your guests, then you write off 100 percent of the tab.

We recommend that you review the flowchart at least once a month for the first year. That way the distinction between the rules will

EXHIBIT 3-9. Recording the Cost of Group Entertainment at Home.

FACTS: Ritter built his own office building and is looking for tenants. He throws a party for friends that would be desirable tenants.

ENTRY IN DIARY:

Tax Reduction Diary		
Circle Month — JAN FEB MAR APR MAY JUN / JUL AUG SEP OCT NOV DEC		**15**
& Day — SUN MON TUE WED THU FRI SAT		

To Do (Priority)
- ☐
- ☐
- ☐
- ☐
- ☐
- ☐
- ☐

T R A N S P O R T A T I O N	**Automobile**		
		Gas & Oil	12
	Check One	Repairs/Main. Wash/Wax	13
	☐ Local	Insurance Tags/Licenses	14
	☐ Out-of-Town	Auto Lease Other	15
	Circle Car # 1 2 3		17
		Total	
		Parking & Tolls	19
	Hired Transportation		
		Airfare	21
	Check One	Skycaps	22
	☐ Local	Auto Rental	23
	☐ Out-of-Town	Bus/Taxi Subway	24
		Total	25

Appointments	Automobile Mileage Bus / Per
8:00	
8:30	
9:00	
9:30	
10:00	
10:30	
11:00	
11:30	
12:00	
12:30 Elliots, Chaums,	
1:00 Gordons, Harpers,	
1:30 Finders, Duffys,	
2:00 Sheppards, Goddings,	
2:30 Quinns, Hamiltons,	
3:00 Hills, Coats, Timkins	
3:30	
4:00	
4:30	
5:00	
5:30	

T R A V E L			
	Where (City) ___ Where ___	Breakfast	31
	Where ___	Lunch	32
	Where ___	Dinner	33
	Why (Business Reason)	Lodging	34
		Tips/Laundry	35
		Other	36
		Total	37

E N T E R T A I N M E N T				
	Who (Name & Title)	Breakfast	41	
		Lunch	42	
	Where Home	Dinner	43	
	Beverages $110 Food $130 Cocktails		44	
	Hairo $30 Bartender $30 Associated		45	
	Why (Business Reason) Prospective Tenants	Home/Other	46	300 —
	for new office	**Total**	47	300 —

E D U C A T I O N			
	Institution/Sponsor	Tuition	71
	Location	Books	72
		Supplies	73
	Subjects	**Total**	74

RESULTS: DEDUCTIBLE BECAUSE RITTER PASSES TESTS 1 AND 2.

TEST 1—Clear showing of commercial motivation: Ritter's invitation established the introduction of the new office building as the reason for the party. In the room where the party was held, Ritter had photographs of the new building posted on a bulletin board. Although none of the individuals attending the party rented space in the new building, Ritter established a clear business motivation for the party.

TEST 2—Meet Five Elements of Substantiation:

1. **Cost:** Ritter has receipts and canceled checks.
2. **Time:** Date at top of diary page.
3. **Description:** Words in diary.
4. **Business purpose:** Words in diary plus invitations and photographs of people around bulletin board.
5. **Business relationships:** Names of individuals who own their businesses and are prospective tenants.

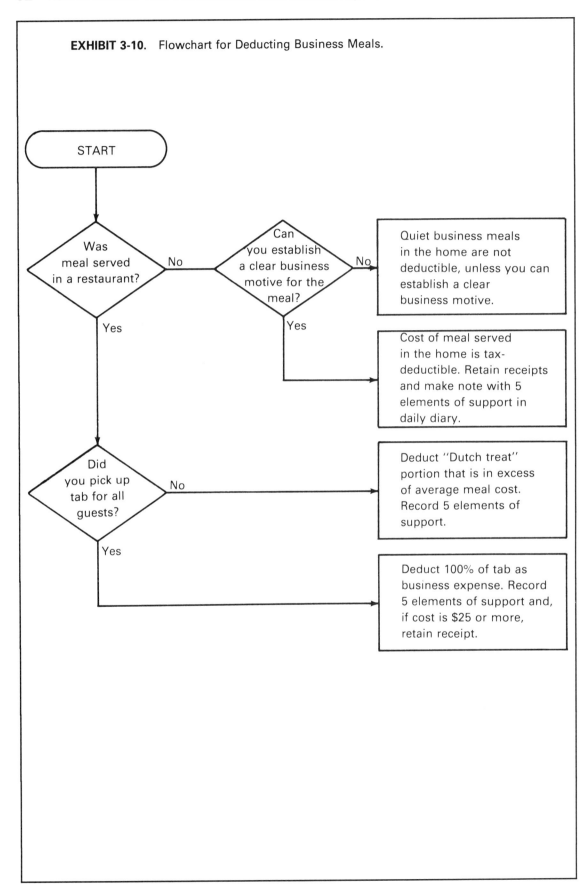

EXHIBIT 3-10.   Flowchart for Deducting Business Meals.

be clearly set in your mind. Moreover, applying the rules will become a matter of habit and will take little time.

HOW TO DEDUCT SOCIAL, ATHLETIC, OR SPORTING CLUB DUES

When you take a client to lunch at the country club, the lunch is tax deductible providing (1) it's incurred in the ordinary and necessary course of business, and (2) you meet the five elements of substantiation.

If you qualify, you may also add a portion of your club dues to your other business deductions. You must use the club primarily for business purposes to qualify for the club dues deduction.

The flowchart in Exhibit 3-11 contains the IRS approved method for determining your club dues deductions. Essentially, your club dues deductions are based on the results of a two-step test. In step one, you determine if the club is used primarily for business.

Primary use determination: Use the decision table in Exhibit 3-12 to classify each day that a club is used as either business or personal. In the column labeled, "Step one day," a "yes" answer indicates a business day. A quiet business meal on a day with no family or personal usage results in a business day. On the other hand, a quiet business meal on a day when another family member uses the club for personal purposes, the day is considered a nonbusiness day.

If the club is used 12 days during a business year, you would consider only the 12 days for purposes of step one. If you have more yes answers than no answers in step one, you have passed the primary purpose test. Once the primary purpose test is passed, you are entitled to a dues deduction, and the amount of that deduction is determined under step two.

Using the decision table in Exhibit 3-12, you determine the percentage of dues that you are allowed to deduct by establishing a ratio the numerator of which is the total of the yes answers, and the denominator of which is the total days of use (business and personal) during the year.

Example: Your dues in a club are $1,200 a year and you use the club 20 days during the year. Fifteen days are for business use under step one (yes answers), and five days are for direct business usage under step two (yes answers). Under step one, you use the club 75 percent of the time for business, so you are entitled to a deduction. The amount of your deduction is determined under step two. You have five days of business usage out of a total of 20 days; therefore, your dues deduction is $300 ($1,200 times 5/20).

Why use the decision table? It is imperative that you use the decision table if you want to apply the IRS approved rules for deducting your club dues. In the decision table, a quiet business meal becomes a directly related business meal for purposes of step two when there is no family usage during that day. Note that associated entertainment, such as golf or tennis only, is business usage under step one when no family member uses the club, but the associated day is never a step two directly related day. Thus, the simplest way to avoid confusion is to always use the decision table for purposes of classifying your club dues deduction.

Working example: Exhibit 3-13 contains a working example for computing a tennis club dues deduction. In the example, the club was used a total of 10 days during the year. The business uses are specified in the second column and the personal uses are specified in the third column. Using the decision table in Exhibit 3-12, the taxpayer passes the step one test because the club is used 60 percent of the time for business purposes. Under step two, the taxpayer determines that 50 percent of the dues is deductible.

What dues are deductible? Your monthly or annual dues are deductible, assuming you passed steps one and two.

Initial membership fees or initiation fees are not deductible at the time you purchase the membership, unless the initiation or initial membership fee has a defined useful life. In the case of a defined useful life, you allocate the cost, less expected salvage, over the period of benefit.

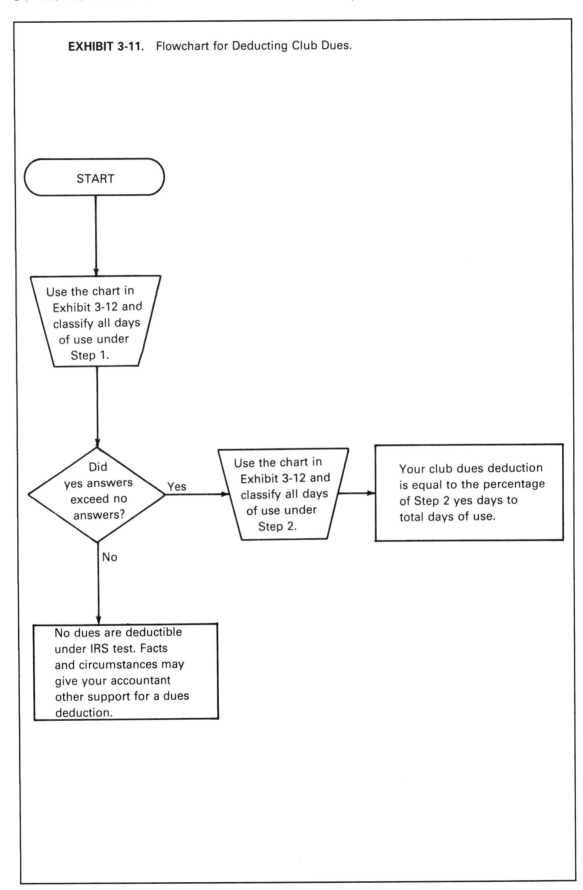

EXHIBIT 3-11. Flowchart for Deducting Club Dues.

EXHIBIT 3-12. Decision Table for Classifying Days of Club Usage.

USAGES FOR DAY

Deductible Business Usage	Any Family or Personal Use	Step 1 Day	Step 2 Day
Quiet business meal	No	Yes	Yes
Quiet business meal	Yes	No	No
Directly related business meal	No	Yes	Yes
Directly related business meal	Yes	Yes	Yes
Associated entertainment only	No	Yes	No
Associated entertainment only	Yes	No	No

EXHIBIT 3-13. Computing the Tennis Club Dues Deduction (Example).

DAY	BUSINESS USE	PERSONAL USE	STEP 1 DAY	STEP 2 DAY
1/01/85	Quiet	Yes	No	No
1/18/85	Quiet	No	Yes	Yes
1/31/85	Direct	Yes	Yes	Yes
2/28/85	Direct	No	Yes	Yes
3/14/85	Associated	No	Yes	No
4/17/85	Associated	Yes	No	No
4/18/85	Quiet	No	Yes	Yes
4/19/85	Direct	Yes	Yes	Yes
4/20/85	Quiet	Yes	No	No
12/9/85	Quiet	Yes	No	No

$$\text{Step 1} = \frac{6 \text{ Yes}}{10 \text{ Total}} = 60\% \text{ business use.}$$

$$\text{Step 2} = \frac{5 \text{ Yes}}{10 \text{ Total}} = 50\% \text{ of dues is deductible.}$$

When the life of the initiation or initial membership fee cannot be determined, which is the usual case, no deductions for the fee are available while you are a member at the club, but you may have a case for gain or loss on sale of your membership.

Business gain or loss: Your percentage of business use during the membership life is determined under step two. You allocate the initiation fee based on the percentage from step two. This is the basis in your initiation fee. Your gain or loss is determined by comparing the selling price, if any, to your initiation fee.

Example: Collins paid $5,000 to become a member in a tennis club. The initiation fee

was a one-time charge and therefore, under IRS rules, had no useful life. Five years after purchase, Collins moved to a new location and gave up his membership in the club. His step two usage during the five years he used the club averaged 80 percent. Since Collins forfeited his membership, he received no money for canceling his membership. Accordingly, Collins has a $4,000 ($5,000 times 80 percent) loss on the disposition of his business membership in the club.

Personal gain or loss: The general tax rule is that personal gains are taxable and personal losses are nondeductible.

Example: In September of 1967 Kendrick purchased a membership certificate in a country club at a cost of $600. She sold the membership certificate in March of 1984 for $15,000. Kendrick used the club not for business, but solely for personal purposes.

During the period that Kendrick was a member of the club, certain capital improvements were made to the club's facilities. The capital improvements were financed out of dues increases which were assessed to each member.

The IRS ruled that the sale was a capital transaction and subject to taxation at the favored capital gains rates. Kendrick's basis in her membership certificate was the amount originally paid ($600) plus any amount she could prove was spent from her dues contributions for capital assets.

Assume $400 was spent from her membership dues for capital improvements, Kendrick's basis would be $1,000 and her taxable gain would be $14,000 ($15,000 minus $1,000 basis).

Personal profit motive: If you expect to make money on a club membership, you have a profit motive. Accordingly, you could claim a deduction for a loss on the sale of a club membership.

Using a non-IRS test for deducting club dues: The "days of usage" test discussed in this section is taken from the IRS regulations and is the usual test applied by IRS examiners. You may, however, have another or more appropriate basis for determining your club dues deduction. A good example would be dollars spent. However, when you deviate from the "days of usage" test, your facts and circumstances for the other basis must be more appropriate than the days of business use. If you have such a circumstance, make sure you review the application of a different basis with your tax advisor.

Reducing chances of audit: If you have heavy entertainment deductions, you may want to attach a schedule supporting your club dues deduction to your Form 1040. If your return is pulled by the computer for audit, the IRS examiner will see a supporting schedule, which discloses that you understand the rules for deducting club dues. This show of understanding may lead the examiner to override

the computer and return your tax file to the not-to-be-audited pile.

HOW TO DEDUCT DUES PAID TO CLUBS OTHER THAN SOCIAL, ATHLETIC, OR SPORTING CLUBS

Business luncheon clubs are not considered social clubs. Professional and civic organizations such as medical associations and the Lions Club are not considered social clubs. Accordingly, you need not meet the "two-step test" to deduct a portion of the dues paid to such clubs. The dues are deductible if the club usage qualifies as an ordinary and necessary business expense.

Business meals served at professional and civic clubs are deductible under the "Dutch treat" rules discussed earlier in this chapter.

NO DEDUCTIONS FOR THE COST OF MAINTAINING AND OPERATING ENTERTAINMENT FACILITIES

Generally, the term *entertainment facility* includes any item of real or personal property that is owned, rented, or used in connection with an entertainment activity. Such facilities include yachts, hunting lodges, fishing camps, swimming pools, tennis courts, and bowling alleys. Airplanes, automobiles, hotel suites, apartments, beach cottages, and ski lodges located in recreational areas may also be included as entertainment facilities but are not subject to the special rules unless the property is used in connection with entertainment. When an automobile or airplane is used for business trips, the expenses for depreciation and operating cost continue to be allowed.

Costs in connection with entertainment facilities include deductions for depreciation, rent, water, electricity, repairs, painting, insurance charges, and salaries or expenses for caretakers and watchmen. Effectively, all expenses for maintaining and operating the facility are disallowed. Ownership expenses that are otherwise deductible, such as mortgage interest and property taxes, continue to be deductible.

Caution: The disallowance applies only to the cost of maintaining and operating the entertainment facility. Expenses for otherwise allowable business entertainment activities and business meals continue to be deductible. For example, the out-of-pocket cost for a dinner at an entertainment facility is deductible, even though the costs of maintaining the facility are not.

No lodging deduction: The disallowance of entertainment cost is extended to the cost of lodging on trips to recreational areas.

Example: Wilson, an outside salesperson, takes a customer hunting for a day at a commercial shooting preserve. The expenses of the hunt, including the hunting rights, dogs, and hunting guide are deductible providing that Wilson meets the test for deducting associated entertainment.

That night Wilson and his customer stay at the shooting preserve's hunting lodge. The cost attributable to the lodging is not deductible.

HOW TO DEDUCT THE COST OF SEASON TICKETS TO SPORTING AND THEATRICAL EVENTS

Season tickets and box seats to theaters and sporting events are treated according to the individual events. If, for example, you hold season theater tickets and are entitled to attend 15 performances during the year, you treat each of the 15 performances separately.

Theater performances and sporting events generally constitute associated entertainment; therefore, you must satisfy the rules of substantiation for associated entertainment. That entails having a substantial and bona fide business discussion before or after the entertainment event and meeting the five elements of substantiation.

Also, when using associated entertainment as a means to increase your business, you need not accompany the person or persons being entertained. You could, for example, give the theater tickets to your clients and send them to the theater alone.

HOW TO DEDUCT THE COST OF ENTERTAINING YOUR SPOUSE

The IRS has a "closely connected" rule, and although it is not stated explicitly, most spouses would be deemed closely connected. This rule permits deducting the expenses of entertaining your spouse as well as the spouse of a business guest, because your spouse is considered to be present as a result of the presence of the business guest's spouse.

In other words, if your business guest brings a spouse, you are entitled to bring yours. Naturally, you must be entertaining the business guest during the ordinary and necessary course of your business, and you must meet the five elements of substantiation. If you have complied with these requirements, then the presence of your spouse to offset the presence of the business guest's spouse results in a deduction for both spouses.

Example: Jones entertains a business customer in the ordinary and necessary course of business and meets the five elements of substantiation. The customer's spouse joins Jones and the customer during the entertainment, because under the circumstances, it is impractical to entertain the customer without the spouse (for example, the customer is from out of town). The cost of entertaining the customer's spouse is deductible. In addition, Jones's spouse joins the entertainment because the customer's spouse is present; therefore, the cost of entertainment allocable to Jones's wife is also deductible as an ordinary and necessary business expense.

Effectively, if the spouse of the prospect or client is present because it is either impractical for the spouse not to be present (out-of-town clients) or because both spouses must be present during the decision-making process (purchase of a new home), then the cost of entertaining both spouses is deductible.

When spouses are present, you must have a clear business purpose rather than a personal or social motivation in incurring the expense. The rationale should be set forth when you meet the five elements of substantiation.

SPECIAL SUBSTANTIATION FOR EMPLOYERS

To obtain a deduction for entertainment expenses, the employer has the burden of support. Effectively, the employer must maintain adequate records and documents that substantiate all expenditures made by an employee for the benefit of the employer.

Thus, the employer must require the employee to submit documentary evidence including an account book, diary, or similar record in which entertainment expenses were entered at or near the time they were incurred.

Essentially, an employer must insist that employees meet all the documentation requirements discussed in this chapter. The submission of a monthly expense report would not be adequate. The employer must be able to prove that the entries were made at or near the time the entertainment expenses were incurred. Thus, in addition to the expense report, the employer should insist on some type of diary record.

Review required: For an employer's accounting procedures to be deemed adequate, the employer must utilize proper internal controls so that employees' entertainment expenses can be verified by a person other than the one incurring the expense.

Hint: The burden of support can be shifted to some extent from the employer to the employee if the employer treats the reimbursements to the employee as additional compensation, subject to withholding.

SPECIAL DOCUMENTATION RULES FOR EMPLOYEES

An employee who makes an "adequate accounting" of his expenses to his employer may be excused from reporting reimbursements and deductions on his return. Also, he may be excused from providing further substantiation of his expenses.

The problem is the term "adequate accounting." That means an employee must meet all the rules for substantiation discussed in this book and submit those documents substantiating the expense, including an account book, diary, or similar record, in which he has entered each expenditure *at or near the time he made it.* In other words, the employee must submit to the employer the same type of records and supporting documentary evidence

that would be required if he were not reimbursed.

When there is a reimbursement arrangement, the employer, not the employee, has the burden of proving the deductibility of entertainment expenses under the "directly related" or "associated" tests.

Big danger—failure to seek reimbursement: If the employee could have been reimbursed, but did not seek reimbursement, he cannot deduct the outlay as a business expense. The deduction is lost forever.

Hint—employment agreement: If an employee will be reimbursed for some expenses but not others, his employment agreement must detail the nature of this arrangement. The IRS assumes that the employer will reimburse the employee for all "ordinary and necessary" business expenses. Only an employment agreement can overcome this presumption.

Example: Farrar works as a salesman for the Tax Reduction Institute. His employment agreement requires him to incur entertainment expenses on behalf of the Tax Reduction Institute. Such entertainment expenses are considered essential in his position. However, his employment agreement requires him to absorb all Tax Reduction Institute entertainment expenses and further states that his salary is considered adequate to absorb such expenses on behalf of the company. Accordingly, Farrar has a legitimate claim to deductible employee business expenses.

Since Farrar wants to deduct the "employee business expenses" for which he was not reimbursed, he must:

1. Submit a statement with his tax return detailing the total reimbursements and a list of all expenses broken down into categories, such as transportation, entertainment, gifts, meals and lodging while away from home.
2. Maintain records and evidence according to the rules discussed in this chapter for substantiating entertainment deductions.

His net deduction is the difference between the expenses incurred and the total reimbursement.

WHY SHAREHOLDER/EMPLOYEES FACE DOUBLE JEOPARDY WHEN THEY FAIL THE DOCUMENTATION REQUIREMENTS

If a shareholder of a one-person or small corporation fails to adequately support reimbursed entertainment expenses, the IRS will disallow the deduction to the corporation and deem the expenses a dividend to the shareholder. Thus, both the corporation and the individual shareholder will be taxed (double taxation).

If you are employed by a corporation in which you own 10 percent or more of the stock, make certain you have a reimbursement arrangement (or nonarrangement) evidenced by written agreement with the corporation. Preferably, such agreement should be approved by corporate resolution.

If you are reimbursed for entertainment expenses, make doubly sure (or you'll be doubly taxed) to meet the substantiation rules discussed in this chapter.

HOW AUTOMOBILES AND AIRPLANES BECOME ENTERTAINMENT FACILITIES AND THEREFORE BE NONDEDUCTIBLE

The IRS broadly defines the term "entertainment facility" to include any item of personal or real property owned, rented, or used by a taxpayer . . . if it is used during the taxable year for, or in connection with, entertainment. This definition includes automobiles and airplanes that are used for entertainment purposes. It means that a deduction for expenditures incurred "with respect to" an automobile that is used for entertainment could be disallowed.

Occasional or incidental use in connection with entertainment will not disallow the expenses of an automobile or an airplane.

However, use of an automobile or airplane for "associated" entertainment could be disallowed.

Essentially, use of an automobile or airplane for "associated" entertainment is treated as personal use. It does not count as business use.

Summary: Most business professionals must involve themselves in business entertainment. Since this is an unavoidable fact of life, and since it is possibly one of your best promotional tools, document it carefully! Take your legitimate tax deductions. After all, you are entitled to them.

TAX REDUCTION CHECKLIST

IRS publication to be obtained:

- Publication 463—*Travel, Entertainment, and Gift Expenses*

Basic rule for all entertainment:

- It must be incurred for ordinary and necessary business expenses.
- It must be documented to meet five elements of substantiation.

The five elements of substantiation are:

- Cost—receipts are required if amount is $25 or more.
- Time of entertainment (e.g., date).
- Description of entertainment and place.
- Business purpose of entertainment and discussion, if any.
- Business relationship of guests entertained.

General types of entertainment:

- Quiet business meal—it has a business purpose, but need not include a business discussion.
- Directly related entertainment—it has a definite monetary or other business purpose and generally includes an active business discussion.
- "Associated with" (goodwill) entertainment—it generally is fun, such as golf, hunting, or the theater, and must precede or follow a substantial and bona fide business discussion.

Hints for quiet business meals:

- They must be served in an atmosphere conducive to business discussion.
- When you pick up the tab for guests, the entire tab is deductible unless you are absorbing a substantial amount of your personal meal expenses.
- Dutch treat lunches in excess of usual personal lunch expenses are deductible.
- When a quiet business meal is served at home, establish clear business (versus social) motive.
- You must meet the five elements of substantiation.
- You need a business reason for the meal, but need not discuss business.

Social, athletic, and sporting club dues:

- Deduction is based on a two-step process.
- Step 1—Business days of use must exceed personal days of use.
- Step 2—If you pass step 1, deduction is based on days of defined directly related usage.

Tickets to theaters, sporting events, and so forth:

- They are deductible when the event follows or precedes a substantial business discussion.
- You need not attend to get a deduction.
- The five elements of substantiation must be met.
- Season tickets are deducted event by event.

Expenses for entertainment facilities:

- They are not deductible.
- The IRS even disallows lodging on hunting trips.

Expenses for entertaining spouses:

- They are deductible if necessitated by business.
- Out-of-town guest's spouse may necessitate your spouse's presence.

- A dual decision by husband and wife may necessitate your spouse's presence.

Expenses for employers, employees and shareholders:

- Employers have burden of proof.
- Employees should keep daily diaries.
- Employers must have adequate expense verification procedures.
- Employees who are entitled to reimbursement but fail to be reimbursed may not deduct such expenses.
- Employees who are partially reimbursed should have a written employment agreement.
- Shareholder/employees should have written employment agreement specifying reimbursement policy of company.

We assume that you would like to combine a little pleasure with your business travel.

Tax law obviously does not say, "combine a little pleasure with business to obtain extra tax deductions while traveling." The law does, however, allow 100 percent deductions for transportation expenses incurred on combined business and pleasure trips when a specified percentage of days are spent on business. Furthermore, you do not need to spend all day on business or at a convention to deduct expenses incurred during that day.

To obtain any deduction for travel, even travel for an all-work/no-play business trip, you must adhere to some very strict documentation requirements.

DEFINITIONS OF TRAVEL AND TRAVEL EXPENSES

Travel expenses differ from local transportation costs. You are "traveling" when you are away from home overnight or for a period of time sufficient to require sleep.

Travel expenses include expenditures for sustaining life on the road, as well as transportation costs to your overnight or "sleep" destination. Thus, costs for airfare, automo-biles, cabs, meals, hotel rooms, and even laundry or dry cleaning are deductible.

To prove that you have been away overnight or long enough to require sleep, you are required to keep all lodging receipts. In addition to showing that you were away on a trip that required sleep, the lodging receipt will let the IRS know whether you were alone or with someone else. Lodging receipts usually show the number of occupants in the room.

Deductible travel expenses on a trip away from home overnight include:

- Air, rail, and bus fares.
- Operation and maintenance expenses for your automobile.
- Taxi fares or other costs of transportation between the airport and hotel, and from one customer to another.
- Baggage charges and transportation costs for sample and display materials.
- Meals and lodging.
- Cleaning and laundry expenses.
- Telephone and telegraph expenses.
- Public stenographer's fees.
- Tips that are incidental to any of these expenses.
- Other expenses incidental to qualifying travel.

In other words, you are allowed to deduct essentially all the expenses of sustaining busi-

4

How to Combine Pleasure With Business and Get a Tax Deduction for Travel Expenses

ness life on the road while you are away from home for a sufficient length of time to require sleep.

WHAT IS AWAY FROM HOME

Generally, your tax home is your principal place of business, regardless of where you maintain your family residence. If you do not have a regular or principal place of business, then your tax home is the place where you regularly reside in a real and substantial sense.

If you do not have a regular place of business or do not regularly live someplace, you are considered an itinerant and your home is wherever you happen to work. Thus, as an itinerant you are never away from home and you may never claim a traveling expense deduction.

If you live and work in the same city, you have no problem with the "tax home" rules and you should merely scan the rest of this discussion and proceed to the next section of this chapter. However, if you live and work in different places, you could have a "tax home" problem.

The IRS does not yet have the power to tell you where to live. Since you choose your "home," the IRS, with the support of the Tax Court, has consistently taken the position that your "tax home" is your principal place of business, not your abode. Accordingly, travel from your home to your business is not deductible.

Exceptions: If you have a principal place of employment and business in one location and you accept temporary work or you have a secondary business at another location, your presence at the second location is deductible as *away from home travel expenses* if it would be unreasonable to expect you to move you and your family to the second location. If you have no principal place of employment, but you are sent on temporary assignments from a city where you maintain a "live-in-home," your real home becomes your "tax home." As you would expect, the IRS has a number of definitions in connection with the exceptions.

What is "temporarily" away from home? Once you have a tax home, the travel expenses to take a "temporary" job at a place where it is impossible to return home each day are deductible. Thus, in this case you deduct breakfast, lunch, dinner, lodging, and other travel expenses. But what is "temporary?" It means employment of a definite, limited duration. Employment for an indefinite period of time, although temporary, will not qualify.

To help you distinguish "temporary" from "indefinite" work, the IRS has issued a revenue ruling which states that you have "temporary" work when you satisfy three requirements:

1. You "clearly demonstrate by objective factors" that you "realistically expected" your employment to last for less than two years and that you would return home at the end of that time;
2. You did, in fact, return home within two years; and
3. Your claimed tax home is your "regular place of abode in a real and substantial sense."

To satisfy the third requirement—that your claimed tax home is your "regular place of abode in a real and substantial sense"—you must prove three further facts:

1. You lived in the claimed tax home while working in its vicinity before taking the temporary job, *and* you maintain bona fide work contacts (such as job-seeking, taking a leave of absence, or operating a second business) in the area of your claimed tax home during your temporary employment;
2. Your living expenses at your claimed tax home are duplicated during your temporary employment because your work requires you to be away from home; and
3. One or more family members continue to live at your claimed tax home, *or* you continue to use your claimed tax home frequently (such as staying there on weekends).

If you can prove all three of these facts, the IRS will allow your deduction. If you can prove only two of these facts, the IRS will give all the facts and circumstances of your case "close scrutiny" in deciding if your deduction is allowable. If you prove only one of these facts, the IRS will turn down your deduction.

Case law by and large follow the IRS's tests; however, the Tax Court has pointed out that "No single element is determinative of the ultimate factual issue of temporariness, and there are no rules of thumb, durational or otherwise. Each case turns on its own facts." If you have circumstances that you think are "temporary," but your facts and circumstances do not fall within the IRS's tests, see your tax advisor immediately.

Factors indicative of "indefinite" work: To qualify for a travel expense deduction, the work at a "temporary" location must be temporary and not "indefinite" or "indeterminate." If you cannot foresee or reasonably predict when the work will end at the time you set out to work at a temporary location, the work is considered "indefinite" and you are not entitled to any travel deductions.

Get proof: If, at the time you accept a "temporary" assignment, you expect the assignment to last less than two years, obtain proof. At the time you accept the employment, have your employer write you a letter or a contract.

Temporary work which turns out to be indefinite: Work could start out as being originally "temporary" because it has a short-lived duration at the outset, but then later become indefinite or indeterminate because the assignment extends beyond the reasonably short period originally anticipated. Such a change of status is generally manifested by some outside indication demonstrating that the assignment will be prolonged, rather than temporary. In this situation, you deduct expenses during the temporary period, but once the assignment becomes indefinite, your deductions stop.

Seasonal employment: You have one, and only one tax home. If you have more than one business location, one will be considered "major" and the other will be considered "minor." Generally, the determination of your "major" business location is based on the total time spent at each location, the degree of business activity in each location, and the relative financial return from each business location. If you travel from your major business location to a minor business location, the travel expenses incurred during the stay at the minor business location are deductible.

Caution—no travel deductions for trips from temporary employment to personal residence: If you are temporarily employed away from your home and you return home on non–working days to visit your family or for other personal reasons, the cost of the trip home is personal and nondeductible. However, the IRS has ruled that the cost of such trips home may be deducted as traveling expenses to the extent they do not exceed either: (1) otherwise deductible expenses that you would have incurred had you remained at the temporary location, or (2) the reasonable and necessary expenses you would have incurred in traveling between the temporary location and your principal location. Thus, if it would cost you more to stay at the temporary location than return home, you get a full deduction for the travel expenses home. On the other hand, if it would cost more to travel home than to stay at the temporary location, your deduction is limited to the cost you would have incurred had you stayed at the temporary location.

Key to deduction—duplicate living expenses: If you do not have any duplicate living expenses, you are not traveling. Your "tax home" follows you from location to location.

Discrimination against singles: The IRS has indicated that it's "probable" that a single person would have more difficulty establishing a "tax home" because it would be difficult for a single person to have duplicate living expenses. Thus, if you are single, you must demonstrate duplicate upkeep costs and regular visits to an abode that you can call your "tax home."

Multiple places of business: If you have regular work at two or more locations, each a "traveling" distance from the other, you must determine which location constitutes your principal place of business. Trips from your residence to your principal place of business are nondeductible commuting costs. But trips from your principal place of business to any secondary business location requiring sleep result in deductible travel expenses. Generally, your principal business location is based on three factors: (1) the total time ordinarily spent by you at each business post, (2) the degree of business activity in each area, and (3) the relative significance of the financial return from each area. Of these, the first factor is considered the most significant.

Second business in your home: If your minor place of business is in the same location where you live, trips from your principal business to your home are not deductible.

Married couple working apart: Where a husband and wife each have a principal business or position at distant locations, the "tax home" of each is where he or she works. Thus, if both live in Washington, D.C., but one works in New York City, that person gets no travel deductions.

Special rules for transportation workers: An airline pilot, railroad employee, or truck driver has his "tax home" at his principal or regular post of duty, regardless of the physical location of his residence. The principal post of duty of an airline pilot is the airport where he departs on scheduled flights. The principal post of duty of a member of a train crew is the terminal where the train begins and ends its runs. The "tax home" of a long lines truck driver is his home terminal.

Special rules for construction workers: The construction worker who is usually employed on job sites in and around the city where he has his "regular place of abode" and maintains his union membership, but who occasionally accepts employment elsewhere for periods of less than two years when work in his home vicinity is unavailable qualifies for travel expense deductions when he accepts "temporary" jobs.

Special rules for professional athletes: Generally, an athlete's "tax home" is the professional team's home town. Thus, while he is in the city where his professional team is located, he does not incur travel expenses. If he lives in another town and commutes to the town where his team is located, the expenses of traveling from his "home" town to

his "tax town" are nondeductible personal expenditures.

Exception: If a professional athlete has a business during the off-season and that business generates more income and takes more time than athletics, the "tax home" becomes the athlete's principal business location. For details, see the earlier discussion on principal place of business.

Special rules for entertainers and actors: The IRS frequently argues that entertainers or actors who have numerous temporary engagements have no "tax home" from which to be away. Generally, the IRS will win such arguments if an actor resides where he performs, or if he has no contact with another location. This happens in cases of circus performers who live with the troupe, or musicians or comedians who stay where they perform.

On the other hand, if an actor or entertainer can demonstrate that he incurs duplicate expenses at a residence where he spends his nontraveling time, the deduction for travel expenses could be allowed even if the number of days spent away from home far exceeds the time spent at home.

To qualify for deductible traveling expenses, actors and entertainers must meet the "temporary" work rules. Such rules are not effective if an engagement is "indefinite."

Once you have a tax home: You must have a tax home in order to have deductible travel expenses. Once you've established the tax home, all expenses incurred on business trips away from your home (when you require sleep) are deductible. Moreover, you may be in a position to have combined business/personal trips.

HOW TO CONVERT WEEKENDS TO TAX-DEDUCTIBLE BUSINESS DAYS

Travel expenses are divided into two components: (1) transportation, and (2) on the road living expenses. You deduct transportation expenses when your "trip" is primarily business. You deduct "on the road" expenses for each business day.

There are five types of business days.

1. Your presence required: If your presence is required at a particular place for a specific and bona fide business purpose, that day is counted as a business day, even though your presence is required for only part of the day and even if, during the normal working hours of the day, you spend more time sightseeing and playing than participating in business activities.

Example: You fly to Hawaii to get a contract signed. The signing takes one hour, and you spend the rest of the day at the beach. You have a business day.

2. Principal activity is business: If you spend the majority of normal working hours pursuing your trade or business, that day is counted as a business day. When you are prevented from engaging in the conduct of your trade or business because of circumstances beyond your control, the day is still counted as a business day, even though you spend the day in the sun.

Example: You drive to Chicago to meet with a client. On the day the meeting is scheduled, your client is run over by a truck. The day is a business day.

3. Convention, meeting, or seminar day: If a convention, meeting, or seminar has at least six hours of scheduled business activities during the day, and you attend at least two-thirds of these activities, your day is considered a business day. (Note—although this rule is from the old foreign convention rules, it has been followed by the courts for domestic conventions.)

4. Travel days are business days: Days in transit are considered business days provided that the travel is by reasonably direct route to the business destination and does not involve substantial nonbusiness diversions.

The need to take a reasonably direct route does not affect your means of transportation. You may take the trip by automobile, airplane, or train, provided that your route is reasonably direct. The days you spend traveling by the direct route are considered business days.

Example: Mary takes three days to drive in a direct route from her home in Phoenix to a convention in Chicago. All three days are counted as business days.

5. Weekends and holidays are business days: Legal holidays or weekends which fall between business meeting dates are counted as business days if you are in a foreign destination. Thus, all on the road expenses for the weekend or holiday are deductible as business travel expenses in that foreign destination.

If you are traveling domestically or in "North America" and the legal holidays or weekends fall between business meeting dates, you are allowed to deduct the lesser of (1) what it would cost to return home and back, or (2) what it would cost to stay at your business destination.

Example: Patterson travels from Buffalo, New York, to Honolulu, Hawaii, on Thursday. She conducts business on Friday, spends Saturday and Sunday waiting for a business discussion on Monday, and returns to Buffalo on Tuesday. Since it would have been more expensive to return to Buffalo, all travel and subsistence expenses during the trip are business and deductible, including the weekend.

Hint: It is extremely important to keep track of the time you spend working or at seminars each day. Make notations in your diary to substantiate the time spent on business every day you are away from home.

For each business day, you are entitled to deduct your "on the road" expenses. Also, the number of business days as compared to the number of personal days will determine how much, if any, of your transportation expenses to your travel destination are deductible.

THREE TAX TRAVEL RULES THAT ALLOW COMBINED BUSINESS AND PLEASURE

To deduct a business trip, the primary purpose of the trip must be business. Traveling for business reasons is subject to the "ordinary and necessary" test. That is, you are allowed to deduct your expenses if the trip is helpful, appropriate, needed, normal, customary, or usual in your pursuit of business. In other words, you must have planned the trip with the possibility of benefiting your business. Therefore, a trip to meet with a prospect is just as deductible as a trip to meet with a client.

When your trip is to a convention, meeting, or seminar, you may deduct the expenses if you can show that attendance benefits or advances the interest of your trade or business. Conventions for social, political, or other purposes are not deductible.

Example: Sam, a dentist, attends a dental convention. Assuming that he meets all the tests for support and business days, Sam has incurred deductible expenses.

Example: Mike, a dentist, attends a Shriners' convention. Mike has taken a personal trip and incurred personal expenses that are not deductible.

Hint: Trips on behalf of charitable organizations may be deductible as charitable contributions.

If you attend a convention as an appointed or elected delegate of a local group, your expenses are deductible if you can demonstrate that your attendance benefits or advances your business interest. It's your business interests that count, not the interests of the group you represent.

Example: Johnson, a lawyer, is a member of the committee that plans the annual State Bar convention. The committee meets at a distant city, and has an agenda showing that the principal purpose of the meeting is to plan the convention. Since Johnson's bar association activity is business related, the expense of his attendance at the committee meeting is tax deductible, even though there is no direct business benefit from the activity at the meeting.

Two types of travel: There are basically two types of travel:

- Travel strictly for business.
- Travel to a convention, meeting, or seminar.

Three destinations: Your travel for business or to a convention, meeting, or seminar is subject to different rules depending on your destination.

- Business trips within the 50 United States and the District of Columbia are subject to the $^{51}/_{49}$ business purpose test.

- Convention, meeting, or seminar trips within the defined North American area are subject to the $^{51}/_{49}$ test.
- Trips on business outside the United States and District of Columbia and trips to conventions, meetings, or seminars outside the defined North American area are considered "foreign" trips and are subject to either the $^{76}/_{24}$ test or the one-week test.

The tests are discussed later in this chapter.

Easy method: When taking a trip where you will combine business and pleasure, always refer to the flowchart in Exhibit 4-1. It's easy to use and it will tell you which rule applies to which trip. Once you know the rules, business trips are much more fun.

Example usage: Assume you are taking a trip to Montreal, Canada, for the purpose of conducting a specific business transaction. The trip will take four days, but the business will take only one. Use the flowchart to determine how much of the "transportation" expenses are deductible.

Result: All (100 percent) of the transportation expenses to and from Montreal are tax deductible. The trip is foreign, and subject to the "one-week" exception, to be discussed in more detail later.

Trip to convention in Montreal: Assume the same four-day trip to Montreal to attend a convention for one day. Which test applies, and how much of the "transportation" expenses can you deduct?

Result: You are subject to the $^{51}/_{49}$ test for a trip to a convention in the North American area. Since you failed to establish the primary purpose of the trip as business based on the days you spent working, you will not be allowed a "transportation" deduction unless you can establish that, in spite of the minor business activity (one day out of four) at your business destination, the trip was still primarily business. We'll discuss this further in connection with the discussion on the $^{51}/_{49}$ test.

Important reminder: Your travel expenses are divided into two components: (1) trans-

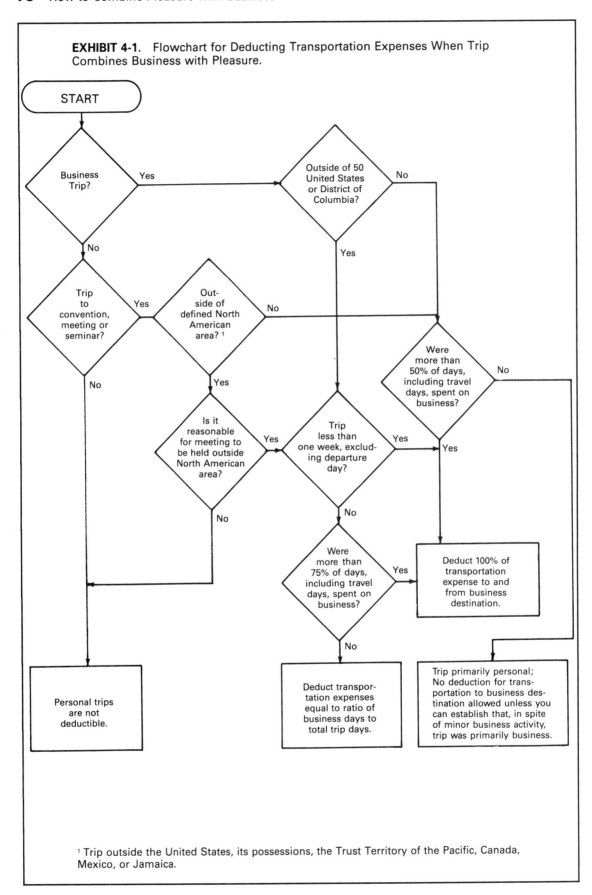

EXHIBIT 4-1. Flowchart for Deducting Transportation Expenses When Trip Combines Business with Pleasure.

¹ Trip outside the United States, its possessions, the Trust Territory of the Pacific, Canada, Mexico, or Jamaica.

portation, and (2) on the road expenses. For each business day, you deduct your "on the road" expenses. When the trip meets the tests outlined in the flowchart in Exhibit 4-1, you deduct 100 percent of the transportation costs. If you fail the tests in Exhibit 4-1, you may end up allocating transportation expense between business and pleasure.

GUIDELINES FOR COMBINING PLEASURE AND BUSINESS ON A TRIP SUBJECT TO THE "⁵¹/₄₉" TEST

The cost of transportation is deductible for "business trips" within the 50 United States and the District of Columbia or "convention, meeting, or seminar trips" within the defined North American area if, and only if, the purpose of the trip is "primarily for business." Conversely, if the travel is primarily for pleasure, none of your travel expenses are deductible, even though you engage in some business activities at the destination. In this case, though, "on the road" expenses attributable to your business activities at the destination are deductible even though the "transportation" expenses are not.

Generally, the primary purpose of a trip is supported by the number of days spent on business versus those spent on pleasure. Hence, the "⁵¹/₄₉" test.

Example: If you take an eleven-day trip subject to the ⁵¹/₄₉ test, you must spend six days on business in order to deduct 100 percent of the transportation expenses, unless you can demonstrate otherwise that the trip was primarily for business reasons.

The question of whether a trip is primarily for business, thereby rendering the "transportation" costs entirely deductible, or primarily for pleasure, thereby rendering the transportation costs entirely nondeductible, is essentially a question of fact; the burden of proof showing the travel as primarily business-related is on you, the taxpayer. The IRS stresses that the amount of time spent on personal activities compared to the time spent on business is an "important factor" in deciding whether a trip is primarily for pleasure or business.

Example: Assume you are in control of your business trips and that you spend one week at a convention in New York City and from there visit your relatives in Connecticut for five weeks. If you live in San Diego, the presumption would be that the trip was primarily for personal reasons since you controlled it and spent only one-sixth of your time at a business convention. Accordingly, the $700 you spent for transportation from San Diego to New York City is not deductible, but the $800 you paid for meals and lodging while attending the convention is deductible.

If your trip is primarily for business and, while at your business destination, you extend your stay for a vacation, make a nonbusiness side trip, or have other nonbusiness activities, you may deduct the travel expenses to and from your destination.

Example: You work in Atlanta and make a business trip to New Orleans. On the way home, you stop in Mobile to visit your parents. You spend $450 for the nine days you are away from home for travel, meals, lodging, and other travel expenses. If you had not stopped in Mobile, you would have been gone six days and your total cost would have been $400. You may deduct $400 for your trip, including the round-trip transportation, to and from New Orleans.

Defined North American area: The North American area includes the Unites States, its possessions, the Trust Territory of the Pacific Islands, Canada, Mexico, and Jamaica. The U.S. possessions include Puerto Rico, Guam, and the U.S. Virgin Islands. The Trust Territory of the Pacific lslands includes American Samoa. Jamaica includes the island of Jamaica, the Morant Cays, the Pedro Cays, and their dependencies.

Technical note: Public law 96-608 authorized the attendance at conventions, meetings, and seminars in the North American area to be treated the same as a convention, meeting, or seminar held in Chicago. The Senate explanation of this law states, "Under the bill, a convention would not be treated as a foreign convention unless it were held outside the United States, its possessions, and the Trust Territory of the Pacific, and Canada and

Mexico . . . as for any other travel expenses, the principal purpose for making the trip must be for business purposes for transportation expenses to be deductible." Current IRS regulations do not yet reflect the changes brought about by this new law.

You may have noted that Jamaica was not included in the Senate explanation. Jamaica was added as a North American convention site as part of a tax treaty which came about after the new law was passed.

Important reminder: The $^{51}/_{49}$ test applies to business trips within the 50 United States and the District of Columbia and to trips for conventions, meetings, or seminars held within the defined North American area. You obtain a deduction for 100 percent of your "transportation" expenses when you have as your *primary* purpose a business reason for a trip.

Caution: The principal motivation for your trip must be either business or attendance, regardless of the daily classifications. Days provide support for your intent; they do not constitute intent.

Hint: Correspondence prior to a trip is good evidence of intent.

GUIDELINES FOR COMBINING PLEASURE WITH A FOREIGN BUSINESS OR CONVENTION TRIP

Congress seems to think trips to foreign destinations are a rotten idea. Certainly, you must spend a lot less time having fun on a foreign trip because to obtain a deduction for 100 percent of your transportation expenses to and from the destination, you must spend 76 percent of your time on business ($^{76}/_{24}$ test) or spend less than one week at the location.

Remember, trips for business within the 50 United States and the District of Columbia and trips for conventions, meetings, and seminars within the defined North American area are subject to the $^{51}/_{49}$ test. Trips outside of these areas are subject to the $^{76}/_{24}$ test, or the one-week test.

Special reasonableness test for conventions, meetings, and seminars held outside the North

American area: No deduction is allowed for expenses allocable to a convention, seminar, or similar meeting held outside the North American area unless, taking certain factors into account, it is "as reasonable" for the meeting to be held outside the North American area as within it. Under this reasonableness standard, the factors to be taken into account are: (1) the purpose of the meeting and the activities taking place at the meeting; (2) the purposes and activities of the sponsoring organizations or groups; and (3) the residences of the active members of the sponsoring organization and the places at which other meetings of the sponsoring organizations or groups have been or will be held.

IRS has yet to propose regulations on the "reasonableness standard." What you have just read is taken from the Senate explanation of the law. When the IRS does set forth its guidelines on what constitutes reasonableness, the general effect will discourage conventions held in foreign locations.

Exceptions to $^{76}/_{24}$ test: You may deduct your travel expenses for a trip into a foreign area using the same rules that apply to U.S. travel if you meet either of the following conditions:

1. You have no substantial control over arranging the trip. You are not considered to have control merely because you have control over the timing of your trip.
2. You are an employee, not related to your employer, and not a managing executive, and you were reimbursed or received a travel expense allowance for the foreign trip.

Executives have control: If you have executive authority and responsibility for arranging your trips and you are not subject to the veto of another, you are deemed to have substantial control over arranging your trips.

Self-employed: If you are self-employed, you are generally regarded as having substantial control over arranging your business trips.

Deduct all transportation: To deduct 100 percent of the transportation costs to and from your business destination in a foreign location, you must either pass the $^{76}/_{24}$ test, which means that 76 percent of your days were spent on business or convention activities (remember, weekends and travel days may count as business days), or spend less than one week at the business or convention location.

Example: You flew from Seattle to Tokyo, where you spent 14 days on business and five days playing, and then flew back to Seattle. You spent one day's flying time in each direction. Your entire trip was more than one week, but only five of the 21 days of your total time abroad (less than 25 percent) were spent in nonbusiness activities. You may deduct as your travel expenses what it would have cost you to make the trip if you had not engaged in any nonbusiness activity. Thus, you may deduct the round-trip airfare and 16 days of meals, lodging, taxis, car rentals, shoe shines, and so forth. You may not, however, deduct the daily "on the road" expenses of the five playtime days.

Failing the $^{76}/_{24}$ test: When you spend more than a week on a foreign trip, and you fail the $^{76}/_{24}$ test, you must allocate your transportation expenses between business and pleasure. The allocation is based on the ratio of business days to total trip days. Thus, if you spend eight days on business (or at conventions and meetings) and four days on pleasure, you may deduct two-thirds of the transportation expenses.

One-week test: The one-week test applies to foreign travel only. Spend one week or less traveling to a foreign destination for either business or a convention, and you may deduct 100 percent of the transportation costs of getting to and from the location. For this test, one week means seven consecutive days including the day of departure, but excluding the day of return.

Example: On Wednesday morning, you leave for a three-day convention in Paris. After the convention, you tour Paris and then return home the following Wednesday evening. Your trip took a total of eight days, but the date of departure from Paris is not counted; accordingly, you may deduct 100 percent of your transportation expenses to and from the convention location.

HOW TO DEDUCT TRAVEL EXPENSES WHEN LOOKING FOR RENTAL PROPERTIES

You are allowed to deduct all travel expenses in connection with your business or income-producing activities. In this section we will travel the sometimes rocky road of looking for rental properties and see what travel expenses are deductible. Depending on your circumstances, the deductible expenses can be:

- Written off "above the line" as business deductions (Schedule C);
- Written off "below the line" as itemized deductions (Schedule A);
- Written off (amortized) over a 60-month period as "start-up expenditures" of an "active" rental business;
- Written off (partially) as part of the depreciable basis of property used in a "passive" rental business; or
- Not written off at all (Oh horror of horrors!).

Exhibit 4-2 provides a road map showing the way to each of these five tax destinations. The business traveler and the nonbusiness traveler take off on different roads, but sometimes reach the same tax destination if they make a purchase. On the other hand, the business traveler sometimes gets a business deduction, whereas the nonbusiness traveler may get an itemized deduction or no deduction at all.

Your tax destination on a property-seeking trip depends on the answers to these questions:

- Are you traveling to expand your existing rental business?
- Have you targeted a specific property for purchase?
- Did you buy the targeted property?
- Is your rental business "active" or "passive"?

Why business gives you a smooth road: A business traveler can write off any properly documented expenses incurred in looking for or attempting to purchase business property. If property is purchased, the travel costs are capitalized as part of its cost. These expenses

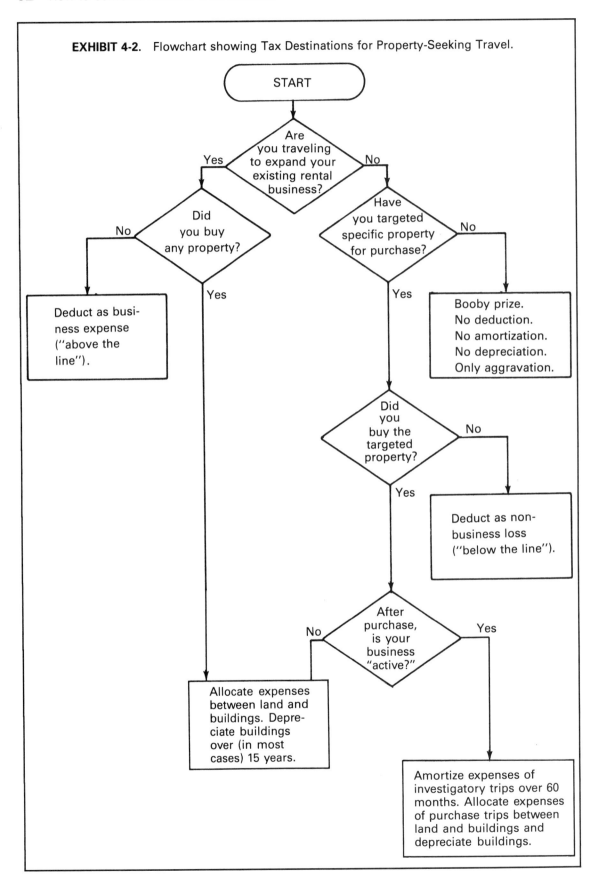

EXHIBIT 4-2. Flowchart showing Tax Destinations for Property-Seeking Travel.

are written off in part as a portion of the property's depreciable basis.

Rocky road for nonbusiness traveler: The road is rockier for the nonbusiness traveler because personal expenses are not deductible. Property-seeking expenditures are considered "personal" until the nonbusiness traveler actually targets a property for purchase. At that point, the traveler is considered to have entered into a profit-seeking "transaction." If the property is not purchased, any further expenses constitute an itemized deduction (called a nonbusiness loss). If the property is purchased, the expenses are capitalized and are written off, in part, as a portion of the property's depreciable basis.

Result: The practical result of being a nonbusiness traveler is that general "investigatory" expenditures are not deductible.

How to be in business: Buy a piece of rental property and you are in business. According to the Tax Court and the IRS, that's all it takes. In fact, the Tax Court even says that you are in business if you inherit that one piece of rental property and hire someone else to manage it for you.

But deducting travel isn't easy: Although there is no trick to establishing that you are in the rental business, you do not automatically get a deduction for property-seeking travel. You must prove that the travel is connected to your *existing* rental business.

Example: Consider the case of Mr. O'Donnell, who owned rental property in Las Vegas. He owned a house and a two-unit apartment building in his own name, and owned three small commercial buildings jointly with his brother. When O'Donnell found out about the rental building for sale in Miami, Florida, he took a trip to look at it. He decided not to buy it, but tried to deduct the cost of the trip as a business expense.

"No soap," said the Tax Court. Being in business one place doesn't give you a tax-deductible ticket to look elsewhere, even though you are looking for the same kind of business. To be deductible, the expense must be for expanding the existing business.

This is business: Mr. and Mrs. Fairey recently did battle with the IRS in the Tax Court, but fared much better than Mr. O'Donnell. Mr. Fairey was a construction worker who planned to retire soon and go into the rental business full time with his wife. The couple already owned five rental properties totaling 21 units in Santa Maria, California.

In May 1977 they spent a day in Palm Springs looking at a rental townhouse. During a vacation in Reno in November 1977 they spent two days looking at rental properties and made an offer to buy one. In May 1978 they again went to Palm Springs and spent three days looking at rental properties. During a November 1978 vacation in Phoenix, Arizona, they spent a day looking at rental properties. In June 1979 they bought two of the rental properties discovered on their 1978 Palm Springs trip.

The Tax Court decided that Mr. and Mrs. Fairey were in the business of "owning rental properties." The expenses of investigating the properties they purchased had to be capitalized, of course, but the expenses attributable to the other investigations that were not purchased were tax deductible.

In other words, Mr. and Mrs. Fairey received tax benefit for all of their property-seeking travel, except the direct vacation portions.

More business: For purposes of obtaining a home office deduction, the Tax Court ruled that Dr. Curphey, who owned and personally managed six rental units (two townhouses, three condominium units, and one single-family residence), was engaged in a business. Apparently, the units were all located in or around the city of Honolulu. Could Curphey have deducted the cost of an island-hopping search for more rental properties?

Facts and circumstances: The answer in Dr. Curphey's case, in Mr. and Mrs. Fairey's case, in Mr. O'Donnell's case, and in your case, depends on the facts and circumstances of each individual case. Factors include the scope and extent of the rental activity, including the amount of time spent on it. Renting a house in Bangor, Maine, probably will not justify a business deduction for travel to San Francisco to look at an office building. On the other hand, owning a rental property in a resort town might justify a business deduction for a trip to that town to look at another rental property there. In addition, lots of out-of-town property hunting will create a broader rental business than traveling only once a year.

Hint: As a practical matter, anyone who owns only one or two rental properties in their local area will have trouble showing that an out-of-town property hunt was part of the existing rental business. But you can still deduct the transportation expenses for local trips in pursuit of your business, including the search for new properties.

How targeting the property gets deductions: Don't just look at property; set your sights on it and go for it! Unless you are in the rental business and are traveling to expand it, you get no deduction for a "general search" or "preliminary investigation." Once you have targeted a specific property, however, you can deduct any expenses, including travel, related to an unsuccessful attempt to buy it. If your attempt is successful, the expenses are capitalized and deducted as explained later.

What is targeting a property? Targeting property means more than just looking at it. That's what poor Mr. O'Donnell found out when he tried to deduct the cost of his trip to Miami. As you will recall from the earlier discussion, the Tax Court didn't think Mr. O'Donnell's trip to Miami was related to his rental business in Las Vegas, so it did not allow him a business deduction. The court also denied him an itemized deduction because he had not entered into a profit-seeking transaction. He was just looking, even though he spent a lot of money doing so.

Don't sightsee: "Just looking" has caused many taxpayers to lose deductions, including one weary traveler who went all over the country looking for a newspaper business and another who flew to Europe, but returned

with only a serious case of jet lag to show for the effort. The IRS says you can't deduct any expenses unless you actually decide what to buy. Although the courts have not explicitly approved this rule, in just about all the cases allowing deductions, the taxpayers had committed themselves to buying a specific property.

The "just looking" rule prevents nonbusiness travelers from deducting the expenses of their first trip to see a property.

HOW TRAVEL EXPENSES FOR A NEW BUSINESS OR EMPLOYMENT ARE TREATED

To obtain deductions for travel expenses you must be in business. That presupposes an existing business or, in the case of an employee, existing employment. Deductions are available when you advance or further your business.

Essentially, tax law allows travel deductions when an expenditure is made in connection with acquiring, rather than retaining or protecting, a business. When you investigate a potential new trade or business, travel costs have been held to be capital costs and nondeductible (although they may qualify as amortizable "start-up expenses").

Job hunting by employees: If you are an employee, you are in the trade or business of rendering services to your employer. If you are an employee and you are seeking employment in a new field unrelated to the services you have performed in the past, you are seeking employment for the first time and the expenses of your job search are nondeductible. Also, if there is no "continuity" between your past employment and your new job search, the expenses of the job search are not deductible.

Expenses incurred by an employee in looking for new employment in his continuing and existing "trade or business" of performing services he previously rendered are deductible. The general travel rules discussed earlier in this chapter are applied to such searches. If the travel is primarily personal, the costs of travel are nondeductible, but expenses incurred during the trip allocable to the job search are deductible. If the trip is primarily business, the expenses are deductible.

Unsuccessful attempt to buy a new business: If you incur travel expenses in looking for a new business, a deduction may be available if you entered into a transaction for profit, but the transaction fell through. This rule was discussed in detail in the previous section of this chapter dealing with travel expenses incurred while looking for rental properties.

HOW TO WRITE OFF CRUISESHIP CONVENTIONS

A new law was born in 1983 as part of the gas tax bill (formally known as the Surface Transportation Assistance Act of 1982). This law allows a $2,000 deduction for cruiseship conventions.

General requirements: The new law permits a deduction of up to $2,000 each year for the expenses of attending conventions, seminars, or similar meetings on cruiseships, provided:

- The meeting is directly related to the active conduct of your business or investment (including tax planning) activities.
- The vessel is registered in the United States.
- All ports of call are located in the United States or possessions of the United States.
- Certain reporting requirements are met (see below).
- The regular "travel and entertainment" substantiation requirements are met.

Special reporting requirements: To deduct the cost of a cruiseship convention, seminar, or meeting, you must attach two statements to your tax return. Failure to attach the statements will cost you a deduction. The first statement must be signed by you and must include:

- Total days of the trip (excluding travel days to and from the cruiseship port).
- Total hours per day you devoted to scheduled business activities.

- The program of scheduled business activities.
- Anything else the IRS requires (when it so requires it by issuing regulations).

The second statement that you must attach to your return must be signed by an officer of the program sponsor (such as an association of accountants, attorneys, bankers, doctors, life insurance underwriters, or real estate professionals). This statement must include a schedule of business activities, verify your attendance and the number of hours you devoted to scheduled business activities, and include any other information that the IRS will require by regulations when it finally issues such regulations.

Amount deductible: Up to $2,000 is deductible per person per year. A husband and wife may each deduct $2,000, provided the expenses of each qualify.

Example: Buy and Sell are a husband and wife widget-selling team who attended a convention sponsored by the Association of Widget Sellers and held during a week-long Caribbean cruise in February 1984 (on a U.S.-registered vessel with ports of call in only the U.S. and U.S. possessions). Each incurs $2,000 of qualifying expenses. The full $4,000 is deductible on their 1984 tax return. The full $4,000 would also be deductible if Buy and Sell went on separate cruises in 1984, provided each cruise qualified.

On the other hand, if only Sell were in the widget-selling business and Buy just came along for the ride, only $2,000 would be deductible, even if Sell had more than $2,000 of qualifying expenses.

Caution: The $2,000 annual limit applies to all cruises beginning in a given taxable year. Depending on how the IRS and the courts interpret this provision, taxpayers who shove off at the wrong time of year could be sunk at tax time.

Example: Weatherford attends a direct-response sales seminar held on the U.S.S. Dollar during the first week of March 1985, incurring qualifying expenses of $2,000. As a result of the seminar, Weatherford's sales improve 500 percent. Encouraged by this success, Weatherford attends another seminar on the U.S.S. Dollar beginning December 31, 1985, and continuing through January 6, 1986. A special deal enabled Weatherford to defer payment until February 1986. The new law, as written, would disallow all expenses of the second trip—forever—because it began in 1985 and Weatherford had already reached the deduction limit in 1985.

HOW TO MAKE TRAVEL EXPENSES OF YOUR SPOUSE DEDUCTIBLE

"Take me along if you love me" is a plea that will not work with the IRS. If your spouse goes with you on a business trip or to a business convention, meeting, or seminar, the expenses attributable to your spouse's travel, meals, and lodging are not deductible *unless you can prove a bona fide business purpose for his or her presence.* Incidental services, such as typing notes or assisting in entertaining customers, are not sufficient to warrant a deduction.

The presence of your spouse must be necessary, not merely helpful, for you to secure a deduction for his or her expenses. Spouse travel has been disallowed when the function of the spouse was to serve only as a "socially gracious" person, to act as a host or hostess at dances and receptions, or to assist a taxpayer in making business acquaintances. Also, the IRS has rules that typing notes for the taxpayer and attending business luncheons and dinners while on the trip is insufficient for deductibility.

If you can demonstrate that the trip is not intended primarily as a vacation for your spouse and that your spouse performed helpful business-related functions while traveling, your spouse's expenses may be deductible even if the services consisted largely of socializing with business acquaintances and their spouses.

Example: Warwick, an officer-director of a tobacco company, was accompanied by his wife on trips he made to Europe to retain the company's ties to existing customers and in order to find new customers. The tobacco company expected Warwick to have friendly social relations with the European customers and en-

tertain them when they came to the United States. While in Europe, Warwick's wife entertained, toured plants, and performed clerical duties for her husband. She did no sightseeing. The court concluded that Warwick's wife's travel was not primarily for pleasure, and that her expenses, reimbursed by the tobacco company, were deductible by Warwick as ordinary and necessary employee business expenses.

Caution: If you have circumstances similar to Warwick's, make sure you review your specific facts and circumstances with your tax advisor before "counting" your tax deductions for your spouse's travel.

Bona fide business: You are likely to get a deduction for your spouse's travel if your spouse has a substantive role in your business. For example, the Tax Court allowed a deduction for an employee who brought his wife on a trip where the wife's function was not only to entertain, but also to assist her husband (a Swedish-born naturalized citizen) in understanding English.

Travel expenses are also less subject to successful challenge by the IRS when the spouse assists you in your trade or business when you are not in travel status. If your spouse is a regular employee of your firm, you have a better chance of deducting your spouse's travel expenses.

Caution: If your spouse is merely an investor, the necessity of his or her presence on your business travel is open to question.

Spouses of employees: If you are an employee, the test of business necessity for your spouse's presence is made in relation to your business, not the business of your employer. Therefore, even if your employer requires you to bring your spouse, the expenses of your spouse may be nondeductible if you cannot prove why your spouse's presence was necessary to the conduct of your business.

Penalty: If the expenses of your spouse's travel are paid by your employer either directly or by reimbursement and you cannot demonstrate business purpose, not only are such expenses not deductible by you, but they are included in your taxable income as additional compensation. If you are a closely held corporation, you could end up in the double jeopardy position of having your spouse's travel expenses passed on to you as a dividend (therefore nondeductible to the corporation) and nondeductible to you (double taxation).

How expenses are disallowed: If the expenses for bringing your spouse are disallowed, the disallowed amount is equal to the increase in cost you incurred because you brought your spouse along.

Example: You travel to Chicago on business in your car and take your spouse with you. No business purpose is served by your spouse's presence. You paid $65 a day for a double room. A single room would have cost $57 a day. You may deduct the total cost of operating your car to and from Chicago, but only $57 a day for your hotel room. In other words, your deductible cost is equal to what the trip would have cost had you not brought your spouse along.

HOW TO SHOEBOX (DOCUMENT) YOUR TRAVEL EXPENSES

To deduct travel expenses, your records must prove:

- The amount you spend daily for such things as transportation, meals, and lodging.
- The dates of your departure and return home from each trip, and the number of days spent on business while away from home.
- Where you traveled, described by the name of the city, town, or similar designation.
- Why you traveled, including the business reason for your travel or the business benefit derived or expected to be gained from the travel.

If you goof and fail to prove the individual elements of your travel expenses, your deduction will be limited to less, perhaps far less, than the money you actually spent. The necessity of properly documenting your expenses cannot be overemphasized.

Evidence required: Besides meeting the four tests, you must have receipts for all lodging expenses while traveling away from home. Remember, you must require sleep in order to qualify for a travel expense deduction. You must also have receipts for any other expenditure of $25 or more.

Audit proof: Although the regulations state that you need not have receipts for expenditures (other than lodging) which are less than $25, keep them anyway. The agent auditing your return will verify your expenses by adding up your receipts, even though you do not need receipts under the IRS regulations. Thus, if the IRS challenges you, your audit life is substantially easier if you have as many receipts as possible, even though they are not required.

Canceled checks: A canceled check will not by itself support a business expenditure without other evidence to show that the check was for a business purpose.

The necessity of a diary or account book: The Internal Revenue Code and the IRS regulations require that travel expenditures be recorded "at or near the time" expenses were incurred. The IRS believes these so-called contemporaneous records have a "high degree of credibility not present with respect to a statement subsequent thereto when generally there is a lack of accurate recall." In other words, these records will help you. Although no special form of record must be maintained, the law expects that you will keep a diary or account book in which entries are made on a daily basis.

A diary or account book does not stand alone to provide substantiation. You must be prepared to produce receipts and paid bills in order to support entries in your diary or account book.

A diary or account book is essential to deduct business travel expenses. Use a diary to list your activities for the day, including all expenditures. Then substantiate the diary with the required receipts.

Exhibit 4-3 shows a well-documented travel day. The taxpayer's appointments are listed in the appointment column. Correspondence prior to the trip exists for some of

EXHIBIT 4-3. A Well-Documented Travel Day (Example).

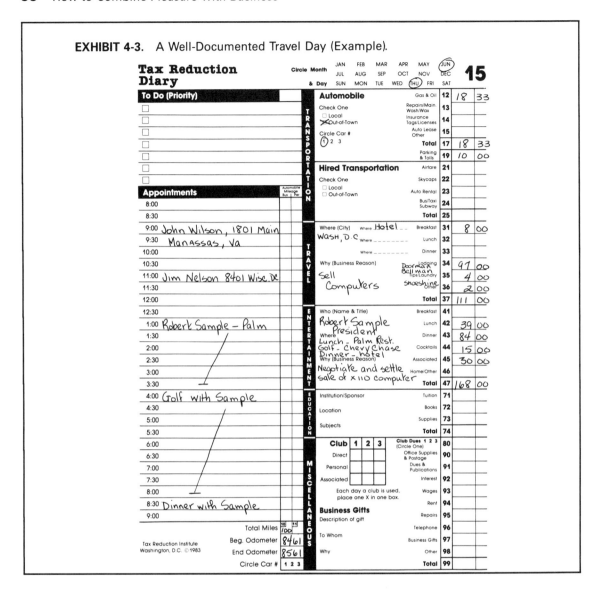

the appointments. The taxpayer incurred two types of expenses. Travel expenses are coded with a "60" and appear at the top of the expense side of the diary. Entertainment expenses are coded "52" and are recorded in the lower portion of the expense side of the diary. The taxpayer keeps receipts for all expenditures, even those which are less then $25 individually. *Reason:* if an audit should occur, it will be easier to convince the auditor that the expenses are bona fide.

Obviously, the taxpayer does not have receipts for tips to the bellman and for tips to the doorman.

The purpose of the trip is noted at the top of today's schedule. The taxpayer went to

Washington, D.C., an out-of-town destination, to sell computers. The individual appointments are listed in the appointment book.

Entertainment expenses are recorded separately: When you incur deductible entertainment expenses while traveling on a business trip, you must meet the five elements of substantiation for entertainment. Those requirements are different from those for travel expenses, and you should review Chapter 3.

Note how the appointment book and receipts are intertwined in Exhibit 4-3 to prove the taxpayer's trip. The hotel bill contains the location where the taxpayer spent the evening. The purchase of gasoline in

Washington, D.C., further proves the taxpayer's arrival. the appointments prove that the taxpayer actually conducted business in Washington, D.C. All told, the *combination* of receipts and business appointments serve to prove and document travel expenses incurred for business reasons.

Special documentation for conventions, meetings, or seminars: Conventions, seminars, and meetings are (1) generally scheduled well in advance, and (2) often located in pleasurable resort areas. In many cases, this entices taxpayers to incur travel expenses partly for business reasons and partly for personal reasons such as sightseeing.

In addition to the necessity of keeping a diary or account book and maintaining the necessary receipts (those for $25 or more and for lodging), you must keep the agenda and related handout materials when you attend a convention, seminar, or meeting.

The IRS says that the "business relationship" test for deducting convention expenses is satisfied if the convention or meeting agenda is related to the taxpayer's position and attendance is for business purposes. The rationale for relying on the meeting agenda is that the agenda often clearly demonstrates how the conference or meeting relates to the taxpayer's business and whether or not the meeting attracted other participants with like business interests or duties. When a meeting is sponsored or conducted by a professional association, the requirements for the deduction are likely to be satisfied. For example, convention expenses of doctors attending medical society or association meetings, lawyers attending meetings of the American Bar Association, and secretaries attending meetings of the National Secretaries Association have all been held deductible.

Hint: Be sure the conference or meeting has a business-enhancing purpose (for example, expanding selling techniques, new medical practice, more effective time management, tax planning, or better office relations).

Thus, the first step you should take when attending a convention, meeting, or seminar is to obtain copies of all agendas, handout materials, and so forth that will help you establish the business purpose of your meeting.

Caution: When a conference, meeting, convention, or seminar is scheduled in a resort area, it is more likely to raise eyebrows at the IRS. You must make sure that you have accumulated the necessary evidence to prove your tax deductions. The agenda and handout materials are essential as the first step. They should be combined with entries in your diary or account book, and you must make sure you obtain the necessary receipts as described in the business travel section.

If possible, and if the convention, meeting, or seminar requires them, make sure you sign attendance sheets. Always put yourself in a position to prove that you actually did attend business meetings.

In determining the number of hours you actually spend on business-related convention or seminar activities, you may not count time spent at parties, receptions, or similar social functions. However, if there is a banquet at which there is a speaker, the time attributable to the speech, if it is business-related, may be counted.

HOW EMPLOYEES SHOULD ACCOUNT TO THEIR EMPLOYERS

Employees should give their employers documentary evidence including an account book, diary, or similar record in which each expense is entered at or near the time it was incurred.

Also, employees must attach receipts when required for all travel expenses.

If an employee is reimbursed for some, but not all, travel expenses, the employee should have a written employment agreement with the employer. Such an agreement should clearly specify which expenses will be reimbursed and which will not. The unreimbursed expenses may then be taken by the employee as unreimbursed business expenses. Such expenses are deducted by the employee using Form 2106.

SPECIAL CARE FOR STOCKHOLDER/EMPLOYEES AND FOR FAMILY EMPLOYEES

An employee is deemed related to his employer if he is a member of the employer's family (sibling, spouse, or lineal descendant) or if he owns, directly or indirectly, more than 10 percent of the company.

To verify the travel deductions of related employees, the employer must have adequate accounting procedures, including adequate internal controls.

In such situations, careful attention to the adequate records requirement is absolutely essential to maintaining deductions. Read and reread the documentation requirements discussed earlier and make sure that a diary or account book is used to keep track of expenditures. Also, double check to make sure that all necessary receipts are available for IRS inspection.

Double taxation for violators: If you are an employee/shareholder in a closely held corporation and you violate the travel rules, you could end up being doubly taxed. First, the IRS will disallow the deduction to the corporation (tax 1). Second, the IRS will tax the reimbursement to you as a dividend (tax 2). Thus, neither you nor the corporation gets a deduction, and you both are taxed on the travel reimbursement.

THE IRS STANDARD MEAL RATE FOR BUSINESS TRAVEL

The IRS has a stingy meal allowance for business travelers that is available without proving actual costs. Substantiation of the time, place, and business purpose of the travel are still required. Taxpayers who can prove larger meal expenses are still allowed to write off their actual expenses.

The $14-a-day limit applies if the traveler is away from home in one general locality for less than 30 days. For stays of 30 days or more in one locality, only $9 a day is allowed.

All or none: You cannot choose the optional rate for some business trips and the actual expenses for other business trips. You must use the optional rates for all trips during the year, or you must use the actual expenses for all trips.

Example: Reed took a five-day business trip in June but forgot to record his meal expenses. He took another five-day business trip in September and recorded expenses of $20 a day. Reed can deduct either $100 (actual method), or $140 (optional method—$14 × 10 days), not $170 (five days at $14 plus five days at $20).

Light eaters benefit: Big eaters—even moderate eaters—won't benefit from this rule if they keep good tax records. In most places, $14 a day does not buy very much food. But business travelers who eat lightly may get a bonus.

Substantiation still required: To claim the optional allowance, business travelers must still keep good contemporaneous tax records proving:

- Time—dates of departure and return, and number of days spent on business.
- Place—names of destinations or localities of travel.
- Business purpose—business reason for the travel or the business benefit expected.

The proposal does not cover business entertainment. It covers only the cost of meals during travel status. You still need receipts, credit card slips, or other documents to prove the cost of meals you buy for business entertainment.

Recommendation: Although most business travelers will get bigger write-offs under the actual expense method, the optional method may provide bigger write-offs for some taxpayers. Keep this method in mind when tax time comes.

TAX REDUCTION CHECKLIST

IRS publication to be obtained:

- Publication 463—*Travel, Entertainment, and Gift Expenses*

Basic rules for all travel expenses:

- Travel expenses must be incurred in the ordinary and necessary course of business.
- Travel expenses must be documented to meet four elements of substantiation.
- You must be away from home long enough to require sleep to be in travel status.

Deductible expenses:

- Air, rail, and bus fares.
- Operation and maintenance expenses for your automobile.
- Taxi fares or other costs of transportation between the airport and hotel, and from one customer to another.
- Baggage charges and transportation costs for sample and display materials.
- Meals and lodging.
- Cleaning and laundry expenses.
- Telephone and telegraph expenses.
- Public stenographer's fees.
- Tips that are incidental to any of these expenses.
- Other expenses incidental to qualifying travel.

Four elements of substantiation:

- The amount of each separate expenditure for travel away from home, such as the cost of transportation and lodging.
  - Receipts are required for individual expenses of $25 or more.
  - Receipts are required for all lodging expenditures.
  - Expenses under $25 may be totaled, if they are listed in reasonable categories such as meals.
- The dates of your departure and return home from each trip, and the number of days spent on business while away from home.
- The destination or locality of your travel, described by name of city, town, or similar designation.
- The business reason for your travel or the business benefit derived or expected to be gained from your travel.

Definition of "tax home":

- Generally, your tax home is your principal place of business.
- If you do not have a principal place of business, your tax home is where you live.
- If you do not have a regular place of business or do not regularly live someplace, you are considered an itinerant and your home is wherever you happen to work.

Definition of temporary work:

- You anticipate and actually work at the temporary location for a period of less than two years.
- You maintain a "regular place of abode in a real and substantial sense."
- You have a business (versus a personal) reason for incurring duplicate living expenses at a location distant from your "tax home."

Definition of business days:
- Days when specific business is conducted.
- Weekends if stay is necessitated by business.
- Travel days in direct route to destination, regardless of mode of transportation.
- Convention days in which you spend at least four hours on bona fide convention activities that benefit your business.

General types of travel:
- 50 United States & D.C. business travel—You must meet the $^{51}/_{49}$ test to deduct all transportation expenses. Fail the $^{51}/_{49}$ test, and you may not deduct any of your transportation expenses.
- North American travel to conventions, meetings, and seminars—You must meet the $^{51}/_{49}$ test to deduct all transportation costs to and from the meeting destination. Fail the $^{51}/_{49}$ test, and you may not deduct any of the transportation expenses.
- Foreign travel (outside the United States if for business, outside the defined North American area if for conventions, meetings, or seminars)—You must pass the $^{76}/_{24}$ test or spend less than a week at the destination in order to deduct 100 percent of the transportation expenses. Fail the $^{76}/_{24}$ test, and you may allocate a portion of the transportation expenses for deduction, based on the number of business days.

Deductible travel when looking for rental properties:
- Active investors write off property-seeking travel as business deductions.
- Passive investors get no write-off for property-seeking travel.
- For properties purchased, active investors write off travel over 60 months.
- For properties purchased, passive investors write off travel over depreciable life.

Travel to hunt for new job:
- Deductible if in same field.
- Not deductible if first job in new field.
- Not deductible if no "continuity" between last job and new job.
- Subject to regular travel rules on business purpose.

Cruiseship conventions:
- Maximum deduction is $2,000 a person per year.
- Must be U.S. vessel making all ports of call in U.S. and U.S. possessions.
- Statements from you and the sponsor must be attached to the return.

Travel expenses for your spouse:
- Usually not deductible—incremental expenses such as lodging for two versus lodging for one are disallowed.
- You must prove a bona fide business purpose for your spouse's presence if you want a deduction.

Special rules for employees:
- Documentary evidence must be submitted.
- If you are reimbursed for some, but not all, travel expense, there should be a written agreement between you and your employer.

Special rules for stockholder/employees:
- Related employees are family members and those who own 10 percent or more of the company.

- Employer must have adequate verification procedures.
- Double taxation for those who violate the rules.

IRS standard meal rate:

- In lieu of actual meal costs—no support necessary.
- $14-a-day limit if you are away from home for less than 30 days.
- $9-a-day limit if you are away from home for 30 days or more.

Business automobiles have been around longer than the Internal Revenue Code and you would think that by this time the rules would be clear and easy to understand. Wrong. The rules are quite complex and there are hundreds of nuances which may bring some horrendous news. And the Tax Reform Act of 1984 doesn't make things any easier even though the 1984 contemporaneous record-keeping requirement was repealed in 1985.

If you do not have a nice, nifty log book to support your business mileage, your relationship with the IRS will clearly be more competitive than cooperative. It makes no difference how you operate your business, whether you are self-employed or a corporation, you must support your business/personal splits.

The Tax Reform Act of 1984 limits the availability of two great tax breaks, the investment tax credit and accelerated depreciation. The Act also installs tough rules for "recapturing" the investment tax credit and accelerated depreciation in certain cases, and stiffens the requirements for employees who claim tax breaks for job-related auto use. These new rules apply to cars purchased after June 18, 1984. This chapter explains both the new rules and the rules for cars purchased before June 19, 1984.

In this chapter we will explore many of the schemes, myths, and real ways to deal with the problems of supporting your business mileage. We will explain why it's almost impossible to have 100 percent business use of your automobile.

We will explain the only known way to actually increase your business mileage, and we will talk about a time-saving approach for supporting your business-use percentages.

If you have been using, or are about to use, the IRS standard mileage rates, we will show you why such rates usually are a "bad joke," how actual auto expenses usually provide far more loot for taxpayers, and some easy ways to make that comparison.

In addition, we will discuss how to take a trip through your garage to look for business-related equipment and tools that may be used on your automobile. We will talk about some seldom applied tax-reducing techniques for use when you dispose of your business automobile, assuming you would like to pick up a little wisdom money at that point.

THE MORE-THAN-50-PERCENT BUSINESS USE TEST

Let's start with the Tax Reform of 1984. This legislation makes it more important than ever for businesspeople to know:

5

Driving Your Automobile for Tax Deductions

- What constitutes—and what does not constitute—business use of an automobile.
- How to increase the business use percentage of an automobile.

The tax stakes: The two biggest tax breaks you can get from using a car for business are the investment tax credit and rapid depreciation write-offs under the Accelerated Cost Recovery System (ACRS).

The investment credit is a wonderful dollar-for-dollar tax reducer. We will discuss this tax break later in this chapter and fully in Chapter 7.

Depreciation is a noncash expense, which is also discussed later in this chapter and is fully discussed in Chapter 6. Under the ACRS depreciation method, you can write off the cost of your business car in just three years.

Congress enacted legislation in 1985 putting new severe limits on these two tax breaks for cars costing more than $11,250.

The test: For cars purchased after June 18, 1984, you must use the car more than 50 percent for business purposes in order to get the investment credit and ACRS depreciation. If business use does not exceed 50 percent, you can claim no investment credit, and depreciation is limited to the straight-line method over a six-year period (i.e., 10% in year 1, 20% in each of years 2 through 5, and 10% in year 6).

Using your car for "production of income" purposes does *not* count as "business" use. A "production of income" use basically means use in your investment activities, such as inspecting your rental properties.

However, if you use your car more than 50 percent of the time for business, you may count "production of income" auto use to figure your investment tax credit and ACRS write-offs. Also, if you fail the more than 50 percent business use test, you still count production of income use in your 5-year straight-line depreciation write-off.

Example 1: You use your car 30 percent in your business and 30 percent for the production of income. Since you did not use the car more than 50 percent in your business, you may not claim any investment tax credit nor may you use ACRS to figure your depreciation. However, you may claim 5-year straight-line depreciation using 60 percent of the cost of the automobile.

Example 2: You use your car 70 percent in your business and 20 percent for the production of income. Since business use exceeds 50 percent, you get the investment tax credit and ACRS depreciation. You may claim the investment credit and ACRS based on 90 percent business use.

What constitutes production of income or investment use is not changed by the new law. Thus, driving to a stockholders meeting was not deductible mileage under the old law and it is still not deductible mileage under the new law.

Moreover, as under present law, you are not entitled to consider mileage driven for "associated" entertainment as business use. Remember, this is "having fun" entertainment, such as taking a hunting trip. Mileage driven for such a trip is still considered personal mileage.

Corporate cars: There are also special new rules for 5 percent owners of corporations and partnerships. If you own 5 percent or more of a corporation or a partnership and that business entity gives you a car to use for personal purposes, any personal use which is treated as compensation to you is not treated as use in the business. Also, leasing a car to or from your corporation or partnership does not qualify as business use.

Annual test: If your business use of post-6/18/84 cars drops to 50 percent or below, you must switch to the straight-line depreciation method. What's worse, even if business use exceeds 50 percent in later years, you can't go back to the rapid ACRS method. You are stuck with straight-line depreciation for the life of the car.

Tough recapture rules: As explained later in this chapter, a reduction in business use of post-6/18/84 cars will trigger "recapture" of depreciation.

Old cars: For business cars purchased before June 19, 1984, you can claim the investment tax credit and 3-year ACRS depreciation even if business use does not exceed 50 percent.

Hint: If you own one car that you purchased before June 19, 1984, and another that you purchased after June 18, 1984, give your new car priority to make sure you satisfy the more-than-50-percent test.

Throughout this chapter we will discuss other rules that apply to cars purchased after June 18, 1984 and new rules for cars purchased after April 2, 1985. The next several sections of this chapter explain in detail the rules on business use in general. These rules apply to all cars regardless of purchase date.

THE MYTH OF 100 PERCENT BUSINESS USE

If you do not live in your office, you do not have 100 percent business use of your car. A corporation will not cure this problem. Moreover, a corporation could make matters worse by resulting in double jeopardy to the owner/employee.

There is a rather shameless tax rule that prohibits a deduction of personal, living, and family expenses. The IRS, it seems, thinks you are living while you are commuting to work. The IRS does not care what type of work you do, how far you travel, what mode of transportation you use, or what type of emergency you are going to face. If you leave from your home to perform your duties, you are considered *going* to work. A trip to work is personal and not deductible.

Example: Dr. Doom lives five miles from his office and 25 miles from the hospital. While on call one night, the good doctor received five different emergency phone calls, all requiring him to drive 25 dreadful miles to and from the hospital to save patients' lives. Trips to the emergency room are considered commuting trips from home to a work location, and Dr. Doom had not one but five nondeductible commuting trips that night.

Tax law does not as yet choose the location of your personal residence. Since the location of your residence is a personal choice, you decide how much personal commuting mileage you want to incur. The IRS believes the differences in distances traveled and amounts spent on commuting are influenced by one's personal preference in place of living

and means of transportation. The rationale goes on to state that to allow a deduction for such expenses would be to allow a deduction for personal expenses. Therefore, all deductions for commuting expenses are disallowed in order to assure similarity of treatment for all taxpayers.

The surprising application of this nasty, ugly, and downright bad word, *commuting*, is that it applies to each and every trip from your home.

Example: Ross, a salesperson, drives 35 miles to his downtown office in the morning, works all day, and drives 35 miles back to his home in the evening for dinner. After dinner, Ross drives 55 miles to meet with a client and then struggles home another 55 miles in the late hours of the night. Ross has not driven a single business mile. He commuted to the office and home, and then he commuted to a secondary work location, the client's, and back home. Accordingly, Ross has driven 180 personal commuting miles that are not deductible.

You may have heard the popular notion that it is a good idea to make a work stop on the way into the office and a work stop on the way home to avoid big chunks of commuting mileage. The IRS has thought of that, too. Stops to see clients on the way to the office or on the way home do not negate your commute to or from your principal office location.

Example: Young regularly works at an office located 10 miles from her personal residence. On any given day, she has duties that require activities in her office as well as at other locations meeting with clients. Tuesday, Young leaves home and drives two miles to visit with a client, goes to her regular office nine miles away, and drives 10 miles directly home for a total of 21 miles round trip. The direct route from Young's personal residence to her regular office is 20 miles round trip. Young has one business mile for the day and 20 nondeductible, personal, commuting miles.

No principal office: What happens when you do not have a place to work from? You may make all your calls and your money by using your automobile, mailing your orders to another city at the end of each day. The IRS has thought of this, too. Your first stop of the day is considered to be your first work location, and your last stop of the day is considered to be your last work location. You have commuting expenses from home to your first work location and from your last work location to your home.

Example: Mitchell, a self-employed salesperson, has no principal work location in the city where he makes his sales calls. At the end of each day, he places all of his sales orders in an envelope and mails them to the corporate office. Mitchell's first stop each day is considered commuting mileage. After his first stop, if he drives to 15 other locations before getting to his last stop, those trips are considered business mileage. But the final trip from the last work location to Mitchell's home is again personal, nondeductible, commuting mileage.

Now suppose that Mitchell meets a client for dinner one evening. Because Mitchell is grubby at the end of the work day he drives home to shower, shave, and change. His trip from home to the dinner meeting and back is considered commuting mileage, and again, as you would expect, it is not tax deductible.

Trips outside your normal work area are deductible: Trips from your home to your office are nondeductible, personal trips. Similarly, if you leave from home and go to another work location, other than your office, you have had a personal, nondeductible trip. The rule applies to your general work area and the way you generally conduct your business. What happens if your office is ten miles away and you have to attend a business meeting in a city located 70 miles away?

Example: Anderson, a self-employed individual, maintains a principal place of work in a downtown office building. In order to attend a business meeting in a distant city, Anderson drives directly from his residence to the distant city located 70 miles away and later that same day returns directly to his residence. Due to the length of time required to make the trip and attend the meeting, it is not reasonable to expect Anderson to stop at the office on the way out of town and on the way back. However, in effect, Anderson is traveling between one work location and another. In Rev. Rul. 55-109, the IRS stated that transportation costs incurred between work locations are deductible business expenses. Therefore, Anderson is entitled to deduct the lesser of (1) the expenses incurred in traveling between Anderson's residence and the business meeting, or (2) the expenses that would have been incurred if Anderson had traveled between his office and the business meeting.

Result: Anderson's trip from home to the distant city was 140 miles. If Anderson had gone to the office and then to the business meeting, the total trip would have been 160 miles. Anderson has 140 business miles for the day.

Minor office at home: If you have more than one office, you have an office which is considered your principal work location and all other offices are considered minor work locations. Trips from principal work locations to minor work locations are tax deductible. However, if the minor work location is located in your home, trips to that location are considered personal, nondeductible trips.

Example: Douglas, an individual, regularly works and resides at home and also makes daily round trips to and from another work location, his principal place of work. No portion of the transportation expenses is deductible.

In addition, with regard to Douglas's work at home (which is considered Douglas's minor place of work), if Douglas, after returning home from the principal place of work, goes to one or more other work locations, the transportation expenses incurred in going from Douglas's home to the first work location and in returning home from the last such location are not deductible.

Trips to temporary job are deductible: If you have a minor or temporary assignment which is beyond the general area of your "tax home" (see Chapter 4) and you return home each evening, the expenses of daily round-trip transportation are deductible. This rule does not apply when your assignment is deemed to be either indefinite or permanent. See our discussion in Chapter 4 for definitions of the word "temporary."

If you think you may have a "temporary" assignment which results in deductible business mileage, see your tax advisor. The rules for this deduction are based on court precedent and are not firmly established. Moreover, there is the question of what is your general area of work. The IRS has ruled that a metropolitan area is treated as a person's general area of work; however, in terms of mileage, the IRS has not prescribed how far the location of the temporary employment has to be from your general work area in order for you to gain deductions for the transportation.

Example: Harris regularly worked in the metropolitan area of Los Angeles. The Tax Court and the appeals court ruled that he could not deduct daily transportation costs for travel to jobs in an adjoining county. The courts had no sympathy for the fact that in commuting from his residence to various jobs, Harris had to travel one-way distances ranging from 50 to 81 miles. The rationale for this decision was that Harris worked generally in the Los Angeles area which is a far-flung metropolitan area and the seemingly large distances are not unusual in Los Angeles.

An easy way to find the right rule: Exhibit 5-1 contains a flowchart for determining your deductible business mileage for trips that originate from your home. The flowchart is easy to use and should take some of the confusion out of these complex rules. In fact, we encourage you to make a photocopy of Exhibit 5-1 and put it in your daily diary for reference.

DOUBLE JEOPARDY FOR 100 PERCENT BUSINESS USE THROUGH INCORPORATION

The common word on the street these days is that the one-person corporation is the saviour of all your tax woes. For the uninitiated, the careless, and the poor record-keepers, one-person corporations can be disastrous. Take the personal use of an automobile, for example. It should be clear that a trip from your home to your office is a personal, nondeductible, commuting trip. It makes no difference whether you take this trip in a leased car, the family car, or the corporate car. Regardless of the vehicle, trips from your home to work locations are commuting miles.

Now here's what happens when an owner/ employee travels from the home to the office in a corporate automobile. First, the trip is a personal, nondeductible, commuting trip. If it is deducted, the corporation will take the tax deduction to reduce the corporate income and pay less tax. When the IRS finds this deduction, it disallows it, resulting in two rather stultifying consequences.

First, the corporation is not allowed a tax deduction. This increases the corporate tax. Second, you, the owner/employee, are considered to have received a constructive dividend; consequently, you will pay tax on the dividend.

The final score is two points for the IRS and none for you. You are double-taxed, once to your corporation and once to your person.

To avoid this rather cavalier treatment of your corporate business automobile, you must have a sharing arrangement with the corporation that allows for your personal use. Under this type of arrangement, the corporation must treat your personal use either as compensation to you or require reimbursement from you. When you treat the personal use as compensation, it is subject to income tax withholding, Social Security, and unemployment taxes. That's why we favor the reimbursement arrangement.

Reimbursement amount: The amount you should reimburse your corporation for personal use should be based on your personal-use percentage. You should take actual expenses of operating the automobile, including depreciation, for each month or specific stated period of time and calculate the amount you owe the corporation. The amount should be set up as a receivable and it should be paid by you before the end of the tax years of both the corporation and yourself. If the years are different, you should reimburse the corporation at least twice each year. A monthly or quarterly reimbursement schedule would be better.

The personal-use percentage of a corporate automobile must be based on the facts and circumstances of each taxpayer. If

EXHIBIT 5-1. Flowchart for Determining Deductible Business Mileage for Trips Originating from Home.

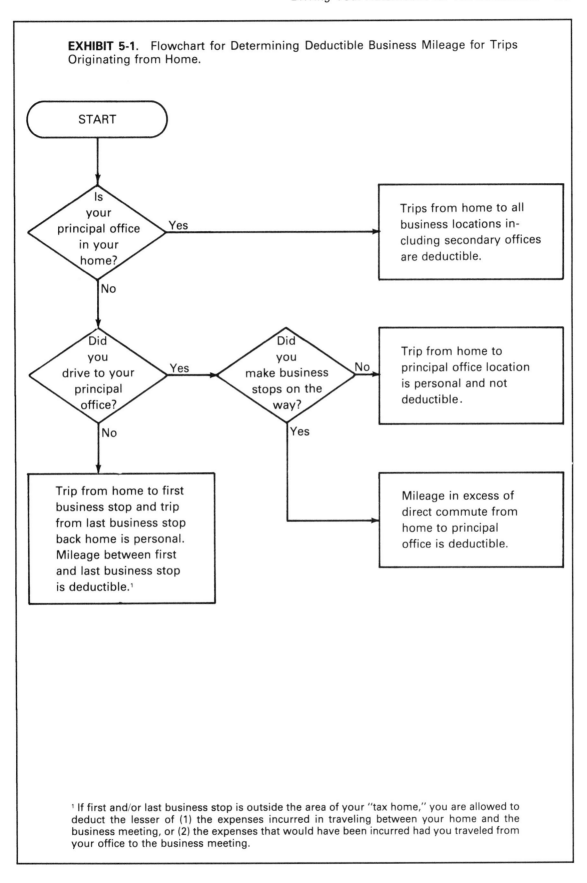

¹ If first and/or last business stop is outside the area of your "tax home," you are allowed to deduct the lesser of (1) the expenses incurred in traveling between your home and the business meeting, or (2) the expenses that would have been incurred had you traveled from your office to the business meeting.

the car is used for personal vacations as well as commuting, both the vacations and the commuting must be considered in developing the appropriate percentage. Careful tax planning and following a sound plan to develop the personal-use percentage is essential to avoid the double-taxation results of disallowance.

Study the rules explained later in this chapter on how to develop a business-use percentage.

Corporate resolution: Whether your corporation will treat personal use of corporate cars by officer/shareholders as additional compensation or expenses requiring reimbursement to the corporation, you should have a corporate resolution. The resolution should set forth the parameters of automobile usage. It should be approved by the automobile user, the company president, and the board of directors. A copy of the resolution should be included in the corporate minutes. An example of appropriate language for such a resolution is contained in Exhibit 5-2. Consult your attorney to be sure you satisfy all technical requirements of your state's corporation law.

WHY TRANSPORTING TOOLS, EQUIPMENT, AND INSTRUMENTS DOESN'T INCREASE YOUR BUSINESS MILEAGE

Commuting costs are never deductible. Your commute between home and work does not become tax deductible even when you haul the tools, equipment, instruments, and other implements necessary for you to perform your work. You get deductions for the cost of transporting equipment only when it costs more to transport the equipment than it would to go to and from your workplace. The mode of transportation does not enter into the computation.

The Supreme Court decided in the *Fausner* case that the "additional expense" approach to determining the cost of transporting tools was the appropriate method. Under this method, you are allowed to deduct only the incremental costs incurred in transporting tools and equipment. Assume that you normally commute by bus, which costs $2. Because you

have to carry tools one day, you drive your automobile, which costs $10. You are not allowed to deduct the difference between the $2 and the $10. It's still a commuting cost; the mode of transportation makes no difference.

Practically the only way to deduct expenses for transporting tools is when it costs more to transport the tools than it would to otherwise commute to and from work. If you had to rent a trailer to carry implements, for example, the cost of the trailer rental would be deductible.

HOW TO INCREASE YOUR BUSINESS MILEAGE PERCENTAGE

For tax purposes, documentation is synonymous with virtue. The upcoming hints on how to increase your business mileage percentages depend in large measure on how willing you are to document your tax deductions.

Make your home your principal place of business and you won't have to drive to work unless you have a really big home.

When your home is your principal place of work and you drive to one or more other places of work, you are driving for business, rather than commuting, and all of your transportation expenses are deductible. Personal usage is, of course, still disallowed, but you will have far less personal usage when you eliminate commuting mileage.

Caution: To make your home office your principal place of business, you must adhere to all the requirements for the home office deduction discussed in Chapter 8, and you must maintain a work activity log and the guest log to substantiate your usages. "Principal place of business" means that you spend most of your time working from your home, and that such work is your biggest revenue producer.

The home office deduction is available if you either meet the "principal place of business" test or use your home in the normal course of business to meet with clients, patients, customers, or prospects. But only the "principal place of business" test for your primary business will reduce your commuting mileage.

EXHIBIT 5-2. Executive Reimbursement for Personal Use of Company Automobiles.

In order to further the continued prosperity of this company and to carry on the necessary business of this company, the officers of this company are furnished automobiles.

The officers are authorized to use the company automobiles for their personal use to a limited extent because it is recognized that to prevent any personal use would not only be impractical but require each officer to own or lease a personal vehicle—a pointless economic burden.

Each officer who uses a company car must provide the company with a record of personal use at the end of each quarter, so that the company may determine the total cost of personal usage. Cost shall be determined by reference to actual expenses, including depreciation. The percentage of personal use shall then be applied to such cost and the resulting amount shall be reimbursed by the officer within a period of 90 days.

Officers who are provided with company cars shall exercise due care and protect the company auto whether the auto is being used for business or personal use.

It is expected that the officers will drive the cars from the office to their homes and that the officers shall garage at their expense, without reimbursement, the company automobiles.

_____   _____
Officer   President

_____   _____
Date   Date

To be included in corporate minutes.

Second business: The way IRS enforces the commuting rules, it could be said that there are two different types of second businesses which could be run from your home—one where the cash transactions take place *within* your home, and one where the cash transactions take place *outside* of your home. If the cash transactions take place inside your home, your home would be your principal place of business for the second-business and mileage you incur from your home for second-business purposes would be considered business mileage. If your home is merely a storehouse, record-keeping, or appointment-making operation, you would be subject to the first and last business stop rules for commuting.

Example: Leneer is an employee during the day and sells cosmetics during the evening. Her cosmetic sales take place in clients' homes, and she does not maintain a home office set up exclusively for the cosmetics business. Leneer has commuting mileage to her first cosmetic stop and from her last cosmetic stop each night.

Home office set up exclusively for the cosmetics business: Assume Leneer properly established a home office deduction for her second business, the cosmetics business. The IRS enforces the commuting rule just as if Leneer had not set up her home office properly. Leneer may win if she desires to go to court and test the IRS's position. However, that's generally an expensive and time-consuming proposition.

Home office is sales center: If the revenue generated from your home office operation is actually received at your home office, you get a different result.

Example: Bennett owns eight rental units which he operates from his home. Tenants make payments to Bennett's home and call at all hours of the night with complaints. Bennett's trips from his home to collect rent and for maintenance are considered business trips and are fully deductible.

Caution: The IRS has not fully sanctioned the Bennett example. It could take the position that Bennett has commuting mileage to and from his first and last business stops from his home office. Our experience in dealing with IRS over this rule has been that it will usually be allowed. Moreover, Congress recently amended the home office rules to state that a home office could be the principal location for any business and be fully deductible. The IRS had taken the position that an individual had only one principal work location, but it was overruled by Congress.

Second job: Mileage from your first work location to your second or minor job is classified as business mileage. But trips to either the first or second job that originate from your home are not deductible.

Hint—don't go home: If you like your home, we suggest you establish it as your principal place of business, and make sure you pay attention to all the details for substantiating a deduction. It's the only known way to sustain 100 percent business use of an automobile.

Home offices of corporations: If you are an owner-employee of a corporation and you want to establish your home office as the headquarters of that corporation, make sure the corporation either leases the home office from you or has an agreement with you that states your compensation is considered adequate for you to find a workplace of your own on behalf of the corporation. Either the rental agreement or the work agreement should be written by your corporate attorney.

A TIME-SAVING APPROACH TO SUPPORTING BUSINESS-USE PERCENTAGES

You're guilty!

The IRS manual on how to audit (and intimidate) taxpayers states, "The use of the automobile by business and professional people is often overstated."

How to keep a daily mileage log: Although the contemporaneous recording requirement was repealed in 1985, you are playing with disaster if you don't keep good records. Good records are produced when you record transactions as they occur. We have an easy way to do this. Exhibit 5-3 shows an excerpt from the Tax Reduction Institute's *Tax Reduction Diary*. Note that next to each appointment is room for you to allocate mileage to business or personal purposes. At the end of each day, you simply tally the miles driven for business and personal purposes and then reconcile the totals with your beginning and ending odometer readings.

You can accomplish the same thing by simply drawing two lines in your appointment book and recording the mileage next to each entry.

By using the *Tax Reduction Diary* (available for $75 from the Tax Reduction Institute), or your own substitute diary, you can meet all the record-keeping requirements for business automobile expenses plus the requirements for travel, entertainment, club dues, and other expenses.

Penalties for noncompliance: You could be found negligent for claiming deductions for amounts unsupported by adequate records. The negligence penalty is stiff. It's 5 percent of the amount of underpayment of tax.

Besides imposing the nondeductible penalty, IRS will assess you interest for the period of underpayment.

Negligence penalties and interest are bad enough, but Congress went an extra step. It has intimated that failure to keep good records for the business use of your vehicle may be fraud.

WHY IRS STANDARD MILEAGE RATES ARE A JOKE

The IRS has been known to pay its own employees more per mile than it allows tax-

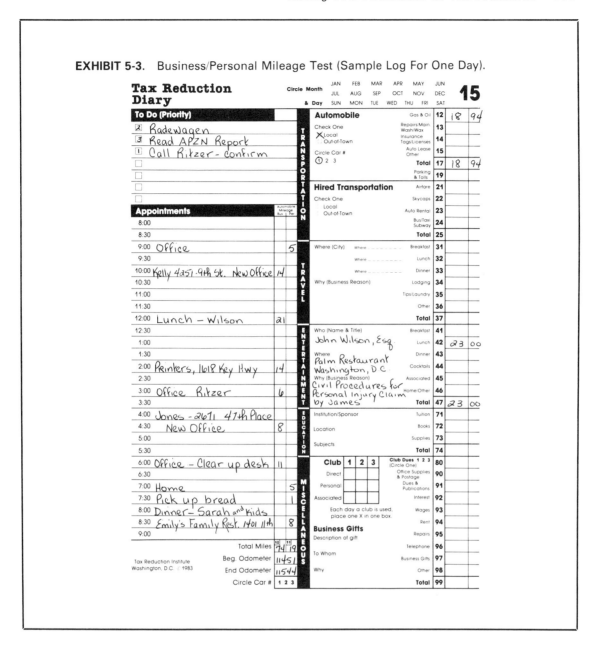

EXHIBIT 5-3. Business/Personal Mileage Test (Sample Log For One Day).

payers to deduct. During the 1980s, for example, the IRS has paid its employees 22½ cents a mile for operating their autos for IRS business. It allows taxpayers to deduct 21 cents a mile on the first 15,000 business miles for 1985.

Hertz corporation, the one that rents all those cars and stops people from running through airports, releases a study at the beginning of each tax year. The Hertz study usually indicates that it costs a whole lot more

to operate a car than the IRS allows lazy taxpayers, those who use standard IRS mileage rates. A recent Hertz study indicated that it costs almost 40 cents, about double IRS rates, to operate a little, tiny, itty-bitty car.

Beware of IRS propositions: IRS optional (or standard) mileage rates were put in place for the lazy taxpayer in the hopes of raising more money for the Treasury. If you do not want to keep track of what it costs you for gas and oil, maintenance and repairs, and other operating costs, you may use IRS optional or standard mileage rates and not have any supporting documents for your operating costs. That trade-off could cost you anywhere from five cents a mile to 95 cents a mile, depending on what type of car you drive.

Optional rates currently in effect: At the time this book was written, the IRS had just released the rates for calendar year 1985. The decision for 1985 was to fleece lazy taxpayers by prescribing these rates:

- 21 cents on the first 15,000 miles, if eligible.
- 11 cents on miles in excess of 15,000.
- 12 cents for charitable activity.
- 9 cents for medical and moving mileage.

The 21 cents a mile is available only for the first 15,000 business miles an auto is driven during a year. Once an automobile has accumulated 60,000 business miles at the maximum standard mileage rate, the automobile is considered fully depreciated and you must switch to 11 cents a mile. Also, the rates are the same whether the car is new or used.

Example: Jones buys a used business car which has 18,000 miles on it at the time of purchase. During the year he drives the car 20,000 miles for business and 5,000 miles for pleasure. His deduction under the IRS optional mileage rate is $3,700 (15,000 @ 21 cents plus 5,000 @ 11 cents).

At the end of the year, the car has 43,000 actual miles on its odometer. A total of 15,000 miles has been claimed at the 21 cents a mile maximum standard mileage rate, and Jones could drive the car 45,000 additional business miles at the 21 cents before being required to switch to 11 cents a mile.

Example: During year 2, Jones drives 15,000 business miles and no personal miles. His deduction for the year is $3,150 (15,000 times 21 cents).

At the beginning of year 3, the automobile has 58,000 actual miles on its odometer. During year 3, Jones drives 55,000

business miles and 5,000 personal miles. His business automobile deduction under the standard mileage rate for the year is 7,550 (15,000 @ 21 cents plus 40,000 @ 11 cents).

At the beginning of year 4, the automobile's odometer shows 118,000 miles. So far, Jones has claimed a total of 45,000 miles at the maximum standard mileage rate of 21 cents. In year 4, he could claim a maximum of 15,000 miles at the maximum rate. If so, he would have to use 11 cents a mile for all business miles incurred after the 60,000 business mile level has been reached.

Must elect optional method in first year: If your automobile is first placed in service for business purposes after December 31, 1980, you are allowed to use the optional method only if you elect that method in the first year that the automobile is placed in service for business purposes. By electing the optional method, you have made an election to exclude your automobile from the Accelerated Cost Recovery System forever.

Switch from optional to actual expense method: If you elected the optional method in the first year you used the car for business and that year was after December 31, 1980, you may elect to use or not to use the optional method in later years, on a yearly basis. If you elect to use the actual expense method rather than the optional method in a later year, you must deduct straight-line depreciation over the automobile's estimated useful life, and you may not take the deductions provided by ACRS.

Cars used for business before January 1, 1981: If you used your automobile for business purposes before January 1, 1981, and you used the "actual cost" method to compute automobile expenses, the useful life of the automobile is the estimated period over which you based the depreciation deduction you calculated under the "actual cost" method. Once that period expires, your automobile is considered fully depreciated and you may not use 21 cents a mile, but you could use 11 cents a mile.

Other limitations: The optional method is not acceptable for (a) vehicles used for hire, such as taxicabs; (b) two or more automobiles used simultaneously, such as in fleet operations; or (c) any vehicle that is leased, rather than owned.

Using two cars: When one person alternates in using two automobiles on different occasions for business purposes, the total business miles of the two automobiles must be combined for purposes of the 15,000-mile annual limitation on the 21-cent mileage rate. One person using two cars is not considered a fleet operation.

In the one-person/two-car case, if one of the automobiles is fully depreciated, the total business miles of the vehicles are not combined for purposes of the 21-cent mileage rate. The fully depreciated automobile may be deducted only at the rate of 11 cents per miles for all of its miles.

Costs included in optional mileage rate: If you compute your automobile expense deduction using the optional rate, that rate is in lieu of all operating and fixed costs of the automobile. Such items as depreciation, maintenance and repairs, tires, gasoline (including all taxes on gasoline), oil, insurance, and registration fees are included in the 21 cents a mile rate. However, parking fees and tolls attributable to use for business purposes may be deducted as separate items. Similarly, the 21 cents a mile rate does not affect any deduction for interest relating to the purchase of the automobile, nor does it affect a deduction for state and local taxes.

Computation note: If your automobile is operated less than 100 percent for business purposes, an allocation is required to determine the business and nonbusiness portion of the taxes and interest deductions. The portion of interest and state and local taxes attributable directly to the operation of the automobile for business purposes is deductible from gross income (either as an employee business expense or in Schedule C). The personal portion of the interest and state and local taxes is deductible only if you itemize deductions.

Special note: The standard mileage rate of 21 cents a mile is available only to employees and self-employed individuals. It is not available to corporations.

Replacement automobiles: If you replace an automobile during the year, the total business miles of both automobiles must be combined in computing the 21 cents a mile deduction, providing that your former automobile was not fully depreciated. However, if the old car was fully depreciated and you want to use 21 cents a mile on the new car, you use 11 cents a mile on the old car and 21 cents a mile on the new car. If you want to use actual expenses for the new car, you may do so and claim 21 cents a mile on the car replaced.

Ownership: When a husband and wife file a joint return, but the auto is in the husband's name and the wife uses it for business, there is generally no problem. The car is considered owned by the couple rather than by a single individual. Also, many states have community property laws in which title to the vehicle does not make much difference. It's still considered owned by both husband and wife.

Caution: Do not borrow a car from a friend or neighbor and expect to deduct 21 cents a mile. If you are not the owner, you are not entitled to deduct the full automobile expenses regardless of the method used. Your deduction is based on your out-of-pocket expenses.

Two businesses and one car: When a husband and wife operate separate businesses and use a jointly owned car, the mileage of both husband and wife must be combined before applying the optional rates. If separate automobiles are used for separate businesses, then separate rates (the full 21 cents), are applied to each separately used car.

Depreciation rate when optional rate is used: If you used the optional method in 1980, 1981, 1982, 1983, 1984 or 1985, your car is considered to have been depreciated at the rate of 7 cents per 20-cent mile for 1980 and 1981, 7.5 cents per 20-cent mile in 1982, and 8 cents per 20.5-cent mile in 1983 and 1984, and 8 cents per 21-cent mile in 1985. If you used the "actual cost" method in any one or more of those years, the rates of 7 cents, 7.5 cents, and 8 cents do not apply to those years. The depreciation rates of 7 cents, 7.5 cents, and 8 cents reduce the basis of your automobile in determining adjusted basis when you sell, trade, or switch to the actual expense method.

Remember, under the optional method your automobile is considered to have a useful life of 60,000 business miles at the maximum standard mileage rate of 21 cents per mile. The depreciation is determined without reference to the age of the vehicle. After 60,000 miles of business use at the maximum standard mileage rate of 21 cents, the automobile is considered fully depreciated. Moreover, an automobile is considered to have been driven no more than 15,000 miles at the 21 cent rate in any one year, even though the actual business mileage of the automobile may be greater.

Exhibit 5-4 contains an example of how you compute basis after using the optional mileage method. You need to determine basis if you're going to sell your car, trade it in, or switch to the actual cost method. Later in this chapter we will discuss how to compute gain or loss. If you use the optional mileage rate, your basis will be determined by a computation similar to that in Exhibit 5-4.

Standard mileage rate for charitable, medical, or moving mileage: There is a different standard mileage rate for charitable, medical, or moving mileage. The 1985 rate for medical and moving is only 9 cents a mile, compared to the business rate of 21 cents a mile. The Tax Reform Act of 1984 increased the charitable rate to 12 cents a mile for tax years after 1984. The reason the rates are lower for these activities is because certain items such as the proportionate share of general maintenance or general repairs, liability insurance, and depreciation may not be taken into account in computing the amount paid for transportation with respect to rendering gratuitous services to charitable organizations, or with respect to medical care or moving expenses.

Thus, your choice is to take either the measly optional rates or your actual out-of-pocket expenses for charitable, medical, or moving mileage.

General problem with the IRS rates: The optional IRS mileage rates are the result of an administrative procedure. The IRS changes that procedure whenever it feels the need or desire. During the past five years, the useful lives of automobiles have changed twice. The 7 cents, 7.5 cents, and 8 cents depreciation rates are new. Previously, there were no guidelines on how you depreciated the automobile when you selected 21 cents a mile.

The frequent changes pose a tax-planning nightmare. If you can't count on the rules, even though you're playing the game, it's impossible to win. Moreover, the IRS optional rates may be far too low for you. The only way to know for sure is to make a comparison, which we will discuss in the next section of this chapter. Meanwhile, should you desire to use 21 cents a mile without making a comparison, you are doing so at your own peril and with your own pocketbook.

HOW TO COMPARE ACTUAL AUTO EXPENSES WITH IRS MILEAGE RATES

Taxpayers who receive W-2's, otherwise known as employees, use IRS Form 2106 to report their business automobile expenses. The form actually encourages you to take the larger of actual expenses or IRS optional mileage rates. However, if you are a taxpayer who files Schedule C, or otherwise do not use Form 2106, you are not asked to make such a comparison and frequently you must operate in the dark.

Exhibit 5-5 contains a sample computation to assist you in comparing actual auto expenses with IRS optional mileage rates.

The example computation in Exhibit 5-5 is based on a taxpayer who drove two cars during the year. Car number 1 was driven 20,000 total miles, of which 18,000 were business miles. Car number 2 was driven 8,000 total miles, of which 4,000 were business miles. This is a case of one taxpayer driving two cars during the year. He may compute actual expenses on each car based on the percentage of business use of each car. In the example, the taxpayer determines that $4,142 would have been lost if IRS optional rates had been used. That computation is as follows:

EXHIBIT 5-4. Computing Basis When IRS Rates Are Used.

FACTS: Norman bought a new car in January of 1982 and used IRS optional mileage rates to compute his deductions for 1982, 1983, and 1984. In 1985, Norman want to sell his automobile. He determined his basis for gain or loss as follows:

Original cost of 1982 car	$9,000
Business use percent	×80%
Business use basis	7,200
Depreciation 1982 (11,000 miles @ 7.5 cents)	(825)
Depreciation 1983 (15,000 miles @ 8 cents)	(1,200)
Depreciation 1984 (12,000 miles @ 8 cents	(960)
Basis	$4,215

Actual expenses	$8,062
IRS rates	(3,920)
Money ahead	$4,142

The example is based on today's cars at today's prices. We assume the cars get 21 miles to the gallon and use bargain gasoline at $1.09 per gallon.

The only sure way to know how much you will save by keeping track of actual expenses is to prepare a worksheet similar to that found in Exhibit 5-5. In some categories, your expenses will be higher or lower than those used in the example. Fill in the numbers for your car and see how you come out. We'll bet you'll be many dollars ahead by using the actual expense method.

Depreciation and cost recovery are explained fully in Chapter 6. After reading Chapter 6, you will have no problem plugging your numbers into the form at the bottom of Exhibit 5-5.

Example: Car number 1 was purchased on December 31, 1984. Its total cost at the time of purchase was $11,650. It was used 90 percent for business during 1985 and its business cost was $10,485 ($11,650 times 90 percent). The investment tax credit was $630. It was claimed in 1984 and 50 percent of that amount ($315) is used to reduce the business cost from $10,485 to $10,710—the depreciable basis. Once this basis is determined, it's merely a matter of applying the percentages from Chapter 6 to determine the depreciation. In 1985, the depreciation was $3,865, deter-

mined by taking the 38 percent ACRS rate for the second year times $10,170.

Total deduction: At the bottom of Exhibit 5-5 is the total auto deduction for 1985. Interest, personal property taxes, parking and tolls are not considered in the IRS optional mileage rate of 21 cents. Accordingly, the numbers are not used for comparing the 21 cents with actual expenses. Therefore, in computing your deduction for the year, take the amounts from the top of the schedule (use the greater of actual or the IRS mileage rate) and add interest, personal property taxes, parking, and tolls to arrive at your total auto deduction.

You must compute to know: Take three minutes to complete a computation similar to that in Exhibit 5-5. It will save you money.

WHY EMPLOYEES WHO ARE REIMBURSED FOR BUSINESS MILES SHOULD CLAIM AUTO EXPENSE DEDUCTIONS IN THEIR TAX RETURNS

If you are an employee who is reimbursed for business mileage by your employer, you should consider reporting the reimbursement as income and deducting your actual auto expenses. If you are reimbursed for your auto expenses, your situation is comparable to a taxpayer who uses IRS standard mileage rates. Your losses can be computed in a manner similar to Exhibit 5-5.

EXHIBIT 5-5. Comparison of Actual Auto Expenses With IRS Mileage Rate (Example Computation for 1985).

	CAR 1	CAR 2
BUSINESS/PERSONAL USE		
Total mileage for business	18,000	4,000
Total mileage for year	÷ 20,000	÷ 8,000
Business %	90%	50%

ACTUAL EXPENSES TO BE COMPARED WITH IRS MILEAGE RATES

	CAR 1	CAR 2
Gas and oil	$ 991	$ 396
Insurance	800	600
Repairs and maintenance	200	200
Tags and licenses	100	80
Wash and wax	130	130
Other	50	50
Total	2,271	1,456
Business %	× 90%	× 50%
Business total	2,044	728
Depreciation (per computation below)	3,865	1,425
Total actual expense	$5,909	$2,153

Actual for comparison	$8,062	
IRS mileage rate for business miles		
First 15,000 miles @ 21 cents	3,150	($4,142 ahead
Miles in excess of 15,000 @ 11 cents	770	with actual
IRS allowance for comparison	$3,920	expenses)

DEPRECIATION

	Make Model	Date Acq.	Total Cost or Basis[1]	Business %	Business Cost or Basis[2]	50% of ITC[3]	Basis for Depr.	Depreciation Method	Prior	This Year
Car 1	RZ 41 VREP	12/31/84	$11,650	90%	$10,485	$315	$10,170	3-yr. ACRS	$2,543	$3,865
Car 2	RZ 42 VREP	6/17/84	$7,732	50%	$3,866	$116	$3,750	3-yr. ACRS	$938	$1,425

[1]From worksheet.
[2]Total × business %.
[3]50% of investment tax credit is used to reduce business cost to the basis for depreciation.

TOTAL AUTO EXPENSE DEDUCTION

Operating expenses—greater of actual or IRS mileage rate	$8,062
Interest (total × business %)	482
Personal property taxes (total × business %)	344
Parking and tolls	320
Total auto deduction	$9,208

However, you could lose more than that shown in Exhibit 5-5. Besides actual expenses of operating the car, you are entitled to an investment tax credit in the year you purchase the car. Your investment tax credit is based on your percentage of business versus personal use. Exhibit 5-6 shows how Belshaw drove his newly purchased car 12,000 business miles during a year in which his employer reimbursed him 21 cents a mile. By using actual expenses and claiming the investment tax credit, Belshaw put $1,077 in his pocket. That's not tax savings, that's *money* in the pocket.

Make the computation: If you are in a situation similar to Belshaw's, make sure you make a computation similar to that in Exhibit 5-6. Do not merely ask your tax advisor to make the computation for you; do it for yourself. Then, if you so desire, have your tax advisor review it. Actually, your tax advisor will review it automatically when putting the information into your tax return.

No deductions when you fail to seek reimbursement: If you could have been reimbursed by your employer for automobile expenses, but you failed to seek reimbursement, you will be denied a deduction for such automobile expenses even though you paid them. The rationale behind this disallowance is that the expenses are not necessary to your business as an employee. The expenses are necessary to your employer. You get no deductions for expenses which you pay on behalf of another.

Employment agreement: If you are reimbursed for some but not all business mileage, make sure your agreement with your employer clearly specifies that your salary is considered adequate to absorb certain types of automobile expenses and that such expenses are incurred on behalf of the company at your expense as part of your employment. The agreement with your employer provides the basis for your deduction of automobile expenses incurred on behalf of your employer.

Reimbursement at less than 21 cents a mile: If you are reimbursed for your auto-mobile expenses at a rate less than the IRS optional mileage rate, you can deduct the difference as an employee business expense. You complete IRS Form 2106 and show the reimbursement as an offset to your 21 cents a mile claim. In such situations, however, you should figure your automobile expenses under both the actual cost method and the IRS optional rate method. Also, do not forget to claim the investment tax credit in the year you purchase an automobile.

Reimbursement in excess of 21 cents a mile is income: If you are reimbursed at a rate greater than 21 cents a mile, the excess is considered taxable income to you unless you prove that your actual expenses are greater. In this situation, you should figure your automobile expense deduction under both the actual expense method and the IRS optional rate method. You will generally find that the actual cost method provides the greater number. Moreover, that number will generally be greater than whatever reimbursement you received from your employer. Thus, you will be entitled to a deduction.

How to handle the new, tougher rules for employees: In the Tax Reform Act of 1984, Congress poured hot motor oil on employees. If you are an employee, you may deduct your car expenses only if the car is required for the convenience of your employer and as a condition of your employment.

Thus, your employer must require you to have a car in order to properly perform the duties of your employment. This requirement is not satisfied merely by your employer's statement that the property is required as a condition of employment.

The IRS will issue regulations on the "condition of employment" requirement. Until then, assume you qualify for a deduction of car expenses if your employer's business requires you to visit clients, patients, customers, or prospects away from your employer's office.

In addition, you should obtain a formal, written employment agreement from your employer specifying the reason you need a car as an employee.

EXHIBIT 5-6. Employee Computation of Auto Expenses in Excess of Employer Reimbursement.

FACTS: Belshaw drove his new car 12,000 business miles, for which his employer reimbursed him 21 cents a mile. Following is Belshaw's computation of total tax benefit he received by claiming the car as an employee business expense.

Total mileage for business	12,000
Total mileage for year	÷ 15,000
Business percent use	80%
Gas and oil	$ 716
Insurance	550
Repairs and maintenance	200
Tags and licenses	100
Wash and wax	130
Other	50
Total out-of-pocket	1,746
Business percent	x 80%
Business out-of-pocket	1,397
Business depreciation	2,192[1]
Business expense	3,589
Reimbursement from employer	(2,520)
Employee business expense	1,069
Tax rate	x 50%
Tax refund	535
Investment tax credit	542
Total cash in pocket	$1,077

[1] Depreciation

MODEL	DATE ACQ	TOTAL COST	BUS %	BUS COST	50% ITC	BASIS FOR DEPR	METHOD	PRIOR DEPR	DEPR THIS YEAR
Z1411 VXPQ	2/14/85	$11,300	80%	$9,040	$271	$8,769	3-yr. ACRS	N/A	$2,192

WHY THE INVESTMENT TAX CREDIT IS MISSED ON MANY AUTOMOBILES

If you buy a new or used automobile for use in a business, even a second business, or for use as an employee, the business portion of the automobile qualifies for the investment tax credit, that wonderful dollar-for-dollar rebate discussed fully in Chapter 7.

Overlooked with optional mileage rates: Many taxpayers overlook the invest-ment tax credit when they use IRS optional mileage rates. If you purchased a new car during any of the past three tax years and used IRS optional mileage rates to deduct your business mileage, make sure you check your prior years' returns to find out if you have taken the investment credit. If not, file an amended return to get your refund. You have three years from the time you filed your return to make changes, and one of the most frequent changes made is a claim for the investment tax credit when IRS optional mileage rates have been used.

Credit if optional mileage rates used: The one tax advantage to using the IRS optional mileage rates is that your available credit could be a little higher than if you use the actual expense method. Choosing the optional rates makes your car "non-recovery property," that is, property for which you cannot use the ACRS rules to figure your depreciation write-offs. As "recovery property," your car is eligible for a 6 percent credit—discussed later in this chapter and fully in Chapter 7. On the other hand, if your car is "non-recovery property," you may choose a five-year useful life for the car and get a credit of 6.67 percent or a seven-year useful life and get a credit of 10 percent.

What to do: If you overlooked the investment tax credit on your present car and have already selected the optional rates, claim the credit using a seven-year useful life (assuming you have reasonable support for a seven-year life). This strategy will give you the 10 percent credit. Even if the credit is later "recaptured"—see the discussion later in this chapter and in Chapter 7—you will have had the interest-free use of the tax refund until the year you pay the recapture tax.

If you have just bought a car and haven't claimed any deductions yet, you should probably use the actual expense method, since using this method will generally increase your total write-offs, as explained earlier in this chapter. However, make sure you always work out the numbers for your particular situation.

Unreported reimbursements cost credit: If you are reimbursed for your business mileage and you do not report that reimbursement in your tax return, you lose the investment tax credit.

Example: Miller drives 10,000 business miles during the year and is reimbursed by his employer at the rate of 21 cents a mile. He purchased a new car costing $10,000 and used it 90 percent of the time for business. Miller was entitled to an investment tax credit of $540. He lost the credit because he failed to claim it in his tax return.

Solution: Miller should have reported $2,000 in automobile expenses and $2,000 in employer reimbursements for a net deduc-

tion of zero. He then would have been entitled to claim the investment tax credit and would have put $540 in his pocket at the end of the year.

The investment tax credit is equal to 6 percent of the "tax cost" of your car. Tax cost will generally equal your basis in the automobile for purposes of determining depreciation. If you elect to expense a portion of your car in lieu of depreciation, the expensed amount reduces your cost for both depreciation and purposes of the investment credit. The special expense election is explained fully in Chapter 6.

If you purchase a new car, your basis for both depreciation and the investment tax credit is equal to your net cost. However, there are three rules which can affect your computation of net cost. First, if you receive a rebate from the manufacturer, the rebate is subtracted from the purchase price to arrive at your net cost. The rebate is not taxable income to you; it's merely a reduction in your car's tax cost.

Second, if you buy a car subject to the gas guzzler tax, you must reduce the amount of your "tax cost" by the amount of that tax.

Third, depending on state law, you could elect to deduct the sales tax in the year of purchase rather than add it to the purchase price of the car. You may or may not have that option. It depends on whether the sales tax is imposed on you as the purchaser or on the seller. In those states where the sales tax is imposed on the purchaser, you have the option of deducting the sales taxes or adding them to the basis of your car. If you claim a deduction for the tax, the business portion of the tax is reflected in the car expense deduction and the non-business portion is reported as an itemized deduction.

If the sales tax is imposed on the seller or retailer, you the customer do not have the option of claiming a deduction for the sales tax. You must treat it as part of the cost of the car.

Trade old car plus cash for new car: If you trade your old car for a new car, your adjusted basis for the new car is determined by taking the basis of the old car and adding any cash boot to it. Cash boot is reduced by manufacturer's rebates, gas guzzler taxes, and if elected, sales taxes.

If the old car was traded in before the expiration of its three-year life for the investment tax credit, a portion of the investment credit had to be recaptured. Fifty percent of the recaptured amount is added to basis for purposes of determining the basis of the new car. See Chapter 7 for further details on the investment tax credit.

Trade old car for used car: If you trade your old car for a used car and there is no recapture of investment tax credit on the old car, your basis for determining investment tax credit is limited to the cash boot you paid.

Sixty-day rule for used cars: If you sell your old car and there is no recapture of investment tax credit and then within 60 days you buy a used car to replace the old car, the transaction is treated the same as a trade. You must reduce the cost of the used car by the adjusted basis of your old car for purposes of figuring the investment tax credit.

Example: You buy a used car for $5,000. You count the entire $5,000 to figure your credit. However, if you bought the used car to replace an old car within 60 days before or after an outright sale of an old car that had an adjusted basis of $4,000, only $1,000 would be counted, regardless of the amount you realized on the disposition of the old car.

If you traded the old car for a used car in a tax-free exchange and paid an additional $700, only the $700 would be counted for purposes of determining your investment tax credit.

If you buy a used car and the recapture rule applies to the disposition of your old car, the basis of the used car for determining the investment tax credit is figured the same as for new property.

HOW TO HANDLE THE LIMITATIONS ON INVESTMENT CREDIT AND DEPRECIATION

Dollar limits on the investment tax credit and depreciation apply to all passenger auto-

mobiles purchased after June 18, 1984. Additional restrictions apply to cars purchased after April 2, 1985. If your car was ordered before the applicable cutoff date, and delivered after the cutoff, you are subject to the rules in effect before the cutoff date.

New investment credit limit: The maximum investment tax credit you can claim for any passenger automobile purchased after June 18, 1984, is $1,000 and $675 for any car purchased after April 2, 1985. To compute your credit, multiply the cost (or basis) of the car by 6 percent, then impose the $1,000 or $675 limit and reduce the lower of the computed amount or the limit to reflect any personal use.

Example: On August 1, 1985, you purchase a $40,000 Mercedes for use in your business. You use the car 60 percent of the time for business and 40 percent for personal driving. Your credit is as follows:

Computed credit ($40,000 × 6%)	$2,400
Maximum credit under new law	$675
Lower of computed or maximum credit	$675
Business use percentage	×60%
Investment tax credit	$405

Recommendation: To get the full investment credit (that wonderful dollar-for-dollar reducer of your taxes), buy cars that cost no more than $11,250 (6% of $11,250 = $675). You may deduct separately and immediately—and thus not count as cost—sales tax, licenses, and tags.

New dollar limits on depreciation: If you purchased a car in 1984 but after June 18, 1984, the maximum allowance you can claim for depreciation is $4,000 in 1984 and $6,000 in any later year. For cars purchased after April 2, 1985, the first year depreciation limit is $3,200 and $4,800 thereafter. In computing depreciation, apply the general rules for depreciation, then impose the limitation and reduce your depreciation to reflect any personal use.

Exhibit 5-7 compares the effect of the latest rules with the effect of the old rules. If

EXHIBIT 5-7. Overview of Old Versus New Rules

FACTS: Car purchased August 1, 1985, for $35,000; used 100 percent for business until 1992.

	Old 1983 Rules	New 1985 Rules
Investment tax credit	$ 2,100	675
1st-year depreciation	8,488	3,200
2nd-year depreciation	12,901	4,800
3rd-year depreciation	12,561	4,800
4th-year depreciation	0	4,800
5th-year depreciation	0	4,800
6th-year depreciation	0	4,800
7th-year depreciation	0	4,800
8th-year depreciation	0	3,000

NOTE: If you are in the 50 percent tax bracket, the value of the above deductions in today's dollars, using an 8 percent interest rate to compute present value, is:

Tax Savings with Old 1983 rules	$17,702
Tax Savings with New 1985 rules	13,725
Cost of new law	$ 3,977

you buy a really expensive car after June 18, 1984, the IRS gets you with a double whammy: First, you lose some investment tax credit. Second, your depreciation deductions are spread out beyond 3 years and, because of the time value of money, are worth less each year you must wait.

Planning pointers: These new dollar limits, combined with the new "more-than-50-percent" business use test explained earlier, make good tax planning more crucial than ever. Keep these pointers in mind:

• Make sure you meet the "more-than-50-percent" business use test. Remember, if you fail the test, you get no investment tax credit and you must use 5-year straight-line depreciation.

• Do not buy cars with a cost (or basis) that exceeds $11,250. Any cost above this amount will require you to defer depreciation deductions; at the same time, you will be losing investment tax credit.

• If you have met these criteria and wish to maximize your deductions, you should then consider using two cars for business.

Beat the New Law by Using Two Cars

Assume, for example, that you purchased two new cars on August 1, 1984, and that you have a choice of driving one or two cars for business. Exhibit 5-8 shows the advantage of using both rather than only one car in this way. Moreover, you increase your investment tax credit by $252. Over 3 years of ownership, your savings in the form of extra tax deductions will be as follows.

	Extra Deductions
1984	$1,508
1985	1,992
1986	1,951
Total	$5,451

What to do: We have a mandate for you. Make a computation similar to that in Exhibit 5-8—using the same format. Compare using one car with two cars. If your spouse works, would it benefit you to swap cars for part of each week?

It is imperative that you do the analysis in Exhibit 5-8 if you want to qualify for new deductions. You must *plan* to get new deductions. Good planning could give you well over $5,000 in new deductions in just 3 years.

What if the second car will be used less

EXHIBIT 5-8. Getting the Maximum Auto Expense Deduction (Case Example)

	One Car	Two Cars	
		Car 1	Car 2
Business/Personal Use			
Total mileage for business	22,000	18,000	4,000
Total mileage for year	÷ 24,000	÷ 20,000	÷ 7,800
Business use percentage	92%	90%	51%
Deduction Calculations			
Gas and Oil[1]	$1,245	$1,038	$ 405
Insurance	800	800	600
Repairs & Maintenance	200	200	200
Tags and Licenses	100	100	80
Wash and Wax	130	130	130
Other	50	50	50
Total operating expense	2,525	2,318	1,465
Business use percentage	× 92%	× 90%	× 51%
Business total	2,323	2,086	733
Depreciation[2]	3,632	3,553	1,091
Total each car	$5,955	$5,639	$1,824
Total two cars		$7,463	
Savings—1984	$1,508[3] ($7,463 − $5,955)		

[1]Based on bargain gasoline costing $1.09 a gallon and cars getting 21 miles a gallon.
[2]Depreciation computed as follows:

	Model	Date Acq.	Cost or Basis	Bus. %	Bus. Cost	50% of ITC	Basis for Deprec.	Depreciation		
								Method	Prior	This Year
For 1 Car	R241	8/1/84	$16,278	92%	$14,976	(449)	$14,527	3-Year ACRS	N/A	$3,632
Car 1	R241	8/1/84	16,278	90%	14,650	(440)	14,210	3-Year ACRS	N/A	3,553
Car 2	R242	8/1/84	8,820	51%	4,498	(135)	4,363	3-Year ACRS	N/A	1,091

[3]In addition, using 2 cars gives extra investment tax credit of $252.

than 50 percent of the time for business? Should you still consider using it? Absolutely.

If the second car in Exhibit 5-8 had been used only 50 percent of the time for business, the owner would have been unable to take investment tax credit on the second car and would have been stuck with that ugly 5-year straight-line depreciation schedule. Even so, the savings from 1984 through 1986 would have been $3,266—which is not chicken feed.

Thus, the only way to know for sure how well you will make out by using one or two cars is to make the computations.

THE LEASING MYTH

There are no tax advantages to leasing an automobile. It is strictly a financial decision. To ensure maximum advantage, you should analyze the bottom line from an after-tax standpoint.

Leasing companies have done a good job selling leases. Somehow, a popular myth has started that leasing gives you tax advantages that a purchase won't. That's wrong. A lease will give you no additional tax advantages.

First of all, because you lease a car does not mean that you do not commute. You must still divide your mileage between business and personal miles. Your lease deduction is equivalent to your business mileage percentage.

Perhaps the biggest menace from leasing is the loss of the investment credit. When you buy an automobile for business use, you are entitled to an investment tax credit. The amount of your credit depends on the percentage of business use. When you lease a car, leasing companies frequently have the option of keeping the credit for themselves or giving it to you. Now, what do you think they are most likely to do?

Leasing is not the answer to increasing your automobile deductions. It may rob you of the investment tax credit, and it will do nothing for your business-use percentage.

Leasing won't defeat new law: If you've been thinking about leasing a business car to beat the limits on the investment credit and ACRS depreciation, forget it. Congress thought of that. The IRS has issued tables that prescribe the deductible percentage of lease payments for business car leases entered into after June 18, 1984. Result: As a lessee, you are stuck with the same limits as an owner.

GUIDELINES FOR DEDUCTING SCREWDRIVERS, BATTERY CHARGERS, AUTO TUNEUP EQUIPMENT, AND SIMILAR TOOLS

Take a trip through your garage, basement, workshed, or wherever you store tools and cleaning supplies. Make a list of the items you use on your car. You will probably find a battery charger, battery cables, and maybe even a battery tester. You might find a tire pump, a vise, a buffer, and a sander. By the time you get to the small tools such as screwdrivers,

pliers, and wrenches, you will note a number you have overlooked in your tax return.

If you do lots of work on your car, you may have equipment that should be capitalized and depreciated. If an item has an original cost in excess of $100, it should be capitalized and depreciated. If the cost is less than $100 for an individual item or a group of small tools, the normal procedure is to expense such items in the year of purchase.

Once you have completed your tour of the tool area, take a trip through your bookcase and see if you've purchased any handbooks on how to take care of your car. Next, proceed to your cleaning supplies and look for upholstery cleaner, chamois, brushes, and other items you might use to clean the car.

Bad news: You have just found some items that should have been claimed in your tax return but were not. What can you do? Since the general tax rule allows you to deduct items only in the year in which you pay for them, you could throw your hands up in the air and say "tough luck." However, another alternative is to simply convert the items from personal to business usage this year and start taking the deductions.

Caution: Only the business portion of the tools is deductible. You must have a basis for making the business determination and determining the appropriate cost to deduct.

Example: Norman has two automobiles, one used exclusively for business and the other used exclusively for personal purposes. The business car was driven 20,000 miles and the personal car was driven 10,000 miles during the year. Norman has two choices for making an allocation of the cost of tools used solely for automobile repairs.

Choice 1: Norman may reason that the tools are used about half the time on one car and half the time on the other. Since one car is a deductible business car and the other is a nondeductible personal car, Norman would deduct 50 percent of the cost—not the wisest choice.

Choice 2: Norman may reason that 20,000 of the 30,000 miles driven during the year were driven for business purposes. This rationale will give him two-thirds of the cost of the tools—a much better choice.

It's a good idea to have receipts, invoices, and canceled checks to back up all of your business expenses. If you fail to get receipts for some of the items found on your tour, make sure you take a photograph of the items to prove their existence. The photographs will not displace the need for receipts, but it will establish the reasonableness of your deduction. Start keeping all receipts and become a "pack rat" today.

RECORDS NEEDED TO SUPPORT YOUR AUTOMOBILE EXPENSES

Even when you drive an automobile around town for business reasons, you should maintain records good enough to meet the nattering travel substantiation rules that apply when you are away from home overnight. For details see Chapter 4.

Without question, the most difficult and most needed support involves your business mileage, which was discussed earlier in this chapter. Here, we will discuss the types of receipts you should obtain to support your transportation expenses.

Gasoline and oil: As a practical matter, you should obtain receipts for each gas and oil purchase. If you forget or otherwise fail to obtain a receipt, make sure you write the purchase in your diary or appointment book.

Reason: Gas and oil receipts will show where you made the purchase. That location will corroborate the entries in your diary or appointment book for business usage. The combination of the appointment book and the receipts establish where you went on business during the day.

At the end of the year when you tally your total purchases, test the gasoline expenses for reasonableness. Divide the total miles by miles per gallon to derive the gallons used during the year. Then multiply the gallons used by the cost of gasoline and check your total for reasonableness. Gas receipts are small and sometimes get lost, but this simple little calculation may increase your deductions.

Banks and major credit card distributors seem to be out of favor with many of the oil companies. Recent policy for most gas stations has been to accept only certain credit cards. However, even if you need to use three or four different credit cards, it is still a good idea to charge your gasoline and oil. That way the credit card companies will do a major portion of the bookkeeping for you.

Repairs and maintenance: Retain all receipts for repairs and maintenance and use them to verify your total mileage—just as the IRS will do.

Tires, batteries, and other replacements: When your motor falls out and you need a new one, what should you do? As a practical matter, accounting for the cost of replacements is a fairly complicated procedure. You would subtract the cost of the original motor, less depreciation, and add the cost of the new motor to the total basis of the automobile. The new motor would then be depreciated under the ACRS system (generally three years).

Actually, the proper tax treatment of replacement items is not entirely clear. Such items usually include tires, batteries, radios, heaters, motors, and so forth. The IRS could, as a technical matter, require you to capitalize such items and thus force delay of your tax recovery via depreciation. Capitalization is a pain in the neck and quite complex, but thankfully, most examining IRS agents will allow a deduction for replacement items.

Washing and waxing: Here again, get receipts. They correspond with your appointment book to give the location of your car at a specific time. If you do your washing and waxing at home, make sure you deduct the cost of supplies purchased for the project. It's unlikely that you would want to go through the trouble of allocating a portion of your water bill, though.

Taxes, licenses, and tags: You usually pay for these items by check. Keep both the canceled check and the receipt for the payment.

Insurance and auto club: If your insurance

policy covers other members of the family, it's highly unlikely that you have 100 percent business usage. At least, that is the IRS's presumption.

Generally, your insurance company will require you to cover other family members, especially if you have teenagers in the family. If that is your situation, make sure you highlight that portion of the policy which requires coverage of everyone, or get a statement from your insurance broker.

The insurance policy should be in the name of the person taking the business deduction. If the corporation owns a car, for example, the insurance policy should be in the corporation's name.

Make sure you retain your policies and canceled checks.

Parking fees and tolls: Parking receipts will establish the physical location of your automobile and will help document the entries in your appointment book. Likewise, tolls establish where your automobile travels during the day. Make sure you obtain receipts for all parking and tolls whenever possible.

Sales tax: When your car is used a percentage of the time for business, you effectively have two cars—a business car and a personal car. If you live in a state where the sales tax is imposed on the purchaser, you may deduct the sales tax on the business car as a business expense and the sales tax on the personal car as an itemized deduction. However, if you live in a state where the sales tax is imposed on the seller or retailer, you do not have the option of claiming a deduction for the sales tax paid on the business car. You must add the cost of the sales tax to the cost of the business car.

You need the automobile purchase receipt for a number of reasons, including the deduction for sales tax. Make sure you retain this receipt for the entire period of time the car is owned and for three years after you sell it. If you trade your car, keep receipts for the car traded and for the new car for as long as the new car is owned and for three years after that, unless that car is also traded.

Personal property taxes: Personal property taxes paid on the business portion of the car are deductible as an operating expense of the automobile. If you use optional IRS mileage rates, personal property taxes are added to the optional rate—they are not one of the components used in making up the rate. On the personal-use portion of your automobile, personal property taxes are deductible as itemized deductions.

Auto registration fees in some states include personal property tax as part of the assessment. If personal property tax is not part of the assessment, you may claim auto registration fees on the business portion of the car only. Such fees are not deductible as itemized deductions.

Interest: Interest paid for financing the purchase of your automobile is handled the same as personal property taxes. If, for example, the loan interest for the year is $400 and you use your car 75 percent of the time for business, $300 is deductible as a business expense. The remaining $100 qualifies as an itemized deduction.

Cost of traffic violations: You do not need any receipts for these, since they are not deductible. Sorry!

Casualty and theft losses: It is extremely difficult nowadays to get a receipt from a thief. If your auto suffers a casualty or theft loss, you will have two different types of losses— the business portion and the personal portion. The unreimbursed business portion of the loss is deductible as a business expense. The unreimbursed personal loss is deductible as an itemized deduction subject to the 10 percent of adjusted gross income floor and the $100 reduction. Thus, the loss must exceed both 10 percent of your adjusted gross income and $100 for you to obtain any benefit from a personal casualty loss.

If you do suffer a casualty or theft loss, make sure you obtain documentation. For a theft loss, you will want a copy of the police report. For a casualty loss, you will want the police report, if any, photographs of the damaged car, and a copy of any insurance checks.

A casualty loss is deductible in the year the casualty occurs. If you expect to be reimbursed by insurance, IRS regulations say you must reduce your loss by the estimated recovery from the insurance company. You deduct in the year of occurrence the net casualty loss as computed on the basis of estimates of recovery. Recent court decisions, however, allow a taxpayer to write off a loss without reduction for the estimated insurance recovery. Under this method, the taxpayer would report the later reimbursement as income. The IRS has not yet announced whether or not it will accept this rule.

The amount of your casualty or theft loss may not exceed the tax basis of your car. Second, the casualty loss may not exceed the loss in fair market value caused by the casualty. Generally, for an automobile, the cost of repairs to the car is acceptable as evidence of loss in value when you are able to show that:

- The repairs are necessary to restore your car to its condition before the casualty;
- The amount spent for such repairs is not excessive;
- The repairs do not take care of more than the damage suffered; and
- The value of your car after the repairs is not greater than the value of your car immediately before the casualty.

SELDOM APPLIED TAX-REDUCING TECHNIQUES TO USE WHEN YOU DISPOSE OF YOUR BUSINESS AUTOMOBILE

Inflation is good for the Treasury. Buy a business car for $10,000, depreciate it to zero in three years, sell it for $10,000, and you pay tax on the $10,000.

The business portion of your automobile is a business asset. When you dispose of a business asset, you will have either a tax gain or a tax loss. How you structure the transaction, as an outright sale or as a trade, will determine the tax impact of getting rid of your old business car.

Now even if you use a designated hitter to help you with your taxes, your accountant will not be around when you get mad at your automobile. And that's usually when you dispose of it. The ultimate cash value of your

automobile may be in jeopardy without a little tax planning to calm you down.

The decision to trade or sell: Let's assume you are about to get mad at your car. You have, in fact, decided that the car will be gone at the end of the week. That decision carries tax implications.

State sales tax: The trade or sell decision could impact the amount of sales tax you pay to your state government. In some states, the sales tax is computed on only the cash boot paid on the trade. If you purchase, you pay the sales tax on the gross purchase price. Some states have no sales tax.

Investment credit: If you trade your old auto for a new auto, your basis for computing the investment tax credit is the cash boot paid plus the tax basis of your old automobile. If you purchase outright, the cash purchase price is used to determine your investment credit.

Tax on outright sale: If you sell your car outright, any gain or loss will be recognized for tax purposes in the year during which the sale took place. If you have a tax loss, you get to deduct the loss in the year of sale. If you have a tax gain, you are allowed to contribute to the U.S. Treasury.

Deferred tax on trade: If you trade in your auto for another one, any gain or loss is deferred, or pushed over, to the new automobile and it is recognized, taxwise, in the depreciation of the newly acquired automobile.

This scenario raises some tactical questions. Would you rather pay tax now, or later? Which is best for you, to sell or trade? It all depends on your facts and circumstances and the only way to know for sure is to make a computation similar to that in Exhibit 5.9.

Johnson spent 46 minutes making the computation in Exhibit 5-9. Was the time well spent? If you could save $458 in 46 minutes, is that time well spent? We think so, and the computation really isn't difficult.

One premise in Exhibit 5-9 (which may or may not be true in your case) is that the trade-in value equals the sales proceeds. Johnson figures he could sell the car outright,

EXHIBIT 5-9. The Trade or Sell Decision (Example Computation).

FACTS: Johnson made the computation in Exhibit 5-10 and determined that he would have a $2,666 tax gain if he sold the old car outright. Johnson plans on purchasing a new car for $11,250. He makes the following computation to determine how much he will save by trading in the old car.

	TRADE OLD CAR	SELL OLD CAR
Purchase price of new car	$11,250	$11,250
Trade-in value or sales proceeds	(7,000)	(7,000)
State sales tax on transaction	255 [1]	675 [2]
Investment credit recapture	167 [3]	167 [3]
Investment credit on new car	(402)[4]	(562)[5]
Tax on gain from old car	1,135 [6]	1,333 [7]
Net Economic Cost	$5,405	$5,863

$458 Saved with trade-in

[1] 6% tax x $4,250 ($11,250 cost − $7,000 trade value).
[2] 6% tax x $11,250.
[3] 2% credit recapture x $8,330 cost of original car (Exhibit 5-9).
[4] 6% credit x $6,705 ($4,250 cash boot x 83.3% business + $3,165 basis of old car).
[5] 6% credit x $9,371 ($11,250 x 83.3% business).
[6] Present value of $2,666 gain (Exhibit 5-9 spread over cost recovery period of new auto (ACRS three years) assuming 10% value of money and Johnson's 50% tax bracket.
[7] 50% tax x $2,666 ordinary gain.

but by the time he took the cost of ads away from his selling price, he would realize the same amount by trading the car for the new one. Johnson also has the election to deduct state sales taxes on the transaction. He lives in a state where sales taxes are imposed on the purchaser, not the seller. Accordingly, he may deduct the sales taxes. A portion of the sales taxes will be deducted as a business expense, and a portion will be deducted as itemized deductions. In Johnson's case, both the business deduction and the itemized deduction produce tax benefit.

Note that Johnson must recapture investment credit regardless of whether the car is traded or sold.

The investment credit on the new car will differ if there's a trade versus a sale. The computations are contained in the footnotes.

Johnson's gain on sale if the car is sold outright is $2,666. Since Johnson lives in the 50 percent tax bracket, his tax on the gain if the car were sold outright would be $1,333.

If the car is traded, the same tax will be paid, but it will be paid in the future. We assume that money will be worth less in the future than it is today. The assumption in Exhibit 5-9 is 10 percent. Basically, the tax of $1,333 is spread over the cost recovery period of the new auto and we assume Johnson chose ACRS for three years. Thus, 25 percent of the tax will be paid during the first year the new car is depreciated, 38 percent will be paid the second year, and 37 percent will be paid the third year. For the second and third years we calculated the present value of the future tax payments. That means in today's dollars, Johnson's future tax would amount to $1,135 rather than $1,333.

You should make a similar computation. If you do not have a calculator which computes present value, you may simply discount the money for what you think it will be worth in the future. The other calculations are quite easy. Just follow the numbers and rationale set out in Exhibit 5.9.

Computing gain or loss: If your auto consists of two parts, a business part and a personal part, your first step in determining your tax gain or loss is to divide the car into its respective parts. The computation in Exhibit 5-10 shows how this is done. You simply add the business miles the car has traveled and compare them with the total miles to derive your business percentage. That's step one.

In step two, you determine the basis of your automobile. See Exhibit 5-10.

If you know the existing basis of your automobile, computing the basis at time of sale is easy. First, subtract the depreciation to the date of sale. Generally, this will be the depreciation in your prior year tax return.

Make sure you add the prior depreciation to find your total depreciation to date. Second, add 50 percent of any investment tax credit that must be recaptured to your basis. Thus, all you must do is subtract depreciation and add 500 percent of any investment credit recapture to determine your new basis.

Finally, you're ready for step three—computing your gain or loss. Here, simply take your net selling price and subtract your basis. The difference will be your gain or loss.

No deduction for personal losses: Note that step three resulted in a $501 tax loss on the personal portion of the car. There is no deduction for personal losses.

EXHIBIT 5-10. Computing Gain or Loss on Disposition of Auto (Example Computation).

STEP 1: Determine Percentages of Business and Personal Use

	BUSINESS MILES	PERSONAL MILES	TOTAL MILES
1983	16,000	4,000	20,000
1984	13,000	2,000	15,000
1985	21,000	4,000	25,000
	50,000	10,000	60,000
	83.3%	16.7%	100%

STEP 2: Determine Basis

	83.3% BUSINESS	16.7% PERSONAL	TOTAL
Original cost (or basis[1])	$ 8,330	$ 1,670	$ 10,000
Depreciation to date of sale	(5,248)[2]	N/A	(5,248)
Add 50% of investment credit recapture	83 [3]	N/A	83
Basis	$ 3,165	$ 1,670	$ 4,835

STEP 3: Compute Gain or Loss

	83.3% BUSINESS	16.7% PERSONAL	TOTAL
Selling price	$ 5,831	$ 1,169	$ 7,000
Basis	(3,165)	(1,670)	(4,835)
Gain (loss)	$ 2,666 [4]	$ (501)[5]	$ 2,165

[1]If car was acquired by trading in another car, refer to earlier discussion on how to compute basis.

[2]ACRS depreciation in 1983 and 1984.

[3]50% × $167 of investment credit recaptured because car was not held for full three-year period. 50% of this recaptured amount is added to basis.

[4]Trade decision should be considered for maximum benefits (see Exhibit 5-9).

[5]Personal loss is not deductible; however, had this been a gain, the personal gain would have been taxable.

Personal gains are taxable: If the computation in step three had resulted in a personal gain, the gain would be taxable. If the automobile were held for more than one year (one year and one day, or longer), the gain would be considered capital gain and taxed at tax-favored capital gain rates.

Capital gain on business portion: When would you be taxed at tax-favored capital gains rates on the business portion of the automobile? Only when the selling price exceeds your original purchase price.

Example: Evans buys a business car for $10,000 and takes $2,500 in depreciation the first year. His tax basis in the automobile is now $7,500.

If Evans sells the car for $9,000, he will have $1,500 of taxable gain. That gain is ordinary income and will be taxed at the regular-income tax rates.

Now let's assume that Evans makes money on his car. He sells the $10,000 car for $11,000 after taking a tax deduction for $2,500 in depreciation. Since Evans's tax basis is $7,500 at the time of sale, he has a $3,500 gain, which is broken down into $2,500 of ordinary income and $1,000 of long-term capital gain (assuming he held the car for at least one year and one day).

The basic rule on gains is that any gain attributable to depreciation of the automobile is taxed as ordinary income. Any gain in excess of the original purchase price, or basis, is taxable as capital gain. The word *probably* is used because capital gains and losses must be grouped together to determine the ultimate tax effect. But if the only transaction of a capital nature that took place that year was the gain on the sale of the automobile, and if the car had been held for more than one year, the $1,000 would be capital gain.

Exhibit 5-11 contains a flowchart of the trade or sell decision. The general rule is that if you are buying or trading for a new car, and the outright sale of your old car would result in a tax gain, you should trade in the old car to get the best tax benefit. On the other hand, if the transaction would result in a tax loss, you are generally better off to sell the old car and purchase the new car outright.

Caution: Always compute the best benefit. Your individual facts and circumstances including where you live will determine the ultimate result of the sell or trade decision. The economic consequences of either choice are not significant, if you do not care about $500. We think you should make the computation.

HOW A DECLINE IN BUSINESS USE REQUIRES RECAPTURE OF INVESTMENT TAX CREDIT

Your depreciation deduction each year is based on your percentage of business use. Your investment credit is first claimed based on your percentage of business use at the time of purchase. If your business use later declines, your investment credit is subject to recapture.

When your business use declines, the percentage reduction is treated as a taxable sale of your car as of the beginning of the taxable year in which your business use declined.

Example: Porter buys a new business car in 1983 for $10,000. He uses the car 100 percent of the time for business in 1983, 70 percent of the time for business in 1984, and 90 percent of the time for business in 1985.

Porter's depreciation deductions are computed as follows:

1983: $10,000 × 25% × 100% = $2,500

1984: $10,000 × 38% × 70% = 2,660

1985: $10,000 × 37% × 90% = 3,330

Total $8,490

Now let's see what happens to Porter's investment tax credit. In 1983 Porter received an investment tax credit of $600 ($10,000 × 6%). In 1984, Porter's business usage percentage drops from 100 percent to 70 percent. The IRS will now recapture $180 of investment credit [$10,000 − $7,000 ($10,000 × 70%) × 6 percent]. In 1985, when Porter's business usage jumps to 90 percent, he receives no additional credit. The declining business use is a one-way road.

EXHIBIT 5-11. The Trade or Sell Decision (Flowchart).

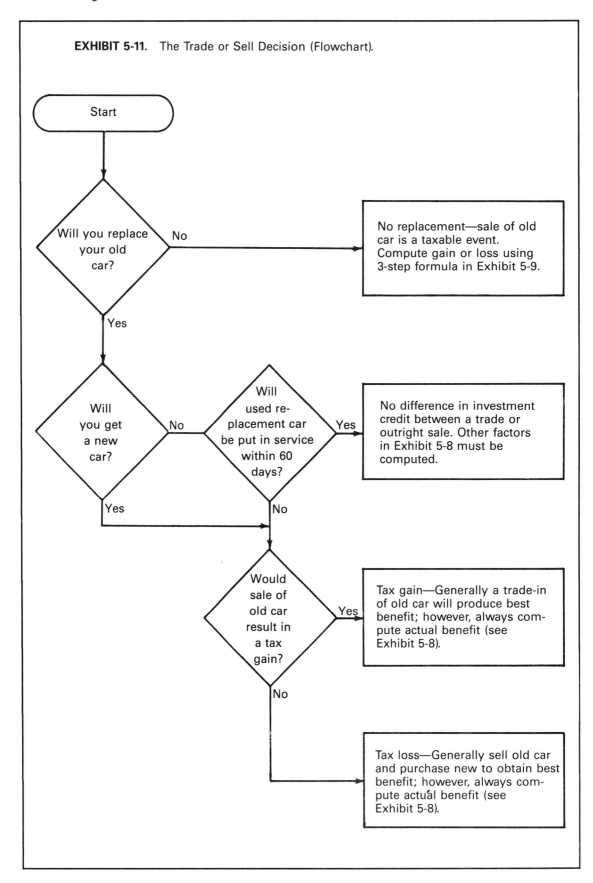

The recapture percentage in Porter's case was 6 percent. When you buy a business car, you are allowed a credit of 6 percent of the car's business cost (business use percentage times total cost) subject to the new $675 limit. For each full 1 year and 1 day you use the car for business, you "earn" one-third (2%) of the credit, so if you sell the car after a year, only 4 percent of the credit is recaptured. However, a reduction in business use is treated as a sale as of the beginning of your taxable year. Thus, in Porter's case, he was deemed to have sold 30 percent of his car on January 1, 1984, less than 1 year after buying the car. Therefore, he had to pay back the full 6 percent credit on $3,000 to Uncle Sam. If Porter's business use did not drop until 1985, he would have had to pay back only 4 percent.

Recapture rules for expense election: You can elect to expense up to $4,000 for cars purchased after June 18, 1984 and $3,200 for cars purchased after April 2, 1985, rather than depreciatae that amount. If you do, you are subject to the same recapture rules as applied to the investment tax credit.

At the time this book was written, IRS had not issued its regulations for "recapturing" any benefit of the expense deduction if property is not used "predominantly in a trade or business" for 2 full taxable years after the property is placed in service.

The Congressional Conference Committee Report which summarized the law indicated that "recapture" would take the form of an addition to income.

Cautionary note: If you claim the special expense election in lieu of depreciation and you expect fluctuations in your business-use percentage, make sure you check with your tax advisor.

NEW RECAPTURE RULE FOR EXCESS DEPRECIATION

Until the Tax Reform Act of 1984, a decline in business use did not trigger the recapture of depreciation. Now, for cars purchased after June 18, 1984, a drop in your business use percentage from above 50 percent to 50 percent or below will trigger recapture of "excess depreciation." "Excess depreciation" is the excess of ACRS deductions actually claimed over depreciation that would have

been claimed on the basis of 5-year straight-line depreciation. "Depreciation recapture" means that the calculated excess amount is reported in your tax return as ordinary income and is subject to regular income tax.

Example: You purchase a business car for $16,279 in July 1984 and use it in your business 100 percent during 1984 and 1985. In 1986, your business use percentage drops to 45 percent. Back in 1984, you claimed an investment tax credit of $977 ($16,279 × 6%). Your ACRS deduction was computed by taking your adjusted basis of $15,791 [$16,279 − $977 × 50%)] times 25 percent ACRS deduction for a total of $3,948. In 1985, your ACRS deduction was $6,000. However, because your business use percentage dropped to 50 percent or below, you had to report $5,064 as ordinary income in 1986. The computation is as follows:

	ACRS	5-Years
1984	$3,948	$1,628
1985	6,000	3,256
Total	$9,948	$4,884

$5,064
Recapture

If you were in the 50 percent tax bracket, the recapture would have cost you additional taxes of $2,532—a horrible thought to contemplate, so plan carefully.

Note: There is no basis reduction for 50 percent of the investment tax credit when computing straight-line depreciation for purposes of recapture.

Planning tip: To get any tax breaks, you must first establish your business use with a daily mileage log. Then make sure that your business use percentage remains approximately the same from the first year through the third full taxable year following the year in which the car is placed in service. Thus, for a car purchased July 1, 1984, you would want similar business use percentages for 1984, 1985, 1986, and 1987.

GUIDELINES FOR CONVERTING A PERSONAL CAR TO BUSINESS USE

If you convert a personal car to business use, you are subject to the lower of cost or market rule for determining basis. Cost is what you paid for the car originally. Market is the fair market value of the automobile on the day you convert it to business use. Generally, a "blue book" value is adequate evidence of market. A better bet would be to take the car to a dealer and have the dealer give you a statement showing the market value of the car at the date of conversion.

Hint: When getting market value, ask for retail value. That's what you would have to pay to purchase the car and what a regular customer would have to pay a dealer.

Example: Assume you purchased a car several years ago for $8,000. Today, that car has a retail book value of $5,000. Your basis for purposes of computing depreciation or cost recovery is $5,000.

No investment credit: If you convert a personal car to business use, you do not get any investment credit. The investment credit applies only to the *purchases* of eligible assets for use in business. When you first purchased your automobile, you purchased it for personal use. Thus, you get no investment credit.

GUIDELINES FOR CONVERTING A BUSINESS CAR TO PERSONAL USE

Form 1040 filers: If you operate your business as an employee or a self-employed individual and you claim your automobile deductions on Form 1040, the transfer of your business car to personal use is not a taxable event, unless you have to recapture some investment tax credit as discussed earlier in this chapter.

Your basis in the automobile for personal use is the same basis you had at the time the car was transferred from business to personal use. Remember, if you sell a personal car at a gain, the gain is taxable. If you sell a personal car at a loss, the loss is not deductible.

Corporate sale to shareholder: If you operate your business as a one-person or controlled corporation and the corporation sells you the corporate car, the transaction must be consummated at fair market value. The corporation is denied capital gain treatment and any gain must be reported as ordinary

income, *if* you intend to use the automobile for business; if not, the corporation will get the capital gains break if the sales price exceeds its original cost. Moreover, if a loss results, the corporation may not deduct the loss.

Thus, the corporate sale of a business automobile to a shareholder is a taxable event. Moreover, the corporation is penalized for such a sale.

If you operate your business as a one-person or a controlled corporation and you want the corporate car because you take good care of it, get the car out of the corporation. You do not get additional tax breaks because the car is owned by the corporation. Essentially, your records must be in the same condition, whether or not the car is owned by the corporation.

AUTOMOBILES AS ENTERTAINMENT FACILITIES

Tax law broadly defines the term "entertainment facility" to include "any item of personal property . . . owned, rented, or used . . . if it is used during the taxable year for, or in connection with entertainment." The IRS has stated that this definition includes automobiles that are used for entertainment purposes.

Basically, the use of an automobile for "associated with" entertainment is treated as personal use. Thus, a trip by automobile to a hunting lodge for a hunting trip would be considered nonbusiness use.

If you have substantial "associated with" entertainment and you use an automobile or an airplane for such entertainment, you could have a significant tax problem. You should have a long discussion with your tax advisor.

If your "associated with" entertainment is only occasional or incidental, you have no problem. Generally, the IRS will ignore occasional or incidental transportation costs.

THE TAX REFORM ACT RULES AT A GLANCE

For a final, quick review of the changes Congress made in 1984 and 1985, review the easy-to-follow flowchart in Exhibit 5-12.

EXHIBIT 5-12. Easy-to-follow Flowchart of New Automobile Rules[4]

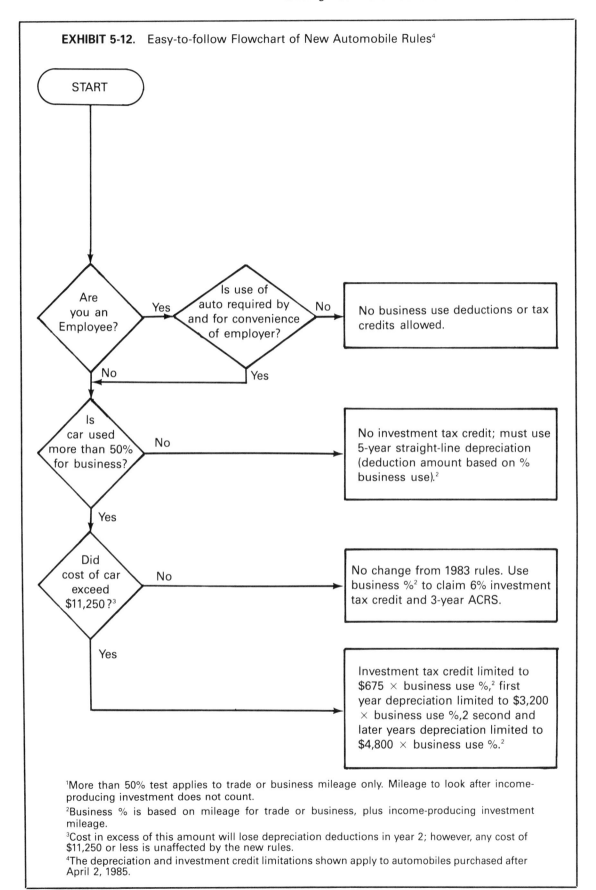

[1]More than 50% test applies to trade or business mileage only. Mileage to look after income-producing investment does not count.

[2]Business % is based on mileage for trade or business, plus income-producing investment mileage.

[3]Cost in excess of this amount will lose depreciation deductions in year 2; however, any cost of $11,250 or less is unaffected by the new rules.

[4]The depreciation and investment credit limitations shown apply to automobiles purchased after April 2, 1985.

TAX REDUCTION CHECKLIST

IRS publications to be obtained:

- Publication 463—*Travel, Entertainment, and Gift Expenses*
- Publication 551—*Basis of Assets*
- Publication 535—*Business Expenses and Operating Losses*
- Publication 583—*Information for Business Taxpayers—Business Taxes, Identification Numbers, Recordkeeping*
- Publication 334—*Tax Guide for Small Business*

Business versus personal mileage:

- If you drive from your home to an office or work location, you do not have 100 percent business mileage.
- You may have more than one commute a day when you return home before going to another work location.
- You must have support for your business mileage percentage—a sound test basis will work.
- You could have 100 percent business mileage if your home is also your principal place of business.
- Corporate ownership of the car will not eliminate personal mileage.
- Leasing does nothing for your business/personal mileage split.
- Usage of business cars for associated entertainment is treated as personal use.

IRS standard mileage rates are not a good deal:

- Usually, actual expenses will far exceed standard mileage rates.
- Trade-off—gas receipts are not necessary when you use IRS standard mileage rates, an expensive price for a few receipts.
- Autos eligible for IRS standard rates include those that
  - Have not been depreciated by an accelerated method.
  - Have not been depreciated using ACRS.
  - Have not taken advantage of additional first-year depreciation.
  - Have not taken advantage of the special expense election.
  - Are not fully depreciated.
- When optional rates are used, the investment tax credit is often overlooked. If you overlooked investment credit during the past three years, file an amended return and get your money back.
- If you use more than one car during a year, you must combine mileage before applying IRS optional rates.
- If you buy a new or used car to replace your old car, you may use optional rates on one car and actual expenses on the other.

Reimbursed employees should claim automobile expenses in their tax returns because:

- They will get the investment tax credit on car purchases.
- Actual expenses will exceed employer reimbursements and tax refunds result.

Investment tax credit on business automobiles:

- Equal to 6 percent of business "tax cost" (limited to $675 after April 2, 1985).
- Applies only in year auto purchased and placed in service for business use.
- Available even if IRS standard mileage rates are used.
- For new-car trades, tax cost on which credit is based is equal to cash boot and basis.
- Available to employees who are reimbursed for business mileage.
- Available on leased cars if lessor so allows.

126

- Early disposition triggers recapture.
- Decline in business use triggers recapture.

Leasing:

- No extra deductions.
- No change in business/personal split.
- Could cost you investment tax credit.

Receipts are necessary for actual automobile expenses:

- Receipts of gasoline purchases and other items establish correspondence between your appointment book and your transportation activities. Therefore, obtain receipts for
  — Gasoline and oil.
  — Repairs and maintenance.
  — Washing and waxing the auto.
  — Licenses and tags.
  — Insurance and auto club.
  — Parking fees and tolls.
  — Sales taxes.
  — Personal property taxes.
  — Interest.
- When you do work on your car at your home, make sure you check in the garage and other locations for tools, equipment, and supplies used.

Disposing of the automobile:

- If you have a tax loss, sell the automobile to take the loss in the year of sale.
- If you have a tax gain, trade the auto to defer gain over the life of the new auto.
- When you trade, you must use the boot to establish the depreciation basis of the newly acquired car.
- Recapture of the investment tax credit must be considered when you want to dispose of the old car.
- If you are a Form 1040 filer, transfer of an auto from business to personal use is not a taxable event at the time of transfer. Subsequent sale and resultant gain, if any, is taxable. Old business basis is transferred to personal computation.
- Corporate sale to related shareholder must be at "fair market value." Moreover, the corporation may not deduct losses or receive tax-favored capital gain treatment on such sales.

New rules in 1985:

- Business use must exceed 50 percent in order to get investment tax credit and three-year ACRS depreciation.
- Daily mileage logs required.
- First-year depreciation (and expensing) limited to $3,200, maximum after first year is $4,800 for cars purchased after April 2, 1985. First year depreciation is limited to $4,000 and subsequent years are limited to $6,000 for automobiles purchased between June 19, 1984 and April 2, 1985.

It used to be lots of fun to argue with the IRS about estimated useful lives and estimated salvage values in trying to justify larger depreciation write-offs. Taxpayers always wanted very short useful lives and very low salvage values. The IRS, of course, wanted just the opposite. But those days of fun and games are gone. Thanks to the Economic Recovery Tax Act of 1981 (ERTA), the old depreciation rules were replaced with a completely new, stream-lined system tilted heavily in favor of the businessperson and investor.

The new system is called the *Accelerated Cost Recovery System*. We'll just refer to "the ACRS rules" in the remainder of this chapter.

Under the ACRS rules, you are allowed to write off specified percentages of your cost of business or income-producing property each year. It is no longer necessary to battle with the IRS. You simply go to a schedule and pick the percentage of cost to write off in a given year. Furthermore, you will no longer have any arguments with the IRS about salvage value, since salvage value is ignored under the new ACRS rules.

The Tax Reform Act of 1984 added a minor complication by extending the write-off period for most real estate acquired after March 15, 1984, to 18 years (from 15 years) and the President signed legislation in October, 1985 extending the write-off period to

19 years. Still, the benefits of real estate depreciation are tremendous compared to the dark days before ACRS.

The 1984 law also added a not-so-minor complication concerning certain property used partly for personal purposes and partly for business purposes. For property covered by this rule, depreciation write-offs are limited—and the investment credit (Chapter 7) lost—if business use does not exceed 50 percent.

Despite the new restrictions added by the new law, the ACRS rules are a boon for business people. In this chapter you will learn:

- The easiest way to understand the ACRS rules.
- What assets are covered by the ACRS rules.
- How to handle personal property write-offs under the ACRS rules.
- How to handle the expensing election for personal property.
- Why the new ACRS rules are so much better than the old depreciation rules.
- How commercial real estate is penalized under the ACRS rules.
- How to profit from ACRS write-offs for income-producing residential property.
- How to write off your costs of making leasehold improvements.
- How to avoid the antichurning trap.

6
How to Cut Your Taxes With the New Accelerated Cost Recovery Rules

• Why big capital gains and big ACRS write-offs don't mix.

THE EASIEST WAY TO UNDERSTAND THE ACRS RULES

Like the old depreciation rules, the ACRS rules provide write-offs for noncash expenses. The theory of depreciation is that a business asset loses value over a period of time and therefore represents a business expense. The old depreciation rules tried—although clumsily—to match actual economic loss with tax write-offs.

On the other hand, the ACRS rules bear no relationship to reality; they are based strictly on the whims of Congress. Under the new rules, your investment in all covered property is written off over fixed recovery periods that are unrelated to and shorter than the actual useful lives of the property. Furthermore, the new rules do not distinguish between new and used property.

The concept called basis: Under the ACRS rules, you write off *100 percent* of the "basis" of depreciable property. Beginning in 1983, your depreciable basis must be reduced by 50 percent of any investment tax credit (Chapter 7). For property acquired by purchase, your depreciable basis is cost less 50 percent of investment tax credit, if any.

Example—basis of purchased investment credit property: You pay $10,000 for a new business car. Your basis for the ACRS write-offs is $9,700 [$10,000 cost − $300 ($600 investment credit × 50%)].

Basis when property is acquired by trade: If you trade property for like-kind property, there is no tax on the transaction. Your basis for deducting the cost of the newly acquired property is equal to the cash you paid plus the basis of the property traded, less one-half the investment credit, if any.

Basis of property traded: Once property is placed in service (generally, ready for and used in business), it is depreciated or recovered over a specified period of time. Any depreciation or recovery deductions claimed are subtracted in determining basis. Thus, the basis of property traded is equal to:

• Cost
• Less 50% of the investment tax credit
• Less depreciation or recovery deductions
• Plus 50% of any investment tax credit recaptured.

Example—basis of property traded: In 1984 you purchase a new business car for $10,000. You use the car 100 percent in your business for two years and two days and then trade the car, plus $7,000 cash, for a new 1986 model. Your basis in the 1984 car is determined as follows:

Original cost	$10,000
Less 50% of investment credit	(300)
Less ACRS deductions in 1984 and 1985	(6,111)
Plus 50% of investment credit recaptured	100
Basis in 1984 car at time of trade	$ 3,689

The basis of your 1986 car for purposes of the investment credit is equal to $10,689 (7,000 cash boot + $3,689 basis in 1984 car traded). Your basis for the 1986 ACRS deduction is $10,368 ($10,689 − 50% of $641 investment tax credit on 1986 car).

Example—ACRS write-off of business car: Assume a business car with a basis of $10,000. Your ACRS tax deduction in the year you buy the car would be $2,500. In the next year, you would deduct $3,800, and the following year, the remaining $3,700. Your total deductions would be $10,000, all based on specified percentages and a three-year recovery period, as prescribed in ERTA.

As you might expect, ERTA does not take away the need to make decisions. In the example above, you could have elected straight-line recovery over three, five, or 12 years. In other words, you could have elected a five-year recovery period and deducted $1,000 in the first year, $2,000 in each of the next four years, and $1,000 in the sixth year. If you're wondering why it takes six years to write off the total expense under the "five-year" election, it's because you are allowed only a half-year's write-off in the first year, so it takes until the sixth year to write off the entire cost—more on this point later.

As you progress through this chapter, you will learn the various elections, pitfalls, and other areas of concern. But for now, suffice it to say that you collect 100 percent of the basis of assets as tax deductions.

It makes no difference how you pay for the assets or how long the assets will last. For example, assume you have a very rich and very kind uncle who sells you a $200,000 building located on land worth $40,000 for nothing down, with no payments of either principal or interest for 20 years. Under the ACRS rules, you would write off the entire $200,000 (you can't depreciate land) over a 19-year period. Thus you would get $200,000 in tax write-offs without spending a penny.

Important reminders: ACRS deductions are noncash expenses. You write off 100 percent of the basis of assets over statutory lives, unrelated to physical lives. The same rules apply to both new and used property. Financing does not affect your write-offs. There are no arguments with the IRS over estimated useful lives or estimated salvage values. These old concepts do not exist with ACRS.

WHAT ASSETS ARE COVERED BY THE ACRS RULES

The ACRS rules apply to almost all business and income-producing property placed in service after 1980. For assets placed in service before January 1, 1981, the old depreciation rules still apply and you keep doing what you were doing on January 1, 1981. Thus, you can still have those wonderful arguments with the IRS about useful lives and estimated salvage values if you have any property you placed in service before January 1, 1981.

Generally, property eligible for the ACRS rules is the same type of property that you could depreciate under the old rules. Thus, the ACRS rules apply to buildings, but not to land.

Certain property is excluded from the ACRS rules. The rules do not apply to leasehold improvements or low-income rehabilitation expenditures. If you elect a depreciation method not expressed in terms of years, such as the unit-of-production method or the income forecast method, you may not use the ACRS rules. Similarly, if you elect the IRS standard mileage rate for your business automobile, you are not eligible for ACRS on that automobile.

Component depreciation extinct—with two exceptions: Under the ACRS rules, component depreciation is eliminated. That is, you may not write off the costs of separate components of a building, such as plumbing or wiring, as you could under the old rules. The new rules require you to write off the expense of the building as a whole. Also, if you make improvements to the building after placing it in service, you must use the same write-off period and method (such as 19-year, straight-line) for the improvements. There are, however, three exceptions to this general rule.

Exception 1—substantial improvement: A substantial improvement to a building is treated as a separate building, rather than as one or more components. Thus, you do not have to use the same write-off method for the substantial improvement as you are using for the remainder of the building. For example, suppose you bought a building today and decided to use straight-line, 19-year recovery. If you make a substantial improvement four years from now, you could write off the cost of the new improvement under any method allowed for a separate building; you would not have to use the straight-line, 19-year method. Later, we will discuss the various permissible methods.

An improvement is defined as "substantial" if

- The amount spent for the improvement over a two-year period is at least 25 percent of the building's adjusted basis (cost), disregarding depreciation and amortization adjustments, and
- The improvement was made at least three years after the building was placed in service.

Exception 2—first improvement after 1980 and before March 16, 1984: As mentioned before, buildings placed in service before 1980 are not eligible for ACRS write-offs. However, post-1980 improvements do qualify. For the first improvement made after 1980 but before March 16, 1984, you may select any write-off period and method (such as 15-year, accelerated) available as of that time. Subsequent improvements made before March 16, 1984, must be depreciated using the same period and method as the first improvement, unless the subsequent improvement qualifies as a "substantial improvement" under Exception 1.

Exception 3—first improvement after March 16, 1984: For most real estate placed in service after March 6, 1984, the shortest write-off period is 18 years. If you make an improvement in June 1984 you may use any write-off period and method (such as 18-year, accelerated) available as of that time. Subsequent improvements must be depreciated using the same period and method as the first post-March 16, 1984, improvement. Note: You may not use 15-year depreciation on post-March 16, 1984, improvements (or 18-year depreciation on post-May 8, 1985 improvements) even if your building was first placed in service at the time the faster write-off period applied.

In short, Exceptions 2 and 3 treat the first improvements made during the applicable periods as though they were separate buildings. You select any depreciation period and method available as of that time and you must use the same period and method on later improvements, unless they qualify as "substantial improvements" under Exception 1.

Example: In 1978 you purchased an office (no land) for $80,000 and elected to depreciate it over 40 years using the straight-line depreciation method ($2,000 a year). In 1981 you spent $5,000 on improvements. This is the first improvement subject to ACRS. You elected a 15-year accelerated write-off for the $5,000. In 1983 you spent $4,000 further improving your office. You must write off the $4,000 using the same 15-year accelerated method you selected for the 1981 improvement.

Note: if you make an improvement in April 1985, the shortest write-off period you can select is 18 years, but you may use either the accelerated or straight-line method.

HOW TO HANDLE PERSONAL PROPERTY WRITE-OFFS UNDER THE ACRS RULES

All tangible personal property falls into one of three classes for purposes of the ACRS rules.

These are three-year property, five-year property, or 10-year property. Most property you use in your business will fall in either the three-year class or the five-year class. You may use the accelerated recovery percentages or you may elect straight-line recovery over various recovery periods. Exhibit 6-1 has a brief listing of assets included in these categories and shows the appropriate recovery percentages.

Four basic rules: Determining your ACRS deductions for personal property is easy. You must follow four basic rules:

1. Determine the basis of the assets to be written off.
2. Group all personal property assets acquired during the year into the appropriate three-, five-, and 10-year classes.
3. Select one method for each class of assets and deduct the appropriate percentage from Exhibit 6-1 for each year the asset is in service in your business.
4. In the year you sell, trade, or otherwise dispose of an ACRS personal property asset, you get *no* ACRS deduction.

Example: In December 1984 you purchased a $16,279 used car for your business and you claim a $6,186 investment tax credit. Your basis for claiming ACRS deductions is $15,790 ($16,279 cost less 50 percent of $977). You choose accelerated recovery for the three-year asset. For 1984, you deduct $3,948 (25 percent times $15,790). For 1985 you deduct $6,000 (38 percent times $15,790). For 1986, you deduct the remaining $5,842 (37 percent times $15,790).

Audit-proof deduction: Even if your automobile will last 45 years, you still recover your cost in the first three years you own it. The IRS can't attack the deduction based on estimated useful life. Furthermore, even if the car's value increased during the time you own it, you are still allowed to write off the full cost over the three-year period.

Half-year convention: In Exhibit 6-1, note how the first year percentages are lower than the percentages for the second year. The first year percentage reflects one-half of one full

EXHIBIT 6-1. Overview of ACRS Rules For Personal Property.

3-Year Assets: Includes automobiles, light-duty trucks, R&D machinery and equipment; and special tools; and all assets with an asset depreciation range (ADR) midpoint life of four years or less.

5-Year Assets: Includes all tangible personal property, including public utility property with a present ADR midpoint of 18 years or less, that is not included in the 15-year, 10-year, or 3-year recovery classes.

10-Year Assets: Includes mobile and modular homes.

Accelerated Cost Recovery Percentages

RECOVERY YEAR	3-YEAR	5-YEAR	10-YEAR
1	25%	15%	8%
2	38%	22%	14%
3	37%	21%	12%
4		21%	10%
5		21%	10%
6			10%
7			9%
8			9%
9			9%
10			9%
	100%	100%	100%

Election of Straight-Line Recovery

CLASS OF PROPERTY	RECOVERY PERIOD
3-Year Assets	3, 5, or 12 Years
5-Year Assets	5, 12, or 25 Years
10-Year Assets	10, 25, or 35 Years

Straight-Line Percentages

YEAR	3-YEAR	5-YEAR	10-YEAR	12-YEAR[1]	25-YEAR	35-YEAR[1]
1	17%	10%	5%	4%	2%	1%
2	33%	20%	10%	9%	4%	3%
3	33%	20%	10%	9%	4%	3%
4	17%	20%	10%	9%	4%	3%
5		20%	10%	9%	4%	3%
6		10%	10%	8%	4%	3%
7			10%	8%	4%	3%
8			10%	8%	4%	3%
9			10%	8%	4%	3%
10			10%	8%	4%	3%
11			5%	8%	4%	3%
12				8%	4%	3%
13				4%	4%	3%
	100%	100%	100%	100%	(2)	(3)

[1]Rounded as specified in IRS Proposed Regulations.
[2]Continues at 4% a year through year 25. Remaining 2% is deducted in year 26.
[3]Continues at 3% a year through year 31, then at 2% through year 35. Remaining 1% is deducted in year 36.
Note: The method selected applies to *all* assets in class and is irrevocable.

year's recovery. You deduct basis equal to the first year percentage regardless of when you purchase personal property.

Example 1: Harris, a calendar year taxpayer, purchases and places in service a new car on January 1, 1984. The car has a basis of $10,000.

Harris chooses accelerated recovery and deducts $2,500 in 1984.

Example 2: Finey, a calendar year taxpayer, purchases and places in service a new car on December 31, 1984. The car has a basis of $10,000. Finey chooses accelerated recovery and deducts $2,500 in 1984.

Hint: Buy personal property during the last part of a tax year to maximize recovery deductions.

Straight-line election: If you have plenty of write-offs now or if you expect your income to creep into higher and higher tax brackets as the years go by, you may wish to use the straight-line method for writing off the cost of personal property. For three-year assets, you may use the straight-line method over three, five or twelve years. For five-year assets, you may use five, twelve, or twenty-five years.

As mentioned earlier, any ACRS method, even the straight-line method, allows only a half-year's write-off in the first year. But unlike the accelerated method, the straight-line method takes one extra year to recover your cost. For example, if you elect to use the straight-line method over three years, your write-off in the first year is only 17 percent. You would write off 33 percent over each of the next two years, and the remaining 17 percent in the fourth year.

Same method for each class in same year: You must use the same method under the ACRS rules for writing off the cost of all personal property in the same class—three-year, five-year, and ten-year—*placed in service during the same year.* For example, if you buy eleven business cars in 1984 and place them all in service during that year, you would have to use the same method for all eleven. If you buy five other cars in 1985, you could use a different method for those five.

No write-off in year of disposition: If you dispose of or retire personal property during the year, you get no write-off for that year. For example, if you bought a business car in 1982 and retired it in December 1985, your write-off for 1985 would be *zero.*

Recapture rules: When you sell personal property at a gain, you must pay regular tax at the full rate to the extent the gain is attributable to your previous write-offs. Thus, the only way to qualify for tax-favored capital gain is to sell personal property for more than you paid for it. When you do get that tax-favored capital gain, you exclude 60 percent of the gain from your income, leaving only 40 percent to be taxed.

Example of regular tax: Fowler purchased a micro computer in 1981 for $10,000. In 1986, after claiming $10,000 of ACRS deductions (note—tax law did not require an adjustment for 50 percent of investment credit in 1981 or 1982), Fowler sells the computer for $10,000. His taxable gain is computed as follows:

Basis for ACRS in 1981	$10,000
ACRS deductions 1981–1985	(10,000)
Basis at time of sale	$ –0–
Net sales proceeds	$10,000
Basis at time of sale	–0–
Gain	$10,000

Since all of the $10,000 gain results from prior ACRS write-offs, Fowler is taxed on the full $10,000. It is treated as or called "ordinary income."

Interest-free loan: The personal property recapture rule acts as a type of interest-free government loan. When you buy and as you use personal property, you are allowed write-offs. When you sell, you pay back the previous write-offs to the extent your gain is attributable to such write-offs.

Example: Assume you have bracket-creeped your way into the 50 percent tax bracket. Further assume that you will continue to live in this creepy bracket for quite some time. This means that every extra dollar you earn is shared 50/50 with Uncle Sam, and every write-off you get is shared 50/50 with Uncle Sam. If you take an ACRS deduction of $10,000, you save $5,000 in taxes. If you sell the property three years later and you have to recapture the $10,000 deduction as ordinary income, you will pay Uncle Sam back the $5,000 you saved previously. In the meantime, you had the use of that $5,000. If the money's use was worth 10 percent a year to you, you would have converted the $5,000 to $6,655 by the time you repay the $5,000 three years later.

Figuring your taxable gain from the sale of personal property is a three-step process. First, you figure the total gain by subtracting the basis from the selling price. Second, you treat all of the gain as ordinary income, to the extent of your previous ACRS write-offs. Third, any remaining gain is taxed as capital gain.

Example of capital gain from sale of personal property: You purchase a business desk in 1982 that has an ACRS basis of $3,000. In 1985 you sell the desk for $5,000. You compute your taxable gain as follows:

Net sales proceeds		$5,000
1982 ACRS basis of desk	$3,000	
ACRS write-offs 1982–1984	(1,740)	
Basis of desk at time of sale		1,260
Total gain on sale of desk		3,740
Amount taxed as ordinary income		1,740
Amount taxed as long-term capital gain		$2,000

If you are in the 50 percent tax bracket at the time of sale, your tax is $1,270 [($2,000 × 40% × 50%) + ($1,740 × 50%)]. Sixty percent of the long-term capital gain is deducted, leaving only 40 percent subject to the 50 percent tax rate.

Capital gain treatment: To qualify for "long-term capital gain" treatment, which gives you the 60 percent deduction, you must have owned the property for a certain period of time. For assets acquired before June 23, 1984, you must have owned the property for one year and one day. For assets acquired after June 22, 1984, you must have owned the property for six months and one day. If you sell the property before the minimum time period, any gain is taxed as ordinary income.

Personal property does not provide a tax shelter: Since ACRS write-offs, both straight-line and accelerated, must be recaptured to the extent of any gain or sale, personal property is not a tax shelter. Tax shelters provide write-offs that do not have to be recaptured

and gains that are treated as tax-favored long-term capital gains.

Best bet—Select accelerated recovery for personal property: Since ACRS write-offs for personal property must be recaptured as ordinary income regardless of whether you elect an accelerated or straight-line method, select accelerated methods to get the money away from the government and into your pockets as soon as possible.

When "best bet" is bad: If you are in a low tax bracket this year and will be in a high tax bracket next year, and the year after, you *might be* better off financially by selecting a straight-line method.

HOW TO HANDLE THE EXPENSING ELECTION FOR PERSONAL PROPERTY

As an alternative to an ACRS write-off, you are allowed a special election for certain personal property you buy for your trade or business. Under the election, you may write off up to $5,000 of the cost of qualifying property you place in service during the year. The limit was scheduled to increase to $7,500 in 1984, but the Tax Reform Act of 1984 postponed this increase until 1988. The new schedule of increases is contained in Exhibit 6-2.

Autos limited to $3,200: 1984 and 1985 tax legislation. The Tax Reform Act of 1984 actually cut back the limit on business autos. For autos acquired after April 2, 1985, the limit is $3,200, the same limit as for depreciation on business cars. The limit will be increased to account for inflation.

Property qualifying for the expense election: In general, property qualifying for the special expense election is *investment credit property* acquired by *purchase* for use in a trade or business. Thus, property acquired for the production of income, instead of for use in a trade or business, won't qualify for the special expense election.

If property eligible for the investment credit is acquired by trade, you count only the cash boot for the special expense election. Investment credit property purchased from a

---

EXHIBIT 6-2. Election to Expense in Year of Acquisition.

TAXABLE YEAR	MAXIMUM AMOUNT
1984	5,000
1985–87	5,000
1988–89	7,500
1990 and thereafter	10,000

---

related party does not qualify for the special expense election.

In lieu of ACRS deductions: The expense election is in lieu of ACRS deductions. In effect, it is merely an accelerated recovery method. If 1984 property eligible for the expense election had a basis of $20,000 and you elect to expense $5,000, your basis for ACRS write-offs is $15,000 ($20,000—$5,000).

Expense election costs investment tax credit: In the above example, $15,000 qualifies for the investment credit. The $5,000 expensed does not qualify.

Economic results: The special expense election gives you an early write-off, but costs you the dollar-for-dollar investment tax credit. Remember, the expense election is available only for the cost of personal property qualifying for the investment tax credit. Assume you are in the 50 percent tax bracket and that after-tax, after-inflation money has a value of 8 percent. What is the economic consequence of electing to expense $5,000? The computation follows:

Money pocketed with ACRS write-offs and investment tax credit:		
Investment credit—year 1: $5,000 × 10%	$ 500	
ACRS refund—year 1: $4,750 × 15% × 50%	355	
ACRS refunds discounted 8%—years 2-5	1,675	
Present value of money pocketed		$2,530
Money pocketed with expense election:		
$5,000 × 50% tax refund		$2,500
Money ahead in real dollars with ACRS and investment tax credit		$30

Best bet: On a real-dollar basis, you are ahead by *not electing* the special expense election. However, the difference between the expense election and ACRS write-offs combined with the investment tax credit is less than 2 percent—not a large number.

How to elect: You make the election on Form 4562, which requires you to describe each property and the portion of each property's cost that you are electing to expense. This election must be made on your *original return*—not an amended return—for the year you placed the property in service. You may not revoke your election without the IRS's consent.

Tricky recapture rule: Any amounts you write off under the expensing election are subject to the recapture rules, just as regular ACRS write-offs are. Thus, you will have to repay Uncle Sam any previous expensing deductions to the extent your gains are attributable to them.

Congress added a tricky new wrinkle to the recapture rule in the Technical Corrections Act of 1982. Under the new law, the IRS is to issue regulations that provide for "recapturing the benefit" of the expensing write-off whenever the property is not used "predominantly in a trade or business" for two full taxable years after the property is placed in service. It is not at all clear how the IRS will apply this rule. It could require you to include any previous expense write-offs in your income proportionate to any decrease in business use of the property.

For example, if you wrote off $1,000 for property you used 100 percent in business, and one year later your business use decreased to 70 percent, the IRS might want you to include $300 (30 percent of $1,000) in your income. What's worse, the IRS could interpret the new law as requiring *full recapture whenever your business use fell below 50 percent.*

Hint: Until further clarification of the new rule, use the expensing election for property you intend to use solely for business purposes for at least two full taxable years after you buy the property.

HOW STRAIGHT-LINE DEDUCTIONS ON REAL PROPERTY TURN INTO CAPITAL GAIN

Real property, unlike personal property, is a tax shelter. Once real property is placed in service, you are allowed tax deductions for depreciation (recovery). The deductions reduce your taxable basis for computing gain or loss. When you sell real property that you have owned for more than one year (or more than six months, in the case of property acquired after June 22, 1984), you are eligible for tax-favored long-term capital gains treatment.

In effect, your real property write-off is dollar-for-dollar. When you sell, your gain attributable to the dollar-for-dollar write-off is 40 cents on the dollar.

Applies to straight-line component only: There are special recapture rules for real property that are discussed later. For now, keep in mind that the trade of a $1 deduction for a 40-cent gain applies to straight-line deductions only.

Example: Exhibit 6-3 illustrates how straight-line deductions turn into long-term gain. During the time Waters owned the building, he deducted $9,450. At the time he sold the building for the exact price he originally paid, he was taxed on $3,780. Thus Waters converted $9,450 of straight-line deductions into long-term capital gain.

Note: Waters used a 15-year depreciation since he bought his property in 1982. Today, Waters would have to use a 19-year schedule. See the next section of this chapter.

Value of money: Waters received his tax refunds in years 1, 2, and 3. He paid tax in year 4. If you consider the time value of money at 8 percent, Waters is $3,632 ahead because he owned depreciable real property.

Tax reduction strategy: Buy depreciable real property to save tax dollars. Depreciable real property, unlike personal property, turns the straight-line write-off component into tax-favored long-term capital gain.

Leverage adds more: Depreciable real property is generally mortgaged. Your write-offs, however, are based on the full cost of the property. The mortgage is ignored for ACRS deductions. Interest on the mortgage is, of course, fully deductible. But the value of leverage is twofold. First, your ACRS write-offs are based on the leveraged cost. Second, your appreciation is based on the leveraged cost.

Example: You buy a depreciable building for $100,000, paying $10,000 down. Your ACRS write-offs are based on $100,000. If the building appreciated 5 percent in the first year, you made 50 percent on your $10,000 investment.

Best bet: If you want Uncle Sam to help increase your net worth, buy appreciating real property that is depreciable using leverage.

HOW THE NEW ACRS RULES FOR REAL ESTATE WORK

Before the ACRS rules were adopted, if you wanted to turn your brains into tapioca, all you had to do was spend some time determining estimated useful lives for real estate. As we have mentioned, you need no longer do that. Lives are determined by law. These changes are terrific improvements over the old system, but these are just the icing. The cake is the faster write-offs now available.

Effective date: The ACRS rules apply to real estate placed in service after December 31, 1980.

Write-off periods: The write-off period can be 15, 18, 19, 35 or 45 years, depending on the type of real estate, the date you placed it in service, and the type of election you made.

On low-income housing the shortest write-off period is 15 years. You can also elect a 35-year or 45-year write-off period.

On real estate other than low-income housing, the shortest write-off period is

EXHIBIT 6-3. How Straight-Line Deductions Turn into Long-Term Capital Gain.

FACTS: Waters, a 50-percent bracket taxpayer, invested $50,000 in his office building three years ago. Of the $50,000, appraisals established that $5,000 was for nondepreciable land and $45,000 was for the depreciable building. Today, after three years of straight-line deductions, Waters sells the property for $50,000, the exact amount he paid originally. Following are the calculations:

BASIS (Total Cost Less Depreciation):

Original cost	$50,000
Less depreciation[1]	(9,450)
Basis	$40,550

COMPUTATION OF CAPITAL GAIN:

Net sales proceeds	$50,000
Less basis	(40,550)
Taxable long-term capital gain	$ 9,450

TAX ON LONG-TERM CAPITAL GAIN:

Taxable long-term capital gain	$9,450
Statutory deduction ($9,000 x 60%)	(5,670)
Gain taxable at ordinary rates	3,780
Tax rate	x 50%
Tax	$1,890

ECONOMIC CONSEQUENCES:

Investment of tax refunds at 8% after-tax yield:

Year 1 ($3,150 deduction – 50% tax x 8% compounded for 3 years)	$1,984
Year 2 ($3,150 deduction – 50% tax x 8% compounded for 2 years)	1,837
Year 3 ($3,150 deduction – 50% tax x 8% compounded for 1 year)	1,701
Less tax on sale (first day of next tax year)	(1,890)
Dollar return resulting solely from depreciation	$3,632

[1]21% under IRS Proposed Regulations.

either 15, 18 or 19 years, depending on when you placed the property in service. If you placed the property in service before March 16, 1984, you can use a 15-year write-off period. If you placed the property in service after March 15, 1984, the shortest write-off period is 18 years. If you placed the property in service after May 8, 1985, the shortest write-off period is 19 years. You can also elect a 35-year or 45-year write-off period, regardless of when you placed the property in service.

Percentage write-offs: The annual write-offs under ACRS are based on one of three methods:

• 200 percent declining balance, with a switch to straight-line when the straight-line method yields a higher deduction. This method applies to low-income housing that you elect to depreci-

ate over a 15-year write-off period. The lower portion of Exhibit 6-4A lists the appropriate percentage write-offs.

• 175 percent declining balance, with a switch to straight-line when the straight-line method yields a higher deduction. This method applies to real estate (other than low-income housing) you placed in service before March 16, 1984, and elected to depreciate over a 15-year write-off period, to real estate (other than low-income housing) you placed in service after March 15, 1984, and elect to depreciate over an 18-year write-off period and to real estate placed in service after May 8, 1985, on which you elect a 19-year write-off period. (At the time this book was written, the IRS had not prescribed tables for determining the appropriate percentage write-offs under the 19-year schedule. The appropriate percentage write-offs under the 18-year schedule are listed in the upper portion of Exhibit 6-4A.)

EXHIBIT 6-4A. ACRS Deduction Tables for Real Estate.

All Real Estate (except Low-Income Housing) Acquired After June 22, 1984 and Before May 9, 1985.

THE APPLICABLE PERCENTAGE IS:
(Use the Column for the Month in the First Year the Property is Placed in Service)

Recovery Year	1	2	3	4	5	6	7	8	9	10	11	12
					The applicable percentage is:							
1	9	9	8	7	6	5	4	4	3	2	1	0.4
2	9	9	9	9	9	9	9	9	9	10	10	10.4
3	8	8	8	8	8	8	8	8	9	9	9	9.0
4	7	7	7	7	7	8	8	8	8	8	8	8.0
5	7	7	7	7	7	7	7	7	7	7	7	7.0
6	6	6	6	6	6	6	6	6	6	6	6	6.0
7	5	5	5	5	6	6	6	6	6	6	6	6.0
8	5	5	5	5	5	5	5	5	5	5	5	5.0
9	5	5	5	5	5	5	5	5	5	5	5	5.0
10	5	5	5	5	5	5	5	5	5	5	5	5.0
11	5	5	5	5	5	5	5	5	5	5	5	5.0
12	5	5	5	5	5	5	5	5	5	5	5	5.0
13	4	4	4	5	4	4	5	4	4	4	5	5.0
14	4	4	4	4	4	4	4	4	4	4	4	4.0
15	4	4	4	4	4	4	4	4	4	4	4	4.0
16	4	4	4	4	4	4	4	4	4	4	4	4.0
17	4	4	4	4	4	4	4	4	4	4	4	4.0
18	4	3	4	4	4	4	4	4	4	4	4	4.0
19	–	1	1	1	2	2	2	3	3	3	3	3.6

Low-Income Housing

THE APPLICABLE PERCENTAGE IS:
(Use the Column for the Month in the First Year the Property is Placed in Service)

Recovery Year	1	2	3	4	5	6	7	8	9	10	11	12
1	13	12	11	10	9	8	7	6	4	3	2	1
2	12	12	12	12	12	12	12	13	13	13	13	13
3	10	10	10	10	11	11	11	11	11	11	11	11
4	9	9	9	9	9	9	9	9	10	10	10	10
5	8	8	8	8	8	8	8	8	8	8	8	9
6	7	7	7	7	7	7	7	7	7	7	7	7
7	6	6	6	6	6	6	6	6	6	6	6	6
8	5	5	5	5	5	5	5	5	5	5	6	6
9	5	5	5	5	5	5	5	5	5	5	5	5
10	5	5	5	5	5	5	5	5	5	5	5	5
11	4	5	5	5	5	5	5	5	5	5	5	5
12	4	4	4	5	4	5	5	5	5	5	5	5
13	4	4	4	4	4	4	5	4	5	5	5	5
14	4	4	4	4	4	4	4	4	4	5	4	4
15	4	4	4	4	4	4	4	4	4	4	4	4
16	—	—	1	1	2	2	2	3	3	3	4	4

Note: Tables do not apply for short taxable years of less than 12 months.

• Straight-line. This method is elective and applies to real estate of all types. For real estate you placed in service after May 8, 1985, the write-off period can be 19, 35, or 45 years. Notice that these write-off periods apply to low-income housing as well as other types of real estate, even though you can use a 15-year write-off period on low-income housing if you choose the 200 percent declining balance method.

Write-offs begin in month property is placed in service: Unlike ACRS write-offs for personal property which start the *year* property is placed in service, the ACRS write-offs for real property start the *month* property is placed in service.

Mid-month convention: For real estate (other than low-income housing) placed in service after March 15, 1984, you get a half-month's depreciation in the month you place the property in service.

Property-by-property election: Unlike personal property which must be grouped by class before selecting *one* ACRS method for all assets in that class, the ACRS rules for real property apply *separately* on a property-by-property basis. You may, for example, select 19 year accelerated recovery for a property placed in service on July 1, 1985, and 35-year straight-line recovery for a property placed in service on July 21, 1985.

Example of 15-year accelerated recovery for real property: Abbot, a calendar year taxpayer, placed a $100,000 building in service on July 27, 1983. Using the table in Exhibit 6-4A, Abbot went to month 7 and determined that he could write off $6,000 in 1983 ($100,000 × 6%). In 1984 Abbot writes off the appropriate percentage based on the month the property was *originally* placed in service. When the property is sold, Abbot must apportion the percentage based on the months the property is in service during the year of sale. If, for example, the property is sold on July 1, 1985, Abbot's write-off for 1985 will be $5,000 ($100,000 × 10% × 6/12).

Straight-line tables: A way to figure straight-line write-offs is to divide your depreciable basis by the number of months in the write-off period, then multiply by the number of months you had the property in service during the tax year. For example, if you bought a $180,000 building and placed it in service in March 1985, your straight-line write-off would be $10,000 ($180,000 ÷ 216 × 10). Let's call this the "precise" way of figuring straight-line depreciation.

The IRS has created some confusion by issuing tables prescribing percentages for

figuring straight-line write-offs for 18-year, 35-year, and 45-year recovery periods. The percentages for 18-year straight-line recovery are rounded in a way that gives you higher write-offs during the first 10 years of ownership than you would get by using the precise way. Exhibit 6-4B has the proposed IRS table for 18-year straight-line recovery.

Example of straight-line recovery under IRS proposed table: Assume you bought a building for $180,000 and placed it in service in March 1985. Your 1985 write-off under the IRS proposed table would be $7,200 ($180,000 × 4%). This is $2,800 less than you could claim by using the precise way described before ($180,000 ÷ 216 × 12 = $10,000).

19-year schedule not issued: When this was written, the IRS had not issued any tables for figuring ACRS write-offs on property subject to 19-year recovery.

Placed in service: Your real property ACRS deductions begin the month real property is placed in service. When a new building is completed and *capable* of being used, it is placed in service. When a used building is purchased, it is placed in service when (1) escrow closes, and (2) it is listed for rent. If not for rent, but for use in your business, the used building is placed in service when you *can* move in and use it in your business.

Converting a personal residence to a rental property: The recovery (or depreciation) period starts the date the owner moves out of the residence and lists it for rent, providing the property is available for occupancy. In other words, the moment the property ceases to be a personal residence and becomes a rental property, the recovery period begins. When a personal residence is remodeled, the recovery period commences the day (1) the renovation is completed, (2) the residence is available for the tenant usage, and (3) it is listed for rent.

Caution: A personal residence is "placed in service" with its first use. If that was prior to January 1, 1981, you must use the old "de-

EXHIBIT 6-4B. Proposed IRS Table for straight-line ACRS write-offs on real estate placed in service after June 22, 1984 and before May 9, 1985.

THE APPLICABLE PERCENTAGE IS:
(Use the Column for the Month in the First Year
the Property is Placed in Service)

Recovery Year	1-2	3-4	5-7	8-9	10-11	12
			The applicable percentage is:			
1	5	4	3	2	1	0.2
2	6	6	6	6	6	6.0
3	6	6	6	6	6	6.0
4	6	6	6	6	6	6.0
5	6	6	6	6	6	6.0
6	6	6	6	6	6	6.0
7	6	6	6	6	6	6.0
8	6	6	6	6	6	6.0
9	6	6	6	6	6	6.0
10	6	6	6	6	6	6.0
11	5	5	5	5	5	5.8
12	5	5	5	5	5	5.0
13	5	5	5	5	5	5.0
14	5	5	5	5	5	5.0
15	5	5	5	5	5	5.0
16	5	5	5	5	5	5.0
17	5	5	5	5	5	5.0
18	5	5	5	5	5	5.0
19	1	2	3	4	5	5.0

Note: Table does not apply for short taxable years of less than 12 months.

preciation" rules when you convert the residence to a rental property. ACRS applies only to assets first placed in service on or after January 1, 1981.

Example of placed in service: Clark purchased a duplex. On January 26, 1975, escrow closed and Clark placed an ad in the local newspaper advertising one side of the duplex for rent. Clark moved into the nonrental side of the duplex. She found no tenants with the first ad, so she ran the ad each week for the next several weeks. Still—no tenants. In April she placed notices in the local store. No tenants. This went on until 1983 when Clark sold the duplex. Was Clark entitled to depreciations from 1975 to 1983? Yes. The property was placed in service when she (1) owned the property, and (2) listed it for rent. It remained in service because she never ceased trying to rent the duplex.

WHY THE NEW ACRS RULES FOR REAL PROPERTY ARE BETTER THAN THE OLD DEPRECIATION RULES

Under the old rules, used real property was in many cases depreciated over a period of 20 years. New real property generally was depreciated over periods of 40 to 60 years.

The old rules limited accelerated depreciation on used buildings to 125 percent of the straight-line rate.

A 18-year or 19-year write-off for a new building was a fantasy under the old rules. Now, you get short write-off periods and accelerated write-offs. Moreover, the same rules apply to both new and used real property.

Exhibit 6-5 uses a $120,000 depreciable building placed in service before March 16, 1984, to illustrate how ACRS makes virtually every real property an instant tax shelter.

EXHIBIT 6-5. Comparison of Old Real Property Depreciation Rates With New Cost Recovery Rates.

ANNUAL DEDUCTIONS

| | NEW COST RECOVERY RULES | | OLD DEPRECIATION RULE | | | |
| | | | USED PROPERTY | | NEW PROPERTY | |
YEAR	175%[1] D.B.	STRAIGHT-LINE[3]	125% D.B. 20 YEARS	STRAIGHT-LINE 20 YEARS	200% D.B. 40 YEARS	STRAIGHT-LINE 40 YEARS
1	$14,400	$ 8,400	$ 7,500	$ 6,000	$ 6,000	$ 3,000
2	12,000	8,400	7,031	6,000	5,700	3,000
3	10,800	8,400	6,592	6,000	5,415	3,000
4	9,600	8,400	6,180	6,000	5,144	3,000
5	8,400	8,400	5,794	6,000	4,887	3,000
6	7,200[3]	8,400	5,794	6,000	4,643	3,000
7	7,200	8,400	5,794	6,000	4,410	3,000
8	7,200	8,400	5,794	6,000	4,190	3,000
9	7,200	8,400	5,794	6,000	3,981	3,000
10	6,000	8,400	5,794	6,000	3,782	3,000
11	6,000	7,200	5,794	6,000	3,592	3,000
12	6,000	7,200	5,794	6,000	3,412	3,000
13	6,000	7,200	5,794	6,000	3,242	3,000
14	6,000	7,200	5,794	6,000	3,080	3,000
15	6,000	7,200	5,794	6,000	2,926	3,000
16-40	0	0	28,963	30,000	55,596	75,000
	$120,000	$120,000	$120,000	$120,000	$120,000	$120,000

[1]Assumes property was placed in service in first month of taxable year and before March 16, 1984.
[2]Rates based on IRS Proposed Regulations.
[3]Point where switch to straight-line is necessary to maximize deductions. IRS Tables make this switch automatically.

Using the accelerated method, you write off 46 percent of the cost of depreciable real property in the first five years.

The first year accelerated ACRS deduction in Exhibit 6-5 is 2.4 times greater than the accelerated rate for used buildings. The straight-line ACRS deduction is 2.8 times greater than the old straight-line depreciation rate for new buildings and 1.4 times greater than the straight-line rate for used buildings.

Total deduction is the same: The maximum deduction in Exhibit 6-5 is $120,000—the depreciable cost of the building. The advantage to ACRS is that you get the deductions earlier. Since money has a time value, the earlier you get the money, the better your economic future. ACRS gives you a healthier economic future. The advantage of 19-year

ACRS is only slightly less than 15-year ACRS. A precise comparison could not be made at the time this book was written because the IRS had not yet prescribed the new tables.

HOW COMMERCIAL REAL ESTATE IS PENALIZED UNDER ACRS

As with a new tax law, there are a few potholes to make things difficult. The major pothole for commercial real estate is that if you use accelerated recovery, the same recapture rule that applies to personal property also applies to commercial real estate. Thus, if you use the 15-year, 18-year, or 19-year accelerated write-off method, *all* your ACRS write-offs are recaptured as ordinary income to the extent of any gain you have when you sell the property. Under previous law, you had to recapture only the excess of accelerated depreciation over straight-line depreciation.

Exhibit 6-6 shows the effect of recapturing 100 percent of your ACRS write-offs when you select the accelerated method. Note that the tax is *more than double* the tax with the straight-line method. The reason, quite simply, is that straight-line write-offs are turned into capital gain at the time of sale, whereas accelerated write-offs are turned into ordinary income. With long-term capital gain, only 40 percent is taxed as ordinary income. The remainder escapes tax.

General rule: For commercial real property, select the straight-line method to maximize tax benefits over the long run. With the straight-line method, none of your gain will be recaptured as ordinary income. You may use the straight-line method over a period of 15, 18, 19, 35, or 45 years. Usually, the shorter write-off period is best.

If you use the straight-line method, and hold the property for the required holding period before selling it, *all of your gain is classified as long-term capital gain, producing a tax on only 40 percent of the gain.*

Example: In January 1984 you buy a commercial property that contains a $90,000 building and elect the straight line method. Five years later, you sell the building for $150,000. Your basis in the building is $58,500 ($90,000 cost − $31,500 write-offs). Your capital gain is $91,500 ($150,000 − $58,500). Of this, only $36,600 ($91,500 times 40 percent) is taxed; the balance is excluded from tax.

Note that the general rule for commercial real property differs from the general rule for personal property. That is, we recommend the accelerated method for personal property and the straight-line method for commercial real property, even though the same recapture rule applies.

There are three reasons for this recommendation. First, remember that full recapture applies to even straight-line write-offs on personal property, whereas straight-line write-offs on commercial real property are not recaptured as ordinary income. Thus, your tax

---

EXHIBIT 6-6. Tax Penalty for Using Accelerated Recovery on Commercial Real Property (Sample Computation).

ASSUMED FACTS: You purchase an office building for $150,000. At the time of purchase, land is valued at $30,000 and the building is valued at $120,000. After five years of ownership, you sell the property for $200,000. You are in the 50 percent tax bracket.

	ACCELERATED RECOVERY		STRAIGHT-LINE RECOVERY	
Sales proceeds		$200,000		$ 200,000
Original cost	$ 150,000		$ 150,000	
Recovery deductions	(55,200)		(42,000)	
Basis of property		(94,800)		(108,000)
Taxable gain		105,200		92,000
Recapture		(55,200)		0
Long-term capital gain		50,000		92,000
Percentage taxed as ordinary income		× 40%		× 40%
Taxed capital gain		20,000		36,800
Recapture		55,200		0
Taxable income		75,200		36,000
Tax rate		× 50%		× 50%
Tax on sale		$ 37,600		$ 18,400

Note: Applies to commercial real property only. Residential income-producing property is subject to a different recapture rule. Property was placed in service before March 16, 1984, so 15-year ACRS write-off period applies.

savings on a sale of commercial real property on which you used the straight-line method are much greater than the savings on the sale of personal property on which you used the straight-line method. Second, you will usually hold commercial real estate for a longer time than you hold personal property, thus allowing the straight-line write-offs to catch up to the write-offs under the accelerated method. Third, as a practical matter, many items of personal property will not result in much, if any, gain on their sale because they have depreciated in value.

Home office: The home office deduction is discussed in Chapter 8. We mention it here because, when you turn a portion of your residence into an office, you have converted residential property to commercial property. However, there are several special rules that must be considered in selecting an ACRS method for your home office. You should review Chapter 8 in detail to select the best method.

HOW TO PROFIT FROM ACRS WRITE-OFFS FOR INCOME-PRODUCING RESIDENTIAL PROPERTY

Definition of residential rental property: A building or structure is considered a "residential rental property" if 80 percent or more of the rental income is from dwelling units. If you occupy a unit, or portion of the structure, the fair market rent for your unit or portion is counted as rental income from a dwelling unit.

Example: You own a four-unit apartment building and occupy one unit as your personal residence. The fair market rent of the unit you occupy is $500/month. You count the $500/month fair market rent in determining if 80 percent of the rental income is from dwelling units.

Dwelling unit: A "dwelling unit" is a house or an apartment used to provide living accommodations to nontransients. Units in hotels, motels, and inns are considered "nonresidential" when they provide living ac-

commodations to transients. A transient is someone who occupies the unit for less than 30 days.

Recapture rule: Unlike commercial real property, where the accelerated method triggers 100 percent recapture, the accelerated method on residential property is far less taxing. As under the old depreciation rules, you are required to recapture as ordinary income only the accelerated write-offs that exceed the allowable straight-line write-offs.

Example: In January 1984 you buy a residential rental property that contains a $90,000 building and elect the accelerated 15-year method. After five years, you sell the building for $150,000. Your basis in the building is $48,600 ($90,000 cost minus $41,400 write-offs), so your gain is $101,400. Since the straight-line method would have produced write-offs of $30,000 ($5/15 of $90,000), the ordinary income recaptured is $11,400 ($41,400 minus $30,000). The remaining gain of $90,000 ($101,400 minus $11,400) is taxed as long-term capital gain.

Increase cash flow: Exhibit 6-7 shows how you benefit by using the accelerated method on income-producing residential properties. In effect, the accelerated method for residential property acts as an interest-free government loan. You get the excess write-offs today and pay them back when you sell the property. The Exhibit assumes a 50 percent tax bracket and a 10 percent return on invested tax savings. The cash flow at the end of eight years is $10,846. If the building is sold, you pay back $4,800. Thus, you earned $6,046 by selecting accelerated recovery.

Best bet: Use accelerated recovery on residential property, unless you have an "alternative minimum tax" problem (discussed later in this chapter).

HOW TAX-FREE SWAPS OF REAL PROPERTY CAN STEP UP DEDUCTIONS

There is no tax on the exchange of business or investment real estate for "like-kind" real estate. A tax-free exchange is a tricky trans-

EXHIBIT 6-7. How New Cost Recovery Rules Increase Cash Flow.

ASSUMPTIONS

- TAX BRACKET 50%
- REFUNDS INVESTED FOR AFTER-TAX RETURN OF 10%
- PROPERTY HELD FOR EIGHT YEARS
- DEPRECIATION BASIS $120,000

YEAR	ACCELERATED COST RECOVERY 15 YEARS	STRAIGHT-LINE RECOVERY OVER 15 YEARS[1]	INCREASED DEDUCTIONS	50% REFUND (PAYMENT)	FUTURE VALUE AT 10%
1	$14,400	$ 8,400	$6,000	$3,000	$ 6,431
2	12,000	8,400	3,600	1,800	3,508
3	10,800	8,400	2,400	1,200	2,126
4	9,600	8,400	1,200	600	966
5	8,400	8,400	0	0	0
6	7,200	8,400	(1,200)	(600)	(799)
7	7,200	8,400	(1,200)	(600)	(726)
8	7,200	8,400	(1,200)	(600)	(660)
	$76,800	$67,200	$9,600	$4,800	$10,846

[1]Rates based on IRS Proposed Regulations.

action and should be monitored by your tax advisor. However, you should know the general reasons for tax-free swaps and the possible tax benefits.

Three reasons for using tax-free swaps: The general reason for entering into a tax-free exchange is that you do not want to have a tax when you dispose of the property. But there are other reasons that you should be aware of. A tax-free exchange can step up your depreciation deductions in two ways for ACRS property and in three ways for non-ACRS property.

1. More depreciation with bigger mortgage: Say you own a building free and clear in which your basis is $100,000. Assume also that the building's fair market value is $100,000. You swap this building for a $200,000 building which has an underlying $100,000 mortgage.

Result: You have swapped equal equities. However, the $200,000 property will give you twice as much depreciation as the $100,000

property. Why? Your basis for depreciation of the property you received includes the mortgage liability as well as your $100,000 carry-over basis.

Extra ACRS deductions: Assume the property you gave up in the exchange was non-ACRS property because you had placed it in service prior to 1981. The additional $100,000 of basis because of the exchange qualifies as ACRS recovery property. Your carry-over basis of $100,000 in the old building must be depreciated using the same method you were using before the exchange.

2. Increasing the building to land ratio: Your building and land are worth $100,000. You have depreciated the building down to $10,000 and the land has a basis of $40,000. You trade for a $100,000 building and land package, in which the building is worth $90,000 and the land is worth $10,000.

Result: In the exchange, you carry-over your $50,000 total basis to the new property. It is allocated $45,000 (90 percent) to the new building and $5,000 (10 percent) to the land. You have stepped up your basis for depreciation from $10,000 to $45,000.

3. Shorter useful life: This works only for non-ACRS property. You swap a building with a remaining useful life of 35 years for one with a useful life of 20 years.

Result: You have stepped up your depreciation deductions by 75 percent.

Best bet: Exchanges can be extremely beneficial. They are also quite tricky. If you are interested in an exchange, make sure you engage your tax advisor to help you with the transaction.

TAX CONSEQUENCES OF ASSET SALES

Keeping all the rules straight for asset dispositions is difficult. The summary flowchart in Exhibit 6-8 will help you capsulize the tax consequences of selling business or investment property.

The ramifications shown in the flowchart were discussed in each of the sections dealing with personal property, commercial real property, and residential real property. Remember, the rules differ with respect to each type of property.

HOW TO WRITE OFF YOUR COSTS OF MAKING LEASEHOLD IMPROVEMENTS

When you make improvements to property that you rent from someone else, you are making a leasehold improvement. You are allowed to write off the cost of the improvement over the term of the lease or the recovery period of the property, whichever is the shorter time.

If the recovery period is the shorter time, you may use either the accelerated or the straight-line method. On the other hand, you may use only the straight-line method if the lease term is less than the recovery period. In determining the recovery period for your improvement, you must use the recovery period of the underlying property.

Example: In January 1985 you add $10,000 in fixtures to an office complex you are leasing. The lease term is for five years. You would amortize the $10,000 over a five-year period, at $2,000 a year. If the lease term were 20 years and the office building were being written off over 18 years, you could use either the straight-line or accelerated method over 18 years.

Best bets: For leasehold improvements which can be written off in 15, 18 or 19 years under an ACRS method, select accelerated recovery. Remember, accelerated recovery triggers recapture of 100 percent of prior recovery deductions *to the extent of gain*. Since there will be no gain when the lease term expires, the improvement generally reverts to the landlord. Thus, select accelerated recovery for maximum economic benefit.

HOW THE PROPER ALLOCATIONS TO LAND, BUILDINGS, AND EQUIPMENT INCREASE DEDUCTIONS

Since land is not depreciable, you want to allocate as little of the cost to land as possible. The next question is, "How much should be allocated to building and equipment?" It depends. For commercial property, allocate as much cost as possible to equipment that qualifies for the investment tax credit. For residential property, allocate as much as possible to building—forget equipment.

Clearing and grading costs: General purpose clearing and grading costs that are necessary to adapt land for a specific use are not eligible for cost recovery. Such expenditures are considered a cost of land. Remember, there is no benefit to having an expenditure classified as land.

Setting a building: Generally, the cost of digging and removing soil for setting of building is treated as part of the recoverable cost of a building. In many cases, a significant and sometimes substantial part of the charges for excavating, grading, and soil removal should be included in the building costs. If handled the right way, the charges step up your de-

EXHIBIT 6-8. Tax Consequences of Asset Sales Overview Flowchart.

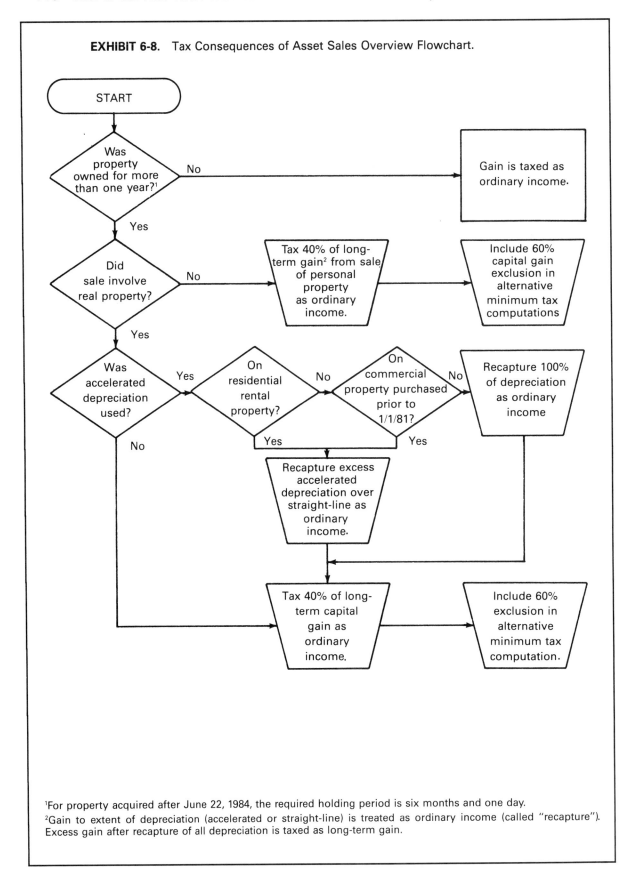

[1]For property acquired after June 22, 1984, the required holding period is six months and one day.
[2]Gain to extent of depreciation (accelerated or straight-line) is treated as ordinary income (called "recapture"). Excess gain after recapture of all depreciation is taxed as long-term gain.

preciation deductions and help you take advantage of the new ACRS breaks.

Example: Marshall built a processing and storage complex. He had to follow certain safety precautions including the setting of buildings at least 70 to 80 feet apart, and no more than 16 buildings could be constructed in the group. Each group had to be separated by at least 500 feet. To provide access between buildings for fork-lift trucks, Marshall had to build a system of roads.

Result: Marshall can depreciate the cost of digging, grading, and removing soil for proper setting of the buildings and the roadways. The costs have a "direct association" with the buildings and roadways. Thus, they are included as part of the depreciable cost of construction.

Landscaping and shrubbery: The cost of landscaping and shrubbery around an office building may be eligible depending on the location of such assets.

- Landscaping and shrubs located immediately adjacent to eligible recovery assets, such as buildings, are eligible because destruction of the building would also destroy the shrubbery.
- If landscaping and shrubbery are located around the perimeter and not adjacent to the building, the costs are capitalized as part of the land and are not recoverable.

Personal property: Chapter 7 on the investment tax credit contains a complete discussion on how to find personal property in a building. Remember, you want to find personal property for commercial buildings, but you do not want to find personal property for residential buildings.

Exhibit 6-9 contains an illustration of three different allocations to land, buildings, and equipment for a commercial property. Review the Exhibit in detail and then consider the following discussion.

Case 1 versus Case 2: The difference between Case 1 and Case 2 is in the cost allocated to land and buildings. Taylor saves $1,100 or 27 percent after tax by allocating $7,000 less to land in Case 1. Thus, in deciding between

allocations to land and building, always allocate as much as possible to the building.

Case 2 versus Case 3: The difference between Case 2 and Case 3 is in the allocation to equipment. Since this is commercial property, the equipment qualifies for the investment tax credit discussed in Chapter 7. Also, equipment is depreciated over five years versus 15 years for a building. However, equipment depreciation must be recaptured in total whereas building depreciation (straight-line method) is not recaptured. Case 3 results in extra *cash* of $1,277, or a 31 percent increase in spendable cash after tax. Thus, in deciding the allocation of cost between equipment and building, always allocate as much as possible to equipment (for commercial buildings only).

Best bet for commercial buildings: Allocate as little as possible to land. Between building and equipment, allocate as much as possible to equipment.

Residential property is different: Exhibit 6-10 shows the importance of initial allocations to land, buildings, and equipment for residential property. As you will see in Chapter 7, the investment tax credit is not available for residential properties. Accordingly, the results for a residential property are different than the results from a commercial property.

Case 1 versus Case 2: The difference between Case 1 and Case 2 in Exhibit 6-10 is in the allocation of cost between land and building. In Case 2, an additional $7,000 was allocated from building to land. By increasing the land cost, you lose $1,306, or 31 percent of your after-tax cash flow. Thus, always allocate as much as possible to building.

Case 2 versus Case 3: The difference between Case 2 and Case 3 in Exhibit 6-10 is in the allocation of cost between equipment and building. An additional $8,000 was allocated from the building to the equipment in Case 3. *Result*: You lose $180, or 4.4 percent of your after-tax cash flow. *Reason*: For residential property, there is no investment tax credit for equipment. Moreover, all depreciation on equipment must be recaptured as ordinary income at the time of sale. Thus, always

EXHIBIT 6-9. Importance of Initial Allocations to Land, Buildings, and Equipment (Commercial Property Example).

FACTS: Taylor, a 50 percent bracket taxpayer, purchases an office property for $70,000 in 1983 and sells it after five years for $100,000.

	CASE 1	CASE 2	CASE 3
Allocations			
Value of land	$ 7,000	$14,000	$14,000
Value of equipment	8,000	8,000	16,000
Value of building	55,000	48,000	40,000
Basis	$70,000	$70,000	$70,000
Cost Recovery[1]			
Year 1	$ 4,807	$ 4,340	$ 4,947
Year 2	5,339	4,872	6,011
Year 3	5,263	4,796	5,859
Year 4	5,263	4,796	5,859
Year 5	5,263	4,796	5,859
	$25,935	$23,600	$28,535
After-tax cash Future value 10%/year			
Year 1[2]	$ 5,159	$ 4,783	$ 6,560
Year 2	3,908	3,567	4,400
Year 3	3,503	3,192	3,899
Year 4	3,184	2,902	3,545
Year 5	2,895	2,638	3,222
Cash in bank	18,649	17,082	21,626
Tax on sale[3]	(13,467)	(13,000)	(16,267)
Net cash (after-tax)[4]	$ 5,182	$ 4,082	$ 5,359

[1] Straight-line recovery for building and accelerated recovery for equipment.

[2] Future value of tax refund and investment credit.

[3] Tax on net sales proceeds. Computation includes recapture of personal property recovery deductions as ordinary income.

[4] Ignores cash received on sales. Figures represent net cash resulting from tax benefits.

allocate cost to building, rather than equipment, when purchasing or building residential property.

Best bet for residential property: Always allocate as much as possible to building. Unlike commercial property, do not split the building between personal and real property. The best results for residential property are obtained when the most cost is allocated to the building.

You must have support for your allocations: Since the allocations produce different tax results, the IRS will be interested in how you determined the allocations. You must have

supporting documents. If you are constructing a building, you should have a cost accounting system in place to keep track of the costs. If you are purchasing a used building, you will need different support.

Using the tax assessor: A common method for allocating basis between land and depreciable assets is to use the ratio employed by the tax assessor. Typically, the tax assessor will assess the land and improvement separately. The assessed values may bear no identifiable relationship to market value of property; nevertheless, the ratios of land/buildings do

EXHIBIT 6-10. Importance of Initial Allocations to Land, Buildings, and Equipment (Residential Property Example).

FACTS: You are in the 50 percent bracket and purchase a rental property in 1982 for $70,000. You own the property for five years and then sell it for $100,000. Following are the cash flow tax results under three different allocations of purchase price to land, buildings, and equipment.

	CASE 1	CASE 2	CASE 3
Allocations			
Value of land	$ 7,000	$14,000	$14,000
Value of equipment	8,000	8,000	16,000
Value of building	55,000	48,000	40,000
Basis	$70,000	$70,000	$70,000
Cost Recovery[1]			
Year 1	$ 7,800	$ 6,960	$ 7,200
Year 2	7,260	6,560	7,520
Year 3	6,630	6,000	6,960
Year 4	6,080	5,520	6,560
Year 5	5,530	5,040	6,160
	$33,300	$30,080	$34,400
After-tax cash flow at 10%			
Year 1	$ 6,281	$ 5,605	$ 5,798
Year 2	5,315	4,802	5,505
Year 3	4,412	3,993	4,632
Year 4	3,678	3,340	3,969
Year 5	3,042	2,772	3,388
Cash in bank	22,728	20,512	23,292
Tax on sale[2]	(17,150)	(16,240)	(19,200)
Net cash (after-tax)[3]	$ 5,578	$ 4,272	$ 4,092

[1] Accelerated recovery on both building and equipment.

[2] Tax on net sales proceeds of $100,000. Computation includes recapture of excess accelerated deductions on building and 100 percent recapture of equipment recovery deductions.

[3] Ignores cash received on sales. Figures represent net cash resulting from tax benefits.

provide an acceptable basis for allocating costs for tax purposes.

Engaging an independent appraiser: Often, you will not obtain the best benefit by using the allocation of the tax assessor. Another approach is to engage an independent appraiser to determine the relative values of land, buildings, and equipment. (Note—the tax assessor does not allocate to equipment.) Your appraiser should be well qualified. The IRS has its own appraisers and may challenge your appraisal. Such challenges are not common, however, when the taxpayer employs a well-qualified appraiser.

Appraisers often find as much as 20 percent of an office building's value in personal property. Thus, even if an appraisal costs $1,000 or more, it can pay big tax savings.

Income analysis: An appraiser may value the entire property using "income analysis," which calculates the earnings potential of a property over its estimated useful life. Calculation of the property's earnings potential may involve assumptions that certain alterations or improvements will be made. This method is generally known as the "building residual technique."

Using the purchase agreement: If the purchase is an arms-length transaction, the IRS generally accepts the contractual allocation for tax purposes. This approach, however, is accepted only if the parties have conflicting or competing interests in the allocation. Arbitrary allocations that cannot be supported by objective evidence or that are based on self-serving instruments will fail if attacked by the IRS.

Best bet: Generally, any purchase of real property will involve an appraisal for purposes of the mortgage. By spending a little extra money at this point, you will have at least two basic documents to work with: (1) the tax assessor's estimates, and (2) the appraisal. If the differences are significant, you should discuss with an appraiser the cost of a more detailed appraisal to give you the results you are looking for.

HOW TO AVOID THE ANTICHURNING TRAP

The new ACRS rules are extremely beneficial to taxpayers. But they are intended to apply only to property purchased and put in use after 1980. The law has various rules to prevent taxpayers from avoiding this restriction. Specifically, the ACRS rules do not apply to real property if:

- The taxpayer, or a person related to the taxpayer, owned the property during 1980.
- The property is leased back to a person who owned it during 1980 or to a person related to that person.
- The property is acquired in various tax-free transactions, such as like-kind exchanges, rollovers of low-income housing, involuntary conversions, or repossessions.

Example: A taxpayer makes a tax-free exchange of depreciable real property acquired before 1981. The taxpayer gives up property with an adjusted basis of $60,000 and also pays $40,000 in cash for like-kind depreciable real property. The acquired property has two separate costs for the purpose of depreciation. The ACRS basis is $40,000. The depreciable basis under the pre-1981 rules is $60,000.

The tax-free exchange can be a very large trap for taxpayers who are not aware of the antichurning rules. As far as the taxpayer is concerned, the property received in the trade is post-1980 property. But, for tax purposes, the property is treated the same as if it were pre-1981 property.

Lesson: When making a tax-free exchange of properties, be sure to trade property you first used after 1980. If you don't, you may be stuck with the pre-1981 depreciation methods. Of course, if you want to go back to the good old days of arguing about useful lives and salvage values, you could be in for a real treat.

Related parties: Another trap you can fall into is the trap of buying from a related party. Note that the antichurning rules apply if you or a person related to you owned the property before 1981. Related parties include spouses, children, grandchildren, parents, grandparents, brothers, and sisters. They also include entities, such as partnerships and corporations, in which you or your relatives have an interest of more than 10 percent. Very complex rules, called attribution rules, apply in determining who is a related person for tax purposes. Therefore, anytime you are dealing with relatives or businesses in which relatives have an interest, make sure you consult your tax advisor.

WHY BIG CAPITAL GAINS AND BIG ACRS WRITE-OFFS DON'T MIX

Congress giveth and Congress taketh away. A year after giving you the ACRS system, Congress took away *some* of its appeal by passing a monstrosity called the alternative minimum tax. To be more precise, Congress passed a monstrous revision of the alternative minimum tax. The idea—if there is one—behind this tax is to penalize people for taking too much advantage of the goodies that Congress gave us in the Economic Recovery Tax Act of 1981.

The full implications of the alternative minimum tax are still being explored. At this point, however, suffice it to say that taxpayers who have large capital gains deductions and large accelerated recovery write-offs in one year may get stuck with this tax. Both the capital gains deduction and the amount of accelerated write-offs that exceed 15-year or 18-year straight-line write-offs are considered "preference items" under thenew law. When the total of your preference items approaches $30,000 for unmarried taxpayers, $40,000 for married taxpayers filing jointly, and $20,000 for married persons filing separately, watch out. You should particularly watch out if you also have some tax shelter investments. Exhibit 6-11 lists the "preference items" under the new law.

NEW, MORE-THAN-50-PERCENT BUSINESS USE TEST

The Tax Reform Act of 1984 restricts ACRS deductions for certain property used 50 percent or less for business purposes. Since these new rules also apply to the investment tax credit, the new rules—and how to handle them—are discussed in the next chapter.

EXHIBIT 6-11. Tax Preferences Defined by the New Alternative Minimum Tax.

Tax preferences most often encountered by individuals include:

- Capital gains deduction (60% of long-term capital gains).

- Excess of accelerated depreciation (or ACRS) on real estate over straight-line write-off. (For accelerated recovery, this is the excess of the accelerated write-off over the straight-line write-off using a 15-year recovery period).

- Excess of accelerated depreciation (or ACRS) over straight-line write-off for personal property *subject to a lease.* For accelerated cost recovery, this is the excess of the accelerated write-off over the applicable straight-line write-off period as follows:

In the case of:	The straight-line recovery period is:
3-year property	5 years
5-year property	8 years
10-year property	15 years

- Dividends excluded by the $100 (or joint $200) dividends received exclusion.

- Excluded interest on All-Savers Certificates.

In addition, these other preferences will affect some individuals:

- The bargain element upon exercise of an incentive stock option.

- Rapid write-offs in excess of the amount allowable under a 10-year straight-line amortization for: 1) research and experimental costs, 2) mining development and exploration expenses, 3) circulation expenses.

- Amortization of certified pollution control facilities in excess of depreciation normally allowable.

- Percentage depletion deductions in excess of the adjusted basis of the property.

- Intangible drilling cost deductions in excess of income from oil, gas, and geothermal properties.

TAX REDUCTION CHECKLIST

IRS publications to be obtained:

- Publication 534—*Depreciation*
- Publication 544—*Sales and Other Dispositions of Assets*
- Publication 551—*Basis of Assets*
- Publication 334—*Tax Guide for Small Business*
- Publication 17—*Your Federal Income Tax*

Overview of cost recovery system (ACRS rules):

- Replaces old depreciation rules and is required for most assets.
- All assets fall in one of the following asset classes:
  — three-year assets—includes automobiles, light-duty trucks, research and development machinery and equipment, and special tools.
  — five-year assets—includes almost all other tangible personal property.
  — 10-year assets—includes mobile homes.
  — 15-year public utility property—a category not applicable to our readers.
  — 15-year real property—real property placed in service before March 16, 1984.
  — 18-year real property—real property placed in service after March 15, 1984.
  — 19-year real property—real property placed in service after May 8, 1985.
- All write-offs are based on accelerated methods over class lives, unless the taxpayer elects to use the straight-line method.

Expense election:

- In 1984 and 1985 you may elect to expense, rather than write off under the ACRS rules, up to $5,000 of the cost of tangible personal property used in your trade or business.
- Expensing is generally a bad idea because it costs you the investment tax credit, discussed in the next chapter.

Assets covered by the ACRS rules:

- Most tangible depreciable property placed in service after 1980 is covered.
- Substantial improvements made to pre-1981 property are also covered by the ACRS rules if the improvements are made after 1980.
- For property used before 1981, the first improvement or component is eligible for the ACRS rules, even if the improvement is not substantial.
- If you elect to depreciate under the unit-of-production method, you are not eligible to use the ACRS rules.

Recapture rules:

- On all tangible personal property, all gain is taxed as ordinary income to the extent of previous write-offs—this is referred to as "recapture."
- You must recapture all previous write-offs as ordinary income when you use the accelerated method for commercial real estate.
- For income-producing residential property, recapture is required only to the extent the previous write-offs exceed the write-offs that would be permitted under the 15-year straight-line method.

Straight-line election:

- For three-year property, you may elect the straight-line method over three, five, or 12 years.
- For five-year property, you may elect the straight-line method over five, 12, or 25 years.

- For 10-year property, you may elect the straight-line method over 10, 25, or 35 years.
- For 15-year real property, you may elect the straight-line method over 15, 35, or 45 years.
- For 18-year real property, you may elect the straight-line method over 18, 35, or 45 years.
- For 19-year real property, you may elect the straight-line method over 19, 35, or 45 years.
- The straight-line method is almost always a good idea for commercial real property—the accelerated method on commercial real property results in all your previous write-offs being taxed at ordinary-income rates.

Antichurning rules:

- For property owned before 1981, there are special rules to prevent you or a related party from taking advantage of the ACRS rules.

Alternative minimum tax:

- May apply if your long-term capital gains deduction and accelerated ACRS write-offs are large—$30,000 for single taxpayers, $40,000 for married taxpayers filing jointly, and $20,000 for married taxpayers filing separately.
- Taxpayers with substantial tax shelter investments may be affected also.

Looking for help in buying business or investment property? Take advantage of the Tax Code, which gives you a purchase rebate ranging from 3.33 percent to 25 percent of your investment. In most cases the credit will be 10 percent. This rebate, called the investment tax credit, is one of Uncle Sam's ways of stimulating economic growth.

There are actually three separate credits. The first is the regular credit, which applies mainly to tangible personal property used for business or investment purposes. The second is the business energy credit, which applies to certain energy-saving business property. The third is the rehabilitation credit, which applies to old or historic buildings.

Although qualifying for the credit is generally pretty easy, Congress has laid a few traps for the unwary, especially those who buy used property or borrow from relatives. In this chapter you will learn how to take advantage of this tax rebate and avoid the traps. Specifically, you will learn:

- What property qualifies for the regular credit, including some commonly overlooked property.
- How to figure your credit.
- How to handle the recapture rules.
- Why used property can cost you big tax savings.
- How to get the credit for property you lease.
- How to get the credit for investment property.

- How the business energy credit works.
- How to get the credit for fixing up old buildings.
- What forms to file, including the form for claiming credits you overlooked in previous years.
- How to handle the new rules added by the Tax Reform Act of 1984.

WHAT PROPERTY QUALIFIES FOR THE REGULAR CREDIT

Machinery and equipment used in your business qualify for the investment credit; buildings do not. That's the general rule. In fact, just about all tangible, depreciable personal property you buy for your business qualifies for the regular investment tax credit.

To be eligible for the credit, the property must:

1. Be depreciable;
2. Have an ACRS recovery period or an estimated useful life of at least three years;
3. Be personal property—or real property used as an integral part of production;
4. Be placed into service during the taxable year; and
5. Be used predominantly within the United States.

Buildings and their structural components do not qualify. The term "building" in-

How to Take Advantage of the Investment Tax Credit

cludes factory and office buildings, apartment houses, residences, warehouses, garages, and barns. The structural components of a building include walls, fixed partitions, floors, permanent floor coverings, windows, doors, plumbing, wiring, central heating and air conditioning, and other components integral to the operation or maintenance of a building.

Technical definition: Property eligible for the regular investment tax credit is technically known as "section 38 property." This property includes:

1. Tangible personal business property, including certain assets that may be classed as fixtures under local law.
2. Certain tangible real-property-like assets (except buildings), which are tied closely to production.
3. Certain research and storage facilities.
4. Elevators and escalators.
5. Single purpose agricultural or horticultural structures.
6. Storage facilities used in connection with the distribution of petroleum or any primary product of petroleum.

The universe of tangible, depreciable personal property that qualifies for the investment tax credit is very large. Thus, you would think that everyone is cashing in on this rebate opportunity. But that's just not so. Many taxpayers buy a used business building and fail to make the proper allocations discussed in Chapter 6. That slight oversight costs taxpayers upwards of 30 percent in after-tax dollars.

Common qualifying investment credit property found in buildings: Neither a building nor its structural components qualify for the investment tax credit. What items that qualify for the investment tax credit are located in a typical office building? Here are just a few:

- Carpeting
- Cleaning equipment
- Draperies and shades
- Office furniture and fixtures
- Removable partitions
- Record vault doors
- Decorative lighting such as chandeliers

- Security and alarm systems
- Intercoms
- Fire extinguishers
- Emergency generators
- Special air conditioning systems (which are not part of the central air conditioning system) to maintain humidity and temperature at a specified level
- Bathroom partitions and accessories such as mirrors and vanities
- Glassware, silverware, kitchen utensils, crockery, and linens
- Appliances
- Mail chutes
- Linen chutes
- Lockers
- Computer floors and connections
- Recessed or acoustical tile ceilings
- Movable walls
- Dumbwaiters, elevators, and escalators
- Kitchen areas, including kitchen units and equipment such as ovens and exhaust systems
- Refrigerators and refrigeration equipment
- Kitchen cabinets and adjustable shelving units
- Kitchen waste compactors, grease traps and retentions
- Kitchen gas piping, drainage and water systems
- Bars
- Billboards, display racks and shelves
- Gardening equipment
- Lighting for exterior of building
- Telephones, switchboards, and intercom systems
- Water heaters
- Water softeners
- Window washing equipment

Caution: When using any checklist, including the one above, you must remember that facts and circumstances, and support, determine qualifying property. Every building is different and the cost elements of each building must be carefully identified, segregated, and supported.

Exceptions to the "buildings" rule: Buildings and their structural components do not qualify for the investment tax credit (unless they are being rehabilitated). The big exception to this rule is "special purpose buildings." Essentially, a "special purpose building" is a structure that is so closely related to the use of "qualified investment credit property" that the structure clearly can be expected to be replaced when the property it houses is replaced. Such structures are treated the same as the equipment they house (even for depreciation purposes). Thus, a special purpose building is generally written off over the ACRS recovery period assigned to the equipment. Often, special purpose buildings are found in the food, textile, and other industries.

Real-property-like assets: If you have property that does not qualify under the liberal definition of "personal property," take another look. There's a good chance that you may still be able to obtain credit.

If the property is (a) an *integral* part of a manufacturing, production, or extraction operation; or (b) an *integral* part of the furnishing of transportation, communications, electricity, gas, water, or sewage disposal services, it qualifies for the credit.

Reminder: Buildings and their structural components do not qualify.

When is property an *integral* part? Only when it's used directly to produce your product or service.

Example 1: Carter builds a fence around his cattle ranch to keep the cattle in. Novice Manufacturing builds a fence around its factory to keep burglars out.

Result: Carter gets the credit but Novice Manufacturing gets no credit. Why? Carter's fence is an integral part of cattle raising. Novice's fence is not an integral part of manufacturing.

Example 2: S.A. Steel Manufacturing constructs a dock to bring materials to its lakeside plant. At the same time, it also constructs a railroad siding for the sole purpose of shipping finished products to the marketplace.

Result: There is credit for the dock, but no credit for the railroad siding. To manufacture the product, it is necessary to transport the raw materials. Thus, the dock is an integral part of the manufacturing process, but shipping the products is not.

Example 3: Rich Company builds an airstrip for its executives who fly in and out on company business. Agony Airlines constructs an airstrip for its passenger service.

Result: Agony gets credit, Rich doesn't. Agony's landing strip is an integral part of providing its passenger service. Rich's airstrip is not part of the manufacturing process.

Lodging facilities—hotels and motels: Transients live in hotels and motels. A transient is defined in tax law as someone who stays for a rental period of less than 30 days. If a hotel or motel has more than 50 percent of its living quarters occupied by transients, the personal property within the hotel or motel qualifies for the tax credit. Thus, beds and other furniture, refrigerators, and stoves used by a 50 percent or more transient occupied hotel or motel are eligible for the investment tax credit.

Vacation homes occupied by transients: If you own a vacation home that is rented to individuals for rental periods of less than 30 days, you probably have a hotel or motel. If so, you should be claiming the investment tax credit.

Reminder: The investment tax credit is a purchase rebate. It is a one-time credit. It's a dollar-for-dollar tax reducer. Make sure you are getting your free government dollars.

COMMONLY OVERLOOKED BUSINESS PROPERTY ELIGIBLE FOR THE CREDIT

When you buy a business desk and place it in a business office, there's usually little trouble identifying the asset as eligible for the investment tax credit. But what happens when that desk is located in your home? The credit is overlooked.

Automobile: It seems hard to imagine that the automobile would be overlooked as a property eligible for the investment tax credit. But it is, for a variety of reasons, such as use of the IRS's standard mileage rates. Many professional tax preparers use a computer program to prepare tax returns. Many of these programs do not identify property as eligible for the credit unless the property shows up on the depreciation schedule. Since the IRS standard mileage rate has depreciation built into it, there is no separate depreciation schedule for the car. As a result, the computer overlooks the car as property eligible for the credit.

Standard mileage rate is not ACRS: If you choose the IRS standard mileage rate (Chapter 5) as the method for deducting your business automobile expenses, you have elected *out of ACRS*. Your investment credit is computed using non-ACRS rates.

Another reason people overlook the credit is the obscure forms and instructions. Thus, people who prepare their own returns many times are simply unaware that the credit exists.

Home business use: Many people do not claim the credit for business property used at home, especially if they do not qualify for the home office deduction. For example, suppose you return home after a busy day and use an office in your home. You do not claim a home office deduction because you use the office for personal purposes 10 percent of the time, and the home office deduction requires exclusive business use. In your office, you have a lamp, a desk, a chair, a calculator, a telephone, filing cabinets, and a typewriter. If you bought the items this year, you can claim a credit for them.

Credit is based on percent business use: If your business car or any eligible investment credit property is used partly for business and partly for personal use, your investment credit is based on business use only. We'll explain this fully when we discuss "How to compute the credit."

What types of business property are commonly found in the home? Exhibit 7-1 contains a list and gives you the credit percentages. Review the list, and ask yourself if you use any of these items for business. If so, make sure you develop a business/personal split, depreciate the items, and claim the investment tax credit in the year of purchase.

HOW TO FIGURE YOUR CREDIT

The credit is based on your *cost*. Property you get by gift or inheritance generally does not qualify for the credit.

Generally, figuring your cost is pretty simple. It's the amount you pay for the property, including any charges for delivery or installation. If you pay in part with borrowed money, the borrowed money counts as long as you are personally responsible for the debt. If you are lucky enough to get a nonrecourse loan, you cannot include the loan amount as part of your cost.

Don't borrow from relatives: If you borrow money from a "related person," none of the loan amount is included as part of your cost, even if you are personally liable on the loan. A related person for this purpose includes your spouse, your children, grandchildren, parents, grandparents, brothers, and sisters. Related persons also include corporations or other entities in which you or other family members have an interest. The rules on related persons are quite complex. In case of doubt, be sure to consult your tax advisor before signing the dotted line.

Trade-ins for new property: If you buy new property on a nontaxable trade-in, your cost includes your adjusted basis in the property you traded in.

Example: You trade your old business car for a new business car. You pay $5,000 boot to make the trade. If your old car had a basis of $7,000 at the time of trade, your investment tax credit is based on $12,000 ($5,000 + $7,000).

Trade-ins for used property: The credit for used property is based on the cost of the property. The cost of used property does not include the basis of any property traded in unless the trade-in caused recapture of investment credit.

Example: You trade your old typewriter for a used electronic typewriter. You pay $10,000 boot to make the trade. If your old typewriter

---

EXHIBIT 7-1. Property Qualifying for the Investment Tax Credit (Selected Examples[1]).

Automobiles —6% credit	**Lamps —10% credit**
Briefcases —10% credit	**Paintings —10% credit**
Bookcases —10% credit	**Pick-up trucks —6% credit**
Burglar alarms —10% credit	**Photocopiers —10% credit**
Calculators —10% credit	**Postage meters —10% credit**
Cameras —10% credit	**Rugs —10% credit**
Carpets —10% credit	**Storage cabinets —10% credit**
Chairs —10% credit	**Tables —10% credit**
Computers —10% credit	**Tape recorders —10% credit**
Credenzas —10% credit	**Telephone answer machines —10% credit**
Desks —10% credit	**Tools —10% credit**
Drapes —10% credit	**Typewriters —10% credit**
File cabinets —10% credit	**Video recorders —10% credit**

[1] Percentages shown are for property eligible for depreciation under the ACRS rules (see Exhibit 7-2).

---

had a basis of $1,000 at the time of trade and you had to recapture investment tax credit because of early disposition, your investment tax credit for the used electronic typewriter is based on $11,000 ($10,000 boot + $1,000 basis).

If no recapture: If, in the above example, there had been no recapture of investment tax credit, your basis for figuring investment tax credit on the used electronic typewriter would be $10,000—the cash you paid.

Special 60-day rule for used property: If you buy similar used property as a replacement within 60 days of the time you dispose of old property, you count as your investment only the amount you spend that is more than the basis of the old property. This rule applies only if there is no investment tax credit recapture on the disposition of the old property.

Example: You buy a used $5,000 machine to replace an old machine within 60 days before (or after) an outright sale of the old machine, which had an adjusted basis of $4,000. There was no recapture of investment tax credit on the sale of the old machine. You count $1,000 for purposes of figuring your investment tax credit.

If the sale of the old machine had resulted in recapture of investment tax credit, your basis for figuring investment tax credit on the used machine (newly acquired) would be $5,000—the amount you paid.

Important reminder: Your basis for cost recovery is different from your basis for the investment tax credit. For cost recovery, you must reduce your basis by 50 percent of the investment tax credit. Similarly, if you must recapture any investment tax credit, you increase your basis by 50 percent of the investment credit recaptured for purposes of determining cost recovery.

Trade of personal-use property for business-use property: Generally, trade-ins are not taxable because they are considered "like-kind" exchanges. For example, trading in your business car for a new business car is a nontaxable exchange. If, however, you trade a personal asset for a business asset, the exchange could be taxable. There is a general tax rule that says losses on personal-use property are not deductible, but gains are fully taxable. The same is true on a trade of personal-use assets for business-use assets. In such a trade, your cost for purposes of determining the investment tax credit is equal to the fair market value of the property traded plus cash boot. If the fair market value of the personal-use property traded is greater than your basis, you have a taxable gain. If less, you have a nondeductible personal loss.

Example: In 1981 you purchased a personal car for $6,000. In 1984 you trade the personal car plus $12,000 for a new business car. The new business car has a fair market value of $20,000 and your old personal car has a fair market value of $8,000. You are taxed on $2,000 ($8,000 value − $6,000 basis). Your basis for purposes of determining the investment tax credit is $20,000 ($12,000 cash boot + $8,000 fair market value of old personal car).

Investment credit ceiling: For new property, there is no limit on the amount of cost that can qualify for the credit. On the other hand, no more than $125,000 of the cost of used property may be counted. The dollar limit applies to the total of all used property you buy during a given tax year. For example, if you bought five pieces of used property during the year for a total of $175,000, only $125,000 would qualify. You may not use the excess amount for any other year.

Expensing limitation: If you elected to use the special expensing deduction discussed in Chapter 6, you must reduce your cost by the amount of the expensing deduction. For example, if you bought a $12,000 office machine and wrote off $5,000, your credit would be based on $7,000 ($12,000 minus $5,000).

Credit percentages: As noted at the beginning of this chapter, the credit ranges from 3.33 percent to 25 percent. Exhibit 7-2 shows the credit percentages for personal property. The percentages that apply to the energy investment credit and the rehabilitation credit are discussed in later sections.

For personal property, the amount of credit depends first on whether the property is "recovery" or "nonrecovery" property, and second, on the property's useful life. Recovery property is property eligible for the ACRS rules. This includes almost all personal property placed in service after 1980.

Nonrecovery property, as you might have guessed, is any property that does not qualify as recovery property. This includes all depreciable property that you placed in service before 1981. About the only nonqualifying post-1980 property would be property for which you use a depreciation method not expressed in terms of years, such as the unit-of-

---

EXHIBIT 7-2. Credit Percentages: Personal Property.

Recovery Property[1]	Credit—As a percentage of cost
3-year assets	6%
All other assets	10%

Nonrecovery Property[1]	Credit—As a percentage of cost
Useful life	
3-5 years	3.33%
5-7 years	6.67%
7 years or more	10.00%

[1] Recovery property is property eligible for depreciation write-offs under the ACRS rules, discussed in the preceding chapter. Generally, this means depreciable property you placed in service after 1980. Nonrecovery property is depreciable property you placed in service before 1981 or that otherwise does not qualify under the ACRS rules (because the unit-of-production method is used, for example).

production method. Also, if you choose the IRS standard mileage rate in the year of acquisition, you have elected not to use ACRS and the automobile is treated as non-ACRS property.

For recovery property, there are only two percentages. The credit for three-year property is 6 percent. For all other recovery property, the amount is 10 percent.

Example: A tape recorder is a five-year asset under the ACRS rules and therefore qualifies for a 10 percent credit. If the tape recorder costs you $1,000, Uncle Sam will give you a tax credit of $100.

Example: A business automobile is a three-year asset under the ACRS rules. If you pay $10,000 for a 100% business car and do not use the IRS standard mileage rates, Uncle Sam will give you a tax rebate of $600.

Basis reduction: In an apparent effort to make modern life even more difficult, Congress recently passed a law requiring you to reduce your basis for depreciation purposes by one-half of your credit. (For certain property eligible for the rehabilitation credit, the basis is reduced by the full amount of the credit—discussed later.) For example, on that $1,000 tape recorder mentioned above, your basis for purposes of the ACRS rules is $950 ($1,000 cost − $50 [50% of $100]). Your basis in that $10,000 business auto is $9,700 ($10,000 − $300 [50% of $600]). The law applies to property placed in service *after 1982*.

Reduced credit election: Instead of reducing your basis by one-half of your credit, you may elect to reduce your credit by 2 percent. This means you would get 4 percent on three-year property and 8 percent on all other property. Thus, to retain your $1,000 basis in the tape recorder, you could elect a credit of $80 (8 percent of $1,000). To retain your $10,000 basis in the business auto, you could elect a credit of $400 (4 percent of $10,000).

Hint: Generally, you should take the full credit unless you have no tax liability to offset.

Business versus personal use: When you use property partly for business and partly for personal purposes, your credit is based on the part of the cost attributable to your business use. For example, if you use your $1,000 tape recorder for business only 70 percent of the time, your cost for purposes of figuring the credit is $700. Thus, your 10 percent credit is $70. Similarly, if you use your business auto only 75 percent of the time for business, your credit is based on $7,500, for a total credit of $450 ($7,500 × 6%).

Hint—Establish business-use percentage: When you use property for business only part of the time, you must take steps to substantiate your business use. It's worth the effort because the cost of such assets determines both the investment tax credit and the ACRS write-offs. Generally, you must do two things:

- Create a work activity log that summarizes your business use.
- Establish additional evidence to support your activity log.

Creating a work activity log is really quite simple. Merely embellish your appointment book or diary to show your business use of an asset, such as a desk. Refer to Chapter 8 on the home office deduction for an example of a work activity log. (Remember, however, that you don't have to qualify for the home office deduction to claim the credit and depreciate property in your home that you use for your business.)

Will IRS believe your appointment book entries? Not unless you have some additional evidence, such as:

- Copies of letters you wrote that have dates corresponding with entries in your appointment book.
- Copies of business letters you received at your home address.
- Business cards with your home phone number and address.
- Telephone bills that show business use.

While none of these types of evidence will prove business use of a desk in your home, they do provide reasonable support when combined with your appointment book entries.

Example: You buy a telephone answering machine and connect it to a telephone line that you use for both business and personal purposes. Keep a log on a test basis showing the number of business and personal phone calls. To corroborate the log, retain several recording tapes. The log forms the basis for determining your percentage of business use. It is supported by the tapes, as well as correspondence that supports your business use. The business portion of the machine's cost qualifies for both the investment tax credit and the ACRS rules.

WHEN CREDIT IS CLAIMED

Remember, the investment credit is a one-time credit. It is allowed only in the year in which you first place qualified property *in service*. It is possible for property to be *placed in service* for purposes of the investment credit prior to the time for which depreciation or cost recovery is allowed. The IRS regulations provide that property is placed in service in the earlier of the following taxable years:

- The taxable year in which depreciation begins; or
- The taxable year in which property is placed in a condition or state of readiness and available for a specifically assigned function.

Example 1: Parts are acquired and set aside for use as replacements for a machine. The credit may be claimed when the parts are received.

Example 2: You buy equipment in late Fall of 1985, but have no need for it until 1986. You merely keep it on hand for use in your business in 1986. *Result:* You take the investment tax credit in 1985.

Exception to the "placed in service" rule: Generally, the investment credit is available only when eligible property is actually placed in service. However, there is a special rule for property with a long construction period. You may claim the investment tax credit for progress expenditures made on qualified investment tax credit property. To qualify for progress expenditure treatment, the investment credit property must meet two conditions:

- It must be reasonable to believe that the property will be investment tax credit property in your hands at the time it is placed in service; and
- It must have a normal construction period of at least two years.

Special rules and tricky computations: To determine the amount of progress expenditures in a given year, you must use engineering or architectural estimates or cost accounting methods. There are special rules if the property is self-constructed. Generally, you should seek good tax advice when claiming the investment tax credit for progress expenditures.

Annual dollar limit: Your credit is limited to your tax liability. If your credit is greater than your tax liability for a given year, you may use any excess against your previous three years' tax liability and the following 15 years' tax liability. (These are called carry-backs and carry-forwards.)

If your tax liability for the year is greater than $25,000, your credit cannot exceed that amount plus 85 percent of your tax liability in excess of $25,000. Most of us, of course, won't have to worry about this limit.

Other taxes: The investment tax credit applies only against your "regular" income tax. It will not reduce your self-employment tax, the minimum tax, the alternative minimum tax, and various other special penalty taxes.

HOW TO HANDLE THE RECAPTURE RULES

When you claim the investment tax credit, you enter into an agreement with Uncle Sam for a credit advance. Uncle Sam gives you the full amount of the investment tax credit at the time you file your tax return for the year in which you place the property in service.

But if you dispose of an asset too soon, Uncle Sam wants some or all of the credit back. If, for example, you dispose of a three-year asset, such as a business car, after only one full year of use, you must give back two-thirds of the original credit you claimed. When you think of it, this isn't such a bad deal at all. It's a bit like getting an interest-free loan from the government. And remember, if you replaced the asset with another business or investment asset, you get *another credit for the replacement asset.*

Recapture percentages: The amount of credit you must pay back depends on whether the property is "recovery" or "nonrecovery" property. Recovery property is covered by the ACRS rules, discussed in the preceding chapter, and generally includes all business or investment assets you placed in service after 1980. Nonrecovery property generally includes all business or investment assets you placed in service before 1981. Exhibit 7-3 shows the recapture percentages for both recovery and nonrecovery property.

Basis recovery: If tax is recaptured on property you placed in service after 1982, one-half of the recaptured amount is added back to your basis for figuring your gain or loss and for figuring your basis on trade-ins.

Example: Assume you bought a copy machine for $10,000 in 1984 for your business. The machine is five-year recovery property, eligible for a 10 percent credit, or $1,000. You placed the machine in service on July 1, 1984. On July 2, 1986, you trade the machine for a new one worth $12,000. Using the chart in Exhibit 7-3, you would see that $600 (60 percent of $1,000) is recaptured. Thus, your 1986

EXHIBIT 7-3. Recapture Percentages.

Recovery Property

Number of full years used before disposition:	RECAPTURE PERCENTAGE	
	3-year property	All other property
0	100	100
1	66	80
2	33	60
3	0	40
4	0	20
5	0	0

Example: Jones bought a typewriter (five-year property) for $500 and claimed a 10 percent credit, or $50. After using it for two years and three months, he sold it. The amount recaptured was $30 (60 percent of $50).

Nonrecovery Property

Number of full years used before disposition	RECAPTURE PERCENTAGE FOR ORIGINAL USEFUL LIFE OF:		
	3-5 years	5-7 years	7 or more years
0	100	100	100
1	100	100	100
2	100	100	100
3	0	50	66.7
4	0	50	66.7
5	0	0	33.3
6	0	0	33.3
7	0	0	0

Example: Smith bought a machine in 1980 for $500, assigned it a seven-year useful life, and claimed a 10 percent credit, or $50. After using it for two years and three months, he sold it. The amount recaptured was $50 (100 percent of $50).

return will show an additional $600 tax attributable to this transaction.

But remember that the new machine is eligible for a 10 percent credit on your 1986 return. Also remember that your basis in the old machine will be increased by one-half the recaptured amount, thus increasing your basis in the new machine. Assuming you used the accelerated method of writing off the cost, your adjusted basis of the old machine is $6,285, computed as follows:

Cost	$10,000
One-half credit	(500)
Depreciable basis	$ 9,500
Depreciation (37%)	(3,515)
Restored basis ($1/2$ recapture)	300
Adjusted basis	$ 6,285

If your cash outlay is $5,000 (trade-in allowance of $7,000), your basis for figuring your new credit is $11,285 ($5,000 cash plus $6,285 adjusted basis of old machine). Therefore, your new credit is $1,128.50 (10 percent of $11,285). Assuming that you have some regular income tax for the current or preceding three years, that tax will be reduced by your $1,128.50 credit. Since your recaptured tax was only $600, you would end up with a rebate of $528.50 ($1,128.50 − $600)!

Watch out for unusual "dispositions": The preceding example shows that the recapture rules can generally be handled pretty easily if you are ready for them. But sales and trade-ins are not the only dispositions that trigger the recapture rules. A list of the most common types of dispositions, as well as transactions that do not constitute dispositions, is contained in Exhibit 7-4. Notice that you can mortgage your property, lease it, put it into a partnership or corporation (provided you have a substantial interest in the partnership or corporation), or sell it and lease it back without triggering the recapture rules. You may also die and leave it to someone without causing any recapture tax. On the other hand, if you give it away or abandon it, you may have to pay tax. You also may pay a recapture tax if the property is stolen or destroyed.

Perhaps the most surprising "disposition" occurs when your business use decreases.

Example: You bought a $100 tape recorder on March 1, 1984, for home use in practicing oral presentations you make in your business. You took a $10 investment tax credit on your 1983 return, since the tape recorder is a five-year asset eligible for the 10 percent credit. In April of 1985 you buy a more deluxe model. Your kids now use the old tape recorder. As a result, you have disposed of the old tape recorder for tax purposes and you must pay back $10 of the credit.

Things get a little more complicated if you continue to use the property for business, but the business use decreases. In the tape recorder example, if your business use had decreased to 50 percent, you would have to pay back only $5.00 of the credit. This is because there was a disposition only to the extent of 50 percent of the property. If your business use had declined to 60 percent, the disposition would have been only 40 percent.

To figure the extent of any disposition resulting from decreased business use, subtract the new percentage of business use from the old percentage and divide the difference by the old percentage. If, for example, you formerly used property 80 percent of the time in business, and you now use it only 60 percent of the time, there has been a 25% disposition. This is determined as follows:

Former use	80%
Current use	60%
Reduction	20%
Percentage disposition equals 25% (20% divided by 80%)	

Use standby status to avoid recapture: Suppose you have a business asset that you need to replace, but the recapture period has not yet expired. If you retain the old asset as a backup for the new asset, there should be no recapture. Property you retain and do not convert to personal use is not considered "disposed of" until it is *permanently withdrawn* from use in your trade or business. Thus, putting an asset in standby status will not trigger the recapture rules.

Example: You use your tape recorder for four and one-half years, then buy a new one. Instead of selling the old one or converting it to personal use, you keep it as a backup in case you have a problem with the new one. No recapture applies in this situation.

EXHIBIT 7-4. Dispositions for Purposes of Recapture Rule.

The following transactions are common types of "dispositions" for purposes of triggering the recapture rule:

- Sales (including "leases" that are disguised sales).
- Trade-ins.
- Decreased business use (e.g., from 80 percent business use to 20 percent).
- Refund of part of price in a later year.
- Casualties and thefts.
- Gifts.
- Retirement or abandonment of property.
- Transfer to a bankruptcy trustee for liquidation.
- Foreclosures.
- Sale of stock by an S Corporation shareholder.
- Sale of partnership interest by a partner.

The following transactions are not "dispositions" for purposes of triggering the recapture rule:

- Transfers because of death.
- Mortgages or giving property as collateral for a loan.
- Leases.
- S Corporation election or revocation of election.
- Change in form of doing business (e.g., from sole proprietorship to corporation).
- Sale and leaseback to seller (even though the seller paid tax on gain).

WHY USED PROPERTY CAN COST YOU BIG TAX SAVINGS

Several special rules limit or deny the investment tax credit when you buy used property.

As mentioned previously, you get no investment tax credit for used property you buy in excess of $125,000 during a year. Used property does not qualify at all for the business energy credit, discussed later. And you may not claim a credit for used property that you lease. These restrictions are fairly well known. Some less commonly known restrictions are the following.

Buying used property from a related person: You do not get any credit for used property you buy from a related person. "Related" has the same meaning here as for the rule, discussed earlier, that denies a credit for money borrowed from a related person—*except* that

brothers and sisters are not related for purposes of this rule. Thus, you cannot borrow from a brother or sister, but you can buy used property from them and get the investment tax credit.

Lesson 1: If you want the investment tax credit, buy only new property from a related person.

Lesson 2: Pay the full purchase price on all investment credit property purchased from a related party; otherwise, you lose the credit to the extent you borrowed from a related party.

Trade-ins: When you buy *used* property on a tax-free trade-in, you cannot include the adjusted basis of your old property as part of your cost for figuring the credit.

Example: Suppose you buy used property for $10,000 and trade in old property with an adjusted basis of $8,000. Assume you are allowed $9,000 on the old property, so you have to pay only $1,000 in cash. Your basis for figuring the credit is $1,000.

Effect of recapture: If your trade-in results in recapture, you are allowed to use the entire adjusted basis of the property in figuring your credit. In other words, your used property is transformed into new property, at least for figuring your credit.

Example: Assume you bought a typewriter for $1,000 in 1983 and claimed a credit of $100. (No reduction in basis was necessary since the property was placed in service before 1984.) Your deductions under the ACRS rules for 1983, 1984, and 1985 totaled $580, giving you an adjusted basis of $420 in 1986, when you traded it in for a used typewriter costing $1,200. You were allowed $600 on the trade-in, so you paid $600 in cash. Since the old typewriter was a five-year asset under the ACRS rules, and you used it for less than five full years, part of your original credit is recaptured as tax. Under these circumstances, you include the $580 adjusted basis of the old typewriter as part of your cost for figuring the credit. Therefore, your credit is based on $1,180 ($580 adjusted basis of old typewriter plus $600 cash).

On the other hand, if you had used the typewriter for a full five years, none of your original credit would have been recaptured and only the $600 cash you paid for the used typewriter would count in figuring your credit.

Obscure 60-day rule: Suppose you heard about the trade-in rule just discussed, so you decided to *sell* the old typewriter and buy a used one. If you bought the used one within 60 days before or after you disposed of the old one, the adjusted basis of the old one would reduce the creditable amount. As a result, your credit would be about the same as on a trade-in!

Example: Suppose you sold your old typewriter for its fair market value of $600 and bought a used one to replace it for $1,200. Remember, your basis in the old typewriter was $580. You would have to subtract this amount from your cash investment of $1,200 to arrive at your basis for determining your credit. Therefore, your credit would be based on $620 ($1,200 cash investment minus $580 basis in old property).

Notice that in this case your credit basis is $20 more than in a trade-in. *Reason*: Your sale for $600 resulted in a $20 taxable gain.

60-day rule and recapture: Suppose your sale of the old typewriter resulted in recapture of tax. As is the case with trade-ins, application of the recapture rules removes the restriction on figuring your basis. Therefore, you figure your credit on the full $1,200 you paid for the replacement property.

Lesson: Whenever you replace business or investment property with used property, you must do some pencil-pushing. If your trade-in or sale will not result in recapture of tax under the rules discussed in the preceding section, you must remember that your credit is reduced by the adjusted basis of your old property. Thus, your purchase rebate is lower than you might have expected. On the other hand, the price break you get by buying used property may be sufficient to overcome your lost tax credit. To complicate matters a bit more, you must also consider the probable costs of maintaining the used property versus the costs of maintaining new property during the time you expect to use it.

HOW TO GET THE CREDIT FOR PROPERTY YOU LEASE

Ordinarily, the investment tax credit is available only to the owner of property. However, a special rule allows you to get the credit for *new* property you lease for use in your business or investments. This break is not available for used property.

Your credit is based on the fair market value, not the cost of the property. If the property is new, however, chances are that the IRS will accept the cost as an accurate measure of fair market value.

Lessor (owner) must elect: In order to get the credit, you must convince the owner to give it to you. Otherwise, the owner will get the credit. To pass the credit on to you, the lessor must do two things. First, the lessor must file a certain statement with you. The statement must include the following information:

- Name, address, and taxpayer identifying number of both the lessor and the lessee (you).
- The local IRS District Director's office.
- A description of the property.
- The date the property was transferred to you.
- The useful life of the property.
- The fair market value of the property.
- If the lessor is leasing the property from someone else (that is, the lessor is subleasing the property to you), the name, address, taxpayer identifying number, and local IRS District Director's office of the owner.

The lessor must file this statement with you on or before the due date of your tax return. Both the lessor and you must sign this statement.

Second, the lessor must notify the IRS in the lessor's tax return by filing a summary of all property on which the lessor has allowed lessees to get the investment tax credit.

Once the election is made, it cannot be revoked.

Recapture rules: If the credit is passed on to you, you are treated as the owner of the property for purposes of the credit. Therefore, the regular recapture rules apply. The length of your lease is irrelevant. Thus, if you were to lease five-year property for a period of only three years, 40 percent of the credit would be recaptured when you stopped using the property.

Special recapture rule: Remember that an owner who claims the investment tax credit must reduce the property's basis for purposes of depreciation write-offs by one-half of the credit claimed. A lessee, however, may not depreciate property. Thus, the lessee has no basis to be reduced. Congress apparently didn't think this was fair. Therefore, it passed a special rule designed to put lessees in roughly the same position as owners who claim the credit. Under this special rule, a lessee must include

one-half of the credit in income over the recovery period under the ACRS rules.

Example: You lease a $10,000 copy machine and claim a credit of $1,000 ($10,000 times 10 percent). You must include $100 in your income over a five-year period beginning in the year in which you claimed the credit. This amount is figured by taking one-half of the credit ($500) and dividing by the ACRS life (5).

As an alternative, you may reduce the credit by 2 percent, just as an owner could do. Thus, instead of claiming the full $1,000 credit on the copy machine, you could claim only $800 ($10,000 times 8 percent) and avoid having to add back the $100 per year into your income.

Recommendation: Taxpayers in the 40 percent or lower bracket should take the full credit. Taxpayers in higher brackets will need to do some figuring, but generally should also take the full credit.

No credit for lease-options: If you buy property by using a lease-option and don't claim the credit when you place the property in service under the lease, you have lost the credit forever. You may not claim the credit after exercising your option to purchase. Therefore, if you want the credit, you must convince the lessor to pass it on to you.

On the other hand, if the lease-option is treated by the IRS as a disguised sale, you may claim the credit for the year in which you place the property in service. You may also claim depreciation write-offs for the property, since the transaction is treated as a sale for all purposes.

HOW THE BUSINESS ENERGY CREDIT WORKS

A special credit is allowed for certain property used in a trade or business. It is not available for investment property. Called the business energy credit, it differs in many respects from the regular credit.

First, the credit is available for structural components of buildings. Second, it is available for residential property. Third, there is no limit on the amount of tax it can offset. Fourth, the credit amount for certain property is 15 percent, for other property it is 11 percent, and for still other property it is 10 percent. The types of qualifying property and the percentage credit available are shown in Exhibit 7-5. Note that certain energy property might also qualify for the regular credit.

Qualifying property is either property that uses fuel other than petroleum products or property that reduces energy use. Regulations define qualifying property in detail. If you plan to install any energy-saving property or property that uses alternative forms of energy, you should definitely consult your tax advisor to determine whether or not the property qualifies for the credit.

Caution: The credit is scheduled to expire in 1985. After 1985, it will be too late to get the credit.

HOW TO GET THE CREDIT FOR FIXING UP OLD BUILDINGS

Congress wants old buildings to look nice. Therefore, a special investment credit is available for fixing up old buildings. For commercial buildings at least 30 years old, the credit is 15 percent of the rehabilitation cost. For commercial buildings at least 40 years old, the credit is 20 percent. And for "certified historic structures," whether commercial or residential, the credit is 25 percent.

What buildings qualify: The credit is available for your rehabilitation expenditures on any building and its structural components if three conditions are satisfied. First, the building must have been substantially rehabilitated. Second, it must have been placed in service before the beginning of the rehabilitation work. Third, at least 75 percent of the external walls must be retained in place as external walls.

The third requirement is that at least 75 percent of the external walls must be retained in place as external walls. An alternative to the third requirement was added by the Tax Reform Act of 1984. The alternative requirement is satisfied if at least half of the external walls are retained in place as external walls, provided:

• At least 75 percent of the existing walls are retained in place as either external or internal walls; and

• At least 75 percent of the existing internal structural framework is retained in place.

You must spend more than $5,000 to qualify for the credit. Furthermore, the amount you spend must exceed the adjusted basis of the building. Otherwise, the building will not have been "substantially rehabilitated."

In addition to the minimum dollar amount, there is a time limit on your spending. You must spend the minimum amount during 24 months. There is an exception to this limitation for so-called "phased rehabilitations." Under the exception, you may spread your payments over a 60-month period if both of the following conditions are met:

• Architectural plans and specifications were drawn before work began.

EXHIBIT 7-5.   Energy Investment Credit Qualifying Property and Percentage Credits.

TYPE OF PROPERTY	PERCENTAGE CREDIT
Solar, wind, or geothermal property	15%
Ocean thermal property	15%
Qualified hydroelectric generating property	11%
Qualified inner city buses	10%
Biomass property	10%

Note: Credit is no longer available after 1985.

• Completion may reasonably be expected during the 60-month period.

Most fix-up expenses will qualify. However, you may not count any acquisition costs or any costs of making enlargements to the building.

Qualifying buildings: As noted above, a building must be at least 30 years old to qualify for the credit, unless it is a certified historic structure (which will probably be at least that old in any case). Also, residential buildings don't qualify unless they are certified historic structures.

Be careful when seeking the credit for a certified historic structure. A certified historic structure must be on the National Register or certified by the Secretary of the Interior as being of historic significance in a registered historic district. For your rehabilitation to qualify, you must obtain the Secretary of the Interior's certification that the rehabilitation is consistent with the historic character of the property and the historical district. If the property is not a certified historic structure but is located in a historical district, you must obtain the Secretary of the Interior's certification that the rehabilitation is consistent with the historical character of the district.

Reduction in basis: As with the regular investment tax credit, the rehabilitation credit requires you to reduce the basis of your property. For certified historic structures, the basis is reduced by one-half of the credit. For other buildings, you must reduce the basis by the *entire* credit allowed. For example, assume you spend $200,000 rehabilitating a 40-year-old building that is not a certified historic structure. Your rehabilitation credit would be $40,000 (20 percent of $200,000), but your depreciable basis would be reduced to $160,000. If the building were a certified historic structure, your credit would be $50,000 (25 percent of $200,000), and your depreciable basis would be $175,000 ($200,000 minus $25,000).

Straight-line method must be used: You cannot use the accelerated method for writing off your costs if you claim the rehabilitation credit. Under the ACRS rules, however, you are allowed to write off your costs over 15 years (if you placed the property in service before March 16, 1984), 18 years (if you placed the property in service after March 15, 1984), or 19 years (if you placed the property in service after May 8, 1985).

Recapture: The recapture rules also apply to the rehabilitation credit. For purposes of those rules, the property is considered five-year property. Thus, the recapture percentages for five-year property will apply to dispositions of rehabilitated buildings. For example, if you sold your certified historic structure after two full years, you would pay $30,000 (60 percent of $50,000).

As with other qualifying property, your basis for purposes of determining gain or loss will be restored when the recapture rules apply. Thus, on your certified historic structure, your basis would be increased by one-half of the recaptured amount, or $15,000.

WHAT FORMS TO FILE

Claiming your credit is generally a pretty easy task. You simply fill out Form 3468 and send it in with your regular Form 1040 or Form 1120. If the recapture rules apply, you must file Form 4255 and pay the tax.

Claiming overlooked credits: There is one more form you should think about filing—the form for an amended return. For individuals, it's Form 1040X; corporations use Form 1120X.

You should think about filing an amended return if you have overlooked property that qualifies for the credit. Check the list on Exhibit 7-1. Then look around your house and office and see if you can find any of those items. If you do and you use any of those items for your business, run down to your local IRS office and get the form you need to file an amended return. Establish the cost of those items by digging your receipts out of your shoebox. (Remember? Keep *all* receipts.)

HOW TO HANDLE THE NEW RULES ON PROPERTY USED PARTLY FOR BUSINESS AND PARTLY FOR PERSONAL PURPOSES

The Tax Reform Act of 1984 adds special rules for certain property placed in service after June 18, 1984. The new law applies to:

- Trucks, motor homes, and vans
- Amusement, entertainment, or recreation equipment such as video tape cameras and recorders, cassette tape players, golf clubs, hunting rifles, and so forth
- Airplanes and helicopters
- Computers, and
- Other property specified by the IRS.

Congress has left it to the IRS's wisdom to subject other property to the new rules. It's an open-ended deal, so you won't know exactly what's subject to the new rules until the IRS gets around to issuing its regulations (give it a year).

However, follow the rules outlined here and no matter what the IRS specifies, you will be covered.

Flowchart: The new rules are somewhat complex and contain a number of exceptions. However, by using the easy-to-follow flowchart in Exhibit 7-6, you will have a good understanding of the new rules.

Generally, two things happen in the flowchart. First, you must have adequate records to support your deductions or they will be disallowed and you may pay negligence penalties.

Second, if business use is greater than 50 percent, you are allowed the regular investment tax credit and you may use the rapid ACRS depreciation tables. However, if business use is 50 percent or less, you are entitled to no investment tax credit, and you must use straight-line depreciation over an excessively long period, based on the "earnings and profits life" of the asset.

The "earnings and profits life" of autos and other motor vehicles weighing less than 13,000 pounds is 5 years. For most other business assets, the earnings and profits life is 12 years. Note, however, that the law allows you to take only a half-year's straight-line depreciation in the year you place an asset in service. Thus, the actual depreciation periods are 6 years and 13 years, respectively.

Planning tip: Even if you must use 6- or 13-year straight-line depreciation, you should

still keep adequate records. Any write-off is better than none at all.

Airplanes: Airplane owners get a special break. Although airplanes are subject to the more-than-50-percent business use test, only 25 percent of the use need be direct business use.

Once the 25 percent direct business use requirement is met, you may count leasing of the airplane to an employee or related party as additional business use. Moreover, if you use the airplane for personal purposes and that personal use is considered compensation to you (i.e., it is shown in your Form W-2), you may treat the compensation as a business use for purposes of meeting the 50 percent test.

Computers: The flowchart also discloses a tricky rule with respect to computers located in your office. Note that any personal use of the computer in a home office could eliminate your home office deduction. Reason: to qualify for a home office deduction, you must use the home office 100 percent of the time for business.

Transfer to personal use: Sole proprietors, self-employed individuals, and employees should not transfer business assets listed in Exhibit 7-6 to personal use until after their "earnings and profits lives" have expired. Transfers to personal use before that time will trigger extremely rough recapture rules.

Recapture rules: As explained earlier in this chapter, any reduction in the business use percentage of an asset results in at least partial recapture of the investment tax credit. The new law does not change this rule. However, the new law adds a tricky depreciation recapture rule for property listed in Exhibit 7-6: If business use decreases from above 50 percent to 50 percent or below, depreciation recapture is triggered. The recapture procedure is identical to that for an automobile (see Chapter 5).

The amount recaptured as ordinary income is equal to the depreciation actually claimed minus depreciation that would have been claimed on the basis of straight-line depreciation over a 6-year period (for autos and other light duty vehicles) and over a 13-

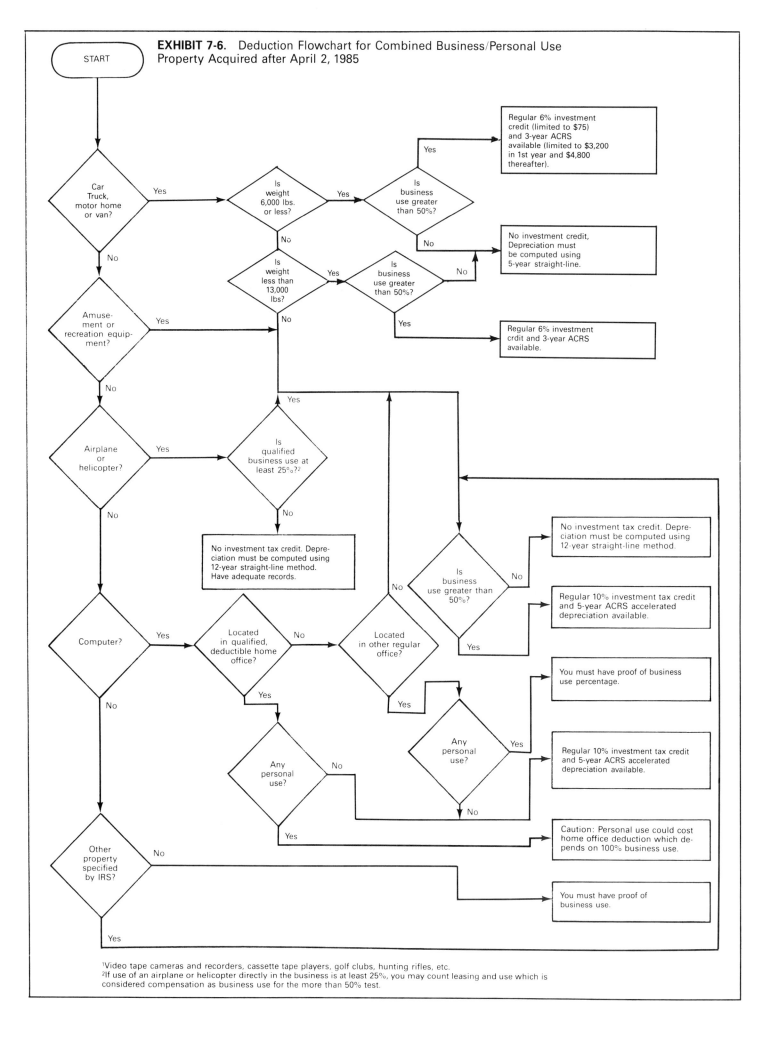

EXHIBIT 7-6. Deduction Flowchart for Combined Business/Personal Use Property Acquired after April 2, 1985

START

Car Truck, motor home or van?

Is weight 6,000 lbs. or less?

Is business use greater than 50%?

Regular 6% investment credit (limited to $75) and 3-year ACRS available (limited to $3,200 in 1st year and $4,800 thereafter).

No investment credit, Depreciation must be computed using 5-year straight-line.

Is weight less than 13,000 lbs?

Is business use greater than 50%?

Regular 6% investment crdit and 3-year ACRS available.

Amusement or recreation equipment?

Airplane or helicopter?

Is qualified business use at least 25%?[2]

No investment tax credit. Depreciation must be computed using 12-year straight-line method. Have adequate records.

Computer?

Located in qualified, deductible home office?

Located in other regular office?

Is business use greater than 50%?

No investment tax credit. Depreciation must be computed using 12-year straight-line method.

Regular 10% investment tax credit and 5-year ACRS accelerated depreciation available.

Any personal use?

You must have proof of business use percentage.

Any personal use?

Regular 10% investment tax credit and 5-year ACRS accelerated depreciation available.

Other property specified by IRS?

Caution: Personal use could cost home office deduction which depends on 100% business use.

You must have proof of business use.

[1]Video tape cameras and recorders, cassette tape players, golf clubs, hunting rifles, etc.
[2]If use of an airplane or helicopter directly in the business is at least 25%, you may count leasing and use which is considered compensation as business use for the more than 50% test.

year period (for most other business assets) using the straight-line method.

Example: You purchase a personal computer for $7,000 and use it 100 percent of the time in your business during the first 3 years of ownership. In year 4, your business use declines from 100 percent to 10 percent. You must first pay the IRS $252 for its recapture of investment tax credit.

Second, you must report $2,317 as ordinary income resulting from the IRS's recapture of excess depreciation. (During the first 3 years you depreciated the computer $3,857 under the 5-year ACRS depreciation tables. Straight-line depreciation during the first 3 years would have been $1,540. The $2,317 difference is "recaptured" as income.)

Don't purge your deductions. Make sure that your business use percentage stays about 50 percent.

Corporations beware: If you operate your business as a coporation, all transfers from the corporation to any other party must be made at fair market value. Furthermore, if the transfer at fair market value results in a tax loss to the corporation, that loss is not tax-deductible if the transfer is to a related party.

Do not lease to your corporation under the new 1984 tax law: If you own more than 5 percent of your corporation, you are subject to a sneaky little rule. To use ACRS depreciation tables, you must use the property in Exhibit 7-6 more than 50 percent of the time for business. "Qualified business use" does not include leasing property to any 5 percent owner, or to anyone related to a 5 percent owner, of a corporation.

Also, qualified business use does not include use of property provided as compensation for the performance of service by a 5 percent owner or related person. Remember, this restriction does not apply to any aircraft if at least 25 percent of the total use of the aircraft consists of other qualified business use.

Example: You purchase a $10,000 personal computer and lease it to your corporation. You may claim no investment tax credit and you must use 13-year straight-line depreciation. Reason: leasing the computer to your corporation is not a qualified business use. However, the computer is used for the production of income. Thus, you can depreciate 100 percent of the cost, but it will take 13 years to get all the deductions to which you are entitled.

New, tougher rules for employees: To deduct any expenses for a truck, van, motor home, video cassette recorder, airplane, or other asset subject to the new rules, an employee must prove that the use of the asset is (1) for the convenience of the employer, and (2) required as a condition of employment.

"Convenience of the employer" simply means that the employer would either have to buy the equipment for you to use or pay you for using your own equipment. Thus, a video cassette player could be required for the convenience of the employer so the employer does not have to purchase a television set and a video tape player for the office.

The use of such equipment must also be required as a condition of employment. Generally, a written agreement spelling out the requirement is best. For example, if use of a video cassette recorder is a condition of your employment, it should be so stated in an employment contract.

How to document combined business/personal use: You must keep good records to get big deductions and credits.

Exhibit 7-7 illustrates a work activity log that could be used for a personal computer. The log is taped next to the computer. Anyone using the computer simply fills in the date, describes the use, records the minutes of use, and signs his or her name. Note that

EXHIBIT 7-7. Activity Log for Personal Computer (Example)

			MINUTES OF USE		
Date	User	Description Of Use	Business	Investment	Personal
9/1/85	John	Play video games	—	—	90
9/2/85	Henry	Cash flow tax shelters	—	120	—
9/3/85	Henry	Update referral file	240	—	—
9/4/85	John	Play vido games	—	—	60
9/4/85	Henry	Record business expenses	120	—	—

minutes of use are broken down between business, investment, and personal use.

Remember, to claim investment tax credit and ACRS depreciation, your business use must exceed 50 percent. However, regardless of how you come out on the 50 percent test, your depreciation deduction is based on the combined business and production-of-income use.

Example 1: You buy a personal computer and use it 40 percent of the time for business and 30 percent for your investments. You must use 13-year straight-line depreciation and you may claim no investment tax credit. Your depreciation calculation is based on 70 percent (40% business plus 30% investment use).

Example 2: You buy a personal computer and use it 60 percent of the time for business and 20 percent of the time for investment purposes. You calculate investment tax credit and 5-year ACRS depreciation using 80 percent of the cost of the computer.

Create a work activity log for computers, video tape cameras and recorders, cassette tape players, golf clubs, hunting rifles, and similar equipment. Use a mileage log for your truck, motor home, or van. Use an hourly flight log for your airplane or helicopter and make sure you describe the business usage in the log.

For assets located in a home office, but used only partly for business (and therefore denying you a home office deductions) make entries in your daily diary. Simply note in your diary the hours spent working and any

hours of personal use so you can develop the business use percentage.

How to make the new law work for you: Look around your home for assets you use for both business and personal purposes. Surveys taken at Tax Reduction Institute seminars indicate that 97 percent of the participants do some work at home. You can qualify for tax breaks if you use assets in your home for business purposes.

What assets do you use at home for your work? Do you take business pictures with your personal camera? Do you watch business video tapes on your personal television set using your personal video tape player? Do you have a room set aside for work at home?

Exhibit 7-8 shows how Joe Wilson found an additional $7,560 in tax deductions and $288 in investment tax credits by using assets in his home for business purposes.

Wilson purchased a bookcase in June of 1975 and used it for personal purposes until January 1, 1984. When he converted the bookcase from personal use to business use, he was subject to the "lower of cost or market rule." Under this rule, Wilson depreciated the lower of what he paid for the bookcase in June of 1975 ($200) or the fair market value of the bookcase on January 1, 1984 ($250).

Also, because the bookcase was purchased before 1981, he was subject to the old rules for depreciation. He selected the 150-percent declining balance method of depreciation over a remaining useful life of 5 years.

Remember, assets purchased during the current year (carpet, drapes, and lamps)

EXHIBIT 7-8. How to Take Advantage of Combined Business and Personal Use Property (Example Computation)

FACTS: Joe Wilson, self-employed, works in his downtown office during the day. On January 1, 1984, he starts working in an office in his home in the evenings. He uses the office 90 percent for business use and 10 percent for personal use. He does not qualify for a home office deductible because he fails the 100 percent business use test. Yet, he is able to put almost $1,000 in his pocket by properly deducting his business assets in his 1984 tax return. During the next 5 years, Joe Wilson will add $7,560 in new deductions to his tax return, plus claim an investment tax credit of $288.

		Cost	FMV[1]	Basis[2]	Depreciation in 1984 Method	Yrs	Amount
Bookcase	6/1/75	$ 200	$ 250	$ 200	DB[3]	5	$ 60
Carpet	8/1/84	2,000	N/A[4]	2,000	ACRS	5	300
Chair	9/1/81	150	50	50	ACRS	5	8
Computer	4/5/83	5,000	3,000	3,000	ACRS	5	450
Desk	6/5/79	500	300	300	DB[3]	5	90
Drapes	8/1/84	1,000	N/A[4]	1,000	ACRS	5	150
File cabinets	2/11/82	200	150	150	ACRS	5	23
Lamps	8/1/84	200	N/A[4]	200	ACRS	5	30
Painting	2/2/82	2,000	1,500	1,500	ACRS	5	225
Totals				8,400			1,336
Business use percentage				x 90%			x 90%
Deductible amounts				$7,560			1,202
Tax brackets							x 53%
Tax savings in 1984							637
Investment Tax Credit (ITC)							288
Cash in pocket—1984							$ 925

[1]Fair market value.

[2]For assets purchased prior to 1984, basis is equal to the lower of cost or market.

[3]150 percent-declining balance—available for assets placed in service prior to 1981.

[4]Lower of cost or market rule does not apply to assets purchased and placed in service during the year.

qualify for ACRS deductions and the investment tax credit. Assets originally placed in service for personal purposes and then converted to business use do not qualify for the investment tax credit.

Summary of new law:

To profit from the new law:

1. Study the flowchart in Exhibit 7-6 and make sure you understand the new rules. They are effective for all assets placed in service after June 18, 1984.

2. Use assets first in your business and then transfer them to personal use, but only after their earnings and profits lives have expired. Remember, the recapture rules for property listed in Exhibit 7-6 are very punitive.

3. Most importantly, develop a work activity log to support your business use.

TAX REDUCTION CHECKLIST

IRS publications to be obtained:

- Publication 544—*Sales and Other Dispositions of Assets*
- Publication 572—*Investment Credit*

Property qualifying for regular credit:

- Tangible personal property used in your business or in connection with commercial investment property qualifies for the credit.
- Buildings and structural components do not qualify, but many items classified as fixtures under local law—such as store counters—do qualify.
- Often overlooked are items located in your home—such as desks, chairs, calculators, typewriters, lamps, and the like—that are used for both business and personal purposes.

Figuring the credit:

- For used property, no more than $125,000 a year is eligible.
- Unlimited amount of new property is eligible.
- Credit is a percentage of cost—from 3.33 percent to 10 percent for the regular credit. See Exhibit 7-2.
- Credit is available once; the year you place the property *in service*, which means *ready for use*, not necessarily actual use.
- Only amounts at risk qualify; money borrowed from a related person (including certain entities, like corporations) is not "at risk."
- On trade-ins of new property, your basis includes the adjusted basis of the property you traded in.
- Eligible amount is reduced by any amount you claim under the special expensing write-off, discussed in the preceding chapter.
- Basis for depreciation write-off is reduced by one-half of your credit, but is restored if recapture rules apply.
- Credit is limited to your regular income tax for the year—not self-employment, or alternative minimum tax—but not more than $25,000 plus 85 percent of your taxes in excess of $25,000 for the year.

Disadvantages of used property:

- On trade-ins, the adjusted basis of your old property is not included in your basis for figuring the credit on used property, unless the recapture rules apply. Same rule applies when you buy used property to replace other property you disposed of within 60 days before or after buying the used property.
- Used property you buy from a relative does not qualify for the credit.
- You are not allowed the credit for used property that you lease.
- Used property does not qualify for the business energy credit.

Handling the recapture rules:

- If you dispose of property before a certain amount of time, you must pay a certain percentage of your original credit as tax in the year of disposition. See Exhibit 7-3.
- Various transactions besides sales and trade-ins constitute dispositions. See Exhibit 7-4.
- Increased personal use is a disposition to the extent of the percentage decrease in business use.
- If recapture rules apply, one-half of the recaptured amount is added to your basis for purposes of determining gain or loss.
- Putting an old asset on standby status may avoid the recapture rules.

Leasing:

- If you lease *new* property, you may get the regular credit—based on the property's fair market value—if the lessor agrees.
- The lessor must file a statement with you and with the IRS.
- You must include a pro rata part of the credit in your income during the property's ACRS write-off period. Alternatively, you may reduce the credit by 2 percent.
- Even if you buy under a lease-option contract—unless it's a disguised sale—the credit is available only if the lessor consents at the beginning of the lease. Credit is not available when you exercise your purchase option.

Investment property:

- The regular credit is available for tangible personal property used in connection with commercial investment property.
- The credit is not generally available for property used in connection with your residential property, but certain exceptions may apply.

Business energy credit:

- A credit of from 10 percent to 15 percent is allowed for certain property used in your business.
- Building components may qualify.
- Property used in connection with investment property does not qualify.
- Types of eligible property are limited and specially defined; generally, includes certain energy-saving property or property using alternative sources of energy.
- Credit expires after 1985.

Rehabilitation credit:

- Credit applies to costs of rehabilitating old buildings.
- Credit is 15 percent for 30-year-old buildings, 20 percent for 40-year-old buildings, and 25 percent for certified historic structures.
- Minimum investment is $5,000 and total expenses must exceed the adjusted basis of the building.
- Expenses must be paid over a period of no more than 24 months, unless work will be done in phases over a 60-month period under plans drawn before the project started.
- Basis of certified historic structure is reduced by one-half of credit.
- Basis of 30-year-old and 40-year-old buildings is reduced by full amount of credit claimed.
- Recapture rules apply as though the buildings were five-year property under ACRS rules.

Forms to file:

- Claim credit on Form 3468.
- Report recaptured tax on Form 4255.
- File refund claim for overlooked credits on Form 1040X. Claim must be filed within three years from due date of return or when return is filed, whichever is later.

New rules for business/personal use property:

- Applies to assets listed on Exhibit 7-6, placed in service after June 18, 1984.
- Business use must exceed 50 percent for you to get investment tax credit and ACRS write-offs.
- If business use is 50 percent or less, no investment tax credit is available and depreciation is taken over "earnings and profits lives" (usually 6 or 13 years) on straight-line basis.

- Reduction in business use from above 50 percent to 50 percent or less will trigger depreciation "recapture."
- "Business use" does not include use for the production of income (i.e., use for investment purposes), leasing between a business entity and a five percent owner or relative, or use provided as compensation for a 5 percent owner or relative.
- Employees get no deductions or credits for property listed in Exhibit 7-6 unless the use is:
  — For the "convenience of the employer," and
  — Required as a condition of employment.
- Take advantage of the new law by converting personal use property to partial business use.
- You must keep good records to support your business deductions.
  — To satisfy this requirement, maintain activity logs.

You could be eligible for a home office income tax deduction. Do you use a portion of your home in the normal course of business or as your principal place of business (for any business)? If so, income tax deductions for an office in your home could put over $1,000 a year in your pocket.

Surveys of professionals who have attended our firm's workshops on business tax deductions reveal that fewer than 12 percent of 20,000 people claimed home office deductions prior to attending our seminars. Surveys taken one year after the seminars showed that more than 50 percent of those professionals not only qualified for, but actually did claim, home office deductions.

A number of factors account for the confusion surrounding the home office deduction. In 1976 Congress passed a law restricting the availability of the home office deduction. The Internal Revenue Service interpreted the law more severely than Congress intended. So, five years later, Congress acted again to pass a law making clear its original intent. That change was retroactive to 1975 and negated some of the stricter aspects of the IRS interpretation.

In this chapter, we will analyze the current laws, discuss the rules, and explain how to document home office deductions.

SIX ECONOMIC REASONS FOR TAKING A HOME OFFICE DEDUCTION

Your home is already a tax-sheltered investment. The current year deductions it produces, however, are limited to mortgage interest and property taxes. (If you suffer a disaster, you may also claim a casualty or theft loss deduction.) By claiming a home office deduction, you increase the amount of your tax-shelter return for at least one and possibly six economic reasons.

Economic reason 1—new deductions: By adding a home office deduction, you deduct otherwise nondeductible expenses for such things as rent, depreciation, cost recovery, heat, light, homeowner's insurance, and repairs and maintenance.

Economic reason 2—reduce Social Security taxes: If you are self-employed, the home office deduction allows you to transfer a portion of your mortgage interest and property taxes from Schedule A (itemized deductions) to Schedule C (business expenses). With Social Security taxes at 11.8 percent in 1985, self-employed taxpayers reporting less than $39,600 in bottom line profit on Schedule C

8

How to Take the Home Office Deduction

will decrease their Social Security tax bills. The reason: Social Security taxes are assessed against the bottom line of the Form 1040 Schedule C. This break becomes more valuable in 1986, when the tax rate rises to 12.3 percent (and the earnings limit rises to approximately $41,700, according to estimates at the time this was written).

Economic reason 3—corporate avoidance of double taxation: If you operate as a corporation, versus being self-employed, the home office deduction may provide you with a way to get money out of the corporation without double taxation and without having the money subject to Social Security taxes. To do this, the corporation rents the home office from you as an individual.

Economic reason 4—eliminate personal commuting mileage: If your home office is the principal place of business for your primary business, placing the principal office in your home eliminates personal, nondeductible mileage to secondary work locations.

Economic reason 5—tax-favored gain: One of the common objections to the home office deduction (and expressed by many tax advisors) is that selling the home results in a taxable event on the home office portion. The fact that this ultimate tax is assessed at tax-favored capital gains rates is often overlooked. In reality, each dollar of depreciation you claim later turns into tax-favored capital gains. Thus, for each dollar of depreciation deducted, you are taxed at the time of sale on 40 cents—60 cents is tax-free.

Economic reason 6—new IRS ruling may allow you to avoid tax on sale of home office: As a result of a new IRS ruling (Rev. Rul. 82-26), you may be in the best shape ever with respect to home office deductions. Following the rules carefully could let you avoid paying *any* tax on the sale of a home with a home office.

In addition to these economic reasons for claiming a home office deduction, consider the following:

- Today's economic climate has caused slower appreciation in the value of homes.
- The value of money continues to decline.

Thus, any gain on your home, if taxable at all, may be much smaller than you had first anticipated.

With the value of money decreasing each year, it is better to be a money grubber today and put the money in your pocket, rather than wait until it declines in value tomorrow. It's also better to take a deduction at today's higher tax rate and then repay that deduction in later years at a lower tax rate. As we move through this chapter, we will discuss many of these elements in more detail.

HOW TO FIGURE THE ECONOMIC VALUE OF A HOME OFFICE DEDUCTION

The exact value of a home office deduction to you depends on how you use the office, your tax bracket, how much your home will appreciate, how long you will keep your home, and whether you are self-employed, a corporation, or an employee.

Exhibit 8-1 shows how a home office deduction puts $1,590 in Snyder's pockets each year. Snyder uses his home office in his production of self-employment income. By establishing the home office deduction, Snyder realizes annual cash savings of $203 from expenses otherwise taken as itemized deductions, $770 attributable to expenses deductible solely because of the home office, and $617 by establishing the home office as the principal work location.

Itemized deduction shift: Snyder is self-employed. With or without a home office deduction, he will deduct mortgage interest and property taxes. But with a home office, Snyder transfers 15.84 percent (the percentage of house space occupied by the home office) of his mortgage interest and property taxes from Schedule A to Schedule C. In Schedule C, the business expense deductions reduce Snyder's business income and his self-employment tax.

Expenses deductible because of home office: Without a home office, Snyder's home-

EXHIBIT 8-1. How Snyder Pocketed $1,590 Each Year from a Home Office Deduction.

FACTS: In 1984 Snyder will be filing a joint tax return with his wife. They earn $45,000 in taxable income per year. That puts them in the 38 percent income tax bracket. Mrs. Snyder earns $25,000 from her job as an employee in town. Mr. Snyder works out of his home and earns taxable income of $20,000 which is reported in Schedule C of his Form 1040.

Expenses deductible as itemized deductions:

Mortgage interest	$10,401	
Real estate taxes	947	
Casualty loss	-0-	
Total	$11,348 × 15.84%[1] Bus.	$1,798
Self-employment tax rate (applicable to $37,800 of 1984 business net profit)		× 11.3%
Benefit of converting a percentage of itemized deductions to business expenses		$ 203[2]

Expenses deductible because of home office:

Utilities	$1,704	
Insurance	310	
Repairs and maintenance benefiting entire residence	600	
Total	$2,614 × 15.84% Bus.	$ 414
Depreciation (Cost Recovery) on business area (15-year straight-line method)		845
Repairs and maintenance to business area		40
Total		1,299
Tax rate (income tax rate of 38%; self-employment tax rate of 11.3%; state tax rate of 10%)		× 59.3%
Benefit of deducting direct expenses of home office		$ 770

Conversion of commuting miles to secondary-work-location miles:

Number of miles commuting to office location per year	4,000
Per-mile operating cost	× 26¢
Commuting cost	$1,040
Tax rate (income tax rate of 38%; self-employment tax rate of 11.3%; state tax rate of 10%)	× 59.3%
Value of home office as principal place of business	$ 617

Total tax benefit of home office	$1,590
Tax refunds invested annually @ 12% for five years—annuity due factor	× 7.1152
Estimated cash flow from home office deduction	11,313[3]
Tax on home office when residence sold	2,788[4]
Net Cash Savings (Loss)	$8,525

[1] Based on square footage in Exhibit 8-5.
[2] Shareholder/employees do not reduce self-employment tax, but if the home office deduction lets you take money out of the corporation tax-free, you benefit by a reduction in both corporate and individual Social Security taxes.
[3] Snyder could have pocketed the entire $11,313 by making himself ineligible for a home office deduction and taking advantage of the tax-free rollover rules. See the discussion on avoiding tax on sale of the home office.
[4] Tax computed in Exhibit 8-2.

owner's insurance, utility bills, and repairs are personal expenses and are not deductible. By establishing a home office, Snyder is able to deduct a percentage of these expenses and depreciate a percentage of his home. The percentage is based on the square footage of the home office area.

What about furniture? Desks, lamps, chairs, file cabinets, and other equipment purposes are eligible for depreciation deductions, even when a home office is not claimed. You can also claim the investment tax credit in the year of purchase, provided you use the equipment more than 50 percent for business. Accordingly, the computation in Exhibit 8-1 does not consider depreciation or the investment tax credit on furniture because such deductions would be available whether or not you claim a home office.

Cash value of commuting mileage: Snyder lives 10 miles from his other office. If the other office were Snyder's principal workplace, he would have a 20-mile nondeductible commute each round trip. With 200 round trips a year, one each working day, Snyder would accumulate 4,000 miles of nondeductible mileage during a tax year at an average cost of 26 cents a mile.

Trips from a primary work location to a secondary work location are deductible. Making the home office his primary work location, Snyder increases his deductible automobile expenses by $1,040 and puts $617 in his pocket.

Caution: Mileage for commuting to your principal job location is never deductible. A home office which is not your principal place of business will not eliminate your commuting mileage, even if you use it in the normal course of business or for a second business.

Snyder nets $8,525: Using taxable income of $45,000 per year, the Snyders purchase a $90,000 new home in 1984 and expect to sell it in 1989 for a whopping $190,000. The Snyders expect to pay tax on the home office portion of the $100,000 in appreciation. After tax, the Snyders pocket a net amount of $8,525 solely because of the home office deduction.

When the Snyders set up the home office, they effectively divided their residence into two components: the living quarters and the office. The Snyders must treat the living quarters as a personal residence. The tax rules for personal residences apply to that portion. The office portion is treated as a commercial office, and the tax rules surrounding a commercial office apply.

Tax rules for personal residence: Proper application of the rules allows you to upgrade your personal residence tax-free. Then, when you retire to fun and sun, you may exclude from taxation up to $125,000 of the taxable gain.

The rollover: When you sell your old home and buy a new home, you are required to avoid income taxes under the tax-free rollover rule. The rollover rule requires you to defer tax on the gain from sale of your old principal residence when you purchase and occupy a new principal residence within 24 months of the sale of the old residence, and when the new residence costs more than you receive from the sale of the old residence.

The $125,000 exclusion: The $125,000 exclusion allows taxpayers age 55 or over to exclude from taxation up to $125,000 of gain from the sale of their principal residence. This once in a lifetime exclusion must be elected by attaching a signed statement to your income tax return. To qualify for the $125,000 exclusion, you or your spouse must be age 55 or over at the date of sale, and you must have owned and occupied the home for three of the five years before sale.

Taxation of home office: If you sell a home which contains a home office, you have sold two properties: (1) an office, and (2) a home. The home office sale is taxed the same as any other sale of commercial real property. If the home office has been in service for at least one year and one day, the proceeds are eligible for tax-favored capital gain treatment. Capital gain treatment allows you to deduct 60 percent of the gain; the remaining 40 percent is subject to regular income taxes.

Exhibit 8-2 shows how the Snyders computed their taxes on the sale of their home

EXHIBIT 8-2. How Snyder Computes Tax on Sale of Home With Home Office.

FACTS: In 1989 the Snyders sell their $90,000 (cost) home for $190,000. Even with appreciation of $100,000, the tax on the home office portion is only $2,788. Compare that with the $11,313 pocketed from the home office and the Snyders are $8,525 better off (Exhibit 8-1).

	TOTAL	RESIDENCE	HOME OFFICE
Projected sales price	$190,000		
Selling expenses	(15,000)		
Projected proceeds from sale	$175,000		
Estimated proceeds due to land	$ 50,000	$ 46,040	$ 3,960[1]
Estimated proceeds due to building	125,000	105,200	19,800[2]
Projected proceeds from sale	$175,000	151,240	23,760
Projected basis at date of sale		(76,536)	(9,240)[3]
Taxable gain		$ 74,704[4]	14,520
Less 60% capital gain deduction			(8,712)
Gain subject to tax			$ 5,808
Tax			$ 2,788[5]

[1] Appraisal established projected sales value of land at $50,000. IRS does not allow lawn or landscaping upkeep expenses as home office expenses. Since building occupies 50% of land area, home office land cost is computed: $50,000 x 15.84% x 50% = $3,960.

[2] Appraisal established projected sales value of building at $125,000. Projected value attributable to home office is $19,800 ($125,000 x 15.84%).

[3] No improvements are projected for five years of ownership. Thus, basis for home office is cost less depreciation computed as follows:

Land $10,000 x 7.92% =	$ 792
Building $80,000 x 15.84% =	12,672
Depreciation $\frac{\$80,000}{15}$ x 15.84% x 5 years =	(4,224)
	$ 9,240

[4] Taxpayer plans on buying more expensive replacement residence and deferring tax to later years.

[5] $5,808 x 48 percent (38 percent Federal tax plus 10 percent state tax).

Note: If Snyder were *not eligible* to claim a home office deduction in the year of sale, the entire gain on sale, including the $5,808 gain attributable to the home office, could be rolled over tax-free with the purchase of a more expensive home.

which contained a home office. Note that the Snyders used the appraisal prepared for the lending institution on behalf of the buyers as a basis for projecting the sales values between land and building.

Special treatment for land: The IRS proposed regulations do not allow lawn or landscaping upkeep expenses as home office expenses. Accordingly, in determining the sales proceeds from land, Snyder uses only the land area directly attributable to the building. That

special computation decreases the percentage of nondepreciable land associated with his home office and saves him money.

You must make a computation: Snyder realized three of the six possible economic benefits from claiming a home office deduction. You may or may not be so fortunate. The only way to know for sure is to make the computation yourself.

Use Exhibits 8-1 and 8-2 as model worksheets to compute your benefit from taking a home office deduction. Do not rely on "off-the-cuff" answers from a tax advisor. Make the computations yourself, have your tax advisor check the computations, and then discuss the merits of claiming a home office deduction.

WHAT DEPRECIATION METHOD TO SELECT

Your home is considered "placed in service" the day you move in and establish it as your principal residence. If you used your home as a personal residence prior to 1981, you are not eligible to use ACRS. You must use the old depreciation rules which were in effect at the time you first used the property as a personal residence.

Depreciable amount: You depreciate the building, not the land. You depreciate only that portion of the building which is used as a home office.

Lower of cost or market rule: If your home was used by you as a personal residence before you decided to take a home office deduction, you are subject to the "lower of cost or market rule." Under this rule, your depreciation or cost recovery deduction is computed using either your cost or the fair market value at the date of conversion, whichever is lower.

Example: You purchased your home in 1975 and used it as a personal residence in its entirety until 1986. During 1986, you establish 20 percent of your home as a home office and use it exclusively for that purpose on a regular basis. In depreciating the 20 percent, you are not allowed to use ACRS; you must use the old depreciation rules that were in effect in 1975 (when you first used the home). Furthermore, if the original cost of your home was $50,000 in 1975 and the fair market value at the date of conversion in 1986 was $90,000, you must use the $50,000 as your cost. You then allocate the cost to land and buildings based on either a tax assessor's statement or an independent appraisal. The portion of the $50,000 allocated to the home office portion of the building is the depreciable amount.

Straight-line or accelerated: Sound tactics dictate using accelerated depreciation whenever possible. Inflation causes money to decline in value; therefore, grab your money as early as possible. Accelerated depreciation or cost recovery allows you to grab your money earlier. But with a home office deduction, the rules are not so simple.

Home office is commercial property: To pick the right depreciation method for a home office deduction, you should read the rules on cost recovery discussed in Chapter 6 and review Exhibit 8-3.

If you purchased and moved into your home before 1981, you are subject to the old depreciation rules. If you select accelerated depreciation, you must recapture as ordinary income the excess accelerated over straight-line deduction. No recapture applies to the straight-line component of your accelerated deduction. In effect, the accelerated deductions act as interest-free government loans. You get the accelerated deductions now and pay back the accelerated deductions later. Therefore, if you are subject to the pre-1981 rules, you will almost always want to select accelerated depreciation.

If you are not eligible for a home office deduction in the year you sell your home, consider your home office eliminated. That's good—IF the home sale is not a taxable event. If the 24-month rollover rule makes the home sale a tax-free event, you should select accelerated recovery to put more money into your pockets.

If you do have taxable gain on the final sale of a home which contained a home office at some time, you must first report any ordinary income from that sale. Ordinary income arises from recapture of depreciation. Thus, if your taxable gain will exceed $125,000, you should select straight-line recovery.

HOW OLDER HOMES ARE PENALIZED BY THE HOME OFFICE

There is an ugly rule, "the lower of cost or market rule," that requires you to depreciate your home office based on the lower of cost or market value at the date you establish the office. Now, let's suppose that you have lived in your home for 10 years and it has appre-

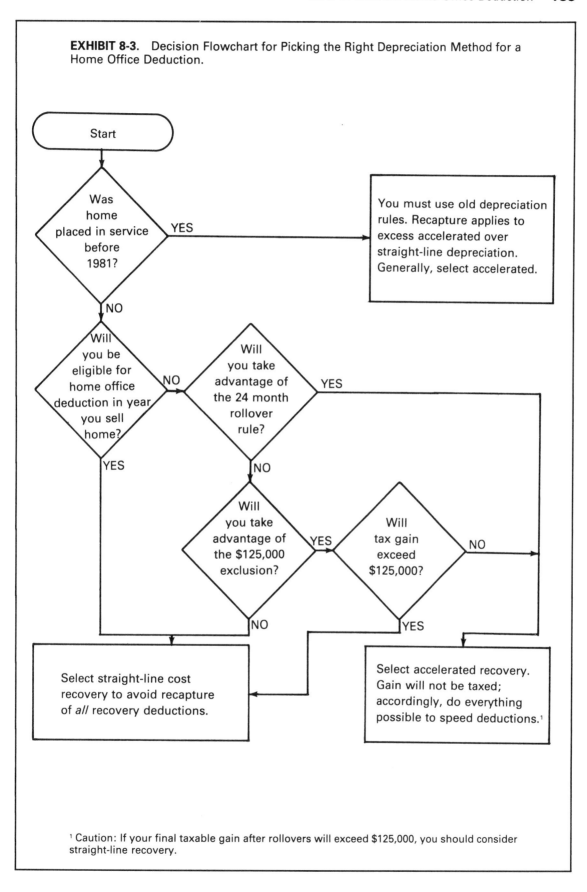

EXHIBIT 8-3. Decision Flowchart for Picking the Right Depreciation Method for a Home Office Deduction.

¹ Caution: If your final taxable gain after rollovers will exceed $125,000, you should consider straight-line recovery.

ciated from its original cost of $45,000 to $100,000. What happens if you establish a home office today?

First, the bad news. Your depreciation deduction is based on the $45,000, but some of that goes to land.

Second, the horrible news. You pay tax on the home office portion using the $45,000 base. If 10 percent of your home was used as a home office, and you sold the home one day after you established the home office, your taxable gain would be $5,500 [($100,000 − $45,000) × 10 percent].

Okay, one day is an exaggeration, but the rules are not. Once you establish a home office, you base your gain on the *lower* of original cost or fair market value on the date you establish the office. Therefore, you must carefully analyze the tax benefits of establishing an office in a home that you have owned for awhile.

AVOIDING TAX ON THE SALE OF A HOME WITH A HOME OFFICE

Remember, when you sell a personal residence that contains a home office, you are effectively selling two assets: your office and your home. IRS recently ruled (Rev. Rul. 82-26) that failure to meet the requirements for taking a home office deduction in the year of sale negates any business allocation for purposes of deferring gain under the tax-free rollover rule.

Example: In 1978 Nelson purchased a used home for $60,000 and established 20 percent of the home as her office. She used the office exclusively for business purposes on a regular basis from 1978 until 1985. At the beginning of 1985 Nelson converts the home office into a gameroom and uses it for personal purposes. (This is a violation of the home office rules; accordingly, she is not eligible to claim a home office deduction in 1985). In December of 1985 Nelson sells the home for $100,000 and purchases a new home for $101,000. Nelson is entitled to a tax-free rollover on the gain from sale of her old principal residence. The entire gain on the sale of the old residence (including the gain attributable to the

home office) is deferred and thus not taxable in the year of sale.

Note: Nelson must reduce the basis in her home for depreciation claimed because of the home office.

Keywords—not eligible: In Nelson's case, the keywords are "not eligible." If Nelson were eligible for the home office deduction, but failed to take it, the IRS could adjust her tax return to include the home office and tax her on the sale of that home office. She must violate one of the three magic rules (discussed later in this chapter) for claiming the deduction in order to convert her home office portion into a personal residence.

The $125,000 exclusion: The IRS reasons differently for the $125,000 exclusion. The exclusion applies only to the portion of your home that was used as a principal residence for three of the last five years. Thus, you will pay tax on the home office portion of your home if you qualified for the deduction for more than two of the last five years.

WHY A CORPORATION SHOULD RENT THE HOME OFFICE

If you operate your business as a regular corporation (not an S Corporation), either you can claim a home office deduction as an employee, or the corporation can rent the home office from you.

If you operate your business as a corporation, one of the things you are looking for is a way to get your money out of the corporation without having it taxed twice, first to the corporation and then to you as an individual. If the corporation leases the home office from you, the corporation gets a deduction for the rent. You receive rental income which is offset by home office expenses.

As a one-person corporation, receiving rent from the corporation is like moving money from your left pocket to your right pocket. The net effect is zero. The bottom line effect, however, is that you achieve a deduction for your home office expenses. Thus, the home office reduces the amount of actual tax you pay.

Moreover, you avoid double taxation. If the money coming out of the corporation for rent would otherwise have been paid to you as a dividend, it would have been taxed first as income to the corporation and second as a dividend to you individually.

Added bonus if your salary is low: If your 1985 corporate officer salary is $39,600 or less, both you and your corporation can reduce Social Security taxes by renting the home office.

Example: Byrne receives a 1985 salary of $39,600 from his one-person corporation. The total Social Security tax on both the corporation (left pocket) and Byrne individually (right pocket) is $5,584. Byrne's salary is dropped to $30,000 and he receives $7,800 in rental income from the corporation for rental of office space located in his home.

Result: Byrne's spendable income increases by $1,100 ($7,800 × 14.10% employer/employee Social Security tax rate). Moreover, Byrne saves income taxes because the home office allows him to deduct otherwise nondeductibles such as homeowner's insurance.

Thus, you will want to have your corporation rent the home office from you if: (1) your salary is below the Social Security maximum or (2) your corporation is paying taxes.

If the corporation does rent, you are subject to the same rules as anyone else claiming a deduction.

HOW THE THREE RULES FOR A HOME OFFICE DEDUCTION WORK

Tax law, in its wisdom, has decreed that capitalism does not take place in your home, which is deemed a personal living expense. However, by legislative grace, you are allowed to claim tax deductions for mortgage interest, property taxes, and casualty losses. The itemized deductions for your personal residence were instituted by Congress, not out of the kindness of its heart, but to stimulate investments in housing.

Tax law also states that you may take a

further tax deduction for a home office if three circumstances exist: (1) you *regularly* use (2) an *exclusive* portion of your principal residence (3) for certain types of *business*.

Qualifying business use: The "certain types of business use" requirement for claiming a home office deduction is that you use the home office:

- As the principal place of business for any of your trades or businesses, including second businesses;
- As a place of business that is used by prospects, clients, or patients in meeting or dealing with you in the normal course of your trade or business; or
- In the case of a separate structure that is not attached to the dwelling unit, in connection with your trade or business.

The three rules (regular, exclusive, and business use) for claiming a home office deduction are quite straightforward, and probably not nearly as threatening as you might have imagined. Still, there are related tax laws that can act like iron fists to hammer down your deductions in certain circumstances.

We will discuss each of the three rules in more detail in just a moment. First, however, a reminder: your home office deduction is limited to the gross income derived from the business use of your personal residence after considering the deductions for mortgage interest, property taxes, and casualty losses.

Limitation on home office deduction: Business deductions with respect to your home office are allowable in the following order and only to the following extent:

1. Mortgage interest and real estate taxes are allowable as business deductions *to the extent of the gross income derived from use of your home office.* Any excess is claimed as itemized deductions.

2. Home office expenses, other than depreciation or cost recovery, are deducted *to the extent that gross income exceeds the deductions allowable in Number 1 above.*

3. If your gross income exceeds the deductions under the above two steps, you are allowed to deduct depreciation or cost recovery *to the extent of gross income.*

Exhibit 8-4 shows how to compute the limitation on the home office deduction.

Now, let's turn our attention back to the three basic rules of regular use, exclusive use, and business use.

Rule 1—regular use: Your facts and circumstances in conducting your business will determine whether or not you use your home office on a regular basis. Regular use means more than occasional or incidental use. Two hours a day, five days a week, has constituted regular usage.

Rule 2—exclusive use: To claim the home office deduction, you must set up a portion of your dwelling unit for business use, and you must use it for no other purpose. The business portion may be used for more than one business, but it may never be used for personal purposes.

When you set aside a full room as the portion of your residence devoted to business use, there is no problem claiming the deduction. But what happens when you set aside an area that is not a distinct physical segment of your home?

Deducting a portion of a room: Gomez set up her home office in various areas of her living room. The room contained furniture used exclusively for business and furniture used exclusively for personal purposes. Because of the size and shape of the living room, it was impossible to put all of the business assets in one segregated area. Gomez was denied a home office deduction because she had not set up a clearly defined "portion" of her home as a business office.

Gomez's failure to have all the assets set up in a clearly defined "portion" of her home was the sole reason she was denied the home

---

EXHIBIT 8-4. How the Limitation on a Home Office Deduction Works.

RULE: The deduction for a home office may not exceed the gross revenue generated from a home office operation.

FACTS: Kaiser runs a part-time consulting business from her home. She earned $5,000 but incurred expenses of $5,680. Kaiser loses $680 of otherwise deductible depreciation.

Gross income from home office activities		$5,000
Expenditures to conduct home office activities:		
Expenses for secretary	$1,000	
Business telephone	800	
Supplies	200	2,000
Gross income derived from home office activities		3,000
Deductions for mortgage interest and property taxes:		
Mortgage interest $8,000 × 20% for home office	1,600	
Property taxes $1,000 × 20% for home office	200	1,800
Limit on further deductions		1,200
Deductions for maintenance and operation of home office:		
Homeowner's insurance $400 × 20% for home office	80	
Utilities $2,000 × 20% for home office	400	
Repairs to outside of home $2,000 × 20% for home office	400	880
Limit on further deductions		320
Depreciation or cost recovery $5,000 × 20% for home office		1,000
Amount of depreciation that is not deductible		$ 680

office deduction. In her previous home, in which she was allowed a home office deduction, she had set up a clearly defined *portion of one room* for her business office.

Hint: If you will use only a portion of a room, keep all business furniture together.

Rule 3—business use: You must use your home office as either a principal office location for one of your businesses or in the normal course of one of your businesses.

First choice—principal business location: The home office deduction is available for any of your businesses. This is a recent change. If you have a first business, second business, and third business, for example, and your home office is the principal location of your second business, you may claim a home office deduction for that second business.

When a single business has more than one office, then one office is the principal office and the other office is the secondary office. In determining which office is the principal business location, the IRS scrutinizes the following facts and circumstances:

- The portion of the total income from business activities that is attributable to activities at each location;
- The amount of time spent in business activities at each location; and
- The facilities available at each location.

To qualify as your principal place of business, your home office must be the focal point of your business activities. The focal point is determined based on those facts and circumstances, and such determination includes where you spend your time working, how much money you make, and what kinds of facilities you have available. If you fail the principal business test, your only other choice for claiming the home office deduction is to use it in the normal course of your business. We will discuss that below; meanwhile, let's concentrate on what your principal place of business is and the advantage of making your home office your principal place of business.

Eliminate personal commuting: Trips from your home to your principal place of business are personal and do not qualify as deductible expenses. Thus, the only way to eliminate commuting mileage is to live close to your office or have your office in your home. If your office is in your home, you will not have to drive to work (unless you have a really big home). But for your home to be your principal place of business, your home must be the focal point of your business activities.

Example: Baie operated a food stand located near her residence. The stand contained no kitchen facilities; accordingly, Baie used the kitchen of her home to prepare food to sell at the food stand. She also used one room of her home exclusively as a business office for keeping books and records related to her food stand. Baie was denied a home office deduction because the food stand was her principal place of business, not her home.

Baie's food stand was the focal point of her business, not her home. The kitchen failed to qualify because it was not used exclusively for business purposes. The bookkeeping chores failed to qualify because the money was not collected at home and the sales took place at the food stand. Remember, to qualify as your principal business location, business transactions must be conducted from the home office.

If you owned six rental properties, for example, and had tenants pay rent to your home office, you would be using the home office as the focal point for your business activities.

Second choice—usage in the normal course of business: If you do not use your home office as your principal place of business, then your only other choice for qualifying for the deduction is to use the home office as a place to meet or deal with clients, patients, and prospects in the normal course of your business. This exception applies only if the use of the home office by your clientele is substantial and integral to the conduct of your business. Occasional meetings are insufficient to make this exception applicable.

Magic words: The magic words for this exception are "meet" or "deal" with clients, patients, or customers. The general connotation given to the term "meet" is to be able to look someone in the eye, press his flesh or kick him in the shin.

Surprisingly, the U.S. Tax Court once ruled that the term "deal" includes contact *by telephone*. However, an appeals court disagreed, and the Tax Court has now changed its interpretation. Thus, to "meet" or "deal" with a client, customer, patient, or prospect in your home office, the individual must be *physically present* in your home office.

Amount of use: How often must you meet with clients, customers, patients, or prospects for such meetings to constitute the "normal course of business"? At a minimum, you must prove that such meetings are ordinary, usual occurrences in your business, not occasional, spur-of-the-moment, or last-minute accommodations to someone's schedule. In other words, home office meetings must be an integral part of the way you do business.

If you have home office meetings only once a week, such meetings may constitute the "ordinary course of business" if you have several meetings on that one day. On the other hand, if you have only one or two home office meetings on any one day, schedule meetings on two or more days each week.

Telephone use is still important: Although telephone contact does not constitute "meeting" or "dealing" with customers, clients, patients, or prospects, keep track of phone calls anyway.

Anyone who regularly uses a home office and uses a home office in the normal course of business will regularly use a home telephone for business purposes. By proving such regular use of your home telephone, you support your claim of regular home office use and use in the "normal course of business."

Separate structure exception: You may qualify for a home office deduction if in connection with your trade or business you use a separate structure which is not attached to your dwelling unit. The separate structure must be used exclusively and on a regular basis in connection with your trade or business. An artist's studio, a florist's greenhouse, and a carpenter's workshop are examples of structures that fall within the separate structure requirements.

With a separate structure, you don't need to meet the "principal-place-of-business" or the "deal-with-customers" test. However, it must be used regularly and exclusively for your business.

Example: Berry operates a floral shop in town. Behind his house is a greenhouse and a garage. In the greenhouse, Berry grows the plants he sells in his shop. In the garage, Berry stores bulbs, fertilizer, and other supplies for making plants grow. Both the greenhouse and garage are used exclusively and regularly in Berry's business. The expenses for the greenhouse and garage are deductible.

WHY EMPLOYEES NEED PERMISSION TO HAVE A HOME OFFICE DEDUCTION

To qualify for home office status as an employee, the work at home must be for the convenience of your employer. Tax law does not define "convenience of your employer," but that basically means whatever you're doing at home must be part of your job. Moreover, it should be part of the work agreement with your employer. That's true even if you run a one-person corporation.

Example: Aab was a cancer researcher who spent four hours a day in a laboratory provided by her employer. The employer did not provide her with an office or desk space where she could do the writing required by her job. Although she probably spent more time writing at home, the court ruled that her principal place of business was the laboratory, since her business was that of cancer research and the laboratory was the focal point of the research.

Thus, the only way Aab could qualify for the home office deduction was if the space in her home was used for the convenience of her employer. That should have been no problem, but Aab had no agreement with her employer. She needed a written agreement with her employer spelling out that she would not be provided with office or desk space where she could do the writing required by her job. The agreement should have stated that she was required to find and pay for the necessary office or desk space to do the required writing.

Hint: If you are an employee and plan to claim a home office deduction because it is for the convenience of your employer, put that understanding in writing, preferably at the time you start employment.

SPECIAL RULES FOR STORAGE SPACE

The home office area includes storage space for inventories of products that will be sold at retail or wholesale prices, but only if the dwelling unit is the sole fixed location of your trade or business for which the inventory is stored. To deduct costs for the portion of your dwelling unit devoted to storage space, the inventory stored therein must be wedded to the business conducted from your home. Furthermore, the inventory stored within your residence must be for use in a trade or business of selling products at retail or wholesale. The storage unit includes only the space actually used for storage; thus, if you store inventory in a portion of the basement, the storage space includes only that area even if you make no other use of the rest of the basement.

There is no escaping the requirement that the inventory stored in your home must be related to a business conducted from your home. Although this restriction has produced some ludicrous results, violate it and you will receive a uniformly hostile review from the IRS.

Example: Garvey was a registered druggist for a pharmacy where he also served as a company officer and shareholder. The pharmacy was physically located in a medical complex, but contained only limited storage space for the drug inventory. Garvey set up a storage area for the drug inventory in the garage attached to his personal residence. The garage was devoted solely to the storage of drugs and Garvey possessed, in accordance with state law, the only keys to the garage, which was kept locked at all times. The court ruled that Garvey was not entitled to a home office storage deduction. In order for Garvey to qualify for the deduction, the dwelling unit in which the inventory storage was located must have been the sole fixed location of Garvey's pharmacy. In this case, the taxpayer had a fixed place of business apart from his personal residence. Accordingly, Garvey was denied a home office deduction for storage space.

Summary of rules: To deduct an expense for storage of inventory, you must meet *all* of the following five tests:

1. The inventory must be kept for use in your trade or business, and
2. Your trade or business must be the wholesale or retail selling of products, and
3. Your home must be the only fixed location of your trade or business, and
4. The storage space must be used on a regular basis, and
5. The space used must be a separately identifiable place suitable for storage.

SPECIAL RULES FOR DAYCARE CENTERS

If you use a portion of your home to provide daycare services for children or for individuals who have attained age 65, or for individuals who are physically or mentally incapable of caring for themselves, you can qualify for a home office deduction. Moreover, the space allocated to daycare need not be used "exclusively." You could, for example, use the space for daycare from 8:00 AM to 5:00 PM, and then for personal purposes the rest of the day and still qualify for a deduction.

Definition of daycare services: Daycare services are services which are primarily custodial in nature; in other words, you are taking care of people. Daycare services may include educational, developmental, or enrichment activities which are incidental to the primary care services. If the services performed in the home are primarily educational or instructional in nature, however, they do not qualify as daycare services.

The determination of whether or not particular activities are incidental to or primarily for care services generally depends on all the facts and circumstances of the case. Educational instruction to children of nursery school age is considered incidental to the care services. Further, educational instruction to children of kindergarten age would ordinarily be considered incidental to the custodial services if the instruction is not in lieu of public instruction under a compulsory state educational requirement. In addition, enrichment instruction in arts and crafts to children, handicapped individuals, or the elderly ordinarily would be considered incidental to the care services.

Licensing requirement: To be eligible for a home office deduction because of daycare services, the daycare center must be appropriately licensed with the state. If no state license is required, then no license need be obtained.

Special allocation formula: In determining the deduction for daycare services, you first determine the appropriate square footage allocation (discussed later in this chapter). Once you have the square footage, you must make a further allocation based on the time that your dwelling is used for providing daycare services. For example, if the daycare portion of your dwelling is used for daycare services an average of 36 hours each week during the taxable year, the fraction to be used for making the allocation required is $^{36}/_{168}$, the ratio of the number of hours of daycare use in a week to the total number of hours in a week.

If the daycare portion of your home is used exclusively for that purpose, no time allocation is required.

HOW TO ALLOCATE SQUARE FOOTAGE

You may use any method that is reasonable under the circumstances to determine the expenses allocable to your home office. For instance, if the rooms in your home are of approximately equal size, you may allocate the general expenses for the unit according to the number of rooms used for business purposes. You may also allocate expenses according to the percentage of the total floor space in the unit that is used for business purposes.

If there are common areas involved in getting to and from your home office area, it may be appropriate to use the net square footage method for the allocation. Under this method you subtract the common areas (such as entries) in computing the square footage space. This method will increase the allocable percentage for home office expenses.

Exhibit 8-5 shows a diagram of the second floor in Snyder's house where his home office was located. To get there, a customer had to enter through the front door and go to the first room at the top of the stairs.

The exhibit analyzes the three choices. Net square footage turned out to be the most favorable. To derive this number, Snyder eliminated the areas where customers and prospects used the same areas as the family. Since Snyder saw a lot of people in his home, his rationale seems appropriate for his circumstances.

EVIDENCE TO SUPPORT A HOME OFFICE DEDUCTION

If you decide that a home office deduction is worthwhile, you must establish the necessary evidence to support your deduction. Remember, the burden is on you to prove that you used the home office in accordance with the rules. You must set up evidence to convince an IRS auditor that you are entitled to a home office deduction.

In developing support for your home office deduction, put yourself in the IRS examiner's place (just for a moment!) and ask, "What documents would convince a skeptic of:

- Exclusive use?
- Regular use?
- Primary business location?
- Dealings with clients, patients, and prospects?
- Revenue sources?
- Expenses?"

Must you be convincing? Absolutely! The IRS automatically views most claims to a home office as unfounded. You must be in a position to assert otherwise; accordingly, here are some helpful suggestions.

Photogaph the office: You use a home office today, but will you use it tomorrow? There's no way to know for certain; therefore, a photograph of your present office will provide proof that the office existed. Establish the vintage of your photograph with a processing date to show when the home office existed.

Finally, make sure that the photographs

EXHIBITS 8-5. Example Computation of Home Office Square Footage.

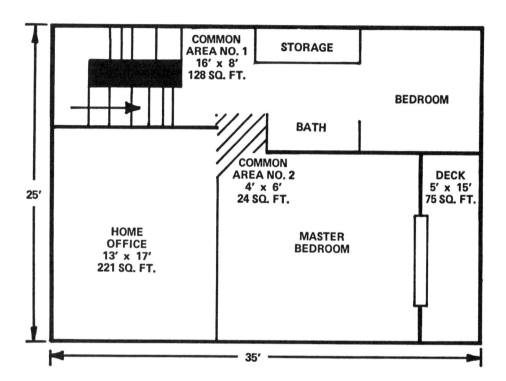

SECOND FLOOR

THREE CHOICES

1. Number of rooms office occupies, divided by total rooms in house.
2. Total square footage office occupies as a percentage of total square footage in house.
3. Net square footage applicable to office use.

COMPUTATION OF NET SQUARE FOOTAGE

Total Square Footage 25′ × 35′ × 2

Floors		1,750
Deduct:		
Common Areas:		
First floor entry and stairway	128	
Second floor stairway and landing	128	
Second floor common area	24	
Deck (not a living area)	75	355
Net Square Footage Base		1,395

ANALYSIS OF CHOICES BASED ON

1. Number of rooms 1/8 — 12.50%
2. Total square footage 221/1675 (1750 — 75 for deck) = 13.19%
3. Net square footage 221/1395 = 15.84%

establish exclusive use. Take close-ups of the bookcase containing only business-related books. Open the file drawers and take photographs of the tabs.

A good photo session will (1) show that the office existed, (2) document when it existed, and (3) support the essential element of exclusive use.

Keep a work activity log: Your home office may be either your primary business location or a place to meet and deal with clients, patients, or prospects. In either case, you must have supporting documents.

A work activity log (embellished appointment book) offers an excellent supporting document to establish where you spend your work time. The log is a journal of daily activities broken down into time periods. Since time is one of the key tests for primary location, you need the log to prove where you spend the most work time. It could disclose, for example, four hours of effort from your home office and two hours from your other office. The log should disclose types of activities at each location such as:

- business phone calls
- client prospect contacts
- types of paperwork
- studying, reading, and so forth.

Exhibit 8-6 contains an example of a work activity log for a typical morning. The log consists of notations in the appointment book. "HO" stands for home office location. "OO" stands for other office location. "CO" stands for client office location. In Exhibit 8-6, the taxpayer spent five hours in his home office, two hours in his other office, and two hours meeting with clients in their offices. He met with Al Lincoln at 10:00 AM in his home office to get a contract signed. That signing is noted in the appointment book.

You should keep the log often enough to establish where you spend your time working and making money. Frequently, test periods will provide a sound basis for your deduction. You can use six week-long test periods if your work activities are relatively consistent from week to week. More test periods are necessary if you have a volatile work pattern.

Caution: Volatile work patterns could negate regular use! To substantiate the home office deduction, you must use the home on a regular basis each and every week, except for vacations and similar absences.

More than one office: Your deductions for business use of your home cannot be more than the gross income from the business use of your home. If you have *one* business operated from two locations (home office and other office), you must divide your income between the locations to figure this limit. The IRS states that you should consider the amount of time you spend at each location in making this division. Your time log is essential in this situation.

Keep a guest book: You must establish use of your home office in the normal course of business. If that involves meeting and dealing with clients, patients, prospects, and colleagues, have them sign a guest book each time they come to your office. It's easy, and it's a terrific supporting document.

Exhibit 8-7 illustrates a typical guest book. Note how Al Lincoln signed the book to corroborate the entry in the appointment book. Also, since Al Lincoln signed the contract in the home office, evidence for income production from the home office is obtained.

Use business cards with a home office phone number: Where can you be reached for business? If you can be reached at either your home office or another office location, your business card should include telephone numbers for both.

Make your name the most prominent item on the business card. List both your general office and home office phone numbers. If you regularly meet clients in your home, have your residence address on the cards.

Make sure you are listed in the white pages of the telephone book and, if allowed by state law, have a listing in the yellow pages.

Establish phone usage: Your home office activities probably include telephone discussions with clients, referral sources, patients, prospects, and colleagues. If you want a deduction

EXHIBIT 8-6. Work Activity Log (Embellished Appointment Book).

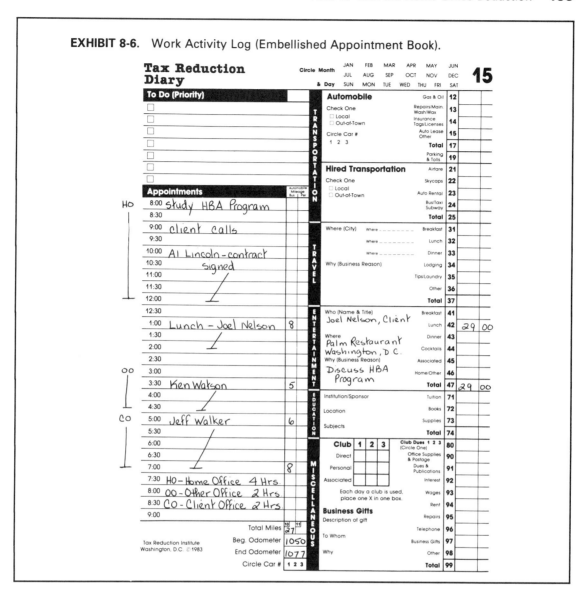

for at least a portion of your phone bill, log in test periods of incoming and outgoing phone calls. A by-product is more support for your regular use in the normal course of business.

When additional phone services are necessary to accommodate your business activities, you have more support for substantial business usage and, of course, deductions for the extra phone charges. Common examples include an answering service, an answer phone, call forwarding, and a separate business line.

Keep business mail: When you operate at least a portion of your business from your home, you will receive mail addressed to the home office. Keep dated correspondence to corroborate entries in your log indicating that you read business mail. A test approach may be appropriate for you and, if used, it should coincide with your activity logs.

Retain receipts and paid invoices: Canceled checks prove that you paid for something. Receipts and invoices support the checks by proving what you paid for.

You have two types of home expenses: (1) those that benefit the entire home, and (2) those solely for the home office.

You need to keep track of both types. You are allowed to deduct a portion of the ex-

EXHIBIT 8-7. Guest Book for Home Office.

Cover: **Inside:**

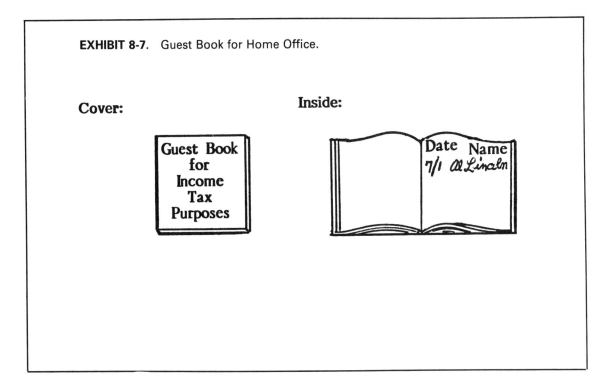

penses that benefit the entire home, and you are allowed to deduct all expenses that benefit the home office. Such expenses include, among others:

- business telephone and allocation of residential phone
- office supplies
- depreciation on office assets
- mortgage interest
- property taxes
- homeowner's insurance
- water, light, and heat
- maintenance
- depreciation (recovery) of a portion of structure based on square footage or rooms.

Business equipment: In your home office you will undoubtedly have a desk, chair, bookcase, lamp, and other equipment for operating your office. Read the chapters on depreciation, cost recovery, and the investment tax credit for details on how to handle business equipment.

HOW TO REPORT THE HOME OFFICE DEDUCTION IN YOUR TAX RETURN

If you file Schedule C with your Form 1040, your home office deduction is no secret to the IRS. In fact, you must check one of those scary boxes to let the IRS know what you are doing. The box asks the question, "Did you claim a deduction for an office in your home?"

If you are claiming a home office as an employee and file the employee business expense form (Form 2106), the IRS is able to zero right in on your home office in your tax return.

Since the home office can't hide in your tax return, make sure you have the necessary supporting documents in your files. Then, reduce your chances of audit selection because of the home office deduction by adding a footnote saying, "Taxpayer regularly uses an exclusive portion of the home in the normal course of business in meeting and dealing with clients and prospective customers. Accordingly, taxpayer has claimed the deduction for an office in the home. Gross revenues from the office exceed expenses, and amounts claimed in the return are in accordance with IRS regulations."

The addition of such a footnote to your tax return tells the audit classifier that you aren't just some schmo—you know what you are doing. Such a note can significantly reduce your chances of audit selection.

SUMMARY

The home office deduction will help line your pockets if you qualify for it and follow the rules for exclusive and regular use. Also, you must determine up front whether your office will be a principal place of business or used in the normal course of business. Once that determination is made, you can start establishing evidence to prove your business usage.

Take the time now to analyze the worth of a home office deduction. It could have more economic value than you think. The only way to know for sure is to make a few computations.

If you decide that a home office deduction is worthwhile, start now to establish the necessary supporting evidence. Remember, the burden of proof is on you. You must be able to convince an IRS auditor that you are entitled to a home office deduction. Get your ammunition ready!

TAX REDUCTION CHECKLIST

IRS publications to be obtained:

- Publication 587—*Business Use of Your Home*
- Publication 523—*Tax Information on Selling Your Home*
- Publication 530—*Tax Information for Homeowners*
- Publication 911—*Tax Information for Direct Sellers*

Basic rules for home office deduction:

- Area is set up for exclusive use.
- Area is used regularly.
- Area is used as
  - Primary business location.
  - Place of business for patients, clients, and customers.
  - Principal office for a second business.

Special rules:

- Employees need written agreement with employer.
- Storage space for wholesale and retail products is exempt from principal business location or place of business for patients, clients, customers tests.
- Daycare centers licensed by state are exempt from exclusive use test.

Limitation on deduction:

- May not exceed income from home office activity.

Economic reasons for taking a home office deduction:

- New deductions for otherwise nondeductibles.
- Reduces Social Security taxes for self-employed reporting business income less than Social Security maximum.
- Reduces double taxation of closely held corporations.
- Eliminates personal nondeductible commuting mileage, if principal office.
- Produces tax-favored capital gain when sold.
- Tax on sale can be avoided if no home office in year of sale.

Tax rules for sale of personal residence:

- Capital gain—if owned and used for more than one year.
- Tax-free rollover—if you purchase and occupy a new principal residence within 24 months of the sale of the old residence; and if the new residence costs more than you receive from the sale of the old residence.
- $125,000 exclusion—if you or your spouse are age 55 or over at date of sale and you have owned and occupied your home for three of the last five years.

Depreciation methods:

- Tax-free rollover—accelerated depreciation or recovery.
- $125,000 exclusion—accelerated depreciation or recovery.
- Taxable sale—pre-1981 home—accelerated depreciation or recovery.
- Taxable sale—post-1980 home—straight-line recovery.

Supporting documents include:

- Photographs.
- Business cards.
- Phone listings and usages.
- Work activity log.
- Guest book.

- Business mail.
- Receipts, invoices, and canceled checks.

Miscellaneous considerations:

- Add a note to reduce chances of audit selection.
- Conversion back to residence may avoid tax.
- Pay attention to square footage allocation to increase deduction.
- Lawn care is not deductible—it may reduce gain.
- Older homes may be penalized.

Uncle Sam will help underwrite the costs of your continuing business education. If you are established in a trade or business and are continuing to get smart, you may write off your educational expenses as business expenses—whether you are self-employed, an employee, or an outside salesperson. Writing off your educational expenses, especially when the education is expensive, is not always easy. There's often a fine line between deductible and nondeductible educational expenses. Being on the right side of the line requires careful attention to documenting the *reasons* for the education, the relationship between the education and your business or profession, and, of course, the amounts of your expenses.

You may be surprised to discover the variety of expenses that you may write off, provided you land on the right side of that fine line. For example, the owner of a small business was allowed to write off the costs of obtaining a pilot's license. An engineer was allowed to write off all costs of getting a master's degree in business administration (MBA). Teachers who wish to become administrators may write off their educational costs. You may even be able to write off the cost of your summer vacation—if you are traveling to get educated.

On the other hand, the IRS often accuses taxpayers of trying to rob the Treasury. Recently, for example, an air traffic controller was not allowed to write off his costs of getting an instrument rating. Real estate agents have been denied write-offs for courses that would allow them to become real estate brokers. And for every deductible summer vacation, at least three are disallowed.

You will learn how to walk that fine line to educational expense write-offs in this chapter. Specifically, you will learn:

- How to meet the qualifying standards for educational write-offs.
- How to prove that education maintains or improves your skills.
- How to write off travel as an educational expense.
- How to write off education while away from home.
- What expenses you can write off.
- How to avoid the local transportation trap.
- How to report educational expenses.

HOW TO MEET THE QUALIFYING STANDARDS

Let's start with the basics. The flowchart in Exhibit 9-1 summarizes the basic requirements for writing off your educational expenses.

9
How to Get Smart With Tax Subsidies for Educational Expenses

Exhibit 9-1 shows the five essential questions you must answer in order to write off your educational expenses. Each of these is discussed separately below. Before moving on to the individual questions, however, let's summarize the requirements.

Summary: You may write off your educational expenses if:

- You have already met the minimum educational requirements for your trade, business, or profession;
- You are established in your trade, business, or profession;
- The education will maintain or improve the skills you need in your existing trade, business, or profession; *or*, the education meets the express requirements of your employer or law as a condition to retaining your status; *and*
- The education will not qualify you for a new trade, business, or profession.

We know that's quite a mouthful. But we wanted to give you a concise statement of the rule for future reference.

Now, let's break down the rule into its five separate parts.

Part 1—Minimum education: You may not write off the costs of obtaining the minimum education required for your trade, business, or profession. The minimum requirements are established by state or local law, certification standards of a profession, standards of a trade, or the requirements of an employer.

Examples of nonqualifying educational expenses are those for courses or training leading to

- A license to sell real estate.
- A license to sell insurance.
- A license to practice medicine, law, or public accounting.
- A license to teach.

Similarly, if you're required to get specific training or education in order to qualify for a certain job, the expenses are not deductible.

On the other hand, once you have met the minimum requirements, it doesn't matter if the requirements are later changed. In fact, education is generally deductible if it is re- quired for you to *maintain* your position. This includes education necessary to meet new requirements imposed after you initially qualified.

Example: A high school hires college graduates who have at least 20 credit hours of education courses. Two years later, the rules are changed to require at least 30 credit hours, and all employees are given five years to meet the new requirements. Expenses for the new courses are deductible, because the employees had already met the minimum educational requirements at the time the new requirements were imposed.

If your trade, business, or profession does not have uniform licensing or certification requirements, your individual situation may require a closer look. Different employers may have different standards. The IRS says that you have not necessarily met the minimum requirements just because you are already employed. For example, you may be hired on a probationary basis and allowed to perform certain tasks, on the condition that you complete certain education. At that point, you would be taken off of probationary status and allowed to perform all of the duties of your position. Until then, you would not be considered as having met the minimum educational requirements for your job. Therefore, you could not write off your expenses for getting the required education.

In other circumstances, the requirements of your particular employer may work to your advantage. Consider the case of Toner.

Toner case: Toner was a parochial school teacher who met the minimum educational requirements of her employer—a high school education. In order to retain her status, Toner was required to take at least six college credits a year until she obtained her bachelor's degree. The public schools, however, would hire only teachers who already had their bachelor's degree. Because of the public schools' requirement, the IRS denied Toner's write-off.

Toner won her case and was allowed her deduction. She proved that a high school education was the minimum standard set by her employer. She was a full-fledged member of her school's faculty. Therefore, her continuing education was required for her to *retain*

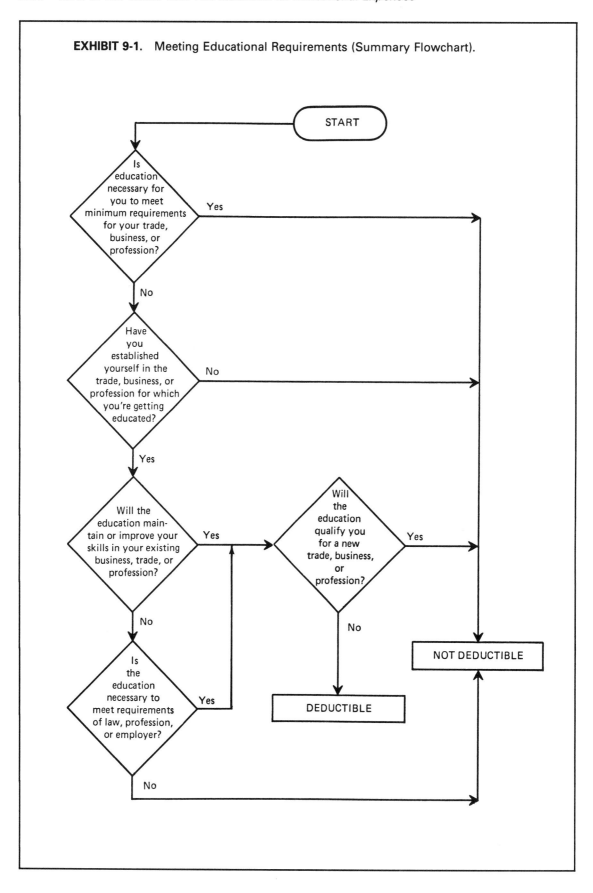

EXHIBIT 9-1. Meeting Educational Requirements (Summary Flowchart).

her position, not meet the minimum requirements for it.

Part 2—Be in business: Since your educational expense write-off is permitted only as a business expense, you must actually be *in business* for your educational expenses to be deductible. In other words, you must be employed or self-employed at the time you incur your educational expenses.

Therefore, you cannot immediately start deducting your continuing education expenses once you have met the minimum educational requirements for your profession. You must actually *begin working* in your profession before educational expenses are deductible. A young attorney named Kohen missed out on some very large deductions because of this failure.

Kohen case: Kohen graduated from law school, took the bar exam, and was licensed to practice law in Pennsylvania. Instead of going into law practice right away, however, Kohen decided to continue his education. When Kohen tried to write off the expense of his post-graduate education (in the law of taxation!), the IRS balked. Kohen went to the Tax Court, but to no avail. Why? Because Kohen was never in business. Kohen had given some free legal advice to members of his family, but the court ruled that this activity fell far short of being in business.

Temporary absences: Vacations, leaves of absence, or other temporary absences from your business will not prevent you from taking an educational expense write-off. The IRS has a general rule that a period of one year or less is okay, provided you resume the same type of work after you finish your educational program. If you do not intend to resume the same general type of work, your education obviously cannot be justified as an expense associated with that work.

Although the IRS uses the one-year rule as a general guideline, your own facts and circumstances may justify a longer absence. The longer you have been in business, the longer and more expensive the education can be. When just starting in business, you may take many short training courses of from one to five days. The IRS will very seldom attack

your deduction for these programs. However, when you start spending lots of money and taking formal courses leading to degrees, you will find it more difficult to justify your deduction. You will find it particularly difficult if you leave your job in order to pursue full-time study. Here are two examples.

Furner case: Furner taught for three years, then resigned to take a year of graduate work. Although Furner did not take a leave of absence, she resumed teaching after completing her studies. Furner's deduction was allowed, since her three years of teaching before her graduate program and her resumption of teaching afterwards proved that she was in the business of teaching.

Reisine case: Reisine, an engineer, was employed for less than one year when he returned to school for an advanced engineering degree. He was not allowed a deduction for the expenses. He failed to show that he was in the business of engineering.

Part 3—Skills: The first two parts of the educational expense test are the preliminaries: you have established that you meet the minimum educational requirements and that you are in a particular business. Now you must prove one of two things: (1) that the education improves or maintains skills you need in your business, or (2) that the education meets the express requirements of the law, or your business, or your employer, in order to retain your position. We will discuss the skills test first.

Many types of education obviously qualify under the skills test. Short courses, programs, seminars, or workshops dealing with current developments in your area will satisfy the IRS. Similarly, refresher courses qualify.

Other types of education may qualify, but are harder to justify because their connection with the improvement of your skills is not so obvious. For example, a deputy district attorney named Kosmal was entitled to write off the cost of Spanish lessons. The reason? Kosmal worked in a community that had many Spanish-speaking people. The lessons improved his ability to interview witnesses and victims in cases he was handling.

On the other hand, a research engineer named Joyce was not allowed a deduction for

French lessons. There was no obvious connection between Joyce's work and the French lessons, and Joyce was unable to prove that there was a connection. Similarly, an insurance company employee named Coughlin was denied a deduction for philosophy, sociology, and economics courses. Again, he was unable to prove that the courses would maintain or improve his business skills.

Cases similar to Joyce's and Coughlin's have reached opposite results where the taxpayers were able to show the necessary connection between the education and their jobs. Remember the magic words, "ordinary and necessary" that are used in the Internal Revenue Code and by the courts. If you can show that your education was "appropriate, needed, helpful, customary, usual, or normal" in your business, you can get a deduction.

Example: Knudtson slipped out of the IRS's grasp when he proved to the Tax Court that his expenses for obtaining a pilot's license were ordinary and necessary business expenses. Knudtson was in the business of rebuilding automobile windshield wiper motors. He bought a plane to allow him to visit suppliers and customers, which were located over a large geographic area. The court, noting that it was particularly important for Knudtson to maintain a close working relationship with his suppliers, said: "Obviously, the expense of owning and operating the plane is *necessary* in the sense that it is *appropriate and needful* to the development of Knudtson's business. It is a *normal and natural response* to the specific conditions under which Knudtson conducts his business." Since Knudtson needed the plane for his business, he also needed to learn how to fly it. Therefore, the court allowed his deduction for flying lessons.

Stoddard case: In another case, Stoddard, a commercial airline pilot who usually flew a DC-9, was allowed to write off his expenses of maintaining and operating a single-engine airplane. Stoddard proved that any plane having seven basic instrument gauges could be used to improve a pilot's basic skills needed to fly the DC-9 on instruments. Having established that he operated the plane for this educational purpose, Stoddard was allowed the deduction.

Part 4—Express requirements: Even though you have met the minimum requirements for your business, you may be required to continue your education at some later time. This might be because of new requirements. Or, as in many professions, you must fulfill certain continuing education requirements. Also, your boss may decide that you need further education—such as computer training—in order to retain your position. In each of these cases, your expenses would be deductible, provided you met the other requirements.

The "express requirements" of the educational expense rules is an alternative to the "skills" part. The reason is simple. If the education is required for you to retain your position, it must be necessary for your business. In short, the IRS cannot second-guess your boss, your state or local legislature, or your professional governing body. Many states now require certain minimum continuing education for various professionals, such as doctors, lawyers, accountants, insurance salespeople, real estate salespeople, and others. If you can establish that you are in one of those professions and can properly document your expenses, you should have no problem justifying your deduction for such courses.

Part 5—New trade or business: The last hurdle on your way to a deduction for educational expenses is sometimes the most difficult. Even if your education improves your skills or is required for you to retain your job, it is not deductible if it is part of a program of study that will qualify you for a new trade or business. It makes no difference whether you actually intend to engage in that new business. Even though you stay in your old job, you still may not deduct the expenses.

The key question is: What is a new trade or business? The IRS and the courts have given us some general guidelines to follow. First, a mere change of duties does not amount to a new trade or business if you are doing the *same general type of work* that you are doing now. Second, an advancement in your business or profession is not considered a change, even though you may be doing somewhat different tasks. Third, the IRS considers teaching and related duties as one trade or business. For example, a classroom teacher may deduct the education necessary to become a guidance counselor or a principal. Here are some specific examples:

- A dentist may deduct all expenses of postgraduate study to specialize in orthodontics.
- A medical doctor may deduct the expenses incurred to specialize in obstetrics.
- A psychiatrist may deduct the expenses of study and training at an accredited psychoanalytic institute that will lead to qualification as a psychoanalyst.

On the other hand, obtaining a law degree or CPA designation is never deductible, even though you do not intend to practice law or public accounting. The same is true of just about any profession in which certification or licensing is required. Obviously, a medical education would not be deductible, even though you're a lawyer who wants to get rich on medical malpractice cases. Similarly, in a recent case, a real estate agent was not allowed to deduct education necessary for becoming a real estate broker. The court decided that since California law required specific education and training for a person to become a real estate broker, it must be a different trade or business from the business of being a real estate agent.

Beckley case: A good example of how the "new trade or business" rule works is the case of Beckley, a special agent for the Federal Bureau of Investigation. Beckley held a pilot's certificate when he started working for the FBI. In his first four years as an agent, Beckley had 20 missions as a pilot. Several of these were aborted because he lacked an instrument rating. To overcome this deficiency, Beckley took courses to obtain his instrument rating. He took further courses and obtained a commercial pilot's certificate and a certified flight instructor's rating.

The court allowed Beckley to deduct all expenses of obtaining his instrument rating, since the training greatly improved his skills as a pilot and special agent for the FBI. The expenses of obtaining the pilot's certificate and flight instructor's rating were not allowed, since these expenses were for new trades or businesses.

Beckley's case dramatizes the importance of good documentation. He was able to cite specific missions completed, as well as those aborted, to show why he needed the additional education.

HOW TO GATHER EVIDENCE TO PROVE THAT EDUCATION MAINTAINS OR IMPROVES YOUR SKILLS

The IRS is only too happy to question your claimed educational expense deduction. The burden of proof is on you, the taxpayer. Hundreds of tax cases on the educational expense deduction have been decided in the past decade. In most cases, the expenses themselves were properly documented, but in many, many cases, taxpayers were unable to document that the education improved their skills or met the express requirements of their jobs. On the other hand, good documentation won deductions.

That's why early consideration of the necessary documentation will spare you lots of headaches. The following paragraphs contain ideas on the types of documentation you should accumulate. Remember, the bigger the deduction, the better the documentation you need.

Prove your business: Can you prove how long you've been in business, or for that matter, that you're in business now? If you can't, you're in trouble right away. Most people will be able to prove this, however. Here's how.

Start by looking at your previous years' tax returns (Form 1040 or 1040A). Remember that little box in the upper right hand corner of the first page, just below the space for your Social Security number? The one that says "Your occupation"? What did you write? What did you list as your business on Schedule C? Since tax returns are signed under the penalty of perjury, the occupation or business that you have listed in the past should be very good evidence.

In addition to tax returns, you should have plenty of other written evidence of your past and present business. You should have your earnings records, all necessary certificates and licenses, business cards, diplomas, account books, diaries or business calendars, "dead" files, and any other types of documents commonly used in your business. All of these should, of course, be kept in permanent files.

Prove your skills or business requirements: The courts use a "common sense" test to determine whether your education

- Maintained or improved your skills.
- Was a requirement for entering your trade, business, or profession.
- Qualified you for a new trade, business, or profession.

This "common sense" test requires you to show the skills needed in your job, the skills you had before your educational program, and the skills you had after completing the program. Always ask yourself this question before taking any educational program: "How will this program help me in my business?" If you cannot answer this question in 25 words or less (and preferably 15 or less), you may have a problem justifying your deduction.

If you can answer this question in 25 words or less, write it down. Then go into more detail. Write down the types of skills you need in your job, the skills that you have, and the skills you believe the education will add or improve.

Example: Whittington, a Realtor, evaluated an MBA program by listing next to each course the skill he would get to make him a better sales manager and real estate broker. Next to "Psychology of Management" he wrote, "Will help me evaluate my management style and apply that style to the needs of my individual agents." Next to "Commercial Law," he wrote, "Will assist me in evaluating contracts, offers, and other legal matters, which face me on a daily basis." Whittington evaluated each course on how it would increase his skills and elevate his position in his existing business.

In some cases, it may be better to evaluate an educational program in terms of its overall business benefit. For example, an MBA program may, as a whole, be more beneficial than would the individual courses, standing alone.

Always keep the words *appropriate, helpful, needed, and useful* in mind. They will help you to look for other evidence to justify your deduction. Here are some ideas on what this other evidence might consist of:

- Magazine and newspaper articles on people in your line of work with credentials similar to the ones you seek.

- Letters and other correspondence from your colleagues that discuss educational needs.
- A letter or statement from your boss, manager, or other supervisor regarding the need for certain types of skills and education.
- Articles, especially from newsletters or magazines in your field, that discuss new developments and the educational needs of people in your profession.

Such evidence will help to establish that the education is appropriate, helpful, needed, and useful.

You may be wondering why all this documentation is necessary. After all, doesn't everybody know what types of education someone in your profession needs? No, they don't, especially IRS agents. Prove it to them. Keep those articles, letters, and anything else pertinent in your shoebox. Then, you will be ready just in case the the IRS questions your deductions. We hope that need will never arise, but we're asking you to be a good scout and be prepared.

HOW TO WRITE OFF TRAVEL AS AN EDUCATIONAL EXPENSE

At the beginning of this chapter, we said you would learn how to deduct the cost of your summer vacation. Well, this is it. That summer vacation just might be deductible if your purpose was to get educated.

Education is more than just sitting in a classroom or studying a book. Travel may be a form of education. Both the IRS and the courts recognize this. The classic example is the language teacher who travels to a foreign country to improve his or her proficiency in that language.

As with all travel, however, the *primary purpose* of your trip must be business.

Major activity must be business: Since travel is generally considered recreation, the IRS and the courts impose a somewhat tougher standard than on other forms of education. Specifically, you must prove that the major part of your activities directly maintain or improve skills you need in your business. Furthermore, simply having your employer's approval will not always justify your write-off.

Diary is crucial: If ever there was a need to keep a detailed diary of your activities, this is it. If you are traveling to get educated, you should write down—every single day—the activities that were educational *and why they were educational*. Also, it is very important to record the amount of time that you spent on these activities each day.

Here are some examples to help you explore the somewhat hazy boundaries of the definition of educational travel.

Example: A medical doctor and his wife specialized in alcoholic patient care and ran a clinic for their patients' treatment. They took a trip around the world to study alcoholism. The expenses were allowed because the trip maintained and improved their skills in conducting their clinic.

Example: Carney, a U.S. Army civil engineer, took a trip to Europe to study European geography. The court held that Carney's study was related to his work; however, it disallowed his expense, because he failed to prove that the major portion of his travel in Europe directly maintained or improved his skills.

Example: Duncan, a grade school math teacher, was not allowed to write off the cost of a 37-day trip to Japan. She was only able to prove that 14 hours of the entire trip were related to maintaining or improving her professional skills.

Example: Smith, a French and Latin teacher, was allowed to write off the cost of a Mediterranean tour. The expenses were primarily for improving and maintaining Smith's skills as a teacher of those subjects.

Example: Bowden, the assistant principal of a school, was not allowed to deduct the cost of a world tour that he and his spouse took. He was unable to prove that he did anything different from what regular tourists do when they travel.

Spouse's expenses: When your spouse travels with you while you're getting educated, you must have a substantial business reason for your spouse's presence in order to claim a deduction for his or her expenses. Further-

more, your spouse's presence will automatically make the trip look more like a personal than a business expense.

HOW TO WRITE OFF EDUCATION WHILE AWAY FROM HOME

Even if your travel itself does not qualify as education, you may write off your expenses of traveling to and from the place where you are getting educated. You are not confined to your own backyard. However, for your traveling expenses to be deductible, your *primary purpose* for the travel must be education.

Whether a trip is primarily personal or primarily educational depends largely on the amount of time you spend on personal activities compared with the time you spend on education.

Example: An executive travels to Chicago to attend a one-week educational seminar, which qualifies as an educational expense. During the week, the executive takes a sightseeing trip, entertains some personal friends, and takes a one-day side trip to Milwaukee. Most of the executive's activities relate to the educational seminar, however. Under these circumstances, the expenses of traveling to and from Chicago are deductible, as are the lodging expenses while in Chicago. The expenses, including travel, meals, and lodging, of the Milwaukee trip are not deductible. Also, any expenses in Chicago that are attributable to personal activities are not deductible.

In contrast to the above example, assume the same facts except that the executive spends five weeks on personal activities after the one-week seminar. Unless the executive can present very strong evidence of a business purpose, the costs of traveling to and from Chicago will not be deductible. The only deductible traveling costs will be meals and lodging allocable to the one week the executive spent attending the seminar.

Part-time study: If you go out of town to study at a university or other institution, your travel costs may be deductible. However, if you don't take a full course load, the IRS may deny your travel deduction on the ground that your trip was primarily personal. For example, if you went to another city to take only one-fourth of a full course of study, the IRS would disallow any deductions for the travel, although you could deduct one-fourth of your living costs while at the university.

IRS Regulations hint that your write-off would be allowed—even for only one course—if you proved that your primary purpose in going out of town to take the course was to help you in your business. For example, a particular course might be given in only one or a few locations. If none of the locations is near you and the course is particularly important for your business, you would have a very good argument that your travel was motivated by business. Documentation, particularly in your diary, would be crucial in this case. You would need to keep a careful record showing the amount of study, as well as class attendance, required. You would also, of course, keep all of your course materials, including all of your assignments and exam papers.

Foreign travel: You may write off your expenses of traveling to a foreign country to get educated. Remember, however, that expenses for attending a convention, seminar, or similar meeting outside the North American area or Jamaica must meet special requirements, particularly the 76/24 test. You should review our earlier chapter on travel if you intend to get educated somewhere other than the United States, its possessions, the Trust Territory of the Pacific Islands, Canada, Mexico, or Jamaica.

WHAT EXPENSES YOU CAN WRITE OFF

Basically, all money you spend to get educated will qualify as an educational expense. The list includes tuition, books, supplies, laboratory fees, and similar items, as well as certain travel and transportation costs. Remember, travel and transportation expenses must meet the substantiation rules discussed in a previous chapter.

Other deductible expenses include the cost of correspondence courses, tutoring, training programs, and any research you do as part of your educational program.

All expenses, out-of-pocket and otherwise, should be supported by receipts. Use checks whenever possible when paying for

items. The check shows what you paid and the receipt shows what it was for. And don't forget to record your educational activities—such as classes, library study, and the like—in your diary.

HOW TO AVOID THE LOCAL TRANSPORTATION PROBLEM

A good way to waste gasoline without getting any additional tax benefit is to go home for dinner before going to class. You may only write off the cost of going from your work to the educational site. Any extra mileage you log because of a trip home is a nondeductible personal expense. In other words, the educational site is treated the same as a second job location for purposes of determining your transportation deduction.

Example: You work 10 miles from your home and normally drive to work each day. Thus, your daily commute is 20 miles. You take a night course at a local university four miles from your office. Thus, if you go straight from your office, your total commute is 24 miles. You may deduct only the four miles between your office and the school.

Now assume that you are hungry so you drive home for dinner and then drive back to the school. You are still limited to the expenses of traveling four miles.

Therefore, you can probably save money—considering the high cost of operating a car—by having a snack before class and saving your big meal until you get home.

Caution: If you attend class on a non–work day, your entire trip is nondeductible, since it is a commuting expense.

Hint: Try to find an excuse for going to the office and working for a while before going to class.

HOW TO REPORT EDUCATIONAL EXPENSES

To get your tax subsidy for education, you must report the expenses to the IRS, and report them properly. Proper reporting depends on whether you are an employee, an outside salesperson, or a self-employed person. Thus, your first step in reporting educational expenses is to determine your employment category.

You are an employee if you are not an outside salesperson and you receive Form W-2. You are an outside salesperson if you do your selling away from your employer's place of business. You are not an outside salesperson if your job requires you to sell at your employer's place of business, even for only a portion of each week. Moreover, if your main duties are service or delivery, you are not an outside salesperson. For example, bread truck drivers, milk truck drivers, and insurance debit agents are not outside salespersons.

You are self-employed if you are your own boss and file Schedule C. You may receive a Form 1099, or no form at all.

Employee reporting: Employees must divide their educational expenses into two categories. First, travel and living expenses are deducted as employee business expenses on Form 2106. These expenses represent deductions from your gross income. Second, expenses for tuition, books, supplies, and other direct costs of the education are deducted as miscellaneous deductions in Schedule A of Form 1040.

We note with regret that itemized deductions are not as good as deductions from your gross income. Itemized deductions help you only if your other itemized deductions for the year exceed your zero bracket amount. Furthermore, since your medical expenses are deductible only to the extent they exceed 5 percent of your adjusted gross income, it is to your benefit to reduce your adjusted gross income.

Therefore, an employee should do some tax planning to ensure getting benefit from tuition, books, and supplies. Make absolutely sure that your itemized deductions exceed the zero bracket amount for the year in which you pay educational expenses.

You would probably like to avoid being selected for audit by the IRS. Improperly reporting your educational expenses can upset the IRS computer and make you a worthy audit candidate. To avoid the delay and expense of an audit, you must report accurately,

completely, and in full accord with the instructions. This requires answering all questions in Part III of Form 2106. These questions are contained in Exhibit 9-2.

In addition, a complete statement should be added to establish exactly why the education improved or maintained your skills, or met a legal or employer requirement. If you have brochures or agendas that further establish the nature of the education, you should attach those to your return as well. The information you include with your return should answer all the questions an IRS auditor may want to ask about your educational expenses.

Reimbursement by employer: If your educational expenses are reimbursed by your employer, you cannot deduct them. On the other hand, you don't include the reimbursement as income—provided the expenses, if they had not been reimbursed, would be deductible. For example, if you took a course that improved your skills and were reimbursed by your employer, the reimbursement would not be income—unless the course was part of a program that would qualify you for a new trade or business.

If you had deductible educational expenses in excess of what your employer reimbursed, you may deduct the excess.

Outside salesperson: An outside salesperson reports all educational expenses as business expenses on Form 2106 and deducts them from gross income. Thus, the outside salesperson need not worry about losing the benefit of educational expenses if other itemized deductions do not exceed the zero bracket amount.

Again, a complete statement should be attached to Form 2106 to explain fully the nature of the educational expenses.

Self-employed: A self-employed businessperson or professional reports educational expenses on Schedule C. Note that Schedule C does not have any questions regarding your educational expenses. Nevertheless, the IRS says you should attach a complete statement to your return. As we will see in the next section, this is almost always a good idea, whether required or not.

HOW TO REDUCE YOUR CHANCES OF AN IRS AUDIT

You should attach a complete statement in support of your educational expenses to your return. The more complete your statement, the better your chances of not being audited. IRS auditors have been waging war over educational expenses for over a decade and are constantly looking for new skirmishes.

All of the questions from Part III of Form 2106 should be answered, regardless of whether you are an outside salesperson, an employee, or a self-employed person. The questions from Part III are, in effect, a partial audit of your return. If your educational expenses are large, IRS computers will flag your return for a little more attention. The first human attention is a reading of the statement supporting your educational expenses. That statement can go a long way toward satisfying the IRS right there. If the IRS is not satisfied at that point, it will call you in for a little discussion.

Answering the questions: Exhibit 9-2 tells how to answer the questions. Make sure you answer the first two questions "no." The first of them asks: "Did you need this education to meet the basic requirements for your business or profession?" The "basic requirements" refer to the minimum requirements for entering your profession, not advancement through the ladders of an organization or profession.

Thus, if you answer "yes," you are telling the IRS that you *don't qualify for the deduction.*

The second question asks: "Will this study program qualify you for a new business or profession?" Again, this question should be answered "no." By answering "yes," you are admitting that your education does not qualify for the deduction.

After asking you these two questions, the form asks you to describe your educational program and its relationship to your job. This should be answered with a detailed statement similar to the one in Exhibit 9-3. The statement in Exhibit 9-3 describes why a sales manager attended a one-semester program to improve his skills. The actual course load is detailed, including the expected improvement resulting from each course. These details are important for two reasons. First, they explain the connection between the taxpayer's business and the courses. Second, they can remove any suspicions that the taxpayer is actually embarking on a new trade or business. The IRS is especially suspicious of accredited courses because they may help the taxpayer get into a new business. Consequently, the statement should attack all arguments the IRS may make in seeking to deny your write-offs.

You need not live in poverty while obtaining your education. Remember that educational expenses are trade or business expenses, which need only be ordinary, necessary, or appropriate. Your travel and trans-

---

EXHIBIT 9-2. How to Answer Questions from Form 2106, Part III.

Part III of Form 2106 has three critical questions. The appropriate answers to these questions can avoid an IRS audit. Here are the questions and the appropriate answers:

- **Question:** Did you need this education to meet the basic requirements for your business or profession?

  Answer: No.

- **Question:** Will this study program qualify you for a new business or profession?

  Answer: No.

- **Question:** If "No," list the courses you took and their relationship to your business or profession.

  Answer: See statement attached (Exhibit 9-3).

EXHIBIT 9-3. Statement to Support Educational Expenses (Example).

Taxpayer, a sales manager, attended a one-semester program at All American University in Anytown, U.S.A., to improve skills in marketing and managing salespersons. Specifically, the courses taken and improvements attained were as follows:

Course 504	Advertising—Ad writing
Course 615	Psychology of Management—New management techniques for handling sales force
Course 621	Advanced Statistics—Mathematical analysis for direct measuring of marketing efforts and results
Course 634	Accounting for Managers—Reading and understanding financial results and reports for application to sales force and comparison to other sales managers

This one-semester, 15-credit hour program was designed especially for sales managers across the country. Although the program was accredited and applicable to degree programs, Taxpayer enrolled for the express purpose of improving skills in an existing job and not as part of a degree program for a new trade or business.

Taxpayer was away from home overnight for 120 days while obtaining the education. Expenses incurred were as follows:

Travel and living expenses		
Airfare, one round-trip ticket	$ 540	
Lodging	2,400	
Meals	2,978	
Other	622	
Total		$ 6,540
Tuition, books, and supplies		
Tuition	3,000	
Books	145	
Supplies	397	
Total		3,542
Grand Total		$10,082

portation expenses cannot be "lavish or extravagant," but first-class airline tickets, for example, are not considered lavish or extravagant. As you can see in Exhibit 9-3, our taxpayer was not lavish or extravagant, but quite obviously did not live poorly, either.

The statement contained in Exhibit 9-3 applies to an employee, an outside salesperson, or a self-employed person. Further details, such as a statement from your employer or a certification that a course is required by law, regulation, or your profession, should be attached to your return whenever possible. Such attachments will go a long way toward establishing why you undertook this program.

If you have a succinct course outline and an overview of the benefits to be derived from a particular course of study, attach these details as well. You need not attach receipts for airfares, lodging, tuition, books, supplies, or any other expenses incurred. The IRS will have fewer problems with those expenses than with the reason you undertook the education.

When you attend meetings and seminars for educational purposes, always retain the workbooks, handouts, and hand written notes you've taken during the course. Such items usually contain a good rationale of why the course benefited you, especially if you spent the time to take detailed notes and used a workbook.

VA reimbursements: You may not deduct educational expenses paid for by Veteran's

Administration benefits. For example, suppose you received $780 of VA benefits, one-half of which is a reimbursement for tuition and books. The other half is for subsistence. You incur $1,000 for tuition and books. Since $390 (50 percent of $780) of the cost is considered paid by your VA benefits, your educational expense deduction is $610 ($1,000 minus $390).

Scholarships: You may not deduct educational expenses paid for by scholarships. The full scholarship benefit is considered to be for education, including the portion for room and board. For example, suppose you received $900 as a scholarship. Tuition, books, room and board, and registration fees were $2,900. Your deduction is $2,000 ($2,900 minus $900).

TAX REDUCTION CHECKLIST

IRS publications to be obtained:

- Publication 508—*Educational Expenses*
- Publication 463—*Travel, Entertainment, and Gift Expenses*
- Publication 535—*Business Expenses*

Qualifying standards for deductible educational expenses:

- You must be in a trade, business, or profession.
- You must undertake the education to
  - Improve the skills you use in your existing trade, business, or profession, or
  - Meet the express requirements of law, regulation, your profession, or your employer.

Disqualifying standards for educational expenses:

- The education must not qualify you for a new trade, business, or profession.
- The education must not enable you to meet the minimum educational requirements for your trade, business, or profession.

Supporting documents needed:

- Receipts and canceled checks are required for tuition, books, supplies, laboratory fees, travel, transportation costs, meals, lodging, and other expenses incurred to take the program.
- Local transportation expenses are subject to the commuting rule: You may deduct only the incremental or excess mileage incurred because of your schooling, but you may never deduct the mileage or other transportation expense when you leave from your home on a nonworking day to get educated.
- Supporting evidence is essential for substantiating why education maintains or improves your skills. Therefore, whenever possible, obtain
  - Newspaper clippings.
  - Written requirements from state law, your profession, or your employer.
  - Job descriptions and work profiles.
  - A written rationale of why you are getting the education.

Reporting expenses in your return depends on whether you are:

- An employee.
- An outside professional.
- A self-employed person.

Employees use Form 2106, but may not receive tax benefits from all expenses:

- Travel, transportation, parking, tolls, and other expenses are deductible from gross income.
- Expenses for tuition, books, lab supplies, and the like are deductible only as itemized deductions. Thus, you get tax benefit only if your other itemized deductions exceed your zero bracket amount.

Outside salespersons and Schedule C taxpayers receive full benefits from educational expenses:

- All expenses are classified as business expenses and deducted from adjusted gross income.
- Outside salespersons report their expenses on Form 2106.

- Self-employed businesspersons and professionals report their expenses on Schedule C.
- A statement should be attached explaining fully all the elements in Form 2106 and, more specifically, why the education maintained or improved skills in an existing business or why it was necessary to obtain the education to satisfy the requirements of the law, a profession, or an employer.

Way back in 1962, Congress decided it didn't like business gifts, so it put a $25 cap on them. After two decades of rapid inflation, what do you suppose the cap is now? $25. Sound bad? Hold on, it gets worse.

Suppose you make your gift to an employee. Unless the employee is related to you, or is a real good friend, the IRS will probably make the employee pay tax on that $25. And, the IRS will say you should have withheld income taxes and Social Security taxes.

What was Congress so upset about when it put the $25 cap on business gifts? Supposedly, fat-cat, wheeler-dealer types were making lavish gifts to their business buddies, who paid no tax on them because gifts aren't taxable. But the wheeler-dealers were deducting the full cost because they claimed that the gifts were given for business reasons.

Whether this supposed abuse was real or imagined, we're stuck with this silly rule. In this chapter, we will explain the rules so you won't fall into the business gift trap. Also, we will show you a few ways to get around this rule. Specifically, we will discuss:

- How to distinguish between business and personal gifts.
- How that miserable $25 ceiling works.

- How to turn business gifts into entertainment expenses.
- How to handle gifts to employees.
- How to profit from cheap gifts.
- How to document your business gifts.

HOW TO DISTINGUISH BETWEEN BUSINESS AND PERSONAL GIFTS

Tax law recognizes that people make some gifts for personal reasons and some for business reasons. Not surprisingly, tax law treats the two differently.

Personal gifts are not deductible because personal expenses are not deductible. Furthermore, a personal gift is subject to the gift tax law. Under the gift tax law, you must pay a tax on the value of the gifts you make. However, you may give up to $10,000 each year to any number of persons without having to pay any gift tax. The person who receives a personal gift has no tax liability, either for income or gift tax.

A business gift, on the other hand, can qualify as an ordinary and necessary business expense. Generally, if you make a gift to a business associate, chances are your primary reason is your own economic benefit, not dis-

10

How to Turn Business Gifts Into Tax-Deductible Dollars

interested generosity. For example, you may give a business associate's son or daughter a wedding present in order to maintain or improve your business relationship with that associate. Under those circumstances, you would have a legitimate business deduction. But that's where the business gift limit comes in. Regardless of how legitimate the expense is, you can deduct only up to $25 of the expense.

In short, any gift to a business associate or a business associate's family will probably be a business gift unless the associate is related to you or is a close personal friend.

HOW THAT MISERABLE
$25 CEILING WORKS

In the good old days before 1962, you could make a business gift in any amount and receive a tax deduction for it. Now, your maximum deduction for business gifts to any one person during a tax year is $25.

To get a deduction for even that measly $25, the gift must be an ordinary and necessary business expense. Generally, it's not hard to meet that test. If making such gifts is customary in your line of work, you should have no problem getting the deduction. Once you have met the ordinary and necessary test, there are five elements of substantiation you must also meet. We'll go over the five elements later in this chapter.

The $25 applies to cost: Suppose you purchased a trinket 15 years ago for $5 and it's now worth $500. If you give it to a business associate, your deductible gift is $5. In other words, what counts is your original cost, not the current value of the gift. What's worse, the person who receives the gift will have a basis of only $5, so if that person sold the trinket for $500, he or she would have a taxable gain of $495.

Gifts to corporations and other entities: A gift to a corporation, partnership, or other entity is not subject to the $25 ceiling. However, if the gift is really intended for a certain individual, the IRS will treat the gift as though you made it to that individual. Therefore, the $25 ceiling will apply. In many cases, gifts to corporations or partnerships will in fact be intended for a particular individual. This will often be true in the case of a small corporation or partnership. It will certainly be true in the case of a one-person corporation.

Gifts to families: You may not avoid the $25 ceiling by making a gift to the business associate's family, or to a member of the family. In the wedding gift example that we used earlier in this chapter, the gift to the son or daughter would be considered a gift to the parent, your business associate. A gift to the business associate's spouse would also be treated as a gift to the business associate.

On the other hand, if you have an independent business relationship with your associate's spouse, you may deduct the cost of gifts (up to the $25 ceiling, of course) to both the associate and the spouse. But be careful. If a gift to one spouse is intended for the other's use, you're back to the $25 ceiling again. For example, suppose Bob and Alice are both business associates of yours. You give Bob a new golf club. You give Alice a dozen golf balls. If Alice is an avid golfer and Bob wouldn't come near a golf course if you threatened him with a gun, both gifts would be treated as Alice's. Your deduction is limited to $25.

Partners—business and marital—treated as one: For purposes of the business gift limitation, you and your spouse and you and your business partners are treated as one taxpayer. That is, any gift your spouse makes to a business associate is considered a gift made by you, and vice versa. This rule applies even though you and your spouse are in separate businesses and even though you each have an independent business connection with the recipient.

A similar rule applies to partnerships. Any gift you make on behalf of the partnership is considered a gift by each of your partners. By the same token, any gift one of your partners makes on behalf of the partnership is considered a gift by you. The result is that a partnership can deduct no more than $25 a year for business gifts to any one individual.

HOW TO TURN BUSINESS GIFTS
INTO ENTERTAINMENT EXPENSES

Tickets to the theater or various sporting or other entertainment events make terrific business gifts. Having just read lots of bad news about the business gift limitation, you may have decided to stop buying these tickets for your business associates. Don't. You are allowed to treat the cost of tickets as either a business gift or a business entertainment expense. The choice is yours, and you can even change your mind and amend your tax return within the three-year statute of limitations.

If you go along to the event, you have no option. You must treat the cost as an entertainment expense. In that case, don't forget that this expense will qualify only as a goodwill expense, since your business discussion may not occur at the event, a nonbusiness setting for tax purposes.

With respect to any consumable item, your expense will be considered an entertainment expense only if you are part of the consumption process. Buying your associate a drink at the bar, for example, can be business entertainment. But buying your associate a bottle of fine wine at the liquor store and presenting it, unopened, for the associate's later consumption, will constitute a business gift. In that case, make sure the wine doesn't cost more than $25.

HOW TO HANDLE GIFTS TO EMPLOYEES

We'll start with the turkeys. It's OK to give turkeys, hams, or other such items to your employees as holiday gifts. You do not have to count the cost of these items as additional compensation to your employees.

Should you give a gift certificate, however, the cash value will be considered compensation. On the other hand, a gift certificate for a turkey is probably OK.

Employee awards: The $25 limit is raised to $400 for the cost of certain gifts to employees. If the gifts are made because of the employee's length of service, productivity, or safety achievement, you may deduct up to $400 for any one employee. You may deduct up to $1,600 of the cost if the gift qualifies as a qualified plan award. To qualify, the award must meet three tests. First, the award must be made because of length of service, productivity, or safety achievement. (This first

requirement is the same as the requirement for the $400 exception mentioned above.) Second, the award must be part of a permanent written plan that does not discriminate in favor of officers, shareholders, or highly paid employees. And third, the average cost of all awards under the plan must be no more than $400 during the year. In other words, if you want to give one employee $1,600, you must give several other employees considerably less than $400.

Considering how complex these special rules on employee awards are, you would think the awards are tax free to the employees. But the IRS says the employees must consider these awards to be compensation unless they can show that you made the awards out of a sense of detached and disinterested generosity. Maybe you made the awards because you wanted to be generous, but chances are that your generosity was inspired by business objectives. Thus, in most cases, the IRS will tax employees on this type of award. It would probably be better to give your employees a nice fat cash bonus at the end of the year. And maybe include a personal note of thanks along with it. They will probably appreciate it more than a gold watch.

HOW TO PROFIT FROM CHEAP GIFTS

Cheap promotional gifts are not subject to the $25 limit. These are items that cost $4 or less and that have your name printed on them, such as pens, desk sets, and plastic bags and cases.

You may also exclude point-of-purchase advertising items such as signs, display racks, or other promotional material to be used on your business premises.

HOW TO DOCUMENT YOUR BUSINESS GIFTS

Business gifts are covered by the same rules as travel and entertainment expenses, explained in previous chapters. If you have read those chapters, you know that substantiating your deduction will cause you some writer's cramps. Here's what you must record:

- Cost of gift.
- Date of gift.
- Description of gift.
- Business reason for gift.
- Name of recipient, title, and business relationship to you.

The most difficult of these five requirements is identifying the business reason. You must describe the benefit you derived or the benefit you expect in the future. Generally, on business gifts, the goodwill factor is the key.

TAX REDUCTION CHECKLIST

IRS publications to be obtained:

- Publication 17—*Your Federal Income Tax*
- Publication 334—*Tax Guide for Small Business*
- Publication 463—*Travel, Entertainment, and Gift Expenses*

Business versus personal gifts:

- Personal gifts are made out of admiration, affection, or other personal reasons.
- Personal gifts are not deductible.
- Business gifts are motivated by the desire for future profit or recognition of past business benefit.

The $25 ceiling:

- Applies to the *cost*, not the *value*, of the gift.
- Gift to a family member of a business associate is considered a gift to the business associate, *unless* you have independent business relationship with the family member.
- Gift to a corporation or other entity is not subject to the ceiling, unless gift is intended for a particular person.
- Gift by one spouse is considered a gift by the other spouse—even if each spouse has independent business relationship to recipient.
- Gift by one partner on the partnership's behalf is considered a gift by each partner.

Turning a business gift into business entertainment:

- Send business associates to the theater or ball game alone and you may treat the cost of the tickets as either entertainment or as a business gift.
- If you make a bad choice in declaring gift as entertainment, or vice versa, you can change your mind any time while your tax return is open to IRS examination.
- Packaged food, packaged beverages, and other items intended for later consumption are always classified as business gifts.

Gifts to employees:

- Holiday turkeys and similar items aren't considered income to employees.
- Gifts worth up to $400 are deductible if given in recognition of length of service, productivity, or safety achievement.

Do estimated taxes give you a headache? Have you ever paid the penalty for under-estimating your taxes? If the answer to either of these questions is "yes," you should read this chapter. Even if the answer is "no," consider this: Each year, millions of people are stuck with penalties for underpaying their estimated taxes, yet many could have avoided it simply by filing the right form—specifically, Form 2210. Unfortunately, many taxpayers are either unaware of this form or don't know how to use it to their advantage. By using the form, you can prove to the IRS that you satisfy one of several exceptions, and there-fore can avoid a penalty for underpaying your 1985 estimated taxes.

Form 2210 is used for escaping the penalty for underpaying *1985* estimated taxes. Because of the Tax Reform Act of 1984, the requirements for paying estimated taxes in *1985* and later years are substantially different for individuals from prior years. The require-ments for corporations in 1986 are the same as prior years. This chapter covers the require-ments for paying 1986 estimated taxes and the means for escaping the penalty for underpay-ing 1985 estimated taxes.

To help you solve the estimated tax puzzle without getting headaches, without paying penalties, and without paying so much as a penny more than necessary, this chapter will discuss:

- Why the IRS collects estimated taxes.
- How to determine if you must pay estimated taxes.
- When you must pay estimated taxes.
- How to use the annualization exception to mini-mize your 1986 estimated taxes.
- How to use your tax records for figuring esti-mated taxes.
- How wage withholding can avoid estimated tax penalties.
- How a husband and wife pay estimated taxes.
- How to avoid the penalty for underpaying 1984 estimated taxes.
- How to handle your corporation's estimated taxes.

WHY THE IRS COLLECTS ESTIMATED TAXES

Our Federal Government feels very uneasy about waiting until April 15 to receive your taxes for the previous year. After all, you may not have the money to pay your taxes in a lump sum on April 15. Moreover, our govern-ment is spending more than it brings in, so it needs to get your tax money earlier to pay its bills on time. Therefore, it has adopted two methods for collecting your money on the installment basis during the tax year.

The first method, familiar to all wage earners, is the income tax withheld from an

11
HOW TO REDUCE YOUR ESTIMATED TAXES WHILE ESCAPING NASTY PENALTIES

employee's earnings. This prepayment system is relatively painless, because most employees have learned to think of their salary in terms of the net amount.

The second method for collecting advance payments of tax is the estimated tax system. If the withholding system does not collect enough of your money, you must also pay estimated taxes. This system applies mainly to taxpayers who are self-employed. Under this system, you must make quarterly payments to the IRS during the tax year, based on your estimated income. In short, you must withhold taxes on yourself, just as employers withhold taxes from employees.

But the self-employed person—or, for that matter, any person whose income is not subject to withholding taxes or whose withholding taxes may fall short of satisfying the law's requirements—has a big problem: How to decide how much, if anything, to pay.

HOW TO DETERMINE WHETHER YOU MUST PAY ESTIMATED TAXES

If you will owe $500 or more of income tax, alternative minimum income tax, and self-employment tax for 1986, the IRS expects you to pay estimated taxes. Note: 1985 was the first year in which the alternative minimum tax is counted in figuring your estimated taxes.

Effect of withheld taxes: Your estimated tax is the total tax you expect to owe for the year, minus your expected withholding. In other words, estimated tax is the amount you would have to pay when you file your Form 1040 for 1986, *if* you didn't pay any estimated tax during the year.

Example: Harvey is a self-employed artist who makes very little money. Harvey's spouse is a corporate executive who makes lots of money so that Harvey can play with his paint set. The Harveys make the following calculation:

Expected joint income taxes	$15,000
Expected self-employment tax	1,000
Total expected taxes	16,000
Less: Expected withholding	(15,800)
Expected balance due with Form 1040	$ 200

The Harveys need not pay any estimated taxes because their expected tax liability is less than $500.

Let's change the above numbers just a little. Suppose the expected withholding taxes were only $12,000. In that case, the expected balance due would be $4,000 ($16,000 minus $12,000), and the Harveys *might* have to pay estimated taxes. In a later section of this chapter, you will find out how estimated taxes can be avoided by increasing a wage earner's withholding taxes.

Exception—Zero tax liability in preceding year: If you had to pay zero taxes for 1985, you won' owe any estimated taxes in 1986. To qualify under this exception, you must have been a U.S. citizen or resident throughout the preceding year and the year must have consisted of a full 12 months.

Example: Briggs was a full-time college student in 1984, but had a summer job. Her boss withheld $300 in taxes. Briggs filed her 1985 return and got a full refund. Since Briggs paid no tax in 1985, she need not pay estimated taxes in 1986, even if she makes a million dollars from self-employment.

WHEN YOU MUST PAY ESTIMATED TAXES

Estimated taxes are paid in four installments, using a Form 1040ES payment voucher, which the IRS gladly supplies. You may pay all of your estimated tax with the first voucher—a terrible idea—or you may pay in four installments.

The installments are due on the following dates:

- April 15 for the three months ending March 31.
- June 15 for the five months ending May 31.
- September 15 for the eight months ending August 31.
- January 15 for the twelve months ending December 31.

If any of these dates falls on a weekend or legal holiday, the due date is the first working day after the weekend or holiday.

You may avoid filing the January 15 voucher if you file your Form 1040 and pay any tax due before January 31. Filing a final return by January 31, however, will not avoid any underpayment penalties for the first three vouchers, as you will see in a later section. The January 31 return simply acts as a filing of the fourth voucher.

Since your final tax payment isn't due until April 15 each year, the early January filing drains some of your cash unnecessarily. As a general rule, you're better off keeping your money for as long as possible, and paying Uncle Sam only when necessary.

HOW MUCH ESTIMATED TAX YOU MUST PAY

The law says that your four installments are payable in equal amounts (even though the installment periods are not equal in length), and must total the *lower* of:

- 80 percent of your current (1986) year's taxes, or
- 100 percent of your preceding (1985) year's taxes.

Total taxes include the regular income tax, the self-employment tax, and the alternative minimum tax (if any).

Example of quarterly payments: Brown's tax bill for 1985 was $10,000 and his tax bill for 1986 will be $16,000. If Brown pays based on his 1986 taxes, his payments will be $3,200, figured this way:

$$80\% \text{ of } \$16,000 = \$12,800$$

$$\$12,800 \div 4 = \$3,200$$

If Brown pays based on your 1985 tax, his payments will be $2,500, figured this way:

$$\$10,000 \div 4 = \$2,500$$

Brown should pay the $2,500 installments and keep the $700 savings ($3,200 − $2,500) working for him instead of Uncle Sam.

Withholding may cover estimated taxes: Remember the Harveys from a previous section of this chapter? We left them with expected taxes of $16,000 and expected withholding of only $12,000. If the Harveys paid $12,000 in taxes for 1985, they need not pay estimated taxes in 1986. Reason: Since withholding counts as estimated tax payments, the $12,000 to be withheld in 1986 covers the Harvey's estimated tax liability for 1986.

HOW TO MINIMIZE YOUR 1986 ESTIMATED TAX PAYMENTS BY USING THE ANNUALIZATION EXCEPTION

As mentioned before, the law says you must make four equal estimated tax payments totaling: 80 percent of your 1985 income taxes, or 100 percent of your 1986 income taxes, whichever is less. Remember, "income taxes" include the regular income tax, the alternative minimum tax, and the self-employment tax.

If your income flow is constant throughout the year, this method might be satisfactory. But if, like many business people, your income flow is erratic, you may have trouble digging up the cash to pay your estimated taxes for a quarter in which your income was low. If you run into this problem in 1986, the "annualization" exception can ease your burden.

Annualized income: The annualization exception allows you to figure an estimated tax installment by using your current income to date as the basis for projecting your total income for the year. Exhibit 11-1 is a worksheet for figuring the annualization exception.

Exhibit 11-2 contains three different annualization factors, corresponding to the first three installment periods. To annualize the income received through the first installment period of January 1 through March 31 (three months, or one-fourth of the year), multiply taxable income by 4. The factor for the installment period ending May 31 (five-twelfths of the year) is 2.4, and the factor for the installment period ending August 31 (two-thirds of the year) is 1.5.

Example: Jennings is a single, self-employed taxpayer. In 1985 Jennings had taxable income and self-employment income of

EXHIBIT 11-1. Worksheet for figuring annualization exception for 1986 estimated taxes

1. Taxable income[1] (or, if greater, alternative minimum taxable income) from January 1 through end of reporting period[2] _____

2. Multiple line 1 by annualization factor[3] ____×____

2a. Result: Annualized taxable income (or alternative minimum taxable income) ═══════

2b. Tax on amount from line 2a[4] _____

3. Self-employment income from January 1 through end of reporting period[2] _____

4. Multiply line 3 by annualization factor[3] ____×____

4a. Result: Annualized self-employment income[5] ═══════

4b. 12.3% of amount from line 4A: _____

5. Annualized taxes: Add lines 2b and 4b _____

6. Multiply line 5 by applicable percentage[6] ____×____

                    6a. Result _____

7. Subtract previous installment(s) from line 6a (_____)

8. Result: Payment required under annualization exception ═══════

[1]Gross income minus exclusions, deductions, and exemptions.

[2]March 31, May 31, or August 31.

[3]For period ending March 31, factor is 4.
For period ending May 31, factor is 2.4.
For period ending August 31, factor is 1.5.

[4]Use Tax Rate Schedules contained in Form 1040 instructions.

[5]Do not enter any amount exceeding the maximum self-employment income taxable in 1986. At the time this was written, the 1986 maximum had not been announced, but was estimated at $41,700.

[6]For the first installment, applicable percentage is 20%.
For the second installment, applicable percentage is 40%.
For the third installment, applicable percentage is 60%.

$20,000. Jennings expects to earn about $37,000 in 1986 because he has several big deals cooking that will pay off during the second half of the year.

Jennings had taxable income (and self-employment income) of $6,250 during the first three months of 1986. He paid his first installment of estimated taxes based on his 1985 taxes of $5,465. Therefore, his first installment was $1,366 ($5,465 ÷ 4). Jennings could have paid 20 percent of his expected 1986 taxes, but this would have amounted to $2,595. (The taxes on his anticipated $37,000 of taxable income and self-employment income equal $12,975.)

During the months of April and May, Jennings earns taxable income and self-employment income of only $400. He still expects those sweet deals to bear fruit later in the year, but he's in a cash crunch right now.

Jennings solves his cash problem by using the annualization exception. Under this exception Jennings pays only $276 as his second installment, instead of $1,366. Total saved: $1,090. Exhibit 11-2 shows how Jennings figured his payment under the annualization exception.

Caution—Savings increase later installments: You can use the annualization exception for later installments, but if you don't qualify, your next regular installment is the regular installment amount *plus the savings on the previous installment(s).* In other words, you must bring your estimated tax payment up to the level they would have been if you hadn't used the annualization exception.

Example: Let's go back to the Jennings case. Remember that Jennings earned a total of

EXHIBIT 11-2. How Jennings saved $1,058 on second estimated tax installment by using annualization exception

1. Taxable income (or, if greater, alternative minimum taxable income) from January 1 through end of reporting period	$ 6,650
2. Multiply line 1 by annualization factor	× 2.4
2a. Result: Annualized taxable income (or alternative minimum taxable income)	$15,960
2b. Tax on amount from line 2a	$ 2,222
3. Self-employment income from January 1 through end of reporting period	$ 6,650
4. Multiply line 3 by annualization factor	× 2.4
4a. Result: Annualized self-employment income	$15,960
4b. 11.8% of amount from line 4a:	$ 1,963
5. Annualized taxes: Add lines 2b and 4b	$ 4,185
6. Multiply line 5 by applicable percentage	× 40%
6a. Result	$ 1,674
7. Subtract previous installment(s) from line 6a	$ (1,366)
8. Result: Payment required under annualization exception	$ 308

         SAVINGS: $1,366 − 308 = 1,058

only $6,650 through May 31, the end of the second installment period. In the third installment period, Jennings earns $17,950, bringing his income for the year to $24,600. This rush of income is far too great to enable Jennings to qualify for the annualization exception. As a result, Jennings must pay the regular installment of $1,366, plus the $1,058 savings from the preceding installment, or a total of $2,424.

HOW TO USE YOUR SHOEBOX FOR FIGURING ESTIMATED TAX PAYMENTS

We believe the easiest and least painful way to keep track of your taxes is to do it in little spurts, such as once a month. If monthly grappling with your tax records is more than you can bear, the estimated tax requirements offer an alternative. To take advantage of the annualization exception, you must have your records broken down for the following periods:

- Three months ending March 31.
- Five months ending May 31.
- Eight months ending August 31.

No special form of records is required. Actually, you need the same supporting documents you need for your Form 1040 at the end of the year. Therefore, all that's necessary is a periodic computation.

HOW PENALTIES ARE FIGURED

If you underpay any required installment of estimated taxes in 1986, you will penalized, unless you satisfy the annualization exception explained earlier. Similarly, if you underpaid any required installment of estimated taxes in 1985, you will be penalized, unless you satisfy one of *three exceptions*, which we will explain later in this chapter.

How the penalty rate is determined: The penalty rate is determined by the IRS, based on the average prime interest rate—rounded to the nearest whole percent—determined by the Federal Reserve Board for the six-month periods ending March 31 and September 30.

The new rates go into effect the following July 1 and January 1, respectively. The rate for the period from January 1 through June 30, 1985, was 13 percent. (The prime rate did not change enough during the year to require a rate change at mid-year.) Unlike penalty rates on other taxes, which are compounded daily, the rates on underpaid estimated taxes are compounded annually.

Daily basis: The penalty is figured on a daily basis, beginning the day following the due date and ending the date of payment.

Example: Wilson forgot to pay his $2,000 estimated tax payment due April 15, 1985. He remembered on May 1. His penalty was $11 ($2,000 × 15/365 × 13%).

Each installment stands alone: You can't avoid a penalty by paying an extra amount in a later installment to make up for a previous underpayment. You are penalized for the period you are underpaid.

Example: Wilson waits until June 15, 1985, to pay the $2,000 that was due on April 15. He cannot bring his account with the IRS current simply by doubling up on his payments, that is, by paying $4,000. He must pay a total of $4,037 to prevent further accrual of interest. The computation follows:

April 15 installment	$2,000
Plus: 61 days' interest @ 13% ($2,000 × 61/365 × 13%)	43
June 15 installment	2,000
	$4,043

Not deductible: Unlike regular interest, the penalty amount is not deductible.

HOW WAGE WITHHOLDING CAN AVOID ESTIMATED TAX PENALTIES

A relatively painless—although expensive—way to avoid estimated tax penalties is simply to increase the withholding taxes on the salaried spouse.

How withholding is treated: Taxes extracted via the payroll withholding process are counted as payments of estimated tax. In a joint Form 1040, each spouse's withholding taxes are counted. You may count withholding in one of two ways in order to avoid the estimated tax penalty: (1) you may take total withholding for the year and allocate it equally to each month; or (2) you may use the actual amounts withheld each month.

Hint: Increase withholding in later months to avoid penalties from earlier months.

Example: The Johnsons paid $10,000 in taxes for 1985. Mr. Johnson is a wage earner, Mrs. Johnson is self-employed. Because of a big jump in Mrs. Johnson's business, the Johnsons will pay a total of $16,000 in taxes for 1986. Since 80 percent of $16,000 is $12,800, the Johnsons' 1986 estimated taxes are equal to their 1985 taxes of $10,000. Mr. Johnson's expected withholding for the year is only $9,000, however. To make up the $1,000 shortfall, the Johnsons must pay four installments of $250 each.

But suppose the Johnsons don't realize they have to pay estimated taxes until October 1986. They can avoid the penalty by having Mr. Johnson's employer increase the withholding so that the total for the year equals $10,000

HOW A HUSBAND AND WIFE FILE ESTIMATED TAXES

A husband and wife may file separate Form 1040s or a joint 1040. Estimated tax vouchers do not control whether a separate or joint tax return is filed.

When vouchers are filed jointly by husband and wife but the final tax is filed in separate Form 1040s, the estimated payments may be divided between the spouses in any way they desire. For example, if you and your spouse paid joint estimated taxes of $10,000, but filed separate Form 1040s, you could take $6,000 and your spouse could take $4,000.

What happens when a husband is mad at his wife or a wife is mad at her husband? The IRS has considered this problem and decided that estimated tax payments made by angry spouses who cannot agree shall be apportioned on the basis of each spouse's tax liability. For example, if you and your spouse made joint estimated tax payments of $10,000, and each had to pay $8,000, the IRS would credit each of you with estimated tax payments of $5,000 if you filed separate returns and could not agree on any other allocation. Thus, each of you would receive a bill from IRS for underpaying your estimated taxes.

When vouchers are filed separately, the husband and wife are treated separately. Overpayment by one may not be used to offset underpayment by the other. Thus, if you and your spouse each filed separate vouchers and you overpaid by $1,000 and your spouse underpaid by $1,000, your spouse would not be credited with your overpayment.

Responsibility for filing estimated taxes rests with each spouse individually. If a husband is required to pay estimated taxes, his wife need not make the payments for him, and vice versa.

HOW TO AVOID THE 1985 ESTIMATED TAX PENALTY BY USING FORM 2210

In 1985 you were required to pay estimated taxes if your 1985 taxes, minus withholding, totaled $500 or more. The IRS expected you to pay four equal installments totaling 80 percent of your 1985 taxes.

Therefore, if the amount of the check you send the IRS when you file your 1985 Form 1040 equals more than 20 percent of your total taxes for 1985, the IRS will send you a bill for underpaying your 1985 estimated taxes—*unless* you file Form 2210 and prove that you satisfy one of the three exceptions to the 1985 estimated tax penalty.

Form 2210: At first glance, Form 2210 doesn't look like a form you would use to escape a penalty. The form is called "Underpayment Of Estimated Tax By Individuals." Since IRS will be happy to figure the penalty for you, you don't really have to file Form 2210 to tell IRS how much of a penalty you owe. The real value of Form 2210 is that you use it to prove you *don't* owe any penalty.

Form 2210 is based on the exceptions to the 1985 estimated tax penalty, as prescribed in the Internal Revenue Code. The form is not, shall we say, a masterpiece of clarity. In fact, taxpayers have been known to call the IRS and ask if they can just pay the penalty and not have to file Form 2210. That's why we have prepared worksheets for you to use. We will show you how to use them in the next section. But first, let's get acquainted with the exceptions to the penalty.

Exception 1—Last year's tax: The first exception allows you to assume that this year's estimated taxes are the same as last year's *actual* taxes (including self-employment taxes). You will not owe a penalty if any installment equals the amount necessary under this assumption. To qualify for this exception, you must have filed a Form 1040 that covered the full 12 months of last year and showed a tax liability.

Exception 2—Tax on annualized income: Good tax records are required to make this computation. Take your income and deductions for the period preceding the installment due, annualize them, and figure the tax based on those amounts.

Note: In 1985 and later years, self-employment taxes are annualized.

Exception 3—Tax on actual income: Under this exception, your estimated taxes are based on your actual income up to that point in the year. If any estimated tax installment equals or exceeds 90 percent of the tax figured on that income, you are not penalized on that installment.

HOW TO FIGURE THE PENALTY EXCEPTIONS FOR 1985 ESTIMATED TAXES

Let's work through a somewhat simplified example to illustrate how to use the penalty exceptions. The numbers are shown in tabular form on Exhibit 11-3.

Working example: Johnson is a single, self-employed taxpayer. In 1984 she had taxable income of $35,700 and self-employment income of $29,540. Her regular income tax was $8,593. Her self-employment tax was $3,338 ($29,540 times 11.3%). Thus, her total tax liability for 1984 was $11,931.

In 1985 Johnson had $50,000 of taxable income. Her regular income tax was $13,889 and her self-employment tax was $4,271 ($36,195 times 11.8%). Thus, her total tax liability for 1985 was $18,160.

EXHIBIT 11-3. How Johnson Avoided Estimated Tax Penalty

	APRIL 15	JUNE 15	SEPT. 15	JAN. 15
1. What the IRS wanted Johnson to pay (20% of 1985 taxes).	$3,632	$3,632 ($7,264 cumulatively)	$3,632 ($10,896 cumulatively)	$3,632 ($14,528 cumulatively)
2. What Johnson could pay—cumulatively— to avoid penalty by using:				
A. Exception 1—Last year's tax (Total: $11,931)	2,983 (25%)	5,966 (50%)	8,948 (75%)	11,931 (100%)
B. Exception 2—Tax based on this year's annualized income	1,850 (20%)	3,634 (40%)	13,256 (60%)	Not Applicable
C. Exception 3—Tax based on this year's income to date of installment	1,852 (90%) ($10,000 income)	3,194 (90%) ($15,000 income)	12,405 (90%) ($40,000 income)	Not Applicable
3. Least amount required—cumulatively—to avoid penalty.	1,850 (Exception 2)	3,194 (Exception 3)	8,948 (Exception 1)	11,931 (Exception 1)

As with most self-employed people, Johnson's income flow during 1985 was not uniform. For the period ending 3/31/85, her taxable income was $10,000. As of 5/31/85, it was $15,000. As of 8/31/85, it was $40,000. Finally as of the end of the year, Johnson had earned a total of $50,000 of taxable income.

If Johnson could have guessed that her taxable income for the year would be $50,000, she would have figured her 1985 tax liability (including self-employment tax) to be $18,160, and would have paid 20 percent of this amount, or $3,632, in each of four installments. These numbers are shown on the horizontal row number 1 in Exhibit 11-3. But, of course, Johnson didn't know how much she was going to earn during 1985, so she used the Form 2210 exceptions to figure the necessary estimated tax payment for each installment. These figures are shown on horizontal rows 2A through 2D on Exhibit 11-3. For her first installment, Johnson determined that Exception 3 (tax based on actual income to date) was the cheapest way to go, so she paid the estimated tax of $1,850. Exception 4 (tax based on actual income to date) was the best bet on her second installment.

For Johnson's third installment, Exception 1 (last year's taxes) was the cheapest route. Exception 1 also was the cheapest route for her fourth installment.

Figuring your estimated taxes: Appendices 1 through 4 are worksheets for figuring the penalty exceptions for 1985 estimated taxes. Appendix 4 is a master worksheet that allows you to determine at a glance which of the exceptions will result in the least tax for each installment. Appendices 1 through 3 show you step-by-step how to figure each exception for each installment. Appendix 1 covers Exception 1, Appendix 2 covers Exception 2, and Appendix 3 covers Exception 3. After reaching the bottom line in each worksheet, fill in the results on the master worksheet, Appendix 4.

Caution: Be sure to file Form 2210 when you file your Form 1040 for 1985. Filling it out should be a snap if you have used our worksheets.

To illustrate how to use these worksheets, we have filled them in for Johnson's case. These are shown in Exhibits 11-4 through 11-8.

HOW TO HANDLE YOUR CORPORATION'S ESTIMATED TAXES

The strategy for paying corporate estimated taxes is to pay your quarterly installments based on the exceptions to the penalty. These

EXHIBIT 11-4. Master Worksheet for Figuring Estimated Tax Exceptions (Example Showing Johnson's Case).

	INSTALLMENTS			
	1st	*2nd*	*3rd*	*4th*
STEP ONE				
Amount Required Under:				
A. Exception 1—Last year's tax	$2,983	$5,966	$ 8,948	$11,931
B. Exception 2—Tax on this year's income annualized	1,850	3,634	13,256	N/A
C. Exception 3—Tax on this year's income to date	1,852	3,194	12,405	N/A
STEP TWO				
Least amount under Step One—If cumulative payments as of the end of each installment period equal or exceed these amounts, you do not owe a penalty.	1,850	3,194	8,948	11,931

EXHIBIT 11-5. Worksheet for Figuring Exception 1 (Last Year's Taxes—Example Showing Johnson's Case).

STEP ONE
Last year's income and self-employment tax from Form 1040. $11,931

STEP TWO
Multiply amount in Step One by percentages shown below.

1ST INSTALLMENT (DUE 1/15/85)	2ND INSTALLMENT (DUE 6/15/85)	3RD INSTALLMENT (DUE 9/15/85)	4TH INSTALLMENT (DUE 1/15/86)
Last year's tax	Last year's tax	Last year's tax	Last year's tax
× .25	× .50	× .75	× 1.00
$2,983	$5,966	$8,948	$11,941

exceptions are similar to the exceptions available to individuals for 1985 estimated taxes. The main difference is a corporation has an Exception 4.

Which corporations must pay estimated tax: If you operated your business through a corporation, the IRS expects you to guess what your corporation's tax will be next year. If the corporation will owe $40 or more, the IRS wants quarterly installments of 22½ percent of the estimated tax. Actually, the IRS forms and publications ask for 25 percent, but the corporation won't be charged with an

EXHIBIT 11-6. Worksheet for Figuring Exception 2 (Tax on Annualized Income—Example Showing Johnson's Case).

	INSTALLMENTS		
	1st	*2nd*	*3rd*
STEP ONE Adjusted gross income from January 1 through end of reporting period.	$12,000	$18,000	$50,000
STEP TWO Multiply amount in Step One by factor shown.	× 4	× 2.4	× 1.5
Result is annualized adjusted gross income.	48,000	43,200	75,000
STEP THREE Itemized deductions from January 1 through end of reporting period.	3,300	4,300	11,300
STEP FOUR Multiply amount in Step Three by factor shown.	× 4	× 2.4	× 1.5
Result is annualized itemized deductions.	13,200	10,320	16,950
STEP FIVE Subtract zero bracket amount from amount in Step Four.	[2,300] 10,900	[2,300] 8,020	[2,300] 14,650
STEP SIX Multiply $1,000 by number of personal exemptions.	1,000	1,000	1,000
STEP SEVEN Add amounts in Steps Five and Six.	[11,900]	9,020	[15,650]
STEP EIGHT Subtract amount in Step Seven from amount in Step Two.	36,100	34,180	59,350
STEP NINE Regular income tax on amount in Step Eight.	8,267	7,537	18,059
STEP TEN Self-employment income from January 1 through end of reporting period.	8,700 × .113	13,700 × .113	35,700 × .113
STEP ELEVEN Multiply amount in Step Ten by self-employment tax rate.	983	1,548	4,034
STEP TWELVE Add amounts in Steps Nine and Eleven.	9,250	9,085	22,093
STEP THIRTEEN Subtract credits from amount in Step Twelve.	[-0-]	[-0-]	[-0-]
STEP FOURTEEN Multiply amount in Step Thirteen by percentage shown.	× .20	× .40	× .60
Result is cumulative payment required under Exception 3 for installment period shown.	$1,850	$3,634	$13,256

underpayment unless the amount falls below 22½ percent. Thus, for corporations, 90 percent—not 80 percent, as required for individuals—is the required cumulative payment for the year. Anything less is an underpayment.

Example: Smith, Inc. expects to owe $1,000 tax next year. Smith, Inc. must pay installments of $225 (22½ percent of $1,000), unless it meets one of the exceptions discussed later.

EXHIBIT 11-7 Worksheet for Figuring Exception 3 (Tax on Actual Income to Date—Examples Showing Johnson's Case).

	INSTALLMENTS		
	1st	*2nd*	*3rd*
STEP ONE Adjusted gross income from January 1 through end of reporting period.	$12,000	$18,000	$50,000
STEP TWO Itemized deductions from January 1 through end of reporting period.	$3,300	$4,300	$11,300
STEP THREE Subtract zero bracket amount from amount in Step Two.	[2,300] 1,000	[2,300] 2,000	[2,300] 9,000
STEP FOUR Multiply $1,000 by number of personal exemptions.	1,000	1,000	1,000
STEP FIVE Add amounts in Steps Three and Four.	[2,000]	[3,000]	[10,000]
STEP SIX Subtract amount in Step Five from amount in Step One.	10,000	15,000	40,000
STEP SEVEN Regular income tax on amount in Step Six.	1,075	2,001	9,749
STEP EIGHT Actual Self-employment income from January 1 through end of reporting period.	8,700	13,700	35,700
STEP NINE Multiply amount in Step Eight by self-employment tax rate.	× .113 983	× .113 1,548	× .113 4,034
STEP TEN Add amounts in Steps Seven and Nine.	2,058	3,549	13,783
STEP ELEVEN Subtract credits from amount in Step Ten.	[-0-]	[-0-]	[-0-]
STEP TWELVE Multiply amount in Step Eleven by 90 percent (.9). Result is cumulative payment required under Exception 4 for installment period shown.	2,058 × .9 $ 1,852	3,549 × .9 $ 3,194	13,783 × .9 $12,405

Note: In figuring its estimated tax for the year, a corporation may consider available credits, such as the investment tax credit, discussed in Chapter 7. Thus, if Smith, Inc. expected an investment tax credit of $600, its estimated tax would be $400 (not $1,000).

When installments are due: The installment dates for a corporation with a taxable year ending December 31 (a calendar year) are as follows:

• April 15 for the three months ending March 31.
• June 15 for the five months ending May 31.
• September 15 for the eight months ending August 31.

• December 15 for the eleven months ending November 30.

Note that the final installment is due one month sooner than the final installment for individuals.

Corporations that use a fiscal year pay in the same increments as above, except that the due dates are measured from the beginning of their fiscal year, not January 1. Each installment is due on the 15th of the following months of the fiscal year:

• Fourth month—for the preceding three months.
• Sixth month—for the preceding five months.
• Ninth month—for the preceding eight months.
• Twelfth month—for the preceding 11 months.

Example: Smith, Inc. has a fiscal year beginning February 1. The estimated tax installments are due May 15, July 15, October 15, and January 15.

How to pay: Unlike individuals, who make estimated tax payments directly to the IRS, corporations pay their estimated tax at either Federal Reserve Banks or authorized commercial banks. Form 503, Federal Tax Deposit, Corporation Estimated Taxes, must be used.

Penalty rate: The penalty rate is the same for corporations as it is for individuals, if the corporation's underpayment falls below 80 percent of the tax for the year. If the underpayment is below 90 percent but at least 80 percent, the penalty rate is only three-fourths the individual rate. For example, if a 16 percent rate applied to individual underpayments, the corporate rate would be 12 percent, provided the corporate underpayments were at least 80 percent of the tax.

Example: Assume Smith, Inc. owed $1,000 for 1984. It should have paid $225 per installment (unless it fit one of the exceptions). If Smith, Inc. paid less than $200 per installment (80 percent), the penalty will apply at the full rate. If Smith, Inc. paid at least $200 per installment (80 percent), the penalty will apply at only three-fourths the regular rate.

Tax reduction strategy—Payment based on exceptions: To minimize corporate estimated taxes, base your payments on the penalty exceptions.

Exception 1—Last year's taxes: Your estimated tax can be based on last year's tax, provided your return covered the full year and showed a liability of at least $1.

Exception 2—Last year's facts, this year's rates: This rule is basically the same as for individuals for 1984 estimated taxes, with one important difference: If last year's return showed a tax of *zero*, you can base your estimate on that fact. In other words, you don't have to pay any estimated tax.

Example: Smith, Inc. expects to have taxable income of $100,000 this year. Last year, Smith, Inc. paid no corporate tax because the tax was wiped out by a previous year's net operating loss. Smith, Inc. will not have any net operating loss carryover to offset this year's tax. Nevertheless, Smith, Inc. may base its estimate on last year's zero tax liability. Thus, Smith, Inc. keeps its $100,000 for the whole year without sharing any of it with the IRS.

Exception 3—Annualized income: This rule is the same as for individuals for 1984 estimated taxes, except that a corporation must pay *90 percent* (not 80 percent) of the tax based on its annualized income.

Exception 4—Seasonal income: Corporations with recurring seasonal income get a special break. Under this rule, such corporations can pay their estimated tax based on annualized income, projected on the basis of their income flow for the preceding three years.

To qualify under this exception, a corporation's taxable income for any consecutive six-month period must have averaged 70 percent of its annual taxable income during each of the past three years. For example, if your corporation earned an average of 70 percent of its annual taxable income during the period from October through March during each of the last three years, it would qualify to use this exception. The steps in the computation are shown in Exhibit 11-9.

If you overpay: If you goof and pay more estimated tax than you should have, you can get a "quick" (within 45 days of filing) refund. You must file your claim after your tax year is over but before your return is due—the 15th day of the third month; for example, March 15 for a calendar year corporation. Use Form 4466.

To qualify, your corporation must have overpaid by at least $500. Furthermore, the overpayment must have been at least 10 percent of the estimated tax. Thus, if you paid $10,000 of estimated tax and discovered that you owed only $9,000, your corporation could get a refund of the $1,000 that you overpaid. On the other hand, your corporation would not qualify if it overpaid by only

---

EXHIBIT 11-8. Worksheet for Figuring Exception for Corporation With Recurring Seasonal Income (Example).

FACTS: Smith, Inc.'s average taxable income for the years 1982, 1983, and 1984 was $100,000. For the July-December period of each year, the average taxable income was $70,000 (70 percent). Thus, Smith, Inc. qualifies for the "recurring seasonal income" exception. The remaining 30 percent of the company's taxable income was spread evenly throughout the first six months of the year for the preceding three years. In 1985 Smith, Inc. expects to have taxable income of $150,000. However, its taxable income through May 31, 1985, was only $30,000. The installment due June 15, 1985, is figured as follows:

STEP ONE   Actual taxable income through May 31. $ 30,000

STEP TWO   Divide by "base period percentage" through May 31, that is, average percentage of annual taxable income for corresponding period for preceding three years.

$$\div \ .25$$
$$\overline{120,000}$$

STEP THREE   Tax on amount from Step Two.   34,950

STEP FOUR   Amount from Step Three times "base period percentage" through June 30.

$$\times \ .30$$
$$\overline{10,485}$$

STEP FIVE   Subtract previous installment.   [6,990]
      Installment due June 15 $3,495

$499. Likewise, it would not qualify if it overpaid by $1,000, but had paid a total of $11,000, since $1,000 is less than 10 percent of $11,000.

Caution—Large corporations: This discussion has assumed your corporation is not "large." It is large if its taxable income during any of the last three years was $1 million or more. If it is large, congratulations. Be sure to consult your tax advisor for special rules on estimated tax payments for large corporations.

TAX REDUCTION CHECKLIST

IRS forms and publications to be obtained:

- Form 1040ES—Estimated Tax for Individuals
- Form 2210—Underpayment of Estimated Tax by Individuals
- Publication 505—Tax Withholding and Estimated Tax
- Form 1120W—Corporation Estimated Tax
- Form 2220—Underpayment of Estimated Tax by Corporations
- Form 4466—Corporation Application for Quick Refund of Overpayment of Estimated Tax
- Publication 542—Tax Information on Corporations

Who must pay estimated tax—Individuals:

- IRS wants you to pay estimated tax if you expect to owe regular income tax and self-employment tax of $500 in 1986.
- No estimated tax payments required if you had no tax liability in 1985.
- Withholding taxes count as payments.
- The alternative minimum tax counts in determining whether you must pay estimated tax.
- See below (last heading) for corporate estimated taxes.

When and how much you must pay:

- Installments are due
  - April 15 for the three months ending March 31.
  - June 15 for the five months ending May 31.
  - September 15 for the eight months ending August 31.
  - January 15 for the twelve months ending December 31.
- Technically, each installment must be at least 20 percent of your total tax liability for the year. But see below for exceptions.
- Use annualization exception in 1985 to pay least amount necessary.

Underpayment penalty:

- Penalty rates are determined every six months. See page 11.
- Penalty is charged on each underpaid installment and compounded on annual basis (simple interest).
- Each installment stands alone; paying extra in a later installment will not avoid interest on previous underpayment.
- Extra wage withholding can avoid penalty because withheld taxes are considered paid ratably during the year.

The three exceptions to the penalty:

- Base payment on 1984 actual taxes—exception applies only if you paid taxes for 1984 and your return covered a full twelve months.
- Base payment on your annualized income for the period covered by the installment due.
- Base payment on actual income for period covered by installment due.

How a husband and wife file estimated tax:

- Vouchers can be filed jointly or separately.
- If separate 1040s are filed but joint vouchers have been filed, you and your spouse may divide the estimated tax payments as you wish.
- If separate vouchers were filed and separate 1040s are filed, each spouse gets credit only for his or her payments.

Corporate estimated tax:

- Corporations that will owe $40 or more must pay installments of 22½ percent (total of 90 percent), unless an exception applies.
- Four penalty exceptions:
  — Exception 1—last year's tax.
  — Exception 2—tax based on last year's income (if zero, no estimated tax this year).
  — Exception 3—tax based on annualized income.
  — Exception 4—tax based on seasonal income.
  — Exception based on actual income is not available to corporations.
- If payment based on penalty exceptions, file Form 2220 with corporate tax return (Form 1120).
- If overpaid by at least $500 and 10 percent, "quickie" refund available by filing Form 4466.

Numerous tax and nontax benefits are available to corporations. On the other hand, because incorporation also has some drawbacks, owners of small businesses have always had to soul-search and pencil-push to decide whether or not to incorporate. This chapter will help you understand the tax angles of incorporating.

One-person businesses: The decision is especially tough for one-person businesses. In many jurisdictions, professionals in law, medicine, real estate, and insurance are allowed to incorporate. Incorporation may or may not, however, limit legal liability—the primary nontax reason to incorporate. In such cases, tax benefits are the main reason for a one-person business to incorporate.

TEFRA makes it tougher: The Tax Equity and Fiscal Responsibility Act of 1982 (TEFRA) makes it even tougher to decide whether or not a one-person business should incorporate. In a later chapter, we compare the benefits of corporate versus noncorporate qualified (tax-free) retirement plans and conclude that TEFRA made these benefits about equal. Therefore, the benefits from retirement plans no longer provide the main tax reason for a one-person business to incorporate.

Facts and circumstances: The incorporation decision can be made only after you reach the bottom line. Then you have to search your soul a bit to decide whether the bottom line (if it favors incorporation) justifies the additional headaches, like keeping corporate minutes and observing other corporate formalities.

Tax benefits: In this chapter, you will learn the many tax benefits available from incorporating. Here's a quick list of benefits discussed in this chapter:

- Income-splitting.
- Tax-free death benefit.
- Converting ordinary income into capital gain.
- Deferred compensation.
- Tax-free medical benefits.
- Tax-free disability insurance.
- Tax-free life insurance.
- Interest-free loans.
- Dividends received deduction.
- Deferring tax on year-end bonuses.

WHY YOU CAN SAVE TAXES BY INCORPORATING

A corporation and its owners, called shareholders, are separate legal "persons." Thus,

12
How to Save Taxes By Incorporating

when a business is operated through a corporation, the earnings are taxed to the corporation, not its shareholders (unless it's an "S Corporation").

The separate tax status of corporations and their shareholders allows two major tax-planning opportunities:

- Lowering the effective tax rate on business income by splitting the income between the corporation and its shareholders.
- Permitting the shareholders to receive various tax-free or tax-favored ("fringe") benefits available to "employees," but not available to sole proprietors or partners.

Control retained: The shareholders control the business, of course, because they own the corporation.

Don't pay yourself dividends: Your silent partner, the IRS, will love you if you incorporate and then pay yourself dividends from corporate earnings. That way, your partner gets two tax bites, once from the corporation and once from you. In the most extreme case, Federal taxes could take 73 percent of marginal corporate earnings—46 percent from the corporation and then 50 percent of the remaining 54 percent from you!

Hire yourself instead: Instead of paying yourself dividends, hire yourself and pay yourself a salary. Although your salary is taxed, the corporation can deduct it, provided it's reasonable. Thus, the corporate earnings are taxed only once if extracted from the corporation as salary, rather than dividends.

Any earnings your corporation does not pay as salary or dividends will accumulate at lower tax rates, allowing a greater buildup of funds. Furthermore, as an employee, you are eligible for various fringe benefits discussed later. In many cases, the tax savings from wearing two hats (as both shareholder and employee) more than justify the additional costs and effort required.

HOW TO SAVE TAXES BY SPLITTING INCOME WITH YOUR CORPORATION

Conducting business through a corporation allows more income to be taxed at lower rates.

If income is split between a corporation and its controlling shareholder/employee, some of the income is taxed in the corporation's lower tax bracket and some is taxed in the shareholder/employee's lower tax bracket. The result is a lower combined tax than the tax on the corporation only or the shareholder/employee only.

Exhibit 12-1 shows the tax savings possible at various income levels when the income is split between a corporation and its controlling shareholder/employee. The remainder of this section suggests some ways that the controlling shareholder/employee (you) can retain the benefits of income that is taxed to the corporation.

Accumulate for expansion: Perhaps the greatest benefit from corporate income-splitting is the ability to accumulate funds for expansion. Exhibit 12-1 shows the tax savings available at various income levels. Exhibit 12-2 is a rather breathtaking example of how an entrepreneur could more than double his savings by incorporating.

Support relatives: Individuals using after-tax dollars to support relatives may reduce their cost by incorporating. This can be done by giving stock to the relatives and paying dividends on the stock. Although the dividends will be taxable (and not deductible by the corporation), the tax will be imposed on the relatives, who presumably are in lower tax brackets than the controlling shareholder/employee.

Better yet, if your relatives are able to work, hire them. The wages, if reasonable, will be deductible by the corporation and taxed in the relatives' lower tax brackets.

Invest in the stock market: Corporations are entitled to a special deduction for dividends received from other corporations. The deduction is 85 percent of the dividend. Thus, in effect, a corporation is taxed on only 15 percent of the dividends it receives.

Example: Simpson, who is in the 40 percent bracket, owns stock that pays dividends of $2,000 a year. Simpson's corporation is accumulating funds for expansion. Simpson's tax on the dividend is $640 [($2,000 − $400

EXHIBIT 12-1. Table Summarizing Income-Splitting Advantages of Corporations.

	TAX ON INDIVIDUAL OPERATING AN UNINCORPORATED BUSINESS			TAX WHERE INCOME IS SPLIT BETWEEN SHAREHOLDER/EMPLOYEE AND CORPORATION					
Taxable Income	Tax (1984) Rates	Effective Rate (%)	Individual Taxable Income	Tax	Corporate Taxable Income	Tax	Combined Tax	Effective Rate (%)	Dollar Savings
$ 30,000	$ 4,818	$ 16.06	$ 25,000	$ 3,565	$ 5,000	$ 750	$ 4,315	14.38	$ 503
40,000	7,858	19.65	25,000	3,565	15,000	2,250	5,815	14.54	2,043
50,000	11,368	22.74	25,000	3,565	25,000	3,750	7,315	14.63	4,053
60,000	15,168	25.28	30,000	4,818	30,000	4,650	9,468	15.73	5,700
70,000	19,368	27.67	30,000	4,818	40,000	6,450	11,268	16.10	8,100
80,000	23,568	29.46	30,000	4,818	50,000	8,250	13,068	16.34	10,500
90,000	27,900	31.00	35,000	6,218	55,000	9,750	15,968	17.74	11,932
100,000	32,400	32.40	35,000	6,218	65,000	12,750	18,968	18.97	13,432
125,000	44,274	35.42	50,000	11,368	75,000	15,750	27,118	21.69	17,156
150,000	56,524	37.68	60,000	15,168	90,000	21,750	36,918	24.61	19,606
175,000	68,900	39.37	75,000	21,468	100,000	25,750	47,218	26.98	21,682
200,000	81,400	40.70	100,000	32,400	100,000	25,750	58,150	29.08	23,250

exclusion) × 40% tax rate]. If the corporation owned the stock, its tax would be only $45 [($2,000 − 85% of $2,000) × 15% tax rate].

Turn ordinary income into capital gain: When a corporation dissolves (liquidates), it pays all its debts and distributes any excess to its shareholders. Generally, the shareholders are allowed to report their profit (i.e., amount received over basis in the stock) as capital gain. This rule allows the shareholder to turn ordinary income into capital gain.

Example: Scott accumulates $10,000 of income a year in his corporation for ten years, saving $8,500 each year after taxes (of 15 percent), and invests the savings at 10 percent (9.85 percent after taxes). The corporation liquidates after ten years, pays its debts, and distributes $140,000 to Scott, whose stock basis is $20,000. Scott has a long-term capital gain of $120,000, of which $48,000 (40 percent) will be taxed at Scott's 50 percent bracket. After taxes, Scott has $116,000 ($140,000 minus $24,000 tax). Had Scott received the $10,000 each year as a dividend or additional salary, he would have kept only $5,000 of it after taxes and received an after-tax return of only 5 percent. At the end of ten years, he

would have accumulated only $66,000, or $50,000 less than the amount he received when the corporation dissolved.

HOW TO SAVE TAXES BY PROVIDING EMPLOYEE BENEFITS FOR YOURSELF

As an employee of your corporation, you are entitled to various benefits not available to a sole proprietor or partner. Some of the major benefits are described below.

Deferred compensation: For years, the qualified (tax-free) retirement plans discussed in another chapter have been the most popular form of deferred compensation for corporate executives (you). With the enactment of the "top-heavy" rules for these plans, the so-called nonqualified deferred compensation arrangements will become increasingly popular as substitutes for the qualified plans. In addition, the lower contribution/benefit limits for qualified plans will make nonqualified plans increasingly popular as supplements to qualified plans.

Under a nonqualified plan, the corporation agrees to withhold, say, $10,000 a year from the shareholder/employee's salary and to pay it at a later time, such as on retirement. The corporation may even agree to invest the

EXHIBIT 12-2. Accumulating Income for Expansion (Example Showing Corporate Advantage).

FACTS: Walker, a swinging single taxpayer, needs $75,000 in the bank three years from today to expand his operation. Although he earns $150,000 a year, Walker spends his money on his lifestyle. Moreover, Walker's combined Federal and state marginal tax bracket is 60 percent, so he can save (or spend) only 40 cents out of every extra dollar he earns. If Walker remains a sole proprietorship, his expansion needs will lop off $60,000 a year from his lifestyle needs. If Walker incorporates, he can save for expansion with less than half the pretax earnings. Here are Walker's computations:

ACCUMULATING $75,000 IN THREE YEARS AS AN INDIVIDUAL

Earnings first year	$ 59,594	
Income taxes (60%)[1]	35,756	
Money invested at 12%		$ 23,838
Earnings second year	59,594	2,859 [2]
Income taxes (60%)[1]	(35,756)	(1,715)[3]
Money invested at 12%		48,820
Earnings third year	59,594	5,858 [2]
Income taxes (60%)[1]	(35,756)	(3,515)[3]
Funds accumulated		$75,001

ACCUMULATING $75,000 IN THREE YEARS AS A CORPORATION

Earnings first year	$ 28,434	
Income taxes (20%)[4]	(5,687)	
Money invested at 12%		$ 22,747
Earnings second year	28,434	2,730 [2]
Income taxes (20%)[4]	(5,687)	(546)[3]
Money invested at 12%		47,678
Earnings third year	28,434	5,721 [2]
Income taxes (20%)[4]	(5,687)	(1,144)[3]
Funds accumulated		$ 75,002

ADVANTAGE TO CORPORATE FORM

ADD'L EARNINGS REQUIRED	INDIVIDUAL	CORPORATION
Year 1	$ 59,594	$28,434
Year 2	59,594	28,434
Year 3	59,594	28,434
TOTAL	$178,782	85,302

$93,480 Corporate Advantage

[1] Walker's federal tax rate is 50 percent and his state tax rate is 10 percent.

[2] Earnings of 12 percent on funds invested.

[3] Tax on earnings of invested funds. Rate is 60 percent for individual; 20 percent for corporation.

[4] Walker leaves only the money needed for expansion in the corporation; the balance is paid in fringe benefits and salary. Corporate tax rates are 15 percent Federal and 5 percent state.

deferred salary and to credit or debit any gains or losses to the shareholder/employee's account.

No current deduction, no current tax: Nonqualified plans use the income-splitting potential of corporations to build up a retirement fund for the shareholder/employee. The plans are called "nonqualified" because the corporation does not get a current deduction for the amount it withholds from the employee's salary.

Thus, the withheld salary is taxed to the corporation, but at the corporation's lower rate, not the shareholder/employee's tax rate. When the accumulated funds are paid out, the shareholder/employee will presumably be in a lower tax bracket.

Hint: The key to avoiding IRS attack is to enter into a deferred compensation agreement with your corporation *before* you perform any services for which your salary will be deferred and to structure your agreement so that you will have no enforceable rights in any fund your corporation may establish. Close consultation with your tax advisor is essential in this area.

Tax-free medical benefits: Special rules permit your corporation to use pretax dollars to pay your medical bills and medical insurance premiums at no tax cost to you. Tax-free benefits include corporate payments of:

- Premiums on accident or health insurance.
- Contributions to a fund to be used for paying accident or health benefits.
- Reimbursement for medical care.
- Compensation for certain permanent injuries.

"Medical care" includes diagnosis, treatment, and prevention of disease, as well as transportation to obtain medical care.

Tax-free benefits are also available to your spouse and dependents.

Caution—no discrimination allowed: If your medical expense reimbursement plan is "self-insured" (benefits are paid by the corporation, not through insurance), benefits won't be tax free if the plan discriminates in favor of any "highly compensated" individual (you). To qualify, the plan must meet certain technical requirements. A plan isn't discriminatory simply because highly compensated employees use the benefits to a greater extent than other employees. Presumably, a plan isn't discriminatory just because the corporation has only one employee (you) to be covered.

Exhibit 12-3 illustrates the benefits of a self-insured medical plan.

Tax-free disability insurance: Your corporation may also pay your disability insurance premiums at no tax cost to you. In addition, you may receive benefits of up to $100 a week tax free if you retire on disability and are permanently and totally disabled. Tax-free benefits are reduced to the extent your income exceeds $15,000.

Tax-free life insurance coverage: A corporation may provide its employees with up to $50,000 worth of group-term life insurance coverage tax free. Employees pay tax on corporation-paid premiums for coverage exceeding $50,000.

The taxable amount is determined under an IRS premium rate table, not on the basis of the actual premiums paid. In the good old days, the IRS table undervalued premium costs, so the taxable premiums were less than the actual premiums paid. Under current market conditions, however, the table generally overvalues the premium costs, with the result that coverage exceeding $50,000 will be taxed at more than the actual cost.

IRS Regulations say that a plan covering less than ten employees can qualify as a "group-term" plan if certain special requirements are met. Presumably, a plan meeting these requirements will qualify even though only one employee is eligible.

Caution—no discrimination allowed: For taxable years beginning after 1983, qualifying plans will also have to satisfy a new rule prohibiting discrimination in favor of any "key employee." Regulations have not yet been issued under this rule.

Loans from your corporation: Suppose you are merrily rolling along, taking advantage of the income-splitting benefits of your corpo-

---

EXHIBIT 12-3. Self-Insured Medical Reimbursement Plan (Example Showing Tax Benefits).

FACTS: Nelson earns $100,000 operating his business as a sole proprietorship. Because he cannot purchase medical insurance due to a pre-existing condition, Nelson is considering incorporation for the tax benefits that could be obtained from a corporate self-insured medical reimbursement plan. He compares the amount of his medical deductions as follows:

	SOLE PROPRIETORSHIP	CORPORATION
Deductible medical expenses:		
Medicine and drugs	$1,400	$1,400
Doctors, dentists, nurses, etc.	2,000	2,000
Hospitals	1,500	1,500
Transportation	200	200
Hearing aids	100	100
Eyeglasses	200	200
Elevator	2,000[1]	2,000[1]
Total	7,400	7,400
Less: 5%[2] of adjusted gross income	(5,000)[2]	-0-
DEDUCTION	$2,400	$7,400

$5,000 Corporate Advantage

[1] Nelson installed an elevator upon advice from doctor. Cost of elevator ($4,000) less increase in value of home ($2,000) is deductible [Riach Frank (CA-9) 62-1 USTC ¶9419, 302 F.2d 374; Rev. Rul. 54-57, 1954 C.B. 67].

[2] In 1983, the floor for deductible medical expenses was increased from 3 to 5 percent of adjusted gross income (Tax Equity and Fiscal Responsibility Act of 1982 § 202).

---

ration by accumulating some of the income for expansion or deferred compensation when, all of a sudden, a meteor crashes into your house and you discover that your casualty insurance expired last week?! Where do you find the money to fix the house? From your bank? Your savings and loan association? A loan shark?

Why not borrow from your corporation? After all, it has all that money piled up, waiting to help you expand your business or pay your retirement benefits. Instead of investing in the stock market or money market, it can invest in you.

If your corporation just gives you the money outright, the money is taxed as a dividend (ordinary income), to the extent the corporation has current and accumulated profits. If the corporation makes a valid loan,

however, you are not taxed of the amount of the loan.

Avoid below-market loans: Until June 6, 1984, interest-free or below-market rate loans were a great benefit to corporate owner/employees. Your corporation could lend you money at no interest and you would not be taxed on the interest-free use of the money.

The IRS never liked this rule, however, and finally convinced Congress to do something about it. What Congress did was pass a law (as part of the Tax Reform Act of 1984) saying that interest-free or below-market rate loans from a corporation to a shareholder are taxed as dividends. This hurts because your corporation can't deduct a dividend it pays you. The amount of the "dividend" is the interest the corporation *could have charged* on an arm's length loan, that is, the market rate. The market rate is 10 percent for the period through the end of 1984.

Starting in 1985 the market rate for loans will be based on the average yield on United States Treasury Bills ("T-Bills"). The IRS will redetermine the rates every six months. Check with your tax advisor for the latest rates.

Because of this new rule, you should make sure your corporation charges you the market rate on loans it makes to you.

Caution: Make sure all corporate loans are currently enforceable and comply with all the formalities of arm's-length loans. Otherwise, IRS will be happy to treat the full amount of the loan as a taxable dividend to you.

Tax-free death benefit: When you die, your beneficiaries can receive the first $5,000 of death benefits from your corporation tax free. This exclusion is available to self-employed persons only if benefits are paid in a lump sum from a qualified (tax-free) retirement plan.

Year-end bonuses: You can defer tax on a portion of your salary if your corporation adopts a policy of paying year-end bonuses, but doesn't pay them until after the end of your taxable year. If your corporation is on the cash basis, it deducts the bonus in the year paid.

Hint: If your corporation adopts a January 31 fiscal year, it can get a current deduction while allowing you to defer tax on the bonus.

Example: Burns Corporation has a January 31 fiscal year. On January 2, 1985, the corporation votes a $10,000 bonus to its sole share-holder and employee, Burns, for outstanding service during the past year. The bonus is paid during that month. The corporation deducts the bonus on its 1985 tax return, due April 15, 1985. Burns reports the bonus on his 1985 tax return, due April 15, 1986.

Caution: IRS loves to treat year-end bonuses as taxable dividends. Careful planning is required.

TAX REDUCTION CHECKLIST

IRS publications to be obtained:

- Publication 334—*Tax Guide for Small Business*
- Publication 542—*Tax Information on Corporations*

Overview of incorporation decision:

- Nontax reasons—such as limited liability—often don't apply to one-person businesses.
- Tax-free retirement plans are no longer the main tax reason for incorporating.
- Individual facts and circumstances must be analyzed with tax advisor.

Two main tax advantages from incorporating:

- Splitting income—this means taking advantage of lower corporate rate by keeping some of income in the corporation and paying some to yourself.
- Permit employee/owner to get tax-free or tax-favored fringe benefits.

Income-splitting possibilities:

- Expand your business.
- Support your relatives by paying them dividends or salaries.
- Invest in stock market—your corporation can deduct 85 percent of the dividends it receives.
- When corporation liquidates, its accumulated income is taxed as capital gain to you.

Employee benefits:

- A nonqualified deferred compensation plan can build a larger retirement nest egg.
- Corporation-paid medical insurance or medical expense reimbursement is tax free to you.
- Corporation-paid disability insurance premiums are tax free to you.
- Corporation-paid life insurance premiums on first $50,000 of coverage is tax free to you.
- Your corporation can be a source of loans, although arm's-length terms should be provided.
- Year-end bonuses can defer income for up to eleven months.

Court cases show how to protect the tax breaks you get from incorporating—tax-free retirement plans, income-splitting plans, and fringe benefits, to name just a few. These cases establish two golden rules to keep you out of tax trouble.

GOLDEN RULE NUMBER ONE

Stay at arm's length. Remember, you aren't running the business anymore; your corporation runs the business. You run the corporation. You also invest in the corporation, lend it money, and (maybe) rent to it. You must act as an executive, a shareholder, a lender, and a landlord.

GOLDEN RULE NUMBER TWO

Make the public know it's dealing with a corporation. Your corporation must have its own bank account, letterhead, telephone listing, and other trappings of an operating business.

If these golden rules become second nature to you, you will keep the tax breaks for which you incorporated. The rest of this chapter explains the golden rules, using examples from court cases, including one classic—the corporate car—and gives practical advice on how to follow the golden rules.

Before we get specific, let's be clear on this point: Incorporating won't make the IRS get after you. The IRS simply uses different weapons against you when you incorporate. Following the two golden rules will protect you against IRS attack.

Now, let's get specific. Here's what the IRS can do if you don't follow the golden rules:

- Tax you directly on the corporate income.
- Penalize the corporation for keeping the wrong kind of income (instead of paying it to you).
- Penalize the corporation for keeping too much profit (instead of paying it to you).
- Tax both the corporation and you on the same income.

These nasties are discussed under separate headings below.

HOW TO AVOID A DIRECT TAX

If you ignore your corporation, the IRS will also ignore it and will tax you directly on the corporate income. On the other hand, the IRS may not tax you just because you incorporated to get tax breaks.

How to Protect Your Corporate Tax Breaks From IRS Attack

The IRS uses three traps for taxing the business owner directly: the sham corporation trap, the assignment-of-income trap, and the reallocation-of-income trap.

Sham corporations: The IRS and the courts ignore corporations that are shams. A corporation is a sham if it doesn't do any business.

In a recent case, Mr. Horn got stuck with all of his corporation's income. Why? The court gave lots of reasons. Specifically, the corporation failed to:

- Obtain credit from a third party (e.g., a bank).
- Pay its own rent, utilities, and overhead.
- Pay its own insurance premiums.
- Get a license in its own name (although required by state law).
- Keep records of its business activities.
- Advertise or have itself listed in the telephone book.
- Let its clients know that it existed.

Mr. Horn didn't follow either of the golden rules. His corporation was just a piece of paper, nothing more. The corporation was a secret to the public. Mr. Horn ran the business. He should have run the corporation and let the corporation run the business.

Assignment of Income: A second trap IRS can use to tax you directly, instead of taxing the corporation, is the assignment-of-income trap. You fall into this trap by violating golden rule number one.

Sign corporation's name: To avoid this trap, make sure you sign contracts in your corporate name. Like this: "Smith, Inc., by John Smith, President." If you sign in your name, you pay tax on the income. It makes no difference that the money goes to your corporation. Two recent cases drive home this point.

Johnson case: Charles Johnson was a terrific basketball player. At least his team, the Warriors, thought so, since it paid him lots of money. Johnson incorporated himself to get some of those tax breaks available through incorporation.

The Warriors paid Johnson's salary directly to his corporation. But the team's owner made Johnson personally sign a contract with the team. When IRS taxed Johnson on the salary, he cried foul and went to the Tax Court. The court upheld the IRS because Johnson signed the contract in his name, not his corporation's name.

Brooks case: William R. Brooks was a terrific life insurance salesman who incorporated himself. He ran into the same problem as Johnson. He signed the contract with the insurance company in his own name. Result: He was taxed directly on the commissions.

Income reallocation: The third trap the IRS can use to tax you directly is the reallocation-of-income trap. By law, the IRS may allocate income among one or more "organizations, trades, or businesses." The IRS has used this power to tax the owner/employee of a personal service corporation, even though the service contracts were in the corporate name. Recently, however, an appeals court ruled that this power doesn't apply when an owner/employee works exclusively for his or her corporation.

Hint: The IRS has used this power only when the corporation was almost a sham. If you follow the two golden rules, your tax breaks should be safe from this third trap.

HOW TO AVOID THE PENALTY ON INVESTMENT AND SERVICE INCOME

If the IRS can't tax you directly by using one of the traps described in the preceding section, it may try to impose one of two penalty taxes on your corporation. The penalties apply if you violate golden rule number one by using your corporation as a pocketbook. This section discusses one of the penalties, which is based on the types of income your corporation earns.

Will your corporation earn commissions, fees, rents, royalties, dividends, or interest? If so, it could owe a 50 percent penalty on that income. This penalty is the "personal holding company" tax. It's easy to avoid, but painful if you don't.

When tax applies: The tax applies when more than 60 percent of your corporate income is "personal holding company income." This assumes that five or fewer people own more than half of your corporate stock; the tax applies only to closely held corporations.

When tax does not apply: The tax won't apply if you limit your corporation's investments and word your contracts the right way.

Investments: Make sure that dividends, interest, rents, and royalties add up to *less than 60 percent* of your corporate income.

Rent exception: Rents don't count against a corporation in the rental business, i.e., if rents make up most of its income. But rents do count if other investment income exceeds 10 percent of total corporate income.

Planning opportunity: Corporations still make dandy tax shelters for investment income if investment income is less than 60 percent of total ordinary income. But rental corporations should not have any investment income.

Contract wording for commissions and fees: Make sure that no contract—oral or written—names or describes the person who will do the work. Also, make sure that no one except your corporation has the right to name or describe that person. The IRS admits that the tax doesn't apply to a one-person corporation just because clients expect the owner/employee to do the work.

Recent example: The IRS tried to slap the personal holding company tax on Thomas P. Byrnes, Inc., a sales representative's corporation. Byrnes had incorporated to set up a tax-free retirement plan. After incorporating, Byrnes made sure his sales representation contract was between his corporation and the client firm.

Under the contract, Byrnes, Inc. could not hire any new salespeople without first discussing the matter with the client firm. Also, the client could require certain training of new salespeople. Finally, the client could end the contract if it thought Byrnes, Inc. wasn't doing a good job.

The IRS claimed that the contract, in effect, designated Byrnes as the person to do the sales work. Therefore, the IRS said, the commissions are personal holding company income. The Tax Court disagreed. The contract protected the client from bad salespeople, but it didn't designate Byrnes to do the selling. Therefore, the tax penalty did not apply. Byrnes followed golden rule number one.

HOW TO HANDLE PAPERWORK AS A CORPORATION

As you can see from the discussion up to this point, paperwork is important. But the paperwork isn't nearly so tough as you might think. Mainly, it's a matter of keeping your corporation's minute book up to date. This means writing up a summary of Board of Directors' meetings. Your lawyer can help you with this.

The rest of the paperwork is mainly a change from having things in your name to having them in your corporation's name. Here's a list of the types of things that should be in the corporation's name.

- Contracts—Make sure no one but your corporation has the right to decide who will do the work.
- Financing—Your personal guarantee may be necessary. That's okay. Just make sure that your corporation is the borrower, not you.
- All bills to clients or customers—Your corporation performs the service. Your corporation sends the bill. The bill should instruct clients to make checks payable to your corporation, not you.
- All accounts—Utilities, suppliers, and the like should be billing your corporation, not you.
- Stationery—Your name can be on the stationery, of course, but your corporate title should be given. ("John Smith, President, Smith, Inc.")
- Advertising, business cards, and telephone book listings—Again, you can be featured, but as chief officer of your corporation.
- Professional licenses, if state law allows—and definitely, if state law requires—corporations to have licenses in the corporate name.

Finally, make sure you get an Employer Identification Number from the IRS. This number is like a Social Security number for organizations. It is used to let IRS computers know that your corporation is a taxpayer separate from you.

HOW TO AVOID TAX ON PROFITS YOUR CORPORATION KEEPS

A violation of golden rule number one could cause a second penalty on your corporation for keeping too much of its profits. This penalty, called the accumulated earnings tax, is used to limit income-splitting. But lots of penalty-free income-splitting is available. Let's see how much.

The $25,000 exemption: A recent law permits a corporation to keep as much as $250,000 of its profits for any reason without penalty. This exemption is cumulative. For example, if your corporation kept $10,000 of its profits in 1982, $2,000 in 1983, and $3,000 in 1984, it could keep as much as $235,000 ($250,000 minus $15,000) in future years.

Service corporations: Certain corporations . are allowed to keep only $150,000 of their profits. This limit applies to corporations run by:

- Health professionals, e.g., doctors, dentists, psychologists.
- Lawyer.
- Accountants.
- Actuaries.
- Performing artists, e.g., actors, musicians, dancers.
- Consultants.
- Engineers.
- Architects.

Business needs permit unlimited accumulation: In addition to keeping as much as $250,000 of profits ($150,000 for service corporations) for *any* reason, your corporation can keep an unlimited amount of profits for the reasonable needs of its business. For example, if your corporation needs to buy a new car, a new desk, whatever, it can accumulate profits in order to make these purchases.

What the IRS allows: The IRS has a list of okay reasons for keeping profits. This is it:

- Business expansion.
- Debt retirement.
- Working capital needs.
- Acquiring another business.
- Lending to suppliers or other customers to protect your business.

What courts allow: The IRS admits that its list isn't exclusive. The courts have accepted other reasons for keeping profits.
These include:

- Retirement plan funding.
- Self-insurance.
- Reserves against contingencies.
- Key-man insurance.

Caution: Having a good reason and proving it are two different things. Make sure your business records prove your business needs. Put your reasons in your corporate minute book. And do it—if at all possible—before the profits are earned.

Example: If your corporation will need a new car next year, hold a Board of Directors meeting now. Discuss why the car is needed and how much it will cost. Resolve to set aside $10,000 (or whatever) of this year's profits to buy the car. Put all this in the minute book.

Now, let's look at IRS's last weapon for denying corporation tax breaks. This weapon is also based on a violation of golden rule number one.

HOW TO AVOID DOUBLE TAX

To most of us, the word "dividend" is good. It means money. Return on investment. Something extra. Happiness.

If the dividend comes from your corporation, however, it's bad. A dividend is profit that's been taxed already—to your corporation—and now it's going to be taxed again—to you, personally. See Exhibit 13-1.

Unintended dividends: IRS has a bad habit of calling certain payments dividends, even though you don't intend them to be. Excessive salaries and rents are two prime examples. Likewise, if your loans aren't valid, your corporation's loan payments will be dividends to you.

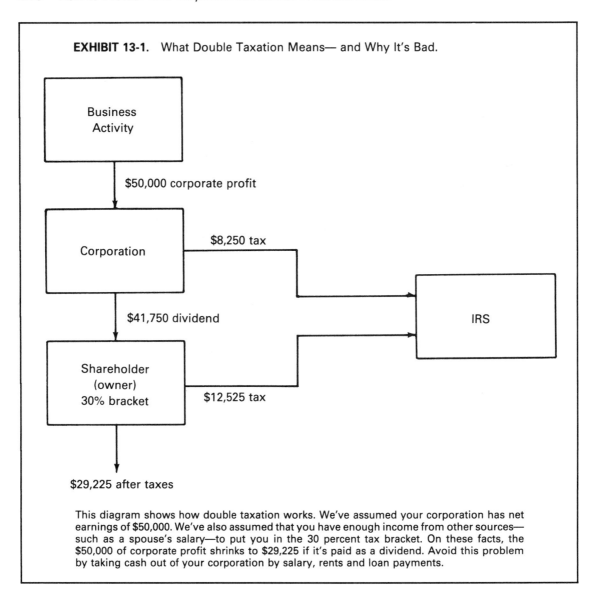

EXHIBIT 13-1. What Double Taxation Means— and Why It's Bad.

This diagram shows how double taxation works. We've assumed your corporation has net earnings of $50,000. We've also assumed that you have enough income from other sources— such as a spouse's salary—to put you in the 30 percent tax bracket. On these facts, the $50,000 of corporate profit shrinks to $29,225 if it's paid as a dividend. Avoid this problem by taking cash out of your corporation by salary, rents and loan payments.

The corporate car—A classic example: Sometimes you're taxed as though you received a dividend even though you didn't get any money. The classic example is the corporation car.

You are taxed on personal use of your corporate car, if you don't reimburse your corporation. You are also taxed if you don't keep good records of your business use. In short, you are taxed because you didn't follow golden rule number one.

Holland case: J. Henry Holland, Jr., was the president (employee) and sole shareholder (owner) of J. Henry Holland Corporation. Holland (employee) used the Holland Corporation's car for both business and pleasure. But neither Holland the employee nor the Holland Corporation kept track of how much was for business and how much was for pleasure. IRS said 22½ percent was for pleasure. Holland couldn't prove otherwise. Result: Both the Holland Corporation and Holland (owner/employee) paid tax on 22½ percent of the car's rental value.

Reimbursement saves tax: It's all right to use the corporate car for personal reasons. Just make sure you keep good records. And reimburse your corporation for the personal use.

Other examples: Always deal at arm's length. The business car example is just that, an example. The IRS will tax you, or your corporation, or both, anytime you violate golden rule number one by getting too cozy with your corporation.

Bargain purchase: Robert Terris and his dad were the only shareholders of a real estate corporation. The corporation bought land, subdivided it, built houses on it, then sold the houses. The corporation gave Robert and his wife a terrific deal on one of its homes. They bought it for $50,000. The home was worth $64,400. The Terrises were taxed on $14,400 of dividend income ($64,400 minus $50,000).

Personal expenses: If your corporation pays a personal expense for you, it's a taxable dividend. For example, you would be taxed if you used corporate funds to take your family to a movie and the corporation would be taxed because it could not deduct the expense.

Loans to your corporation: As the next section points out, it's a good idea to lend money to your corporation when you start it. In that way, you can get cash out of your corporation without paying a double tax.

But tax law says IRS can treat the loan repayments as taxable dividends to you. This won't happen if your loan is handled like any arm's-length deal. The IRS has said that you're on safe ground if you:

- Charge the prime lending rate.
- Make interest payable at least once a year.
- Don't lend more than three times than the amount you paid for your stock.
- Make sure your corporation pays on time.

These points were in IRS Proposed Regulations that were never finalized, but they are the most current guidelines available as of this writing.

Usually, you can avoid the double tax by hiring yourself, renting from yourself, and borrowing from yourself. The next two sections explain how.

HOW TO GET CASH OUT OF YOUR CORPORATION WITHOUT TAX PENALTIES

To avoid double taxation and the accumulated earnings tax, get cash out of your corporation by paying yourself a reasonable salary, renting to your corporation, and lending to your corporation. The following section discusses your salary negotiations. First, let's look at renting and lending to your corporation.

Rent to your corporation: Become your corporation's landlord. It's usually a good idea for you to keep business real estate in your name. Rent it to your corporation for a fair price; otherwise, any excess rent will be a dividend to you. And your corporation won't be allowed to deduct the excessive rent.

Any rent you get will be ordinary income to you. But your corporation will deduct it—provided it's a fair amount. Thus, you avoid double tax.

Caution: Because of the Tax Reform Act of 1984, renting certain items to (or from) your corporation will prevent you from claiming the investment tax credit and rapid depreciation under the ACRS rules. See the last section of Chapter 7 for details.

Lend to your corporation: Another way to extract cash is to lend your corporation money when you incorporate. Some of the cash you put in your corporation will be for stock. But make some of the cash a loan. In fact, three-fourths of your capital contribution can be by loans. (And this is a conservative estimate.)

For example, if you plan to put $20,000 in your corporation, make $5,000 a payment for stock and $15,000 a loan. The loan payment will be part interest and part principal. The corporation deducts the interest and you pay tax on it. The corporation can't deduct the principal, but you get it back tax free.

HOW TO NEGOTIATE A REASONABLE SALARY

Your corporation deducts your pay "package"—salary, medical benefits, life insurance premiums, pension plan contributions, and the like. But, if your pay is "unreasonable" (excessive), your corporation can't deduct the excess amount. And you will be taxed on the excess amount as a dividend.

Small corporations and the IRS have been battling for years over what is "reasonable" pay. There is no formula. It's purely a fact question.

To set up your pay package, negotiate with your corporation. This sounds silly, but that's what you have to do. You wear three hats: your greedy executive hat, your corporate director hat, and your shareholder (owner) hat. As executive, you want as much as you can get. As shareholder, you don't want all the corporate profits siphoned off by greedy executives. As a corporate director, you want to give your executives an incentive to work hard but you must protect the shareholder's investment. If you think of the situation in this light, you will probably "negotiate" a reasonable pay package.

Make sure the pay package spells out who pays for what out-of-pocket expenses, such as travel and entertainment. Also, you should agree to reimburse the corporation for any personal use of the corporate car.

Once the deal is struck, put it in writing. Hold a Board of Directors meeting and approve the contract. Write up the minutes of the meeting, explaining why the contract is fair—how great John Smith is and why, what a good job he has done in the past, how this deal will give him even more incentive, how this deal is competitive for your corporation's line of business. Be specific.

Then get to work.

SUMMARY

IRS isn't any tougher on corporations than individuals. It just has different weapons. These weapons shouldn't keep you from incorporating, Just remember to follow the two golden rules. This means keeping your corporation at arm's length from you and making sure the public and your creditors know they are dealing with a corporation.

TAX REDUCTION CHECKLIST

IRS publications to be obtained:

- Publication 334—*Tax Guide for Small Business*
- Publication 542—*Tax Information on Corporations*

Two golden rules to avoid trouble:

- Keep your corporation at arm's length.
- Make the public know it's dealing with a corporation.

How IRS attacks corporate tax breaks:

- Direct tax on business owner.
- Penalty tax on corporation for personal holding company income.
- Penalty tax on corporation for unreasonable accumulation of income.
- Double tax—first on your corporation, then on you.

Avoid direct tax by:

- Putting business assets and accounts in corporate name.
- Signing corporate name to contracts.
- Presenting yourself as corporate executive, not self-employed person.

Avoid personal holding company tax by:

- Wording contracts to avoid designating a particular corporate employee (such as you) to perform services.
- Not having more than 60 percent of corporate income from "passive" sources—dividends, interest, rents, and royalties.

Avoid accumulated earnings tax by:

- Establishing good business reasons for accumulating more than $250,000 (or $150,000 for certain service corporations).

Avoid double tax by:

- Not using corporate assets for personal purposes unless you reimburse corporation.
- Making sure all transactions between you and your corporation are for fair value.

Get cash out of corporation without double tax by:

- Renting to your corporation for fair market value.
- Making arm's-length loans to your corporation—see text for details.
- Taking a reasonable salary for your services as employee.

For both self-employed and incorporated businesspeople, tax-free retirement plans are the greatest invention since depreciation. Contributions to a tax-free plan are deductible, earnings build up in the plan free of tax, and benefit payments after retirement are taxed at favorable rates.

Before the Tax Equity and Fiscal Responsibility Act of 1982 (TEFRA) was passed, there were many differences between corporate and self-employed tax-free retirement plans. Thanks to TEFRA, most of these differences are eliminated for years *after 1983*. You will learn the new rules under TEFRA in this chapter, as well as the one major difference that still applies.

Specifically, you will learn:

- Why tax-free retirement plans are great shelters and great investments.
- Who may set up a tax-free corporate plan.
- Who may set up a tax-free self-employed plan.
- What types of tax-free retirement plans you can have.
- How to decide what investment form to use.
- How to control your investments.
- How much you can contribute to your tax-free plan.

- How you can borrow money from your tax-free plan.
- Why your tax-free plan will be "top heavy" and what this will mean to you.
- How to avoid harsh penalties.
- When you can get your retirement benefits.

Employees: Although this chapter focuses on one-person and closely held businesses, we will discuss, where pertinent, the effect of employees on tax-free retirement plans.

First, let's discuss what's so great about tax-free retirement plans.

WHY TAX-FREE RETIREMENT PLANS ARE GREAT TAX SHELTERS AND GREAT INVESTMENTS

Contributions to a tax-free plan save taxes two ways.

Contributions are deductible: First, contributions to a tax-free plan are, within limits, deductible from gross income ("above the line") and therefore reduce taxable income dollar-for-dollar. This benefit can be seen in two related, but different ways:

How to Maximize Your Return From Tax-Free Corporate and Self-Employed Retirement Plans

- As increasing the amount available for savings.
- As increasing the amount you can afford to save.

Example: Let's take two 50 percent bracket taxpayers, Green and Baker, who both want to establish a retirement savings plan. Green has decided to sock away $15,000 a year, come hell or high water, even if it requires some hardship, like giving up his annual Acapulco trip or reducing his grubstake for the gaming tables at Monaco.

Baker, on the other hand, has kids to send to college, sickly parents to take care of, and a mortgage with a big appetite. Thus, despite Baker's high income, she can't find $15,000 to save each year, no matter how deep she digs.

For Green, a tax-free retirement plan increases the amount available for savings (or for trips to Acapulco and Monaco). Each annual $15,000 contribution yields a $7,500 (50 percent of $15,000) tax refund that Green could put into a taxable plan.

For Baker, a tax-free retirement plan increases the amount she can afford to save—doubles it, in fact. With a taxable plan, Baker would be able to save only $7,500 out of $15,000 of earnings available for savings because taxes cut the available savings in half.

With a tax-free retirement plan, Baker could save the entire $15,000 because she can deduct the entire $15,000 from income. In effect, Uncle Sam gives her (or, to be more precise, doesn't take away) an extra $7,500 to use for savings. For the Bakers among us, that's a terrific deal.

Tax-free compounding: The second reason tax-free plans are great investments is that the income accumulates tax free. The effect of tax-free compounding is almost magical. In fact, when you work out the numbers on your calculator, you may blink, shake your head, clear the entry, and do the calculation all over again.

You will be amazed to discover that the numbers come out the same way no matter how many times you compute them. Don't get new batteries. Don't throw your calculator in the garbage can. It isn't lying to you. See Exhibit 14-1.

WHO MAY SET UP A TAX-FREE CORPORATE PLAN

Tax-free corporate plans are set up, as the name implies, by a corporation. Thus, if you are incorporated, your corporation can set up a plan for you, its employee. If you have other employees, they must also be covered, provided they meet certain minimum requirements. The added cost of covering other employees is a big factor in deciding whether to establish a tax-free retirement plan and what kind of plan to establish.

WHO MAY SET UP A SELF-EMPLOYED PLAN

Tax-free self-employed plans are for self-employed people who are not incorporated. The rules covering these plans also apply to businesspeople who are incorporated, but who have elected to be taxed under the special rules of Internal Revenue Code Subchapter S.

You are eligible for a tax-free self-employed plan if you have self-employment income. This is the income figured on Schedule C for sole proprietors and Form 1065 for partners. It is also the income reported on Schedule SE, Computation of Social Security Self-Employment Tax.

WHAT TYPES OF TAX-FREE RETIREMENT PLANS YOU CAN HAVE

The three major types of tax-free retirement plans are:

- Defined contribution plans.
- Defined benefit plans.
- Combined plans.

These three types apply to both corporate and self-employed plans. In other words, there are corporate defined contribution plans and self-employed defined contribution plans; there are corporate defined benefit plans and self-employed defined benefit plans; finally, there are corporate combined plans and self-employed combined plans.

In defined contribution plans, each par-

EXHIBIT 14-1. Tax-Free Retirement Plans Are Great Investments (Example).

	GREEN				BAKER	
	Taxable plan only	vs.	Tax-free retirement plan	plus	Taxable plan	Taxable plan	vs.	Tax-free retirement plan
Annual investment	$15,000		$15,000		$7,500[1]	$7,500[2]		$15,000[3]
After-tax yield	5%[4]		10%		5%[4]	5%[4]		10%
Accumulation after 25 years	$715,906		$1,475,206		$357,953	$357,953		$1,475,206
Tax on distribution	-0-		($628,450)[5]		-0-	-0-		($628,450)[5]
After-tax accumulation	$715,906		$846,756		$357,953	$357,953		$846,756
Total after-tax accumulation	$715,906		$1,204,709			$357,953		$846,756
Extra savings with tax-free retirement plan	N/A		$488,803 (68% more than taxable plan only)			N/A		$488,803 (136.5% more than taxable plan)

[1] $15,000 deduction times 50% tax rate equals additional $7,500 available for saving.
[2] $15,000 pretax earnings times 50% tax rate equals $7,500 available for saving.
[3] $15,000 deduction makes entire $15,000 of pretax earnings available for saving.
[4] 5% equals 10% yield times 50% tax rate.
[5] Tax using ten-year averaging rule.

ticipant in the plan has a separate account. Each year, a specific sum is placed in the account and invested for the participant's benefit. The annual contribution is based on a specific (defined) formula; for example, 10 percent of annual salary. The retirement benefit is based on whatever amount is in the participant's account at retirement. Thus, the risk of investment loss and reduced retirement benefits is on the participant.

In defined benefit plans, each participant is entitled to a specific annual benefit at retirement, which can be a specific dollar amount (such as $2,000 a month) or a specific amount based on a formula (such as 5 percent of annual salary times years of service). The actual amount set aside each year is actuarially determined to meet the guaranteed benefit at retirement. This amount can be considerably greater than a contribution to a defined contribution plan if the participant is close to retirement age.

In combined plans, each participant is covered by both a defined contribution plan and a defined benefit plan. In general, greater benefits are available under combined plans than under separate plans.

HOW TO DECIDE WHAT INVESTMENT FORM TO USE

Almost any financial institution is willing to take your money. After all, in this brutally competitive world of ours, a financial institution seldom has the opportunity to put a lock on a customer. Though tax-free retirement plans offer this opportunity better than many other mechanisms, you can avoid a lock by understanding the various funding methods and investment options.

There are basically two funding methods for building up your retirement fund. You may:

• Put your money into a trust or custodial account.

• Purchase annuity contracts from an insurance company.

Trusts and custodial accounts: Under the trust arrangement, a formal, legal document is drawn to transfer legal title to the money you put in the plan to a trustee, who agrees to invest your money for your benefit. The trustee is paid a fee for this service and is subject to the strict rules that apply to all fiduciaries.

Trustees are often banks, trust companies, savings and loan institutions, insurance companies, brokerage houses, and other types of financial institutions. For corporate plans, the trustee can be an individual, even a corporate officer (you), if approved by the IRS.

Since 1984, the same rule has applied to self-employed plans. However, if you are the only employee, you court tax disaster by being the trustee (or custodian—see below) of your tax-free retirement plan. It's better to use a professional trustee, such as a bank. Let the bank do the paperwork. You can concentrate on making money.

A custodial account serves the purpose of getting your money into the hands of a fiduciary, a necessary element of a tax-free plan. Although less formal than a trust, for tax purposes, custodial accounts are treated the same as trusts.

Annuities: A nontransferable annuity contract may be purchased from a life insurance company. Under such a purchase, there is no necessity for a trust or custodial account. You may purchase the traditional forms of annuities that pay you a fixed monthly income for life or a guaranteed monthly income for a fixed period of years. You also may invest in variable annuity contracts in which the return is governed by fluctuations in the value of assets purchased by the insurance company. Nontransferable "face amount certificates" issued by investment companies operating under the Investment Company Act of 1940 (mutual funds) are also included in the annuity category.

Before May 1, 1982, a third option was available for self-employed plans. You could have purchased U.S. Retirement Bonds. They were discontinued in 1982 because they were a bad deal (low yield). Existing bonds are subject to the same conditions as they were when purchased.

Deciding how to fund your tax-free plan and what investments to use requires an analysis of several factors, including desired return, flexibility, safety, simplicity, convenience, and expense.

Annuities are very safe, very cheap, and very simple, offer a fair return and some flexibility. Guaranteed returns are pretty low, but some annuities have been yielding an actual return of 11 to 12 percent recently. And if you are careful not to touch your money, you may be able to switch from one plan to another plan you like better (although switching may require you to pay an early-withdrawal penalty to the company).

Trust and custodial accounts offer the most flexibility and the highest return. The types of investments are almost unlimited, including stock, stock options, bonds, annuities, government securities, certificates of deposit, commercial paper, mutual funds, real estate, and even retirement bonds.

If you shop wisely, you should be able to find a financial institution that offers a plan that suits your needs. The advantage to using a financial institution is that it will already have a "master" plan that has wormed its way through the IRS approval process, and that will save you money. A "master" plan is a standard form of plan, with a related form of trust or custodial agreement, and administered by the financial institution as the funding medium to provide standardized benefits.

There also is such a thing as a "prototype" plan. It differs from the master plan in that it is not administered by the organization that sponsors it. Prototype plans are most often used by owner-employees and partnerships who want to use the plan for the entire organization.

HOW TO CONTROL YOUR INVESTMENTS

Before handing your money over to a financial institution, brokerage firm, or insurance company, consider a self-directed account. With a self-directed account, usually in the form of a trust or custodial account, you still part with your money. But you retain control over how it's invested.

Warning: Effective for 1982 and thereafter, self-directed plans—both corporate and self-employed—may not invest in "collectibles," which include gold or other precious metals, gems, works of art, stamps, coins, liquor, antiques, oriental rugs, or any similar items IRS includes in regulations to be issued.

Self-directed plans are relatively new, but are becoming very common. Almost all of the major brokerage houses have such plans. Many insurance companies have plans where you have substantial flexibility with your investment portfolio.

Once you select your investment portfolio, you can change your mind. You may tailor your self-directed portfolio to your investment objectives and shift as the market conditions change, or as your own needs dictate.

Before rushing out to start a self-directed plan, you should consider the cost of such a plan and whether you have the time to pay proper attention to your investment portfolio.

Fees for opening and maintaining a self-directed fund may be substantial. One plan, for example, costs $25 to open, a minimum of $80 to maintain, plus commissions on all sales and purchases. On the other hand, at least one discount broker charges only $25 per year to maintain the plan after an initial fee of $25 to open it. So it could pay to shop around a bit.

"Family" plans: An attractive alternative to using a full-bore, self-directed plan is to invest in a plan offered by a company that operates a "family" of "no load" (no commission) mutual funds and allows you to shift your money among the various funds whenever you wish. Such a fund family might include a stock market fund, a large-firm growth stock fund, a small-firm growth stock fund, and a long-term bond fund. This type of plan gives you convenience, simplicity, diversification, flexibility, low cost, and the promise of a high yield, if you are "shifty" enough.

Look for return: Do not investigate just one investment for your plan. That's like dealing with unguided missiles. It will cause a substantial degreening of your investment portfolio.

Why is it so important to shop around for a good investment? It's really quite simple. The better interest rate you are able to earn, the more money you will have at retirement. If, for example, you were comparing investments with the yield of 8 percent to investments with a yield of 12 percent, and you were able to make annual contributions of $15,000, there would be a mind boggling difference in the amount of money in the fund at age 60 (35 years later). At a measly 8 percent return, your total accumulation after 35 years of contributing $15,000 would be $2,584,752. At 12 percent interest, the accumulation would amount to $6,474,953. That little 4 percent difference adds up to almost $4 million!

Exhibit 14-2 shows the projected growth of tax-free retirement plan contributions of $15,000 per year at a 12 percent simple interest rate. As you can quickly see from Exhibit 2, consistent contributions will amount to a sizeable fund in a short period of time. Interest rate differences can have a massive impact on your projected balance, so make

---

EXHIBIT 14-2. Projected Growth.

This chart shows how your tax-free retirement plan fund will grow with annual contributions of $15,000 deposited on the first business day of the year, earning 12% simple interest.

AGE WHEN ACCOUNT IS ESTABLISHED	PROJECTED PRE-TAX BALANCE AT AGE 60
25	$6,474,953
30	3,619,990
35	2,000,008
40	1,080,787
45	559,196
50	263,231
55	95,293

---

sure you investigate all of the available possibilities.

HOW MUCH YOU CAN CONTRIBUTE TO YOUR TAX-FREE PLAN

As we mentioned earlier, there are three general types of tax-free retirement plans available under both corporate plans and self-employed plans: (1) defined contribution, (2) defined benefit, and (3) combined plans. Because of TEFRA, the contribution limits are *identical* for corporate and self-employed plans.

Exhibit 14-3 shows the contribution limits for defined benefit plans and defined contribution plans. Note that the Exhibit uses the term "contribution/*benefit*" limits, rather than just "contribution" limits. The reference to "benefit" is just a reminder that the permitted contribution for a defined *benefit* plan is an actuarially determined amount, the amount needed to fund a certain retirement *benefit*, for example, $2,000 a month. Thus, the limit for defined benefit plans is expressed in terms of the maximum benefit; the actual dollar amount you can stash away is determined by actuarial factors, such as your age.

The maximum contribution for combined plans is not shown on Exhibit 14-3. Suffice it to say that somewhat larger contributions are permitted for combined plans than for either defined contribution plans or defined benefit plans. However, if you will be

subject to the top-heavy rules—and you probably will be—combined plans will offer no advantage. The top-heavy rules are discussed later in this chapter.

Post-1983 contribution/benefit limits for both self-employed and corporate plans: The maximum contribution to a defined contribution plan is 25 percent of compensation, but not more than $30,000. The maximum benefit that can be funded under a defined benefit plan is 100 percent of average compensation for the employee's high three years, but no more than $90,000. A combined plan permits somewhat greater contributions, except for top-heavy plans, discussed later.

Figuring self-employed plan contribution limits: Under the old (pre-1984) rules, contributions to a self-employed plan were based on "earned income," which generally was the same as self-employment income. Under the new rules, self-employment income, for puposes of determining how much can be stashed into a self-employed plan, is computed "with regard to" the permissible deduction for self-employed plan contribution.

IRS hasn't issued any regulations on the new rules as yet, but it looks like the new rules require self-employed people to pretend they work for a salary. The "salary" plus the self-employed plan contribution can't exceed the self-employment income. To figure the maximum contribution, divide self-employment income by 1.25.

EXHIBIT 14-3. Contribution/Benefit Limits for Tax-Free Retirement Plans.

TYPE OF PLAN	CONTRIBUTION/BENEFIT LIMIT
Defined contribution plan limits: maximum annual additions[1]	Lesser of (i) $30,000, or (ii) 25% of compensation[2]
Defined benefit plan limits: maximum annual benefit that can be funded[3]	Lesser of (i) $90,000, or (ii) 100% of average compensation for high 3 years

[1] "Annual additions" are:
- Employer contributions; plus
- The *lesser of:*
    (i) employee contributions in excess of 6 percent of compensation, or
    (ii) one-half of the employee contributions; and
- Forfeitures.

[2] For the self-employed, "compensation" is determined with reference to the amount deductible and therefore will be less than self-employment income. Thus, a self-employed person with self-employment income of $100,000 can make a $20,000 contribution to a defined contribution plan. See text.

[3] The actual dollar amount of the annual contribution is computed actuarially, based on the assumption that benefits will be payable in the form of a straight life annuity (e.g., $90,000 a year for life) and that payments will begin after the recipient reaches age 62 and by the time he or she reaches age 65. Actual benefits, and the time they begin, may differ from these assumptions, but actuarial adjustments are made so that the annual contribution will be the amount needed to fund the assumed benefits.

Example: Larry Bucks is a self-employed salesperson who has a defined contribution self-employed plan. If Larry's 1984 self-employment income is $100,000, Larry's maximum contribution will be $20,000, not $25,000. This is because Larry must pretend he draws a salary, and compute his contribution on the basis of the "salary." The contribution and salary cannot exceed the self-employment income. Thus, if Larry's self-employment income is $100,000, his deemed "salary" is $80,000 and his maximum contribution is $20,000 (25 percent of $80,000).

HOW YOU CAN BORROW MONEY FROM YOUR TAX-FREE PLAN

TEFRA changed the rules on permissible loans from qualified plans. The new rules, which apply to loans made after August 13, 1982, loosen the restrictions on self-employed plan loans, but tighten the rules generally.

Before TEFRA, a business owner could not, as a practical matter, borrow from the business's self-employed plan. The loan was taxed as an outright distribution and, if it was made before the owner reached age 59½, an additional 10 percent penalty tax was tacked on. To scorch the earth a little more, the law also labeled such loans as "prohibited transactions" (no-no's) and imposed another 5 percent tax, plus a 100 percent tax if the money wasn't restored soon enough. Finally, the owner who got the loan could not have any contributions made to the plan on his or her behalf for five years.

In contrast, corporate owners could borrow from their plans if the loans were "reasonable." To be reasonable, a loan would have to:

- Be available to all plan participants on a more or less equal basis.
- Not be available in greater amounts to officers, shareholders, or highly paid employees.
- Be made under specific provisions in the plan.
- Bear a reasonable interest rate.
- Be adequately secured.

The new rules, while retaining the definition of "reasonable," put limits on:

- The amounts of permitted loans.
- The repayment period.

Limit on loan amounts: The new rules permit loans (including amounts outstanding on existing loans) of as much as one-half of the borrower's nonforfeitable interest in the plan, up to a ceiling of $50,000. Thus, the most anyone can borrow is $50,000. A "floor" of $10,000 also applies. Thus, any plan participant can borrow up to $10,000.

Repayment limits: Under the new rules, the terms of all loans must require repayment within five years, except for "home loans." A home loan is a loan used to buy, build, rebuild, or rehabilitate the principal residence of a participant or members of the participant's family. These include the spouse, parents, grandparents, children, grandchildren, and brothers and sisters.

Mortgage loan exception: Congress's Conference Committee agreed that "investments," including residential mortgage loans, will not be covered by the above restrictions on dollar amounts and repayment period if they:

- Are made "in the ordinary course of an investment program."
- Do not exceed the fair market value of the property purchased with the loan.

This exception does not apply, however, to loans benefiting officers, directors, or owners of the business sponsoring the plan.

Caution—earth still scorched: Although Congress was nice enough to repeal some restrictions on loans from self-employed plans, it managed to avoid changing the "prohibited transaction" rule. Thus, loans from self-employed plans to an "owner-employee" (someone with more than a 10 percent interest in the business) are still subject to the 5 percent/100 percent penalty mentioned above.

Result: Because of the "prohibited transaction" rule, owners of small businesses still may not borrow from their self-employed plans.

Thus, until Congress gets around to changing the "prohibited transaction" rule, the availability of loans will continue to be an advantage of corporate plans.

Exhibit 14-4 summarizes the new rules.

WHY YOUR TAX-FREE PLAN WILL BE "TOP HEAVY" AND WHAT THIS WILL MEAN TO YOU

If the TEFRA story ended with the new loan rules, the ending would be reasonably happy, despite Congress's apparent oversight in not repealing the prohibited transaction rule on self-employed plan loans to owner/employees. Unfortunately for many small businesses, Congress went on (overboard, some might say) to create a new category of tax-free retirement plans, which apply to both corporate and self-employed plans, called "top-heavy" plans. The "top-heavy" rules went into effect in 1984.

Why your plan will be top heavy: Top-heavy plans are plans in which more than 60 percent of the benefits are for "key employees." "Key employees" include, among others, owners of more than a 5 percent interest in the business.

Thus, all qualified plans covering one-person businesses will be top heavy. Many (and probably most) qualified plans covering small businesses with only a few non–owner/employees will also be top heavy. This chapter and this book is written for the business with fewer than ten owners.

Employee protection: Congress apparently thought that employees covered by top-heavy plans are particularly subject to unfair treatment if they aren't among the top-heavy group. The top-heavy rules try to protect these employees by:

- Requiring certain minimum contributions and benefits.
- Requiring accelerated vesting (nonforfeitability) of benefits for "non-key employees."

Effect on business with employees: The top-heavy rules will very much affect businesses with employees. The costs associated with

EXHIBIT 14-4. Flowchart Showing Rules on Loans from Tax-Free Retirement Plans After August 13, 1982.[1]

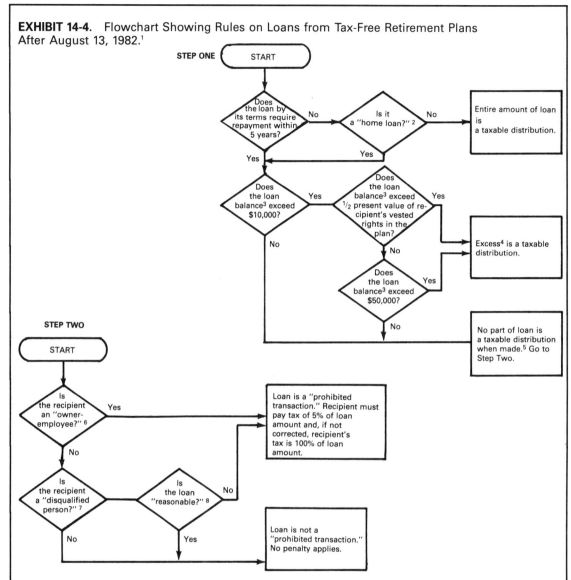

[1] Loans outstanding on 8/13/82 that were renegotiated, extended, revised, or renewed after that date are not treated as made after 8/13/82 if they were *required to be repaid and were repaid before 8/13/83.*

[2] This is our term for a loan used to acquire, construct, reconstruct, or substantially rehabilitate a dwelling unit used (or to be used within a reasonable amount of time) as a *principal residence* of the recipient or a member of the recipient's family. Members of the family include the spouse, descendants (children, grandchildren, etc.), ancestors (parents, grandparents, etc.), and brothers and sisters.

[3] Loan balance is the amount of the new loan and the outstanding balance of all loans from all plans of the same employer, including amounts outstanding on 8/13/82.

[4] Taxable amount is the loan balance minus the *lesser of:*
  • $50,000, or
  • One-half the present value of recipient's vested rights under the plan.

[5] Tax will apply to any amounts not in fact repaid within five years, except for loans falling under the "principal residence" exception.

[6] An "owner-employee" is the owner of an unincorporated business or a 10%-or-more owner of a partnership. Congress has not gotten around to changing the prohibited transaction rules to put self-employed persons on a par with incorporated persons.

[7] Disqualified persons include, among others, the trustee of the plan, a 50%-or-more owner of the business sponsoring the plan, and members of the owner's family.

[8] "Reasonable" is defined in text.

meeting the new requirements could be staggering. In fact, at least one authority says the top-heavy rules could cause "the demise of small employer plans."

Hint: Take heart. Congress certainly didn't intend to kill small employer plans. If Congress becomes convinced that the top-heavy rules might cause that result, it is likely to modify them.

Effect of one-person business: Although there are no employees to be protected, a plan covering a one-person business is subject to the top-heavy rules. The three main restrictions affecting the one-person business are:

- Distributions from the plan must begin by the time you reach 70^1/2, even though you have not yet retired.
- Any premature withdrawals (i.e., withdrawals made before you reach age 59^1/2, unless you manage to die or become disabled) are zapped with an extra 10 percent tax (in addition to the regular tax on distributions).
- No extra benefits or contributions are available for combined plans.

If these rules look familiar, they should, since they applied to self-employed plans before TEFRA. Now, of course, they apply to both top-heavy self-employed plans and corporate plans. Thus, for the one-person business, the rules don't make much of a difference from a tax standpoint.

The top-heavy rules could affect costs, however, since TEFRA requires all plans to have top-heavy provisions, just in case a plan becomes top heavy. Thus, all new plans will have to include top-heavy provisions and existing plans will have to be amended to include such provisions.

HOW TO AVOID HARSH PENALTIES

As a closely held or one-person business, there are severe penalties for taking your money out of your plan early, or playing with it while it is in the plan. Any money you withdraw early is called a premature distribution. A premature distribution is one made before you reach age 59^1/2, unless you become totally disabled or die. The penalty is 10 percent of the

amount distributed. Added to this penalty is your regular income tax resulting from the distribution. You include the entire distribution in taxable income.

Example: Morrison, age 58, a 50 percent bracket taxpayer, took his money out of his retirement plan. Morrison had accumulated $315,000 in his plan before taking the premature distribution. Morrison immediately began to feel the forces of evil when IRS took 10 percent of the distribution, or almost $31,500, right off the top. But the real pain came when Morrison included the amount in taxable income—IRS took $157,500 more in tax. Thus, Morrison walked away with $126,000 from a fund which had accumulated $315,000.

Caution: You can have a premature distribution in lots of ways besides an outright cash payment. If you pledge an interest in your plan or take out a loan against the plan, the amount of the pledge or loan is a premature distribution, unless you satisfy the loan rules discussed earlier.

You also get taxed on any prohibited transaction you have with your plan. A good rule of thumb is that any transaction you have with your plan is prohibited. A major exception is a loan satisfying the rules discussed earlier. But remember: For *self-employed* plans, loans are prohibited regardless of how reasonable the terms.

The tax on prohibited transactions is 5 percent of the amount involved in the transaction. Then, if you don't set things right—by giving the money back, for example—IRS slaps a *100 percent tax* on you.

How to transfer your money from one plan to another: Very carefully. The golden rule is never touch the money yourself; always allow plan administrators to do it for you. Once you have fondled the money, you have had a premature distribution, and, as you know, you will be taxed brutally.

WHEN YOU CAN GET YOUR RETIREMENT BENEFITS

As a one-person or closely held business, you are entitled to take your benefits from the plan anytime after you reach age 59½ or when you become totally disabled. When you are getting ready to die, you may be considered totally disabled—but check the rules.

Once you are eligible, benefits may be paid in a lump sum or in installments over one of the following periods: (1) your life; (2) a fixed period not exceeding your life expectancy; (3) your and your spouse's joint lives; or (4) a fixed period not exceeding your and your spouse's joint life expectancy.

You must have received your benefits by April 1 of the year following the year in which you reach age 70-1/2, or must at least start receiving benefits under one of the above payout plans by that time.

After your death, any remaining benefits must be paid within five years, or, if you tied the plan to your surviving spouse's life, within five years after your spouse's death. If you selected one of the options under which benefits are paid over a fixed period, the five-year limitation does not apply; benefits simply continue until the end of the fixed period.

Tax planning is essential when you are trying to take a large amount of money out of a retirement plan. There are a number of arrangements you can make that will reduce the tax burden, but all such arrangements should be reviewed carefully with your tax advisor. The two basic options are the lump sum and the installment plan.

Lump sum: One of the most common ways to take your money out, and probably the most expensive one, is to use a lump-sum distribution. If you do choose lump-sum distribution, tax law allows you to ease the burden by a special ten-year averaging formula. That's what was used in Exhibit 14-1. The actual computation is done on Form 4972. If you established your plan before 1974, the part of a lump-sum payment attributable to pre-1974 years could be taxed as a long-term capital gain.

You also may roll your lump-sum distribution into an IRA plan to avoid current taxation. However, you will not be allowed to use the 10-year averaging formula when benefits are paid from your IRA.

Installment plan: If you do not opt for the lump-sum distribution, you can vary the amount that you withdraw from your retirement plan each year, or set up an annuity type of account to get an equal income each year. In either event, you pay tax as the money in the plan is paid to you.

You and your tax advisor should definitely discuss the ins, outs, pros, and cons of all the possible payout arrangements. You worked too hard to build your retirement fund to allow IRS to get a big chunk of it.

TAX REDUCTION CHECKLIST

IRS publications to be obtained:

- Publication 542—*Tax Information on Corporations*
- Publication 560—*Tax Information on Self-Employed Retirement Plans*
- Publication 575—*Pension and Annuity Income*

Why tax-free retirement plans are great investments:

- Contributions are deductible.
- Earnings compound tax free.
- Payments receive favorable tax treatment.

Who may set up a tax-free retirement plan:

- Self-employed (file Schedule C) may set up a self-employed tax-free retirement plan.
- Corporate employees (including owner/employees) may set up a corporate tax-free retirement plan.

Types of tax-free retirement plans:

- Defined contribution—Amount put into the plan is defined (for example, 10 percent of annual salary).
- Defined benefit—Amount to be paid at retirement is defined (for example, 70 percent of average annual salary for life).
- Combined plans—Participants are covered by both a defined contribution and a defined benefit plan.

Investment options:

- Money can be put into trust, custodial account, or annuity contract.
- Banks, savings and loans, brokerage firms, and insurance companies all offer plans.
- You may control investments through a "self-directed" plan.

Contribution limits:

- For defined contribution plans, you may contribute up to 25 percent of compensation, but not more than $30,000.
- For defined benefit plans, you may contribute enough to fund a benefit of 100 percent of average compensation for high three years, but no more than a benefit of $90,000 a year.

Borrowing from the plan:

- Corporate employees, including owner/employees, can borrow from the plan if terms are reasonable.
- Owner/employees may not borrow from their self-employed plans—this is the only major difference between corporate and self-employed plans.

Top-heavy plans:

- Almost all small business plans—and all one-person business plans—will be top heavy.
- Special restrictions, designed to protect employees, apply to top-heavy plans.
- Effect on one-person businesses is minor—mostly paperwork costs.
- Effect on small businesses with employees could be devastating.

Harsh penalties:

- Ten percent penalty on distributions of plan funds before you reach age $59^1/_2$, unless you become disabled or die.

- Possible 100 percent penalty for improperly dealing with your money while it is in your plan.

Getting your money:

- Basic options are lump-sum payment or installment payments.
- Lump-sum payments are taxed under a special 10-year averaging rule.
- Installment payments are taxed as you receive the payments, under regular tax rules for annuities.
- You may defer tax by putting the funds into an IRA.

In this chapter you will learn some surprising things about Individual Retirement Accounts, affectionately known as IRAs.

Chances are you've seen advertisements by banks, S&Ls, insurance companies, and brokerage firms who want you to put your money in their IRA plans. Maybe you've ignored the ads because you and your spouse are already covered by a self-employed or corporate retirement plan. Or maybe you think the amount you can salt away in an IRA is just too piddling to bother with.

In the Economic Recovery Tax Act of 1981 (ERTA), Congress made significant changes in the IRA rules. In light of these changes, you may be surprised to find that IRAs deserve a fresh look. Always considered a mouse-poor country cousin to the rich corporate plans and self-employed retirement plans, IRAs can now do a lot more for you than you may think.

HOW TAX MAGIC BUILDS YOUR IRA SAVINGS

IRAs give you the same general tax benefits as corporate and self-employed retirement plans, although in lower dollar amounts. First, you can deduct the contributions you make to your IRA. Second, the earnings of the IRA

accumulate tax free. These two tax advantages add up to an enormous investment advantage, as shown in Exhibit 15-1.

Just as with a corporate or self-employed plan, you don't pay any taxes on the contributions or earnings in your IRA until you start receiving distributions. You'll probably be in a lower tax bracket then, so your tax bill shouldn't send you into cardiac arrest. If you're lucky enough (or smart enough) to still be in a high tax bracket at that time, your tax advisor should be able to help you work out a plan to dull the tax bite. In any case, as Exhibit 15-1 illustrates, you'll still be ahead of the game even if Uncle Sam takes a full 50 percent bite.

WHY YOU CAN HAVE AN IRA

Until ERTA came along, you couldn't have an IRA if you were covered by another retirement plan. Now, anyone who works is eligible. It makes no difference if your employer also has a retirement plan for you, you may have an IRA in addition to the employer's plan. Similarly, you may have both a corporate or self-employed plan and an IRA.

If you receive "compensation" in a taxable year, you may contribute to an IRA for that year. "Compensation" includes wages, sal-

How to Maximize Your Return From Tax-Free Individual Retirement Accounts

EXHIBIT 15-1. That Old Tax Magic.

IRA contributions build up surprisingly fast because your contributions are deductible and the earnings are not taxed until you take them out. If you were in the 50 percent tax bracket, you would need to make $2,000 in order to put away $1,000 in a taxable retirement plan. And one-half of your plan's annual earnings would be taxed. With an IRA, the $2,000 goes into the plan free of tax and the earnings build up free of tax. Let's compare the yield of an IRA with a taxable plan, using assumed pretax yields of 10 percent and 15 percent and assuming your IRA fund is taxed at 50 percent (an extremely high estimate) when you receive your benefits.

10 PERCENT PRETAX YIELD			15 PERCENT PRETAX YIELD		
End of Year	*Taxable Plan*	*IRA*	*End of Year*	*Taxable Plan*	*IRA*
1	$ 1,050	$ 2,200	1	$ 1,075	$ 2,300
5	5,526	12,210	5	5,808	13,485
10	12,578	31,875	10	14,147	40,607
15	21,579	63,545	15	26,118	95,161
20	33,066	114,550	20	43,304	204,887
25	47,727	196,694	25	67,978	425,586
Less tax	$ 0 (already taxed)	$ 98,347 (assume 50 percent)	Less tax	$ 0 (already taxed)	$212,793 (assume 50 percent)
Return after taxes	$47,727	$ 98,347	Return after taxes	$67,978	$212,793

aries, tips, commissions, professional fees, bonuses, and any other income you receive for services. "Compensation" also includes "net income from self-employment," that is, the amount on which you pay self-employment tax. Beginning in 1985, alimony also qualifies as compensation. Interest, dividends, rents, royalties, and other "passive" or "unearned" income is not compensation.

Just about everyone can use an IRA. Though the leisure class doesn't need a retirement plan and the unemployed may have more immediate needs, the working stiffs among us, including the self-employed, can benefit from an IRA.

HOW MUCH YOU CAN SALT AWAY IN YOUR IRA

You can salt away up to $2,000 each year in an IRA and deduct that amount from your gross income. You can't salt away more than your compensation. If, for example, you earn $1,000, the maximum amount you can put in an IRA is $1,000.

Spousal IRAs: If your spouse does not receive any "compensation," you can salt away—and deduct—up to $2,250 a year, provided that at least $250 is put in a separate IRA for your spouse, and provided you file a joint return.

Employer plans: When employer-sponsored retirement plans permit, participants may deduct their voluntary contributions to the plan as IRA contributions. These contributions, however, may not exceed the $2,000 ($2,250 for spousal IRAs) or the 100%-of-compensation limits.

Excess contributions: You get zapped with a 6 percent tax if you put more money into your IRA than the amount allowed. And you get re-zapped with that 6 percent tax each year you let the excess contribution stay in your IRA. But there is no tax if you take the excess amount and the earnings attributable to it out of the IRA before your tax return is due.

When contributions may be made: You may

make a deductible contribution to your IRA at any time up to and including the day (*without* regard to extensions) your tax return is due. And you may even set up the IRA plan at the eleventh hour. These rules allow you to do some very last minute tax planning.

Example: You file your 1984 tax return at 11:59 PM on April 15, 1985. At 11:00 PM, you contributed $2,000 to an IRA. You get a $2,000 deduction in your 1984 return. Remember, however, that even if you get a filing extension to, say, August 15, you must make your IRA contribution by April 15, 1985 to get a deduction on your 1984 tax return. (This change was made by the Tax Reform Act of 1984.)

Caution: IRA contributions must be made in cash, check, or money orders, except for "rollovers," discussed later.

HOW YOU CAN USE YOUR IRA

Exhibit 15-1 proves that an IRA can produce a much bigger nest egg than a taxable retirement plan. But, a corporate or self-employed plan can produce even bigger eggs, since you can make larger contributions to these plans. For example, in 1983, under a profit-sharing self-employed plan, you can contribute the lesser of $15,000 or 15 percent of your earnings from self-employment, so if you make $50,000 a year, you can put $7,500 a year in your self-employed plan. In 1984 the limits go up to $30,000 or 25 percent. Why bother with an IRA, then? There are a number of ways an IRA can help you.

Supplement other retirement plans: Before ERTA was enacted in 1981, you couldn't have an IRA if you were already covered by a retirement plan, including a self-employed plan. Now, you can supplement your other plan with an IRA. With a $15,000 contribution to a profit-sharing self-employed plan and an IRA, you can squirrel away up to $17,000 in 1983 ($17,250 if you have an uncompensated spouse). In 1984 the number goes up to $32,000 ($32,250 if you have an uncompensated spouse). As Exhibit 15-1 shows, a mere $2,000 per year IRA contribution, compounded at 15 percent for 25 years, will pro-

duce $425,586 before taxes, a tidy little supplement to your other retirement savings.

Compensated spouse: Whether self-employed or employed by a third party, your spouse also can put away up to $2,000 a year in an IRA.

This additional retirement savings opportunity could provide an incentive for non-compensated spouses to obtain either full-time or part-time employment. Many families have decided that it isn't worthwhile for a house-husband or housewife to obtain employment because there isn't much left of this second income after taxes, commuting costs, work clothes, childcare, and lunches. With an IRA, taxes on the second income can be chopped by as much as $1,000 a year (for families in the 50 percent bracket) and retirement savings increased by as much as $2,000 a year.

In the extreme case where the second income is exactly $2,000, and all of it is stashed in an IRA, taxes are zero (i.e., $1,000 less than a 50 percent bracket taxpayer would pay on $2,000 of income), yet $2,000 is added to the retirement kitty.

If your spouse is already employed and covered by a retirement plan, is an IRA worthwhile? Well, there's that extra tax deduction and retirement savings, of course, but maybe you don't think these benefits justify parting with your cash when you could use it right now for something special, like a Caribbean cruise.

Before you reject the idea of an IRA, though, take a look at your spouse's retirement plan. Are the benefits vested? That is, could any or all of the benefits be lost if your spouse quits work or gets canned because management wants "new blood"? Is the plan adequately funded or is it funded at all? What assurances do participants have that benefits will be paid even if the company goes down the tubes? These are not pleasant questions, but they ought to be asked when pondering whether or not an employed spouse should have an IRA.

Partners and employees: If your self-employment income is from a partnership or if you have any employees in your business, self-employment plans get complicated. Maybe you've gone over these problems with your tax advisor and decided that a self-employed plan isn't for you.

You can have an IRA whether or not you have any partners or employees. The IRA is yours. Partners and employees don't enter into the picture at all. Therefore, even if the existence of partners or employees shuts you out of self-employed plan benefits, you can still have the benefits of an IRA.

Rollovers: A "rollover" into an IRA is a useful device for deferring the tax on distributions from other tax-free retirement plans. (You can also use a rollover to change your IRA investments. We will cover that type of rollover later.) A "rollover" is simply a transfer to one or more IRAs of the money or other property you received in certain kinds of distributions from other tax-free retirement plans. These distributions include lump-sum and terminated plan distributions, provided the amounts distributed are the employee's entire interest in the plan. If the lump-sum distribution is from a self-employed plan, it qualifies for a rollover only if the recipient is at least age 59½ or permanently disabled. Also, the recipient of a bond distributed by a qualified bond purchase plan may redeem the bond and roll the proceeds over into an IRA.

Let's look at two examples of how a rollover can defer taxes.

Example (1): Fifteen years ago, at age 45, you signed up for a self-employed plan that called for a lump-sum payment of your entire interest at age 60. Now you're about to get the money, but since you're still making loads of money, the tax bite is going to be deep and painful. You may defer all taxes on the distribution by rolling the money into an IRA that will make a taxable distribution in future years.

Example (2): Your spouse worked faithfully for Downtubes, Inc. for 15 years, but Downtubes is going out of business and terminating its retirement plan. Your spouse can defer tax on the retirement distribution by putting the money into an IRA that will distribute the money in future years.

Caution: Any rollover must occur within 60 days after the employee gets the money or else the entire distribution is taxed.

The normal IRA rules don't apply to rollovers. You don't get any deduction for the rollover (although keeping the distribution out of your gross income in the first place is like getting a deduction). The $2,000 per year contribution limit does not apply, so you can roll over the entire distribution. Furthermore, the "cash only" rule on contributions does not apply, so if the distribution is in property other than cash, you can simply transfer the property to the IRA. Finally, a rollover has absolutely no effect on your regular contribution limit, so you can still contribute up to $2,000 to an IRA in a year when you had a rollover.

Hint: You are not required to rollover the entire distribution. You can keep some of the money and rollover the rest of it. The amount you keep is taxed like your other ordinary income. The amount you rollover into an IRA is not taxed until it is paid to you at some future date or dates.

HOW TO DECIDE WHAT INVESTMENT FORM TO USE

As you have undoubtedly noticed, every investment institution in the United States is stalking your IRA money. Deciding how to invest depends on the risk you are willing to accept in return for a possible higher tax-free yield. You may want to control the IRA yourself or have it professionally managed. There are a variety of options, and Exhibit 15-2 will give you an overview of the investment possibilities.

Types of accounts: There are two basic types of accounts you can put your IRA money in:

- Trusts or custodial accounts.
- Annuities.

The trusts and custodial accounts are quite similar, so we've lumped them into one category. Basically, the trust or custodial account is a written agreement between you and the custodian or trustee. You hand your IRA money over to the custodian or trustee, who invests the money for you. The trustee or custodian is usually a bank. (Even the IRAs of-

---

EXHIBIT 15-2. IRA Investment Options.

TYPE OF INVESTMENT	AVAILABLE FROM	TYPES OF FEES CHARGED
Savings accounts and Certificates of Deposit	Banks and thrift institutions	Annual maintenance fee
Mutual funds, including money-market, stock, bond, option, and combinations[1]	Brokerage houses or directly from mutual funds	Set up and annual maintenance fee. "Load" funds also charge commissions. "No load" funds do not.
Stocks, bonds, options, real estate, oil and gas[2]	Brokerage houses	Set up, maintenance, and commissions
Annuities[3]	Insurance companies	Annual maintenance fee. "Front-load" plans require percentage charge at beginning. "Back-load" plans require percentage charge if funds are withdrawn.

[1] Fund "families" allow switching between various types of funds.
[2] "Self-directed" accounts allow you to control investment decisions.
[3] Variable annuities function much like mutual funds.

---

fered by brokerage houses usually use a bank as custodian or trustee.) Annuities are available only from insurance companies.

Until May 1, 1982, a third plan was available. These plans were called U.S. Individual Retirement Bonds. These were discontinued because of their low rate of return. Any bonds purchased before their discontinuance are subject to the terms in effect at the time of purchase.

Hint: Although you will pay a premature withdrawal penalty if you cash them in, you can re-invest the proceeds into another IRA or tax-free retirement plan without tax penalty. This strategy might pay off in the long run if you can find a better return in another IRA plan.

Now, let's discuss some investment possibilities for your IRA funds. Except for the annuities, all these investment options would be available by using the trust or custodial account form.

Rule of thumb: The IRA is a tax-sheltered investment. Do not put tax-favored investments into your tax-sheltered IRA.

Example: Putting municipal bonds into an IRA would clearly be irrational since it would convert tax-exempt income to taxable income. Although the interest would be tax-free while the bonds were in the account, the money would be taxed when paid to you.

Collectibles not allowed: Congress probably did you a favor when it made collectibles such as gold and diamonds ineligible for IRA investments. Gold and diamond investments give rise to capital gains and you have nothing in that investment to compound (such as interest). Thus, you are probably better off keeping gold and diamonds under a mattress, rather than in an IRA.

Savings instruments: Everyone wants your money. The banks, thrift institutions, and credit unions will offer you Certificates of Deposit with a choice of maturities and interest rates. Generally, there is no charge for opening the account, and a small annual maintenance or management fee. The money is simply put into a savings certificate, and the only thing you have to be aware of is the early-withdrawal penalties.

Insurance companies: Most insurance companies offer individual retirement annuities. The big selling point is that they guarantee you a certain amount of income each year after you retire. The payout, per $1,000 you invest, is based on average life expectancies as well as the value of the investments purchased with premiums. In recent years, the yields have been very competitive.

No-load mutual funds: Firms like the Fidelity Group, the Dreyfus Service Corporation, T. Rowe Price, and the Vanguard Group—to name just a few—offer IRA investors several professionally managed funds without sales charges.

Other Investments: It is not necessary for you to put your money in staid, old income stocks or high-yielding bonds. Many firms provide investment vehicles where you can take lots of risks. You may even invest in real estate. Formerly, the real estate had to be bought with cash. Since 1981, however, an IRA can borrow to obtain income-producing real estate.

With all these options, the final decision will depend on what you feel most comfortable with. We lean toward high-income, reasonably secure investments for IRAs. The speculative growth investments are more appropriate once you've built a solid financial foundation.

HOW TO CONTROL YOUR INVESTMENTS

Many brokerage firms, including discount brokerage firms, offer "self-directed" IRA accounts. These accounts are much like other brokerage accounts, except the funds are kept in accounts separate from non-IRA funds. There is also a legal prohibition against leveraging with IRA funds, and that rules out such things as trading on margin and commodity futures contracts. As noted above, however, income-producing real estate may be financed. These accounts look good to those of us who sob when we think of losing control of our money for several years. We pay for the privilege of retaining this control, usually $25–$50 a year, plus commissions on any transactions we direct. To us, these fees look like a small price to pay for restful nights.

HOW TO MOVE YOUR IRA MONEY

The law does not require that IRA money deposited with one custodian must stay there. IRAs give you a bit of extra flexibility not possible with corporate or self-employed plans. Once a year, you may withdraw funds from one IRA and transfer them to a different IRA you like better. The transfer of funds from one custodian to another must be completed under the rollover rules.

Warning: Don't hold on to the funds too long. Get the rollover money out of your hot little paws by the 60th day after you withdraw it, or you will get burned with the 10 percent penalty tax on "premature distributions," plus you get scorched with the regular income tax because the "distribution" is added to your taxable income. Now if all this doesn't sound bad enough, get this: If you do, in fact, put the money into another IRA after the 60th day, the $2,000 (or 100 percent of compensation) limitation applies, so the excess is an "excess contribution" taxed at 6 percent (unless you yank the excess out of the new IRA before your tax return is due).

Caution: Make sure that you wait a full year (one year and one day) before starting another rollover. Count from the day you received the money in the first rollover. If you don't wait the full year, you'll have the same headaches as we just described: a "premature distribution" and possibly an "excess contribution."

Even if you accomplish the rollover without falling into any of these traps, you still may have to pay a penalty to the plan sponsor for a premature withdrawal. For example, if your IRA is with a bank that has your money in a 30-month savings certificate and you withdraw the money before 30 months are up, you may have to pay a penalty to the bank.

The words to live by when planning an IRA-to-IRA rollover are "be careful." Rollovers are, at best, a fall-back strategy to be used only when necessary. A better strategy is to invest in an IRA with built-in flexibility.

Before selecting your plan, make sure it has been approved by the IRS. Also, make sure your plan sponsor furnishes you with the required disclosure statement, which includes the plan's projected growth, the charges, and the amount—if any—of guaranteed return.

HOW TO AVOID PENALTIES

Premature distributions: As with corporate and self-employed plans, the money you have in your IRA is pretty much locked in, except for the limited fondling allowed by the "rollover" rules.

Unless you are dead or permanently disabled (defined as almost dead under tax law), you or your beneficiaries can't get any money from your IRA (except for money you're going to rollover into another IRA) until you reach age 59½. If you do, it's a "premature distribution" and you get zapped with a 10 percent tax on the amount distributed, plus the regular tax resulting from the distribution. Warning—you're treated as receiving prematurely all amounts in your IRA that you pledge as security for a loan. And things could be worse.

Partial rollovers allowed: Before 1983, you were required to transfer the entire amount. Now, you can withdraw funds from one IRA, keep some of the funds, and transfer the rest to another IRA. You will pay tax on the amount you keep, of course. You will also pay the 10 percent penalty for premature distributions if you are under age 59½.

Hint: Instead of taking physical possession of your money, have your IRA funds transferred from your present custodian or trustee directly to your new custodian or trustee. This

type of transfer is allowed at any time. *You are not limited to once per year.*

Prohibited transactioms: The IRA rules also prohibit you from any improper playing with your IRA. As unpleasant as the tax treatment of premature distributions is, the treatment of "prohibited transactions" and borrowing against an annuity is downright torture. You should assume that any transaction you have with your IRA is prohibited except: (1) putting money in; (2) taking any excess contribution out; or (3) withdrawing funds to be rolled over into another IRA. Specific examples of prohibited transactions between you and your IRA include:

- Sales, exchanges, or leases of property.
- Loans or extensions of credit.
- Furnishing of goods, services, or facilities.

If you do any of these naughty things, here's what happens: THE ENTIRE FAIR MARKET VALUE OF YOUR IRA IS TREATED AS THOUGH IT HAD BEEN DISTRIBUTED TO YOU ON THE FIRST DAY OF THE YEAR AND THE IRA LOSES ITS TAX EXEMPTION AS OF THAT DATE. If this happens, you will moan and whine with good cause because three very bad things will happen:

- You will be taxed on all income earned by the IRA during the year.
- The fair market value of the assets in the IRA as of the beginning of the year will be included in your ordinary gross income.
- If you are under 59½ and not disabled, you will have to pay the 10 percent "premature distribution" tax on the entire fair market value of the assets in the IRA.

Example: Larry is an able-bodied and sane (although not very bright) 47-year-old, 50 percent bracket taxpayer (Mom was kind to him), with an Individual Retirement Account containing $50,000 worth of assets at the beginning of the 1984 tax year. During 1984 Larry sells the IRA $100 worth of stock—a prohibited transaction. The $50,000 IRA earns $5,000 during 1984. Larry will owe Uncle Sam:

- A tax of $2,500 (50 percent of $5,000) on the amount the IRA earned during the year.
- A tax of $25,000 (50 percent of $50,000) on the "deemed distribution" of the assets.
- A tax of $5,000 (10 percent of the $50,000) on the "premature distribution" of the assets.

Grand total: $32,500 in taxes.

Assuming Larry can get his money from the plan sponsor without having to pay an early-withdrawal penalty (a nontax penalty), Larry will have $22,500 ($50,000 minus $32,500) from his IRA after taxes.

When you can and must get your money: You are entitled to start receiving your IRA benefits when you reach age 59½ or become permanently disabled. You may receive them all in one lump sum (although you probably shouldn't) or in installments.

If you elect to receive installments, your benefits must be paid over one of the following periods: (1) your life; (2) a fixed period not exceeding your life expectancy; (3) your and your spouse's joint lives; or (4) a fixed period not exceeding your and your spouse's joint life expectancy.

You must start to receive your benefits by the end of the year in which you reach 70½, and you must receive a certain minimum amount. If you don't, you pay a penalty of 50 percent on this "excess accumulation." Furthermore, you may not continue to contribute to your IRA in the year you reach 70½, or in any later year. A contribution at that time is an excess contribution, taxed at 6 percent for each year you let it stay in your IRA.

Exception: If an IRA consists of voluntary contributions to an employer-sponsored plan, the regular payout requirements don't apply. Distributions of these voluntary contributions is governed by the employer's plan. However, the "no-contribution after reaching age 70½" rule does apply.

Payouts after death: If you die before you receive all your IRA benefits, the remaining benefits must be paid within five years of your death or, if the plan is tied to your and your spouse's joint lives, within five years of your spouse's death. If you had already selected a fixed payout period, the five-year rule does not apply; benefits can be paid over the remainder of that period.

HOW TO PROFIT FROM EARLY WITHDRAWALS

Suppose you do not want to put your money away forever. Is an Individual Retirement Account (IRA) a good place for temporary storage? As noted above, you are slapped with a 10 percent penalty on any funds you prematurely withdraw from an IRA. Is it possible to withdraw your money early, pay the 10 percent penalty, and still come out ahead?

Once you reach age 59½, you may start withdrawing funds from an IRA without incurring that nasty 10 percent penalty. Are there any strategies you should consider when taking your money out of an IRA?

This section will answer both of these questions. First, we will discuss how long you must keep your money in an IRA in order to come out ahead. Second, we will explore some tax strategies for taking the money out of an IRA.

Don't be afraid of the penalty: The possibility of having to pay a 10 percent penalty tax on early withdrawals, albeit most distasteful, should not inhibit you from starting an IRA. In a relatively short time, the tax benefits of an IRA will outweigh the penalty. Remember, your contributions to an IRA are made with pretax dollars, and any earnings on your investment accumulate tax free. Under these favorable conditions, it doesn't take long for a penalized IRA to out-perform a taxable investment. Thus, there's no need to wait until retirement to reap the benefits from an IRA.

Example: At the beginning of this year, you start contributing $2,000 annually to an IRA. You are able to get 12 percent for your money, and you leave it undisturbed for eight years. At the end of eight years, you withdraw the entire amount and pay the penalty and taxes when you are in the 30 percent tax bracket. You would be left with $16,530 from your original $16,000 investment.

Disastrous? Hardly. Compare the results if you had not used an IRA. To begin with, your annual $2,000 investment in the 30 percent bracket would be only $1,400 per year, after taxes. You would be taxed each year on any interest received, so a 12 percent pretax yield would be an 8.4 percent after-tax yield. That means that $1,400 gaining 8.4 percent for eight years would amount to $16,377. Thus, even after all penalties and all taxes, you made more money in the IRA.

Earlier break-even: The break-even point comes even earlier for those in higher tax brackets. If you are in the 50 percent tax bracket, an annual investment in an IRA would begin to out-perform a comparable taxable investment in only five years. The moral of the story is that unless you are planning a major expenditure over the next several years, such as purchasing a house or funding your children's education, don't hesitate to open an IRA.

Moral: The longer you can afford to leave your IRA undisturbed, the better. But you don't need to wait until retirement to come out ahead on your investment. Even over relatively short periods, however, the average person can expect to do better with an IRA than without.

HOW BENEFITS ARE TAXED

Benefits are taxed as you receive them, just as with corporate and self-employed plans. The special 10-year income averaging plan for corporate and self-employed plans is not available for IRAs; only the regular five-year income averaging plan is available. Therefore, careful tax planning is essential for handling the distributions. Your tax advisor can help you adopt a plan suitable to your specific circumstances.

Warning: Aggregate payments to you at the end of any year after you reach age $70^{1}/_{2}$ must equal a certain minimum amount. If they don't, the difference between the minimum amount and the amount you have received up to that time is called an "excess accumulation." You get choked with a 50 percent tax on this amount. The computation of the minimum amount depends on when you start getting

payments, your life expectancy, and the value of your IRA interest.

Taking it out after retirement: What is the best way to withdraw funds once you retire? As slowly as possible. Unless you need the money, you should try to take out the minimum allowable each year. As noted above, you must begin making withdrawals by age $70^{1}/_{2}$, and the minimum amount will be determined based on IRS life expectancy tables for your age and sex. A $70^{1}/_{2}$-year-old single male, for example, can be expected to live, on average, for approximately another eleven years. Therefore, the IRS would require you to take out $^{1}/_{11}$ of the total amount in your account the first year, $^{1}/_{11}$th the second year, and so on. If you are married, you may be able to withdraw over a longer period based on the life expectancy of your spouse.

Hint: The money remaining in your IRA continues to accumulate earnings tax free, even after you begin withdrawals.

Example: You are 60 years old and you have contributed $2,000 to an IRA for 30 years, receiving a 12 percent annual return. Today your account is worth $540,585. For the sake of simplicity, let's say you have 20 years in which to make your withdrawals. In year one, you withdraw $^{1}/_{20}$th, or $27,029.

The money left in your fund is still earning interest at 12 percent and by the end of the year has grown to $575,183. Thus, you have earned more than you took out. The second year your withdrawal is $30,272, but at the end of year two, your account has grown to $610,300. And on and on. By the tenth year, your withdrawal will be over $76,000, and your fund will be worth almost $850,000. By the time you make your 20th and last withdrawal, an amount exceeding $270,000, you will have received a total payout over the years in excess of $1,800,000!

Dying is even better: Since distributions from an IRA do not qualify for either capital gains or special 10-year averaging income tax benefits, it is less attractive tax-wise for an individual to take a distribution while living and more attractive to defer distribution until after death. If you can die with some of your IRA fund still intact, the first $100,000 of death benefit payments can be received by your beneficiaries free of any estate tax. To qualify, the benefit must be paid over a 36-month minimum period or longer.

WHAT FORMS TO FILE

None. Well, almost. You ordinarily don't have to file any special forms for your IRA. Your contributions are reported on your regular Form 1040. When you start to receive distributions, the income will be reported on Form 1040 (as the law stands now, anyway).

The only time you have to file any special form is when you've been naughty and have to report (and pay tax on) an excess contribution, a premature distribution, a prohibited transaction, or an excess accumulation. The form to file is Form 5329. May you never have to.

TAX REDUCTION CHECKLIST

IRS publications to be obtained:

- Publication 590—*Tax Information on Individual Retirement Arrangements*
- Publication 575—*Pension and Annuity Income*

Three tax advantages:

- Contributions are deductible.
- Earnings build up tax free.
- Benefits are taxed when you are in a lower tax bracket.

Who is eligible for an IRA:

- Anyone who earns "compensation"—including wages, salaries, tips, commissions, professional fees, bonuses, net income from self-employment, and alimony.
- You can be covered by a corporate, self-employed, government, or other retirement plan and still be eligible.

Contribution limits:

- General limit is $2,000 a year, but not more than 100 percent of compensation.
- Spousal IRA—if spouse has no compensation, you can contribute $2,250 a year. At least $250 must be in spouse's name.
- If you put in more than allowed, you must pay a 6 percent penalty on the excess and withdraw it to avoid further penalty.

Other contribution rules:

- Contributions may be made for a taxable year up to the day (*not* including extensions) your tax return is due.
- Contributions, except for rollovers, must be in cash.

Some uses for IRAs:

- Supplement other retirement plans.
- Provide retirement benefits for compensated spouse.
- Avoid complications with partners and employees.
- Defer tax on payments from other retirement plans.

Investment possibilities:

- Two forms for IRAs:
  - Trusts or custodial accounts.
  - Annuities.
- Don't put tax-favored investments in an IRA.
- Collectibles, such as stamps, coins, precious metals, and the like, are not permitted as investments for an IRA.
- Certificates of Deposit are available from banks, savings and loans, credit unions, and similar institutions.
- Annuities are available from insurance companies.
- Mutual stock, bond, and money market funds—both "load" and "no-load"—are available from many brokerage firms.
- Other investments, including real estate, are offered by some firms.
- Self-directed accounts allow you to control your investments.

Moving your IRA money:

- You may move your money once a year without tax penalty if you reinvest in another IRA within 60 days after you get the money from your old IRA.
- You may move your money as often as you like by arranging a direct transfer between custodians or trustees.

Harsh penalties:

- Unless you die or become permanently disabled, no distributions are allowed before you reach age $59\frac{1}{2}$—penalty is 10 percent of distribution, plus regular income tax.
- Any dealings with your money (except rollovers) are prohibited—you pay tax on full value of IRA, plus 10 percent premature distribution penalty if you haven't reached age $59\frac{1}{2}$ or become disabled.
- A certain minimum benefit must be paid to you by the end of the year in which you reach age $70\frac{1}{2}$—anything less than the minimum is an excess accumulation, taxed at 50 percent.
- Early withdrawal could still be advantageous because of tax-free compounding.

Tax on benefits:

- Benefits are taxed as received.
- Five-year income averaging can be used—special 10-year averaging is not available.
- If benefits are paid over a 36-month or longer period after you die, no estate tax applies to the first $100,000 of benefits.

Income averaging is a great way to get some extra spending money to celebrate an especially good income year. This tax break helps keep you out of high tax brackets when you have an unusually good year. Furthermore, careful timing of your income, deductions, exclusions, and credits will help you get maximum benefits from income averaging.

The Tax Reform Act of 1984 makes it a little harder to qualify for income averaging for tax years beginning after December 31, 1983. Thus, for most of you, the new rules apply to your 1984 and later tax years, so this chapter covers the new rules only.

Under the new rules, you can use income averaging if your current year's income is 40 percent more than your average income over the previous three years, provided this difference is more than $3,000. Many of you will qualify under these new rules.

In short, income averaging is a terrific tax deal that is often overlooked. To make sure you don't overlook the benefits of income averaging, this chapter will cover:

- Who is eligible for income averaging.
- How to figure your averageable income.
- How to handle changes in marital or filing status.

- How changes in previous years' returns affect income averaging.
- How to plan for income averaging benefits.

WHO IS ELIGIBLE FOR INCOME AVERAGING

Only individuals are allowed to use income averaging. To be eligible, an individual must pass two tests: a citizenship or residence test and a support test. Almost everyone reading this book will pass.

Citizenship or residence test: You will pass the first test if you were a citizen or resident of the United States throughout your last five taxable years. In other words, anyone who was a nonresident alien during any of the last five taxable years does not qualify.

If you and your spouse file a joint return, your spouse must pass the test also.

Support test: To pass the support test, you must have provided at least 50 percent of your support during each of the three years preceding the year for which you want to use income averaging. These three years are called "base years." The year for which you want to use income averaging is called the "computation year."

16
How Income Averaging Saves Tax Dollars

If you were married during any of the three base years, you and your spouse together must have provided at least 50 percent of your combined support. Thus, if you were going to school, taking care of babies, or goofing off during any of those base years, but your spouse provided 50 percent or more of the family's support, you will still qualify for income averaging in the computation year.

If you don't pass this general support test, you may still qualify for income averaging if you fit any one of three exceptions.

Under the first exception, you must have reached age 25 before the end of your computation year, and you must not have been a full-time student for three years after you reached age 21. For example, if you graduated from college in 1980 at the age of 22, spent three years lounging around your parents' house, then made a pile of money in 1984, you would still be eligible for income averaging.

For tax purposes, a full-time student is one who attends school full time for at least five calendar months during a tax year. The five months need not run consecutively. For example, you could attend three months during one winter and two months during the following fall, drop out, and still be considered a full-time student during that year. Whether or not you are enrolled "full time" depends on what your school considers to be full-time status. Although a full-time course of study may include some night classes, the IRS does not consider you a full-time student if you attend classes only at night.

If you don't make the first exception, you still have two left. Under the second exception, you will qualify for income averaging if more than 50 percent of your taxable income for the computation year was from work you did in large part during two or more of the previous three years (that is, base years). For example, assume you have just earned $300,000 in royalties from an invention that you spent the last three years working on. In that case, you would qualify for income averaging.

We call this second exception the "major accomplishment" exception. This term is not used in the IRS regulations, but court cases suggest that the exception applies only to ma-

jor accomplishments, such as inventions or artistic works that take longer than one year to produce. On the other hand, working on *yourself* is not the kind of work contemplated by this exception. For example, spending years honing your acting skills before striking it rich in a major motion picture does not qualify as work leading to your computation year income.

Finally, if you fail the first two exceptions, you have one last chance. We call the third exception the "sponge off your spouse" exception. This exception applies if you are filing a joint return for your computation year and you provided 25 percent or less of the combined adjusted gross income of you and your spouse. For purposes of this exception, community property law is ignored. Only your actual earnings are considered to be your contribution, even though, under community property law, half of your spouse's income would be considered your income. For example, if your spouse earns $75,000 and you earn $25,000, the exception applies, even though community property law would treat half of the earnings as yours and half as your spouse's.

Disqualification for electing foreign income benefits: You may not use income averaging in any year in which you elect any of the following benefits: the foreign earned income exclusion, the foreign housing exclusion or deduction, or the exclusion for income from sources within U.S. possessions or Puerto Rico.

Exhibits 16-1 and 16-2 summarize the eligibility requirements.

HOW TO FIGURE YOUR AVERAGEABLE INCOME

The idea behind income averaging is to prevent a steep climb in your tax bracket in a year when you had an unusually steep climb in taxable income. To oversimplify, this is done by taxing the steep increase in taxable income as though you had received it over a four-year period, instead of in a single year. The result is that the steep increase will be taxed at a lower rate.

Definitions: To better understand how income averaging works, you will need to know a few basic definitions.

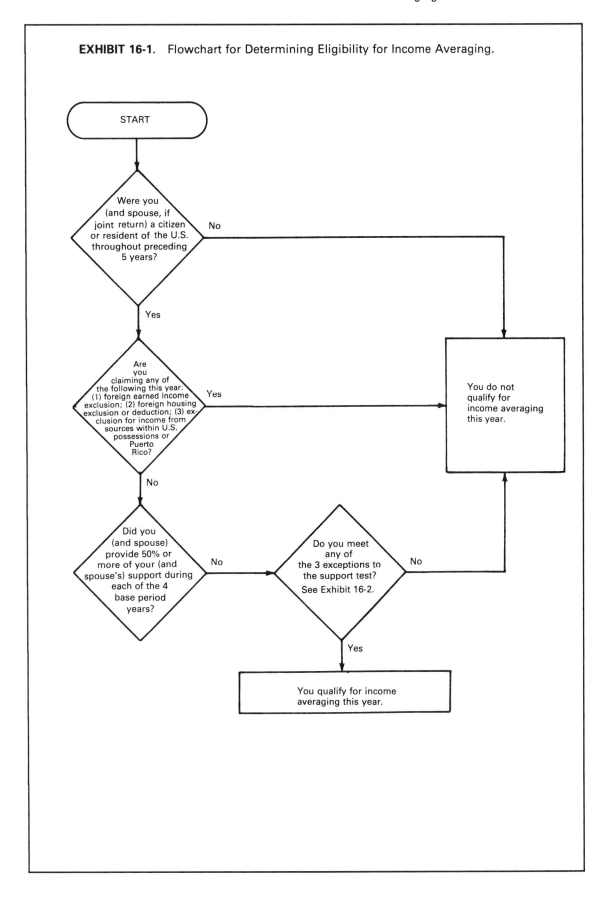

EXHIBIT 16-1. Flowchart for Determining Eligibility for Income Averaging.

EXHIBIT 16-2. Flowchart for Support Test Exceptions.

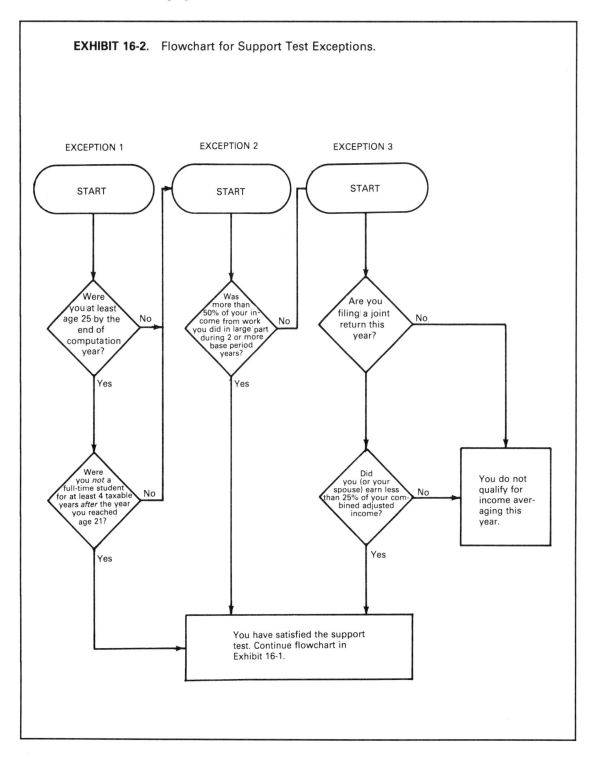

"Computation year"—The computation year is simply the taxable year in which you want to use income averaging. For example, if you are doing your 1985 tax return, your computation year is 1985.

"Base year"—A base year is any of the three years immediately preceding your computation year. For example, if your computation year is 1984, your base years are 1983, 1982, and 1981.

"Base period" and "Base period income" —The term base period means the entire three base years, and the term base period income means your income during the entire three-year base period.

Averageable income concept is critical: Now that we've explained a few basic terms, let's move to the main definition in the income averaging process, the definition of averageable income. This definition is critical because the averageable income determines how much of a break you get from income averaging. In simplest terms, averageable income is your taxable income for the computation year minus 140 percent of your average *base period income.*

Many people will be able to use the simple formula in the above paragraph. However, almost every tax calculation requires a few adjustments. Exhibit 16-3 shows the three necessary adjustments. If you do not receive any income from outside the U.S., do not have a self-employed retirement plan, and do not live in a community property state, these adjustments will not be necessary. If, however, any of these three facts apply to you, you may need to adjust your taxable income as shown in Exhibit 16-3. We will discuss each of these adjustments below.

Adjustment 1—Foreign income: As we mentioned earlier, you may not use income av-

eraging if you elect to take advantage of tax breaks available from foreign-source income. Thus, if you use income averaging, you must include foreign-source income in figuring your averageable income. In many cases, you will be much better off if you use the foreign income breaks than if you use income averaging. However, you must work out the numbers both ways in order to be sure.

Adjustment 2—Tax-free retirement plan distributions: If you are an owner-employee with a tax-free retirement plan and you receive a premature distribution, you must subtract the amount of this penalized distribution from your taxable income for purposes of income averaging. You will still pay tax on the premature distribution, of course, but you may not use income averaging to determine that tax.

Adjustment 3—Community property adjustment: If you and your spouse file a joint tax return, the community property laws present no problem to you. But when you file separate returns, you may have to adjust your taxable income, as described below.

If you and your spouse live together at any time during the year, you may include only the income that you earned, but not more than your one-half share of the community income. For example, if your spouse made $40,000 and you made $20,000, you would

---

EXHIBIT 16-3. Adjusted Taxable Income for Computation Year*.

1. Taxable income $_____
2. Plus: Income from sources outside U.S. or from U.S. possessions or Puerto Rico   _____
3. Minus: Premature distributions from a tax-free retirement plan, if you are an owner-employee   _____
4. Minus: Community income adjustment, if you are filing a separate return   _____

               Adjusted taxable income $_____

* Adjusted taxable income for the computation year and for the base years is figured the same way, but adjustments may be necessary for the base years because of different filing status or different marital status. (See Exhibits 16-5 and 16-6.)

only include the $20,000 of income that you earned when figuring your averageable income. On the other hand, your spouse could include only $30,000 in figuring averageable income, even though your spouse earned $40,000.

If you and your spouse lived apart for the entire year, you would include in your taxable income all of your earnings, even if they were more than your share of the community earned income. No adjustment would be necessary in that case.

Earned income includes wages, salaries, and fees. If you are in a business in which property and money—as well as services—are important, no more than 30 percent of the net income counts as earned income. So-called passive income, such as interest, dividends, pensions, annuities, and capital gains, do not count as earned income. Rental income is not considered earned income unless you perform personal services in connection with the rental.

Once you have made the above adjustments—adding back your foreign-source income, subtracting premature distributions, and subtracting the community income adjustment—the result is "adjusted taxable income." This number is the first step in determining averageable income.

Base period income: As mentioned before, the base period is the three taxable years before your computation year and your base period is your income during those years. In determining your base period income, you make the same adjustments that you made in figuring your adjusted taxable income for the computation year. However, if your marital or filing status in any base year was different from your marital or filing status in the computation year, you must apply special rules, which are discussed in the next section of this chapter. For the moment, we will ignore those adjustments.

$3,000 minimum: After you have figured your adjusted taxable income for your base period years, divide by three to find your average base period income. Multiply this average by 1.4 and subtract the result from the average base period income. The result is your "averageable income." See Exhibit 16-4.

If this amount exceeds $3,000, you may use income averaging.

At this point, you may wish to review Exhibits 16-3 and 16-4 again. These exhibits give you a quick and easy overview of the necessary computations. Stripped of their adjustments, these Exhibits show that you may use income averaging if your computation year's income is more than 140 percent of your average income over the preceding three years, provided the difference is more than $3,000. Having thus gotten your bearings, you are now ready to tackle the adjustments required when your computation year's marital or filing status differs during any base year.

HOW TO HANDLE CHANGES IN MARITAL OR FILING STATUS

If you have been married to the same person for the last four years and have filed joint returns during each of those years, you will have no problem in figuring your averageable income. Likewise, if you have been single for the past four years, you will have no problem. You will simply use the information in your tax returns that cover the four base periods.

However, if your marital or filing status for the computation year was different from your marital or filing status during any base period year, an adjustment will probably be necessary.

Why adjustment is necessary: The idea behind the following rules is to allow you to figure your base period income in the same way as you figured your computation year income. For example, if you were single during each of the three base period years and you earned $20,000 each year, then you married someone also earning $20,000 a year, your computation year income would be $40,000 (assuming you file jointly), and you would get a big break from income averaging. This type of situation was obviously not what was intended when the income averaging law was passed. Thus, in this example, your spouse's income during the base period would be added to your income during the base period (assuming your spouse was also

---

EXHIBIT 16-4. Averageable Income

1. Adjusted taxable income for computation year. (See Exhibit 16-3.) $ _____

2. Base period income (adjusted taxable income for all three base period years) _____

3. Divide amount from line 2 by 3 ÷ 3

3a. Average base period income _____

4. Multiply above amount by 1.4 × 1.4   [_____]

5. Subtract amount on line 4 from amount on line 1. $ _____

Result is averageable income. If this amount is more than $3,000, you may use income averaging.

---

single during that time). As a result, you would not be eligible for income averaging.

Most of us can see the fairness and simplicity behind the idea of adjusting the base period income to account for filing status or marital status changes. In practice, however, the rules can get pretty complex. Under these rules, you are required to compute your income in as many as six different ways, in each of the three base period years, and then to pick the highest number for figuring your adjusted taxable income each year. But don't panic. Most people will not have to make this many adjustments.

A simplified guide through the adjustment maze: Exhibits 16-5 and 16-6 summarize the adjustment rules. Exhibit 16-5 shows how to compute base year income under the three methods we will describe below. Exhibit 16-6 is a flowchart that correlates your computation year status with your base year status and tells you which of these methods to use. We will describe how to use these two Exhibits as we discuss the rules.

Before we move on, let's pause for a minute to make sure we know where we are and where we've been. The rules we are discussing are designed to determine the taxable income in any given base year. These numbers may be further adjusted as shown on Exhibit 16-3 (which can be used to figure both your computation year income and your income in each base year).

The three methods: You must use at least

two of the following three methods to determine your base year income when your marital or filing status is different in your computation than it was in any given base year. The highest of the amounts figured under these methods is the amount you use for your base year income. The three methods are as follows:

1. Your separate income for the base year.
2. 50 percent of the joint income of you and your former spouse in the base year.
3. *If you are filing a separate return this year, add your separate income in the base year to the separate income of your current spouse in the computation year, and divide by two.*

If you are filing a joint return for the computation year and your spouse was married to someone other than you, your spouse must also use these three methods.

To figure your separate income during any base year, allocate income and deductions between you and your former spouse on the basis of your respective adjusted gross incomes. *If your adjusted gross income was 85 percent or more of the combined adjusted gross incomes of you and your former spouse, you could take all of the deductions.*

Working example: Let's use Exhibits 16-5 and 16-6 to work through an example. We have assumed that you were married to a different spouse during the base year and that you filed a joint return showing $50,000 of income and $10,000 of personal exemptions and itemized

EXHIBIT 16-5. Computing Base Period Income Under the Three Methods (Example).

	YOU[1]	FORMER[1] SPOUSE	JOINT[1] RETURN	PRESENT[2] SPOUSE
Form 1040 adjusted gross income	$40,000	$10,000	$50,000	$12,000
Exemptions and itemized deductions	8,000[3]	2,000[3]	10,000	2,000[3]
Taxable income	$32,000	$ 8,000	$40,000	$10,000

[1] Base year numbers
[2] Computation year numbers
[3] Allocated based on ratio of adjusted gross income. If you had made 85 percent or more of the adjusted gross income, all exemptions and itemized deductions would have been yours.

Method 1: Your separate taxable income as computed ($40,000–8,000) = $32,000

Method 2: Fifty percent of joint amount with former spouse ($32,000 + 8,000) × 50% = $20,000

Method 3: Fifty percent of the sum of your separate taxable income added to your new spouse's taxable income ($32,000 + 10,000) × 50% = $21,000

deductions. Further, your former spouse's earnings during that year were $10,000 and your earnings were $40,000. Finally, we assumed that your present spouse earned $12,000 *in your computation year.* Under Method 1 (your separate taxable income), you would include $32,000 as taxable income for the base year. Notice that $8,000 of the $10,000 of exemptions and itemized deductions were allocated to you, since you earned 80 percent of the combined adjusted gross incomes of you and your former spouse. Had you earned 85 percent or more of the combined adjusted gross incomes, you would have gotten all the exemptions and deductions.

To determine which of the three methods applies, check the flowchart in Exhibit 16-6. If we assume that you and your present spouse plan to file separate returns this year, the flowchart tells us that you must use the largest of the three amounts shown. If we assume that you plan to file jointly this year, the flowchart tells us that you must use the larger of Methods 1 or 2. Note also that if your present spouse was also married in the base period year, your present spouse would need to make the same calculations.

Need for records: If adjustments are required, you must be able to prove that you

are using the correct numbers for the base period years. Circumstances such as a divorce can pose serious obstacles to obtaining copies of joint tax records. You can get a copy of your previous years' returns by filing Form 4506 with the IRS Service Center where the original tax return was filed.

But the tax return alone may not be enough. You must be able to prove the deductions for the base years as well. Failure to prove your income and deductions may cause you to lose the benefits of income averaging.

HOW TO PLAN FOR INCOME AVERAGING BENEFITS

Income averaging benefits can be more than just an unexpected, pleasant surprise in an unusually good year. By careful planning, you may get income averaging benefits you otherwise might have lost. Furthermore, you should weigh the benefits of income averaging against the benefits of installment sales and the benefits of the foreign income exclusion.

Election permits planning: To use income averaging, you must file Schedule G. Since income averaging is elective and not auto-

EXHIBIT 16-6. Flowchart for Base-Year Income (Applying the Three Methods to Your Status).

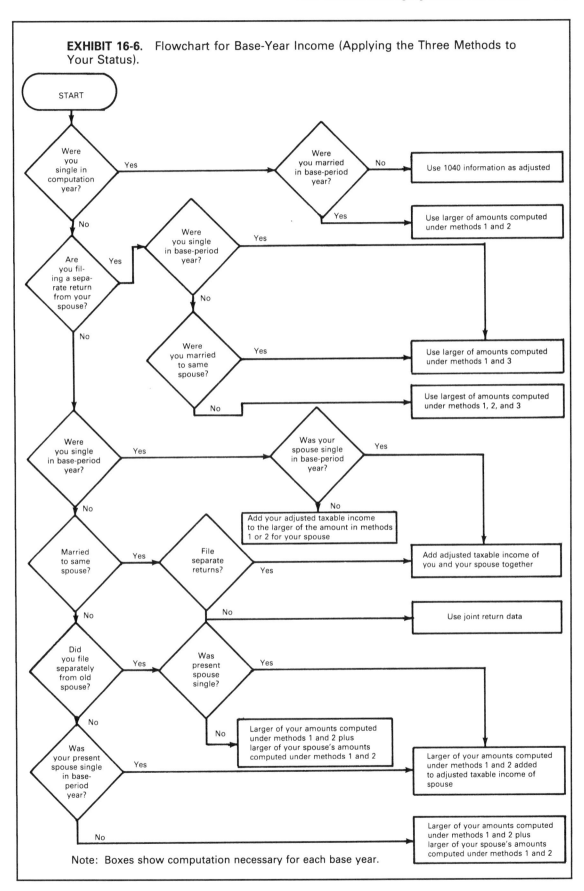

Note: Boxes show computation necessary for each base year.

matic, some taxpayers lose the benefits of income averaging because they fail to make the election. However, for the savvy taxpayer, the election requirement allows flexibility. For example, if you are planning to sell some property for a large capital gain, you may decide to make an installment sale to spread your tax over ten years, fifteen years, or longer, instead of recognizing all your gain in one year, even though you could use income averaging by so doing.

Whether or not you use income averaging in a particular year, you may change your election by filing an amended return within three years from the date you filed your original return. (If you filed early, the three years don't start until the date your return was due. If you were more than a year late in paying your taxes, you have two years from the date of payment in which to amend your return.)

This ability to change your election allows you to use the wisdom of hindsight one, two, or three years after making the initial election. Your situation might have changed enough to warrant a change of mind.

Making a bad year worse can make your tax situation better: No one wants to take a financial beating, but financial beatings can sometimes be tax blessings. A year in which you have a net operating loss can set you up very nicely for income averaging the following year. If your previous years were good years but your current year is a loss year, you can carry your loss back to the three preceding taxable years. Not only will this strategy give you cash in the form of a tax refund, but it will also give you a better shot at qualifying for income averaging next year. Therefore, if your pocketbook can stand it, you should consider accelerating deductions into your current taxable year and deferring income into the upcoming taxable year.

Making a good year better can make your tax situation better: Everyone loves the tax years when the money just keeps rolling in—until tax time rolls around. Income averaging can take some of the edge off of your tax bill. In fact, since the effect of income averaging is to tax your extra income in a lower bracket than it would ordinarily be taxed, you should consider accelerating some of your income into

the current year and deferring your deductions until the following year in order to take maximum advantage of this effect.

WORKSHEET AND EXAMPLE COMPUTATION

Exhibit 16-7 is an example showing how to use the income averaging worksheet. The example is based on the following facts.

O'Neill is a single taxpayer whose taxable income averaged $20,000 over a three-year period. O'Neill's career takes a sharp upward turn in the fourth year, when O'Neill's taxable income is $40,000. During the four base years and the computation year, O'Neill did not have any income from non-U.S. sources, nor did he receive any premature distributions from any self-employed retirement plans. Therefore, O'Neill didn't have to make any adjustments in his taxable income for the computation year or any of the base years. O'Neill referred to Exhibit 16-4 and determined that his averageable income was $12,000 (140 percent of O'Neill's average base period income of $20,000 was $28,000. He subtracted this from his adjusted taxable income for the computation year of $40,000. The result was $12,000 of averageable income.) O'Neill saved $332 because of income averaging.

HOW CHANGES IN OTHER YEARS' RETURNS AFFECT INCOME AVERAGING

If a change is made in the IRS's favor on a previous year's return, you must revise your figures and file an amended return for your computation year. Thus, if the IRS disallows a deduction or credit on a previous year's return, you must amend your return for your computation year. On the other hand, if you amend a previous year's return to take a deduction or credit you previously overlooked, you should also amend your return for the computation year. The lower income in the previous year will increase your averageable income and therefore reduce your taxes.

Example: Assume the IRS found a mistake in one of your base years, resulting in addi-

EXHIBIT 16-7. How O'Neill Saved $684 by Using Averaging.

1.	Averageable income times .25	$ 3,000	
2.	Average base period income times 1.4	28,000	
3.	Total of amounts in lines 1 and 2	31,000	
4.	Community property adjustment (for separate returns)	-0-	
5.	Total of amounts in lines 3 and 4	$31,000	
6.	Tax on amount in line 5*		$ 6,453
7.	Tax on amount in line 3*	6,453	
8.	Tax on amount in line 2*	(5,465)	
9.	Subtract amount in line 8 from amount in line 7	$ 988	
10.	Multiply amount in line 9 by 3		2,964
11.	Tax on regular taxable income (unadjusted) for the current year. (This applies only if you received a premature distribution from a tax-free retirement plan.)	N/A	
12.	Tax on difference between regular taxable income and premature distribution from tax-free retirement plan	N/A	
13.	Subtract amount in line 12 from amount in line 11		N/A
14.	Add amounts in lines 6, 10, and 13. Result is tax under income averaging method		$ 9,417**

*Use Tax Rate Schedules for current year.

**Savings are $332 ($9,749 regular tax minus $9,417 tax using income averaging).

tional taxable income of $10,000. This would reduce your averageable income. On the other hand, a $10,000 decrease in taxable income for a base year will increase your averageable income.

Effect on previous years' returns: Income averaging will not, in itself, affect your previous years' returns. If more than three years have passed since you filed your return, IRS may not stick you with additional tax for those years (assuming you didn't commit fraud or leave out more than 25 percent of your income). However, in figuring your averageable income, you must use the corrected numbers for your base years. For example, if you reported $6,000 of taxable income three years ago, but you should have reported

$6,500, you must use the full $6,500 in figuring your averageable income, even though IRS can't tax you on the extra $500).

Losses in future years: If you have a loss in a future year, you may carry the loss back three years and get tax refunds for those years. If the losses are carried back to base years, you should amend your computation year's return because the lower base period income will increase your averageable income. This produces a lower tax under income averaging. On the other hand, if you carry a loss back to your computation year, you must amend your return, since the loss will reduce—or eliminate—your averageable income.

TAX REDUCTION CHECKLIST

IRS publications to be obtained:

- Publication 506—*Income Averaging*
- Publication 555—*Community Property and the Federal Income Tax*
- Publication 54—*Tax Guide for U.S. Citizens Abroad*
- Publication 570—*Tax Guide for U.S. Citizens Employed in U.S. Possessions*
- Publication 593—*Income Tax Benefits for U.S. Citizens Who Go Overseas*
- Publication 516—*Tax Information for U.S. Government Civilian Employees Stationed Abroad*

Individuals eligible for income averaging:

- You must have been a U.S. citizen or resident for the computation year and all three base years.
- You must have provided at least 50 percent of your own support unless you satisfy one of the following exceptions:
  — You are at least 25 years old in your computation year, and you were not a full-time student for any three tax years after you reached age 21.
  — Over 50 percent of your taxable income for the computation year was from work you did in large part during two or more base years.
  — You file a joint return in the computation year, and you did not provide more than 25 percent of the combined adjusted gross income of you and your spouse.

Benefits of income averaging and definitions:

- Income averaging prevents a steep increase in your income from causing a steep increase in your tax bracket.
- Computation year is the year in which you want to use income averaging.
- Base year is any of the three years before your computation year.
- Base period is three base years.
- Base period income is your total income over the three base years.

Determining your averageable income:

- To use income averaging, you must have averageable income of more than $3,000.
- In the computation year, adjust your taxable income for
  — Income from sources outside the U.S. or income from U.S. possessions.
  — Income earned under community property laws, if you are married and filing a separate return.
  — Premature distributions received as an owner/employee under a self-employed retirement plan.
- Taxable income for any base year may not be less than zero.

Effect of your filing or marital status on income averaging:

- If your marital status or filing status for the computation year differs from any of the three base years, you must make adjustments so that all four years are on the same basis.
- If you were single in the computation year and all base years, you merely use your taxable income as a starting point for each year.
- If you were married to the same person in both your computation year and any base year, you filed joint returns with your spouse in the base year, and you file a joint return in your computation year, your base year taxable income is simply your joint taxable income for that year.
- If you were married to the same person in both the computation year and any base year, you filed separate returns in your base year, but you and your spouse file a joint return in the computation year, you merely add

your separate taxable incomes together to put each period on the same basis.

- If you and your spouse were single during any base year, were married during the computation year, and filed jointly for the computation year, you merely add your base year incomes.
- If you do not meet any of these situations for any base year, refer to the flowchart in Exhibit 16-6 to determine which of the three methods shown in Exhibit 16-5 must be used.

Planning for income averaging:

- Accelerating deductions and deferring income to make a bad year even worse can increase income averaging benefits by reducing the base period income.
- Accelerating income into your computation year and deferring deductions and credits until a later year can save taxes by increasing your averageable income.

Effect of changes in other years:

- You must maintain tax returns for all base years and be ready to prove your income and deductions.
- The IRS may not change your tax liability for returns more than three years old, but may make changes for purposes of figuring your income averaging benefits.
- You must use your correct taxable income for base years. Therefore, if you have had a net operating loss or if the IRS has changed your taxable income, you must amend your computation year's return and use the corrected numbers for income averaging.

Would you like to take $1,000 right off the top of your tax bill without spending any extra money? Would you like to give your over-18-year-old son or daughter a part-time job and get a tax credit for it? Or get a rebate from the government for payments to your parents, inlaws, and other family members? You can if you pay for the care of your under-15-year-old children, certain disabled dependents, or disabled spouse so that you can work—either for yourself or for an employer.

The Internal Revenue Code gives you a credit for at least 20 percent of such payments. That's 20 cents back on every dollar you spend. And, you will be eligible for the credit even if you pay certain relatives for these services. There are limits on the amount of the credit, as well as an "earned income" limitation you'll need to know about. Special rules apply if you're divorced or separated, or if your spouse is disabled or a full-time student.

This tax break is the *child and disabled dependent care credit*. It's a meat and potatoes provision that can mean tax savings to you for expenses you probably would pay anyway.

This chapter will show you the rules, point out some surprising applications so that you won't miss any money-saving opportunities,

explain the special rules, and help you avoid pitfalls. It also will show you how to report and document the expenses to ensure that you get the credit due you.

HOW TO UNDERSTAND THE BASICS

The general rule gives you a tax credit for your "employment-related expenses" if you "maintain a household" in which one or more "qualifying individuals" live. The amount of the credit depends on your income and the number of qualifying individuals you have. Taxpayers with adjusted gross incomes under $10,000 get a credit of 30 percent of their employment-related expenses, with a maximum credit of $720 for one qualifying individual and $1,440 for two or more qualifying individuals. The credit is reduced by one percent for each $2,000 of adjusted gross income over $10,000. For taxpayers with adjusted gross incomes over $28,000, the limits are 20 percent of their employment-related expenses, with a maximum credit of $480 for one qualifying individual and $960 for two or more qualifying individuals. Exhibit 17-1 shows the maximum percentages and dollar limits. *In our examples in this chapter, we have*

17

How the Rebate Program for Dependent Care Works

EXHIBIT 17-1. Child and Disabled Dependent Care Expenses: Increased Credit

You may receive a tax credit for child and disabled dependent care expenses you incur to permit you to work. the new law allows up to $4,800 ($2,400 if you have only one child or disabled dependent) to be counted in figuring the credit. The amount of the credit ranges from 20 percent to 30 percent of these expenses, depending on the amount of your income. The table below shows the percentage applicable to various income levels and the maximum credit available.

| ADJUSTED GROSS INCOME | | | MAXIMUM CREDIT— | MAXIMUM CREDIT— |
OVER	BUT NOT OVER	PERCENTAGE CREDIT	ONE QUALIFYING PERSON[1]	TWO OR MORE QUALIFYING PERSONS[2]
$ 0	$10,000	30%	$720	$1,440
10,000	12,000	29%	696	1,392
12,000	14,000	28%	672	1,344
14,000	16,000	27%	648	1,296
16,000	18,000	26%	624	1,248
18,000	20,000	25%	600	1,200
20,000	22,000	24%	576	1,152
22,000	24,000	23%	552	1,104
24,000	26,000	22%	528	1,056
26,000	28,000	21%	504	1,008
Over $28,000		20%	480	960

[1] Based on maximum qualifying expenses of $2,400.
[2] Based on maximum qualifying expenses of $4,800.

assumed that the 20 percent limit applies. If your adjusted gross income is $28,000 or less, consult Exhibit 17-1 to see what percentage limit applies to you.

The credit, when added to your other credits, may not exceed the amount of your tax. In other words, the credit may reduce your tax to zero, but not below. Most people would settle for that!

The two final limitations are:

- Qualifying expenses may not exceed your earned income or your spouse's earned income, whichever is less.
- You and your spouse must file a joint return to get the credit, unless special rules (discussed later) apply.

These are the rules in a nutshell. Special rules, including those for separated and divorced persons, are discussed later, as is a special opportunity for those in a position to use relatives as care-providers. But let's turn now

to three critical phrases: "maintain a household," "qualifying individual," and "employment-related expenses."

HOW TO "MAINTAIN A HOUSEHOLD"

Your employment-related expenses can be applied toward the credit only if you maintain a household. Thus, the key questions are:

- What is a household?
- Whose household is it?
- What does it mean to maintain one?

This part of the law is pretty simple in most cases. A household for tax purposes is what most of us would think it is: the place where we live. More specifically, it is the principal place of abode. It must not only be your qualifying individual's principal place of abode; it must also be *yours*. Thus, if your disabled dependent, dear old Aunt Sally, lives in the apartment you maintain upstairs, you can't get a credit for any payments you make for her care while you work. That's because Aunt Sally's household must also be yours in order for you to get the credit. Get yourself a larger apartment and give Aunt Sally a room in it. It's cheaper to maintain one big apartment than two smaller ones, and you'll save a few hundred dollars in taxes to boot.

If a person is temporarily absent because of illness, education, business, vacation, military service, or custody agreement, the person is still treated as a member of your household. So even if Junior spends the summer on his grandparents' farm, you are considered to be maintaining his household during that time.

Single parents: Suppose that you're a single parent who shares an apartment or house with another single parent, and you each have one or more qualifying individuals living with you. IRS regulations specifically say that each family is treated as a household. In other words, you can share living, sleeping, and eating areas with others and still qualify for the credit if you maintain your separate household.

Now that we know what a household is, how do you maintain one? Again, the answer is what you probably would expect. You maintain a household when you (or you and your spouse) furnish over one-half (50 percent) of the household costs. These costs include amounts paid for

- Mortgage interest.
- Property taxes.
- Rent.
- Upkeep and repairs.
- Property insurance.
- Food consumed on the premises.

Costs of maintaining a household *do not include* amounts paid for

- Mortgage principal.
- Clothing.
- Education.
- Medical treatment.
- Vacations.
- Life insurance.
- Permanent improvement, betterment, or replacement of property.

Remember that *you*, or you and your spouse, must furnish the costs of maintaining your household. If you are one of those very few lucky folks who have rich parents or inlaws, don't let them exercise their generosity by springing for one of the household costs listed here. If they insist on spending their money on you, get them to send you to Bermuda for a couple of weeks or to pay for that deck you've been wanting to add to the house. You'll get the same economic benefit and not risk losing any credit.

HOW TO FIND A "QUALIFYING INDIVIDUAL"

Your employment-related expenses qualify for the credit only if you maintain a household that includes one or more qualifying individuals. Qualifying individuals include the following:

- Your dependent who is under age 15. (See our later discussion for a special rule that permits certain divorced or separated taxpayers to treat a child as a qualifying individual even though they can't claim a personal exemption for the child.)
- Your dependent (any age) who is physically or mentally incapable of self-care.
- Your spouse who is physically or mentally incapable of self-care.

Dependents: A dependent is anyone you may claim as a personal exemption. The rules, although a bit involved, are easy to apply. Five tests must be satisfied:

- **Support**—You must provide more than half of the person's support during the year. Support includes the value of the person's lodging; the cost of food, clothing, medical care, and the like; and the person's share of the household expenses.
- **Gross income**—The person must not have gross income of $1,000 or more. This rule does not apply to your children who are under the age of 19 or full-time students. A disabled person is a qualifying individual despite having gross income of $1,000 or more, provided that person meets the other four dependency tests.
- **Member of household or relationship**—The person must either be a member of your house-

hold for the entire year or be related to you. The person is considered to be a member of your household even though he or she is temporarily absent.

- **Citizenship**—The person must be a U.S. citizen, resident or national, or a resident of Canada or Mexico for some part of your taxable year.
- **Joint return**—The person must not file a joint return.

It's not likely you'll miss out on the credit because a person isn't a dependent. Remember, the qualifying individual must live in your household for you to get the credit. Most people you allow to live in your home will meet the "member of household or relationship" test as well as the "citizenship" test. If the qualifying individual is your under-15-year-old child, it's unlikely the child will have provided more than half of his or her support and even less likely that he or she will file a joint return.

Disability: If the person you want to claim as a qualifying individual isn't your under-15-year-old child, the person must be a dependent or spouse, physically or mentally incapable of self-care. IRS regulations say that a person is physically or mentally incapable of self-care if a physical or mental defect causes that person

- To be incapable of caring for his or her hygienic or nutritional needs, or
- To require the full-time attention of another person for his or her safety or the safety of others.

A person also qualifies if he or she is physically handicapped or mentally defective and, for that reason, requires the constant attention of another person. But a person isn't considered incapable of self-care simply because of an inability to engage in any "substantial gainful activity," to do normal housework, or to care for the children.

Daily basis: A person's status as a qualifying individual is determined on a daily basis. Thus, if your dependent child turns 15 on June 30, only the employment-related expenses incurred up to that date may be used for figuring the credit. On the other hand, if you have a dependent with a physical or mental defect or handicap that causes episodes of incapacity, the employment-related expenses you incur during times of such incapacity qualify for the credit.

WHAT "EMPLOYMENT-RELATED EXPENSES" ARE

When you maintain a household for one or more qualifying individuals, you will get the credit if you have employment-related expenses. Whether or not the expenses are employment-related depends on why you pay them and the types of services you receive.

Purpose must be gainful employment: The purpose must be to allow you to be gainfully employed. Expenses you incur while *actively searching* for work also qualify, because their purpose is to permit you to be gainfully employed. Thus, if you looked for work from January to June and worked for the rest of the year, all the expenses you paid during the year may qualify.

Gainful employment includes *self-employment* and may consist of service *within your own home*. So the amounts you pay someone to look after the little ones in the playroom—while you work in the study—qualify for the credit.

Gainful employment does not include, however, volunteer work at a nominal rate or for no salary. Therefore, you may not take a credit for expenses you pay someone to take care of the baby while you sell candy at the volunteer firemen's carnival. Nor does gainful employment include a hobby, as the Tax Court informed an unhappy taxpayer who wanted a credit for expenses paid while pursuing an art career. The court thought the taxpayer was just dabbling, since she kept no records, made no systematic efforts to market her work, and in general did very little to convince the court that she cared whether she made any money or not. And, the employment must be *your* employment. Thus, another unhappy taxpayer was unable to get a credit for childcare expenses he paid to enable his ex-wife to work.

TYPES OF SERVICE COSTS UNDERWRITTEN BY UNCLE SAM

Two general types of expenses qualify as employment-related. The first type is expenses for household services, if attributable in part to the care of a qualifying individual. Household services are those performed "in or about" your house for "ordinary and usual services necessary for the maintenance of" your household. Thus, amounts you pay your cook or maid will qualify if part of the duties include cleaning or cooking for a qualifying individual.

Qualifying payments to household workers include the extra costs you incur for their meals and lodging. For example, if you moved into a larger apartment to provide an extra bedroom for your maid, the extra rent and utilities are included as employment-related expenses.

Caution: If you pay a household worker more than $50 a quarter, you will be liable for Social Security (FICA) taxes. The taxes are reported and paid quarterly on Form 942. The combined rate for you and the employee is 14.1 percent of the compensation in 1985. You should withhold the employee's share, which is 7.05 percent. The remaining 7 percent is your share. In 1986 the combined rate goes up to 14.3 percent.

You will also be liable for Federal unemployment tax (FUTA) if you pay the employee more than $1,000 in wages during any calendar quarter. In addition, if you paid the employee more than $1,000 in any calendar quarter *last* year and you pay the employee *any* wages this year, you are liable for FUTA taxes. The rate is 3.5 percent of the first $7,000. But take heart! The FICA and FUTA taxes you pay are also employment-related expenses and are counted in figuring your credit. (Household workers are exempt from income tax withholding, so you don't have to worry about that.) Get Publication 15, *Employer's Tax Guide, (Circular E).*

"Care of" expenses: The second type of legitimate expense is "for the care of" a qualifying individual. For these expenses to qualify, their *primary purpose* must be for a qualifying

individual's "well-being and protection." "Care of" services need not be rendered in your home to qualify. Until 1982, expenses for out-of-home care were allowed only if the qualifying individual was your under-15-year-old dependent child. Beginning in 1982, expenses for out-of-home care of a qualifying individual who regularly spends eight hours a day in your home are eligible for the credit. The new law makes it clear that dependent care centers providing out-of-household services must be in compliance with state and local regulations in order for costs to qualify for the credit.

Just about any expenses you would ordinarily think of as "for the care of" a person will qualify for the credit. However, certain expenses are generally *not* considered to be for the care of a qualifying individual. These include

- Food.
- Clothing.
- Education.
- Transportation.

In some circumstances, even these expenses may qualify. This will occur when the expenses are inseparably a part of the manner in which the care is provided. For example, nursery schools typically include food and educational activities as part of their total child care service. The full amount of the nursery school's expenses will qualify. But for first-graders and above, educational expenses will not qualify. If your grade-schooler is in a before-school or after-school daycare program, however, the expenses you pay for these programs will qualify. And, if there is no separate charge for food or beverages provided in the program, you do not have to reduce the qualifying amount by the estimated value of the food and beverages.

Allocating expenses: As a general rule, if a portion of an expense is for household services or for the care of a qualifying individual, but a portion is for other purposes, you must allocate the expense between the qualifying and the nonqualifying portion. But if the nonqualifying expense is "minimal or insignificant" and the remainder of the expense qualifies, no allocation is required. Thus, the entire expense qualifies. Here's how this rule works in practice.

Example: You have two children, ages nine and 15. In order to be gainfully employed, you hire a full-time housekeeper to take care of the children, clean, cook, and drive you to and from work. The chauffeuring part takes only about 30 minutes a day. Do you have to allocate a part of the salary to the chauffeuring service? Do you have to allocate part to the care of the 15-year-old, who is not a qualifying individual? No. The entire salary you pay will qualify for the credit. (Remember, of course, that with only one qualifying individual in your household, the maximum credit is $480.)

All right, maybe your cook/housekeeper doesn't drive you to and from work. Or maybe you just have someone look after the kids and not do any household chores. The significant lesson from the above example is that the full salary qualifies even though only one of your two children is a qualifying individual.

A final point about qualifying expenses: Most of us try to get our goods and services cheap. But we don't want our loved ones in the hands of just anyone. Are you limited to the cheapest services available? No. As long as the expenses otherwise qualify, they won't be disallowed simply because you could have gotten the services cheaper, or even for free. Doesn't your family deserve the best?

HOW TO APPLY THOSE NASTY LIMITATIONS

Now that you've learned the basic rules and a few applications that may have surprised you, it's time to learn the basic limitations.

Annual dollar limit: The amount of employment-related expenses you use to figure the credit is $2,400 if you have one qualifying individual and $4,800 if you have more than one *at any time during the year*. Thus, if you had one qualifying individual in your household during the year and you had $3,000 of employment-related expenses, your credit may not exceed 20 percent of $2,400 (not $3,000),

or $480 ($2,400 times 20 percent). If you had two qualifying individuals, your credit would be $600 ($3,000 times 20 percent). If you had two qualifying individuals and employment-related expenses of $5,000, your credit could not exceed 20 percent of $4,800 (not $5,000), or $960 ($4,800 times 20 percent).

Example: Your dependent son, Jack, turned 15 on June 30. From January 1 through June 30, you had $2,400 in employment-related expenses for Jack. What's your credit?

Your credit in this case is 20 percent of $2,400, or $480. You don't have to prorate the $2,400 limit over the year, even though Jack was no longer a qualifying individual after the first half of the year. It follows from this example that if disabled Aunt Sally were also a qualifying individual for the first half of the year before she got well, and you had $2,400 of employment-related expenses for her, you would claim the full $960 credit for Jack and Aunt Sally.

Example: Both Jack and Aunt Sally were qualifying individuals for the entire year, but you had $4,000 of employment-related expenses for Aunt Sally and only $800 for Jack. What's your credit?

Your credit is 20 percent of $4,800, or $960. There is no per-person limitation on the amount of employment-related expenses that may qualify. And, when reporting your employment-related expenses for the year, you don't have to show the amounts paid for each qualifying individual. But there's one case where the law isn't clear.

Example: Jack was a qualifying individual through June 30. You had $2,400 of employment-related expenses for him. Aunt Sally became a qualifying individual on July 1, and you had $2,400 of employment-related expenses for her. What's your credit?

Good question. IRS regulations say that the $4,800 limitation applies if you had two or more qualifying individuals "at any one time" during the year. Does this mean that you must have had at least two qualifying individuals at the same time, even for only a day, in order to claim the full credit? Neither Form 2441 (on which you claim the credit) nor any instructions take this possibility into account. You must list on the form the name of each qualifying individual and the amount paid to each person who provided care. You are not required to show the periods during which the qualifying persons qualified, nor are you required to break down the amounts of employment-related expenses for each person. Until there is more guidance on this point, you're probably justified in using the $4,800 limit if you had more than one qualifying individual during the year, even though you never had more than one at a time.

Earned income limitation: In addition to the dollar limitation, the amount of employment-related expenses you may take into account is limited to your earned income. If you are married, the limit is the *lesser of* your earned income or your spouse's. (In some cases, you are not considered "married." See the later discussion regarding divorced and separated taxpayers.)

Earned income means wages, salaries, tips, any other employee compensation, and net earnings from self-employment (bottom line of Schedule C).

This means that no matter how much you earn, *you won't qualify for the credit if your spouse has no earned income, even though your spouse does volunteer charitable work, is self-employed but hasn't turned a profit yet, or has been looking for work but hasn't found any yet.*

Example: You have one qualifying individual for whom you pay $1,600 of employment-related expenses. You had $30,000 in earned income. Your spouse started a business and had only $1,000 in net earnings. Your credit is 20 percent of $1,000, or $200.

HOW STUDENT AND DISABLED SPOUSES GET A BREAK

A special rule applies in figuring the earned income limitation if your spouse is physically or mentally incapable of self-care or is a full-time student.

You will recall that your spouse is a qualifying individual if he or she is physically or mentally incapable of self-care. If your spouse

is your only qualifying individual, your credit can be as much as $480.

Your disabled spouse probably won't earn any money. If the earned income limitation applied, your credit would be zero, because your spouse's earned income was zero. Congress avoided this absurd result by providing that your spouse is deemed to have earned income of $200 for each month that he or she is a qualifying individual. Thus, if your spouse is disabled for the entire year, his or her earned income will be twelve times $200, or $2,400. Your maximum credit would be 20 percent of $2,400, or $480. If you have another qualifying individual in addition to your spouse, the deemed earned income is $400 per month, or $4,800 a year, giving you a maximum credit of 20 percent of $4,800, or $960.

Congress also apparently wanted to encourage education, because the same rules apply for each month that your spouse is a full-time student.

Example: You have a three-year-old child who is your only qualifying individual. You pay $2,500 in employment-related expenses for her during the year. Your spouse was a full-time student for 10 months and worked during the other two months, earning $1,000. Your earned income was $30,000. Your spouse is deemed to have earned $200 a month for 10 months, or $2,000. This plus the $1,000 equals $3,000. Your credit is 20 percent of $2,400, or $480. (Remember the dollar limitation!) If your spouse had not worked at all, your credit would be 20 percent of $2,000, or $400.

To be a full-time student for this purpose, your spouse must have been a full-time student during five calendar months of the year. Thus, if your spouse was a full-time student for only four months, he or she would not be deemed to have any earned income. Note, however, that the five months don't have to be consecutive.

"Full-time" status depends primarily on the school's policy for full-time enrollment. IRS regulations say that a full-time course of study may include some night courses, but IRS does not consider attendance exclusively at night to be a full-time course of study. So even if your spouse is a "full-time" night student, he or she will not be deemed to have any earned income.

A final point to keep in mind is that the study must be at an "educational institution"—that is, a school with a regular faculty, an established curriculum, and an organized body of students in attendance. Schools such as correspondence schools do not qualify.

WHY YOU NEED EXTRA DOCUMENTATION FOR DISABLED DEPENDENTS

If you claim a credit for the care of your disabled spouse or dependent, you have special documentation problems.

Documenting support: If your qualifying individual is a dependent, you must first establish dependency. Remember the five tests: (1) support; (2) gross income; (3) member of household or relationship; (4) citizenship; and (5) joint return. The support test is the most critical. The dependent's share of food and the value of his or her housing are included as support costs. You will have to estimate these amounts based on the number of people in your household. Make sure that you save all grocery bills and have canceled checks and receipts for all support expenses.

Documenting disability: In establishing your spouse's or dependent's physical or mental disability, take a hint from IRS regulations, which state that, on request, you must furnish information detailing the nature and period of the physical or mental incapacity, *including necessary information on the nature of the physical or mental incapacity from the attending physician.* Don't wait until audit time to get the doctor's statement! Get it now! Make sure the statement tells when the disabling condition began and its period of existence. The statement should also say that your dependent or spouse

- As a result of a physical (or mental) defect is incapable of caring for his or her hygienic or nutritional needs, or requires the full-time attention of another person for his or her own safety (or the safety of others); or
- Is physically handicapped (or mentally defective) and therefore requires the constant attention of another person.

If your spouse or dependent has been declared incompetent by a judge, you should, of course, have a certified copy of all pertinent court papers.

How to treat the overlap with medical expenses: In some cases, expenses that qualify as employment-related will also qualify as medical expenses, which are available as itemized deductions. Can you use the same expenses for both? Not surprisingly, IRS regulations say no. You can use some of the expenses in figuring the credit and some in figuring your itemized deductions, but you may not use the same expenses for both purposes.

When you have an expense that may be classified as either a medical expense or an employment-related expense, your fingers will have to walk through the computations to find the best deal. You must consider your tax bracket, the 5 percent medical threshold, and the 20 (to 30) percent credit.

Example: You are in the 40 percent bracket and have bad teeth. Your dentist charged you a fortune and you are well above the 5 percent medical limitation. You incurred dependent care expenses of $5,000 for one dependent. Such expenses may be classified as either medical expenses or dependent care expenses. Which do you prefer?

Actually, there are several choices. One, you may classify the full $5,000 as dependent care expenses and reduce your tax by a measly $480 ($2,400 × 20%). That would be silly, of course, since you would not have used $2,600 for any tax advantage. If you claimed the remaining $2,600 as medical expenses, you would further reduce your taxes by $1,040 ($2,600 × 40% tax bracket). Thus, your total savings under this option would be $1,520 ($480 for dependent care plus $1,040 medical deduction). A third possibility is to classify the full $5,000 as a medical expense and reduce your tax by $2,000 ($5,000 expense × 40% tax bracket). We like the third choice best.

In many cases, you will find it difficult to qualify for the medical expense deduction because of that awful 5 percent floor. In those cases, you will usually be better off claiming the maximum possible as a dependent care expense.

WHAT TO DO WHEN YOU ARE SEPARATED OR DIVORCED

If you are married at the end of the year, you and your spouse must file a joint return in order to get the credit for child or dependent care. This rule will be significant in those rare cases when it would otherwise be advantageous to file separate returns.

Your year-end marital status will determine if you are subject to the joint return requirement and whether your credit will be limited by the lower of your or your spouse's income. Any custody arrangements will have a big impact on whether or not you may claim the credit.

If you're legally married at the end of the taxable year, you will have to file a joint return to get the credit. The amount of employment-related expenses you may take into account is the lesser of your or your spouse's earned income.

On the other hand, if you are divorced at the end of the taxable year, neither the joint return requirement nor the earned income limitation applies to you. You are considered divorced if you and your spouse are separated under a decree of divorce (often called a "partial divorce") or separate maintenance. If you're separated but not divorced at the end of the taxable year, you will be treated as married unless you meet *all* the following requirements:

- You file a separate return for the year.
- You maintain a household for more than half the taxable year as the principal place of abode of a qualifying individual.
- You furnish over half the cost of maintaining the qualifying individual's household for the year.
- You have a spouse who is not a member of the household at any time during the last six months of the taxable year.

That last requirement is the hard one. If you and your spouse separated any time after the first six months of the taxable year and you are not legally separated under a court decree, you and your spouse must file a joint return to get the credit. The amount of the credit is limited by the lower of your earned incomes.

Special dependency rule: Divorce settlements frequently entitle the noncustodial parent to the dependency exemption for the couple's child or children. But entitlement to the exemption does not give the noncustodial parent the child care credit. The child care credit is based on the need to have the child cared for while a taxpayer works. Obviously, the child does not interfere with a noncustodial parent's ability to work, because the child is living with the custodial parent.

But can the custodial parent claim the credit? Recall that for a child to be a qualifying individual, you must be able to claim a dependency exemption for the child. The divorce settlement says that the noncustodial parent gets the exemption. So are both parents out of luck? No. Congress foresaw this problem and decided that the divorced parent who keeps the child the longer time may qualify for the credit, providing that the child

- Is under age 15 or is physically or mentally incapable of self-care.
- Receives over half of his or her support during the year from one or both parents.
- Is in the custody of one or both parents for more than half the taxable year.

The significance of this rule is that even though you are not entitled to claim a child as a dependent, you may still be entitled to the dependent care credit if you have custody for a longer time during the year than the other parent. If your spouse has custody for the longer time, you are not entitled to any credit.

Extra documentation required: The special rules for divorced and separated parents that we have been discussing make documentation even more important. Make sure that you have documented the cost of maintaining the qualifying child's household and that you have furnished over half that cost. This is especially important if you receive child support. Keep careful records of the following:

- Mortgage interest.
- Property taxes.
- Rent.
- Utilities.
- Upkeep and repairs.
- Property insurance.

- Food consumed on the premises.

Make sure you do not use child support or alimony for any of the expenses listed above. Use it for your child's clothes, medical care, and even child care. You can get the credit because the expenses are *your* expenses and *you* paid them, even if the money came from someone else. If you are not legally separated under a court decree, observe the joint return requirement and the earned income limitation that apply to both your income and your spouse's, *unless* you fit the "living apart" exception. The hard part of the "living apart" exception is proving that your spouse was not a member of your household for the last six months of the taxable year. The most direct proof are sworn statements from neighbors, friends, and even relatives who have personal knowledge of your separation. If you have moved into a new house or apartment, a deed or lease in your name only will be helpful.

Proving your qualification under the special dependency rule should not be especially difficult. The one thing you must guard against is an agreement that calls for equal custody for each spouse. The law makes no provision for splitting the credit between the parents, so make sure your agreement provides that either you or your ex-spouse has custody for the longer time. If you agree to let your ex-spouse have custody for a longer time, get the dependency exemption, because you will not qualify for the credit.

HIRING YOUR INDEPENDENT RELATIVES AS CARE-PROVIDERS

It's expensive to have someone care for a child or disabled dependent five or more days a week, 52 weeks a year, while you work. Maybe it's more expensive than the $2,400 or $4,800 limits. Is there a way that you can ensure good care for your little ones or Aunt Sally, get your full credit, and not have to pay more than the $2,400 or $4,800 it takes to get the full credit? There may be. Consider the following.

Example: Your married son, who turns 19 this year, lives nearby and attends a local community college. Most of his classes are at night, so he's available to take care of Aunt Sally during the day while you and your spouse work. He and Aunt Sally get along well. He provides her meals, keeps her company, and helps make her comfortable. In short, he does exactly what you would pay someone else to do if your son were not available. But your son doesn't demand as large a salary as an outsider. He is willing to settle for the $2,400 maximum creditable amount. If you pay your son, who needs the money for school and other expenses, $2,400 to take care of Aunt Sally, and your son files a joint return with his working wife, you will be entitled to the credit.

Example: You have two preschoolers who must be cared for during the day while you and your spouse work. You would have to pay an unrelated person at least $100 a week ($5,200 a year) to take care of them. Your sister, who lives in your neighborhood and has a preschooler of her own, would be happy to care for them at her house. If she does and you pay her up to $4,800 during the year, will you get the credit? Yes.

The credit is allowed for payments to any relative who cares for your children or disabled dependents, providing the relative is not a dependent or your child who has not reached age 19 by the end of your taxable year. Thus, in the examples given, you have provided care for your loved ones, provided extra money for other loved ones, and saved yourself money.

Caution: This opportunity is available only if the relative performs the same services you would have hired someone else to do. You do not get any credit for amounts that exceed the amount you would pay someone else. Any excess is treated by the IRS as a gift.

Getting a tax break to pay a relative to care for your loved ones is almost too good to be true. But it is true, so take advantage of this situation if you can.

WHY SPECIAL DOCUMENTATION IS IMPORTANT WHEN YOUR RELATIVE IS THE CARE-PROVIDER

Technically, no special rules apply to substantiating your credit when a relative is the care-provider. But because the IRS almost always casts a more inquiring eye on transactions between relatives, it won't hurt to take some special precautions.

First, make sure the salary you're paying is no more than you would pay someone else to do the same work. If the nondependent relative is to be the exclusive or primary care-provider, check with others first and find out what they would charge. Get a written statement from them, if possible. If the relative will be providing only occasional care, make sure you pay no more than you generally pay others for the same services.

Second, if the services are to be provided in your home and your relative will be an employee under the rules discussed earlier in this chapter, make doubly sure you pay your FICA and FUTA taxes and file the necessary forms.

Third, consider an employment contract. Nothing fancy, just write out the duties and the salary, sign it, date it, and have your relative sign and date it. Do this *before* the services are performed.

Fourth, always pay by check and base your payment on either an employment contract or a timesheet—and preferably both. Detail the services provided if payment is based on hours worked.

A FEW HINTS ON REPORTING AND DOCUMENTING YOUR EXPENSES

You report the credit on Form 2441. Basically, the form requires three kinds of information.

Qualifying persons: You must report the names, birthdates, and relationships of all qualifying persons and the number of months they've lived with you during the year. This information should not cause you a problem.

If the qualifying person has a disability, make sure you gather extra support, as discussed previously in this chapter.

Providers of care: You must list the name, address, and relationship to you (if any) of each person or firm that provided care during the year, as well as the period of time when each provided care. In addition, if any person was your employee and provided services in your home, you must list that person's Social Security number on the form, and you must have copies of all payroll records and reports. If possible, keep a copy of business cards and stationery from commercial care-providers. If the care-providers were individuals, the law requires you to record any address changes.

Amounts: You must list the amounts paid to each care-provider. Here, the substantiation is similar to all other deductible or creditable expenses: canceled checks (to prove you paid and how much you paid) and receipts (to prove what for).

Receipts should consist of a billing in the form of a time summary from individuals you employed for work in your home. The time summary should detail the nature of the tasks performed. Make absolutely certain that a relative submits a time summary.

Always pay by check. Don't get caught in the bind of the taxpayer who claimed that he paid over $1,000 of his child care expenses in cash. The Tax Court allowed only $45, because his only substantiation was a canceled check for that amount.

If you're required to pay FICA or FUTA taxes for a household worker, as discussed earlier, make sure you file Form 942 and Form 940. Keep all payroll records and reports in your shoebox.

TAX REDUCTION CHECKLIST

IRS publicatioms to be obtained:

- Publication 503—*Child and Disabled Dependent Care*
- Publication 15—*Employer's Tax Guide (Circular E)*

Definition of a qualifying individual:

- Child under age 15 whom you claim as a dependent.
- Child for whom you had custody for the longer period during the year if you were divorced, legally separated, or separated under a written agreement. The child also must have
  — Received over half of his or her support from the parents.
  — Been in the custody of one or both parents for more than half the year.
  — Been under age 15 or physically or mentally unable to care for himself or herself.
- Your spouse who is mentally or physically unable to care for himself or herself.
- Any person unable to care for himself or herself whom you can list as a dependent or could have listed as a dependent except that he or she had income of $1,000 or more.

Allowable expenses for credit computation:

- Domestic services in the home:
  — Laundry.
  — Cooking.
  — Cleaning.
- Services outside the home for a child:
  — Day camp.
  — Daycare.
  — Nursery school.
- Payments to relatives not claimed as dependents.

Expenses not allowed:

- Tuition for first grade or higher.
- Payments to dependents.
- Payments claimed as medical expenses. You must choose how you want to classify such expenses—as medical expenses or as child and dependent care expenses.

The tax credit:

- Maximum credit:
  — $720 for one qualifying individual when earned income is $10,000 or less ($2,400 × 30 percent).
  — $480 for one qualifying individual when earned income is $28,000 or more ($2,400 × 20 percent).
  — $1,440 for two or more dependents when earned income is $10,000 or less ($4,800 × 30 percent).
  — $960 for two or more qualifying individuals when earned income is $28,000 or more ($4,800 × 20 percent).
  — If earned income is between $20,000 and $30,000, consult chart in Exhibit 17-1.
- Limitation: Claimed expenses may not exceed the earned income of the lower-earning spouse unless that spouse is either a full-time student or mentally or physically incapable of self-care.

- Spouse must file joint return in order to claim credit, unless divorced or legally separated under a divorce decree. See text for special rule where spouses were separated during the last six months of the tax year.

Special documentation problems:

- When you claim the credit for a disabled dependent or spouse.
- When you are separated or divorced.
- When paying relatives for services.

Hiring your spouse or dependent child can save tax dollars and increase your family's wealth. In many small businesses, the whole family pitches in to make the business successful. In other cases, dependent children earn allowances for taking out the garbage, dusting, mowing the grass, or doing other nonbusiness chores. In this chapter you will learn how to turn these situations into big tax savings.

Hiring your child to do business chores can turn that nondeductible allowance into deductible wages, saving you self-employment and income taxes, relieving some of your financial burden of supporting the child, and allowing greater savings for college or other advanced education. Hiring your spouse can save self-employment taxes and income taxes, as well as permit a greater accumulation of retirement savings.

You can get these savings with surprisingly little paperwork, other than the excellent records you should always keep to substantiate your tax deductions and credits. Hiring your spouse or your dependent child is perfectly legitimate tax planning, not a gimmick. Although this opportunity will not be available to everyone, it is absolutely wonderful for those who qualify. To help you learn why these techniques work and how they work, this chapter will explain:

- Why you can benefit from hiring your dependent child.
- Who is a dependent.
- How to preserve your dependency exemption.
- Why you should comply with child labor laws and a simple way to do so.
- Why you can benefit from hiring your spouse.
- How to select the right salary for your spouse and child.
- How to nail down your family tax breaks with proper documentation.
- What forms to file.

WHY YOU CAN BENEFIT FROM HIRING YOUR DEPENDENT CHILD

Let's assume that you pay your child an allowance of $20 each week, provided the child performs certain household chores, such as taking out the garbage. During the 52 weeks of the year, you would pay your child $1,040—and not a penny of it would be deductible, since the expense was purely personal.

Now, let's assume that you pay your child for business chores, such as maintaining correspondence files. Each week, the child spends enough time to warrant a wage of $20. At the end of the year, you have paid wages for 52

18

How to Increase Your Wealth by Hiring Your Spouse and Your Dependent Child

weeks totaling $1,040—every penny of it deductible as a business expense.

Your financial situation has not changed, except that now the Federal Government is helping to subsidize your weekly payments to your child. You are still giving the child the $20 a week, but now it is classified as a salary for performing business chores, rather than an allowance for performing personal chores.

Income tax savings: The effect of this change is to give you a tax deduction for money that you would have spent anyway. If you are in the 33 percent tax bracket (28 percent Federal and 5 percent state), this $1,040 will mean tax savings of $343.20. And that's not all.

Self-employment tax savings: Assuming your child is under the age of 21, your deduction can also save you self-employment (Social Security) taxes if your self-employment income (together with any employee wages you earn) is less than the maximum amount to which the self-employment (Social Security) tax applies. In 1985, for example, the $1,040 deduction means self-employment tax savings of $122.72 ($1,040 × 11.8 percent tax rate). Thus, between the income tax savings and the self-employment tax savings, you have managed to pocket an extra $465.92 ($343.20 plus $122.72).

Obviously, the higher the salary you pay your child, the more tax you save. However, you will also want to preserve your $1,040 personal exemption for the child, since the exemption saves you $343 ($1,000 times 33 percent tax rate). The next two sections tell how.

HOW TO PRESERVE YOUR DEPENDENCY EXEMPTION

To claim someone as a dependent for tax purposes, that person must satisfy five tests. Generally, minor children pass these tests with flying colors. When you hire your child to do business chores, however, and pay the child a fair wage, you could have a problem with the support test. We will discuss this problem in the following section. First, however, let's review the other four tests.

Member of household relationship test: Your child very easily passes this test because he or she is related to you. Furthermore, a legally adopted child and a stepchild are considered to be related to you.

You can claim any other minors—such as foster children—as exemptions if they live with you for the entire year and are members of your household. However, you may not claim foster children as exemptions if you receive payments from a public agency.

Citizenship: Your child must be a U.S. citizen, resident, or national, or a resident of Canada or Mexico for some part of the year. If either you or your spouse was a U.S. citizen when your child was born, your child passes the citizenship test.

No joint return: You may not claim a dependency exemption for anyone who files a joint return with his or her spouse. Thus, if your 18-year-old son is married and files a joint return with his spouse, you may not claim him as an exemption even though you provided 100 percent of his support.

Earnings test: Generally, you cannot claim a dependency exemption for anyone whose income for the year is $1,040 or more. This rule does not apply, however, if your child is under the age of 19. Also, the rule does not apply if your child was a full-time student during some part of five months of the year, which need not be consecutive. Full-time status is generally determined by the school your child attends, but the IRS will not consider your child a full-time student if the child attends only night classes. A child may, however, be considered full-time even though some night classes are included in the child's schedule. Correspondence and employee training courses do not qualify as school programs.

HOW TO PASS THE SUPPORT TEST

The fifth test your child must pass to be your dependent is called the support test. Under this test, you must provide more than half of your child's support. Ordinarily, this isn't much of a problem. However, if you pay your child fair wages for a fair day's work, and your child is foolish enough to spend the money on such items as food, clothing, and medicine, your dependency exemption could be jeopardized.

Control spending: A wonderful tax rule says that your child can earn an unlimited amount and still be your dependent if you pay the support costs. Thus, you could pay your child $1 million and still claim the exemption if the child didn't use the money for support expenses. Therefore, the key to preserving your exemption is making sure you pay over half of the child's support.

You must provide necessities: Most state laws require parents to provide minor children with the necessities. Thus, make sure that your child spends wages for items other than food, shelter, and clothing. Note—the state law definition of "necessities" is generally much more restrictive than tax law. For example, recreational expenses are tax law support costs, but not "necessities" in most states.

Support items: The IRS lists the following as support items:

- The fair rental value of the lodging you provide the child.
- A share of the household expenses, such as food.
- Medical and dental care.
- Clothing.
- Education.
- Recreation.
- Transportation.
- "Similar necessities."

That last item—similar necessities—leaves a little room for argument. Don't put yourself in a position where you have to argue about the definition of "similar necessities." By the same token, don't give the IRS a chance to argue about it. Leave yourself a cushion for safety. Let's discuss how to do that.

Figuring your support costs: Obviously, determining how much it costs to support a child is no easy task. You might avoid this task by making sure your child saves all of his or her earnings. But since the child is bound to spend some money on support items, such as food

(from a fast-food restaurant, for example), clothing, transportation, and recreation, you would have to pay the child an allowance as well as wages. Many of us are simply unable to afford this strategy. For us, tackling the chore of determining child support costs is unavoidable.

As we suggested in an earlier chapter, becoming a pack rat will help you survive—and prosper—in our tax climate. Exhibit 18-1 contains a list of items you will need to document in order to prove how much it costs to support your child. Make sure your shoebox is stuffed with receipts and other documentary evidence proving the cost of each of these items.

You must also prove that you paid for over 50 percent of these items. Using your checkbook or credit card is the most convenient way of proving that you paid. For many items, of course, you will use cash. Ideally, you should record these expenses in your diary.

Providing a cushion: Once you have figured the support costs, pay as much of them as you can afford. This strategy will achieve two highly desirable results. First, you minimize the risk of losing the dependency exemption. Second, you maximize your child's savings, which will accumulate faster than your savings because the child will pay much less tax, if any at all.

For example, the total support costs in Exhibit 18-1 totaled $7,730. Let's assume the child paid the following expenses:

• Recreation	$ 350
• Books	100
• Dance lessons	30
• Camp	300
• Musical instruments	90
• Tuition	50
• Sports	280
• Total	$1,200

In this example, the child paid only 16 percent ($1,200 divided by $7,730) of the support costs. The parents paid the rest, and ensured their dependency exemption.

Tax-saving note: The $1,200 was going to be spent regardless. By hiring the child, the $1,200

EXHIBIT 18-1. Worksheet for Protecting Dependency Exemption (Example).

DESCRIPTION OF EXPENSE	AMOUNT
Lodging (Fair Market Value of space provided)	$3,600
Tuition	50
Singing lessons	25
Recreation	350
Entertainment	50
Transportation	200
Food	1,300
Books	100
Dance lessons	30
Medical care	220
Health insurance	120
Camp	300
Clothing	500
School supplies	30
Musical instruments	90
Dental care	85
Baby-sitters	400
Sports	280
Total	$7,730

Note: Your dependent child must *expend less than 50%* of his or her support for you to claim a dependency exemption. The child *may earn more than 50%* but *must not absorb more than 50%* of his or her living expenses for you to be entitled to the dependency exemption.

becomes deductible. Effectively, Uncle Sam paid a big part of the $1,200.

WHY YOU SHOULD COMPLY WITH CHILD LABOR LAWS AND A SIMPLE WAY TO DO SO

Government regulation permeates our lives. In fact, some people find the amount of Federal, state, and local paperwork terrifying, not to mention expensive. Sometimes, however, paperwork helps you save taxes.

So it is with the child labor laws. The main reason for complying with these laws is to stay out of trouble with Federal and state—and possibly even local—child labor agencies. But complying with these laws adds a tax benefit: additional substantiation for your deduction. Thus, complying with child labor laws can actually put money into your pocket.

Now, how do you comply? We asked the staff of the U.S. Department of Labor how businesspeople could determine whether or not it would be legal to employ their children in a certain manner. For example, it might not be legal to have your 17-year-old child deliver pamphlets from your automobile, whereas it may be perfectly all right to have the child deliver pamphlets by using a bicycle for transportation. The advice of the people at the Department of Labor is simply this: ask. We agree with this advice wholeheartedly. One of us took on the task of summarizing and simplifying the various child labor laws, so that we could pass them on to you. We ordered summaries to be delivered to our door. When the summaries arrived, we had to hire two burly delivery specialists to haul them in for us. Each of them sustained serious injuries in doing so. That's when we asked the Department of Labor for assistance.

We're stretching things, of course, but the point is well taken. The best way to determine whether or not your plan is legal is to ask the people responsible for enforcing the law.

Prepare a letter similar to the one in Exhibit 18-2, asking the Administrator of the

EXHIBIT 18-2. Sample Letter to Obtain Opinion as to Compliance With Child Labor Laws.

Administrator
Wage-Hour Division
Employment Standards Administration
U.S. Department of Labor
200 Constitution Avenue, N.W.
Washington, DC 20010

Dear Sirs:

I would like to employ my 10-year-old daughter to assist me in my business. Before I employ her, I would like your opinion as to the legality of her employment under the Child Labor Laws.

My daughter's duties as an employee would be performed both in my home and in my office. In my home, my daughter would:

- Clean a home office area;
- Maintain a set of business files; and
- Record financial information in a ledger book.

After school on Wednesdays and Thursdays, I would drive to the school and transport her to the office. At the office, she would:

- Maintain a set of business files;
- Maintain the outside grounds;
- Post entries on a calendar and a map; and
- Clean the office.

Please send me your opinion as to the legality of employing my daughter to perform any or all of the above services.

Sincerely,

Wage-Hour Division if the employment plans you have for your child are legal. Try to be specific. Outline the duties and hours, the place or places where the work will be performed, and the age of the child.

You should send a similar letter to your state government. Your local government probably won't have any child labor laws, but you should ask, anyway. You will find a list of the names, addresses and telephone numbers of the Labor Commissioners of each state in the Appendix of this book. Your letter to the state government should be identical to the one you send the Feds, unless your state has special requirements for seeking a legal opinion. Finally, make sure you retain copies of your letters in your shoebox.

Consult the flowchart in Exhibit 18-3 for an overview of the benefits of hiring your child.

WHY YOU CAN BENEFIT FROM HIRING YOUR SPOUSE

If you are self-employed, hiring your spouse can give you several benefits. First, you get a very loyal employee dedicated to the well-being of your business. Second, you save self-

EXHIBIT 18-3. Flowchart for Self-Employed Hiring Dependent Children Under Age 21.

NOTE: If child is over age 20, child's wages are subject to Social Security and Unemployment taxes. Dependency exemption may be claimed, however, if child earns less than $1,000 or is a full-time student, you provide more than one-half of a child's support, and child does not file joint return.

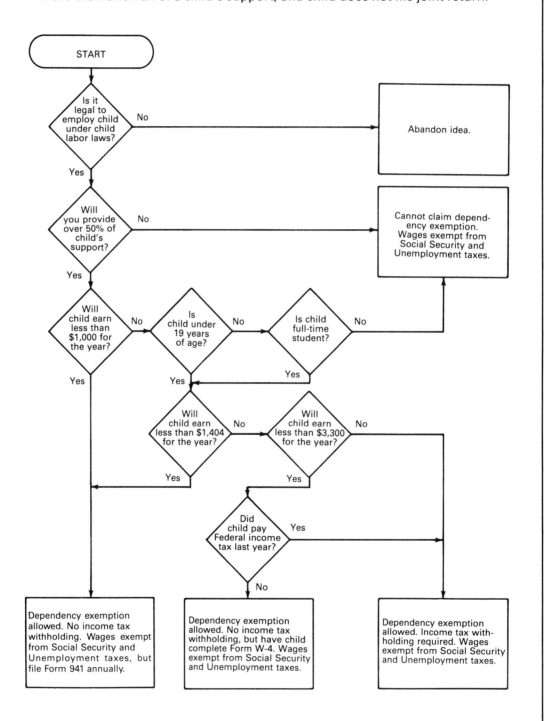

employment taxes. Third, you save income taxes, because your spouse will be eligible for the full IRA deduction, the full deduction under your self-employed retirement plan, and various fringe benefits available to employees.

Self-employment savings: Wages paid by you to your spouse are not subject to Social Security taxes. Therefore, if your current earnings are less than the Social Security maximum—or if they will be after your deduction for wages to your spouse—you will save Social Security taxes.

Example: You earn $35,000. A $10,000 deduction for wages paid to your spouse will reduce your self-employment income by $10,000. The $10,000 paid to your spouse by you is exempt from self-employment tax. In 1985 your savings are $1,180 ($10,000 × 11.8% tax rate)!

Hold still, the news gets even better.

IRA contribution: As you learned in a previous chapter, anyone who works may contribute to an IRA, up to $2,000 a year (unless the person earns less than $2,000, in which case the maximum is the person's earnings). You also know that a spousal IRA only permits a contribution of $2,250. Thus, employing your spouse will allow your family an additional $1,750 ($2,000 − $250) IRA contribution. The tax savings on this $1,750, for a person in the 33 percent tax bracket is $577.50 ($1,750 × 33% tax rate). And, of course, the earnings on that additional $1,750 compound tax-free in the IRA account.

Self-employed retirement plan: In addition to the IRA contribution, your spouse could be covered by your self-employed retirement plan, which you learned about in a previous chapter. The maximum deductible contribution is 25 percent of the employee's pay, up to a maximum of $30,000—starting in 1984. Thus, if you paid your spouse $10,000 in wages, your family could get an additional $2,500 ($10,000 × 25%) tax deduction.

Fringe benefits: As an employee, your spouse will be eligible for many tax-free or tax-favored fringe benefits. The one that's most likely to have the biggest impact on your family's economic well-being is the medical reimbursement plan. Under such a plan, the employer deducts payments of an employee's medical expenses, but the employee does not pay tax on these payments. In short, medical bills are paid with pretax dollars.

Better yet, the medical reimbursement plan can cover you and the children. Thus, the entire family's medical bills could be paid with pretax dollars.

Note: As a self-employed taxpayer, you may not cover yourself under a medical reimbursement plan. By hiring your spouse and providing dependent coverage, you avoid this rule and obtain coverage.

Example: Your family's medical bills—including insurance premiums—are about $2,000 a year. With an adjusted gross income of $35,000 a year, your medical expense deduction is only $250, because the 5 percent floor is $1,750 ($35,000 income × 5%). On the other hand, the $2,000 of medical expenses are legitimate business deductions if paid under a medical reimbursement plan. This $2,000 saves you $660 ($2,000 × 33% tax rate). This is $577.50 more than the savings from the medical expense deduction [$660 − ($250 × 33% tax rate)].

Summary: Exhibit 18-4 is an example of the savings possible by hiring your spouse and child. Note that the example does not include a tax-free retirement plan, since many families with the income shown could not afford to sock away the additional amount permitted under such a plan. Nevertheless, the cash savings in the example amount to a whopping $2,519 (39.5 percent).

HOW TO SELECT THE RIGHT SALARY FOR YOUR SPOUSE AND CHILD

You may be wondering whether the IRS is going to go for all of this tax saving, especially when you're keeping your tax saving within the family. Make no mistake about it; the IRS does look more closely at transactions between family members. However, even the IRS admits that wages paid to your spouse and minor

EXHIBIT 18.4. Example of Benefits of Hiring Spouse and Child. (1984)

BEFORE: Sole proprietor with no employees. $2,000 of medical expenses. Has IRA plan.

AFTER: Hires spouse for $10,000 salary and child for $2,000 salary. Sets up medical reimbursement plan. Spouse sets up IRA.

BEFORE		AFTER
$ 50,000	Gross business income	$ 50,000
(15,000)	Business deductions	(15,000)
-0-	Medical reimbursement plan	(2,000)
-0-	Salary to child	(2,000)
(2,250)	IRA deduction	(2,000)
-0-	Spouse's IRA deduction	(2,000)
32,750	Adjusted gross income	27,000
(10,000)[1]	Itemized deductions	(9,638)[2]
(3,000)	Personal exemptions	(3,000)
19,750	Taxable income	14,362
2,416	Income tax	1,479
3,955 [3]	Self-employment tax	2,373 [4]
$ 6,371	Total taxes	$ 3,852

$2,519 savings

[1] Medical expense deduction for $2,000 of medical expenses is $362.50 [$2,000 - (5% of $32,750 adjusted gross income)].

[2] Since medical expenses were deducted from gross income, the itemized deductions do not include the $362.50 medical expense deduction included in the left-hand column.

[3] $35,000 × 11.3 percent rate.

[4] $21,000 × 11.3 percent rate. The $35,000 of business earnings are reduced by $2,000 of medical expenses, $2,000 salary to child, and $10,000 salary to spouse.

children are deductible if they meet the same requirements as wages paid to strangers.

One of the easiest ways to set the wage is to find out what wage you would have to pay an unrelated person to do the same work. If, for example, the work is to be done in your office, call an employment agency for temporaries and find out the fees for that work.

You should inquire from several sources. For example, if you're trying to set the wage for office work, call at least three employment agencies. If possible, obtain written quotes. In any case, be sure to write down the results of your survey. Record the date, the firm you called, and the quote. Keep these records in your shoebox.

IRS tests: To be deductible, the salary must be "reasonable." The IRS says this means, in general, the amount that would be paid for similar services by businesses similar to yours and under similar circumstances. That's why you should try to find out the amount charged by an outside service. In setting the salary, be sure to make an allowance for the experience (or inexperience) and ability of your spouse or child.

The IRS lists ten factors it considers in deciding whether or not a salary is reasonable:

- Duties performed.
- Volume of work.
- Type and amount of responsibility.
- Complexity.
- Amount of time required.
- General cost of living in the area.
- Ability and achievements.
- Comparison of the amount of salary with the amount of business income.

- Your pay policy as to all employees (if there are any others).
- Pay history of the employee.

Seven-year-old employee: You're wondering how old a child must be for you to justify paying a tax-deductible salary. There is no fixed limit, provided the child is capable of doing the work assigned. The youngest employee we've found in a court case was seven years old. In that case, the court allowed a deduction of $1,200 for wages paid in 1972. The child in that case did various clean-up work in his parents' business. The parents in that case documented the child's duties and the actual work the child did. So should you— see the next section.

HOW TO NAIL DOWN YOUR FAMILY TAX BREAKS WITH PROPER DOCUMENTATION

You already know some of the required documentation. You know your shoebox should have copies of the letters you sent to the child labor authorities and the quotes you received (or your notes) from unrelated parties who provide similar services.

You should consider a third item, an employment contract. Nothing fancy, just an outline of the work that will be done, the hours of work, the salary, and any other terms that you believe are important in your situation. Sign the agreement, date it, and put it in your shoebox. But don't forget about it. Unforeseen circumstances may arise that require your spouse or child to do work you didn't anticipate. In that case, be sure to check the agreement to see whether it covers that work. If it doesn't, amend the agreement.

Timesheet is critical: The documents we've discussed so far just lay the groundwork for the really critical document. The documents discussed earlier will establish what your spouse or child is supposed to do. To get your deduction, you must also be able to prove what work was actually done. The best way we know is to use a timesheet.

Exhibit 18-5 is an example. It is not elaborate, but it has sufficient details to back up your deduction. Note that the timesheet con-

tains a brief description of the work performed and the amount of time spent on the work. These are the most important elements.

Pay by check: The easiest way to prove you actually paid the wages is to pay by check. Even if your spouse or child is planning to put the money into savings, draw the check to your spouse's or child's order. Making a direct payment into your child's or spouse's savings or other account could give an auditor an excuse for disallowing your deduction on the ground that the payments were actually gifts.

WHAT FORMS TO FILE

As you have seen, getting these tax benefits requires some initial paperwork. Keeping the timesheets will, of course, be a continuing task, but you probably would do the same thing if you hired a stranger. The paperwork to file with the government is minimal, however.

Social Security number: If your child does not have a Social Security number yet, by all means get one. This establishes the child as a separate taxpayer—in a paperwork sense— from you and your spouse.

Employment taxes: As we mentioned earlier, your spouse and your child are exempt from Social Security taxes and unemployment taxes (FICA and FUTA). File Form 941 annually and indicate that the wages are exempt.

Income tax withholding: If you will pay wages of less than $1,404, you will not have to withhold income taxes. If you will pay wages of $3,300, your child (or spouse) will have to complete Form W-4. You will not have to withhold taxes on your child, however, if your child did not pay any Federal income tax last year. Assuming you and your spouse filed jointly last year and paid at least $1 in taxes, you will have to withhold taxes from your spouse.

If you will pay your child $3,300 or more, you have to withhold income taxes. If you are

EXHIBIT 18-5.   Dependent Child's Business Services and Wage Summary Sheet.

MONTH _____   **CHILD'S NAME** _____

DAY OF WEEK (MON; TUES)	DAY	DESCRIPTION OF TASKS PERFORMED	HOURS WORKED
_____	___	_____	_____
_____	___	_____	_____
_____	___	_____	_____
_____	___	_____	_____
_____	___	_____	_____
_____	___	_____	_____
_____	___	_____	_____

TOTAL HOURS WORKED _____

× HOURLY RATE _____

TOTAL WAGES PAID WITH CHECK NO. _____ _____

required to withhold, you should obtain Circular E from your local IRS office.

Caution—Corporate businesses: The Social Security tax break is not available if you operate your business as a corporation. The corporation will have to pay Social Security and Unemployment taxes on your spouse and child.

Spouse in the corporation: While there are other advantages to having your spouse work in your corporation, there is no tax-saving on the wages paid to your spouse. The earnings are included in your joint return. Moreover, Social Security taxes must be paid by both your corporation and spouse.

Children in the corporation: If your children work for your corporation, Social Security taxes are paid by both the corporation and the child. The corporation also pays Unemployment taxes and may have increased premiums for workers compensation insurance. Yet, if your tax bracket is over 20 percent, there are savings.

Pencil-push: If your corporation wants to hire your children, calculate the actual tax savings before the hire date.

TAX REDUCTION CHECKLIST

IRS publications to be obtained:

- Publication 334—*Tax Guide for Small Business*
- Publication 583—*Information for Business Taxpayers—Business Taxes, Identification Numbers, Recordkeeping*
- Publication 15—*Employer's Tax Guide (Circular E)*

Benefits of self-employed hiring dependent child:

- Save self-employment taxes.
- Save taxes on business income because of wage deduction.

Benefits of self-employed hiring spouse:

- Save self-employment tax.
- Permit full $2,000 IRA contribution.
- Permit 25 percent ($30,000 maximum) deduction for spouse under your self-employed retirement plan.

Benefits of corporation hiring spouse or dependent child:

- No savings from wages paid to spouse.
- Save difference between increased payroll taxes and combined tax bracket of parent and corporation for wages paid to dependent child.

Definition of a dependent child:

- Meets five tests for dependency exemption.
- Can earn $1,040 or more and still be claimed if child is
  — Under age 19, or
  — Full-time student.

Preserving your dependency exemption:

- Keep a record of all support items and your payments of them.
- Make sure you pay more than one-half of the support expenses—leave a large margin for error.
- Support includes expenses for lodging, tuition, recreation, food, clothing, medical care, among others.

Selecting the right salary:

- Object is to pay no more than what you would pay an unrelated person for the same services.
- Get quotes from outside employment agencies.
- Consider experience and ability of child when deciding amount of pay.

Complying with child labor laws:

- Write a letter to the Federal, state, and—if applicable—local labor law officials, outlining the details of the child's proposed employment.
- This technique provides tax documentation and keeps you out of trouble with the child labor officials.

Substantiation:

- Prepare a simple employment contract.
- Make sure your child and your spouse keep timesheets showing dates, hours worked, and duties performed.
- Always pay by check.

Filing requirements for self-employed:

- File Form 941 annually and indicate that spouse's and child's wages are exempt from employment taxes (FICA and FUTA).
- No income tax withholding if wages are less than $1,404 a year.
- No withholding if wages are less than $3,300 and child paid no taxes last year, but Form W-2 should be completed and kept in shoebox.
- Income tax withholding is required for wages of $3,300 or more a year.

Until the last few years, the word "noncompliance" was seldom heard in connection with taxes. When tax time came along, we filled out the forms, made out our checks, and sent them in by April 15. Most of us still follow this law-abiding ritual.

But lately, we've heard many a discouraging word about the sad state of taxpayer compliance. Magazine and newspaper articles about the "underground economy" have become commonplace. Supermarket shelves carry books by so-called "tax protesters" telling us we don't have to pay taxes because the U.S. isn't on the gold standard, or because the tax law is unconstitutional, or because the earth is flat, or whatever. And slick operators put ads in the newspapers during the last two weeks in December, promising us a $25,000 tax write-off for a $5,000 investment.

With all this tax cheating going on and budget deficits rising faster than the Mississippi in springtime, it's no wonder Uncle Sam, through his duly appointed agent, the IRS Commissioner, is doing something about it. Unfortunately, this something doesn't just affect the kooks, cheats, and assorted other black-hat bozos; it affects all of us law-abiding folks, too. Therefore, we have devoted this chapter to taxpayer compliance issues that will prob-

ably affect nine out of 10 of us in the next few years. Specifically, we will cover:

- How new tax laws have created a compliance stampede
- How to avoid the big new penalty
- What to do about tax shelters
- How not to be a tax protester
- How to take the IRS to court
- Why you should file your returns on time
- What you must report to the IRS about other taxpayers
- What others must report to the IRS about you

HOW NEW TAX LAWS HAVE CREATED A COMPLIANCE STAMPEDE

Several major tax laws have bombarded us in the last few years. However, provisions dealing with taxpayer compliance came in dribs and drabs. Then the real bomb hit—the Tax Equity and Fiscal Responsibility Act of 1982 (TEFRA). Through TEFRA, Congress has armed the IRS Commissioner with an expanded arsenal of weapons. In addition, Congress has authorized a larger posse of IRS agents to pursue those bozos who are not paying their fair share of income taxes.

How to Keep the IRS Posse From Lynching You

What does this mean for us law-abiding citizens in white hats? Saddle up, and get ready to ride a bumpy trail that includes a confusing new penalty for underpaying taxes, new reporting requirements, and new or increased taxes for failing to file required reports.

HOW TO AVOID THE BIG NEW PENALTY

The most innovative, bewildering, and potentially dangerous new law is the penalty for substantial understatement of income tax liability. The penalty is effective for understatements occurring after 1982.

Substantial understatement: If the IRS Sheriff decides that the tax due Uncle Sam—as shown on an individual tax return—is understated by more than $5,000, the penalty may be imposed. The $5,000 threshold also applies to S Corporations and personal holding companies. If you are lucky enough to owe more than $50,000 of taxes, the threshold amount is 10 percent of your correct tax liability. For example, if you owed $60,000 of taxes, the penalty would not apply unless you reported taxes of less than $54,000. For corporations, the threshold amount is $10,000 (or 10 percent of the tax liability, if greater than $10,000).

Penalty: The penalty is 10 percent of the understatement.

Although the threshold for substantial understatement is high, you are likely to cross that threshold at some point in your tax-paying life, because:

- The understatement relates to the aggregate of all items on a return, not just an isolated item or transaction
- A large potential tax liability may result from an isolated transaction if the IRS decides that it was improperly reported

Avoiding the penalty: If the understatement in tax liability is not the result of a tax shelter item, you may avoid the penalty in either of two ways:

- Disclosing in your tax return—or in a statement attached to your tax return—all the relevant facts affecting the transaction that results in the understatement, or
- Showing that you have substantial authority for your claim

Choice 1—Disclosure: You are given absolution from the new understatement penalty if you confess your sins to IRS by flagging your claim in your tax return. In other words, you must tell the IRS there may be a problem with one of your deductions, exclusions, or credits. Although you will sidestep the new penalty, you are almost certain to spend some time with the lynching party, since the confession will probably cause the IRS to audit your return. If, after examination, the IRS disagrees with your tax claims, it will assess back taxes and interest. Also, it may look at other items in your return which might have been overlooked if you hadn't flagged your return.

How to disclose: The IRS says that for most tax claims you must attach a separate statement to your return, specifically identifying the claim. You will have to put a caption on the statement. It should look something like this:

DISCLOSURE STATEMENT UNDER SECTION 6661 OF THE INTERNAL REVENUE CODE

In addition to this caption, your statement must contain enough facts to let the IRS know what the problem is. As an alternative, your tax advisor can describe the legal issue raised by your claim.

A separate statement will not always be necessary. For certain items, simply reporting those items on the proper tax form will be enough to flag them for the IRS. However, the IRS decides which items fall into this category. To let the public know which items these are, the IRS will publish rulings from time to time. Consider your disclosure adequate if you reported the following items properly on your individual return (Form 1040):

- Medical expenses—Schedule A (itemized deductions)

- Taxes—Schedules A or C (trade or business expenses)
- Interest expense—Schedule A
- Contributions—Schedule A
- Casualty and theft losses—Schedules A or C, and Form 4684
- Legal fees—Schedule C
- Specific bad debt charge-off—Schedule C
- Repair as opposed to capital expenditure—Schedule C
- Sale or exchange of principal residence—Form 2119
- Employee business expense—Form 2106
- Moving expenses—Form 3903

For any of the above items that qualify as trade or business expenses of a corporation, disclosure will be adequate if the corporation reports them properly on its corporate return (Form 1120 or 1120S). In addition, corporations needn't report the following items on a separate disclosure statement:

- Reserve for bad debts—Schedule F
- Reasonableness of officers' compensation—Schedule E

Choice 2—let the posse catch you: If you decide that the hazards of confessing are too great, you may wait for the posse. If the Sheriff decides to slap on the new penalty, you can defend yourself by proving that your claim was supported by substantial authority.

Definition of substantial authority: Congress dealt law-abiding citizens the unkindest cut of all by deliberately refusing to tell what authority is "substantial." Instead, in one of the most outrageous buck-passing moves in tax history, Congress left it to the courts to frame a definition of substantial authority.

Obviously, the lack of guiding light will certainly put you out on a ledge with the judge. A court can decide issues only when there is a case before it. Thus, a hapless taxpayer will have to be a judicial guinea pig before a precise standard for substantial authority can be established, if, in fact, a precise standard can ever be established. Meanwhile, you are forced to second-guess both the IRS (which initiates

the penalty) and the courts (which determine whether the penalty is correctly imposed).

To complicate things further, different courts have different attitudes regarding the weight of authority. For example, many experienced lawyers believe that the Claims Court views an argument based on equity more favorably than either the Tax Court or the U.S. District Court, even when the argument seems to defy a literal reading of the Internal Revenue or Regulations.

What the IRS says is substantial authority: The IRS hasn't made much of an effort to define substantial authority. However, the IRS has made it clear that substantial authority means authority that makes your case something more than simply arguable. Also, authority is not substantial if your claim is "fairly unlikely to prevail" in court.

The IRS has tried to quantify the standard of substantial authority. It says that if your claim is supported by a Federal district court decision, but three Federal appeals courts support the IRS, you don't have substantial authority for your claim. But you do have substantial authority if there's only one Federal appeals court decision against your Federal district court decision. Apparently, the IRS hasn't decided whether two appeals court decisions will offset one district court decision.

Delicious agony of choice: In short, then, if you are planning a transaction not supported by absolutely binding authority, you are faced with a Hobson's choice to avoid the understatement penalty:

- Either confess by flagging the return and face the unpleasantness that follows, or
- Get caught and hope that the IRS will accept the authority you relied upon as substantial.

You may feel as though you've just come face to face with the Grim Reaper. You have. The new law places a heavy burden on law-abiding taxpayers, particularly since the result of goofing (even in good faith) turns you into a black-hat.

The law does provide for IRS forgiveness, however. Before we talk about the circumstances when the IRS will forgive you for understating your taxes, let's discuss the special rules on understatements resulting from tax shelter items.

WHAT TO DO ABOUT TAX SHELTERS

What you have just read was the opening shot. Now for the bomb. Suppose the Sheriff decides that the transaction causing an understatement of taxes was a tax shelter item? The new law defines tax shelter item as an item arising from a partnership or other entity, plan, or arrangement with the principal purpose of avoiding or evading Federal income taxes.

If you cannot prove that the item was not a tax shelter item, the disclosure exception is not available. In other words, you cannot absolve yourself simply by flagging the item in your tax return. Furthermore, it is not enough to show that you had substantial authority for your claim. You must also show that you reasonably believed your treatment of the item was "more likely than not" the correct treatment.

The "more likely than not" test is more difficult to pass than the substantial authority test. Congress believes that if "the principal purpose of the transaction is the reduction of taxes, it is not unreasonable to hold participants to a higher standard than ordinary taxpayers."

The IRS says you pass the "more likely than not" test if you rely on your tax advisor's advice that you have a better than 50 percent chance of winning your case in court, and *if* your tax advisor's reasoning is sound. If your tax advisor is a dunce, you're out of luck. Obviously, you would be much better off if you could simply avoid the tax shelter label.

Avoiding tax shelter status: To avoid tax shelter status, you must prove that the principal purpose of the transaction was not tax avoidance. However, many transactions have dual purposes. If you buy a residential rental house, for example, you would be looking for both appreciation in value and the tax benefits resulting because of increased deductions. To avoid tax shelter classification of your rental house, you must prove that your profit motives were more important than your tax

avoidance motives. This subjective determination can be made, short of mind reading, only by examining all facts and circumstances of the transaction.

Shoebox: To avoid tax shelter classification, you must stuff your shoebox with documentation demonstrating your profit motives. This should include letters and memos to real estate salespeople, lawyers, accountants, and others with whom you're dealing. Note that such self-serving documentation is never conclusive as to motive, but it is certainly better to have it than not. Also, documentation discussing tax advantages should be avoided.

IRS forgiveness: Congress granted IRS the power of total absolution for taxpayers who understate their taxes. The IRS may waive all or any part of the understatement penalty if a taxpayer shows there was reasonable cause for the understatement and that the taxpayer made the claim in good faith. This rule applies in both tax shelter cases and non–tax shelter cases.

Thus far, the IRS has given little indication of how it will apply this provision. In non–tax shelter cases, the IRS says it will forgive taxpayers who file an amended return satisfying the disclosure rules discussed previously, even though the return is filed after its due date. In short, if you encourage the IRS to audit you—even though you do it late— the IRS will forgive the penalty for understating your taxes. In tax shelter cases, the IRS says it will forgive you if you amend your return, confess that your original return was wrong, *and pay* the additional tax.

Counting on the IRS to forgive you is a little like entrusting your chickens to a fox. Furthermore, in view of the strong Congressional intent of demanding fierce compliance, it remains to be seen how forgiving the IRS will be when it hears such pleas. Your best bet for avoiding the new penalty is to have great documentation and sound authority for your tax claims.

HOW NOT TO BE A TAX PROTESTER

Don't be a tax protester. The IRS Sheriff has a new weapon to use against tax protesters.

Whether or not you actually owe any tax, the IRS can slap a $500 penalty for filing a "frivolous" tax return.

The posse will chase any return which, on its face, does not contain sufficient information to determine the correct tax, or a return containing information indicating that the tax shown is substantially incorrect. The IRS can impose the penalty only if the taxpayer's position is frivolous or if the taxpayer desires to delay or impede the administration of tax law.

The new law does not define frivolous. However, the penalty will not apply where there is a valid dispute over interpretation of tax law. Congress aims the penalty primarily at those who try to alter tax forms, or claim "war tax," "gold standard," or other unauthorized deductions.

In short, don't be a whacko. Fill out your return completely. Claim all deductions and credits you believe you're entitled to. But don't be cute.

HOW TO TAKE THE IRS TO COURT

Besides the penalty for frivolity, the IRS can fine taxpayers for aiding and abetting tax understatement and promoting tax shelters. These latter two penalties are aimed mainly at tax and investment advisors. But they could apply to anyone, including you.

Congress provided a way for honest taxpayers like you to take the IRS to task for falsely accusing you of one of these three tax sins. By first paying 15 percent of the penalty and filing a refund claim within 30 days after assessment by the IRS, you may file a refund suit in U.S. District Court.

Advisors only: Although this review is available to anyone who aids or abets tax understatement, it is not available if you are slapped with the substantial understatement penalty. Thus, you can seek relief only when you do it to someone else, not to yourself. To obtain relief from the substantial understatement penalty, you must either file a claim in the United States Tax Court, or pay the entire penalty and file a refund suit in U.S. District Court.

WHY YOU SHOULD FILE YOUR TAX RETURN ON TIME

Paperwork costs money. The IRS has been worried because it has to spend $75 to identify taxpayers who fail to file tax returns. In the new law, Congress made sure the IRS is reimbursed for such cost—plus a little extra. For those lazy bozos who don't file tax returns within 60 days of the due date (including extensions), the IRS may impose a penalty equal to the tax due, but not more than $100. You can avoid this penalty by showing that your failure to file was because of some reasonable cause.

WHAT YOU MUST REPORT TO IRS ABOUT OTHER TAXPAYERS

Uncle Sam drafts private citizens to serve with the IRS posse. Unlike military draftees who are paid, members of the IRS posse are required to serve without pay. Moreover, posse members must absorb their own expenses, such as for paperwork.

Information on employee wages: For years, employers have had to tell the IRS how much they paid their employees each year. The report is made on Form W-2 (Form W-2P for annuities, pensions, and retirement pay) and must be filed with the Social Security Administration (which sends it to the IRS) by the end of February. Employers also must file quarterly reports of wages on Form 941E, and pay withheld taxes.

Business expenses—$600 rule: In addition to reporting employee wages, businesspeople must now report certain payments totaling $600 or more in a year to any nonemployee. These payments include:

- Fees, commissions, salaries, and any other compensation
- Interest, rents, royalties, and pensions
- Any other amounts representing gains or profits

For example, if you paid your tax advisor $600 or more for tax advice on business transactions, you must tell IRS.

The reports, which are made on Forms 1096 and 1099, must include the recipient's name, address, taxpayer identification number, and the amount paid. For an individual, the taxpayer identification number is the Social Security number. Corporations and other entities are assigned a taxpayer identification number by the IRS. The penalty for failing to provide the correct taxpayer identification number is $50 for each failure (up to a maximum of $50,000 in one year).

1983 revision: Until 1983 the "$600 rule" did not apply to payments to corporations. For example, if your tax advisor was incorporated, you would not have to report your fees under the old rule. Starting in 1983, business taxpayers must report fees or other compensation of $600 or more for personal services, even though the service-provider is incorporated. Thus, you will now have to report fees of $600 or more to your incorporated tax advisor.

Increase in penalties: If asked to serve with the IRS posse, it's an offer that's hard to refuse. For taxpayers who must file information returns, the penalty for failure to file without reasonable cause has been increased from $10 per failure (maximum of $25,000) to $50 per failure (new maximum of $50,000). Substantially more severe penalties are imposed if the failure to file is because of intentional disregard of the rules.

Backup withholding in 1984: Beginning in 1984, if the person you pay does not tell you his or her taxpayer identification number, or if the number given is obviously incorrect, you must withhold 15 percent of the payment. A taxpayer identification number is obviously incorrect if it has more or less than 9 digits.

WHAT OTHERS MUST REPORT TO IRS ABOUT YOU

The IRS discovered that many bozos were escaping the posse because they didn't report taxable income to the IRS. To remedy this, Congress passed the new law to draft many new recruits into the IRS posse to help the IRS find these bozos.

Brokers: To catch those not reporting their capital gains transactions, the new law requires securities brokers to report transactions that result from their services.

The new law gives the IRS authority to expand its posse by drafting other dealers, barter exchangers, and others who (for consideration) regularly act as middlemen. Under the new requirements, the defined category of brokers must:

- Report gross proceeds from transactions carried on by customers, and
- Furnish information statements to the IRS and customers by January 31 of the year following the year of reporting.

Penalty: If such statements are not furnished by the defined brokers, the penalty is $50 per statement up to a maximum of $50,000 for the year. The new rule applies to transactions after 1982.

Real estate brokers: The IRS has not yet drafted real estate brokers into its posse. But IRS is thinking about it.

State and local governments: The IRS wants to know about your tax refunds. In this novel provision, Congress authorized the IRS to press state and local governments into service to help chase bandits who received tax refunds that should have been reported as taxable income. The refunding agencies are now required to file information returns for any refund of more than $10 to any individual taxpayer. As you would expect, state and local jurisdictions are not enthusiastic, since providing this information to the IRS can be costly indeed. For instance, Maryland estimated that at least $300,000 must be allocated for reporting this information to the IRS.

NEW REQUIREMENTS IN 1985

In the Tax Reform Act of 1984, Uncle Sam tightened the compliance noose even more. Here are the two changes likely to affect you.

Mortgage interest: Uncle Sam wants to make sure you aren't exaggerating your mortgage interest deduction. Therefore, starting in 1985, anyone who, in the course of a trade or business, receives mortgage interest from an individual amounting to $600 or more must report to Uncle Sam. The report must include the individual's name, address, Social Security number, the amount of interest, and anything else the IRS prescribes. Note: This new rule applies to existing mortgages as well as 1984 mortgages.

Failing to report to the IRS will result in a $50 penalty for each required return. Also, the person paying interest will be fined $50 for failing to give the recipient his or her Social Security number.

For most of you, the effect of this new rule will be minimal: You will simply have to give your Social Security number—and perhaps some other information—to your mortgage-holder. If, however, you *receive* mortgage payments from one or more individuals in the course of your business, check with your tax advisor to make sure you satisfy the IRS's requirements.

Charitable contributions: If you make a charitable contribution of property after 1984 and want to claim more than $5,000 as a deduction, you must get a written appraisal from a qualified appraiser. Also, you must file an appraisal summary, signed by the appraiser, with your tax return.

The $5,000 limit applies to each item of property that you donate. You don't *have* to get an appraisal if you donate several dissimilar items, none of which is worth more than $5,000. However, if you give similar items, such as rare books, the $5,000 limit applies to their aggregate value.

Conclusion: Congress has given its blessing to the compliance stampede. The Commissioner of Internal Revenue has been given a green light to chase noncompliers with renewed vigor. Perhaps the only true winners in this legislation are the lawyers who will be defending the words "substantial authority" and "more likely than not."

It's much too early to tell what all this means to us law-abiding citizens, but here are some certainties:

- If you're paying anyone else for anything, the new laws will not only cause increased anxiety, but also increased, costly paperwork.
- You and your tax advisor will have to work harder to make sure your tax claims are supported by substantial legal and factual authority.
- You will need a much better, fatter shoebox.

TAX REDUCTION CHECKLIST

IRS publications to be obtained:

- Publication 15 —*Employer's Tax Guide (Circular E)*
- Publication 583—*Information for Business Taxpayers—Business Taxes, Identification Numbers, Recordkeeping*
- Publication 556—*Examination of Returns, Appeal Rights, and Claims For Refund*

Substantial understatement penalty:

- May apply when you understate your taxes by more than $5,000.
- For non–tax shelter items, avoid penalty by disclosing claim on your return, or having substantial authority for your claim.
  - Disclosure invites IRS audit.
  - Having "substantial authority" requires detailed reasoning by tax advisor.
- Penalty, if it applies, is 10 percent of understatement.

Tax shelter items:

- Substantial understatement penalty on tax shelter items is avoided by showing
  - Substantial authority, and
  - Reasonable belief that your claim had a better than 50 percent chance of winning in court.
- Tax shelters are any plans designed mainly for tax avoidance, rather than economic gain.

Tax protesters:

- IRS can fine you $500 for filing a frivolous return.
- A return claiming "war tax," "gold standard," "unconstitutional," or something else equally goofy is frivolous.

Going to court:

- Special procedures allow you to contest IRS fines in court.

Reporting on others—$600 rule:

- Applies to payments of $600 or more in connection with your business.
- Types of payments include fees, commissions, salaries, interest, rents, royalties, and pensions.
- You must report recipient's name, address, and taxpayer identification number.
- Beginning in 1984, you must withhold 15 percent of the payment if the recipient provides you with an obviously incorrect taxpayer identification number.
- IRS will fine you for not following these rules.

Reports on you:

- Your broker must report your stock and bond transactions.
- State and local governments must report your tax refunds.
- Financial institutions must report your interest and dividends.

No one in the land likes a tax audit except perhaps a revenue agent. But, as a reader of this book, you are undoubtedly in one of those unfortunate categories where you can almost count on an examination of your tax return. The reason, quite simply, is that your return is likely to contain a large number of difficult to support deductions. That does not mean that your return is in error, but it does mean that you are in a class of taxpayers where errors are commonplace.

You probably don't want to cuddle a tax collector. You may be a little concerned about an examination of your return, how it would be conducted, and what you could do to avoid the possibility of being selected in the first place. You need to know what steps are necessary to handle the audit process. This chapter details many of the steps taken by the IRS, defensive tactics you should use, and other information to help you survive a tax audit.

WHAT THE IRS KNOWS ABOUT YOU

There's an itty bitty computer chip in Martinsburg, West Virginia, telling IRS auditors all about you. It is collecting information from your bank, your employer, and other businesses and individuals that pay you money.

When the information from another party does not match your information, your return comes to someone's attention.

The road to Martinsburg: You do not send your tax return to Martinsburg, West Virginia. The postman delivers your return to one of 10 regional IRS Service Centers where it enters the IRS "pipeline." A Service Center is a monolith that looks like a standard industrial park: office buildings, loading docks, storage areas, and computers—lots and lots of computers.

There are some people at the service center too, but in the pipeline, people are not very important. They're just servants to the computer.

The bar-coded envelope you receive with your tax return is fed into computerized equipment which sorts envelopes by type of return at the rate of 30,000 envelopes per hour. Uncoded envelopes are sorted by hand.

Hint: Use the bar-coded envelope to speed up your refund check.

Return analysis: In the second step in the pipeline, human beings check the return for completeness and make sure that the infor-

20
Why Knowledge Is Your Only Defense Against the IRS

mation is entered properly. They also make sure that the returns are properly signed.

Use pre-addressed label to speed refunds: There's a common myth that if you use the pre-addressed label you are going to assist IRS in selecting your return for audit. That's hogwash. The code preceding the taxpayer's Social Security number indicates that the Social Security number has been verified as correct. The "cr" number at the center top is merely a postal carrier route number. The code in the upper-right-hand corner of the pre-addressed label simply designates the IRS district where the taxpayer filed last year. That's all the pre-addressed label represents. Audit codes are assigned later, in Martinsburg. Therefore, help the IRS save the time and trouble of re-verifying and re-creating the codes to speed up your refund check.

Arrange tax schedules to speed up refunds: Individual tax returns are processed more quickly if they are arranged in the following sequence: Form 1040, Schedules A, B, C, D, E, F, G, R, RP, SE, and Forms 2119, 2440, 2441, 3468, 4136, 4625, 4797, 5329, 5695, 6251, and Schedule W. Other forms and schedules should follow in alphabetical and numerical order behind those listed.

On to Martinsburg: Once your return has been keypunched by the regional Service Center, it is entered on a magnetic tape. The magnetic tapes are flown daily to Martinsburg, West Virginia—the IRS National Computer Center. In effect, Martinsburg is the end of the pipeline, and it accumulates data from over 170 million tax returns each year. Exhibit 20-1 lists the types of tax returns filed in 1982.

In mid-1983, IRS replaced the six aging IBM computers with a new $10 million NAS 90-60 computer made by Hitachi of Japan. The new computer system enables IRS to match the returns of individual taxpayers against bank statements and other reports of income from employers, brokerage houses, banks, savings and loans, and companies paying dividends.

Form W-2: If you work as an employee, your employer probably withholds Federal income taxes using a form that is filed with the IRS. At the end of each year, your employer sends a detailed report describing all the information contained in your W-2. That information is correlated with information reported in your tax return.

Form 1099: IRS also wants to know about miscellaneous income. Employers who pay more than $600 to independent contractors must report such payments to IRS using a Form 1099. Banks and savings and loans report your interest earnings using Form 1099. If you take money from a gambling casino, the gambling casino must report, and possibly withhold, some of your money. The reports are filed with IRS.

You are a statistic: Each time you file a tax return it is processed by the mammoth computers in Martinsburg. Your return is matched against other taxpayers with similar characteristics to determine if you are a little unusual. Should you have any abnormalities, you will be invited to visit with your friendly tax collector.

Identifying fraudulent return preparers: The Service Centers, while processing returns, extract information about your tax preparer. The objective of this program is to identify tax preparers who engage in fraudulent practices. It is designed to protect the innocent, uneducated, and uninformed individual taxpayers against fraudulent tax advisors. It is also designed to increase compliance by those taxpayers who look for unscrupulous tax preparers.

The IRS has not only your tax return, but also evidence from other sources which can be used to police your return. If you fail to report income from a bank, for example, IRS computers could catch that error. Computer programs also grade the logic in your return. If, for example, you report a loss of $50,000, but your savings account increases by $30,000, IRS computers identify your return as being somewhat unusual.

Before discussing the actual audit selection process, let's turn our attention to the individuals you are likely to meet at the IRS.

EXHIBIT 20-1. Tax Returns Filed

	1978	1982
Individual Income Tax Returns	87,405,000	95,482,000
Declaration of Estimated Tax	8,103,000	31,863,000
Corporate Tax Returns	2,349,000	2,950,000
Partnership Tax Returns	1,205,000	1,561,000
Employment Tax Returns	25,541,000	25,835,000
Other	12,032,000	12,678,000
Total	136,635,000	170,369,000

WHY TAX AUDITORS ARE DUMBER THAN REVENUE AGENTS

In your initial dealings with IRS, you run into one of three individuals: (1) taxpayer service representative; (2) tax auditor; or (3) revenue agent. The lowest form of IRS life is the taxpayer service representative and the highest form of life is, of course, the revenue agent. Tax auditors fall in between.

Taxpayer service representatives: When you call the IRS information service to get a question answered, you talk to a taxpayer service representative. A taxpayer service representative is someone with a two-year associate degree—two years of college in any field, with no requirement for any accounting or tax courses. These are the people who answer your tax questions.

The reps do get some training. Three days of classroom training is required for reps who assist persons wishing to file Form 1040A. There's also a 20-day basic training course for the people who answer the phones. After the basic training, an individual is IRS qualified to answer phone-in questions.

Compare this with your CPA's training. The CPA must have an accounting degree with at least 24 semester hours of accounting courses, and is required to pass a rigorous examination. Many individuals studying for the CPA examination spend six months getting ready for the exam. Yet, can you call your CPA and get an off-the-cuff answer to your question? Not often; usually the CPA will need to do some research and get back to you later.

Between January 1 and April 24, IRS receives approximately 22 million telephone calls.

There must be a lot of people out there with extreme patience willing to put up with being "on hold" for a considerable period of time. The IRS claims it makes a quality check of telephone responses and that its overall accuracy rate is 98 percent. If that's true, IRS receives an abundance of simple questions.

In a recent check made by the authors, a question was asked about the depreciation component used by IRS in figuring the 21-cents-a-mile standard mileage rate. We got three correct answers and 24 incorrect answers. Similar studies have been conducted by other organizations and no one has found a 98 percent accuracy rate. The best we've been able to find is a 42 percent accuracy rate.

Call the IRS at your own peril: The IRS does not stand behind its answers. If it answers your question incorrectly, you're stuck. It is your responsibility to know that the answer is wrong!

Tax auditors: Your tax return will be examined either by a tax auditor or a revenue agent. If you are going down to IRS to present your information, you will in all likelihood be visiting a tax auditor. To qualify for this esteemed position, a tax auditor must have a four-year college degree—in anything. Tax auditors generally start at a salary of $14,000 and can advance to a salary of $27,000. Before advancing to a salary of $20,000, a tax auditor must have completed six semester hours of accounting courses.

For those unfamiliar with accounting majors, six semester hours covers the "Principles of Accounting." Technicians generally refer to this as the bookkeeping courses. The difficult accounting courses start after an accountant completes the first six semester hours, which are prerequisite to the more difficult courses.

No thinking allowed: The office auditor is generally not required to interpret guidelines nor engage in research. The issues in contention are clearly defined by the classifier before the returns are assigned to the individuals. The entire scope of the audit is set by the classifier, and any expansion beyond that set by the classifier must be approved by the group manager.

Many office audits do not involve any planning for the tax examination. IRS guidelines set forth several conditions which could require pre-contact examination planning for office audits. If your return involves determination of inventories and cost of goods sold, some pre-examination planning is warranted. If the auditor will have to make a net worth determination, pre-planning is required. Also, if you have a power of attorney on file at the local IRS office, tax auditors are required to do pre-contact research. In many cases, however, the first time the office auditor looks at your return is when you walk through the door, or very shortly before that.

Basic problem: Tax auditors are not well versed in tax law. They do not spend a lot of time studying the law, nor do they have the background necessary to interpret the law. Accordingly, the tax auditor's examination is conducted in strict accord with IRS guidelines. Those guidelines interpret IRS policy and are designed to make the tax auditor function like a robot. Very little imagination, skill, or reasonableness is involved.

Direct verification of records: Tax auditors are good at taking your receipts, adding them up and comparing them to your tax return. Differences are usually proposed as adjustments. Tax auditors generally audit:

- Business expenses.
- Bad debts.
- Basis of property.
- Auto repair shops.
- Barber shops.
- Beauty shops.
- Bowling alleys.
- Cafes.
- Restaurants.
- Delicatessens.
- Grocery stores.
- Laundromats.
- Motels.
- Professional persons.
- Appliance service and salespersons.
- Service stations.
- Small building contractors.
- Truckers.
- Farmers.

Last year IRS examined 1.6 million income, estate, and gift tax returns. Of that total, tax auditors performed 65 percent of the examinations. Yet, tax auditors comprise a small percentage of IRS personnel, as shown in Exhibit 20-2.

Revenue agents: Revenue agents must have a four-year college degree and a minimum of 24 semester hours of accounting. Experience can be substituted for the 24 hours of accounting.

IRS does not recruit all "A" students. Many of the revenue agents squeak through college with "C" averages. The "A" students are snapped up by the big accounting firms. That leaves IRS with a pool of "B" and "C" students.

The IRS hires these individuals and gives them a happy place to work. Like the Army, IRS develops a special sense of loyalty. Revenue agents are expected to be and usually are good soldiers. That's important. For the IRS system to work, revenue agents must believe that it is *their* IRS, right or wrong. They learn tax law the way IRS teaches it and wants them to see it.

Revenue agents go through extensive training at IRS to learn the way IRS wants things done. They handle complex returns which require full use of their accounting skills. Unlike the tax auditor, the revenue agent sets the entire scope of the examination.

Revenue agents generally start at a salary of $17,000 and can move through the ranks to a salary of $46,000. Once above the salary level of $46,000, revenue agents are usually promoted to administrative responsibilities.

EXHIBIT 20-2. IRS Personnel Summary.

Examination Specialists	
Revenue Agents	13,313
Tax Auditors	4,821
Other	3,963
Appeals	1,693
Tax Fraud	3,517
Data Processing	22,586
Collection	13,453
National Office	4,651
Other	15,838
Total	83,835

What's better—tax auditor or revenue agent? Generally, the smarter and longer someone has been with IRS, the better the audit is conducted. Remember, the purpose of the audit is simply to determine the correct tax liability—no more, no less.

Revenue agents are trained to use their full accounting skills and knowledge of the Internal Revenue Code. Tax auditors are not so trained. Arbitrary judgments and decisions are often made by tax auditors, whereas revenue agents exercise more judgment developed through knowledge, training, and experience.

You do not get to choose the auditor you would like. Generally, if you are going down to IRS, you will be visiting with a tax auditor. If IRS is coming out to visit you, you will be dealing with a revenue agent.

CHANCES OF AN IRS AUDIT

Once you've submitted your tax return to the IRS regional Service Center, you have entered the pipeline leading to the "audit lottery." The first principle of the audit lottery game is that the odds are heavily stacked in your favor. It's like Russian roulette, with a gun firing about once every 63 times.

The more you make, the better your chances of being audited. Exhibit 20-3 shows the odds of being audited at various levels.

TPI = Total Positive Income: The IRS developed a new audit phrase in 1979 called "Total Positive Income" (TPI). Your TPI is the sum of your wages, dividends, interest, rents, and other income items—without taking into account any losses or other negative income. If your TPI was $50,000 or more in 1982, your chances of audit were 5.68 percent. If you had TPI of $24,000 and filed a simple return, your chances of audit were only .57 percent.

TGR = Total Gross Receipts: If you operate as a small business or independent contractor and attach Schedule C to your tax return, IRS will select your return for audit based on "Total Gross Receipts" (TGR). Like TPI, TGR includes only positive income. Deductions are not considered in this selection process.

Big corporations have the best chance of an audit: Corporations with assets of $100 million and over have a 66.73 percent chance of being audited. The reason is simple. The more money passing through an entity, the better the chances of finding mistakes, and the larger the adjustments.

In 1982 IRS spent about $1 billion on its audit staff and collected $11.7 billion. That's not a bad return on investment.

How much does the IRS collect? Revenue agents collect more than tax auditors. With Total Positive Income of $10,000–$25,000 on a simple return, revenue agent audits netted Uncle Sam an average of $2,520 in additional tax and penalty per return examined. Tax auditors collected only $579 per return ex-

EXHIBIT 20-3. Chances Of An IRS Audit.

INCOME RANGE	TOTAL RETURNS	PERCENT AUDITED
Form 1040		
TPI[1] $10,000–$25,000 simple	21,189,000	.57
TPI $10,000–$25,000 complex	11,251,000	2.45
TPI $25,000–$50,000	17,668,000	2.90
TPI $50,000 and over	3,305,000	5.68
Schedule C		
TGR[2] Less than $25,000	1,831,000	1.68
TGR $25,000–$100,000	1,747,000	3.97
TGR $100,000 and over	921,000	5.94
Subchapter S Corporations	547,000	1.60
Regular Corporations		
Assets Under $100,000	1,035,000	2.79
Assets $100,000–1 million	870,000	4.49
Assets $1–10 million	185,000	12.59
Assets $10–100 million	30,000	23.86
Assets $100 million and over	6,000	66.73

[1] Total Positive Income
[2] Total Gross Receipts

amined. Exhibit 20-4 lists the results for audits conducted in 1982 (the latest year for which this information is available).

When looking at Exhibit 20-4, note how the no-change percents vary between revenue agents and tax auditors. Persons earning Total Positive Income of $50,000 and over, for example, received no-change letters 9 percent of the time from revenue agents, but 29 percent of the time from tax auditors. A no-change letter means the IRS accepts the return as filed.

Big corporations pay more: Revenue agents nailed large corporations for an average additional tax and penalty of $1.5 million in 1982. Note that only 3 percent of the large corporations got no-change letters.

TWENTY-THREE WAYS TO INCREASE YOUR CHANCES OF AN IRS AUDIT

If you are worried because IRS has not yet audited your return, here are some things you can do to speed up the selection process.

1. Make more money: As you saw in Exhibit 20-3, the more you make, the better your chances of audit. Obviously, if you combine the making of more money with larger deductions, you will be able to speed up the process even more.

2. File your tax return late: Late filed returns are subject to special scrutiny at IRS. The scrutiny starts at the regional Internal Revenue Service Center and continues in Martinsburg.

3. Talk about your taxes: Keep a still tongue in your mouth about your taxes. Tattle-tales get paid for squealing to the IRS. The IRS pays finks a 10 percent commission on additional tax collections. Over $15 million is collected by the IRS each year through the tattle-tale system.

4. Write sloppily and illegibly: If you are blessed with poor penmanship, you increase your chances of being audited. Sloppily prepared returns require interpretations, and such interpretations heavily increase the probability of a return being selected for audit. In fact, you may be asked to decipher your return in person.

5. Fail to answer IRS questions: If you don't answer the questions on your tax form, IRS computers will kick out your return. Once your return has been kicked out, you will receive a letter of notification asking what answer you desire for a particular question. Your answer receives extra scrutiny.

6. Claim unallowable deductions: Prior to computer processing at the regional Service Center,

EXHIBIT 20-4. Average Tax And Penalty Per Return Examined By IRS.

Income Range	AVERAGE ADDITIONAL TAX AND PENALTY			NO CHANGE PERCENT	
	Revenue Agent Audits	*Tax Auditor Audits*	*Service Center Audits*	*Revenue Agent Audits*	*Tax Auditor Audits*
Form 1040					
TPI[1] $10,000–$25,000 simple	$ 2,520	$ 579	$248	13	19
TPI $10,000–$25,000 complex	2,731	555	291	12	17
TPI $25,000–$50,000	3,057	648	336	10	20
TPI $50,000 and over	10,841	1,705	468	9	29
Schedule C					
TGR[2] Less than $25,000	4,042	895	451	15	21
TGR $25,000–$100,000	4,526	1,362	427	12	21
TGR $100,000 and over	11,901	2,563	620	10	22
Subchapter S Corporations	4,803			37	
Regular Corporations					
Assets under $100,000	2,465			31	
Assets $100,000–$1 million	4,268			23	
Assets $1–10 million	16,681			18	
Assets $10–100 million	78,969			9	
Assets $100 million and over	1,455,348			3	

[1] Total Positive Income
[2] Total Gross Receipts

your return is manually reviewed for obviously unallowable items. There are approximately sixty such unallowable items, seven of which are identified in Exhibit 20-5.

Once an unallowable item is identified by the Service Center, you are sent a letter asking for money, clarifying information, or additional information. If the item can be resolved by correspondence, your return is processed in the normal fashion. If not resolved by correspondence, your return is transferred to a District Office for audit.

7. Invest in a fraudulent tax shelter: At the end of 1982, IRS was examining 284,828 returns with tax shelter issues. That is an increase of 36,000 returns over the prior year. As a result of the examinations, the IRS collected tax and penalties totaling $954.2 million.

The Tax Equity and Fiscal Responsibility Act of 1982 (TEFRA) contained provisions to curb promotions of tax shelters and expedite processing of partnership returns. The Act provides penalties for the promotion or sale of schemes involving

gross valuation overstatement or false or fraudulent representation of material matters. The Act gives the IRS the right to stop any person from selling abusive tax shelters.

Before investing in any tax shelters, make sure your tax advisor reviews the shelter in detail. There are a number of tax shelters which are perfectly legal. The problem is selecting the legal from the illegal ones.

8. Prepare your own tax return, especially if it's complex: Choosing to do your own tax return can increase your chances of being selected for audit. The IRS instructions are complex, and keeping track of tax problems is almost a full-time job. When no paid preparer signs the return, the obvious conclusion is that you must have completed the tax return yourself. If the return is somewhat complex, the IRS figures that you must have done it wrong.

9. Select a dishonest tax preparer: The Service Center, while processing returns, extracts information for the Return Preparers Program. The objectives of this program are to identify, examine,

EXHIBIT 20-5. IRS Unallowable Items Program (Sample IRS Explanations).

Explanation 14   Gambling Winnings

Your Form 1040 has been adjusted to include the income shown on the Form W-2G attached to your return.

Explanation 33   Medical Expenses—Personal

Your medical expenses on Schedule A have been adjusted because items such as health club dues, diet foods, funeral expenses, maternity clothes, and meals or lodging (unless provided by a hospital or similar institution for medical care) cannot be deducted. (See Publication 502.)

Explanation 34   Federal Taxes

The Federal taxes on Schedule A cannot be allowed. Taxes that cannot be deducted include Federal income tax, social security and railroad retirement taxes, the Social Security tax you paid for a personal or domestic employee, Federal estate and gift taxes, customs duties and Federal excise taxes on automobiles, tires, telephone service, and air transportation.

Explanation 37   Automobile License, Registration, Tag Fees or Taxes

The deduction for automobile license, registration, tag fees, or taxes on Schedule A has been disallowed. These amounts may be shown as personal property taxes only if your State charged them annually and in an amount based on the value of your automobile. Since your State does not charge the fees and taxes this way, they are not personal property taxes and cannot be allowed.

Explanation 39   Personal Legal Expenses

The legal expenses on Schedule A cannot be allowed because expenses for wills, trusts, adoption, divorce, and other items not connected with the production of income are not deductible.

Explanation 45   Sale or Purchase of Personal Residence

The expenses incurred in the sale or purchase of your residence on Schedule A cannot be allowed because closing costs (for example, settlement and legal fees) or realtor commissions are not deductible. (See Publication 523.)

Explanation 80   Loss on Sale of Personal Residence or Property

The loss on the sale of your residence or other property used for personal purposes is not deductible.

investigate, and prosecute return preparers who engage in fraudulent practices.

The wrong preparer is incompetent, thoroughly dishonest, or has otherwise incurred the wrath of the IRS. There's no way to know if you have selected the wrong preparer until it's almost too late. However, there are a number of indicators that should give you a clue. Problem preparers may suggest you take deductions for which you have no support.

To locate problem preparers, the IRS sends out its agents disguised as taxpayers (not a difficult task since IRS agents pay taxes too). Once the IRS identifies a problem preparer, it activates its program. An invitation is issued to a substantial number of the target's clients inviting them down for an audit. The general idea behind the problem preparers program is simply to drive that problem preparer out of business. A large number of audits generally does the trick.

10. Die: As grizzly as it might sound, should you have the audacity to die, you will almost certainly be selected for audit scrutiny. In 1982 there were 8,000 estate tax returns with gross estates of $1 million and over. Of that total, 68.59 percent were audited. That's the single largest audit category.

11. Claim more than 14 withholding allowances: As a result of TEFRA, Congress required IRS to issue regulations enabling taxpayers to match their withholding more closely with their expected tax liabilities. The IRS complied with the law but also issued regulations that require employers to report all employees who claim in excess of 14 withholding allowances or exemptions from withholding. There is a $500 civil penalty for filing false wage withholding information. The IRS has been aggressively pursuing those penalties and the identification of employees who file incorrect withholding allowances.

12. Claim a casualty loss: Casualty loss deductions are difficult to compute and much more difficult to support. The loss is measured by taking the fair market value of the asset before and after the casualty. But the loss deduction cannot exceed what you paid for the item in the first place.

Many taxpayers lack records supporting the cost of items stolen or destroyed by casualty. Consequently, the IRS has a strong record of disallowing casualty loss deductions.

13. Claim a business loss for a hobby: On September 9, 1982, the IRS instituted a special "hobby loss" test for the Austin and Andover Service Centers. Returns showing losses on Form 1040 Schedules C and/or F during the years 1976 through 1981 are being selected for special test audits. Basically, if the return reports losses in four out of five years (six out of seven for horse-related activities), the IRS will be looking at the return. However, returns with potential adjustments of less than $1,000 will be disregarded for the test.

A "hobby loss" examination is a complex and difficult examination. If your return reports losses from business activities for four out of the past five years, make sure you review the contents of Chapter 1 regarding the "profit motive."

14. Claim travel and entertainment deductions: The IRS auditor starts with the assumption that you're probably cheating on your travel and entertainment expenses. The auditor knows that you're probably not a great record-keeper, and have failed to meet the five elements of substantiation required for all travel and entertainment. Moreover, auditors do not get to claim much travel and entertainment expense; accordingly, there's a certain amount of jealousy in this area of tax law.

The only way to defend your deductions for travel and entertainment is to have adequate documentation. It doesn't take a great deal of time, as explained in the travel and entertainment chap-

ters. But make sure you give it attention, for the IRS will be giving it attention when your return is pulled for audit.

15. File as a self-employed individual: A recent IRS study of the "underground economy" estimates unreported income from individual business activities at $26 billion. According to the study, this includes doctors who prefer cash and contractors who work "off the books."

The problem with the IRS unreported income program is that it is difficult to tell the black hats from the white hats. Last year, IRS identified more than 37,729 returns with unreported income, reflecting a noncompliance rate of 89 percent. IRS has instituted 360 projects to help identify unreported income.

Essentially, if you are self-employed, your chances of an IRS audit escalate. Keep good records and make sure all income is reported in your return.

16. Become a tax-exempt mail-order minister: One of the tax scams the IRS has hit hard during the past few years is that of mail-order ministers. The scam involves setting up a church and donating all money earned to the church. The flock consists of the taxpayer's children. Since churches are tax-exempt, the minister and his family live tax free—supposedly. In recent years, the IRS has won a number of cases against mail-order ministers. Many have been sent to jail, where they'll have extra time to count their blessings.

17. Claim that the only legal tender is gold: Some taxpayers actually scribble across their return, "U.S. dollars are worthless. Therefore, I didn't earn anything and I have no taxes to declare." In Orange County, California, there is a self-styled minister who preaches an unusual gospel which goes like this: "Since a U.S. dollar cannot be redeemed in gold, it is therefore corrupt and not real; and therefore nobody owes any taxes." Last year this minister was charged with tax and mail fraud, sentenced to eight years in prison and fined $92,000. He is still free on appeal, but the IRS happily reports that the several hundred people who used to attend his weekly meetings shrank to four in the week after he was sentenced.

18. Claim that the U.S. Federal income tax is unconstitutional: After more than 60 years of Federal income taxation, there are still individuals out there claiming that the Federal income tax is unconstitutional. Generally, such individuals end up in jail.

19. Claim charitable deductions other than those supported by canceled checks: If you claim large charitable deductions for property donations, your tax return will catch the IRS reviewer's eye. The IRS requires supporting statements to be submitted with your return for property donations (including second-hand merchandise). If you donate a painting, furniture, clothing, realty, or securities, attach a statement to your return describing the property, the date of the gift, and how you valued the property. If you are making a gift which has a fair market value in excess of $200, review the aspects of the gift with your tax advisor before claiming it on your return. Also, read the next section of this chapter—how to reduce your chances of an IRS audit.

20. Create an illegitimate family trust: There are legitimate private trusts, but what we are talking about here is a scheme which on the surface meets the law, but in fact does not pass the IRS test of being legal in both substance as well as form.

In an illegitimate family trust, you contribute all of your assets (including your house and car) to the trust. The trust then becomes the taxpaying entity, rather than you, since you purport to have nothing for IRS to tax.

Now, the clincher. You perform services as trustee of the trust. Since all of the trust's costs are deductible, you have the trust pay all of your personal living expenses.

Obviously, such trusts are not proper. The only people who usually benefit from these transactions are the promoters who set them up and charge you a fee. Generally, a family trust set up as we've just described has no chance of escaping IRS scrutiny, a high chance of being challenged, and strong odds of being harshly treated when its bogus nature is exposed.

21. Claim a bad debt deduction: A bad debt deduction is a good audit choice, because most tax-payers are unfamiliar with the legal requirements involved. Such a deduction must be based on an enforceable debt evidenced in writing and then a realistic effort to collect. A realistic effort includes collection agencies and so forth. Until that effort has been exerted, the debt is not deductible. Many individuals do not make the necessary effort to collect; accordingly, the IRS reaps rewards by auditing bad debt deductions.

22. Join a bartering club: During the past several months, IRS auditors have been completing a "barter" questionnaire as part of every audit. Essentially, the IRS is looking for individuals who swap services but don't report the value of the services for income tax purposes. If we, for example,

offer to do your tax return in exchange for your painting our office, we should both report taxable income. Our taxable income would be measured by the fair value of the tax services given to you. Your income should be measured by the same amount.

Obviously, catching that type of barter is extremely difficult for the IRS.

But there is another kind of barter that is very public, and the IRS has been actively going after it. We're referring to barter companies that bring people together for barter purposes and collect fees for their matchmaking efforts. The IRS has been attempting to get the mailing lists of such membership clubs and those of related clearing-houses and associations. When such lists are obtained, the IRS audits all the names on the lists.

Hint: There is nothing wrong with bartering. If you belong to a bartering club and are earning credits, report the credits as income. When you incur valid business expenses, report the expenses on your tax return.

23. Make an interest-free loan to a relative: Interest-free loans to relatives are dangerous. If you are planning such a transaction, make sure you seek the advice of your tax advisor. Also, if you do make an interest-free loan to a relative, know that you have stepped up a couple of rungs on the audit ladder.

NINE WAYS TO REDUCE YOUR CHANCES OF AN IRS AUDIT

The odds are that your tax return will not be selected for audit on a random basis. Most tax returns are audited because they look like good audit prospects. The audit-wise taxpayer knows that the computer kicks out the return for audit and that a human being (called a classifier) reviews the return before an audit is actually started. If your return preparation and organization convinces the auditor or classifier that you are not a good prospect for audit, your chances of being audited are minimal.

1. Mail your return by registered mail, return receipt requested: If the IRS regional Service Center fails to receive your tax return, you automatically increase your chances of being audited. To make sure you're not taking unnecessary chances, send your return by registered mail, return receipt requested.

2. Send changes of addess to the IRS: The IRS likes to know where you are and appreciates being notified of any change of address. Moreover, if you use the pre-addressed label from IRS, you will speed up processing of your return.

3. Make sure your tax return is neat: Your tax return does not have to be typed, but it must be neat and easy to read. Legible tax returns create an impression of attention to detail. Also, all signatures should be affixed where requested.

4. File all elections: There are certain tax breaks and options that require the filing of an election. Sometimes the filing can be done by merely picking a method of reporting. It's generally better to attach separate statements for all elections made in a tax return. This further supports attention to detail and shows an understanding of tax law.

5. Report all income: The IRS has implemented various unreported income audit programs. Make sure your tax return: first, reports all income earned by you, and second, identifies the income by source. If you receive a 1099 for consulting services, report the income on a supporting schedule and include the taxpayer ID number from the 1099. Since the IRS already has the information from the 1099, you will reduce your chances of audit selection by enabling the IRS to match the 1099 with your tax return.

6. Make sure your return is mathematically accurate and that all questions are answered: Triple check your tax return before sending it to the IRS. Mathematical errors or unanswered questions in your tax return will lead to a "correspondence audit," and that in turn could lead to an office or field examination.

7. Have your return prepared by a competent tax preparer: The signature of a Certified Public Accountant or Tax Attorney will help minimize your chances of an audit examination.

8. Break income and expenses into small segments: Income reported to the IRS on a 1099 should be separated from other income not so reported. The separation will help IRS determine that you have indeed reported all income earned. Also, break down expenses as far as possible to explain to the IRS examiners exactly what was involved in the expenses. If, for example, you had promotional expenses of $10,000 and that's all that appeared in your tax return, your chances of audit would be significant. However, should your promotion be broken down between travel, advertising, and entertainment expenses, you may reduce the chance of audit.

9. Add supporting schedules and documentation where necessary: If you have a deduction or an expense which is unusual or exceptionally large, at least add a supporting detailed schedule explaining what happened. If, for example, you incurred a large casualty loss, attach the details of the casualty loss to your tax return. The details you attach should satisfy the audit steps that the IRS auditor would take during an examination. Your tax advisor will know what those steps are, and can assist you in putting together your statement.

HOW RETURNS ARE SELECTED FOR IRS AUDIT

Generally, there are four ways that your return can be brought to the attention of an IRS examiner. First, if you claim obviously unallowable deductions, that fact will emerge during the preliminary screening of your tax return at the regional Service Center. Second, if your return contains a deduction which is a target of IRS, your return will be selected for audit. Third, your return could be selected on a purely random basis for the IRS statistical pool. Fourth, your return could be selected because of a high statistical probability that it contains audit adjustments.

1. Unallowable deductions: Upon receipt by the regional processing center, your return is reviewed by human beings for a number of reasons. One review involves looking over your return for obviously unallowable items. Exhibit 20-5 contains standard IRS explanations of unallowable items. If your return contains such an unallowable item, you would receive an identical paragraph telling you why that item was unallowable.

2. Targeted areas: Earlier, we gave you 23 ways to increase your chances of an IRS audit. These were taken from published targeted areas of IRS concentration. If your return contains items which appear on this list, that alone might cause its selection.

3. Statistical studies: Most tax returns are selected for audit because they have a high probability of containing errors. In order to determine which returns have that high probability, IRS uses a statistical sampling program known as the "Taxpayer Compliance Measurement Program" (TCMP). Statistics generated by TCMP audits are used to classify other returns.

Perhaps the most horrible experience you can ever face in your tax lifetime is to be subjected to one of the TCMP audits. This audit is conducted under the assumption that you are a liar. You have to answer for everything you did during the year. The scenario goes something like this:

The IRS examiner asks, "What is your name?"

You answer and think to yourself that your name was listed on your tax return. Why the question?

"Can you prove it?"

Now you are a little concerned, but you think to yourself, "Pacify the auditor." So you proceed to haul out your driver's license, birth certificate, and Social Security card.

"I see your return shows that you are married. Can you prove it?"

Now you are getting a little more than dubious. You go to your file and drag out your marriage license, bring your spouse in for scrutiny, and otherwise work to satisfy this auditor's seemingly insatiable thirst for proof.

The questioning continues about your children, your employer, and every single line item in your entire tax return. That's right, you have to prove every single item that appears in your entire tax return. This could take weeks or even months, and it will cause you great anxiety.

As a member of the TCMP fraternity, you are in a very select club. Your chances of undergoing a TCMP audit are one-half of one-tenth of one percent (0.0005).

Statistical probability for change: Based on TCMP audits, IRS programs its computers in Martinsburg, West Virginia, to select the majority of tax returns for audit. The computer program is affectionately referred to as the Discriminate Function System (DIF).

The audit selection criteria are based on every line item of your tax return. If you fall outside of a norm, claim a deduction the IRS is interested in, or otherwise have some abnormality that comes to the attention of the audit selection process, your return is the subject of an audit invitation.

Your return receives a DIF score. Returns with high DIF scores are sent to District Of-

fices for review. Essentially, all the District Office receives along with your return is an IRS audit file label (see Exhibit 20-6).

Once the IRS audit labels are received by the District Offices, they are sorted into two groups. Group one labels are sent to classifiers who will identify audit areas for tax auditors. Group two labels are sent to IRS revenue agents for audits.

All the classifier or revenue agent has from the computer is a score. The exact items to be audited are determined either by the classifier or the revenue agent. At this point, any notes or other information attached to your tax return become extremely important. A high DIF score accompanied by good explanations could result in no audit examination whatsoever.

The IRS audit file label contains a lot of information, but the only information of significance to the audit is the DIF score. The rest of the information is used for logistics. There is a 14-digit number just to keep track of your tax return. There are codes for the status of your audit: started, in process, 30-day letter, or 90-day letter.

INITIAL CONTACT BY THE IRS

Letters from the IRS never seem friendly. The audit letter is no exception, although the IRS claims that it has been working on making audit letters friendlier.

If your audit letter is generated by a tax auditor, it will contain standard paragraphs that tell you what records you need for the audit. Tax auditors have over 300 standard paragraphs to choose from. Exhibit 20-7 contains four standard paragraphs that are used by tax auditors to tell you what records you need for the audit.

Reminder: You are dealing with a tax auditor when you are going down to IRS. When they are coming out to see you, you are generally dealing with a revenue agent.

Once you receive the audit notice, and if it contains standard paragraphs, make sure that you have the necessary supporting records before reporting to the audit. If you need additional time to get your records together, IRS will generally allow you a reasonable pe-

EXHIBIT 20-6. IRS Audit File Label.

```
POD 01 TPI 003 SCORE 1000                40000001
10000-000-00000-0 479-54-8093             8212 12
MARSHALL, SENSENEY GRETCHEN JR                 02
                                              101
49203                   041586                2501
```

POD 01	=	Geographical Post of Duty
TPI 003	=	Total Positive Income over $10,000, but under $25,000; simple nonbusiness return; standard deduction claimed; no income from partnerships; no Schedule C or F.
Score 1000	=	DIF Score
40000001	=	Serial Number; eight digit number. First two digits equal district code and the remaining six digits are in sequential order.
10000-000-00000-0	=	14-digit code; from left to right

Digits	Items
2	District Office
1	Class of tax
2	Document code
3	Numeric day of year
3	Block number
2	Serial number
1	Last digit of year
14	

479-54-8093	=	Social Security number
8212	=	Tax year 1982 ended December 31
12	=	Status of audit (in process, 30-day letter, 90-day letter, etc.)
02	=	Source of audit code such as computer identified by DIF score
101	=	Activity code for type of return (1040) and income level
49203	=	Zip code
041586	=	Statute of limitations date April 15, 1986
2501	=	Assignment code for type of auditor (tax auditor)

riod of time. The audit notice will suggest that the audit take place within two to three weeks after you receive the letter. Extensions are not uncommon and are relatively easy to get.

Revenue agent letters: If your return is large or contains complex transactions, you could be audited by a revenue agent. If so, the revenue agent may not tell you exactly what records you need for the audit. The agent's letter will merely state that he would like to look at the records on your business premises, and could you have them available.

EXHIBIT 20-7. Standard Paragraphs Used By IRS Auditors That Tell You What Records You Need For the Audit.

Medical and Dental Expenses

1. Insurance policies on which you deducted the cost of premiums paid. Include your records for payment of these premiums.
2. Itemized receipts for drugs and medicine showing the person for whom the drugs and medicine were purchased. Canceled checks alone are not acceptable.
3. Canceled checks, receipts or statements for all medical and dental expenses showing the person for whom each expense was incurred.
4. Statement from insurance company showing any expense reimbursed or paid directly by it.
5. Statement to show cost and medical requirement for special equipment or education expense.

State and Local Income Taxes

1. Copies of state and local income tax returns for the year ended 19__.
2. Copy of Federal income tax return for the year ended 19__.
3. Canceled checks and receipts showing taxes paid.

Sales Taxes

1. If you chose to deduct your actual sales tax rather than the amount from the optional state sales tax tables, please provide receipts showing the sales tax you paid.

Real Estate and Personal Property Taxes

1. Verification of legal ownership of the property.
2. Canceled checks and receipts for taxes paid.
3. If you sold or purchased real property, a copy of the settlement statement.
4. Identification of any special assessments deducted as taxes, and an explanation of their purpose.

Note: IRS has standard information requests for each item under audit. Chapters in this book that deal with specific deductions contain both the IRS documentation requirements and suggestions from the authors.

ELEVEN STEPS TO GET READY FOR THE AUDIT

The time to get ready for an IRS audit is while you are preparing your tax return. It is at that point when your information should be organized for further scrutiny. Questionable items, if any, should be supported by tax memorandums or other information from your tax advisor.

We assume, however, that you did not prepare for the audit while preparing your return. The 11 steps contained in this section will help you get ready for the audit.

1. Don't panic: The notice that IRS wants to audit your tax return is not indicative of anything wrong with your return. It's simply a request by the IRS to find out if your tax return was properly prepared and to determine the proper amount of tax—no more, no less. Generally, you will be notified of the audit by mail, although you could be telephoned. If by mail, you'll be asked to make telephone contact with the examiner.

2. Burden of proof is on you: Tax law requires you to prove that your deductions are valid and that you have paid the proper amount of tax. The IRS need prove nothing. When going through your records and getting ready for the audit, make sure you keep in mind that the "burden of proof is on you." None of that "innocent until proven guilty" business.

3. Review your tax return: If the audit is being conducted by a tax auditor and you have been told to have certain information for the audit, retrace all of the detailed information line-by-line to your tax return. If there are any weak points, discuss them with your tax advisor.

If you are getting ready for a revenue agent examination, you do not have the luxury of knowing exactly where the revenue agent will look. Accordingly, you want to trace line-by-line everything on your tax return back to your supporting documents. Basically, your purpose is to make sure you can find the information when you are asked for it.

4. Handle the first step yourself: You can pay your tax advisor to handle the tax audit for you, or you can handle it yourself. We believe the most productive is for you to handle the initial examination, and then, after narrowing down the points, to bring in your tax advisor.

Consult with your advisors, however, before going into the audit. You need to know what items are vulnerable, and what supporting documents you are expected to have. A practical advisor can tell you the areas where your return is vulnerable.

If you engage your advisor to go with you, you will be paying fees. The fees could be substantially more than any proposed IRS adjustment. You will be much better off going through the initial stages of the audit by yourself, and then bringing your tax advisor in to dismiss the case.

5. Dress normally: Do not make a special trip to Goodwill Industries to buy clothes for your audit. Dress and act normally during the entire audit. Do not plead poverty or stupidity. Excuses don't help.

6. Be on time: IRS examiners are graded on efficiency. If you are late for your appointment and cause the auditor to be inefficient, you start the audit in an antagonistic environment. Moreover, you have given the auditor extra time to scrutinize your records before the audit begins. Frequently, office auditors will have only 15 to 20 minutes to look over your return before you arrive. If you are late, you've expanded that time and irritated the tax auditor. Best bet: Be early.

7. Bring organized information: Make sure you are prepared to deliver documents and answer questions for the auditor. If you receive notification from the IRS about the documents you need for the audit, make sure those are organized so that you can not only answer the questions, but deliver the supporting documents quickly. This helps the examiner complete the audit more efficiently, get a better grade from his or her superiors, and bring the whole unpleasant task to a quick conclusion.

8. Don't volunteer information: Do not say something like, "I've always done it that way." Such a response will open up the same question for the past three years. A statement such as, "I wrote the book for social purposes, not necessarily to make lots of money," could, due to lack of profit motive, negate any deductions for writing the book (see Chapter 1).

Do not elaborate; answer only the questions asked. Be concise, and if the question does not appear to be relevant, ask why it is being asked. In your information package, bring only the documents requested in the invitation letter, and do not volunteer any information concerning those documents during the audit process. When asked specific questions, answer them, but do not elaborate.

Do not arrange to have some dangling ends for the auditor to find. If it is easy for the auditor to find something wrong, the immediate conclusion is that there must be lots of other things wrong in your return.

9. Do not praise the agent: There are times when flattery may get you somewhere, but not with IRS auditors. In fact, flattery may work against you. If the agent's superior comes into the room, do not praise the examining agent to the superior. It may indicate to the superior that the agent is too soft or has missed some big adjustments.

10. Do not dump paper: Do not gather all of your records into a big gunny sack, march into the IRS office, throw the documents on the agent's desk, and say, "You do it." The agent will do it, and do it to you. The average agent works on 20 cases at a time. When you dump paper on the desk, the agent's case load drops to one. The load of one is maintained for as long as it takes to go through all of your pieces of paper and establish your appropriate adjustments.

11. Don't give in: The IRS Audit Manual states, "Hasty agreement to adjustments and undue concern about immediate closing of the case may indicate a more thorough examination is needed." If you appear to be a soft touch, the IRS will look for larger contributions from you.

There are other reasons why you may want to argue. First of all, the agent examining your tax return may be wrong about the adjustments. If you have reason to believe the agent is incorrect, argue your point tastefully all the way through the examination and do not give in. You may then ask for a meeting with the agent's supervisor, explain your circumstances and the reason why you think the adjustments are improper, and you may get better results.

On the other hand, you may want to go through the audit yourself and narrow down the adjustments for discussion with your tax advisor. Then, you can arrange for a meeting with the supervisor bringing along your tax advisor. Many individuals handle the audit this way and come out very well. First, there is no one who knows your business like you. Second, your tax advisor knows the tax law. The two of you, together, can effect a timely settlement after the initial audit process is completed.

THE AUDIT

The actual audit is not nearly as bad as you may imagine. You will be tense, of course, and that's good because you want to be constantly alert.

The audit starts with some standard questions—standard for IRS, but not for you. The questions will make you somewhat nervous because you may not understand some of them.

Generally, the questions will deal with bartering income, unreported income, and similar types of items. If you do not understand a question, make sure you have the auditor explain the question to you, by example.

After the first three to seven minutes of answering standard questions, the auditor will start looking at specific records. If yours is an office audit, you were informed of the specific records needed for the audit. You can also obtain from your tax advisor the standard examination procedures used by IRS auditors. An example is contained in Exhibit 20-8.

Generally, the office auditor will add all the receipts you have for a specific deduction and then compare the total of the receipts to your tax return. Remember, the burden is on you to prove that you are entitled to the tax deductions you've claimed.

If you are missing receipts but can otherwise prove a deduction through alternate computations, make sure you have a detailed computation available for examination by the auditor.

There is a lot of psychology involved in an audit of your tax return. From your standpoint, you want to answer all questions yes or no. Let the auditor determine the scope of the audit and what documents are needed to verify the deductions. You should absolutely never take the lead. Be polite, but always let the auditor dictate the direction of the audit.

Do not volunteer information. If there is favorable information with respect to a transaction being questioned by the auditor and you feel that information would help your situation, you should bring this to the auditor's attention. However, you should never bring it to the auditor's attention unless it relates directly to the item being questioned and the determination so far has been unfavorable to you.

If you are handling the initial examination yourself and you feel that the audit is going over your head, feel free to say to the auditor that you do not feel you can handle this audit yourself and you need your tax advisor by your side. The audit will be stopped and you will be allowed to bring your advisor.

If the audit starts to go down trails you're unfamiliar with, such as a net worth computation (Exhibit 20-9), stop the audit at that

EXHIBIT 20-8. Standard Examination Procedures Used By IRS Auditors.

Audit Steps To Verify Medical Expenses

1. Verify amounts claimed and determine that the deduction has been taken in proper year.
2. Ascertain whether any insurance reimbursement has been made or is expected.
3. Segregate medicines so that the proper limitations can be applied.
4. Determine that the percentage limitation, the maximum amount limitation, and the dependency qualification have been correctly applied.
5. Determine that the expense was incurred primarily for the diagnosis, cure, mitigation, treatment or prevention of disease, or for the purpose of affecting any structure of the body.

Medical Expenses Paid To	Verified	Per Return	Adjustment	Source Document
DRXY	$500	$1000	$500	MEDICARE PAYMENTS CHECKS/RECEIPTS

Audit Steps To Verify Taxes Claimed as Itemized Deductions

1. Verify amounts claimed and determine that the deduction has been taken in proper year.
2. Determine whether the tax is of the type deductible in accordance with the rules and regulations.
3. Ascertain that no foreign income taxes have been claimed as a deduction where election has been made to claim the foreign tax credit.
4. Verify that the taxpayer has not claimed duplicate deductions for taxes, i.e., itemized deductions and rental expense.
5. Verify that any proration of current real estate taxes in the year of purchase or sale is correct.

Taxes Paid To	Verified	Per Return	Adjustment	Source Document
YYA Mortgage Co.	$600	$2000	$1400	COMPUTER PRINTOUT CHECKS/BANK RECORDS

point and ask to bring your tax advisor to the next session.

Assuming you have navigated the audit and narrowed the potential adjustments to a few items, your next step should be to contact your tax advisor for a review of the potential adjustments. If your tax advisor believes that the IRS is incorrect, there are a number of steps which can be taken. By waiting until this point to involve your tax advisor, you will save yourself professional fees. Moreover, you will be taking maximum advantage of your tax advisor.

One key point about the audit is that you

do not have to agree with the audit findings. There are several steps which may be taken after the initial examination. You may take the steps either by yourself or with your tax advisor. We recommend taking these steps with your tax advisor.

POST-AUDIT MOVES

After the initial examination, you may set up an appointment with the auditor's supervisor. Generally, this meeting should be attended by

EXHIBIT 20-9. Net Worth Computation (Example).

ASSETS	1983	1984
Cash in bank.	$ 2,000	$ 1,500
Equipment	10,000	15,000
Personal residence	20,000	20,000
Personal furniture .	5,000	5,000
Total Assets .	$37,000	$41,500
LIABILITIES		
Notes payable—equipment	$-0-	$ 4,000
Mortgage payable—residence	10,000	8,500
Accumulated depreciation .	8,000	9,000
Total Liabilities .	$18,000	$21,500
Net Worth	$19,000	$20,000
Net Worth at the beginning of the year		19,000
Increase in net worth.		$ 1,000
Add: Personal expenses		4,500
		$ 5,500
Deduct: Veterans pension .		1,200
Adjusted gross income as corrected		$ 4,300
Adjusted gross income per return		2,000
Understatement of adjusted gross income		$ 2,300

you and your tax advisor. You understand your business and your tax advisor understands tax law. The two of you form a good team.

When meeting with the supervisor or other IRS representative, your tax advisor should be thoroughly familiar with and able to factually substantiate your case.

If a 30-day letter has been sent to you as a result of an office examination, you can respond within 15 days and meet with a supervisor, or you can respond after 15 days but within 30 days and meet with an IRS appeals officer. Generally, IRS wants you to meet with a supervisor before going to appeals.

Exhibit 20-10 contains the income tax appeal procedures as outlined by the IRS.

If you are unable to agree with the supervisor, you will then receive a 30-day letter. You must respond within 30 days to this letter. If the adjustments proposed resulted from an office examination, your response may be by telephone or in writing. If you do respond by telephone, make sure you send a confirming letter to IRS so that you have documentary evidence that you were responsive.

If the change in tax exceeds $2,500 for any one taxable period and the examination

was a "field" examination, you must respond to the 30-day letter with a written protest. That protest should be put together by your tax advisor.

At the Appeals conference within the IRS, you will have an informal meeting among yourself, your tax advisor, and an IRS Appeals Officer who will not have previously examined your case. In other words, it's something like a fresh start.

Why you should go with your tax advisor: Have you ever had the opportunity to evaluate your tax advisor? There is really only one forum, and that is in actions on your behalf against the IRS. If you want the opportunity to evaluate how good your tax advisor is, go along for all meetings regarding your return. You need not say anything during such meetings, and in fact, you can grant your tax advisor full "power of attorney" to handle everything.

If you are unable to settle at the end of the audit, after supervisory review, or after meeting with the Appeals Officer, you may take your case to court. You can, if you like, handle the case yourself if it involves attacks

EXHIBIT 20-10. Income Tax Appeal Procedure.

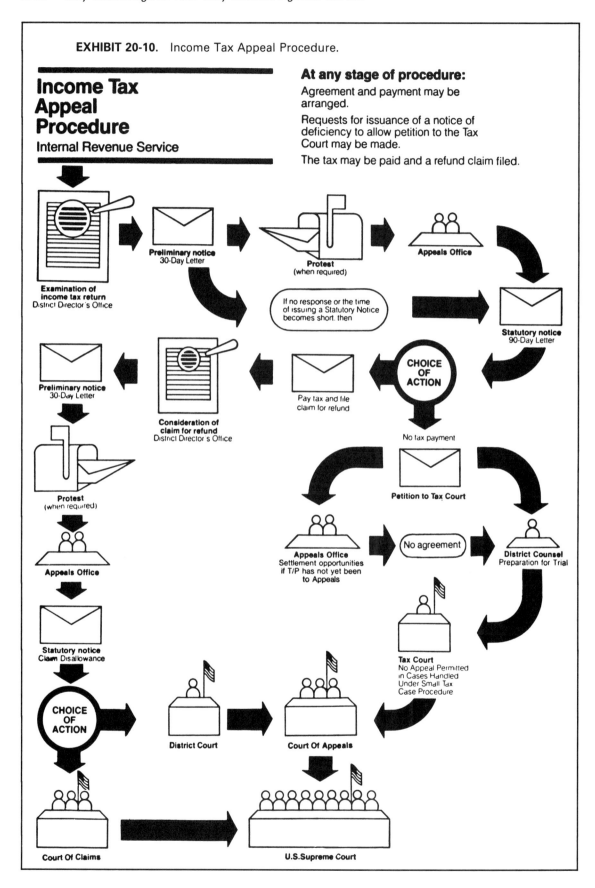

of less than $5,000. You can take it to a small claims division of the Tax Court.

At this stage, however, it is recommended that you definitely engage a tax advisor, preferably a Tax Attorney.

There are different courts where you can appear and different moves you can make. However, your facts and circumstances will dictate the best choice for you. That's why it's imperative that you engage good tax advisors before proceeding in the courts.

Exhibit 20-11 reveals the IRS trial record in Tax Court and compares the results from 1978 and 1982. Remember, the Tax Court is only one of the available courts.

WHEN YOU CAN SUE THE IRS

If you can establish that you had to go to court because IRS was unreasonable, you can collect reasonable litigation costs, including attorneys' fees and expert witness fees. The maximum award you could receive is limited to $25,000. The awarding of litigation cost ap-

plies to all Tax Court cases in the Federal courts, including the United States Tax Court. This provision terminates in 1985.

BEWARE OF SPECIAL AGENTS

If an IRS auditor shows up with a partner, there may be a possibility that the government suspects fraud. Ask the examining agent to explain to you who the other individual is and why that person is present. If the term "special agent" comes up, break off the session and call your attorney. Special agents examine fraud cases.

An examining agent may likewise pursue fraud. If you suspect an examining agent is gathering information to divulge to a special agent, break off the session and contact your attorney.

If the case involves fraud, the IRS has the burden of proof. If you think there is any possibility that the IRS is auditing you for fraud, break off the session and contact your attorney.

EXHIBIT 20-11. IRS Trial Record In Tax Court.

	1978		1982	
	Number	*Percent*	*Number*	*Percent*
Small Tax Cases				
Decided For Government	262	54.0	554	48.6
Decided For Taxpayer	50	10.3	129	11.3
Mixed Decisions	173	35.7	458	40.1
Tax Cases Other Than Small Tax Cases				
Decided For Government	271	47.9	446	51.0
Decided For Taxpayer	66	11.6	83	9.5
Mixed Decisions	229	40.5	346	39.5

TAX REDUCTION CHECKLIST

IRS publication to be obtained:

- Publication 556—*Examination of Returns, Appeal Rights and Claims for Refund*

What the IRS knows about you:

- IRS Forms W-2 are matched with your return.
- IRS Forms 1099 are matched with your return.
- You are a statistic—compared to other statistics for abnormalities.
- Your tax preparer's tax record.

How to speed up your tax refund:

- Use bar-coded reply envelope.
- Use pre-addressed label.
- Arrange tax schedules in sequence (letters followed by numbers).

You must have knowledge of tax law:

- If IRS answers are incorrect, that's too bad; you are responsible for knowing that the answer was incorrect.
- The only way to know if an IRS auditor is competent is to be aware of the tax law yourself.

IRS personnel:

- Taxpayer service representatives—answer your phone questions, but not responsible for any incorrect answers. Two years of college—any field.
- Tax auditors—conduct office audits. Scope of audit set by someone else. Follow IRS guidelines. Four years of college—any field.
- Revenue agents—conduct field audits. Set scope of audit. Interpret tax law. Four years of college—accounting majors.
- Special agents—investigate fraud.

Ways to increase your chances of audit:

- Make more money.
- File your return late.
- Talk about your taxes.
- File a tax return that's sloppy and illegible.
- Fail to answer questions asked in your return.
- Claim unallowable deductions.
- Invest in a fraudulent tax shelter.
- Prepare your own tax return.
- Select a dishonest tax preparer.
- Die.
- Claim more than 14 withholding allowances.
- Claim a casualty loss.
- Claim a business loss for a hobby.
- Claim travel and entertainment deductions.
- File as a self-employed individual.
- Become a tax-exempt mail-order minister.
- Claim that the only legal tender is gold.
- Claim that the U.S. Federal income tax is unconstitutional.
- Claim charitable deductions for donations of property.
- Create an illegitimate family trust.
- Claim a bad debt deduction.
- Join a bartering club.

• Make an interest-free loan to a relative.

Ways to reduce your chances of an IRS audit:

• Mail your return by registered mail, return receipt requested.
• Send change of address to the IRS.
• Make sure your tax return is neat.
• File all tax elections.
• Report all income by taxpayer ID number.
• Make sure your return is mathematically accurate and that all questions are answered.
• Have your return prepared by a competent tax preparer.
• Break income and expenses into small segments.
• Add supporting schedules and documentation where necessary.

How returns are selected for audit:

• Unallowable deductions program.
• Targeted deductions (See ways to increase your chances of an IRS audit).
• Taxpayer compliance measurement program statistics.
• High Discriminate Function System (DIF) score.

Steps to get ready for an audit:

• Don't panic.
• Burden of proof is on you.
• Review your tax return.
• Handle the first step yourself.
• Dress normally.
• Be on time.
• Bring organized information.
• Don't volunteer information.
• Do not praise the agent.
• Do not dump paper.
• Don't give in.

Steps in the audit process:

• Letter of notification.
• Appointment.
• Standard questions.
• Answer questions yes or no.
• Narrow potential adjustments to few items.
• Do not give in.
• Bring in tax advisor for next meetings.

December is a time for parties, goodwill, peace on earth . . . and tax planning. With one exception, tax-planning opportunities for calendar year taxpayers will end at the stroke of midnight on December 31. Act now or pay later; specifically, April 15, next year. This chapter explains:

- Why year-end tax planning can save you money.
- How to defer income until next year.
- How to take deductions and credits this year.
- How to save taxes without spending any money.
- How to earn tax-free income next year.
- Why December tax shelters could leave you cold.
- How to save taxes on stock transactions.
- How to reduce this year's taxes by acting next year.

WHY YEAR-END TAX PLANNING PAYS BIG DIVIDENDS

Good tax planning starts before a tax year begins, not just before it ends. But two reasons make it wrong to suppose that this year's tax planning should be over by December 1.

New laws: First, tax planning never ends. New laws are passed, new rulings are issued, new court cases are decided, financial circum-stances change. These developments require revision of tax strategies. Recent major changes are the Tax Equity and Fiscal Responsibility Act of 1982 (TEFRA), the Economic Recovery Tax Act of 1981 (ERTA), the Technical Corrections Act of 1982, the Social Security Amendments of 1983, the Tax Reform Act of 1984 and the Import Interest Act of 1985.

Special year-end opportunities: Second, the end of the year brings special tax-planning opportunities that aren't available at other times. The right actions can defer income recognition for a full year and accelerate deductions and credits by a full year.

The remainder of this chapter suggests various ways you can reduce your tax liability by acting in December of this year (plus one way of doing it by acting before April 15 next year). These suggestions are subject to this caveat:

The effect of any tax strategy on your tax liability depends on *your* situation, not Diamond Jim Brady's or Freddy the Freeloader's. Knowing your tax situation requires pushing your pencil. Study last year's tax return, this year's records, and next year's financial plans. This is hard. So is paying more taxes than you should.

How to Wring Out Tax Savings at Year's End

Defer income; accelerate deductions and credits: The primary focus of year-end planning concerns:

- Deferring income.
- Accelerating deductions and credits.

Example: Quick and Dead each have $600 of potential income that could be deferred until January and $400 of potential deductions that could be taken in December. Quick acts. Dead doesn't. Both are in the 50 percent tax bracket. Quick saves $500 in taxes (50 percent of $600 income deferred plus 50 percent of $400 deductions taken). Dead does not rest in peace.

HOW TO DEFER INCOME TO NEXT YEAR

Cash basis taxpayers are taxed for the year they receive income. Receive income now and pay tax on April 15, next year. Receive it in January and pay on April 15, the following year. Waiting an extra month to get the money gives you an extra year to use it. For most people, that's a pretty good trade-off. Here are some ideas on how to do it.

Sell short: If you hold stock and want to take your profit now, but don't want to pay tax on it next year, sell short. For tax purposes, the sale is not made until next year, even though you locked in your gain this year. Your broker can handle the details.

Make a one-installment sale: Installment sales offer many benefits, including income deferral. Although installment sales usually have several payments and often extend over several years, an installment sale can consist of only one payment. Therefore, if you want (and can get) your money in one lump sum, consider an installment sale in which the buyer pays the purchase price next year.

Hint: Your business judgment may dictate having the buyer make a substantial down payment now. You can do this and still defer tax on the remainder of the gain.

Defer interest: You can defer interest income by investing in a short-term Certificate of Deposit (C/D), repurchase agreement (repo), Treasury Bill, or other investment vehicle that doesn't credit interest until the end of the term. If the maturity date is after December 31, the interest will not be taxable this year.

Bill in January: An easy way to defer income is to send bills so that they are not received until January.

Take bonuses and commissions in January: Delaying bonuses and commissions until January may also enable you to defer the income until the following year.

Caution: The IRS gets jealous if you hold on to your money too long. The "constructive receipt" rule lets the IRS pretend you received income if the money was available to you. Commissions and bonuses pose a special problem, because you usually have no control over when you become entitled to a bonus or commission. To trip up the IRS, you need a sympathetic boss or escrow agent. If a bonus or commission isn't payable until January, you obviously don't have a right to it until then, so you won't be taxed on it this year. Maybe you'd like to drop a copy of this page on your boss's or escrow agent's desk . . .

HOW TO GET DEDUCTIONS AND CREDITS THIS YEAR

Cash basis taxpayers get deductions or credits for the tax year of payment. Therefore, to get deductions and credits for this year, spend some money now. This section suggests some tax-saving ways to spend your money.

Short of cash? Charge it! Payments made by third-party charge cards (such as VISA, MasterCard, and the like) *are deductible in the year of the charge, not the year in which you repay the company.* You can even charge a charitable contribution.

Caution: If you use a seller's charge card (such as Sears or J.C. Penney), *you get no deduction until you pay the bill.*

Get sick: If you had substantial medical expenses during the year, get sick.

TEFRA makes it much tougher to deduct medical expenses because:

- The separate deduction for medical insurance premiums is eliminated.
- The floor on medical expenses is raised to 5 percent of adjusted gross income (AGI); that is, you deduct medical expenses only to the extent they exceed 5 percent of AGI.

Therefore, if your medical expenses are likely to exceed 5 percent of this year's AGI, strongly consider paying any outstanding bills before year's end. Also, consider having that check-up, dental work, or other medical care you've been putting off. Make sure you pay for it this year, of course.

Don't get sick: If your medical expenses are low this year, bundle up, stay dry, and avoid drafts. Postpone medical expenses until next year so that you have a fighting chance of exceeding the 5 percent floor.

Improve your home: Your home may be your greatest tax shelter. Be nice to it. "Points" paid on a mortgage loan to improve your principal residence are fully deductible in the year paid, if you are lucky enough to live in an area where the payment of points is an "established business practice." (Who isn't so lucky?)

Watch out for loan sharks. You can only deduct the amount generally charged in your area. Any excess payment is amortized over the period of the loan.

Caution: If the lender takes the points out of the loan proceeds, the IRS may try to deny the deduction. Pay for the points at closing with a check and have the lender pay you the full loan proceeds.

Conserve energy: It's going to be a cold winter in many parts of the country and energy prices are still on the rise. If your home was built before April 20, 1977, Uncle Sam will help you save energy by giving you a tax credit of 15 percent of the first $2,000 (that is, $300) you spend—before January 1, 1986—for buying and installing insulation and energy-saving devices, such as caulking, weather-stripping, storm or thermal windows and doors, furnace replacement burners, among others, on your

principal residence. Since the credit is cumulative, the maximum for any year is $300 minus the energy credits you received in previous years.

Caution: The credit is allowed for the year of payment *and installation*, so don't just buy them before December 31; install before then, too. If you are short of funds, finance the purchase with a home improvement loan. If you get stuck with points, at least you can deduct them. See above.

Be charitable: December is a traditional time for charitable giving. Dig deep. It will make you feel better, now and on April 15. You don't need cash to be charitable. Donate appreciated property. You get your deduction, avoid tax on the potential gain, and keep the cash in your pocket.

Caution: Make sure you give to an organization, not an individual, and make sure it is a qualifying organization. In case of doubt, check on whether the organization has IRS approval. Most charitable organizations are required to ask the IRS for a tax exemption letter. Churches are the main exception. If the organization has an IRS letter saying that contributions to it are deductible, your deduction won't be challenged. IRS Publication 78 has a list of IRS-approved charitable organizations.

Prepay state taxes: If you pay estimated state or local income taxes, paying your January installment now will give you a deduction for this year. The same rule applies to early payments of state and local property taxes, provided you are currently liable for them (even though they won't be overdue until sometime next year).

Buy business property: Buying property for your business in December will give you a full year's depreciation under the Accelerated Cost Recovery System (ACRS) method now in effect under ERTA. It will also give you a full year's investment tax credit. Qualifying property includes business cars, desks, filing cabinets, lamps; in short, any *tangible personal* *property* used in your business. The credit is 6 percent for cars and 10 percent for just about everything else.

HOW TO SAVE TAXES WITHOUT SPENDING MONEY

As the last section illustrates, you usually have to spend some money to accelerate deductions and credits. Here are two ideas for saving without spending.

Claim casualty losses even if insurance claim is not settled: If you suffered a casualty or theft loss this year, consider claiming the loss on this year's return, even though you may receive an insurance settlement next year. Although IRS Regulations prohibit this, recent court cases allow it. By making the claim on this year's return, you get to use your tax savings for a year. However, you will be taxed on your return for next year on any insurance settlement you receive next year. For example, if you suffer a loss in 1985 and deduct it on your 1985 return (April 15, 1986), any insurance money you get in 1986 will be taxed on your 1986 return (April 15, 1987).

Establish a self-employed plan: Self-employed persons save taxes two ways with self-employed retirement plans (Keogh plans):

- Contributions to a self-employed retirement plan are tax deductible.

- Money placed in a self-employed retirement plan accumulates tax free.

If you establish a plan *before the end of this year*, you can get a *deduction for this year*, as long as you *make your contribution before this year's income tax return is due*. Therefore, you can get a deduction for this year even if you can't afford a contribution this year.

HOW TO HANDLE YEAR-END STOCK DEALS

Reviewing your stock portfolio in December could pay tax dividends in April. Capital gains and losses are "netted" (combined) in computing taxes. This process opens up some tax-saving opportunities. Timing is the key.

Long-term gains are good: The maximum tax rate on long-term gains is 20 percent (40% of 50%, the highest tax bracket). Therefore, if you must have a capital gain, make it long-term. You must hold the asset for at least six months and a day to get a long-term gain.

Short-term losses aren't so bad: Short-term losses can be deducted from ordinary income, up to a maximum of $3,000 a year, saving a 50 percent bracket taxpayer as much as $1,500 (50 percent of $3,000). Therefore, if you have some clunkers you've held for less than six months, sell before the losses become long-term (and only half as "good" —see below).

Don't mix long-term gains with short-term losses: Short-term losses must be offset against long-term gains. This is wasteful, since the gains will produce a 20 percent tax at most. Short-term losses should be used against ordinary income, which can produce a 50 percent tax. Therefore, if you have, or will have, short-term capital losses this year and a potential long-term gain you are itching to take, sell short. The gain will be locked in but won't be taxable until next year.

Do mix short-term gains with long-term losses: Short-term gains are taxed as ordinary income. This is bad. Long-term losses can be used to offset up to $3,000 of ordinary income, but it takes $6,000 of long-term losses to do it. This isn't good. However, long-term losses can be used to offset short-term gains dollar-for-dollar. This is great. Therefore, you should try to have short-term gains and long-term losses in the same year.

Example: Rogers is a 50 percent bracket taxpayer with $6,000 of long-term losses this year and a potential of $6,000 of short-term gains. If Rogers doesn't sell this year, his losses will save taxes of $1,500 [50 percent of (½ of $6,000)]. If he sells for short-term gain, his losses will save taxes of $3,000 (50 percent of $6,000).

Hint: If you like the "gain" stocks and want to hold on to them, you can sell them and immediately buy replacement stocks. (The "wash sales" rule applies to losses only.)

WHY DECEMBER TAX SHELTERS COULD LEAVE YOU IN THE COLD

TEFRA gave the IRS posse more rope for lynching promoters of abusive tax shelters and the suckers who invest in them. It's all part of the compliance stampede touched off by TEFRA. The IRS Commissioner (Sheriff) talks mighty mean, promising to lead his posse into the tax shelter badlands. The IRS has a full-blown tax shelter program going.

December is traditionally a time for marketing questionable tax shelters to taxpayers anxious for a quick fix for their tax situations. The above facts suggest that you should think more than once, more than twice, and maybe more than three times before you invest in a December tax shelter—or any tax shelter, for that matter.

Don't be deduction-wise and penalty-foolish. Take your time. The best tax shelters, in terms of investment potential and tax legitimacy, are generally marketed early in the year. Definitely get competent tax and financial advice from professionals who are not connected with the tax shelter's promoter. The time and money will be well spent.

HOW TO SAVE THIS YEAR'S TAXES NEXT YEAR

How can you save this year's taxes next year? By opening an Individual Retirement Account (IRA), that's how. Unlike self-employed retirement plans, which must be established before year's end in order to get a deduction for this year, an IRA can be established and funded anytime before April 15, of next year, and you will still get a deduction for this year.

IRAs are now available to anyone who works, whether self-employed or an employee, and even if you are covered by another retirement plan. The maximum deduction per year is $2,000 (or, if less than $2,000, 100 percent of compensation). Although there are tax penalties for early withdrawal of IRA funds, the magical effect of tax-free compounding makes IRAs excellent places for temporary storage of funds. An earlier chapter discusses IRAs in detail.

TAX REDUCTION CHECKLIST

IRS publications to be obtained:

- Publication 17—*Your Federal Income Tax*
- Publication 526—*Charitable Contributions*
- Publication 538—*Accounting Periods and Methods*

Why year-end planning is important:

- New laws require a review of your tax situation at year's end.
- Certain planning opportunities are available only at year's end.

Defer income until next year:

- Make a short sale of stock.
- Make a one-installment sale.
- Put money in investments that will credit interest next year.
- Pay bills in January.
- Take bonuses and commissions in January.

Get deductions and credits this year:

- Use a third-party credit card (such as VISA or MasterCard) if you are short of cash.
- If medical expenses to date exceed 5 percent of your adjusted gross income, pay any outstanding bills this year.
- "Points" paid on a home improvement loan are deductible in the year of payment.
- Tax credit is allowed for cost of insulation and energy-saving devices paid for and installed in current year (until December 31, 1985).
- Make charitable donations—cash, check, charge, or property.
- Prepay state taxes, if they are due now, even though they won't be overdue until next year.
- Buy business property—get full year's investment tax credit and accelerated depreciation.

Save without spending:

- Claim casualty losses even though you expect an insurance settlement next year.
- Establish a self-employed retirement plan, even though you can't afford a contribution until next year.

Year-end stock deals:

- Don't mix long-term gains and short-term losses.
- Sell for long-term losses to offset short-term gains.

December tax shelters:

- The IRS crackdown on abusive tax shelters makes those last-minute tax shelters extremely hazardous.
- Always consult independent financial and tax advisors before investing.

Save this year's taxes next year:

- IRA can be established any time until return date next year; contributions next year can be deducted on tax return for this year.

Nothing, absolutely nothing, will relieve you of your tax liability—not even death. In this life, there are two certainties. First, you are going to die. Second, Congress will continue to pass new tax laws. The only difference between these two certainties is that death will not become worse with the passage of each new law.

You can be sure that with each meeting, Congress will increase the number of new tax regulations. You can also be assured that each new law will bring infinitely more baffling reporting requirements. The trend in Congress is to do nothing to increase your comprehension of tax laws.

To avoid economic madness, you have two choices. One, you can spend all of your time, and we mean *all* of your time, studying the tax laws to make sure your silent partner, the tax collector, is not getting more than a fair share of your profits. Or two, you can spend some of your time and hire others to spend all of their time doing the research for you, to advise you about the tax effects of your actions.

WHY YOU NEED AN ADVISOR

We would like to squelch the idea of doing taxes yourself. You might think that you can pick up ideas from friends (hitchhiking), read some books, and get some other ideas that will help you take care of all of your tax matters. Unfortunately, there is no hope for hitchhikers. If you have a friend who gets tax advice from a tax professional, that advice is based on your friend's facts and circumstances. It may be totally inappropriate to your circumstances. To rely on such information would be to squeeze yourself into the mental world of the simple-minded.

The IRS has a plan to exploit backward taxpayers. The backward taxpayer is normally someone who does it himself or uses a tax preparer (not an advisor). The backward taxpayer situation is devastating if you have any money to worry about.

How do you decide whether to use a tax preparer or to do it yourself? If you are not making any money, do not plan on making any money in the future, and have no rich uncles, aunts, cousins, brothers, or sisters, then you may consider doing your tax return yourself. Otherwise, there is only one prudent way to approach your taxes—that is, to guide your tax advisor along the murky waters of your financial affairs. Then, and only then, will you be in a position to protect yourself. There are far too many matters, too many complications, too many exceptions, and too many elections for one individual to keep track of,

How to Find and Use a Tax Advisor

unless you spend all of your time doing just that.

Finding and choosing a well-qualified advisor may be compared to the traumatic experiences of trying to find a good medical doctor. With a doctor, you place your life in his or her hands. With a tax advisor, you place your ability to pay the doctor in the tax advisor's hands.

WHY YOU SHOULD KNOW THE LAW

Your tax advisor is not with you every day. But every day you make decisions pertaining to your tax situation. If you are ignorant of the law, you will *not* recognize the problems, and you will blunder.

You cannot wait for a year-end visit with your tax advisor to correct your blunders.

Every day is tax day. Since you don't want (nor could you afford) a tax advisor looking over your shoulder every day, you must have enough knowledge to be your own advisor.

Knowledge leads to efficient use of an advisor: If you know absolutely nothing about tax law, your tax advisor will have to spend part of each session giving you an introductory class on the law—an expensive way to get basic tax knowledge.

Knowledge lets you evaluate your advisor: This is the single most important reason why you must know tax law. How do you know whether your tax advisor is worth a penny unless you know something about the tax law?

Your tax advisor will be only as good as you are. You must have enough knowledge to know when and how to use your tax advisor. Moreover, you must be able to evaluate your tax advisor's competency level.

Knowledgeable taxpayers create aggressive advisors: If you are handling someone else's affairs, you will naturally be more conservative than you would be if you were handling your own affairs. Tax advisors suffer the same problems. They are often much more conservative giving you advice than they would be with their own tax returns.

Think of yourself as the coach and your tax advisor as one of the players on your financial team. You may not be able to throw the ball 50 yards, but your quarterback, the tax advisor, has that ability. Your job is to know when to tell your tax advisor to throw the ball.

Set up a program of self-study: Since you need a knowledgeable tax advisor, worth the money you pay, and since you can't look over your advisor's shoulder every day, set up a self-study program immediately. By reading this book, you have taken some important first steps. You will also want to attend seminars and keep up to date with a tax newsletter.

Remember, your profits are divided between you and the IRS. You must be knowledgeable about your partnership agreement—the Internal Revenue Code—to ensure that your tax advisor understands how this partnership agreement with the IRS affects you.

THE PERFECT TAX ADVISOR

There is an expensive way and a less expensive way, but no cheap way, to get tax advice. If you are paying less than $100 a year for someone to take care of your taxes, you are not getting tax advice.

There are two types of tax individuals in this world, the tax gopher and the tax hound.

Tax gophers merely put information onto tax returns. In effect, tax gophers act as robots, with little forethought or hindsight. They merely read and follow IRS Form 1040 instructions. If you could find a programmed computer, you would get the same result.

Tax gophers are nothing more than rodents and ought to be eradicated. You do not get tax advice from such individuals—you get a tax return. Normally, such individuals are part-timers who do not study tax laws, exceptions, applications, or any other aspects that will benefit you in your tax planning.

The tax hound, however, is someone who can sniff out a tax transaction. But a tax hound is only as good as his master—you. You must have enough tax knowledge to take advantage of your tax hound. You must lead the old dog to the appropriate spot, give him a whiff of the transaction, and then set him free. Only then will you have a chance of catching your prey—tax deductions.

Your specialist: You want a tax advisor who specializes in your type of business. That's the most important thing. You wouldn't go to a podiatrist for heart surgery! Likewise, you must find a tax advisor who specializes in your business.

If you are a small business corporation selling insurance, you want a tax advisor with at least ten other clients who are small business corporations selling insurance. A tax advisor with fifty such similar businesses is preferable.

All tax advisors have some specialty. There are specialists in corporate taxation, small business taxation, estate tax, real estate taxation, or family practice. There is no such thing as a "good generalist" in the tax advisor world.

A true specialist is not common. In each major metropolitan area, there are probably only a couple of true specialists in your area of business.

Get the best: You ought to have the best tax advisor in the nation. That doesn't mean the most famous. Famous ones usually give lousy service, so they are really not the best. The best will cost more—maybe $175 an hour, fully tax-deductible. But the difference in confidence, competence, and aggressiveness is worth it.

Education: Your tax advisor ought to be the accountant's accountant, or the lawyer's lawyer. Better yet, your tax advisor ought to be the tax accountant's accountant and the tax lawyer's lawyer. You find such a person by finding those who practice and teach the other professionals.

Later in this chapter we will give you 25 questions to help you find such a person.

Service: Lousy service is lousy service. Your tax advisor should provide good service. He should meet reasonable deadlines, return phone calls promptly, and not hand you off to unqualified junior assistants.

Few individuals knowingly tolerate lousy service from their auto mechanics. Yet, many of these same individuals put up with lousy service from their tax advisors for years. Don't do it. If your advisor is giving you lousy service, find someone else.

Integrity: You want an honest tax advisor. Everyone ought to be honest. Dishonest tax advisors end up on the IRS "problem preparers list." If your preparer ends up on this black list, it could mean big problems for *you!*

PROFILES OF POSSIBLE TAX ADVISORS

Unfortunately, bad tax advisors do not sport black hats and droopy mustaches. Anyone, from the senile or the idiot to the brilliant, can assume the label tax advisor or tax preparer. All that's necessary is to go down to the local government agencies and get a license. That license is only a business license. It has no relationship whatsoever to competence.

There are basically seven types of tax people. We'll reserve the word *advisor* until later. The types we will discuss in this section are:

- Commercial preparers
- Independent preparers
- Accountants
- Enrolled agents
- Certified public accountants
- Tax attorneys
- CPA/tax attorneys

This hierarchy proceeds from the least desirable to the most desirable.

Commercial preparers: The cheapest, most incompetent person you can employ is a commercial preparer. Now don't get us wrong; there is a need for commercial preparers. *But commercial preparers are not tax advisors.*

Most individuals employed by commercial preparers are oblivious to tax laws. They do not have accounting or tax backgrounds, and often they have no formal education. Pay scales for the "worker bees" at a commercial preparer are slightly above the minimum wage, sometimes less. The usual training for such individuals is one day to six weeks during which they learn how to fill out the forms, but not much more.

We rank commercial preparers only slightly ahead of doing it yourself.

Independent preparers: Independent preparers are those individuals who set up a little sideline business each tax season to do income taxes. Their background in taxes comes from reading newspaper articles, a few small tax books, and various IRS forms and publications. Individuals in this classification do not subscribe to the major tax services or read court cases and other interpretations of tax law. When engaging such a person to help you with your taxes, you will get one of two types of individuals.

First, you may get an individual who will allow slightly fewer deductions than an IRS agent would allow. The IRS recently instituted a new program to stab bad tax preparers, so ultra-conservative independent preparers will make sure that they do not anger the IRS. Accordingly, your tax return will not be prepared in a manner that benefits you the most.

Second, you could encounter an imaginative and supercreative dishonest independent preparer. The IRS dubs such preparers "problem preparers" and is definitely interested in their activities, often sending out scouts disguised as taxpayers to see what types of dishonest deductions are being offered. Such creative individuals may add a new baby to your family, even though they have never met your spouse. Sometimes they will offer to throw an extra tithe into the collection plate, even though they have never been to your church. When the IRS goes after these guys, it audits all of their clients.

Accountants: In this category are year-round, full-time businesses concerned primarily with bookkeeping and taxes. Individuals in this type of business may or may not have a good tax background, though it is possible to find an excellent tax advisor among this group.

Most often, however, you will not be so blessed. Tax *preparation* is a seasonal business, whereas tax *advice* is a year-round business. An accountant running a year-round business and a tax preparation business is not a tax advisor. Careful attention *will* have to be paid if you select an individual in this category to be your tax advisor.

There is no competency standard for accountants who are not in the enrolled agent or certified public accountant classifications. When discussing your tax situation with this type of individual, you might ask why the ac-

countant never bothered to become a CPA or an enrolled agent. There may be valid reasons, but cast a suspicious eye on employing such an individual to handle your tax affairs.

Enrolled agent: We are flogging our way up the ladder of expertise. An enrolled agent is one of three categories of people eligible to represent you before the IRS. (The other two are attorneys and CPAs.)

There are two ways to become an enrolled agent: first, pass an IRS test, or second, have at least five years experience as an IRS auditor.

An enrolled agent who has passed the special test given by the IRS could be a good bet. The test has been dubbed by some to be more difficult than the tax portion of the CPA examination. A great deal of skill and expertise in tax law is required to pass the test. An individual carrying the enrolled agent designation is expected to have a high degree of skill and expertise in tax matters.

However, having the designation "enrolled agent" does not, by itself, make a particular agent competent. As with all professions, you have about a 10 percent chance of finding a competent advisor in this group. There are about 15,000 enrolled agents nationwide; you can usually find them listed in the yellow pages under "tax preparation services."

Beware of enrolled agents who have spent more than five years with the IRS. Such individuals may turn out to be overly conservative and dwell on why things cannot be done, instead of finding legal ways to get them done.

Certified public accountants: You are now approaching the heavy thinker category, or at least that's where you're supposed to be. CPAs must pass a rigorous examination to obtain that designation and are considered by most standards to be competent accountants. That does not necessarily mean they are competent tax experts.

Myth—CPAs are tax experts: Certified public accountants may work for a school system, the government, private industry, or a public accounting firm. In any of these areas, an individual could possess the CPA designation and have little or no tax experience. There are approximately 200,000 CPAs in the United States, but fewer than 20,000 are full-time tax specialists. The others specialize in some other area.

Tax attorneys: An attorney does not specialize *before* getting a law degree. Specialization comes later. Attorneys who specialize in the tax law receive a Masters degree in taxation. Generally, that is a two-year program completed after the three years of law school.

You do not want a patent attorney preparing your tax return. The areas of law are completely unrelated, and one sure way to get in trouble with the IRS is to use someone who does not know anything about tax law.

Also, tax attorneys may work for the government, an educational institution, or private industry, or in some other area where daily practice does not concentrate on tax matters.

Tax attorney/CPA: Some tax advisors are both tax attorneys and certified public accountants. Many of these individuals are members of the American Association of Attorney/CPAs, an organization located in Mission Viejo, California (714-768-0336).

The designation tax attorney/CPA does not in itself make that person an excellent advisor for you. There are many tax attorney/CPAs who do not specialize in taxation on a daily basis. Remember, you want someone who specializes in the tax situation for people in your type of business.

The rankings: If you rank tax advisors from the top of the pyramid to the bottom, the top category is the tax attorney/CPA combination, providing that this individual practices taxes on a regular basis and has done so for a number of years. You should pick this individual only if his expertise is in your area of business.

Following close behind the tax attorney/CPA is the tax attorney or CPA who specializes in taxation. To differentiate between these groups, experience is the most important factor. The more experience with your types of business transactions, the better your tax advisor. Your daily personal and business transactions must influence the type of advisor you seek.

In day to day transactions, CPAs are the leaders over tax attorneys. CPAs cannot go to court and are therefore less enthralled with the possibilities of esoteric transactions and more intrigued by the pragmatic transactions.

After attorneys and CPAs, enrolled agents are next in line and far outdistance the remainder of the pyramid. If you can find a tax attorney, certified public accountant, or enrolled agent who is familiar with your business and who thinks like you, you have a good bet for a tax advisor!

TWENTY-FIVE QUESTIONS TO HELP SELECT A TAX ADVISOR

Hiring a tax advisor is an integral part of your business. Your first step is to initiate a search process to find tax advisors worth interviewing.

Business colleagues: Do your business colleagues have excellent tax advisors? If so, ask them for recommendations. Ask for specifics and pin them down as to why they are making the recommendation. Many times this turns out to be a good source for identifying at least one tax advisor to interview. But don't stop there. Get more than one prospect.

Call professional societies such as your state association of attorneys and CPAs. Find out who teaches tax courses to other specialists—specialists in your area of business. Note authors of books and articles that deal with your areas of business interest. Review court cases for attorney names. Look for editors of trade journals. This step in your search will find you the specialist's specialist.

Your area or nationwide? The best may not be available in your home town. But look there first, and look to other areas only after you have exhausted all possibilities in your own backyard.

No credential alone is adequate for selection of a tax advisor. Some lawyers with Masters degrees in taxation are complete idiots. A person may not teach or write about taxes but may be an excellent tax advisor.

Since there is no one credential or attribute that makes for a good tax advisor, you must interview the individuals before making a selection. During the interview process, ask questions that will give you the information you need to select the best possible tax advisor. Following are 25 questions which should help you get started.

1. What type of formal education do you have? Generally, the basic education should be strong. Advanced formal education in tax areas is desirable. But education by itself is not indicative of whom you should or should not hire. It is only one of 25 reasons why you should select a certain tax advisor.

2. Did you pass your professional certification examination on the first try? Approximately 6 percent of the CPAs in this country pass the CPA examination on the first try. Approximately 60 percent of the lawyers pass the bar examination on the first try. You are asking this question to determine the level of your tax advisor's motivation. Someone motivated, at least right after receiving a formal degree, will pass the examination the first time.

3. How many years have you been actively engaged in a tax practice? You are looking for experience. Exclude years teaching or working in specialties other than taxation.

4. How many clients do you handle personally? You do not want a tax advisor with three clients. Similarly, if your tax advisor has a thousand clients, how much of the work is passed on to junior associates? You are looking for someone who is busy with the tax law, but not so busy your problems won't receive proper attention.

5. How many clients do you have that are in my business? This is an extremely important question. Show the prospective tax advisor your last year's tax return and ask for comments. If you have real estate investments, ask the tax advisor how many clients have rental properties. You are looking for a tax advisor who is familiar with your type of return and who has had extensive experience with your type of business.

6. Do you specialize in some aspect of taxes? This question is a corollary to question 5. If you are a small corporation and your tax advisor specializes in estates and trusts, you could have a problem. You are looking for

someone who specializes in areas which include your tax situations.

7. How many times have you represented taxpayers in disputes with the IRS? This question has a twofold impact. First, you are trying to determine if the prospective advisor is at least moderately aggressive and does have some clients who face IRS challenges. Second, you are looking for an advisor who can rebuff challenges and obtain "no change" letters from the IRS. "No change" letters will be an indication of an advisor's competency. You want to know the advisor's batting average.

8. How many times have you represented taxpayers at the IRS appeals level? Again, you want to know the batting average. What you are looking for here is an indication of persistence. You reach the IRS appeals level after having dealt with the IRS at the audit level. You want a tax advisor who not only locates the proper deductions for you, but is persistent if the IRS questions your correct deductions.

9. How many times have you fought tax cases in court? If you are talking to an attorney, you will want answers similar to those sought in questions 7 and 8. CPAs can qualify to represent you before the Tax Court, and you should ask a CPA if he or she is qualified to do so. If the answer is yes, that individual has spent some time studying. You might also ask if the CPA actually fights the cases. Often, CPAs qualified to practice before the Tax Court do not do so because *that forum* is generally *handled better* by attorneys.

10. What continuing education courses or seminars did you attend during the past two years? Look for courses pertinent to your problems. Look for courses about new tax laws. You want your advisor to be completely up to date, and you want him or her to be studying your types of problems. Many continuing educational courses have no relationship to professional expertise (e.g., time management). Obviously, there is nothing wrong with a time management course, but your question regards technical expertise.

11. Have you taught any tax courses during the last two years? To whom were they taught? You are looking for a tax advisor who is teaching tax courses to other tax advisors— tax courses that are pertinent to your tax problems. If someone is teaching a tax course, you can assume that person has spent more time studying the material than those who attend the class.

12. Have you written any tax articles during the past two years? If so, obtain a copy and read them. Find out if they relate to problems you encounter in your business. If the articles are easy to read, you may have found a tax advisor with whom you can communicate. Also, writing an article takes research. You want a tax advisor who spends at least some time doing tax research.

13. What tax and business periodicals do you subscribe to? You are looking for more than the basic major tax services such as those sold by Commerce Clearing House or Prentice-Hall, Inc. Ask for a tour of the library. Note the size and professionalism of the library. The more you see, the better you like it. The basic multivolume services are essential. In addition, you should see speciality services on pension and profit sharing, incorporation, and others. Look for those that relate to your tax questions. You should see bound volumes of past court cases. You should see newsletters, tax journals, and other periodicals that relate to your tax problems.

14. What resources do you use to review private letter rulings? Although private letter rulings are at the low end of the precedential scale, along with IRS publications, access to such rulings is necessary for much tax research. If the materials are "in-house," rather than "out-of-house," you can bet your prospective tax advisor does tax research.

15. What trade publications do you subscribe to? You are looking for a tax advisor who is familiar with your personal and business problems. If the tax advisor subscribes to the same trade publications you use in your business, you can assume that advisor knows something about your business tax situation. The more clients your prospective advisor has

that are in the same business as you, the more important the trade publications.

16. Do you use the computer as a research tool? Many tax advisors subscribe to a computer service called "LEXIS." There are other similar computer tools. Such tools enable a tax advisor to plug keywords into a computer terminal and research those keywords through a multiplicity of tax documents. Such computer access is used primarily by those involved in heavy tax research.

17. What is the latest status of the . . . ? You want a tax advisor who is up to date, and stays up to date. We mentioned earlier in this chapter that you need to have enough tax knowledge to be able to evaluate your tax advisor. Before setting up interviews, review some of your research materials for recent tax developments. Pick out two or three items of extreme importance to you. Ask the prospective tax advisor questions and find out if he knows the answers, or is familiar with the recent developments.

18. Do you own any . . . investments? If part of your tax problems relate to investments, you want a tax advisor that not only understands your investments, but also makes such investments himself.

19. Have you ever paid a tax return preparer's penalty? If so, what for? Were any of the individual penalties more than $100? Penalties are imposed on tax preparers because of willful misconduct or endorsement and negotiation of a taxpayer's refund check. Also, there are penalties over $100 for fraud, and intentional misstatement of a taxpayer's tax liability. Such penalties could be an indication that this prospective tax advisor ignores tax laws. You do not want such an advisor.

20. Do you recommend accelerated depreciation? Generally, a good tax advisor will recommend taking all deductions possible today. We believe all taxpayers should use accelerated depreciation on equipment. Similarly, residential real estate should be depreciated using an accelerated method. On commercial real estate, you should use straight-line depreciation unless you are involved in exchanges. Read the chapters in this book that deal with depreciation before discussing the accelerated methods with a prospective tax advisor. Then, measure his response with the discussion in this book.

21. How many times during the year must I bring in my tax information? If the answer to this question is once, look for a different advisor. You should meet with your tax advisor at least twice a year; once to get your tax return done, and at least once for advanced planning, probably sometime in late September or early October. Also, the advisor should encourage you to bring in all significant transactions for discussion, before entering into them. Periodic phone consultations should be encouraged.

22. How should I bring in my tax information? A good tax advisor will have preprinted forms and questions which you can use to organize your information. The use of such forms cuts down on the advisor's fee, and helps order both your and your tax advisor's thinking. The form should include spaces for not only numbers, but also questions.

23. Do you offer investment advice? You are hiring a tax advisor, not an investment banker. Obviously, while your tax advisor is looking over your tax information, he should note low investment returns and call them to your attention. But, he should not recommend individual investments. There are people who do that for a living. Obtain your investment advice from investment people, obtain your legal advice from legal people, and obtain your tax advice from tax people.

24. Will you do the research on my tax questions? If your prospective tax advisor has a staff, it's important to know who will do the research. If a subordinate will do some of the research, it's important to know how much supervision will be given and if the final product will be reviewed extensively by your prospective tax advisor. If a subordinate does the work, the fees should be lower, but the output may be less than desirable. If your tax advisor is a good people manager, subordinate research may be preferable. You need to know

if you are hiring the prospective tax advisor in total, or partially. If partially, how partially.

25. What is your fee and how do you bill? You want to know not only what the charge is for the tax return, but for all other services. Is a five-minute phone conversation billed, and at what rate? How much will be billed for just the tax returns? How much for the tax returns and five phone conversations during a year? How much for two two-hour consulting sessions during a year? How much for research? Once you get the fee estimate, ask for it in writing.

The final proof: Once you've hired your tax advisor, you'll find out if you chose the right person. Is the advisor:

- easy to work with?
- competent?
- aggressive?
- earning the fee?

Are you paying less taxes?

Final word: You must be master of the situation when hiring a tax advisor. You are the one creating the financial transactions and asking for tax interpretations. Therefore, you must know enough about tax law to converse with your tax advisor. The more you know, the better tax advisor you will find and the better tax help you will receive.

FEES TO EXPECT AND HOW TO KEEP THEM TO A MINIMUM

There is an axiom that the only ridiculous prices in this world are those not paid. Keeping that in mind while interviewing prospective tax advisors, you should not be too shocked at some of the prices.

Fees do not necessarily bear a direct relationship to the competency of the tax advisor; however, they are often a good indicator. Some CPAs and tax attorneys are able to command fees of up to $200 an hour. In most cases, such professionals have staffs to complement their imaginations, and your effective billing rate per hour may be substantially less. In many cases you can find good tax attorneys and CPAs who bill as low as $75 per hour or lower.

Sole practitioners with one or two non-professional staff members often have billing rates as low as $50 an hour, and sometimes even lower than that. If these figures seem on the high side to you, you can drop to the next category, that of enrolled agents.

Enrolled agents frequently charge less than CPAs and tax attorneys, with fees ranging from $10 an hour up to $75 an hour. Hourly rates, although they may appear high on the surface, are not necessarily indicative of the total cost of helping you with your tax problems. There are a number of things you can do to speed up the cycle and reduce your charges for competent tax advice.

The first step in keeping your fees to a minimum is to walk through a typical cycle for a tax year. Ask the practitioner how much it will cost just for preparation of the return with three one-hour counseling sessions during the year, assuming there is no need for research on the side. This gives you a good overview of what to expect at the end of the year. Always obtain a written estimate of the cost in order to put the fee in perspective and facilitate communication with the practitioner should fees exceed that amount.

It will be difficult to get a fixed fee. Tax charges depend on the facts and circumstances of particular situations. Most tax advisors charge by the hour, and total time billed fluctuates according to your facts and circumstances. However, you should set maximum research charges for any particular project before giving the project to a tax advisor. You might state, for example, that the practitioner is authorized to spend two hours reviewing the situation and if it cannot be resolved within that two-hour billing period, to ask for clearance before proceeding.

Always put time constraints on a research project. If you submit it on Monday and expect it a week from Monday, make that clear in a written document. That does two things for you. First, it keeps the fee down. Second, it makes sure you get the information when you need it.

The codes of professional ethics for both lawyers and accountants say that fees should be clearly stated by written agreement. Essentially, professionals are responsible for agreeing with their clients on the fee as early as possible. Agreements prevent misunderstandings, big shocks, and build good relations.

Once you get a fee estimate, you can do a number of things to keep costs to a minimum. First, thoroughly organize your tax information for the practitioner. One of the questions to ask during the interview is what type of input information is required. This gives you an indication of the practitioner's organization and ability to extract good tax information from you.

Second, take the steps necessary to use your tax advisor effectively during the year. The golden rule is never spend any significant money before you ask your tax advisor. Always ask your tax advisor about a divorce or separation. Always consult with your tax advisor when planning real estate transactions.

The real value of a tax advisor shows up in a structuring of transactions. There are hundreds of hidden pitfalls in the Internal Revenue Code that can be avoided with planning. The purpose of an advisor is to help you plan so that you do not tumble into the pits.

Be prepared: The real point in using a tax advisor is to generate a little action. Your tax advisor has seen thousands of involved arrangements and should be able to spew forth data that enables you to keep more of your hard-earned money. But *you* must put your tax advisor in this position. *You* must ask questions in a succinct manner to speed up the cycle and get the most benefit from the process. Always review the tax law before you consult with your tax advisor, and then consult with your tax advisor before you enter into any involved arrangement and before you commit any money.

Finally, make it a point to consult with your tax advisor during late September or early October. Bring in your numbers for the year-to-date and estimates for the remainder of the year. You should be pleased with the tax-saving ideas your tax advisor presents at this session.

TAX REDUCTION CHECKLIST

Why you need a tax advisor:

- To understand complex tax laws.
- To ensure a complete and accurate return.
- To obtain assistance before transactions are consummated.
- To obtain tax-planning ideas.

Why you should know the law:

- Your tax advisor is not with you every day.
- Knowledge leads to efficient use of an advisor.
- Knowledge lets you evaluate your advisor.
- Knowledgeable taxpayers create aggressive advisors.

Types of tax advisors:

- Commercial preparers and tax return factories are not tax advisors; however, they do a good job of moving numbers from your input data to your tax return.
- Independent preparers often work during the tax season only and have rather poor backgrounds in total tax knowledge.
- Accountants and bookkeeping services may or may not have a good tax background, depending on the nature of their business activities.
- Enrolled agents are required to pass a special test given by the IRS and usually have a credible degree of skill and expertise in tax matters.
- CPAs and tax attorneys must be sorted to find tax specialists—then you will have a true tax expert.

Finding possible tax advisors to interview:

- Ask business colleagues for references.
- Look in your home town first.
- Call professional societies and ask for advisors who teach other advisors in your tax area of interest.
- Note authors of books and articles that deal with your areas of business interest.
- Review court cases for attorney names.

Questions to ask a potential tax advisor:

- What is your formal educational background?
- Did you pass your professional certification exam on the first try?
- How many years have you been active in tax practice?
- How many clients do you handle personally?
- How many clients do you have that are in my business?
- Do you specialize in some aspect of taxes?
- How many times have you represented taxpayers in disputes with the IRS?
- How many times have you represented taxpayers at the IRS appeals level?
- How many times have you fought tax cases in court?
- What tax courses did you take during the last two years?
- Have you taught any tax courses in the last two years?
- Have you written any tax articles during the last two years?
- What tax and business periodicals do you subscribe to?
- What resources do you use to review private letter rulings?
- What trade publications do you subscribe to?
- Do you use the computer as a research tool?
- What is the latest status of . . . (law, ruling, etc.)?

- Do you own any . . . (real estate, oil & gas, etc.) investments?
- Have you ever paid a tax return preparer's penalty?
- Do you recommend accelerated depreciation?
- How many times a year must I bring in my tax information?
- How should I bring in my tax information?
- Do you offer investment advice?
- Will you do the research on my tax questions?
- What is your fee and how do you bill?

Keeping fees to a minimum:

- Get the fee quote in writing.
- Restrict research time.
- Demand answers within specific time frames.
- Thoroughly organize and summarize your information.

Using the tax advisor:

- Always use a tax advisor to structure financial transactions.
- Consult your tax advisor anytime you have involved arrangements.
- Always consult your tax advisor sometime during the months of September or October.

Appendixes

APPENDIX 2. Worksheet for Figuring Exception 2 (Tax on Annualized Income).

	INSTALLMENTS		
	1st	*2nd*	*3rd*
STEP ONE Adjusted gross income from January 1 through end of reporting period (March 31, May 31, August 31).	$_____	$_____	$_____
STEP TWO Multiply amount in Step One by factor shown. Result is annualized adjusted gross income.	× 4	× 2.4	× 1.5
STEP THREE Itemized deductions from January 1 through end of reporting period (March 31, May 31, August 31).			
STEP FOUR Multiply amount in Step Three by factor shown. Result is annualized itemized deduction.	× 4	× 2.4	× 1.5
STEP FIVE Subtract zero bracket amount ($3,400 for married filing jointly; $2,300 for single or head of household; $1,700 for married filing separately) from amount in Step Four.	[ ]	[ ]	[ ]
STEP SIX Multiply $1,000 by number of personal exemptions.			
STEP SEVEN Add amounts in Steps Five and Six.	[ ]	[ ]	[ ]
STEP EIGHT Subtract amount in Step Seven from amount in Step Two.			
STEP NINE Regular income tax on amount in Step Eight.			
STEP TEN Self-employment income from January 1 through end of reporting period (March 31, May 31, August 31).			
STEP ELEVEN Multiply amount in Step Ten by self-employment tax rate (11.3% in 1984).	× .113	× .113	× .113
STEP TWELVE Add amounts in Steps Nine and Eleven.			
STEP THIRTEEN Subtract credits from amount in Step Twelve.	[ ]	[ ]	[ ]
STEP FOURTEEN Multiply amount in Step Thirteen by percentage shown. Result is cumulative payment required under Exception 3 for installment period shown.	× .20	× .40	× .60

APPENDIX 3. Worksheet for Figuring Exception 3 (Tax on Actual Income to Date).

	INSTALLMENTS		
	1st	2nd	3rd
STEP ONE Adjusted gross income from January 1 through end of reporting period (March 31, May 31, August 31).	$___	$___	$___
STEP TWO Itemized deductions from January 1 through end of reporting period (March 31, May 31, August 31).	$___	$___	$___
STEP THREE Subtract zero bracket amount ($3,400 for married filing jointly; $2,300 for single or head of household; $1,700 for married filing separately) from amount in Step Two.	[___]	[___]	[___]
	___	___	___
STEP FOUR Multiply $1,000 by number of personal exemptions.	___	___	___
STEP FIVE Add amounts in Steps Three and Four.	[___]	[___]	[___]
STEP SIX Subtract amount in Step Five from amount in Step One.	___	___	___
STEP SEVEN Regular income tax on amount in Step Six.	___	___	___
STEP EIGHT Actual self-employment income from January 1 through end of reporting period (March 31, May 31, or August 31).	___	___	___
STEP NINE Multiply amount in Step Eight by self-employment tax rate (11.3% in 1984).	x.113 ___	x.113 ___	x.113 ___
STEP TEN Add amounts from Steps Seven and Nine.	___	___	___
STEP ELEVEN Subtract credits from amount in Step Ten.	[___]	[___]	[___]
STEP TWELVE Multiply amount in Step Eleven by 90 percent (.9). Result is cumulative payment required under Exception 4 for installment period shown.	x .9 ═══	x .9 ═══	x .9 ═══

APPENDIX 4. Master Worksheet for Figuring Lowest Estimated Tax Payments.

	INSTALLMENTS			
	1st	*2nd*	*3rd*	*4th*
STEP ONE				
Amount Required Under:				
A. Exception 1—Last year's tax	$____	$____	$____	$____
B. Exception 2—Tax on last year's income at this year's rates and using this year's exemptions	____	____	____	____
C. Exception 3—Tax on this year's income annualized	____	____	____	N/A
D. Exception 4—Tax on this year's income to date	____	____	____	N/A
STEP TWO				
Least amount under Step One—If cumulative payments as of the end of each installment period equal or exceed these amounts, you do not owe a penalty.	____	____	____	____

APPENDIX 5.   STATE LABOR COMMISSIONERS

Alabama
Allen Pate
Commissioner
Department of Labor
State Administrative Building
Suite 600
Montgomery, Alabama 36130
(205-832-6270)

William R. Heatherly
Director
Department of Industrial Relations
Industrial Relations Building
Montgomery, Alabama 36130
(205-832-3626)

Alaska
Jim Robison
Commissioner
Department of Labor
P.O. Box 1149
Juneau, Alaska 99811
(907-465-2700)

Arizona
Daniel R. Ortega, Jr.
Chairman
Industrial Commission
1601 West Jefferson Street
P.O. Box 19070
Phoenix, Arizona 85007
(602-255-4411)

Arkansas
Dewey Stiles
Director (Designate)
Department of Labor
1022 High Street
Little Rock, Arkansas 72202
(501-375-8442)

California
Victor V. Veysey
Secretary (Designate)
Department of Industrial Relations
State Building
525 Golden Gate Avenue
San Francisco 94102
(mailing address: P.O. Box 603
San Francisco, California 94101)
(415-557-3356)

Colorado
Ruben A. Valdez
Executive Director
Department of Labor and Employment
251 East 12th Avenue, Room 304
Denver, Colorado 80203
(303-866-6521)

Connecticut
P. Joseph Peraro
Commissioner
Labor Department
200 Folly Brook Boulevard
Wethersfield, Connecticut 06109
(203-566-5160)

Delaware
Dennis C. Carey
Secretary
Department of Labor
State Office Building
820 North French Street, 6th Floor
Wilmington, Delaware 19801
(302-571-2710)

District Of Columbia
Matthew Shannon
Director
Department of Employment Services
Employment Security Building
500 C Street, N.W., Suite 600
Washington, D.C. 20001
(202-639-1000)

Florida
Wallace Orr
Secretary
Department of Labor and
  Employment Security
Suite 206, Berkeley Building
2590 Executive Center Circle, East
Tallahassee, Florida 32301
(904-488-4398)

Georgia
Sam Caldwell
Commissioner
Department of Labor
State Labor Building
254 Washington Street, S.W.
Atlanta, Georgia 30334
(404-656-3011)

Guam
Lloyd Umagat
Director
Department of Labor
Government of Guam
Box 23548, GMF
Guam, M.I. 96921
(477-9821 or 9822 or 8626)

Hawaii
Dr. Joshua C. Agsalud
Director
Department of Labor and Industrial
  Relations
825 Mililani Street
Honolulu, Hawaii 96813
(808-548-3150)

Idaho
Sam Nettinga
Director
Department of Labor and
  Industrial Services
Room 400, Statehouse Mail
317 Main Street
Boise, Idaho 83720
(208-334-2327)

Illinois
E. Allen Bernardi
Director
Department of Labor
Alzina Building, 5th Floor North
100 North First Street
Springfield, Illinois 62706
(217-782-6206)

Indiana
Howard E. Williams
Commissioner
Division of Labor
State Office Building, Room 1013
100 North Senate Avenue
Indianapolis, Indiana 46204
(317-232-2655)

Iowa
Allen J. Meier
Commissioner
Bureau of Labor
Capitol Complex
307 East 7th Street
Des Moines, Iowa 50319
(515-281-3606)

Kansas
Jerry Shelor
Secretary
Department of Human Resources
401 Topeka Avenue
Topeka, Kansas 66603
(913-296-7474)

Kentucky
Thelma L. Stovall
Commissioner
Department of Labor
U.S. 127, South Building
Frankfort, Kentucky 40601
(502-564-3070)

Louisiana
Ulysses W. Williams
Secretary
Department of Labor
1045 State Land and Natural
  Resources Building
P.O. Box 44094
Baton Rouge, Louisiana 70804
(504-342-3011)

Maine
William Malloy
Commissioner
Department of Labor
20 Union Street
Augusta, Maine 04330
(207-289-3788)

Maryland
Dominic N. Fornaro
Commissioner
Division of Labor and Industry
501 St. Paul Place
Baltimore, Maryland 21202
(301-659-4179)

Massachusetts
Paul J. Eustace
Secretary of Labor
Executive Office of Labor
1 Ashburton Place, Room 2110
Boston, Massachusetts 02108
(617-727-6573)

William M. Shipps
Commissioner
Department of Labor and Industries
State Office Building
Government Center
100 Cambridge Street, Room 1100
Boston, Massachusetts 02202
(617-727-3454)

Michigan
S. Martin Taylor
Director
Department of Labor
309 North Washington
P.O. Box 30015
Lansing, Michigan 48909
(517-373-9600)

Minnesota
Steve Keefe
Commissioner
Department of Labor and Industry
Space Center, 5th Floor
444 Lafayette Road
St. Paul, Minnesota 55101
(612-296-2342)

Missouri
Mr. Terry C. Allen
Chairman
Labor and Industrial Relations
  Commission
P.O. Box 599, 1904 Missouri
  Boulevard
Jefferson City, Missouri 65102
(314-751-2461)

Montana
David L. Hunter
Commissioner
Department of Labor and Industry
35 South Last Chance Gulch
Helena, Montana 59601
(406-449-3661)

Nebraska
Ronald E. Sorensen
Commissioner
Department of Labor
550 South 16th Street, Box 94600
State House Station
Lincoln, Nebraska 68509
(402-475-8451)

Nevada
Frank McDonald
Commissioner
Labor Commission
505 East King Street, Room 602
Carson City, Nevada 89710
(702-885-4850)

Mr. F.E. "Bill" DuBois
Director
Department of Industrial Relations
1390 South Curry
Carson City, Nevada 89710
(702-885-3328)

New Hampshire
Dennis E. Murphy, Jr.
Commissioner
Department of Labor
19 Pillsbury Street
Concord, New Hampshire 03301
(603-271-3171)

New Jersey
Roger A. Bodman
Commissioner
Department of Labor
Labor Industry Building, Rm. 1303
John Fitch Plaza
P.O. Box CN 110
Trenton, New Jersey 08625
(609-292-2323)

New Mexico
Mr. R.C. Brooks
Commissioner
Labor and Industrial Commission
509 Camino De Los Marquez,
  Suite 2
Santa Fe, New Mexico 87501
(505-827-9870)

New York
Ms. Lillian Roberts
Commissioner of Labor
Department of Labor
State Campus, Building 12
Albany, New York 12240
(518-457-2741)

North Carolina
John C. Brooks
Commissioner
Department of Labor
Labor Building
4 West Edenton Street
Raleigh, North Carolina 27601
(919-733-7166)

North Dakota
Orville W. Hagen
Commissioner
Department of Labor
State Capitol
Bismark, North Dakota 58505
(701-224-2661)

Ohio
James Harris
Director
Department of Industrial Relations
2323 West Fifth Avenue
Columbus, Ohio 43215
(614-466-3271)

Oklahoma
William R. "Bill" Paulk
Commissioner
Department of Labor
State Capitol Building, Suite 118
Oklahoma City, Oklahoma 73105
(405-521-2461)

Oregon
Mary Wendy Roberts
Commissioner
Bureau of Labor and Industries
1400 S.W. 5th
Portland, Oregon 97201
(503-229-5210)

Pennsylvania
Barry H. Stern
Secretary
Department of Labor and Industry
1700 Labor and Industry Building
7th and Forster Streets
Harrisburg, Pennsylvania 17120
(717-787-3757)

Puerto Rico
Hector Hernandez Soto
Secretary of Labor
Department of Labor and Human
  Resources
Edificio Prudencio Rivera Martinez
505 Munoz Rivera Avenue
Hato Rey, Puerto Rico 00918
(809-754-5353)

Rhode Island
Romeo A. Caldarone
Director
Department of Labor
220 Elmwood Avenue
Providence, Rhode Island 02907
(401-277-2741)

South Carolina
Edgar L. McGowan
Commissioner
Department of Labor
3600 Forest Drive, P.O. Box 11329
Columbia, South Carolina 29211
(803-758-2851)

South Dakota
Judith Meierhenry
Secretary
Department of Labor
Capitol Lake Plaza
Pierre, South Dakota 57501
(605-773-3101)

Tennessee
Mr. Francis S. Guess
Commissioner
Department of Labor
501 Union Building
Nashville, Tennessee 37219
(615-741-2582)

Texas
Allen R. Parker, Sr.
Commissioner
Department of Labor and Standards
Box 12157, Capitol Station
Austin, Texas 78711
(512-475-3499)

Utah
Walter T. Axelgard
Chairman
Industrial Commission
160 East 300 South
P.O. Box 5800
Salt Lake City, Utah 84110-5800
(801-530-6817)

Vermont
Jeffrey L. Amestoy
Commissioner
Department of Labor and Industry
State Office Building
Montpelier, Vermont 05602
(802-828-2286)

Virginia
Mrs. Azie Taylor Morton
Commissioner
Department of Labor and Industry
P.O. Box 12064
Richmond, Virginia 23241
(804-786-2376)

Virgin Islands
Richard M. Upson
Commissioner of Labor
Department of Labor
P.O. Box 890, Christiansted
St. Croix, U.S. Virgin Islands 00820
(809-773-1994)

Washington
Sam Kinville
Director
Department of Labor and Industries
General Administration Building
Olympia, Washington 98504
(206-753-6307)

West Virginia
Lawrence Barker
Commissioner
Department of Labor
Capitol Complex
1900 Washington Street, East
Charleston, West Virginia 25305
(304-348-7890)

Wisconsin
Howard F. Bellman
Secretary
Department of Industry, Labor
  and Human Relations
201 East Washington Avenue
P.O. Box 7946
Madison, Wisconsin 53707
(608-266-7552)

Wyoming
Mr. Vernie E. Martin
Commissioner
Department of Labor and
  Statistics
Hathaway Building
Cheyenne, Wyoming 82002
(307-777-7261)

How to Increase Your NET WORTH

- Work harder and make more money
- Decrease your standard of living
- REDUCE YOUR TAXES.

If you want to increase your net worth, the best way to do it without increasing your work load or decreasing your standard of living is to reduce your taxes.

The fact that you purchased this book proves that you are eager to protect more of your hard-earned money from being lost in Uncle Sam's annual April game.

But wait. . .Congress is making a habit of changing the tax laws in each new session, and the courts and IRS are constantly coming up with new interpretations of the tax laws. How are you going to keep up with all of these changes? More importantly, what source are you going to rely on for providing you with vital tax information?

Your accountant alone cannot reduce your taxes. **You** must know the tax laws and how to apply them in order to help your accountant help you.

Write-off is the source you can rely on for the most up-to-date, comprehensive tax and financial planning information.

Write-off is a monthly, 12-page, fully annotated newsletter published by the Tax Reduction Institute in Washington, D.C.

Each month, **Write-off** presents an in-depth analysis of major tax and financial planning issues. In addition, **Write-off** keeps you on track with the latest happenings in IRS and in the courts.

Try **Write-off.** We know you will benefit from every issue. If, however, after reading three issues you are not completely satisfied with **Write-off,** we will refund your entire subscription fee. That means there's absolutely no risk involved. Send your subscription order today.

- -

I want **Write-off** now. I understand that **Write-off** is guaranteed to help me or you'll refund my entire subscription price (providing I let you know in three months).

Enter my subscription for:

- ☐ 1 Year (12 Issues) - $84
- ☐ 2 Years (24 Issues) - $160
- ☐ 3 Years (36 Issues) - $225
- ☐ Check Enclosed
- ☐ Charge ☐ Visa ☐ Mastercard
- ☐ Am. Express

Mail Subscription To:
WRITE-OFF
1901 18th St., N.W.
Washington, D.C. 20009

Card No. _____ Exp. date _____

Signature _____

Send subscription to:

Name _____

Company _____

Address _____

_____

City _____ State _____ Zip _____

3 Dynamic One-Day Workshops

- **Expert information**
- **Outstanding speakers**
- **Topics that reach right into your pocket and save you money**
- **All guaranteed to be a success!**

Choose One - Or Choose Them All

Tax Reduction Workshop: Past participants report discovering $5,000 in additional business tax deductions. Current tax laws and valuable tips for documenting and deducting business related expenses. Targeted to the self-employed, small business, commission-based and fee professionals. Saves taxes and makes more money.

Real Estate Investment Strategies Workshop: For real estate professionals, investors, home buyers and home sellers. New tax benefits of owning and renting homes and apartments, plus hidden changes made by court decisions and IRS. Maximizes the tax shelter of owning real estate.

Financial Planning Workshop: Independent, unbiased information on tax advantaged investments. The tax consequences of all investment decisions and how to integrate inflation and taxes into a successful plan. Get expert advice for your investment decisions.

Guaranteed To Be A Success

Just having the best, most complete, up to date workshops on tax deductions isn't enough. You're not looking for 6-½ hours of technical, dull tax education. We know that.

That's exactly why businesses and professional associations all across the country feature one or more TRI seminars in their educational programs. Over 250 each year.

Audience Ratings — 95.6% Excellent

They know they're getting fast-paced, entertaining programs. They know they can count on TRI for seminars that:

- are important to their people
- won't waste their time
- are fun as well as informative
- are worth more than 100 times the investment

And they know they'll get evaluations of 95.6% "excellent" or above and hear comments like:

"Best seminar I've attended. Well prepared, useful information, excellent teaching methods."

"Just what I wanted and have needed for years."

"Excellent, informative, humorous. Worth more than 100 times the registration fee."

Created by the Nation's Leading Tax Experts

TRI is an educational organization. TRI's staff presents seminars, writes books, and publishes newsletters on tax and financial planning.

TRI's only product is knowledge.

Recognized as the "nation's leading tax experts," the professional staff consists of expert certified public accountants and financial planners, experienced tax attorneys and investment bankers, former IRS tax law specialists, and professional educators.

TRI speakers are all top tax and financial planning experts with years of hands-on, practical experience and outstanding speaking abilities. Typical comments from participants are "knowledgeable," "articulate," "sincere," "easy to understand," and "humorous."

TRI staff members are featured on *CBS Evening News, CBS News Nightwatch, Money Matters,* and *Consumer Reports* (by the Council of Better Business Bureaus), and quoted in the *Wall Street Journal, Money, Changing Times, Fortune, Forbes,* and *the Washington Post.*

You Get Proven Promotional Materials — At No Extra Cost

And Satisfaction Is Guaranteed

We are so certain of the value of these workshops that we guarantee each participant's satisfaction.

If, for any reason, a participant does not feel the workshop was worth the price, we handle the 100% refund of his or her registration fee—at no cost to you.

It's Worth Looking Into

Fill out the coupon and mail today.
Or call 202-328-6908 (collect).